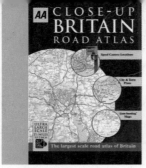

Atlas contents

1st edition October 2006

© Automobile Association Developments Limited 2006

Ordnance Survey® This product includes mapping data licensed from Ordnance Survey® with the permission of the Controller of Her Majesty's Stationery Office. © Crown copyright and database rights 2006. All rights reserved. Licence number 399221.

All rights reserved. No part of this publication may be reproduced, stored in a retrieval system, or transmitted in any form or by any means – electronic, mechanical, photocopying, recording or otherwise – unless the permission of the publisher has been given beforehand.

Published by AA Publishing (a trading name of Automobile Association Developments Limited, whose registered office is Fanum House, Basing View, Basingstoke, Hampshire RG21 4EA, UK. Registered number 1878835).

Mapping produced by the Mapping Services Department of The Automobile Association (A02720a).

ISBN-10: 0 7495 4984 X
ISBN-13: 978 0 7495 4984 8

A CIP catalogue record for this book is available from The British Library.

Printed in Italy by Canale & C. S.P.A, Torino.

The contents of this atlas are believed to be correct at the time of the latest revision, it will not contain any subsequent amended, new or temporary information including diversions and traffic control or enforcement systems. The publishers cannot be held responsible or liable for any loss or damage occasioned to any person acting or refraining from action as a result of any use or reliance on material in this atlas, nor for any errors, omissions or changes in such material. This does not affect your statutory rights. The publishers would welcome information to correct any errors or omissions and to keep this atlas up to date. Please write to the Atlas Editor, AA Publishing, The Automobile Association, Fanum House, Basing View, Basingstoke, Hampshire RG21 4EA, UK.
E-mail: roadatlasfeedback@theaa.com

A&E hospitals derived from data supplied by Johnsons.

Petrol station information supplied by Johnsons.

Information on National Parks in England provided by The Countryside Agency.

Information on National Nature Reserves in England provided by English Nature.

Information on National Parks, National Scenic Areas and National Nature Reserves in Scotland provided by Scottish Natural Heritage.

Information on National Parks and National Nature Reserves in Wales provided by The Countryside Council for Wales.

Information on Forest Parks provided by the Forestry Commission.

The RSPB sites shown are a selection chosen by the Royal Society for the Protection of Birds.

National Trust properties shown are a selection of those open to the public as indicated in the handbooks of the National Trust and the National Trust for Scotland.

National Cycle Network information supplied by Sustrans Limited www.sustrans.org.uk 0845 113 0065.

Marina information supplied courtesy of Noble Marine (Insurance Brokers) Ltd. www.noblemarine.co.uk

Crematoria data provided by The Cremation Society of Great Britain.

Information on fixed speed camera locations provided by Origin technologies.

Central London mapping in this atlas produced by the Mapping Services Department of The Automobile Association. Schools address data provided by Education Direct. One-way street data provided by © Tele Atlas N.V. The Post Office is a registered trademark of Post Office Ltd in the UK and other countries. The boundary of the London Congestion Charging Zone supplied by Transport for London.

Channel Islands update information supplied by David Moran.

Tram and Metro system logos used by kind permission of Nottingham Express Transit, Midland Metro, Metrolink (Manchester), Tyne & Wear Metro and Subway (Glasgow).

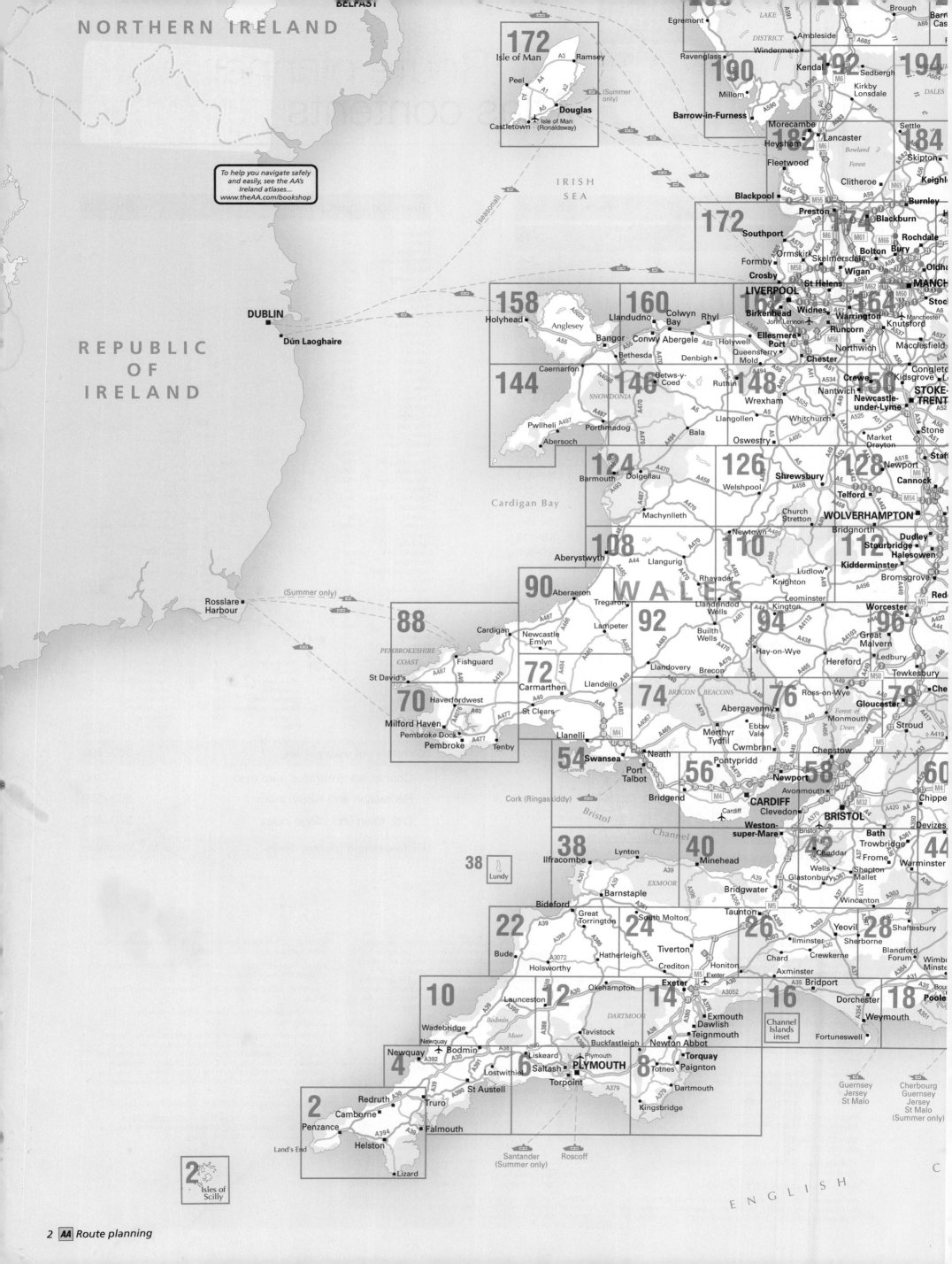

NORTHERN IRELAND

BELFAST

REPUBLIC
OF
IRELAND

DUBLIN
Dún Laoghaire

Rosslare
Harbour

(Summer only)

Cork (Ringaskiddy)

IRISH
SEA

To help you navigate safely
and easily, see the AA's
Ireland atlases...
www.theAA.com/bookshop

172
Isle of Man
Peel
Ramsey
Douglas
Castletown   Isle of Man
(Ronaldsway)

(Summer only)

190
Millom
Ravenglass
Windermere
Ambleside
Barrow-in-Furness

192
Kendal
Sedbergh
Kirkby
Lonsdale

194
Settle
Skipton

182
Morecambe
Heysham
Lancaster
Fleetwood

184

172
Blackpool
Preston
Southport
Formby
Crosby
Ormskirk
Skelmersdale

Clitheroe
Blackburn
Blackburn
Burnley
Rochdale
Bolton   Bury
Wigan

LIVERPOOL
Birkenhead
Widnes
Ellesmere
Port
Queensferry
Mold
Runcorn
Warrington
Manchester
MANCH
Knutsford
Stockport

158
Holyhead
Anglesey
Llandudno
Colwyn
Bay
Rhyl
Bangor
Conwy Abergele
Bethesda
Denbigh

160
Holywell
Chester
Northwich
Macclesfield
Congleton
Kidsgrove

144
Caernarfon
Snowdonia
Pwllheli
Porthmadog
Abersoch

146
Betws-y-Coed
Ruthin

148
Wrexham
Llangollen
Bala
Oswestry
Whitchurch

150
Crewe
Nantwich
Newcastle-
under-Lyme
**STOKE-
ON-TRENT**
Stone
Market
Drayton

124
Barmouth
Dolgellau
Welshpool

126
Shrewsbury
Church
Stretton

128
Telford
Newport
Cannock

108
Aberystwyth
Llangurig

110
Newtown
Rhayader
Ludlow
Knighton
Leominster

112
Bridgnorth
WOLVERHAMPTON
Dudley
Stourbridge
Halesowen
Kidderminster
Bromsgrove
Red

WALES

90
Aberaeron

92
Tregaron
Lampeter
Llandrindod
Wells
Builth
Wells

94
Hay-on-Wye
Brecon
Kington

Worcester
Great
Malvern
Ledbury
Tewkesbury

96

88
Cardigan
Newcastle
Emlyn
St David's
Fishguard

72
Carmarthen
Llandovery
Llandeilo

74
BRECON BEACONS
Abergavenny
Ross-on-Wye
Hereford

76
Monmouth
Forest of
Dean
Stroud
Gloucester

78
Che

Cardigan Bay

PEMBROKESHIRE
COAST

70
Haverfordwest
Milford Haven
Pembroke Dock
Pembroke
St Clears
Tenby

Llanelli

54
Swansea
Gower
Port
Talbot

56
Neath
Pontypridd
Bridgend
Merthyr
Tydfil
Ebbw
Vale
Cwmbran

58
Newport
Avonmouth
Chepstow

60
Chippe

CARDIFF
Cardiff
Clevedon
Weston-
super-Mare

42
BRISTOL
Bath
Trowbridge
Frome
Warminster

44
Devizes

Bristol
Channel

38
Ilfracombe
Lynton
Barnstaple
Bideford

40
Minehead
EXMOOR
Bridgwater
Taunton

Cheddar
Wells
Shepton
Mallet
Glastonbury

26
Wincanton
Yeovil

28
Shaftesbury
Sherborne
Blandford
Forum

Lundy

22
Bude
Great
Torrington
Holsworthy

24
South Molton
Tiverton
Hatherleigh
Crediton

Ilminster
Chard
Crewkerne
Axminster

Wimbo
Minster

38

10
Launceston
Okehampton

2
Tavistock
DARTMOOR
Buckfastleigh

14
Exeter
Exmouth
Dawlish
Teignmouth
Newton Abbot
Honiton

16
Channel
Islands inset
Dorchester
Bridport
Weymouth
Fortuneswell

18
Poole

22
Wadebridge
Newquay
Bodmin
Bodmin
Moor
Liskeard
Saltash
PLYMOUTH
Torpoint

6

8
Totnes
Torquay
Paignton
Dartmouth
Kingsbridge

Guernsey
Jersey
St Malo

Cherbourg
Guernsey
Jersey
St Malo
(Summer only)

4
Newquay
Redruth
Truro
St Austell
Lostwithiel

2
Penzance
Camborne
Helston
Falmouth
Land's End
Lizard

2
Isles of Scilly

ENGLISH

Route planner

Legend:

- Motorway
- Toll motorway
- Primary route dual carriageway
- Primary route single carriageway
- Other A road
- Vehicle ferry
- Vehicle ferry - fast catamaran
- National Park or scenic area
- **140** Index to maps in road map section

To help you navigate safely and easily, see the AA's France and Europe atlases...
www.theAA.com/bookshop

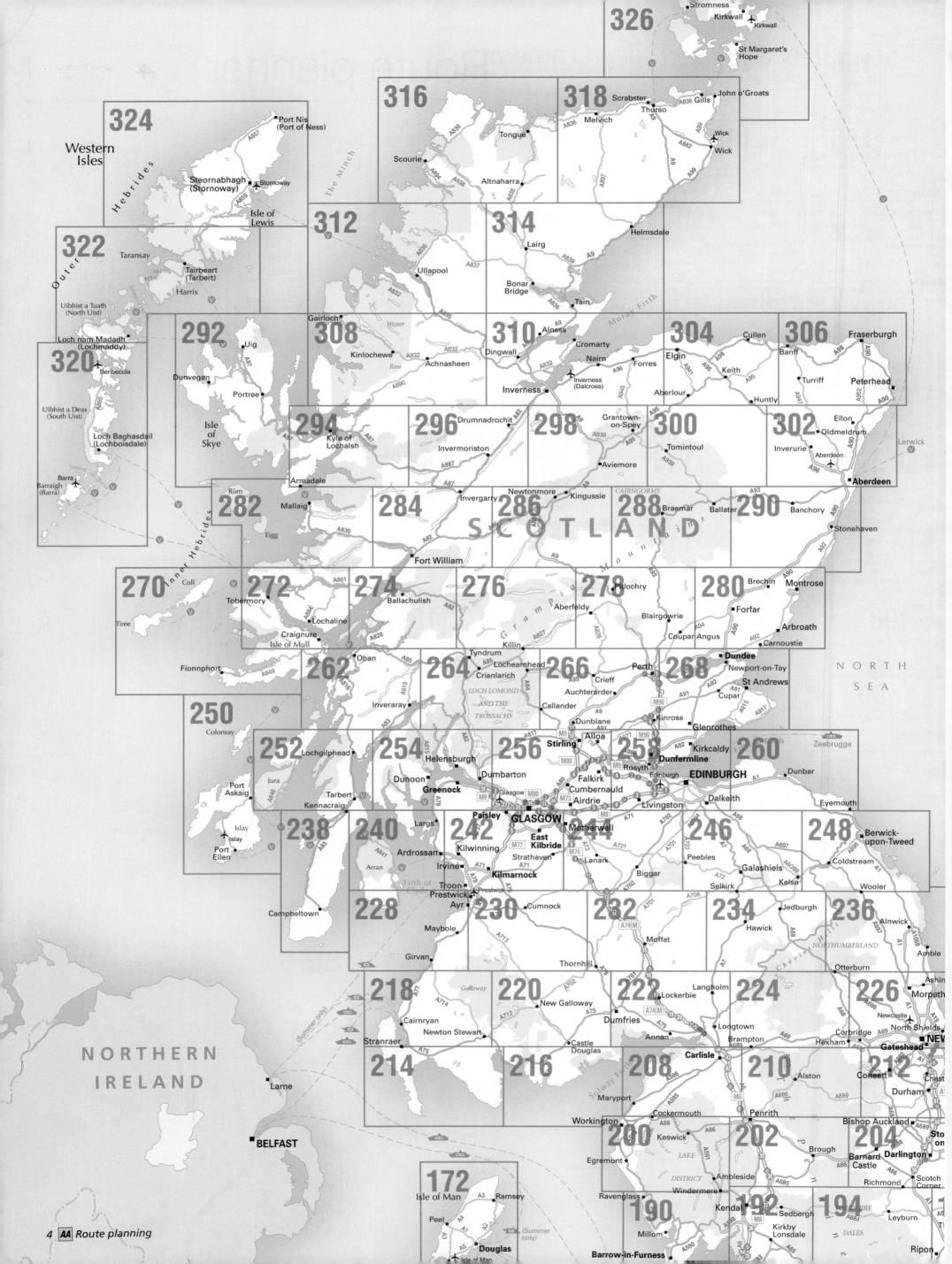

Road safety and fixed speed cameras

First, the advice you would expect from the AA – **breaking the speed limit is illegal and can cost lives**.

Keeping to the speed limit is not always easy and it only takes one momentary lapse of concentration to break the law. The AA Motoring Trust estimate that in 2005 more than 3 million drivers in the UK were fined for doing just that and that 26% of all households in Britain have received a speeding ticket.

Most fixed speed cameras are installed at accident 'black spots' where four or more fatal or serious road collisions have occurred over the previous three years. It is the policy of both the police and the Department for Transport to make the location of cameras as well known as possible. By showing speed camera locations in this atlas the AA is identifying the places where extra care should be taken while driving. Speeding is illegal and dangerous and you MUST keep within the speed limit at all times.

There are currently more than 3,000 fixed speed cameras in Britain. The map on this page gives an overview of where speed cameras occur in Britain and the road mapping in this atlas identifies their on-the-road locations.

 Gatso™　 **Truvelo™**　 **SPECS™**　 **Traffipax™**

Camera locations – read this before you use the atlas

1　The speed camera locations were correct at the time of finalising the information to go to press.

2　Camera locations are approximate due to limitations in the scale of road mapping used in this atlas.

3　In towns and urban areas speed camera locations are shown only on roads that appear on the road maps in this atlas.

4　Where two or more cameras occur close together a special symbol is used to indicate multiple cameras on the same stretch of road.

 This symbol is used on the mapping to identify **individual** camera locations

 This symbol is used on the mapping to identify **multiple** cameras on the same stretch of road

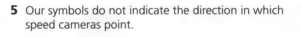

5　Our symbols do not indicate the direction in which speed cameras point.

6　On the mapping we symbolise more than 3,000 fixed camera locations. Mobile laser device locations cannot be shown.

Traffic signs giving orders

National speed limit applies

Speed limits can vary depending on the type of road and your vehicle. See *The Highway Code* rule 103.

30 Maximum speed

Information signs

Area in which cameras are used to enforce traffic regulations

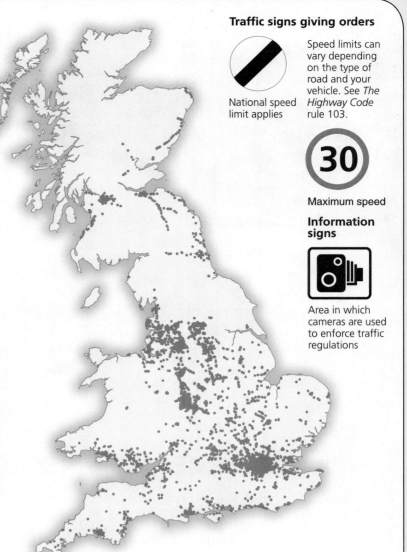

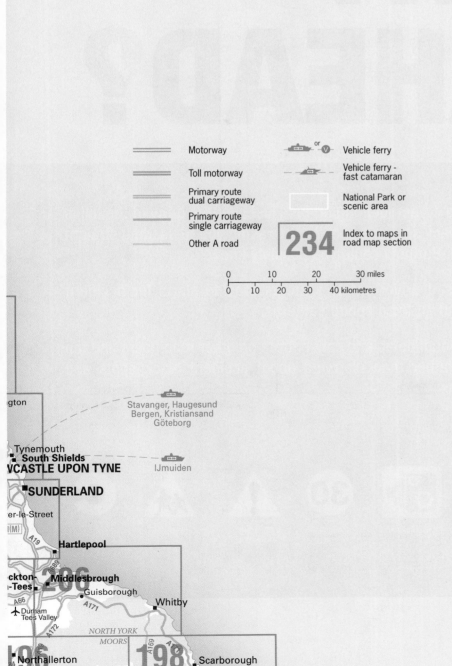

Motorway

Toll motorway

Primary route dual carriageway

Primary route single carriageway

Other A road

or ☐ Vehicle ferry

Vehicle ferry - fast catamaran

☐ National Park or scenic area

234 Index to maps in road map section

0　10　20　30 miles
0　10　20　30　40 kilometres

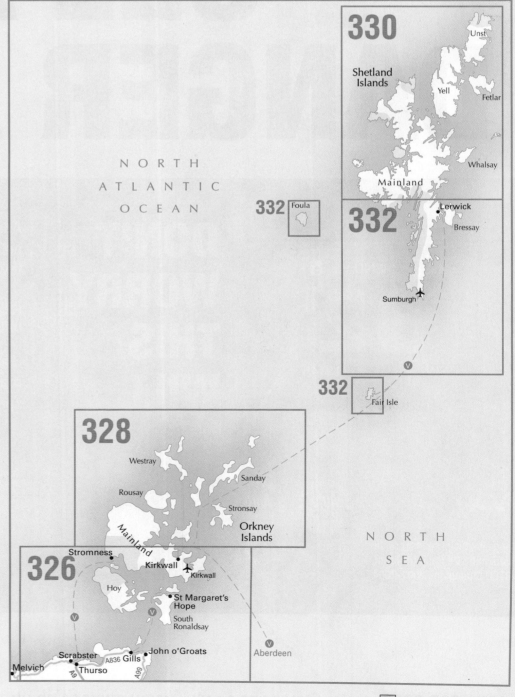

SEE ANY DANGER AHEAD?

DON'T WORRY, THIS WILL

Apart from the corner looming up fast, just over the brow of the hill is an accident black spot and speed camera and you're heading straight towards them. But how could you possibly know?

pogo GPS-based driver safety systems provide alerts for accident blackspots and all fixed speed cameras.

Use one and you'll be able to concentrate on other road users and the road ahead, rather than worrying about accident black spots and speed cameras.

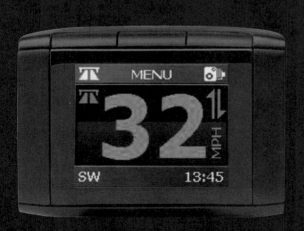

Road safety and mobile speed cameras

Breaking the speed limit is illegal and can cost lives. The AA advises drivers to follow the legal speed limit at all times.

Both the AA Motoring Trust and the Government believe that speed cameras should be operated within a transparent system. By providing information relating to road safety and speed hotspots, the AA believes that the driver is better placed to be aware of speed limits and can ensure adherence to them, thus making the roads safer for all users. For this reason the AA has compiled a list of more than 3,000 regularly policed mobile camera sites, based on official Department for Transport and regional Safety Camera Partnership sources.

The police also deploy mobile cameras at "exceptional sites", at new sites and also at roadworks where temporary speed limits apply. Due to the nature and purpose of mobile speed control devices the list cannot be exhaustive or completely accurate all of the time and **we advise drivers to always follow the signed speed limits**.

Speed limits

Type of vehicle	Built-up areas*	Elsewhere: Single carriageways	Elsewhere: Dual carriageways	Motorways
	MPH	MPH	MPH	MPH
Cars & motorcycles (including car derived vans up to 2 tonnes maximum laden weight)	30	60	70	70
Cars towing caravans or trailers (including car derived vans and motorcycles)	30	50	60	60
Buses & coaches (not exceeding 12 metres in overall length)	30	50	60	70
Goods vehicles (not exceeding 7.5 tonnes maximum laden weight)	30	50	60	70†
Goods vehicles (exceeding 7.5 tonnes maximum laden weight)	30	40	50	60

These are the national speed limits and apply to all roads unless signs show otherwise.
**The 30mph limit applies to all traffic on all roads in England and Wales (only class C and unclassified roads in Scotland) with street lighting unless signs show otherwise.*
†60 if articulated or towing a trailer

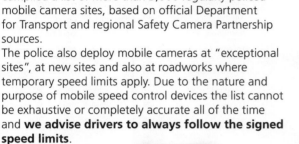

Britain's speed camera regions

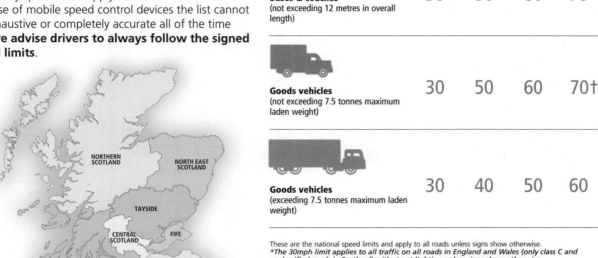

Road number	Location	Speed limit (mph)
ENGLAND		
Avon and Somerset		
M32	Bristol Stadium	60
A4	Anchor Rd, Bristol	30
A4	Keynsham Bypass (at A4175 jct, Durley Hill)	50
A4	Newbridge Rd, Bath	30
A4	Portway, Bristol (near Sea Mills)	50
A4	Portway, Bristol (near A4176 Bridge Valley Rd)	30
A4	Totterdown Bridge, Bristol	30
A30	Cricket St Thomas	50
A30	East Chinnock	30
A30	Roundham	40
A30	Sherborne Rd, Yeovil	30
A30	Hospital Roundabout, Yeovil	40
A37	Wells Rd, Bristol (near St John's La)	30
A37	Chilthorne Domer (eastbound)	60
A37	Emborough	50
A37	Fosse Way (north of Podimore Roundabout)	60
A37	Gurney Slade (northbound)	30
A37	Lydford, near Hornblotton	60
A37	Lydford	40
A37	Shepton Mallet	30
A37	Wells Rd, Bristol (near A4174 Airport Rd)	30
A38	Aztec West, Patchway (near Bradley Stoke Way)	40
A38	Bridgwater Rd, Bedminster Down, Bristol	40
A38	Churchill to Lower Langford	40
A38	Cross	40
A38	Bedminster Down Rd/West St, Bristol	30
A38	Bedminster Down Rd, Bristol (near Bishopsworth Rd)	40
A38	Cheltenham Rd/Gloucester Rd, Bristol (near Cranbrook Rd)	30
A38	East Reach/Toneway, Taunton	30
A38	Gloucester Rd, Patchway (near Highwood Rd)	40
A38	Gloucester Rd North, Patchway (near B4057 Gypsy Patch La)	40
A38	Redhill	50
A38	Stokes Croft, Bristol	30
A38	Bathpool	30
A38	Gloucester Rd, Bristol (near B4052 Ashley Down Rd)	30
A38	Heatherton Grange, Bradford-on-Tone	50
A38	North Petherton	30/40
A38	Pawlett (southbound)	50
A38	Rooks Bridge (eastbound)	30
A38	Taunton Rd, Bridgwater	30
A38	Wellington Rd, Taunton	30
A38	West Huntspill (northbound)	30
A39	Ashcott	30
A39	Bilbrook	30
A39	Chewton Mendip	30
A39	Coxley	40
A39	Green Ore (southbound)	50
A39	Walton	30
A39	Bath Rd, Horsey	40
A39	Bath Rd, Bridgwater	30
A39	North Broadway, Bridgwater (near A38, Taunton Rd)	30
A39	Quantock Rd, Bridgwater	30
A39	North Broadway/Broadway/ Monmouth St, Bridgwater	30
A46	Tormarton	60
A46	Dunkirk	50
A46	North of Nailsworth	40
A46	Shurdington	30
A303	Buckland St Mary	50
A303	Downhead (near Ilchester)	50
A303/A358	Southfields Roundabout	60
A303/A3088	Cartgate Roundabout	70
A357	Templecombe	30
A358	Ashill	60
A358	Donyatt	30
A358	Greenway Rd, Taunton	30
A358	Henlade	40
A358	Hornsbury Mill	40
A358	Pen Elm (3km west of Taunton)(southbound)	40
A358	Priorswood Rd, Taunton	30
A358	Staplegrove Rd, Taunton	30
A359	Mudford (northbound)	30
A361	Doulting	30
A361	Durston	40
A361	Frome Bypass	60
A361	Othery	30
A361	Pilton	30
A361	West Pennard	30
A362	Terry Hill (near A366 jct)	40
A367	Green Park Rd, Bath	30
A367	Wells Rd, Radstock	30
A367	Bear Flat, Bath	30
A369	Abbots Leigh	40
A369	Martcombe Rd, Easton-in-Gordano	60
A370	Beach Rd, Weston-super-Mare	30
A370	Cleeve Village	30
A370	Station Rd/Bristol Rd, Congresbury	30
A370	Flax Bourton (near B3130)	30
A370	Long Ashton Bypass, Bristol end	40
A370	Herluin Way, Weston-super-Mare (near Winterstoke Rd)	50
A370	Somerset Ave, Weston-super-Mare (M5 to A371)	50
A370	Winterstoke Rd, Weston-super-Mare	30
A371	Draycott	30
A371	Priestleigh (southbound)	40
A371	Sidcot La, Winscombe (near A38)	30
A372	Aller	30
A378	Curry Rivel	30
A378	Wrantage	40
A403	Avonmouth Docks	40
A420	Church Rd, Redfield, Bristol	30
A420	Clouds Hill Rd/Bell Hill Rd, St George, Bristol	30
A420	High St/London Rd, Warmley, Bristol	30
A420	Lawrence Hill, Bristol	30
A420	Old Market, Bristol (near Temple Way/Bond St)	30
A420	Two Mile Hill Rd/Regent St, Kingswood, Bristol	30
A420	Wick/Tog Hill	60
A432	Kendleshire	40
A432	Badminton Rd, Bristol (near A4174 Avon Ring Rd)	40
A432	Fishponds Rd, Bristol (near B4048 Lodge Causeway)	30
A432	Fishponds Rd, Bristol (at B4469 Muller Rd)	30
A432	Fishponds Rd, Bristol (near B4469 Royate Hill)	30
A432	Stapleton Rd, Bristol (near A4320 Easton Way)	30
A432	Station Rd/B4059 Stover Rd, Yate	30
A3027	North St/East St, Taunton	30
A3029	Avon Bridge, Bristol	40
A3039	Devonshire Rd, Weston-super-Mare	30
A3088	Lysander Rd, Yeovil	30
A3259	Monkton Heathfield	30
A4018	Black Boy Hill/Whiteladies Rd, Bristol	30
A4018	Catbrain (near Cribbs Causeway)	40
A4018	Cribbs Causeway (at jct 17 M5)	30
A4018	Falcondale Rd, Westbury-on-Trym, Bristol	30
A4018	Park Row/Perry Rd, Bristol	30
A4018	Passage Rd, Bristol (near B4057 Crow La)	40
A4018	Westbury Rd, Bristol (near B4054 North View)	30
A4018	Whiteladies Rd into Queens Rd, Bristol	30
A4044	Temple Way, Bristol	30
A4162	Sylvan Way/Dingle Rd/Canford La, Bristol	30
A4174	Avon Ring Rd (near M32 jct 1)	50
A4174	Avon Ring Rd, Bromley Heath (east of Overndale Rd)	50
A4174	Filton Rd/Avon Ring Rd (near Coldharbour La)	50
A4174	Hartcliffe Way, Bristol	30
A4174	Hengrove Way/Airport Rd, Bristol (near Creswicke Rd)	40
A4174	Station Rd, Filton (near Great Stoke Way)	40
A4320	St Philips Causeway, Bristol (near A4 Bath Rd)	30
B3124	Walton Rd, Clevedon	30
B3130	Stockway North/Chapel Ave, Nailsea	30
B3130	Wraxall	30/40
B3133	Central Way, Clevedon	30
B3139	Chilcompton	30
B3139	Mark Causeway	30/40
B3140	Coast Rd, Berrow	30
B3141	East Huntspill	30
B3151	Compton Dundon	30
B3151	Ilchester	30
B3151	Somerton Rd, Street	30
B3153	Keinton Mandeville	30
B3170	Shoreditch Rd, Taunton	30
B3440	Locking Rd, Weston-super-Mare	30
B3440	Locking Rd/Regent St/Alexandra Pde, Weston-super-Mare	30
B4054	Avonmouth Rd, Bristol	30
B4054	Linden Rd, Westbury Park, Bristol	30
B4054	Shirehampton Rd, Sea Mills, Bristol	30
B4056	Southmead Rd, Bristol	30
B4057	Gypsy Patch La, Stoke Gifford (near Hatchet Rd)	30
B4057	Winterbourne Rd, Great Stoke (near B4427)	50
B4058	Frenchay Park Rd, Bristol	30
B4058	Winterbourne Hill/High St, Winterbourne	30
B4059	Goose Green Way, Yate	30
B4060	Station Rd/Bowling Hill/ Rounceval St, Yate/Chipping Sodbury	30
B4061	Bristol Rd, Thornbury	30
B4465	Staplehill Rd/High St, Fishponds, Bristol	30
B4465	Broad St, Mangotsfield, Bristol	30
-	Bradley Stoke, Little Stoke La	30
-	Bristol, Bishport Ave, Hartcliffe	30
-	Bristol, Broadwalk, Knowle	30
-	Bristol, Hawkfield Rd, Hartcliffe (near A4174 Hengrove Way)	30
-	Bristol, Kingsway, St George	30
-	Bristol, Long Cross, Lawrence Weston	30
-	Bristol, Northumbria Dr, Westbury Park	30
-	Bristol, Redcliffe Way	30
-	Bristol, Stoke Hill/Stoke Rd, Clifton (near Saville Rd)	30
-	Bristol, Sturminster Rd, Stockwood	30
-	Bristol, Whitchurch La (near Dundry Rd)	30
-	Bristol, Whitchurch La/Hareclive Rd, Bishopsworth	30
-	Taunton, Cheddon Rd	30
-	Taunton, Chestnut Dr	30
-	Taunton, Lisieux Way	30
-	Taunton, Trull Rd	30
-	Watergore, Harp Rd (near Over Stratton)	50
-	Yeovil, Combe St	30
Bedfordshire and Luton		
A5	Battlesden	60
A5	Hockliffe	40
A5	Kensworth (near B4540)	60
A6	High St, Clapham (near Highbury Grove)	30
A6	High St, Clapham (near Mount Pleasant Rd)	30
A6	New Bedford Rd, Luton (near Alexandra Ave)	30
A6	New Bedford Rd, Luton (near Brook St)	30
A6	Pulloxhill	60
A6	Silsoe	60
A6	Silsoe (near Gravenhurst turn)	60
A421	Aspley Guise	60
A421	Brogborough	50
A428	Bromham Rd, Bedford	30
A428	Goldington Rd, Bedford	30
A505	Leighton Buzzard Bypass (near Grovebury Rd)	60
A505	Park Viaduct, Luton	30
A505	Tilsworth	60
A507	Shefford Bypass	60
A603	Cardington Rd, Bedford (near Mareth Rd)	30
A603	Cardington Rd, Bedford (near Lovell Rd)	30
A603	Willington	40
A1081	Airport Way, Capability Green, Luton	70
A1081	Airport Way, Gipsy Lane, Luton	60
A4146	Billington Rd, Leighton Buzzard	30
A5120	Ampthill Rd, Flitwick	30
A5120	Dunstable Rd, Flitwick	30
A5120	Bedford Rd, Houghton Regis	40
A5120	Station Rd, Toddington	30
A5134	High St, Kempston	30
B530	Houghton Conquest	60
B531	Bedford Rd, Kempston (Bunyan Rd to Beatrice Rd)	30
B1040	Potton Rd, Biggleswade	30
-	Bedford, Park Ave	30
-	Bedford, Roff Ave	30
-	Bromham, Stagsden Rd	30
-	Cranfield, High St	30
-	Luton, Crawley Green Rd (near Devon Rd)	30
-	Luton, Crawley Green Rd (near Leygreen Cl)	30
-	Luton, Dunstable Rd (near Beechwood Rd)	30
-	Luton, Leagrave High St (near Emerald Rd)	30
-	Luton, Leagrave High St (near Pastures Way)	30
-	Luton, Waller Ave (near Chester Ave)	30
-	Luton, Waller Ave (near Chiltern Gdns)	30
-	Luton, Whitehorse Vale	30
Cambridgeshire		
A1	Little Paxton to Southoe (northbound)	NSL
A1	South of Carpenter's Lodge Roundabout (B1081, south of Stamford)(northbound)	NSL
A14	Bottisham (westbound)	NSL
A14	Bythorn/Molesworth (eastbound)	NSL
A14	Ellington (eastbound)	NSL
A14	Fen Ditton	NSL
A14	Girton to jct 31 (A1307) (westbound)	NSL
A14	East of jct 35 (A1303) (westbound)	NSL
A14	North-east of jct 36 (A11) (eastbound)	NSL
A14	2km west of A1 to Brampton Hut Roundabout (eastbound)	NSL
A14	Jct 16 to 17 (eastbound)	NSL
A14	Jct 18 to 19 (westbound)	NSL
A14	Jct 23 (Spittalls Interchange) (eastbound)	NSL
A15	London Rd, Peterborough (New Rd to Rivergate)	30
A15	Paston Pkwy, Peterborough (northbound)	NSL
A47	Soke Pkwy, Peterborough (eastbound)	NSL
A47	Thorney Toll (and to west)	NSL
A141	Clews Corner	NSL
A141	At B1040 jct, south of Warboys (southbound)	NSL
A141	Wimblington/ Doddington Bypass	NSL
A142	Soham Bypass (southbound)	NSL
A142	Witchford Bypass (eastbound)	NSL
A605	Kings Dyke (west of Whittlesey)	40
A1073	Masons Bridge/Steam House Farm (north of Eye) (northbound)	NSL
A1123	Bluntisham, at Hedgerows Nursery	NSL
A1123	Houghton Hill, St Ives, east of B1090 (eastbound)	40
A1123	Wilburton bends to east of village	40
A1307	Bartlow Crossroads (dual carriageway)	NSL
A1307	Hills Rd, Cambridge (Gonville Pl to Worts' Cswy)(southbound)	30
A1307	Linton Bypass (westbound)	NSL
B645	Tilbrook bends	40
Cheshire		
A50	Knutsford Rd, Grappenhall, Warrington (B5157 Heath Field Park to Cliff La)	30
A50	Manchester Rd/Toft Rd, Knutsford (Woodvale Rd to Garden Rd)	30
A50	Long La, Warrington (Fisher Ave to Longfield Rd)	30
A54	Kelsall Rd, Ashton	60
A56	Camsley La, Lymm (Deans La to M6 overbridge)	40
A57	New Manchester Rd, Paddington, Warrington (Larkfield Ave to Greymist Ave)	40
A523	London Rd, Poynton (South Park Dr to Clifford Rd)	30
A532	West St, Crewe (Marshfield Ave to Peel St)	30
A533	Booth La, Middlewich	40
A533	Northwich Rd, Runcorn (Chester Rd to Rivington Rd)	30
A537	Buxton Rd, near Wildboarclough (100m north-west of Buxton Old Rd to 100m west of A54)	50
A5019	Mill St, Crewe	30
A5032	Chester Rd, Whitby, Ellesmere Port (A5117 to 130m south of Dunkirk La)	30
A5034	Mereside Rd, Mere	60
A5104	Hough Green, Chester (Cliveden Rd to Curzon Park)	30
B5071	Gresty Rd, Crewe (South St to 500m south of Davenport Ave)	30
B5078	Sandbach Rd North, Alsager (The Avenue to Leicester Ave)	30
B5082	Middlewich Rd, Northwich (East Ave to Pullman Dr)	30
B5132	Overpool Rd, Ellesmere Port (Sutton Way to Netherpool Rd)	30
B5463	Station Rd, Little Sutton	30
B5470	Rainow Rd, Macclesfield (Fence Ave to Well La)	30
-	Burtonwood, Lumber La (Green La to Melrose Ave)	30
-	Ellesmere Port, Overpool Rd (Wycliffe Rd to Fairview Rd)	30
-	Runcorn, Astmoor Rd (Lister Rd to Chadwick Rd)	40
-	Runcorn, Boston Ave (Morval Cres to Heath Rd)	30
-	Runcorn, Clifton Rd (Greenway Rd to Beaufort Close)	30
-	Runcorn, Halton Rd (Daresbury Expressway overbridge to Boston Ave)	30
-	Runcorn, Heath Rd (Halton Rd to Boston Ave)	30
-	Runcorn, Warrington Rd (Manor Park to Eastgate Rd)	30
-	Warrington, Battersby La, Howley (A49 roundabout to A574 March House La)	30
-	Warrington, Harpers Rd, Fearnhead (Pasture La to Freshfield Dr)	30
-	Warrington, Lovely La, Whitecross (Monks St to Clap Gates Rd)	30
-	Widnes, Birchfield Rd (Pit La to Rose View Ave)	30
-	Widnes, Hough Green Rd (Liverpool Rd to Arley Dr)	30
-	Widnes, Prescot Rd, Hough Green (Hough Green Rd to borough boundary)	30
-	Wilmslow, Hough La (northern end)	30
-	Winsford, Bradford La (either side of School Rd)	40
-	Winsford, St John's Dr/ Woodford La (Brunner Pl to Grove Cl)	30
Cleveland		
A135	Yarm Rd, Eaglescliffe	30
A171	Charltons (near Margrove Park)	50
A171	Ormesby Bank, Ormesby	30
A172	Marton Rd, Middlesbrough (Longlands to St Lukes)	30
A172	Marton Rd, Middlesbrough (St Lukes to Marton crossroads)	40
A172	Dixons Bank, Nunthorpe (Guisborough Rd to Captain Cook's Cres)	40
A174	Carlin How	30
A177	From Savacentre to county boundary, Stockton-on-Tees	50/60
A178	Coronation Drive, Hartlepool	40/30
A178	The Front, Seaton Carew	30
A179	Easington Rd/Powlett Rd, Hartlepool	30/40/50
A689	Stockton Rd, Hartlepool (from Sappers Corner)	50/40
A1027	Bishopton Ave, Stockton-on-Tees	40
A1032	Acklam Rd, Brookfield (Blue Bell to Crematorium)	40
A1032	Acklam Rd, Linthorpe	30
A1042	Kirkleatham La, Redcar	30/40
A1085	High St, Marske-by-the-Sea	30
A1130	Acklam Rd, Thornaby-on-Tees	30
A1130	Mandale Rd, Acklam	30
B1269	Redcar La, Redcar	30
B1274	Junction Rd, Stockton-on-Tees	30
B1276	Seaton La, Hartlepool	30
B1276	Station La, Seaton Carew	30
B1380	High St, Eston	30
B1380	Ladgate La, Marton (Marton crossroads to Ormesby Rd)	40
B1380	Normanby Rd, Ormesby	30
-	Acklam, Trimdon Ave	30
-	Billingham, Thames Rd	30
-	Billingham, White House Rd	30
-	Dormanstown, Broadway	30
-	Eston, Church La	30
-	Eston, Normanby Rd	30
-	Hartlepool, Catcote Rd	30
-	Hartlepool, Owton Manor La	30
-	Hartlepool, Oxford Rd	30
-	Hartlepool, Raby Rd	30
-	Hartlepool, Throston Grange La	30
-	Hartlepool, Winterbottom Ave	30
-	Hartlepool, Wynyard Rd	30
-	Marske, Redcar Rd	30
-	Normandy, Bankfields Rd	30
-	Normandy, Flatts La	30
-	Park End, Ormesby Rd	30
-	Redcar, Greenstones Rd	30
-	Redcar, West Dyke Rd	30
-	Stanghow, Stanghow Rd	30
-	Stockton-on-Tees, Bishopton Rd West	30
-	Stockton-on-Tees, Darlington La	30
-	Stockton-on-Tees, Harrowgate La	30
-	Thornaby-on-Tees, Cunningham Ave	30
-	Thornaby-on-Tees, Thornaby Rd	30
Cumbria		
M6	Jct 36 to 40	NSL
A6	London Rd, Carlisle	30
A6	Milnthorpe Rd, Kendal	30
A6	Shap Rd, Kendal	30
A6	Scotland Rd, Penrith	30
A6	Garnett Bridge north to Hollowgate	60
A6	Thiefside (south of High Hesket)	60
A7	Westlinton crossroads	60
A65	Burton Rd/Lound Rd, Kendal	30
A65	Devil's Bridge, Kirby Lonsdale	40
A65	Hollin Hall to Hornsbarrow, Kirkby Lonsdale	60
A66	Brough Hill, Warcop	60

Road number	Location	Speed limit (mph)
A66	Brigham/Broughton to Bridgefoot	60
A66	Crackenthorpe	60
A66	Dubwath/Bassenthwaite Lake	60
A66	Sandford road ends	60
A66	Troutbeck/Mungrisdale	60
A69	Aglionby (west of Warwick, single carr)	60
A69	Scarrow Hill (near Lanercost)	60
A74	Floriston (Todhills to River Esk)	70
A590	Bouth road ends	60
A590	Heaves Hotel/Levens/Gilpin Bridge	70
A590	Haverthwaite/Backbarrow	60
A590	Newland, Ulverston	60
A592	Rayrigg Rd, Bowness	30/40
A595	Greenhill Hotel, Red Dial	60
A595	Loop Rd, Whitehaven	40
A595	West Woodside/ Curthwaite jct	60
A595	Wigton Rd, Carlisle	30
A595	Wreaks End, Broughton-in-Furness	60
A596	Micklethwaite	60
A683	Cautley to Middleton	60
A685	Appleby Rd, Kendal	30
A686	Edenhall to Gilderdale Forest	60
A5087	Ulverston	30
B5277	Lindale Rd, Grange-over-Sands	30
B5299	Dalston Rd, Carlisle	40
-	Barrow-in-Furness, Abbey Rd	30
-	Barrow-in-Furness, Michelson Rd	30
-	Carlisle, Blackwell Rd/Durdar Rd	30

Derbyshire

Road number	Location	Speed limit (mph)
A6	Allestree, Derby	30
A6	Bakewell	30
A6	Belper	30
A6	London Rd, Derby	30
A6	Taddington to Buxton	50
A52	Ashbourne Rd, Derby	30
A52	Main Rd, Brailsford	30
A52	Mackworth, Derby	40
A53	St John's Rd, Buxton	30
A61	Main Rd, Shirland	30
A511	Station Rd, Hatton	30
A514	Derby Rd, Chellaston	30
A514	Swadlincote to Hartshorne	40
A514	Swadlincote	30
A514	Ticknall	30
A608	Smalley	30
A609	Kilburn Rd, Belper	30
A609	Kilburn to Horsley Woodhouse	30
A616	Clowne	30
A616	Cresswell	30
A617	Bramley Vale	40
A617	Glapwell to Pleasley	60
A618	Rotherham Rd, Killamarsh	30
A623	Stoney Middleton	30
A626	Marple Rd, Chisworth	30
A632	Bolsover (west)	30
A632	Langwith Rd, Bolsover	30
A632	Matlock	30
A632	Chesterfield Rd, Matlock	40
A5111	Raynesway, Derby (near West Service Rd)	n/a
A5132	Twyford Rd, Willington	40
A5250	Burton Rd, Derby	30
A5250	Burton Rd, Littleover, Derby	30
A6005	Draycott to Breaston	30
A6005	Draycott Rd, Borrowash	40
A6005	Nottingham Rd, Borrowash	30
A6007	Codnor to Heanor	30
A6016	Primrose La, Glossop	30
A6175	Holmewood	30
A6187	Sheffield Rd, Hathersage	30
A6187	Hope	30
B5008	Burton Rd, Repton	40
B5010	London Rd, Shardlow	30
B5036	Cromford Hill, Cromford	30
B5353	Park Rd, Newhall, Swadlincote	n/a
B5353	Union Rd/High St, Swadlincote	30
B6013	Far Laund, Belper	40
B6019	Alfreton Rd, Pinxton	30
B6051	Newbold Rd, Chesterfield	30
B6051	Newbold Rd, Newbold, Chesterfield	n/a
B6052	Whittington, Chesterfield	n/a
B6053	Eckington Rd, Staveley	30
B6057	Chesterfield Rd, Dronfield	n/a
B6062	Chinley	30
B6158	Green La, Coal Aston	30
B6179	Little Eaton	30
B6179	Lower Kilburn	40
B6179	Lower Kilburn to Little Eaton	50
B6179	Ripley to Marehay	30
B6419	Shuttlewood Rd, Shuttlewood	30
-	Bolsover, Mansfield Rd, Hillstown	30
-	Bolsover, Portland Ave	30
-	Borrowash, Victoria Ave	30
-	Brimington, Troughbrook Rd, Hollingwood	30
-	Charlesworth, Long La	30
-	Chesterfield, Ashgate Rd	30
-	Chesterfield, Boythorpe Rd	30
-	Chesterfield, Brockwell La	30
-	Chesterfield, Hawksley Ave	30
-	Chesterfield, Linacre Rd	30
-	Chesterfield, Old Rd	30
-	Chesterfield, Pennine Way	30
-	Chesterfield, Whitecotes La	30
-	Denby, Loscoe-Denby La	30
-	Denby, Street La	30
-	Derby, Acorn Way	40
-	Derby, Blagreaves La	30
-	Derby, Haven Baulk La, Littleover	30
-	Derby, Kedleston Rd	30
-	Derby, Ladybank Rd	30
-	Derby, Sinfin La	30
-	Derby, Stenson Rd	30
-	Derby, Stenson Rd, Stenson Fields	40
-	Derby, Wood Rd, Chaddesden	30
-	Derby, Wragley Way	30
-	Draycott, Sawley Rd	30
-	Ilkeston, Corporation Rd	30
-	Ilkeston, Quarry Hill Rd	30
-	Langley Mill, Cromford Rd	30
-	Langley Mill, Upper Dunstead Rd	30
-	Long Eaton, Draycott Rd, Sawley	30
-	New Whittington, Handley Rd	30
-	Old Brampton, Ashgate Rd	30
-	Pleasley, Newboundmill La	30
-	Ripley, Peasehill Rd	30
-	Ripley, Steam Mill La	30
-	Risley, Bostock's La	30
-	Shirland, Park La	30
-	Swadlincote, Church Ave	30
-	Swadlincote, Common Rd, Church Gresley	30
-	Swadlincote, Hearthcote Rd	30
-	Swadlincote, Midland Rd	30
-	Swadlincote, Sandcliffe Rd	30
-	Swanwick, Sleetmoor La	30

Devon and Cornwall

Road number	Location	Speed limit (mph)
A30	Chiverton Cross (A390/A3075 jct)	60
A30	Highgate	70
A30	Highgate Hill (A392 jct)	70
A30	Monkton	70
A30	Sowton	40
A30	Temple	60
A38	Lee Mill	70
A38	Near Lower Clicker (B3251 jct, south-east of Liskeard)	70
A38	Deep Lane jct, Plympton	70
A38	Smithaleigh (4km west of Ivybridge)	70
A38	Smithaleigh (overbridge) (4km west of Ivybridge)	70
A38	Wrangaton-Bittaford straight	70
A39	Barras Moor (near Perranarworthal)	60
A39	Perranarworthal	40
A39	Valley Truckle, Camelford	30
A361	Ashford	50
A361	Eastern Ave, Barnstaple	30
A361	Knowle	40
A361	Knowle (Westerland)	30
A361	Wrafton	30
A374	Plymouth Rd, Plymouth	40
A374	Antony Rd, Torpoint	30
A376	Ebford	30
A376	Exeter Rd, Exmouth	30
A377	Copplestone	30
A377	Western Rd, Crediton	30
A377	Alphington Rd, Exeter	30
A379	Brixton	30
A379	Dartmouth Rd, Paignton	30
A379	The Strand, Starcross	30
A379	Teignmouth Rd, Teignmouth	30
A379	Babbacombe Rd, Torquay	30
A379	Yealmpton	30
A380	Newton Rd, Kingskerswell	40
A381	East St, Newton Abbot	30
A385	Totnes Rd, Collaton St Mary	30
A385	Ashburton Rd, Totnes	30
A386	Chub Tor (2km south of Yelverton)	60
A386	Outland Rd, Plymouth	30
A386	Roborough Down, Plymouth	60
A386	Tavistock Rd, Plymouth	40
A388	Kelly Bray (north of Callington)	30
A390	Penstraze (1.5km east of A39)	60
A390	Sticker Bypass	60
A394	Kenneggy Downs (near Praa Sands)	40
A396	Rewe	30
A396	Exeter Rd, Stoke Canon	30
A3015	Topsham Rd, Exeter	30
A3047	Trevenson Rd, Pool, Camborne	30
A3047	Tuckingmill, Camborne	30
A3058	Trewoon	30
A3064	St Budeaux Bypass, Plymouth	30
A3074	Carbis Bay, St Ives	30
A3075	Rosecliston, near Newquay	60
B3165	Crewkerne Rd, Raymonds Hill (near A35)	30
B3174	Barrack Rd, Ottery St Mary	30
B3183	Heavitree Rd, Exeter	30
B3183	New North Rd, Exeter	30
B3212	Dunsford Rd, Exeter	30
B3212	Pinhoe Rd, Exeter	30
B3213	Wrangaton village	30
B3233	Bickington Rd, Barnstaple	30
B3250	North Hill, Plymouth	30
B3284	Liskey, Perranporth	30/60
B3344	Station Hill, Chudleigh	30
B3396	Milehouse Rd, Plymouth	30
B3416	Glen Rd, Plympton	30
B3432	Novorossisk Rd, Plymouth	40
-	Avonwick village	30
-	Castle-an-Dinas, (4km east of St Columb Major)	60
-	Exeter, Buddle La	30
-	Exeter, Exwick La	30
-	Fraddon village	30
-	Ivybridge, Exeter Rd	30
-	Paignton, Colley End Rd	30
-	Paignton, Preston Down Rd	30
-	Plymouth, Beacon Park Rd	30
-	Plymouth, Church Hill, Eggbuckland	30
-	Plymouth, Devonport Rd, Stoke	30
-	Plymouth, Eggbuckland Rd	30
-	Plymouth, Glen Rd	30
-	Plymouth, Grenville Rd, St Judes	30
-	Plymouth, Haye Rd, Elburton	30
-	Plymouth, Honicknowle La	30
-	Plymouth, Lipson Rd	30
-	Plymouth, Mannamead Rd	30
-	Plymouth, Molesworth Rd	30
-	Plymouth, North Prospect Rd	30
-	Plymouth, Pomphlett Rd	30
-	Plymouth, Shakespeare Rd, Honicknowle	30
-	Plymouth, Southway Dr	30
-	Plymouth, St Levan Rd	30
-	Plymouth, Tamerton Foliot Rd	30
-	Plymouth, Union St	30
-	Plymouth, Weston Park Rd	30
-	Plymouth, Wolseley Rd	30
-	Saltash, Callington Rd	30

Dorset

Road number	Location	Speed limit (mph)
A30	Babylon Hill (1.5km east of Yeovil)	70
A30	Long Cross, Shaftesbury	30
A31	East of Boundary La Roundabout, St Leonards	70
A35	Sea Rd South, Bridport	50
A35	Christchurch Bypass	70
A35	Lyndhurst Rd, Christchurch	60
A35	Friary Press, west of Dorchester	60
A35	Kingston Russell	60
A35	Baker's Arms Roundabout, Lytchett Minster, to roundabout with A350	70
A35	Organford	70
A35	Upton Rd, Poole	40
A35	Near Sherford/Slepe	60
A35	Vinney Cross (near Uploders)	60
A35	Whiteway Cross (2.5km west of Kingston Russell)	60
A35	Woodbury Cross (1.5km east of Bere Regis)	60
A37	Staggs Folly (near Chalmington)	60
A37	Long Ash La, Frampton	60
A37	Wardon Hill (near Frome St Quintin)	60
A37	Holywell Cross, Holywell	60
A338	Spur Rd (north of Hurn)	70
A338	Wessex Way, Cooper Dean, Bournemouth	50
A348	Ringwood Rd, Bear Cross, Bournemouth	40
A349	Gravel Hill, Poole	40
A350	Holes Bay Rd, Poole	50
A350	Poole Rd, Poole	60
A350	Shaston Rd, Stourpaine	30
A350	Upton Country Park to A35 jct	70
A352	Dorchester Rd, Wool	30
A354	Dorchester Rd, Ridgeway Hill (3km south of A35)	60
A354	Dorchester Rd (Manor Roundabout to Weymouth Hospital)	30
A354	Dorchester Rd, Redlands, Weymouth	40
A354	Buxton Rd, Weymouth	30
A354	Dorchester Rd, Upwey	30
B3065	Pinecliff Rd, Poole	30
B3065	The Avenue, Poole	30
B3073	Christchurch Rd, West Parley	30
B3073	Oakley Hill, Wimborne Minster	30
B3074	Higher Blandford Rd, Broadstone, Poole	30
B3082	Blandford Rd (near Badbury Rings)	60
B3092	Colesbrook, Gillingham	40
B3157	Chickerell Rd, Weymouth	30
B3157	Portesham	30
B3157	Lanehouse Rocks Rd, Weymouth	30
B3157	Limekiln Hill, West Bexington	50
B3369	Sandbanks Rd, Poole	30
B3369	Shore Rd, Poole	30
-	Blandford Forum, Salisbury Rd	30
-	Bournemouth, Branksome Wood Rd	30
-	Bournemouth, Carbery Ave	30
-	Bournemouth, Littledown Ave	30
-	Bournemouth, Petersfield Rd	30
-	Bournemouth, Southbourne Overcliff Dr	30
-	Ferndown, Wimborne Rd West, Stapehill	40
-	Poole, Herbert Ave	30
-	Poole, Old Wareham Rd	30
-	Portland, Weston Rd	30
-	Upton, Poole Rd	30
-	Weymouth, Dorchester Rd	30

Durham Constabulary area

Road number	Location	Speed limit (mph)
A66	Bowes Moor/Galley Bank/Greta Bridge	n/a
A67	Conniscliffe, Darlington	n/a
A167	North Lodge, Chester-le-Street	n/a
A167	North Rd, Darlington	n/a
A167	Whitesmocks and Tollhouse Rd, Durham	n/a
A690	Low Willington up to West Rd, Crook	n/a
A690	West Rainton, Durham	n/a
A1086	Horden south to county boundary	n/a
B6280	Yarm Rd, Darlington	n/a
B6168	Annfield Plain (A692 to A693)	n/a
B6282	Etherley, Bishop Auckland	n/a
B6284	Ediscum Garth, Bishop Auckland	n/a
B6288	Spennymoor to A167 Croxdale	n/a
-	Darlington, McMullen Rd	n/a
-	Durham, Finchale Rd	n/a
-	Peterlee, Essington Way	n/a

Essex

Road number	Location	Speed limit (mph)
A12	Overbridge, near Kelvedon interchange	70
A13	High St, Hadleigh (towards London)	30
A13	London Rd, Leigh-on-Sea	30
A13	North Shoebury	n/a
A13	Bournes Green Chase, Southend-on-Sea	30
A13	Southchurch Blvd, Southend-on-Sea	n/a
A112	Sewardstone Rd, Waltham Abbey	n/a
A113	High Rd, Chigwell	30
A120	Harwich Rd, (Wix Arch Cottages to Cansey La, Goose Green)	n/a
A120	Horsley Cross (south-west to Park Rd)	n/a
A121	Goldings Hill, Loughton (at Monkchester Cl)	30
A121	High Rd, Loughton	n/a
A121	Farm Hill Rd, Waltham Abbey	n/a
A126	London Rd, Grays	30
A126	Montreal Rd, Tilbury	30
A126	London Rd, West Thurrock	30
A128	High St, Chipping Ongar	n/a
A128	Brentwood Rd, Ingrave/ Herongate	30
A129	Crays Hill, Basildon	30
A129	Southend Rd, Billericay	n/a
A129	London Rd, Rayleigh	30
A129	London Rd, Wickford	30
A129	Southend Rd, Wickford	n/a
A130	Long Rd, Canvey Island	30
A130	Canvey Way, South Benfleet	n/a
A133	Clacton Rd, Elmstead Market	30
A133	Colchester Rd, (near Weeley)	n/a
A134	Nayland Rd, Great Horkesley	40
A137	Wignall St, Lawford	30
A414	Malden Rd, Danbury	n/a
A1016	Waterhouse La, Chelmsford	30
A1017	Swan St, Sible Hedingham	30
A1023	London Rd, Brentwood	30
A1023	Shenfield Rd, Brentwood	30
A1025	Second Ave, Harlow	40
A1025	Third Ave, Harlow	40
A1060	Lower Rd, Little Hallingbury	n/a
A1090	London Rd, Purfleet	30
A1090	Tank Hill Rd, Purfleet	30
A1124	Lexden Rd, Colchester	30
A1158	Southbourne Grove, Westcliff-on-Sea	30
A1168	Rectory La, Loughton	30
A1169	Southern Way, Harlow	40
A1232	Ipswich Rd, Colchester	n/a
A1235	Cranes Farm Rd, Basildon (at Honywood Rd)	40
B170	Chigwell Rise, Chigwell	n/a
B170	Roding La, Loughton	n/a
B172	Coppice Row, Theydon Bois	n/a
B173	Lambourne Rd, Chigwell	n/a
B184	Snow Hill, Great Easton	40
B186	South Rd, South Ockendon	30
B1002	Ingatestone High St, Ingatestone	30
B1007	Laindon Rd, Billericay (near School Rd)	30
B1007	Stock Rd, Billericay	30
B1007	Galleywood Rd, Chelmsford	n/a
B1007	Stock Rd, Chelmsford	40
B1008	Broomfield Rd, Chelmsford	30
B1013	Main Rd, Hawkwell	30
B1013	Southend Rd, Hockley/Hawkwell	30
B1013	High Rd, Rayleigh	n/a
B1013	Hockley Rd, Rayleigh	30
B1014	Benfleet Rd, South Benfleet	30
B1018	The Street, Latchingdon	30
B1018	The Causeway, Maldon	30
B1019	Maldon Rd, Hatfield Peveral	30
B1021	Church Rd, Burnham-on-Crouch	n/a
B1022	Maldon Rd, Colchester	30
B1022	Shrub End Rd, Colchester	30
B1022	Maldon Rd, Heckfordbridge	30
B1022	Colchester Rd, Maldon	30
B1022	Maldon Rd, Tiptree Heath	30
B1027	St Osyth Rd, Alresford	40
B1027	St John's Rd, Clacton-on-Sea	30
B1027	Valley Rd/Old Rd, Clacton-on-Sea	30
B1027	Pump Hill, St Osyth	30
B1027	Brightlingsea Rd, (near Wivenhoe)	40
B1028	Colchester Rd, Wivenhoe	30
B1028	The Avenue, Wivenhoe	30
B1033	Frinton Rd, Kirby Cross	30
B1256	Coggeshall Rd, Braintree	n/a
B1335	Stifford Rd, South Ockendon	40
B1352	Main Rd, Harwich	30
B1383	London Rd, Newport	30
B1383	Cambridge Rd, Stansted Mountfitchet	n/a
B1389	Colchester Rd, Witham	30
B1389	Hatfield Rd, Witham	30
B1393	High Rd, Epping	30
B1393	Palmers Hill, Epping	30
B1441	London Rd, Clacton-on-Sea	30
B1441	Clacton Rd, Weeley Heath	n/a
B1442	Thorpe Rd, Clacton-on-Sea	30
B1464	London Rd, Bowers Gifford	30
-	Aveley, Purfleet Rd	30
-	Aveley, Romford Rd	n/a
-	Basildon, Ashlyns	30
-	Basildon, Sandon Rd, Barstable	30
-	Basildon, Clayhill Rd	30
-	Basildon, Felmores	30
-	Basildon, High Rd, Langdon Hills	30
-	Basildon, Durham Rd, Laindon	30
-	Basildon, Nightingales, Laindon	30
-	Basildon, Wash Rd, Laindon	30
-	Basildon, Rectory Rd, Pitsea	30
-	Basildon, Vange Hill Dr	30
-	Basildon, Wickford Ave	30
-	Basildon, Whitmore Way	30
-	Billericay, Mountnessing Rd	30
-	Braintree, Coldnailhurst Ave (Alexander Rd towards Church La)	30
-	Brentwood, Chelmsford Rd	30
-	Brentwood, Eagle Way (Clive Rd to Warley Rd)	30
-	Buckhurst Hill, Buckhurst Way/ Albert Rd	30
-	Canvey Island, Dovervelt Rd	30
-	Canvey Island, Link Rd	30
-	Canvey Island, Thorney Bay Rd	30
-	Chadwell St Mary, Brentwood Rd	n/a
-	Chadwell St Mary, Linford Rd	30
-	Chadwell St Mary, Riverview	30
-	Chelmsford, Baddow Rd	30
-	Chelmsford, Chignall Rd	30
-	Chelmsford, Copperfield Rd	30
-	Chelmsford, Longstomps Ave	30
-	Chelmsford, New Bowers Way, Springfield	30
-	Clacton-on-Sea, Burrs Rd	30
-	Clacton-on-Sea, Kings Parade	30
-	Clacton-on-Sea, Marine Parade East,	30
-	Clacton-on-Sea, St Osyth Rd, Rush Green	n/a
-	Colchester, Abbot's Rd	30
-	Colchester, Avon Way	30
-	Colchester, Bromley Rd	30
-	Colchester, Old Heath Rd	30
-	Daws Heath, Daws Heath Rd	30
-	Eastwood, Green La (at Kendal Way)	30
-	Eastwood, Western Approaches (at Rockall)	30
-	Grays, Blackshots La	30
-	Grays, Lodge La	30
-	Harlow, Abercrombie Way (towards Southern Way)	40
-	Harlow, Howard Way	40
-	Hullbridge, Coventry Hill	30
-	Leigh-on-Sea, Belton Way East (Marine Parade to Belton Gdns)	30
-	Leigh-on-Sea, Belton Way West	30
-	Leigh-on-Sea, Blenheim Chase	30
-	Leigh-on-Sea, Grand Parade/Cliff Parade	30
-	Leigh-on-Sea, Hadleigh Rd	30
-	Leigh-on-Sea, Highlands Blvd	30
-	Leigh-on-Sea, Manchester Dr	30
-	Leigh-on-Sea, Mountdale Gdns	30
-	Leigh-on-Sea, Western Rd	30
-	Loughton, Alderton Hill	30
-	Loughton, Loughton Way	30
-	Loughton, Valley Hill	n/a
-	Maldon, Fambridge Rd	30
-	Maldon, Holloway Rd	30
-	Maldon, Mundon Rd	30
-	Prittlewell, Kenilworth Gdns	30
-	Prittlewell, Prittlewell Chase	30
-	Rayleigh, Bull La	30
-	Rayleigh, Downhall Rd	n/a
-	Rayleigh, Trinity Rd (near Church Rd)	30
-	Rochford, Ashingdon Rd	30
-	Rochford, Rectory Rd	30
-	Shoeburyness, Ness Rd	30
-	Southend-on-Sea, Bournemouth Park Rd	n/a
-	Southend-on-Sea, Hamstel Rd	30
-	Southend-on-Sea, Lifstan Way	30
-	Southend-on-Sea, Western Esplanade	30
-	Southend-on-Sea, Woodgrange Dr (at Sandringham Rd)	30
-	South Woodham Ferrers, Hullbridge Rd	30
-	South Woodham Ferrers, Inchbonnie Rd	30
-	Stanford le Hope, London Rd	30
-	Stanford le Hope, Southend Rd, Corringham	30
-	Stanford le Hope, Springhouse Rd, Corringham	30
-	Theydon Bois, Piercing Hill	n/a
-	Thorpe Bay, Barnstable Rd	30
-	Thorpe Bay, Thorpe Hall Ave	30
-	Waltham Abbey, Paternoster Hill	n/a
-	Westcliff-on-Sea, Chalkwell Ave	30
-	Westcliff-on-Sea, Kings Rd	30
-	Wickford, Radwinter Ave	30
-	Witham, Powers Hall End	30
-	Witham, Rickstones Rd	30

Gloucestershire

Road number	Location	Speed limit (mph)
A38	Twigworth	40
A40	Andoversford	60
A40	The Barringtons	60
A40	Gloucester Rd, St Marks, Cheltenham	40
A40	Churcham	50
A40	Farmington	60
A40	Hampnett	60
A40	Hazleton	60
A40	Northleach	60
A40	Whittington/Andoversford	60
A46	Ashchurch	30
A46	North of Nailsworth	40
A417	Burford Junction (Cirencester)	70
A417	Dartley Bottom (north-west of Cirencester)	70
A417	Gloucester Rd, Corse	40
A417	Lechlade on Thames	40
A417	Maisemore	30
A417	North of Hartpury	40
A419	Oldends La to Stonehouse Court, Stonehouse	40
A429	South-west of Bourton-on-the-Water	60
A429	Fossebridge	40
A430	Hempstead Bypass, Gloucester	40
A435	Colesbourne	60
A436	Near jct with B4068	60
A4013	Princess Elizabeth Way, Arle, Cheltenham	30
A4013	Princess Elizabeth Way, Hester's Way, Cheltenham	30
A4019	Uckington	50
A4136	Brierley	40
A4136	Harrow Hill (near Drybrook)	40
A4136	Little London	40
A4151	Steam Mills, Cinderford	30
A4173	Near St Peter's School, Tuffley, Gloucester	30
B4008	Bristol Rd, Olympus Park area, Quedgeley	30
B4008	Bristol Rd, Hardwicke (south of Tesco roundabout)	40
B4008	Gloucester Rd, Stonehouse	30
B4060	Wootton-under-Edge/Kingswood (at school)	30
B4215	South-east of Rudford	50
B4215	South of Newent Bypass	50
B4221	Kilcot Village	40
B4221	Picklenash School, Newent	30
B4228	Old Station Way, Coleford	30
B4228	Perrygrove, south of Coleford	40
B4633	Gloucester Rd, Cheltenham (south-west of St Georges Rd)	30
-	Cheltenham, St Georges Rd	30
-	Cheltenham, Swindon La	30
-	Cheltenham, Wyman's Lane	30
-	Cirencester, Chesterton La	30
-	Gloucester, Abbeymead Ave	30
-	Gloucester, Barrow Hill, Churchdown	30
-	Minchinhampton Common	40
-	Siddington	30
-	Tewkesbury, Gloucester Rd	40

Greater Manchester

Road number	Location	Speed limit (mph)
A6	Buxton Rd, Hazel Grove	30
A6	Buxton Rd, High Lane	30
A6	Stockport Rd, Manchester	30
A6	Wellington Rd North, Stockport	30
A34	Kingsway, Cheadle	40
A34	Birchfields Rd, Rusholme, Manchester	30
A34	Kingsway, Manchester	40
A49	Wigan Rd, Standish	30
A49	Warrington Rd, Marus Bridge, Wigan	30
A56	Jubilee Way, Bury	30
A56	Manchester Rd, Bury	30
A56	Walmersley Rd, Bury	30
A56	Bury New Rd, Manchester	30
A56	Chester Rd, Old Trafford (at White City Way)	30
A56	Bury New Rd, Prestwich	30
A56	Whalley Rd, Shuttleworth	30
A57	Liverpool Rd, Eccles	30
A57	Manchester Rd, Hyde	30
A57	Mottram Rd, Hyde	30
A57	Hyde Rd/Manchester Rd, Manchester	30
A58	Lily La, Bamfurlong, Abram	30
A58	Liverpool Rd, Ashton-In-Makerfield	30
A58	Wigan Rd, Bolton	40
A58	Angouleme Way, Bury	30
A58	Bolton Rd, Bury	30
A58	Rochdale Rd, Bury	30
A58	Bury and Bolton Rd, Radcliffe	30
A58	Halifax Rd, Rochdale	30
A62	Oldham Rd, Failsworth	30
A62	Oldham Rd, Manchester	30
A62	Oldham Way, Oldham	50
A560	Shaftesbury Avenue,Timperley, Altrincham	40
A560	Crookilley Way, Stockport	50
A571	Pemberton Rd, Winstanley, Wigan	30
A571	Victoria St, Wigan	30
A572	Chaddock La, Astley, Tyldesley	30
A572	Newton Rd, Lowton (near Leigh)	30
A573	Wigan Rd, Golborne	30
A574	Warrington Rd, Leigh	30
A575	Walkden Rd, Worsley	30
A579	Atherleigh Way, Leigh	50
A580	East Lancashire Rd, Leigh	70
A580	East Lancashire Rd, Swinton/ Worsley	50
A626	Marple Rd, Offerton, Stockport	30
A627	Chadderton Way, Chadderton	40
A635	Ashton Old Rd, Manchester	30
A635	Mancunian Way, Manchester	40
A635/A6018	Stamford St, Stalybridge	30
A662	Ashton New Rd, Manchester	30
A663	Broadway, Failsworth	40
A664	Rochdale Rd, Manchester	30
A664	Manchester Rd, Castleton, Rochdale	30
A665	Bury Old Rd, Prestwich	30
A665	Cheetham Hill Rd, Manchester	30
A665	New Rd, Radcliffe	30
A665	Higher La, Whitefield	30
A665	Radcliffe New Rd, Whitefield	30
A666	Blackburn Rd, Bolton	30
A666	St Peter's Way, Bolton	50
A666	Manchester Rd, Swinton	30
A667	Ringley Rd West, Whitefield	30
A670	Mossley Rd, Ashton-under-Lyne	30
A673	Chorley New Rd, Bolton	40
A676	Bolton Rd, Hawkshaw	30
A676	Bolton Rd West, Holcombe Brook, Ramsbottom	30
A676	Stubbins La, Ramsbottom	30
A680	Edenfield Rd, Rochdale	30
A5014	Talbot Rd, Stretford	30
A5079	Slade La, Levenshulme, Manchester	30
A5103	Princess Pkwy (near M60 jct 5)	50
A5103	Princess Rd, Manchester	30
A5106	Chorley Rd, Standish	30
A5143	Bridge La, Bramhall	30
A5143	Jacksons La, Hazel Grove	30
A5145	Edge La, Stretford	30
A5181	Mosley Rd, Trafford Park	30
A5209	Crow Orchard Rd, Shevington Moor	30
A5209	Almond Brook Rd, Standish	30
A6010	Alan Turing Way, Manchester	30
A6010	Pottery La, Manchester	30
A6017	Ashton Rd, Bredbury, Stockport	40
A6033	Todmorden Rd, Littleborough	30
A6044	Hilton La, Prestwich	30
A6044	Sheepfoot La, Prestwich	30
A6045	Manchester Rd, Heywood	30
A6045	Heywood Old Rd, Middleton	30
A6046	Hollin La, Middleton	30
A6053	Dumers La, Radcliffe	30
A6104	Victoria Ave, Blackley, Manchester	30
A6144	Warburton La, Partington	30
A6144	Harboro Rd, Sale	30
A6144	Old Hall Rd, Sale Moor	30
A6145	Hulton La, Bolton	30
B5158	Lostock Rd, Urmston	30
B5160	Park Rd, Bowdon	30
B5165	Park Rd, Timperley, Altrincham	30
B5166	Ashton La, Ashton upon Mersey	30
B5166	Styal Rd, Heald Green, Gatley	30
B5206	Upholland Rd, Billinge	30
B5213	Church Rd, Urmston	30
B5217	Seymour Grove, Old Trafford	30
B5218	Upper Chorlton Rd, Chorlton cum Hardy	30
B5237	Bickershaw La, Bickershaw, Abram	30
B5239	Bolton Rd, Aspull	30
B5239	Haigh Rd, Aspull	30
B5239	Dicconson La, Cooper Turning, Bolton	30
B5375	Miles La, Shevington	30
B5397	Dane Rd, Sale	30
B6101	Strines Rd, Marple	30
B6167	Gorton Rd, Reddish	30
B6177	Stamford Rd, Mossley	30
B6194	Broad La, Rochdale	30
B6196	Ainsworth Rd, Bury	30
B6196	Church St, Ainsworth, Bury	30
B6196	Cockey Moor Rd, Ainsworth, Bury	30
B6196	Hardy Mill Rd, Bolton	30
B6199	Plodder La, Farnworth	30
B6213	Bury Rd, Tottington	30
B6213	Turton Rd, Tottington	30
B6214	Brandlesholme Rd, Bury	30
B6214	Helmshore Rd, Holcombe, Ramsbottom	30
B6214	Longsight Rd, Holcombe Brook, Ramsbottom	30
B6215	Brandlesholme Rd, Greenmount, Ramsbottom	30
B6222	Bury Rd, Rochdale	30
B6225	Milnrow Rd, Littleborough	30
B6225	Wildhouse La, Milnrow	60
B6226	Chorley Old Rd, Bolton	30/50
B6292	Ainsworth Rd, Radcliffe	30
B6292	Starling Rd, Radcliffe	30
B6377	Shawclough Rd, Rochdale	30
-	Aspull, Scot La	30
-	Bolton, Stitch-Mi-La	30
-	Bury, Croft La, Hollins	30
-	Bury, Radcliffe Rd	30
-	Bury, Walshaw Rd	30
-	Cheadle, Birdhall La	30
-	Cheadle, Councillor La	30
-	Cheadle, Schools Hill	30
-	Cheadle Hulme, Carr Wood Rd	30
-	Hazel Grove, Chester Rd	30
-	Heywood, Bury Old Rd	30
-	Heywood, Queens Park Rd	30
-	Horwich, Lever Park Ave	30
-	Leigh, Queensway	30
-	Manchester, Blackley New Rd, Crumpsall	30
-	Manchester, Hazelbottom/ Waterloo St, Cheetham Hill	30
-	Mellor, Longhurst La	30
-	Pendlebury, Langley Rd	30
-	Radcliffe, Stand La	30
-	Rochdale, Bagslate Moor Rd	30
-	Rochdale, Caldershaw Rd	30
-	Rochdale, Smithybridge Rd, Smithy Bridge	30
-	Romiley, Sandy La	30
-	Sale, Glebelands Rd	30
-	Sale, Hope Rd	30
-	Sale, Norris Rd	30
-	Salford, Belvedere Rd	30
-	Stockport, Dialstone La, Offerton	30
-	Stockport, Harrytown, Bredbury	30
-	Stretford, Kings Rd	30
-	Trafford Park, Westinghouse Rd	30
-	Westhoughton, The Hoskers	30

Hampshire and the Isle of Wight

Road number	Location	Speed limit (mph)
A27	Portchester to Titchfield	30/40
A27	Parkgate to A3024	30/40
A30	Blackwater	30/40
A33	Riseley to Basingstoke	50
A33	Western end of flyover (M271) to Mayflower Roundabout, Southampton	50
A325	Farnborough/Aldershot, Hawley La to Cranmore La	30/40/60/70
A325	Whitehill to county boundary near Farnham	30/40/60
A334	Wickham, A32 to B2177	n/a
A335	Eastleigh	30/40
A337	Lymington Rd/Christchurch Rd, New Milton	30/40
A337	Pennington, Lymington to Balmerlawn, Brockenhurst	30/40/50/60
A338	Fordingbridge to county boundary	40/60
A338	Ringwood to Ibsley	40/60
A340	Pamber End to Tadley	30/60
A2047	Fratton Rd, Portsmouth	30
A3020	Blackwater (IOW)	n/a
A3020	Blackwater Rd, Newport (IOW)	40
A3021	York Ave, East Cowes (IOW)	30
A3024	A27 to city centre, Southampton	30/40
A3054	Binstead Hill, Binstead (IOW)	30
A3054	Fairlee Rd, Newport (IOW)	30/40
A3054	High St/Lushington Hill, Wootton Bridge (IOW)	30/40
A3055	High St/New Rd, Brading (IOW)	30
A3056	Blackwater (IOW)	n/a
B2177	A334 to Winchester Rd, Bishop's Waltham	n/a
B3037	Fair Oak to Eastleigh	30/40
B3055	Brockenhurst to A35	30/40
B3321	Adelaide Gr/Victoria Gr, East Cowes (IOW)	30
B3395	Sandown to Yaverland (IOW)	30
-	Basingstoke, Tobago Close	30
-	Newport, Staplers Rd/Long La (IOW)	30
-	Portsmouth, Clarence Esplanade/Esplanade	30

Hertfordshire

Road number	Location	Speed limit (mph)
A41	North Western Ave, Watford (near East Dr)	40
A119	North Rd, Hertford (at St Josephs School)	30
A411	London Rd, Bushey (150m west of Merry Hill Rd)	30
A411	Hempstead Rd, Watford (at Glen Way)	30
A414	St Albans Rd, Hemel Hempstead (near Rant Meadow)	40
A414	Hertingfordbury Rd, Hertford (west of Valeside)	40
A505	Cambridge Rd, Hitchin (100m south-west of Queenswood Dr)	40
A600	Bedford Rd, Hitchin (at Times Close)	30
A600	Bedford Rd, Hitchin (75m south of north jct of Wellingham Ave)	30
A602	Stevenage Rd, Hitchin	40
A602	Broadhall Way, Stevenage (A1072 to 200m east of Broadwater Cres)	40
A602	Monkswood Way, Stevenage (100m north of Broadhall Way)	40
A1000	Barnet Rd, Garwick Corner, Potters Bar (at Wagon Rd)	40
A1057	Hatfield Rd, St Albans (near Beechwood Ave)	30
A1057	St Albans Rd West, Hatfield (near Poplar Ave)	40
A1170	High Rd Wormley, Wormley	30
A4125	Sandy La, Northwood (180m south of Batchworth La)	40
A4125	Eastbury Rd, Watford	30
A4251	London Rd, Bourne End (near Lauries Cl)	40
A5183	Frogmore, Park Street (south of St Albans)	30
A6141	London Rd, Baldock (at Hillcrest)	30
A6141	Letchworth Gate, Letchworth (250m north-west of Baldock La)	60
B156	Goffs La, Broxbourne (at Goffs School)	30
B176	High St, Cheshunt (near Warwick Dr)	30
B197	North Rd, Stevenage (south of Rectory La)	30
B487	Redbourn La, Hatching Green, Harpenden (at Oakfield Rd)	30
B487	Queensway, Hemel Hempstead (near Highfield La)	40
B488	Icknield Way, Tring (at Little Tring Rd)	40
B556	Mutton La, Potters Bar (near Albermarle Ave)	30
B1502	Stanstead Rd, Hertford (east of Foxholes Ave)	30
B5378	Allum La, Borehamwood (at Lodge Ave)	30
B5378	Shenleybury, Shenley (150m either side of Shenleybury cottages)	40
-	Cheshunt, Hammondstreet Rd (Peakes La to Hammond Close)	30
-	Hoddesdon, Essex Rd (at Pindar Rd)	30
-	Letchworth, Pixmore Way (50m east of Shott La)	30
-	Royston, Old North Rd (York Way to Orchard Rd)	30
-	South Oxhey, Hayling Rd (Gosforth La to Arbroath Green)	30
-	St Albans, Sandpit La (at Gurney Court Rd)	30
-	Stevenage, Clovelly Way (Scarborough Ave to Eastbourne Ave)	30
-	Watford, Radlett Rd	30
-	Watford, Tolpits La (at Scammell Cl)	30
-	Watford, Whippendell Rd	30
-	Welwyn Garden City, Heronswood Rd (south of Linces Way)	30
-	Welwyn Garden City, Howlands (at garages at entrance to hospice)	30

Humberside

Road number	Location	Speed limit (mph)
M180	West of River Trent	70
A16	Louth Rd, Grimsby	30
A18	Barton Street, Central (north-east Lincs)	60
A18	Barton Street, North (north-east Lincs)	60
A18	Barton Street, South (north-east Lincs)	60
A18	Doncaster Rd, Scunthorpe	40
A18	Queensway, Scunthorpe	40
A18	Wrawby	30
A46	Clee Rd, Cleethorpes	30
A46	Laceby Rd, Grimsby	30
A46	Weelsby Rd, Grimsby	30
A46	Laceby Bypass	70

Road number	Location	Speed limit (mph)
A63	Castle St, Kingston upon Hull	40
A63	Daltry Street Flyover, Kingston upon Hull	40
A63	Melton	50
A159	Ashby Rd, Scunthorpe	30
A159	Messingham Rd, Scunthorpe	30
A161	Belton	30
A163	Holme upon Spalding Moor	30
A164	Leconfield	30
A165	Beeford	30
A165	Kingsgate, Bridlington	30
A165	Coniston	40
A165	Freetown Way, Kingston upon Hull	30
A165	Holderness Rd, Kingston upon Hull	40
A165	Skirlaugh	30
A180	Great Coates junction	70
A614	Airmyn Rd, Goole	30
A614	Holme upon Spalding Moor	40
A614	Thorpe Rd, Howden	30
A614	Middleton on the Wolds	30
A614	Shiptonthorpe (north of roundabout)	60
A614	Shiptonthorpe (south of the village)	60
A1031	Tetney Rd, Humberston	30
A1033	Thomas Clarkson Way, Kingston upon Hull	40
A1033	Main St, Thorngumbald	30
A1033	Withernsea	30
A1035	Hull Bridge Rd, Beverley	30
A1038	Quay Rd/St John's St, Bridlington	30
A1077	Barton-upon-Humber	30
A1079	Barmby Moor	50
A1079	Beverley Rd, Kingston upon Hull (Desmond Ave to Riverdale Rd)	30
A1079	Beverley Rd, Kingston upon Hull (Sutton Rd to Mizzen Rd)	40
A1079	Bishop Burton	30
A1084	Bigby High Rd, Brigg	30
A1105	Anlaby Rd, Kingston upon Hull	30
A1105	Boothferry Rd, Kingston upon Hull	40
A1136	Cromwell Rd, Grimsby	30
A1136	Great Coates Rd, Grimsby	30
A1174	Dunswell	30
A1174	Woodmansey	30
A1243	Louth Rd, Grimsby	30
B1203	Waltham Rd, Grimsby	30
B1206	Wold Rd, Barrow-upon-Humber	30
B1207	High St, Broughton	30
B1230	Gilberdyke	40
B1230	Newport	40
B1231	Anlaby Rd, Kingston upon Hull	30
B1232	Beverley Rd, Hessle	30
B1237	Leads Rd, Kingston upon Hull	30
B1237	Saltshouse Rd, Kingston upon Hull	30
B1238	Main Rd, Bilton, Kingston upon Hull	30
B1240	Station Rd, Preston	30
B1242	Hollym Rd, Hornsea	30
B1398	Greetwell	40
B1501	Grange La South, Ashby, Scunthorpe	30
-	Belton, Westgate Rd	30
-	East Halton, College Rd	30
-	Grimsby, Cromwell Rd	30
-	Hessle, Beverley Rd	30
-	Immingham, Pelham Rd	30
-	Kingston upon Hull, Bricknell Ave	30
-	Kingston upon Hull, Bude Rd	30
-	Kingston upon Hull, Greenwood Ave	30
-	Kingston upon Hull, Hall Rd	30
-	Kingston upon Hull, John Newton Way	30
-	Kingston upon Hull, Marfleet La	30
-	Kingston upon Hull, Marfleet Ave	30
-	Kingston upon Hull, Priory Rd	30
-	Kingston upon Hull, Spring Bank West	40
-	Kingston upon Hull, Wawne Rd	30
-	Scunthorpe, Ashby Rd	30
-	Scunthorpe, Cambridge Ave	30
-	Scunthorpe, Cottage Beck Rd	30
-	Scunthorpe, Doncaster Rd	40
-	Scunthorpe, Luneburg Way	30
-	Scunthorpe, Moorwell Rd, Yaddlethorpe	30
-	Scunthorpe, Rowland Rd	30
-	South Killingholme, Top Rd	30

Kent and Medway

Road number	Location	Speed limit (mph)
A2	Dunkirk to Upper Harbledown (eastbound)	70
A2	Guston (A256 to A258)	60
A2	London Rd, Rochester (opposite Lancelot Ave)	40
A2	Lydden (Wick La to Lydden Hill, coastbound)	70
A20	London Rd, Addington (Trottiscliffe Rd to Ryarsh Rd)	50
A20	Dover Rd/Archcliffe Rd, Aycliffe, Dover (eastbound approach to Western Heights roundabout)	70/40
A20	London Rd, Ditton (Bell La to Teapot La)	40
A21	Key's Green (Kipping's Cross to Beech La)	60
A21	Sevenoaks Bypass, Hubbard's Hill (southbound, Didben La to Morleys roundabout)	70
A21	Sevenoaks Bypass (northbound, Dibden La to Cold Arbor Rd)	70
A21	Castle Hill, Tonbridge	60
A25	Seal Rd, Sevenoaks (near Mill Pond)	30
A26	Maidstone Rd, Hadlow (Great Elms to Lonewood Way)	40
A28	Ashford Rd, Bethersden (near Kiln La)	40
A224	Tubs Hill, Sevenoaks (The Drive to Morewood Close)	30
A225	Sevenoaks Rd, Otford (Warham Rd to Old Otford Rd)	30
A226	Chalk, Gravesend	50
A226	Higham	40
A226	Shorne	50
A227	Culverstone Green	30
A227	Istead Rise	40
A227	Meopham Green	30
A228	Ratcliffe Highway, Chattenden	40
A229	Hartley Rd/Angley Rd, Cranbrook (Turnden Rd to High St)	40
A229	Bluebell Hill, Maidstone (Tyland La to Chatham Rd)	50
A229	Loose Rd, Loose, Maidstone (Linton Rd to Lancet La)	40/30
A229	City Way, Rochester	30
A249	South Street (Chalky Rd to Rumstead La)	70
A249	Chestnut Street (northbound, near slip rd to A2 Key St roundabout)	70
A256	Betteshanger	70
A256	London Rd, Dover	30
A256	Haine Rd, Haine (Manston Rd to Spratling St)	40
A256	Tilmanstone	70
A258	Dover Rd, Ringwould (north of Church La)	50
A259	Guldeford La (south-west of Brookland)	60
A259	High St, New Romney (near West St)	30
A259	St Mary's Bay (near Jefferstone La)	40
A262	High St, Biddenden	30
A268	Queen St, Stohurst	30
A289	Medway Tunnel, Chatham (near Vanguard Way)	50
A290	Blean	30
A291	Canterbury Rd, Herne (Lower Herne Rd to A299)	30
A292	Mace La, Ashford (Wellesley Rd to Mill Court)	30
A299	Canterbury Road West, Cliffsend	30
A2033	Dover Rd, Folkestone (Wear Bay Rd to Southern Way)	30
A2990	Thanet Way, Swalecliffe, Whitstable (east of Chestfield roundabout)	60
B258	Barn End La, Wilmington, Dartford	30
B2015	Maidstone Rd, Nettlestead Green (near Station Rd)	40
B2017	Badsell Rd, Five Oak Green (Whetstead Rd to Capel Grange Farm)	30
B2067	Woodchurch Rd, Tenterden	30
B2071	Littlestone Rd, New Romney (Warren Rd to Marine Parade)	30
B2097	Maidstone Rd, Rochester (Horwood Close to Valley View)	30
B2205	Mill Way, Sittingbourne (Tribune Dr to Cooks La)	30
-	Bromley Green, Ashford Rd (at Sugar Loaf Crossroads)	60
-	Chatham, Street End Rd	30
-	Chatham, Walderslade Rd (Snodhurst Ave to Chestnut Ave)	30
-	Cobham, Sole St (near Scratton Fields)	30
-	Gillingham, Beechings Way (Bradbourne Ave to Beechings Green)	30
-	Hartley, Ash Rd	30
-	Herne Bay, Mickleburgh Hill	30
-	Longfield, Hartley Rd/Ash Rd	30
-	Maidstone, Rough Common Rd, Rough Common	30
-	Margate, Shottendane Rd	30
-	New Ash Green, Ash Rd	30
-	Rainham, Maidstone Rd (Drury Dr to Thames Rd)	30
-	Teynham, Lower Rd (Station Rd to New Cottages)	30

Lancashire

Road number	Location	Speed limit (mph)
A6	Bolton Rd, Chorley	30
A6	Bay Horse Rd, Galgate	60
A6	Garstang Rd, Broughton (north of M55)	40
A6	Garstang Rd, Fulwood, Preston (north of Blackpool Rd)	30
A6	Garstang Rd, Fulwood, Preston (south of M55)	30
A6	Greaves Rd, Lancaster	30
A6	Scotforth Rd, Bailrigg, Lancaster (near Burrow La)	50
A6	North Rd, Preston	30
A6	Ringway, Preston	30
A56	Albert Rd, Colne	30
A56	Burnley Rd, Colne	30
A56	Leeds Rd, Nelson	30
A59	Gisburn Rd, Gisburn	60
A59	Liverpool Rd, Hutton	50
A59	New Hall La, Preston	30
A65	Cowan Bridge	40
A570	Southport Rd, Scarisbrick (at Brook House Farm)	40
A581	Southport Rd, Ulnes Walton	40
A583	Church St, Blackpool	30
A583	Whitegate Dr, Blackpool (near Waterloo Rd)	30
A584	Promenade, Blackpool	30
A584	Lytham Rd, Warton	30
A584	West/Central Beach, Lytham	30
A587	East/North Park Dr, Blackpool	30
A587	Fleetwood Rd, Blackpool	30
A587	Rossall Rd, Cleveleys	30
A588	Head Dyke La, Preesall/Pilling	60
A588	Lancaster Rd, Cockerham (at Gulf La)	60
A666	Blackburn Rd, Darwen	30
A666	Bolton Rd, Darwen (near Cross St)	30
A666	Duckworth St, Darwen	30
A671	Whalley Rd, Read	30
A674	Preston Old Rd, Cherry Tree, Blackburn	30
A675	Belmont Rd (north of Belmont village)	50
A675	Belmont Rd (south of Belmont village)	50
A675	Bolton Rd, Abbey Village, Chorley (Dole La to Calf Hey Bridge)	60
A680	Rochdale Rd, Edenfield	40
A682	Burnley Rd, Crawshawbooth	30
A682	Colne Rd, Brierfield	30
A682	Gisburn Rd, Gisburn	60
A682	Gisburn Rd, Barrowford (near Moorcock Inn)	60
A682	Long Preston Rd, north of Gisburn	60
A683	Morecambe Rd, Lancaster	30
A5073	Waterloo Rd, Blackpool	30
A5085	Blackpool Rd, Lane Ends, Preston	30
A5209	Course La/Ash Brow, Newburgh	30
A6068	Barrowford Rd, Barrowford	50
A6114	Casterton Ave, Burnley	30
A6177	Grane Rd, Haslingden (west of Holcombe Rd)	50
A6177	Haslingden Rd/Elton Rd, Blackburn	50
B5192	Preston St, Kirkham	30
B5251	Pall Mall, Chorley	30
B5254	Leyland Rd, Penwortham, Preston (Talbot Rd to A59)	30
B5254	Leyland Rd/Watkin La, Lostock Hall	30
B5256	Turpin Green La, Leyland	30
B5266	Newton Dr, Blackpool (near Church St)	30
B5269	Whittingham La, Goosnargh	40
B6231	Union Rd, Oswaldtwistle	30
-	Belmont, Egerton Rd	60
-	Blackburn, East Park Rd	30
-	Blackburn, Whalley Old Rd (west of railway bridge)	30
-	Blackpool, Dickson Rd (Queen St to Pleasant St)	30
-	Briercliffe, Burnley Rd	30
-	Darwen, Lower Eccleshill Rd	30
-	Nelson, Netherfield Rd	30
-	Preston, Lytham Rd	30
-	Preston, St George's Rd	30
-	St Annes, Church Rd/Albany Rd (near High School)	30

Leicester, Leicestershire and Rutland

Road number	Location	Speed limit (mph)
A1	Empingham	70
A1	Stretton	70
A5	B4455 towards Wibtoft	n/a
A5	Watling St (south of A426)	60
A5	Watling St, Hinckley (M69 to A47)	50
A5	Watling St, Hinckley (B578 to M69)	60
A5	Watling St, Sharnford (Highcross to B4114)	70
A6	Abbey La, Leicester	40
A6	Derby Rd, Loughborough	30
A6	Glen Rd/Harborough Rd, Oadby	40
A6	London Rd, Leicester (at Knighton Drive)	30
A6	Loughborough Rd, Birstall	40
A47	Billesdon Bypass	50
A47	Glaston Rd, Morcott	50
A47	Hinckley Rd, Earl Shilton	30
A47	Hinckley Rd, Leicester	30
A47	Humberstone Rd, Leicester	30
A47	Peterborough Rd, Barrowden	60
A47	Uppingham Rd, Bisbrooke	60
A47	Uppingham Rd, Houghton on the Hill	40
A47	Uppingham Rd, Skeffington	50
A47	Uppingham Rd, Tugby	50
A50	Groby Rd, Leicester	40
A50	Groby Rd/Leicester Rd, Glenfield, Leicester	40
A50	Woodgate, Leicester	30
A50	Hemington/Lockington	70
A426	Leicester Rd, Lutterworth	60
A426	Leicester Rd, Glen Parva, Leicester	40
A426	Lutterworth Rd, Dunton Bassett	50
A426	Lutterworth Rd, Whetstone	60
A444	Atherstone Rd, Fenny Drayton	60
A444	Main St, Twycross village	30
A444	Norton Juxta Twycross	60
A447	Hinckley Rd, Cadeby	60
A447	Wash La, Ravenstone	40
A512	Ashby Rd, Loughborough	30
A512	Ashby Rd Central, Shepshed	40
A563	Colchester Rd, Leicester	30
A563	Attlee Way, Leicester	30
A563	Hungarton Blvd, Leicester	30
A563	Krefeld Way, Leicester	40
A563	New Parks Way, Leicester	30
A563	Glenhills Way, Leicester	30
A594	St Georges Way, Leicester	30
A606	Broughton	60
A606	Stamford Rd, Barnsdale (east of Oakham)	60
A606	Stamford Rd, Tinwell (west of A1)	60
A607	Melton Rd, Leicester	30
A607	Melton Rd, Waltham/Croxton Kerrial	60
A607	Melton Rd, Waltham on the Wolds	60
A607	Newark Rd, Thurmaston, Leicester	70
A607	Norman Way, Melton Mowbray	30
A4304	Lubbenham Hill, Market Harborough	40
A5199	Bull Head St, Wigston	30
A5199	Leicester Rd, Wigston	30
A5199	Welford Rd, Leicester	30
A5460	Narborough Rd, Leicester	40
A6004	Alan Moss Rd, Loughborough	30
A6030	Wakerley Rd/Broad Ave, Leicester	30
A6121	Stamford Rd, Ketton	30
B568	Victoria Park Rd, Leicester	30
B581	Broughton Way, Broughton Astley	30
B582	Little Glen Rd, Blaby	30
B590	Rugby Rd, Hinckley	30
B591	Loughborough Rd, Charley (3km south-east of Shepshed)	60
B676	Saxby Rd, Freeby	60
B4114	Leicester Rd/King Edward Ave, Enderby/Narborough	40
B4114	Sharnford	30
B4666	Coventry Rd, Hinckley	30
B5003	Ashby Rd, Norris Hill (west of Ashby-de-la-Zouch)	40
B5010	London Rd, Shardlow	30
B5350	Forest Rd, Loughborough	30
B5350	Nanpantan Rd, Loughborough	30
B5366	Saffron La, Leicester	30
B6416	East Park Rd, Leicester	30
-	Barrow-upon-Soar, Sileby Rd	30
-	Blaby, Lutterworth Rd	30
-	Broughton Astley, Station Rd	30
-	Hinckley, Brookside, Burbage	n/a
-	Ibstock, Leicester Rd	30
-	Leicester, Fosse Rd South	30
-	Shepshed, Leicester Rd	30
-	Woodhouse Eaves, Maplewell Rd	n/a

Lincolnshire

Road number	Location	Speed limit (mph)
A15	Ashby Lodge	60
A15	Aswarby	60
A15	B1191 to Dunsby Hollow	60
A16	Burwell	40
A16	Tytton La, Boston	60
A16	North Thoresby	60
A17	Fleet Hargate	60
A17	Hoffleet Stow (near B1181)	60
A17	Moulton Common (south of B1357)	60
A52	Bridge End	60
A52	West of Swaton	60
A52	Ropsley	60
A153	Billinghay	40
A153	Tattershall	50
A158	Scremby to Candlesby	60
A631	Dale Bridge near West Rasen	n/a
A631	Hemswell Cliff	60
B1188	Branston	30
B1188	Canwick (at Highfield House)	60
B1188	Potterhanworth (near B1178)	60

London

Road number	Location	Speed limit (mph)
M11	Chigwell	n/a
M25	West Drayton	n/a
M25	Colnbrook	n/a
M25	Spelthorne Borough (jcts 13-14)	n/a
M25	Wraysbury	n/a
M25	Runnymede	n/a
M25	Egham	n/a
M25	Byfleet	n/a
A1	Upper St, Islington	n/a
A1	Holloway Rd, Upper Holloway	n/a
A2	Old Kent Rd	n/a
A3	Kennington Park Rd, Kennington	n/a
A3	Clapham Rd, South Lambeth	n/a
A3	Kingston Rd, Roehampton	n/a
A3	Kingston Bypass	n/a
A4	Great West Rd, Chiswick/Brentford/Hounslow	n/a
A5	Edgware Rd, Cricklewood	n/a
A5	The Broadway, West Hendon	n/a
A10	Great Cambridge Rd, Edmonton	n/a
A10	Stamford Hill, Stoke Newington	n/a
A11	Bow Rd, Bow	n/a
A11	Mile End Rd, Stepney	n/a
A12	Eastern Ave, Romford	n/a
A13	Alfred's Way, Barking	n/a
A13	Ripple Rd, Barking/Dagenham	n/a
A20	Lewisham Way, New Cross	n/a
A20	Lee High Rd, Lewisham	n/a
A20	Sidcup Rd, Eltham/New Eltham	n/a
A20	Sidcup Bypass, Sidcup	n/a
A21	Bromley Rd, Catford	n/a
A21	Bromley Rd, Downham	n/a
A22	Godstone Rd, Purley/Kenley	n/a
A23	Brixton Rd, Brixton	n/a
A23	Brixton Hill, Brixton	n/a
A23	Streatham High Road, Streatham	n/a
A23	Thornton Rd, Croydon	n/a
A24	High St Colliers Wood, Tooting	n/a
A40	Westway, Paddington/Shepherd's Bush	n/a
A40	Western Ave, Perivale	n/a
A40	Western Ave, Greenford	n/a
A40	Western Ave, Northolt	n/a
A40	Western Ave, Ruislip	n/a
A102	Homerton High St, Hackney	n/a
A107	Cambridge Heath Rd, Bethnal Green	n/a
A107	Upper Clapton Rd, Clapton	n/a
A107	Clapton Common, Stamford Hill	n/a
A109	Bounds Green Rd, Bowes Park	n/a
A109	Oakleigh Rd South, Friern Barnet	n/a
A110	Enfield Rd, Enfield	n/a
A112	Chingford Rd, Walthamstow	n/a
A112	Hoe St, Walthamstow	n/a
A118	Romford Rd, Forest Gate	n/a
A124	Barking Rd, East Ham	n/a
A124	Barking Rd, Plaistow	n/a
A200	Creek Rd, Greenwich	n/a
A202	Camberwell New Rd, Camberwell	n/a
A202	Vauxhall Bridge Rd, Westminster	n/a
A205	Brownhill Rd, Catford	n/a
A205	Stanstead Rd, Catford	n/a
A205	Upper Richmond Rd, Putney/Roehampton	n/a
A205	Mortlake/East Sheen	n/a
A206	Woolwich Church St, Woolwich	n/a
A206	Beresford St, Woolwich	n/a
A206	Woolwich Rd, Belvedere	n/a
A206	Erith Rd, Belvedere	n/a
A207	Bellegrove Rd, Welling	n/a
A207	Great Western Rd, Westbourne Park	n/a
A208	Court Rd, Eltham	n/a
A208/A205	Well Hall Rd, Eltham	n/a
A212	Westwood Hill, Sydenham	n/a
A213	Croydon Rd, Penge	n/a
A214	Elmers End Rd, Beckenham	n/a
A214	Trinity Rd, Wandsworth	n/a
A215	Denmark Hill, Camberwell	n/a
A215	Beulah Hill, Upper Norwood	n/a
A217	London Rd, Mitcham	n/a
A217	Garratt La, Wandsworth	n/a
A219	Fulham Palace Rd, Fulham	n/a
A219	Scrubs La, Willesden	n/a
A221	Penhill Rd, Blackfen	n/a
A222	Long La, Addiscombe	n/a
A222	Bromley Rd, Beckenham	n/a
A224	Sevenoaks Way, St Paul's Cray	n/a
A232	Cheam Rd, Sutton	n/a
A233	Main Rd, Biggin Hill	n/a
A234	Beckenham Rd, Beckenham/Penge	n/a
A234	Crystal Palace Park Rd, Sydenham	n/a
A239	Central Rd, Morden	n/a
A240	Kingston Rd, Tolworth/Stoneleigh	n/a
A298	Bushey Rd, Raynes Park	n/a
A307	Kew Rd, Kew	n/a
A307	Richmond Rd, Kingston upon Thames	n/a
A312	Harlington Rd West, Feltham	n/a
A312	Uxbridge Rd, Hampton	n/a
A312	Near Southall	n/a
A315	High St, Brentford	n/a
A315	Kensington Rd, Kensington	n/a
A402	Holland Park Ave, Notting Hill	n/a
A404	Hillside, Harlesden	n/a
A404	Harrow Rd, Wembley	n/a
A404	Watford Rd, Harrow	n/a
A406	Barking Relief Rd, Barking	n/a
A406	Southend Rd (North Circular), Walthamstow/South Woodford	n/a
A406	North Circular Rd, Finchley	n/a
A406	North Circular Rd, Dollis Hill	n/a
A406	North Circular Rd, Neasden/Stonebridge	n/a
A408	Cowley Rd, Uxbridge	n/a
A408	Cowley Rd, Cowley	n/a
A408	High Rd, Cowley	n/a
A408	Stockley Rd, West Drayton	n/a
A410	Uxbridge Rd, Harrow Weald	n/a
A410	Fryent Way, Kingsbury	n/a
A501	Euston Rd	n/a
A503	Seven Sisters Rd, Finsbury Park/South Tottenham	n/a
A1010	Fore St, Edmonton	n/a
A1020	Royal Docks Rd, Beckton	n/a
A1020	Royal Albert Way	n/a
A1112	Rainham Rd, North Dagenham	n/a
A1153	Porters Ave, Becontree	n/a
A1199	Woodford Rd, South Woodford	n/a
A1206	Manchester Rd, Isle of Dogs	n/a
A1206	Westferry Rd, Poplar/Isle of Dogs	n/a
A1400	Woodford Ave, Gants Hill	n/a
A2043	Kingston Rd, Kingston upon Thames	n/a
A2043	Cheam Common Rd, North Cheam	n/a
A2043	Malden Rd, Cheam	n/a
A2206	Southwark Park Rd, Bermondsey	n/a
A2212	Burnt Ash La, Plaistow, Bromley	n/a
A2215	Peckham Rye	n/a
A3205	Battersea Park Rd, Battersea	n/a
A3212	Chelsea Embankment, Chelsea	n/a
A3212	Millbank, Westminster	n/a
A3216	Sloane St, Belgravia	n/a
A3220	Latchmere Rd, Battersea	n/a
A4000	Horn La, Acton	n/a
A4006	Kenton Rd, Kenton	n/a
A4006	Kingsbury Rd, Kingsbury	n/a
A4020	Uxbridge Rd, Shepherd's Bush	n/a
A4020	Uxbridge Rd, Southall	n/a
A4020	Uxbridge Rd, Hayes	n/a
A4090	Alexandra Ave, South Harrow	n/a
A4127	Greenford Rd, Greenford	n/a
A4127	Greenford Rd, Southall	n/a
A4140	Honeypot La, Queensbury	n/a
A4180	Ruislip Rd, Yeading	n/a
B155	Belmont Rd, Harringay	n/a
B160	Larkshall Rd, Chingford	n/a
B178	Ballards Rd, Dagenham	n/a
B205	Salter Rd, Rotherhithe	n/a
B213	Abbey Rd, Abbey Wood	n/a
B213	Lower Rd, Belvedere	n/a
B214	Albany Rd, Walworth	n/a
B218	Brockley Rd, Brockley/Crofton Park	n/a
B221	Kings Ave, Clapham Park	n/a
B238	Peckham Rye	n/a
B266	Brigstock Rd, Thornton Heath	n/a
B272	Beddington La, Croydon	n/a
B272	Foresters Dr, South Beddington	n/a
B278	Green La, Morden	n/a
B279	Tudor Dr, Morden Park	n/a
B282	West Barnes La, Raynes Park	n/a
B286	Martin Way, Morden	n/a
B302	Royal Hospital Rd, Chelsea	n/a
B358	Sixth Cross Rd, Strawberry Hill	n/a
B415	Kensington Park Rd, Notting Hill	n/a
B450	Ladbroke Gr, Notting Hill	n/a
B472	Joel St, Northwood Hills/Eastcote	n/a
B483	Park Rd, Uxbridge	n/a
B1421	Ockendon Rd, Upminster	n/a
B1459	Chase Cross Rd, Collier Row	n/a
B2030	Coulsdon Rd, Coulsdon	n/a
-	Balham, Atkins Rd	n/a
-	Beckenham, Wickham Way,	n/a
-	Bedfont, Hatton Rd	n/a
-	Bexleyheath, Pickford La	n/a
-	Brixton, Herne Hill Rd	n/a
-	Coulsdon, Portnalls Rd	n/a
-	Cricklewood, Crest Rd	n/a
-	East Wickham, King Harolds Way	n/a
-	Eltham, Glenesk Rd	n/a
-	Eltham, Rochester Way	n/a
-	Grove Park/Lee, Burnt Ash Hill	n/a
-	Hainault, Manford Way	n/a
-	Hanworth, Castle Way	n/a
-	Harefield, Church Hill	n/a
-	Harrow, Harrow View	n/a
-	Harrow, Porlock Ave	n/a
-	Hayes, Kingshill Ave	n/a
-	Herne Hill, Sunray Ave	n/a
-	Honor Oak, Brenchley Gdns	n/a
-	Hornchurch, Parkstone Ave	n/a
-	Hornchurch, Wingletye La	n/a
-	Kenton, Woodcock Hill	n/a
-	Morden Park, Hillcross Ave	n/a
-	North Kensington, Barlby Rd	n/a
-	North Kensington, Chesterton Rd	n/a
-	North Kensington, Latimer Rd	n/a
-	North Kensington, St Helen's Gardens	n/a
-	Old Malden, Manor Dr North	n/a
-	Peckham Rye	n/a
-	Peckham, Linden Gr	n/a
-	Romford, Brentwood Rd	n/a
-	Sidcup, Faraday Ave	n/a
-	South Ruislip/Eastcote, Field End Rd	n/a
-	Southall, Lady Margaret Rd	n/a
-	St Helier, Morden, Middleton Rd	n/a
-	Upminster, Hall La	n/a
-	Upminster, Ingrebourne Gdns	n/a
-	West Dulwich, Alleyn Park	n/a
-	West Kensington, Holland Villas Rd	n/a
-	Wimbledon, Ridgeway Pl	n/a
-	Wood Green, White Hart La	n/a

Merseyside

The introduction of mobile safety cameras is under consideration.

Norfolk

Road number	Location	Speed limit (mph)
A10	Stow Bardolph	60
A10	Tottenhill/Watlington	60
A11	Attleborough Bypass	60
A11	Ketteringham	70
A11	Roudham Heath (A1075/B1111)	70
A11	Thetford (A134 roundabout)/Croxton	60
A11	Wymondham/Besthorpe	70
A12	Hopton on Sea	70
A17	Terrington St Clement	60
A47	East Winch	60
A47	Emneth	60
A47	Honingham/Easton	60
A47	Lingwood/Acle	50
A47	Mautby/Halvergate	60
A47	Narborough	60
A47	Postwick	70
A47	Pullover Roundabout, King's Lynn	70
A47	Scarning	60
A47	Swaffham/Sporle	60
A47	Terrington St John	70
A47	Tuddenham	70
A47	Wendling/Fransham	60
A47	West Bilney	60
A140	Aylsham	60
A140	Dickleburgh Moor	60
A140	Erpingham	60
A140	Harford Bridge, Norwich	30
A140	Newton Flotman/Stoke Holy Cross/Swainsthorpe	60
A140	Long Stratton/Tivetshall St Mary	60
A140	Roughton	40
A140	Saxlingham Thorpe	40
A140	Scole Bypass	70
A140	St Faiths	60
A143	Belton/St Olaves	60
A143	Billingford/Brockdish	60
A143	Haddiscoe (bends)	30
A146	Hales	60
A148	South Wootton, King's Lynn	40
A148	Bodham	60
A148	Fakenham Bypass	60
A148	Pretty Corner (near A1082/Sheringham)	60
A148	Thursford/B1354	50
A149	Caister Bypass	70
A149	Catfield/Potter Heigham	40
A149	Catfield	60
A149	Hunstanton	30
A149	Kings Lynn (A10/A47 to B1145)	60
A149	Knights Hill, King's Lynn	60
A149	Crossdale Street to Thorpe Market	60
A149	Sandringham	60
A149	Wayford Bridge East (west of Stalham)	50
A149	Wayford Bridge West/Smallburgh	50
A1065	Hempton	50
A1065	Hilborough	60
A1065	South Acre	60
A1065	Weeting	60
A1066	Roydon & Diss	30
A1066	Rushford	60
A1066	Mundford Rd, Thetford	40
A1066	South Lopham	60
A1067	Bawdeswell	50
A1067	Morton/Attlebridge	60
A1075	East Wretham (heath)	60
A1122	Swaffham/Beachamwell	60
A1151	Rackheath/Wroxham	60
B1108	Earlham Rd, Norwich	30
B1110	Beetley/Hoe	60
B1113	Wreningham/Ashwellthorpe	50
B1149	Horsford Woods (north of Horsford)	60
B1150	Scottow	50
B1150	Westwick	50
B1152	Bastwick/Billockby	60
B1332	Ditchingham	50
-	Caistor, Ormesby Rd	30
-	Dereham, Swanton Rd	60
-	Drayton/Thorpe Marriot, Reepham Rd	50
-	Norwich, Gurney Rd	30
-	Norwich, Plumstead Rd/Rd East	30
-	Wymondham (A11) to B1113 (Wreningham/Bracon Ash)	50

Northamptonshire

Road number	Location	Speed limit (mph)
A5	DIRFT to county boundary	n/a
A5/A428	DIRFT Logistic Park triangle (M1, jct 18)	n/a
A5	Long Buckby/Watford/Kilsby	n/a
A6	Burton Latimer Bypass	n/a
A14	Polwell Lane overbridge	n/a
A43	Duddington/Collyweston/Easton on the Hill	n/a
A43	Kettering	n/a
A43	Little Cransley (near Broughton)	n/a
A45	High St, Flore	n/a
A361	Daventry Rd, Kilsby	n/a
A361	Welton	n/a
A422	Brackley Bypass	n/a
A427	Oakley Rd, Corby	n/a
A427	Weldon Rd, Corby	n/a
A428	East Haddon	n/a
A428	Bedford Rd, Little Houghton	n/a
A428	Brafield on the Green	n/a
A428	Harlestone Rd, Northampton	n/a
A508	Broad St, Northampton	n/a
A508	Cattle Market Rd, Northampton	n/a
A508	Harborough Rd, Northampton	n/a
A508	Stoke Bruerne to Yardley Gobion	n/a
A509	Kettering Rd, Isham	n/a
A605	Barnwell	n/a
A605	Oundle Bypass	n/a
A605	Oundle to Warmington	n/a
A605	Thorpe Waterville	n/a
A4500	Ecton Brook	n/a
A5076	Mere Way, Northampton	n/a
A5095	Kingsley Rd/Kingsthorpe Gr, Northampton	n/a
A5095	St Andrew's Rd, Northampton	n/a
A5193	Harrowden Rd, Wellingborough	n/a
A5193	London Rd, Wellingborough	n/a
A6003	Kettering to Great Oakley	n/a
A6014	Oakley Rd, Corby	n/a
A6116	Brigstock	n/a
A6116	Steel Rd, Corby	n/a
B569	Station Rd, Irchester	n/a
B569	Wollaston Rd, Irchester	n/a
B576	Desborough	n/a
B576	Rothwell	n/a
B4525	A43 to A422	n/a
B5385	Main St, Watford	n/a

Northumbria

Road number	Location	Speed limit (mph)
A1	Berwick Bypass at Dunns jct	60
A68	Colt Crag (reservoir)	60
A69	Haltwhistle Bypass	60
A69	Nafferton (near B6309) (eastbound)	70
A69	Two Mile Cottage, Hexham	70
A167	Stamfordham Rd, Newcastle	30
A182	Houghton Rd, Houghton-le-Spring	30
A183	Chester Rd/Broadway, Sunderland	30
A186	City Rd, Newcastle (at Beamish House)	30
A186	West Rd, Denton Burn, Newcastle (at Turret Rd)	40
A186	Westgate Rd, Newcastle (at Elswick Row)	30
A189	Haddricks Mill Rd, South Gosforth	30
A189	High Pitt, Cramlington	70
A189	Spine Rd, Cramlington	70
A191	Whitley Rd, Longbenton	30
A193	Church Bank, Wallsend	30
A194	Newcastle Rd, Simonside	40
A196	Blackclose Bank, Ashington	30
A690	Durham Rd, Houghton-le-Spring (at Stony Gate)	50
A690	Durham Rd, Sunderland	30
A694	At Winlaton Mill, Rowlands Gill	40
A694	Station Rd, Rowlands Gill	30
A695	Crawcrook Bypass	60
A695	Prudhoe	40
A696	Belsay village	30
A696	Blaxter Cottages, Otterburn	60
A696	Kirkwhelpington	60
A696	Otterburn Monkridge	60
A697	Heighley Gate, Morpeth	60
A697	Wooperton	60
A1018	Ryhope Rd, Sunderland (at Irene Ave)	30
A1058	Jesmond Rd, Newcastle (at Akenside Terr)	30
A1068	Amble Industrial Estate	30
A1147	Gordon Terr, Stakeford	30
A1171	Dudley La, Cramlington	30
A1290	Kier Hardie Way, Sunderland	30
A1300	Prince Edward Rd, Harton/Cleadon Park	30
A6085	Lemington Rd, Lemington, Newcastle	40
A6127	Durham Rd, Barley Mow, Birtley	30
B1288	Leam Lane, Gateshead (at A195)	40
B1296	Sheriffs Hwy, Gateshead (at QE Hospital)	30
B1296	Sheriffs Hwy, Gateshead (at Split Crow Rd)	30
B1298	New Rd, Boldon Colliery	30
B1301	Dean Rd, South Shields	30
B1301	Laygate, South Shields (at Eglesfield Rd)	30
B1316	Lynn Rd, North Shields	30
B1318	Bridge St, Seaton Burn	30
B1426	Sunderland Rd, Felling	30
B1505	Great Lime Rd, West Moor, Longbenton	30
B6315	Hookergate La, High Spen	30
B6317	Main Rd, Ryton	30
B6317	Whickham Highway, Whickham	30
B6318	Military Rd, Whitchester (east of Harlow Hill)	60
B6318	Military Rd, Whittington Fell (west of A68)	60
B6324	Stamfordham Rd, Westerhope, Newcastle (A1 to Walbottle Rd)	40
B6918	Woolsington Village	30
-	Ashington, Station Rd	30
-	Blaydon, Shibdon Bank	30
-	Boldon Colliery, Hedworth La/Abingdon Way	40
-	Crawcrook, Greenside Rd	30
-	Dinnington, Dinnington Rd (north of Brunton La)	60
-	Felling, Watermill La	30
-	Gateshead, Askew Rd West	30
-	Harton, Harton La	30
-	Hebburn, Campbell Park Rd	30
-	Longbenton, Coach La	30
-	Newcastle, West Denton Way (east of Hawksley)	40
-	New Silksworth, Silksworth Rd at Rutland Ave	30
-	North Shields, Norham Rd	30
-	South Shields, Nevison Ave, Whiteleas	30
-	Sunderland, North Hylton Rd at Castletown Way, Southwick	40
-	Sunderland, North Moor La, Farringdon	40
-	Sunderland, Springwell Rd	30
-	Sunderland, Warwick Ter	30
-	Wallsend, Battle Hill Dr	30
-	Whickham, Fellside Rd	30

North Yorkshire

There is currently no safety camera partnership.

Nottinghamshire

Road number	Location	Speed limit (mph)
A52	Clifton Blvd, Nottingham	40
A52	Grantham Rd, Radcliffe on Trent	40
A52	Derby Rd, Nottingham	30
A60	Doncaster Rd, Carlton in Lindrick	30
A60	Cuckney/Market Warsop	30
A60	Nottingham (south)	30
A60	Ravenshead	50
A609	Ilkeston Rd/Wollaton Rd/Russel Dr/Trowell Rd, Nottingham	30
A611	Derby Rd, Annesley	30
A611	Hucknall Rd, Nottingham	30
A612	Nottingham Rd, Southwell (Halloughton to Westgate)	30
A614	Ollerton Rd/Burnt Stump, Arnold, Nottingham	60
A616	Ollerton Rd, Caunton	60
A617	Chesterfield Rd South, Mansfield	30
A620	Welham Rd, Retford	30
A631	Beckingham Bypass	60
A631	West of Beckingham	60
A631	Flood Plain Rd, east of Gainsborough	60
A6005	Castle Blvd/Abbey Bridge/Beeston Rd/University Blvd, Nottingham	30
A6008	Canal St, Nottingham	30
A6130	Gregory Blvd, Nottingham	30
A6130	Radford Blvd/Lenton Blvd, Nottingham	30
A6200	Derby Rd, Nottingham	30
B679	Wilford La, West Bridgford	30
B682	Sherwood Rise/Nottingham Rd/Vernon Rd, Nottingham	30
B6004	Strelley Rd/Broxtowe La, Broxtowe	30
B6004	Oxclose La, Arnold, Nottingham	40
B6010	Nottingham Rd, Giltbrook, Eastwood	30
B6040	Retford Rd, Worksop	30
B6033	Bath La/Ravensdale Rd, Mansfield	30
B6166	Lincoln Rd/Northgate, Newark	40
B6326	London Rd, Newark	30
-	Hucknall, Nottingham Rd/Portland Rd/Annesley Rd	30
-	Newark, Hawton La, Balderton	30
-	Nottingham, Beechdale Rd	30
-	Nottingham, Bestwood Park Drive West	30
-	Nottingham, Ridge Way/Top Valley Drive	30
-	Nottingham, Wigman Rd	30
-	Rainworth, Kirklington Rd	30

South Yorkshire

Road number	Location	Speed limit (mph)
A18	Carr House Rd/Leger Way, Doncaster	40
A18	Epworth Rd (Slay Pits to Tudworth) (near Hatfield Woodhouse)	NSL
A57	Sheffield Rd/Worksop Rd, Aston	40/60
A57	Mosborough Parkway, Sheffield	NSL
A57	Worksop Rd, Aston/Todwick	60
A60	Doncaster Rd, Tickhill	NSL
A60	Worksop Rd, Tickhill	30/60
A61	Park Rd, Cutting Edge, Barnsley	30
A61	Chesterfield Rd/Chesterfield Rd South, Sheffield	30/40
A61	Halifax Rd, Sheffield	30/40
A61	Penistone Rd, Sheffield	30
A614	Selby Rd, Thorne	NSL
A618	Mansfield Rd, Wales Bar, Wales	40
A628	Dodworth	40/60
A628	Cundy Cross to Shafton Two Gates, Barnsley	30/40
A628	Barnsley Rd, Penistone	40
A629	New Wortley Rd, Rotherham	40
A629	Hallwood Rd/Burncross Rd, Burncross, Chapeltown	30
A629	Wortley Rd/Upper Wortley Rd, Rotherham	30/40
A629	Wortley	NSL
A630	Balby Flyover to Hill Top, Doncaster	30/40/60
A630	Centenary Way, Rotherham	40/50
A630	Doncaster Rd, Dalton/Thrybergh	30/40/60
A630	Wheatley Hall Rd, Doncaster	40
A631	Bawtry Rd/Rotherham Rd, Hellaby/Maltby	30/40
A631	Bawtry Rd, Brinsworth, Rotherham	40
A631	Bawtry Rd, Wickersley/Brecks	40
A631	West Bawtry Rd, Rotherham	50
A633	Rotherham Rd, Athersley South, Barnsley	30
A633	Rotherham Rd, Monk Bretton, Barnsley	40
A633	Barnsley Rd, Wombwell	30/40
A633	Sandygate, Wath upon Dearne	30
A635	Doncaster Rd/Saltersbrook Rd, Barnsley	30/40/60
A638	Bawtry Rd, Doncaster	40
A638	Great North Rd/York Rd, Doncaster	40/50
A6022	Swinton	30
A6101	Rivelin Valley Rd, Sheffield	40
A6102	Manchester Rd/Langsett Rd, Hillsborough/Deepcar	30/40
A6109	Meadow Bank Rd, Rotherham	40
A6123	Herringthorpe Valley Rd, Rotherham	40
A6135	Ecclesfield Rd/Chapeltown Rd, Ecclesfield/Chapeltown	40
B6059	Kiveton Park/Wales	30/40
B6089	Greasbrough Rd/Greasbrough St, Thorn Hill/Greasbrough	40
B6096	Wombwell to Snape Hill	30
B6097	Doncaster Rd, Wath upon Dearne	30/60
B6100	Ardsley Rd/Hunningley La, Barnsley	30
B6411	Houghton Rd, Thurnscoe	30
B6463	Stripe Rd, Tickhill	NSL
-	Armthorpe, Hatfield La/Mill St	30
-	Armthorpe, Nutwell La	30
-	Barnsley, Pogmoor Rd	30
-	Bolton Upon Dearne, Dearne Rd	30
-	Doncaster, Melton Rd/ Sprotbrough Rd	30
-	Doncaster, Thorne Rd, Wheatley	30
-	Doncaster, Urban Rd	30
-	Finningley, Hurst La	40/60
-	Grimethorpe, Brierley Rd	30
-	New Edlington/Warmsworth, Broomhouse La/Springwell La	30/60
-	Rawmarsh, Haugh Rd	30/40
-	Rawmarsh, Kilnhurst Rd	30
-	Rotherham, Fenton Rd	30/60
-	Stainforth, Station Rd	30
-	Wath upon Dearne, Barnsley Rd	40

Staffordshire

Road number	Location	Speed limit (mph)
A5	From M6 jct 12 to A460/A4601	50
A5	South Cannock, A460/A4601 to A34, Churchbridge	50/30
A5	South Cannock, from A34 (Churchbridge) to B4154 (Turf Pub island)	60/70/60/30
A5	Brownhills, from Hanney Hay/ Barracks La island to A461	60/70/60
A5	From A461 to A5127/A5148	70
A5	From A5127/A5148 to A38	60
A5	From A38 to Hints La, Tamworth	50/40
A34	Talke, from A500 to A5011	30/60
A34	Newcastle-under-Lyme to Talke, from B5369 to A500	40/70
A34	Newcastle-under-Lyme (north), from B5369 to B5368	40
A34	Newcastle-under-Lyme (south), from Barracks Rd (A527) to Stoke City boundary (signed)	40
A34	Trent Vale, from A500 to London Rd Bowling Club	30/40
A34	Stone Rd, Hanford, from A5035 to A500	40/30
A34	Stone	50
A34	North of Stafford, from A513 to Lloyds island/Eccleshall Rd, Stone (B5026)	40/30
A34	From A5013 to A518, Stafford	30
A34	Queensway, Stafford	40
A34	Stafford (south), from A449 to Acton Hill Rd	30/40
A34	Cannock (north), from north of Holly La to A34/ B5012 roundabout	30
A34	Cannock (south), through Great Wyrley from A5 to Jones La	30
A34	Cannock (south), from Jones La to county boundary	30/50/30
A38	From London Rd, Lichfield (A5206) to A5121, Burton upon Trent	70
A38	From Weeford island (A38) to Bassetts Pole island	70
A50	Kidsgrove, from city boundary to Oldcott Dr	30
A50	Victoria Rd, Fenton, Stoke-on-Trent, from Leek Rd to City Rd	30
A51	Weston, from New Rd to 500m north-east of Sandy La	60/40/50
A51	Pasturefields, from south of Amerton La to south of Hoomill La	50
A51	Rugeley (north), from Bower La to jct with A460/B5013	40/30
A51	Rugeley (south), from jct with A460/B5013 to Brereton island (A513)	30/40
A51	From Armitage La, Rugeley to A515 near Lichfield	60
A51	From A5127 (Birmingham Rd) to Heath Rd, Lichfield	30/40/60
A51	Tamworth Rd/Dosthill Rd, Tamworth, from south of Peelers Way to Ascot Dr	30
A52	Stoke-on-Trent (east), from A5272 to A522	30/40
A53	Blackshaw Moor (north of Leek)	50
A53	Longsden, from Dunwood La jct to Wallbridge Dr, Leek	60/40/30
A53	Leek New Rd, Endon, from Nursery Ave to Dunwood La jct	40/30/40/60
A53	Leek New Rd, from A5272 (Hanley Rd) to B5051 at Endon	30/40
A444	Stanton Rd, Burton on Trent, from St Peters Bridge to Derbyshire boundary	30
A449	Stafford (south) from A34 to Gravel La	30
A449	Penkridge, from Lynehill La to half mile north of Goodstation La	40
A449	Gailey, from Rodbaston Dr to Station Dr	60/70
A449	Coven, from Station Dr (Four Ashes) to M54	70/40
A449	Stourton	60/50/40
A449	Stourton to county boundary	40
A454	Trescott, from Brantley La to Shop La	50
A458	From Six Ashes Rd, Six Ashes to Morfe La, Gilberts Cross	40/50
A460	Sandy La/ Hednesford Rd, from A51 to south of Stile Cop Rd, Rugeley	30
A460/A4601	Wolverhampton Rd, Cannock from Saredon Rd to Longford island	40/30
A511	Burton upon Trent (north), from Anslow La to A5121	40/30
A511	Burton upon Trent (south), from A5121 to Derbyshire boundary	30
A518	Weston to Uttoxeter	60
A518	Stafford, from M6 to Bridge St	30
A518	Stafford, from Riverway to Blackheath La	30/40
A519	Woodseaves, from Moss La to Lodge La	30
A519	Clayton Rd, Newcastle-under-Lyme, from A53 to roundabout at Northwood La	40
A520	Weston Rd, Longton, from A50 north to city boundary	30
A520	Sandon Rd, Stoke-on-Trent, from Grange Rd to A50	30
A522	Beamhurst (near Uttoxeter), from Fole La to Grange Rd	50/40
A4601/A460	Wolverhampton Rd, Cannock, from Longford island toward jct 11 to Saredon Rd	30/40
A4601	Cannock, from A34 (Walsall Rd) to Longford island	30
A4601	Old Hednesford Rd, from A5190 (Lichfield Rd) to A460 (Eastern Way)	30
A5005	Lightwood Rd, Stoke-on-Trent, from A520 to A50	40/30
A5013	Eccleshall Rd, Stafford, from A34 to M6	30
A5035	From A34 (Trentham) to A50 (Longton)	30
A5121	Burton upon Trent, from B5108, Branston to Borough Rd	50/40/30
A5121	Burton upon Trent, from Byrkley St, Horninglow, to Hillfield La, Stretton	30/40
A5127	Lichfield, from Upper St John St to Burton Rd	30
A5189	Burton upon Trent, from Wellington Rd (A5121) to Stapenhill Rd (A444)	30/40
A5190	Cannock Rd, Burntwood, from Attwood Rd to Stockhay La	30
A5190	Cannock, from Five Ways island to Hednesford Rd	30/40/60
A5272	Dividy Rd from A52 to B5039	30
B5027	Stone Rd, Uttoxeter from Byrds La to Springfield Rd	30
B5044	Silverdale, Newcastle-under-Lyme, from Sneyd Terrace to B5368	30
B5051	Stoke-on-Trent, from Sneyd Hill to Brown Edge	30
B5066	From B5027 to Hall La, Hilderstone	30
B5066	Sandon Rd, Sandon, from A51 to Salt La	60
B5066	Sandon Rd, Stafford, from A513 to Marston Rd	30
B5080	Pennine Way, Tamworth, from B5000 to Pennymoor Rd	30/40
B5404	Tamworth, from Sutton Rd to A4091	40/30
B5404	Watling St, Tamworth, from A51 to A5	30
B5500	Audley, from Barthomley Rd to Park La	30
B5500	Bignall End (near Audley) from Boon Hill Rd to Alsager La	30/40
-	Burntwood, Church Rd from Rugeley Rd to Farewell La	30
-	Burton upon Trent, Rosliston Rd, from A5189 to county boundary	30
-	Burton upon Trent, Violet Way/ Beaufort Rd, from A444 to A511	30
-	Cannock, Pye Green Rd, from A34 (Stafford Rd) to Brindley Rd	30
-	Cheadle Rd, from Uttoxeter Rd to Quabbs La	30
-	Crackley, Cedar Rd, from Crackley Bank to B5500 (Audley Rd)	30
-	Cresswell, Sandon Rd, from Saverley Green Rd to Uttoxeter Rd	40
-	Hednesford, Rawnsley Rd, from A460 to Littleworth Rd	30
-	Stoke-on-Trent, Oxford Rd/Chell Heath Rd, from A527 to B5051	30

Suffolk

Road number	Location	Speed limit (mph)
A11	Barton Mills	50
A11	Chalk Hall, Elveden	NSL
A11	Elveden	NSL
A11	Elveden crossroads	40
A11	Worlington	NSL
A12	Blythburgh	40
A12	Kelsale	NSL
A12	Little Glemham	30
A12	Little Glemham, (north)	50
A12	Lound	NSL
A12	Marlesford	40
A12	Melton	40
A12	Saxmundham	NSL
A14	Exning	NSL
A14	Newmarket	NSL
A14	Rougham	NSL
A134	Barnham	40
A134	Little Welnetham	30
A134	Long Melford	NSL
A134	Nowton	40
A137	Brantham	30
A140	Thwaite	50
A140	Wetheringsett	40
A143	Bury St Edmunds	30
A143	Chedburgh	30
A143	Stanton	40
A143	Stanton Bypass	40
A143	Highpoint Prison, Stradishall	40
A144	Ilketshall St Lawrence	NSL
A146	Barnby Bends	NSL
A154	Trinity Ave, Felixstowe	40
A1065	Eriswell	40
A1065	Mildenhall	NSL
A1065	North of RAF Lakenheath	NSL
A1071	Boxford	40
A1071	Lady La, Hadleigh	NSL
A1088	Honington	30
A1092	Cavendish	30
A1092	Clare	30
A1092	Skates Hill, Glemsford	40
A1101	Flempton	30
A1101	Mildenhall	30
A1101	Shippea Hill	50
A1117	Saltwater Way, Lowestoft	30
A1120	Stonham Aspal	30
A1156	Nacton	40
A1156	Norwich Rd, Ipswich	30
A1214	London Rd, Ipswich	40
A1302	Bury St Edmunds	30
A1304	Golf Club, Newmarket	NSL
A1307	Haverhill	40
B1078	Barking	30
B1078	Needham Market	30
B1106	Fornham St Martin	30
B1113	Bramford	40
B1115	Chilton	40
B1384	Carlton Colville	30
B1385	Corton	30
B1438	Melton Hill, Woodbridge	30
B1506	Kentford	40
B1506	Moulton	NSL
-	Felixstowe, Grange Farm Ave	30
-	Felixstowe, High Rd	30
-	Ipswich, Ellenbrook Rd	30
-	Ipswich, Foxhall Rd, St Clements	30
-	Ipswich, Landseer Rd	30
-	Ipswich, Nacton Rd	30
-	Ipswich, Ropes Dr, Kesgrave	30

Surrey

Road number	Location	Speed limit (mph)
A31	Hogs Back, Guildford (central section)	60
A31	Hogs Back, Guildford (eastern section)	60
A308	Staines Bypass, Staines	50
-	Staines, Kingston Rd	30

Sussex

Road number	Location	Speed limit (mph)
A24	Broadwater Rd, Worthing (near Cecilian Ave)	30
A27	Hammerpot, Angmering (north side)	70
A27	Firle Straight, Firle	60
A27	Upper Brighton Rd, Lancing (near Grand Ave)	40
A27	Holmbush, Shoreham	70
A29	Westergate St, Aldingbourne (at Elmcroft Pl)	30
A29	Westergate St, Aldingbourne (at Hook La)	30
A29	Shripney Rd, Bognor Regis (northbound)	40
A259	Hotham Way, Bognor Regis	30
A259	Main Rd, Fishbourne	30
A259	Marine Dr, Saltdean	30
A270	Old Shoreham Rd, Hove (at Amherst Cres)	30
A271	North Trade Rd, Battle	30
A272	Midhurst Rd, Tillington	40
A280	Patching	40
A281	Guildford Rd, Horsham	30
A283	Northchapel	30
A283	Lower St, Pulborough	30
A285	Station Rd, Petworth	30
A2032	Littlehampton Rd, Worthing (near Little Gables)	30
A2038	Hangleton Rd, Hove (at Nevill Rd)	30
A2270	Eastbourne Rd, Willingdon	40
A2280	Lottbridge Drove, Eastbourne	40
B2093	The Ridge, Hastings	30
B2100	Crowborough Hill, Crowborough	30
B2104	Ersham Rd, Hailsham	30
B2111	Lewes Rd, Lindfield, Haywards Heath	30
B2138	Lower St, Fittleworth	30
B2166	Aldwick Rd, Bognor	30
-	Bognor Regis, Chalcraft La	30
-	Brighton, Carden Ave, (at Carden Cl)	30
-	Brighton, Falmer Rd, Woodingdean	30
-	Crawley, Gatwick Rd (near Hazlewick Flyover)	30
-	Crawley, Gossops Dr	30
-	Crawley, Manor Royal (at Faraday Rd)	30
-	Heathfield, Hailsham Rd	30
-	Horsham, Pondtail Rd (at Haybarn Dr)	30
-	Horsham, Pondtail Rd (at Pondtail Cl)	30
-	Hove, New Church Rd (at Wish Rd)	30
-	Hove, Shirley Dr (at Onslow Rd)	30
-	Hove, Shirley Dr (at Shirley Rd)	30
-	Worthing, The Boulevard	30

Thames Valley

Road number	Location	Speed limit (mph)
A4	Bath Rd, Beenham	60
A4	Bath Rd, Burnham	50
A4	Bath Rd, Hungerford	60
A4	Bath Rd, Kintbury	60
A4	Bath Rd, Speen, Newbury	60
A4	Bath Rd, Tilehurst, Reading	40
A4	Berkeley Ave, Reading	30
A4	London Rd, Earley	40
A4	London Rd, Slough	40
A4	Sussex Pl, Slough	30
A5	Bletchley	70
A5	Wolverton	70
A30	London Rd, Sunningdale	30
A34	Kennington	70
A34	Radley	70
A40	Cassington	60
A40	Forest Hill	70
A40	Oxford Rd, Denham	30
A40	West Wycombe Rd, High Wycombe	30
A41	Buckland	70
A41	Gatehouse Rd, Aylesbury	30
A41	Tring Rd, Aylesbury	30
A44	Over Kiddington	50
A44	London Rd, Chipping Norton	40
A308	Braywick Rd, Maidenhead	40
A322	Bagshot Rd, Bracknell	40
A329	Kings Rd, Reading	30
A329	London Rd, Wokingham	30
A329	Vastern Rd, Reading	30
A329	Wokingham Rd, Reading	30
A330	Brockenhurst Rd, Sunninghill	40
A338	Hungerford	50
A361	Burford Rd, Chipping Norton	30
A361	Little Faringdon	60
A404	Marlow Bypass, Little Marlow	70
A404	Marlow Hill, High Wycombe	30
A412	North Orbital Rd, Denham	40
A413	Buckingham Rd, Aylesbury	30
A413	Gravel Hill, Chalfont St Peter	30
A413	Hardwick	60
A413	Swanbourne	60
A413	Walton St, Aylesbury	30
A413	Weedon	60
A413	Wendover Rd, Aylesbury	30
A413	Wendover Bypass, Wendover	60
A417	Charlton Rd, Wantage	30
A417	Faringdon Rd, Stanford in the Vale	30
A418	Oxford Rd, Tiddington	30
A420	Headington Rd, Oxford	30
A420	London Rd, Oxford	30
A421	Standing Way, Woughton on the Green, Milton Keynes	70
A421	Tingewick Bypass, Tingewick	70
A421	Wavendon	60
A422	Newport Rd, Hardmead	60
A422	Radclive/Chackmore	50
A422	Stratford Rd, Buckingham	30
A422	Stratford Rd, Wroxton	60
A509	Emberton Bypass	60
A509	Newport Pagnell	70
A4010	Aylesbury Rd, Monks Risborough	30
A4010	New Rd, High Wycombe	30
A4074	Dorchester	60
A4074	Nuneham Courteney	50
A4095	Bampton Rd, Curbridge	40
A4095	Witney Rd, Freeland	40
A4130	Nuffield	60
A4130	Remenham Hill	40
A4155	Castle Hill, Reading	30
A4155	Shiplake	30
A4157	Oakfield Rd, Aylesbury	30
A4183	Oxford Rd, Abingdon	30
A4260	Banbury Rd, Rousham	60
A4260	Banbury Rd, Shipton-on-Cherwell	50
A4260	Oxford Rd, Kidlington	30
A4260	Steeple Aston	60
B480	Watlington Rd, Blackbird Leys, Oxford	30
B3349	Barkham Rd, Barkham	30
B3430	Nine Mile Ride, Bracknell	50
B4009	Ewelme	50
B4011	Bicester Rd, Long Crendon	30
B4011	Piddington	60
B4017	Drayton Rd, Abingdon	30
B4034	Buckingham Rd, Bletchley	30
B4494	Leckhampstead	60
B4495	Church Cowley Rd, Oxford	30
B4495	Windmill Rd, Oxford	30
-	Bracknell, Opladen Way	30
-	Great Missenden, Rignall Rd	30
-	High Wycombe, Sawpit Hill, Hazlemere	30
-	High Wycombe, Holmers Farm Way	30
-	Maidenhead, Greenways Dr	30
-	Milton Keynes, Avebury Blvd	30
-	Milton Keynes, Midsummer Blvd	30
-	Milton Keynes, Silbury Blvd	30
-	Reading, Park La	30
-	Slough, Cippenham La	30
-	Slough, Buckingham Ave	30
-	Slough, Parlaunt Rd	30
-	Witney, Corn St	30

Warwickshire

Road number	Location	Speed limit (mph)
A5	Grendon to Atherstone	50
A5	Clifton Fisheries, near Churchover	60
A46	Stratford northern Bypass, near Snitterfield	60
A46	Kenilworth Bypass at Stoneleigh	70
A47	The Long Shoot, Nuneaton	40
A423	Banbury Rd, near Fenny Compton	60
A423	Southam Rd, Ladbroke	60
A423	Coventry Rd, Marton village	30
A423	Oxford Rd, south of Marton	60
A425	Radford Rd, Radford Semele	40
A426	Rugby Rd, near Stockton	60
A428	Rugby Rd, Binley Woods	30
A428	Church Lawford	40
A428	Long Lawford	40
A429	Ettington Rd, south of Wellesbourne	60
A435	Birmingham Rd, Mappleborough Green	40
A435	The Boot, Mappleborough Green, Redditch	40
A439	Near Fishermans Car Park, Stratford-upon-Avon	50
A439	Near Hampton Lucy turn, 3km north-east of Stratford-upon-Avon	50
A452	Greys Mallory, near Bishop's Tachbrook	60
A452	Europa Way, Royal Leamington Spa	60
A3400	Shipston Rd, Alderminster	40
A3400	London Rd, Little Wolford	60
A3400	Stratford Rd, north of Henley in Arden	40
A3400	Birmingham Rd, Pathlow	50
A4189	Warwick Rd, Henley-in-Arden	30
A4189	Henley Rd, Lower Norton	60
B4089	Arden Rd, Alcester	30
B4100	Near jct with B4455 (near Warwick Services)	60
B4100	Banbury Rd, south of Gaydon	60
B4101	Broad La, Tanworth in Arden	40
B4102	Arbury Rd, Nuneaton	30
B4112	Ansley Rd, Nuneaton	40
B4113	Coventry Rd, Nuneaton	30
B4114	Lutterworth Rd, Burton Hastings	60
B4114	Coleshill Rd, Church End	60
B4114	Coleshill Rd, Ansley Common (near Chapel End)	30
B4455	Fosse Way, south of Princethorpe	60
-	Coleshill, Station Rd	30
-	Nuneaton, Donnithorne Ave	30
-	Rugby, Clifton Rd/Vicarage Hill	30
-	Warwick, Primrose Hill	30

West Mercia

Road number	Location	Speed limit (mph)
A5	Aston	NSL
A5	Moreton Bridge (1.5km south of Chirk)	NSL
A5	West Felton	NSL
A40	Pencraig	50
A41	Albrighton Bypass	40/60
A41	Chetwynd	NSL
A41	Prees Heath	NSL
A41	Ternhill	40
A41	Whitchurch Bypass	NSL
A44	Bromyard Rd, Worcester	30
A44	Wickhamford	40
A46	Cheltenham Rd, Beckford	50
A46	Evesham Bypass	NSL
A49	Ashton	NSL
A49	Dorrington	NSL
A49	Harewood End	40
A417	Parkway (south of Ledbury)	40
A442	Crudgington	40
A456	Blakedown	30
A456	Newnham Bridge	30
A458	Morville	40
A458	Much Wenlock	30
A458	The Mount, Shrewsbury	30
A465	Allensmore	NSL
A483	Pant	30
A491	Sandy La (west of M5, jct 4)	NSL
A491	Stourbridge Rd (south-east of Hagley)	50
A4103	Lumber La to Lugg Bridge (north-east of Hereford)	NSL
A4103	Newtown Cross	40
A4103	Ridgeway Cross	NSL
A4103	Stifford's Bridge to Storridge	50
A4104	Drake St, Welland	30
A4104	Marlbank Rd, Welland	30
A4110	Three Elms Rd, Hereford	30
A5064	London Rd, Shrewsbury	30
B4096	Old Birmingham Rd, Marlbrook	30
B4211	Church St, Great Malvern	30
B4349	Clehonger	NSL
B4373	Castlefields Way, Telford	40
B4373	Wrockwardine Wood Way, Oakengates, Telford	40
B4386	Mytton Oak Rd, Shrewsbury	30
B4638	Woodgreen Dr, Worcester	30
B5060	Castle Farm Way, St George's, Telford	40
B5061	Holyhead Rd, Snedshill, Telford	30
B5062	Sundorne Rd Shrewsbury	30
B5069	Gobowen Rd, Oswestry/Gobowen	30
-	Hereford, Yazor Rd	30
-	Newport, Wellington Rd	30
-	Redditch, Birchfield Dr	30
-	Redditch, Coldfield Dr	40
-	Redditch, Studley Rd	30
-	Shrewsbury, Longden Rd (rural)	30
-	Shrewsbury, Monkmoor Rd	30
-	Telford, Britannia Way, Hadley	30
-	Telford, Hollinsgate, Hollinswood	30
-	Telford, Stafford Park 1	40
-	Telford, Trench Rd	30

West Midlands

Road number	Location	Speed limit (mph)
A41	Warwick Rd	30
A452	Collector Rd, Castle Bromwich/ Kingshurst	50
A4034	Birchfield La, Oldbury/ Blackheath	40
A4036	Pedmore Rd, Dudley	40
A4040	Bromford La, Gravelly Hill/Ward End	30
A4123	Birmingham New Rd, Wolverhampton/Dudley (northbound)	40
A4600	Ansty Rd, Coventry	40
B425	Lode La, Solihull	30
B4114	Washwood Heath Rd, Washwood Heath	30
B4121	Barnes Hill, Selly Oak	40
B4121	Shenley La, Selly Oak	40
B4135	Cranford St/Heath St, Smethwick	30
-	Solihull, Widney Manor Rd	40
-	Wolverhampton, The Droveway	30

West Yorkshire

Road number	Location	Speed limit (mph)
A58	Easterley Rd, Leeds	n/a
A61	Scott Hall Rd, Leeds	n/a
A64	York Rd, Leeds	n/a
A65	Otley Rd, Guiseley	n/a
A65	Kirkstall Rd, Leeds	n/a
A65	Rawdon Rd, Rawdon (near Yeadon)	n/a
A629	Halifax Rd, Cullingworth	n/a
A629	Elland Bypass	n/a
A629	Keighley Rd, Ogden (near Halifax)	n/a
A629	Ovenden Rd, Halifax	n/a
A629	Skircoat Rd/Huddersfield Rd, Halifax	n/a
A636	Denby Dale Rd, Wakefield	n/a
A638	Dewsbury Rd, Wakefield	n/a
A638	Ossett Bypass	n/a
A642	Horbury Rd, Wakefield	n/a
A643	Morley	n/a
A646	Halifax Rd, Todmorden	n/a
A647	Great Horton Rd, Bradford	n/a
A647	Stanningley Bypass	n/a
A652	Bradford Rd, Batley	n/a
A657	Calverley	n/a
A657	Leeds Rd, Shipley	n/a
A657	Town St, Rodley	n/a
A660	Far Headingley, Leeds	n/a
A6036	Bradford Rd, Northowram	n/a
A6120	Ring Road Farsley, Farsley (near Pudsey)	n/a
A6186	Asdale Rd, Durkar (near Wakefield)	n/a
B6144	Haworth Rd, Daisy Hill, Morley	n/a
B6145	Thornton Rd, Thornton	n/a
B6154	Waterloo Rd, Pudsey	n/a
B6154	Tong Rd, Wortley	n/a
B6269	Cottingley Cliffe Rd, Cottingley (near Shipley)	n/a
B6273	Wakefield Rd, Kinsley	n/a
B6380	Beacon Rd, Bradford	n/a
-	Bradford, Gain La	n/a
-	Bradford, Moore Ave	n/a
-	Huddersfield, Long La, Dalton	n/a
-	Leeds, Broad La, Sandford	n/a
-	Middleton, Middleton Ring Road	n/a

Wiltshire and Swindon

Road number	Location	Speed limit (mph)
M4	Approx 6.9km east of jct 15	70
M4	Jct 15	70
M4	Approx 1.8km west of jct 15	70
M4	Approx 3km east of jct 16	70
M4	Approx 8.4km west of jct 16	70
M4	Approx 3.1km east of jct 17	70
M4	Approx 8.3km east of jct 17	70
A4	Froxfield	40
A4	West Overton	60
A30	Fovant	40
A30	The Pheasant	60
A36	Brickworth (near A27 jct)	60
A36	Hanging Langford	60
A36	Knook	50
A36	South of Whaddon	60
A36	Wilton Rd, Salisbury	30
A36	Stapleford to Steeple Langford	60
A303	Chicklade	50
A303	West of Winterbourne Stoke	60
A303	Willoughby Hedge (1.5km west of A350)	60
A338	Boscombe	40
A338	Near Little Woodbury (1.5km south of Salisbury)	30
A338	Near Southgrove Copse (1.5km south of Burbage)	60
A342	Andover Rd, Ludgershall	30
A342	Chirton to Charlton	60
A342	Lydeway	50
A346	Chiseldon Firs	60
A346	Whitefield (5km south of M4)	60
A350	Heywood	60
A350	Pretty Chimneys	70
A354	Coombe Bissett	40
A360/A344	Airmans Corner	60
A361	Devizes to Beckhampton	60
A361	Inglesham	60
A361	Near jct with B3101, west of Devizes	70
A361	Southwick	30
A361	Frome Rd, Trowbridge	30
A363	Trowbridge Rd, Bradford-on-Avon	30
A363	Trowle Common	40
A363	Woodmarsh, North Bradley	30
A419	Near Covingham, Swindon	70
A419	Cricklade	70
A419	near Broad Blunsdon	70
A420	Giddeahall to Ford	60
A3026	Tidworth Rd, Ludgershall	40
A3028	Larkhill Rd, Durrington	40
A3102	Lyneham	30
A3102	Oxford Rd, Calne	30
A3102	Sandridge Rd, Melksham	30
A3102	Wootton Bassett	30
A4259	Near Coate, Swindon	50
A4259	Queens Dr, Swindon (at Rushton Rd)	40
A4361	Broad Hinton	60
A4361	Swindon Rd, Wroughton	30
A4361	Uffcott crossroads	60
B390	Maddington Farm, west of Shrewton	60
B3098	Bratton	30
B3105	Hill St/Marsh St, Hilperton	30
B3106	Hammond Way, Hilperton	30
B3107	Holt Rd, Bradford-on-Avon	30
B4006	Marlborough Rd, Swindon	40
B4006	Swindon Rd, Stratton St Margaret	30
B4006	Whitworth Rd, Swindon	30
B4040	Leigh	50
B4041	Station Rd, Wootton Bassett	30
B4143	Bridge End Rd, Swindon	30
B4192	Liddington	50
B4289	Great Western Way, Swindon (near Bruce St Bridges)	40
B4553	Tewkesbury Way, Swindon	40
B4587	Akers Way, Swindon	30
-	Corsham, Park La	30
-	Swindon, Ermin St	30
-	Swindon, Moredon Rd	30
-	Swindon, Merlin Way	30
-	Trowbridge, Wiltshire Dr	30

SCOTLAND

Central Scotland

Road number	Location	Speed limit (mph)
M9	At M876 (northbound)	n/a
M9	Polmont (northbound)	n/a
M9	Stirling (northbound)	n/a
M80	Denny (northbound)	n/a
M876	Torwood, Larbert (northbound)	n/a
A9	Dunblane (southbound)	n/a
A82	Crianlarich	n/a
A706	Linlithgow Rd, Bo'ness	n/a
A907	Cambus	n/a
A908	Devonside, Tillicoultry	n/a
A908	Sauchie	n/a
A993	Dean Rd, Bo'ness	n/a

Dumfries and Galloway

Road number	Location	Speed limit (mph)
A74(M)	Multiple sites	70
A7	Langholm	60
A75	Multiple sites	60
A76	Closeburn to Thornhill	60
A76	Glasgow Rd, Dumfries	30
A77	Balyett (south of Innermessan)	60
A77	Cairnryan	30
A77	Whiteleys (2.5km south of Stranraer)	60
A701	Moffat	30
A701	St Ann's	60
A709	Burnside (1.5km east of Lochmaben)	60
A711	Beeswing	50
A711	Kirkcudbright	30
A716	Stoneykirk	60
A718	Craichmore (1km north of B798)	60
B721	Eastriggs	30

Fife

Road number	Location	Speed limit (mph)
A91	Deer Centre to Stratheden (Hospital) jct	n/a
A91	Guardbridge to St Andrews	n/a
A92	Cadham (Glenrothes) to New Inn (near A912/A914 jct)	n/a
A92	Cardenden overbridge to A910 jct	n/a
A92	Cowdenbeath to Lochgelly	n/a
A92	Freuchie to Annsmuir (south of A91 jct)	n/a
A92	A91 jct to 1.5km north of Fernie	n/a
A92	Rathillet (south) to Easter Kinnear (1km south-west of B946)	n/a
A823	St Margaret Dr, Dunfermline	n/a
A823	Queensferry Rd, Dunfermline	n/a
A907	Halbeath Rd, Dunfermline	n/a
A911	Glenrothes to Leslie	n/a
A911	Glenrothes to Milton of Balgonie	n/a
A914	Forgan (near A92) to St Michaels (A919 jct)	n/a
A914	Kettlebridge	n/a
A914	Pitlessie to Cupar	n/a
A915	Checkbar jct (Kirkcaldy) to B930 jct	n/a
A921	Esplanade, Kirkcaldy	n/a
A921	High St/The Path, Kirkcaldy	n/a
A921	Rosslyn St, Kirkcaldy	n/a
A921	St Clair St, Kirkcaldy	n/a
A955	Methilhaven Rd, Buckhaven	n/a
A955	Methilhaven Rd, Methil	n/a
A977	Fere Gait, Kincardine	n/a
A985	Culross (west) to Valleyfield	n/a
A985	Admiralty Rd, Rosyth	n/a
A985	Waulkmill (east of Crombie) to Brankholm (Rosyth)	n/a
B914	Redcraigs to Greenknowes (east of A823)	n/a
B920	Crosshill to Ballingry	n/a
B933	Glenlyon Rd, Leven	n/a
B942	East of Colinsburgh	n/a
B980	Castlandhill Rd, Rosyth	n/a
B981	Broad St, Cowdenbeath	n/a
B981	Dunnikier Way, Kirkcaldy	n/a
B9157	Orrock to Kirkcaldy	n/a
B9157	White Lodge jct to Croftgary	n/a
-	Dunfermline, Townhill Rd	n/a
-	Glenrothes, Formonthills Rd	n/a
-	Glenrothes, Woodside Rd	n/a
-	Glenrothes, Woodside Way	n/a
-	Kirkcaldy, Hendry Rd	n/a

Lothian and Borders

Road number	Location	Speed limit (mph)
A7	Crookston (near B6368)	60
A7	Galashiels, Buckholmside to Bowland	NSL
A7	Hawick	30
A7	Stow to Bowland	30
A8	Ratho Station, Edinburgh	40
A68	Jedburgh	30
A68	Soutra Hill	NSL
A70	Balerno (Bridge Rd to Stewart Rd)	30
A71	Breich	30
A71	Polbeth	30
A72	Castlecraig (near Blyth Bridge)	NSL
A72	Innerleithen Rd, Peebles	30
A72	Holylee (near Walkerburn)	NSL
A90	Burnshot flyover to Cammo Rd, Cramond Bridge, Edinburgh (southbound)	40
A697	Greenlaw and southern approach	30
A697	Ploughlands to Hatchednize (either side of B6461)	NSL
A697	Orange La (at B6461)	NSL
A697/8	Coldstream	30
A698	Ashybank (3km east of A6088)	NSL
A698	Near Crailing	NSL
A699	Maxton village	40
A701	Blyth Bridge to Cowdenburn (1km north-east of Lamancha)	NSL
A701	Rachan Mill, Broughton to A72	30
A702	Bruntsfield Pl, Edinburgh (Thorneybauk to Merchiston Pl)	30
A702	Comiston Rd, Edinburgh (Oxgangs Rd to Buckstone Dr)	40
A702	Dolphinton north to Medwyn Mains	NSL
A703	Eddleston and approaches	30
A703	Leadburn south to Shiplaw	NSL
A703	Edinburgh Rd, Peebles	30
A703	Peebles north to Milkieston	30
A705	Longridge Rd, Whitburn to East Whitburn	30
A706	Whitburn (at Cairnie Pl)	30
A720	City Bypass, east of Gogar roundabout, Edinburgh	50
A899	South of Deer Park roundabout (M8 jct 3) Livingston	50
A899	From Lizzie Bryce roundabout to Almond interchange, Livingston	50
A901	Lower Granton Rd, Edinburgh (Granton Sq to Trinity Rd)	30
A6091	Melrose Bypass	NSL
A6105	Gordon and approaches	30
B701	Frogston Rd West, Edinburgh (Mounthooly Loan to Mortonhall Gate)	40/60
B6374	Galashiels, Station Bridge to Lowood Bridge	30
B7069	West Main St, Whitburn	30
-	Edinburgh, Muirhouse Parkway	30
-	Edinburgh, West Approach Rd, from Morrison St link to Dundee St	40
-	Edinburgh, West Granton Rd	30

North East Scotland

Road number	Location	Speed limit (mph)
A90	Mid Stocket Rd to Whitestripes Ave roundabout, Aberdeen	40
A90	Newtonhill to South Damhead, Kincorth, Aberdeen	70
A90	South Damhead to Mid Stocket Rd, Aberdeen	40
A90	Fraserburgh to B9032 jct	60
A90	South of Leys (near Ellon) to Blackhills (near Longhaven)	60
A90	Upper Criggie (3km south-west of A92 jct) to Mill of Barnes (2.5km south-west of A937 jct)	70
A90	North Rd, Peterhead (A982) to 1km south-east of Crimond	60
A92	Johnshaven to Inverbervie	60
A92	Kinneff, north to Mill of Uras	60
A93	Aboyne	30
A93	Banchory, east from caravan site	40
A93	Banchory, west from church	30
A93	Cambus O'May to Dinnet	60
A93	Dinnet to Aboyne	60
A93	Kincardine O'Neil, south-east to Haugh of Sluie	60
A95	Cornhill	30
A95	Keith to Davoch of Grange	60
A96	Great Northern Rd, Aberdeen	30
A96	Haudagain Roundabout to Chapel of Stoneywood, Aberdeen	30
A96	B9002 jct to A920 at Kirkton of Culsalmond	60
A96	Mosstodloch to Lhanbryde (east)	60
A96	Fochabers to Forgie	60
A98	Banff	30

Road number	Location	Speed limit (mph)
A98	Mill of Tynet to Barhill Rd jct, Buckie	60
A98	From Carnoch Farm Rd, Buckie to Cullen	60
A98	Fochabers to Mill of Tynet	60
A941	Elgin to Lossiemouth	60
A941	Elgin to Rothes	60
A944	Westburn Rd, Aberdeen	30
A947	Fyvie to Tulloch	60
A947	Whiterashes to Newmacher	60
A948	Ellon to Auchnagatt	60
A952	New Leeds to A90	60
A956	King St, Aberdeen	30
A956	Wellington Rd, Aberdeen	40
A978	St Machar Dr, Aberdeen	30
B9040	Silver Sands Caravan Park, Lossiemouth to B9012 jct	60
B9077	Great Southern Rd, Aberdeen	30
B9089	Kinloss north-east to Roseisle Maltings crossroads	60
-	Aberdeen, Beach Blvd	30
-	Aberdeen, Springhill Rd	30
-	Aberdeen, West Tullos Rd	40

Northern Scotland

Road number	Location	Speed limit (mph)
A9	Cuaich, north-east of Dalwhinnie	n/a
A9	Near Dalwhinnie	n/a
A9	North of Dalwhinnie jct	n/a
A9	Daviot	n/a
A9	Caulmaillie Farm, near Golspie	n/a
A9	South of The Mound (Loch Fleet near Golspie)	n/a
A9	Altnasleanach, near Inverness	n/a
A9	North Kessock jct	n/a
A9	Near Fearn jct, south of Tain	n/a
A82	North of Temple Pier, Drumnadrochit	n/a
A82	Near Kings House Hotel, Glencoe	n/a
A82	Invergarry Power Station	n/a
A82	Alltsigh Youth Hostel, north of Invermoriston	n/a
A82	Near White Corries, Rannoch Moor	n/a
A87	West of Bun Loyn jct (A887)	n/a
A95	Drumuillie, near Boat of Garten	n/a
A95	North of Cromdale	n/a
A95	Congash Farm, near Speybridge, Grantown-on-Spey	n/a
A96	Auldearn Bypass, western jct	n/a
A96	Auldearn Bypass, eastern jct	n/a
A96	West of Allanfearn jct (near Culloden)	n/a
A96	Gollanfield	n/a
A99	Hempriggs, south of Wick	n/a
A834	Near Fodderty Bridge, west of Dingwall	n/a
A834	Strathpeffer Rd, Dingwall	n/a
A835	Inverlael straight, south of Ullapool	n/a
A939	Ferness to Grantown-on-Spey	n/a
B9006	Sunnyside, Culloden	n/a

Strathclyde

Road number	Location	Speed limit (mph)
M74	Jct 11 (Happendon), northbound	70
M74	Jct 13 (Abington), northbound	70
A70	East Tarelgin (approx 5km west of Ochiltree)	n/a
A73	Carlisle Rd, Airdrie	n/a
A76	near Lime Rd, New Cumnock	n/a
A78	Main Rd, Fairlie	n/a
A82	Bridge of Orchy	n/a
A82	Dumbarton Rd, Milton	n/a
A85	5.5km west of Tyndrum	n/a
A89	Forrest St, Airdrie	n/a
A89	Glasgow Rd, Bargeddie, Coatbridge	n/a
A706	South of Forth	n/a
A730	Blairbeth Rd, Rutherglen	n/a
A730	Glasgow Rd, Rutherglen	n/a
A730	Mill St, Rutherglen	n/a
A737	New St/Kilwinning Rd, Dalry	n/a
A749	East Kilbride Rd, (Cathkin Rd (B759) to Cairnmuir Rd)	n/a
A761	Glasgow Rd, Paisley near Newtyle Rd	n/a
A807	Balmore Rd, Bardowie	n/a
A809/A810	Drymen Rd/Duntocher Rd, Bearsden	n/a
A814	Cardross Rd, Dumbarton	n/a
A814	Glasgow Rd, Clydebank	n/a
A815	near Ardkinglas (near A83 jct)	n/a
B749	Craigend Rd, Troon	n/a
B768	Burnhill St, Rutherglen	n/a
B803	Coatbridge Rd, Glenmavis	n/a
B814	Duntocher Rd, Clydebank (Singer Rd to Overton Rd)	n/a
B8048	Waterside Rd, Kirkintilloch	n/a
-	Barrhead, Aurs Rd	n/a
-	Bishopbriggs, Woodhill Rd	n/a
-	Coatbridge, Townhead Rd	n/a
-	East Kilbride, Maxwellton Rd at Kirkoswald	n/a
-	Johnstone, Beith Rd	n/a
-	Neilston, Kingston Rd	n/a
-	Newton Mearns, Mearns Rd	n/a

Tayside

Road number	Location	Speed limit (mph)
A9	Near Inveralmond Industrial Est, Perth	70
A9	Tibbermore jct	70
A9	Broom of Dalreoch (B9141) to Upper Cairnie (B934)	70
A9	Near Balnansteuartach (approx 1.5 miles west of Blair Atholl)	60
A90	Quilkoe jct (B9128) to Finavon	70
A90	Forfar Rd, Dundee (near Fountainbleau Dr)	40
A90	Kingsway, Dundee	50
A90	Strathmartine Rd roundabout to Swallow roundabout, Dundee	50
A90	M90 jct 11 to Inchyra	70
A90	West of Longforgan village	70
A91	Milnathort to Devon Bridge	60
A92	Arbroath to Montrose	60
A92	East Dock St, Dundee	40
A92	Greendykes Rd, Dundee (Arbroath Rd to Craigie Ave)	30
A93	Guildtown to Blairgowrie	60
A93	Old Scone to Guildtown	60
A94	Scone to Coupar Angus	60
A822	Crieff to Braco	60
A923	Blairgowrie to Tullybaccart (Sidlaw Hills)	60
A933	Colliston northwards to Redford	60
A935	Brechin to Montrose	60
A972	Kingsway East, Dundee (to Pitairlie Rd)	40
A977	Kinross to Crook of Devon	60
B961	Drumgeith Rd, Dundee	30
B996	Kinross to Kelty	60
-	Dundee, Broughty Ferry Rd	30
-	Dundee, Charleston Dr	30
-	Dundee, Laird St	30
-	Dundee, Old Glamis Rd	30
-	Dundee, Perth Rd	30
-	Dundee, Strathmartine Rd	30

WALES

Mid and South Wales

Road number	Location	Speed limit (mph)
M4	3km east of jct 24, Llanmartin overbridge	70
M4	Approx 5km east of jct 32, Cherry Orchard overbridge	70
M4	1km east of jct 32, Rhiwbina Hill overbridge	70
M4	1.1km east of jct 33, Llantrisant Rd overbridge	70
M4	2km east of jct 35 (overbridge)	70
M4	Jct 36 overbridge	70
M4	1.5km east of jct 37 (overbridge)	70
M4	Toll Plaza	50
A40	From 1.2km east to 100m west of Bancyfelin jct	70
A40	Buckland Hall, near Bwlch	60
A40	Johnstown (Carmarthen west)	70
A40	Opposite Llangattock Lodge (southeast of Abergavenny)	70
A40	Llanhamlach	60
A40	Llansantffraed	60
A40	Mitchel Troy	70
A40	Rhosmaen (B4302 jct to national speed limit)	40
A40	Scethrog	60
A40	Trecastle	40
A40	White Mill	60
A44	Forest Bends (5km south-east of Llandegley)	60
A44	Gwystre	60
A44	Llanbadarn Fawr, Aberystwyth	30
A44	Llanfihangel-nant-Melan	60
A44	Sweet Lamb (west of Llangurig)	60
A48	M4 jct 49 north to Bristol House layby	70
A48	From 1.8km west to 300m east of Foelgastell jct	70
A48	From 1.7km west to 300m east of Llanddarog jct	70
A48	From 700m east to 2.2km west of Nant-y-caws jct	70
A48	Dinas Baglan, Baglan	30
A48	Bonvilston	40
A48	Browcastle (2km south-east of Bridgend)	40
A48	Castleton	50
A48	Cowbridge Bypass	70
A48	Cross Hands to Cwmgwili	40
A48	Cwmgwili, (Pontarddulais Rd jct to Bristol House layby)	70
A48	Langstone	40
A48	Clasemont Rd, Morriston, Swansea	30
A48	Berryhill, Newport	50
A48	Parkwall (north-east of Caldicot)	60
A48	Bolgoed Rd, Pontarddulais	30
A48	Carmarthen Rd, Pontarddulais	30
A48	Fforest Rd, Fforest, Pontarddulais	30
A48	Margam Rd, Port Talbot (at Rhanallt St)	30
A48	Peniel Green Rd, Llansamlet, Swansea (near Station Rd outside TOTAL Garage)	30
A48	St Nicholas	30
A438	Three Cocks	40
A449	Near Coldra (near Cats Ash overbridge)	70
A449	Llandenny	70
A449	Llantrisant (south of Usk)	70
A458	Cefn Bridge	60
A458	Llanfair Caereinion (Neuadd Bridge)	60
A458	Trewern	40
A465	Near Clydach	50
A465	Llanfoist near Abergavenny	60
A465	West of Llanfoist, near B4246 jct	60
A465	Pandy	40/50
A465	Triley Mill (near Llantilio Pertholey)	60
A466	High Beech Roundabout to Old Hospital, Chepstow	40
A466	Llandogo	30
A466	Dixton Rd, Monmouth	30
A466	Hereford Rd, Monmouth	30
A466	Redbrook Rd, Monmouth	30
A466	St Arvans	30
A466	Tintern	30
A467	Abertillery	30
A467	Blaina	40
A467	Danygraig, Risca	70
A467	Warm Turn	30
A468	Machen village	30
A468	Caerphilly Rd, Rhiwderyn	30
A469	Lower Rhymney Valley Relief Rd	70
A469	Tir-y-Birth, north of Hengoed	30
A470	Abercynon (southbound)	70
A470	Aberfan (overbridge)	70
A470	Aberduhonw (2km east of Builth Wells)	60
A470	Near Alltmawr (south of Builth Wells)	60
A470	Beacons Reservoir (near A4059 jct)	60
A470	Ysgiog (4km south of Builth Wells)	60
A470	Overbridge north of Cilfynydd	70
A470	Storey Arms (Brecon to Merthyr Tydfil, 2km north of A4059)	60
A470	Erwood	30
A470	Erwood (south)	60
A470	Llandinam to Caersws jct	40
A470	Llandinam village	40
A470	Llanidloes to Llandinam	60
A470	Llyswen	30
A470	Manor Way, Cardiff	40
A470	Newbridge to Rhayader	60
A470	Newbridge on Wye	30
A470	North Rd, Cardiff	30
A470	Rhydyfelin (overbridge, Dynea Rd)	70
A470	Near Taffs Well	70
A472	Hafodyrynys Hill, Crumlin	30
A472	Hafodyrynys	30
A472	Maesycwmmer	30
A472	Monkswood	60
A472	Little Mill, Pontypool	30
A472	Usk Bridge to Old Saw Mill	30
A472/A4042	Pontymoel Gyratory (elevated section)	50
A473/A4063	Bridgend Inner Bypass	30
A473	Bridgend Rd, Llanharan	30
A473	Bryntirion Hill, Bridgend	30
A473	Main Rd, Church Village	30
A473	Penybont Rd, Pencoed	30
A474	Glanaman	30
A474	Glanffrwd Estate jct to 40mph speed limit, Garnant	30
A474	Graig Rd, Alltwen	40
A474	Commercial St, Rhydyfro	30
A474	Heol Wallasey jct, Ammanford to NSL, Portamman	30
A474	Heol-Y-Gors, Cwmgors	60
A474	Penywern Rd, Neath	30
A475	Pentrebach, Lampeter	40
A475	Lampeter (central)	30
A475	Llanwnnen	40
A476	Carmel north to NSL, Temple Bar	30
A476	Cross Hands Roundabout to the Phoenix Inn, Gorslas	30
A476	Erw Non jct to Clos Rebecca jct, Llannon	30
A476	Heol Bryngwilli, south of Cross Hands (mobile near static)	30
A476	Llannon Rd/Bethania Rd, Upper Tumble	30
A476	Stag & Pheasant, south of Carmel	40
A476	The Gate, Gorslas	40
A476	Ffairfach	30
A476	Thomas Arms, Llanelli to NSL, Swiss Valley	30
A477	Cosheston	40
A477	Llanddowror	30
A478	Clunderwen	30
A478	Llandissilio	30
A478	Pentlepoir	30
A479	Bronllys	30
A482	Cwmann (south)	30
A482	Cwmann (north)	30
A482	Lampeter (central)	30
A482	Lampeter Rd, Aberaeron	30
A482	Llanwrda	n/a
A483	near Abbeycwmhir jct	60
A483	Carmarthen Rd, Fforest Fach	30
A483	Garthmyl	60
A483	Midway Bends, Llandrindod Wells to Crossgates	60
A483	NSL to Llandeilo Bridge, Ffairfach	30
A483	North of Crossgates	60
A483	Refail Garage, Garthmyl	50
A483	Rhosmaen St, Llandeilo (King St to Bypass roundabout),	30
A483	Tycroes to Villiers jct, Ammanford	30
A483	Carmarthen Rd, Cwmdu, Swansea	40
A483	Fabian Way, Swansea (western end)	30
A484	Bronwydd	40
A484	Burry Port (all of the 30mph area)	30
A484	Cenarth	30
A484	Cwmffrwd (first bend on entering from the north)	40
A484	Cynwyl Elfed	30
A484	Danybanc jct to St Illtyds Rise jct, Pembrey	30
A484	North of Pembrey	60
A484	Pentrecagel	40
A484	Rhos	30
A484	Sandy Rd, Llanelli (Wauneos Rd to Denham Ave)	30
A484	Saron (outside school)	40
A484	Saron	40
A484	Trostre Roundabout to Berwick Roundabout, Llanelli	60
A484	From B4309 jct to NSL, Idole	40
A484	From 80m west of New Rd jct east to NSL, Newcastle Emlyn	30
A485	Alltwalis	40
A485	From A482 jct to NSL, Cwmann	30
A485	Llanllwni	40
A485	Llanybydder (north)	30
A485	Llanybydder (south)	30
A485	Peniel	40
A487	Bow St	30
A487	Aberaeron (central)	30
A487	Aberystwyth (central)	30
A487	Eglwyswrw	30
A487	Furnace	40
A487	Llanrhystud (southern approach)	40
A487	Llanarth	40
A487	Llanfarian	30
A487	Newgale	30
A487	Newport	30
A487	Penglais Hill/Waunfawr, Aberystwyth	40
A487	Penparc	40
A487	Rhydyfelin	40
A487	Rhyd-y pennau	30
A487	Tal-y-bont	30
A489	Caersws jct to Penstrowed	60
A489	Glanmule (at garage)	60
A489	Penstrowed to Newtown	60
A489	West of Hafren College, Newtown	40
A4042	Llanover	60
A4042	Mamhilad	70
A4043	Cwmavon Rd, Abersychan	40
A4043	St Lukes Rd, Pontnewynydd, Pontypool	30
A4046	College Rd, Ebbw Vale	30
A4046	Ebbw Vale (near Tesco)	40
A4046	Waunllwyd	30
A4047	Beaufort Hill/Hing St, Brynmawr	30
A4048	Argoed	30
A4048	Blackwood (Sunnybank)	30
A4048	Hollybush	30
A4048	Blackwood Rd, Pontllanfraith	30
A4048	Cwmfelinfach village	30
A4049	Bryn Rd, Pontllanfraith	30
A4050	Jenner Rd, Barry	30
A4051	Cwmbran Dr, Cwmbran	60
A4054	Cardiff Rd, Merthyr Vale	30
A4054	Cardiff Rd, Upper Boat	30
A4054	Cilfynydd Rd, Cilfynydd	30
A4054	Edwardsville (near Treharris)	30
A4054	Cardiff Rd, Mt Pleasant (south of Merthyr Vale)	30
A4054	Oxford St, Nantgarw	30
A4054	Pentrebach Rd, Pontypridd	30
A4055	Gladstone Rd, Barry	30
A4058	The Broadway, Pontypridd	30
A4058	Hopkinstown Rd, Hopkinstown, Pontypridd	30
A4059	New Rd, Mountain Ash	30
A4061	Cemetery Rd, Ogmore Vale	30
A4063	Maesteg Rd/Bridgend Rd,Pont-Rhyd-y-cyff, Maesteg	30
A4063	Bridgend Rd, Pen-y-fai	30
A4063	Sarn Bypass near jct with Bryncoch Rd	50
A4066	Broadway	40
A4066	Llanmiloe	40
A4066	Marsh Rd, Pendine	30
A4067	Abercraf	60
A4067	Crai	60
A4067	Mumbles Rd, Swansea (Sketty La to St Helens Sports Ground)	40
A4068	Bethel Rd, Cwmtwrch (near Ystalyfera)	30
A4068	Heol Gleien, Cwmtwrch (near Ystalyfera)	30
A4069	Station Rd, Brynamman (county bdy to Remploy factory)	30
A4069	Brynamman Rd, south of Brynamman	30
A4069	Broad St, Llandovery (A40 south to NSL)	30
A4069	Llangadog (south)	30
A4069	Llangadog (east)	30
A4069	Station Rd, Llangadog (north)	30
A4075	Carew	30
A4075	Pembroke	30
A4076	Johnston	30
A4076	Steynton	30
A4093	Gilfach Rd, Hendreforgan, Gilfach Goch	30
A4093	Glynogwr (approx 2.5km east of A4061)	30
A4102	Goatmill Rd, Merthyr Tydfil	30
A4106	Newton Nottage Rd, Porthcawl	30
A4106	Bridgend Rd, Porthcawl	40
A4106	The Porthway, Porthcawl	n/a
A4107	High St, Abergwynfi	30
A4109	Main Rd, Aberdulais	n/a
A4109	Dulais Rd, south of Seven Sisters	30
A4109	Glynneath	30
A4109	Main Rd, Crynant	30
A4118	near Swansea Airport	60
A4119	Mwyndy Cross, Llantrisant	50
A4120	Aberystwyth	30
A4138	From the 30mph limit at Hendy to the B4297, Talyclun	40
A4138	Loughor Bridge to 40mph limit, Hendy	30
A4139	Pembroke	30
A4139	Pembroke Dock	30
A4139	Tenby	30
A4216	Cockett Rd, Cockett, Swansea	30
A4221	Caehopkin	60
A4222	Abertin Rd, Cowbridge	30
A4222	Primrose Hill, Cowbridge	30
A4222	Maendy	30
A4222	Cowbridge Rd, Pontyclun	30
A4226	Five Mile La, Barry	40
A4226	Five Mile La, Moulton	40
A4233	Ferndale (at Highfield)	30
A4233	Oakland Terr, Ferndale	30
A4233	The Parade, Ferndale	30
B4181	Coity Rd, Bridgend	30
B4181	Coychurch Rd, Bridgend	30
B4223	Gelli Rd, Gelli (Rhondda)	30
B4223	Maindy Rd/Pen-Twyn Rd, Ton Pentre (Rhondda)	30
B4235	Gwernesney, near Usk	60
B4236	Ponthir Rd, Caerleon	30
B4236	Llanfrechfa	30
B4236	Carleon Rd, Ponthir	30
B4237	Cardiff Rd, Belle Vue, Newport	30
B4237	Chepstow Rd, Newport (near Aberthaw Rd)	30
B4237	Chepstow Rd, Newport (near Royal Oak Hill)	40
B4237	Wharf Rd, Newport	30
B4239	Lighthouse Rd, Maes-glas, Newport	30
B4242	Pont-Nêdd-Féchan	40
B4245	Caldicot Bypass	30
B4245	Leechpool (near Caldicot)	60
B4245	Magor Rd, west of Llanmartin	30
B4245	Magor (west)	30
B4245	Undy	30
B4245	Caldicot Rd, Rogiet	30
B4245	West of Rogiet (at Green Farm bend)	40
B4246	Foundry Rd, Abersychan	30
B4246	Varteg Rd, Abersychan	30
B4246	New Rd, Garndiffaith	30
B4248	Garn Rd, Blaenavon	40
B4251	Kendon Hill, Oakdale	30
B4254	Church Rd, Gelligaer	40
B4254	Pengam Rd, Penpedairheol (near Gelligaer)	30
B4254	Gelligaer Rd, Trelewis	30
B4257	Wellington Way, Rhymney	30
B4262	Heol Isaf, Radyr, Cardiff	30
B4265	Llantwit Major Bypass	50
B4265	St Brides Major	30
B4265	St Brides Rd, Wick	30
B4267	Leckwith Rd, Cardiff	30
B4267	South Rd, Sully	30
B4273	New Rd, Ynysybwl	30
B4275	Abercynon Rd, Abercynon	30
B4275	Park View Ter, Abercwmboi	30
B4275	Miskin Rd, Mountain Ash	30
B4275	Penrhiwceiber Rd, Penrhiwceiber	30
B4278	Dinas Rd, Dinas (near Tonypandy)	30
B4278	Gilfach Rd, Tonyrefail	30
B4278	Penrhiw-fer Rd, Tonyrefail	30
B4281	Cefn Rd, Cefn Criwber	30
B4281	High St, Kenfig Hill, Pyle	30
B4282	Bridgend Rd and Castle St, Maesteg (centre of 2.15km section)	30
B4282	Measteg Rd, Bryn	30
B4283	Heol Fach, North Connelly, Pyle	30
B4290	Burrows Rd, /Pen-yr-Heol, Skewen, Neath	30
B4290	New Rd, Jersey Marine	30
B4291	Birchgrove Grove, Birchgrove	30
B4293	Devauden	30
B4295	Cwmbach Rd, Cockett, Swansea	30
B4295	Gowerton to Penclawdd	40
B4295	New Rd, Crofty	30
B4295	Penclawdd to Llanrhidian	60
B4296	Goetre Fawr Rd, Killay, Swansea	30
B4296	Grovesend	30
B4296	Pentre Rd, Waungron	30
B4297	Capel Hendre (Nant yr Arw jct to the Parc Hendre jct)	30
B4297	Cleviston Park to Park La, Llangennech	30
B4297	Fforest	30
B4297	Llanedi (north of Pontarddulais)	30
B4297	Llwynhendy (Capel Soar to the Police Station)	30
B4297	Loughor Bridge Roundabout to Station Rd, Bynea	40
B4301	Bronwydd	30
B4302	Talley	30
B4303	Dafen Roundabout to Felinfoel Roundabout, Llanelli	30
B4304	Copperworks Roadbridge to Morfa Roundabout, Llanelli	40
B4304	Lower Trostre Rd Roundabout to Trostre Rd Roundabout, Llanelli	30
B4306	Heol Y Banc, Bancffosfelen	30
B4306	Llangendeirne	30
B4306	Llanon Rd, Pontyberem	30
B4308	Penmynnydd (east of Trimsaran)	40
B4309	Five Roads	30
B4310	Heol Caegwyn, Drefach	30
B4310	Station Rd, Nantgaredig	40
B4312	Johnstown, Carmarthen (from The Square south to NSL)	30
B4312	Llangain	30
B4312	St Clears Rd, Johnstown, Carmarthen	30
B4314	Pendine	30
B4314	Narberth	30
B4317	Carway (east)	30
B4317	Carway (west)	30
B4317	Heol Capel Ifan, Pontyberem	30
B4317	Myrtle Hill, Ponthenry	30
B4317	Station Rd, Pontyberem	30
B4320	Hundleton	30
B4322	Pembroke Rd, Pembroke Dock	40
B4325	Neyland	30
B4328	Trevaughan, Whitland	30
B4333	Aber-arad, Newcastle Emlyn	30
B4333	Cynwyl Elfed (north)	30
B4333	Hermon	40
B4336	Llanfihangel-ar-Arth	30
B4336	Pontwelly, Llandysul	30
B4436	Northway, Bishopston	40
B4337	Llanybydder	30
B4337	Talsarn	40
B4347	Newcastle (near Monmouth)	30
B4350	Glasbury to Hay-on-Wye	60
B4436	Pennard Rd, Kittle (near Bishopston)	40
B4459	Llanfihangel-ar-Arth (south)	30
B4459	Pencader	30
B4459	Pencader (south)	40
B4478	Letchworth Rd, Ebbw Vale	30
B4486	Steelworks Rd, Ebbw Vale	30
B4487	Newport Rd, Cardiff	30
B4488	Pencisely Rd, Cardiff	30
B4489	Llangyfelach Rd, Treboeth, Swansea	30
B4489	Swansea Rd, Llangyfelach, Swansea	30
B4511	Bedwellty Rd, Aberbargoed (at Coedymoeth Rd)	30
B4511	Penylan Rd, Argoed	30
B4521	Hereford Rd, Abergavenny	30
B4524	Corntown	30
B4556	Cae'r bryn, near Ammanford	30
B4556	Norton Rd, Penygroes	30
B4556	Penygroes Rd, Blaenau (east of Cae'r bryn)	30
B4556	Penygroes Rd, Gorslas	30
B4560	Llangynidr Rd, Beaufort, Ebbw Vale	30
B4591	Cromwell Rd, Risca	30
B4591	Pontymister, Risca (at Welsh Oak pub)	30
B4591	High Cross, Newport (near jct 27)	30
B4591	Risca Rd, Pontymister, Risca (opposite power station)	30
B4595	Brynteg Hill, Beddau	30
B4596	Caerleon Rd, Newport (south of M4)	30
B4596	Caerleon Rd, Newport (east of Beaufort Rd)	30
B4598	Horse and Jockey (near Abergavenny)	60
B4598	Llancayo	60
B4598	Porthycarne St, Usk	30
B4599	Ystradgynlais	30
B4603	Clydach Rd, Ynystawe	30
B4603	Pontardawe Rd, Clydach	30
B4622	Broadlands Link Rd, near Bridgend	30
B4623	Mountain Rd, Caerphilly	30
-	Abergwili (Ambulance Station to the Bypass roundabout)	30
-	Abertillery, Gwern-Berthi Rd	30
-	Ammanford, New Rd/ Pantyffynnon Rd	30
-	Ammanford, Dyffryn Rd, Saron	30
-	Ammanford, Saron (at Saron School)	30
-	Ammanford, Saron Rd (at Saron Church)	30
-	Barry, Barry Rd	30
-	Barry, Buttrills Rd	30
-	Barry, Holton Rd	30
-	Beddau, Gwaunmiskin Rd	30
-	Betws, Betws Rd (near Ammanford)	30
-	Betws, Maesquarre Rd	30
-	Blaenavon, Upper Coedcae Rd	30
-	Bridgend, Brackla Way, Brackla	30
-	Bridgend, Heol-y-Nant, Cefn Glas	30
-	Bridgend, Llangewydd Rd, Cefn Glas	30
-	Bridgend, Merlin Cres, Cefn Glas	30
-	Bridgend Industrial Estate, Kingsway	30
-	Bridgend Industrial Estate, North Rd	30
-	Bridgend Industrial Estate, South Rd	30
-	Bridgend Industrial Estate, Western Ave	30
-	Bridgend, Pen-Y-Cae La	30
-	Briton Ferry, Old Rd	30
-	Brynna, Brynna Rd	30
-	Caerleon, Usk Rd	30
-	Caerleon to Usk road (Apple Tree Farm, north of Garth)	60
-	Caldicot, Chepstow Rd	30
-	Cardiff, Colchester Ave, Penylan	30
-	Cardiff, Cyncoed Rd	30
-	Cardiff, Maes-y-Coed Rd, Heath	30
-	Cardiff, Circle Way, Llanedeyrn	30
-	Cardiff, Excalibur Dr, Thornhill	30
-	Cardiff, Heol y Deri, Rhiwbina	30
-	Cardiff, Rhiwbina Hill	30
-	Cardiff, Rhyd-y-Penau Rd	30
-	Cardiff, Lake Rd East, Roath	30
-	Cardiff, Lake Rd West, Roath	30
-	Cardiff, Wentloog Ave, Rumney	30
-	Cardiff, St Fagans Rd	30
-	Cardigan (north)	30
-	Carmarthen, Lime Grove Ave/ Fountain Head Terrace	30
-	Cefn Criwber	30
-	Cefneithin (west of Gorslas)	30
-	Church Village, Church Rd, Ton-teg	30
-	Church Village, Pen-yr-Eglwys	n/a
-	Church Village, Station Rd	30
-	Clydach, Vardre Rd	30
-	Coity, Heol Spencer	30
-	Cwmbran, Avondale Rd	30
-	Cwmbran, Greenforge Way	30
-	Cwmbran, Henllys Way	30
-	Cwmbran, Llanfrechfa Way	30
-	Cwmbran, Maendy Way	30
-	Cwmbran, Chapel St, Pontnewydd	30
-	Cwmbran, Thornhill Rd	30
-	Cwmbran, Ty Canol Way	30
-	Cwmbran, Ty Gwyn Way/ Greenmeadow Way	30
-	Cwmgwili	30
-	Cwmgwili, Thornhill Rd	30
-	Deri, New Rd	30
-	Dinas Powys, Pen-y-Turnpike Rd	30
-	Drefach, Heol Blaenhirwaun	30
-	Drefach, Heol Caegwyn	30
-	Ebbw Vale, Cwmgovilon, Beaufort	30
-	Ebbw Vale, Gwaun Helyg Rd, Willowtown	30
-	Ebbw Vale, Newchurch Rd	30
-	Ebbw Vale, Reservoir Rd, Rassau	30
-	Fochriw, Olgivie Ter	30
-	Foelgastell (west of Gorslas)	30
-	Forden	30
-	Gelli, (Rhondda), Gelli Industrial Estate	30
-	Gilwern, Cae Meldon (aka Ty Mawr La)	30
-	Gorseinon, Frampton Rd	30
-	Haverfordwest, Merlin's Bridge	30
-	Haverfordwest, New Rd/ Uzmaston Rd	30
-	Llanbradach	30
-	Llandysul (central)	30
-	Llanelli, Denham Ave	30
-	Llanelli, Heol Goffa (A476 to A484)	30
-	Llanharan, Brynna Rd	30
-	Llantrisant, Cross Inn Rd	30
-	Llantwit Major, Llanmaes Rd	30
-	Maesteg, Heol-Ty-Gwyn	30
-	Maesteg, Heol Ty With	30
-	Merthyr Tydfil, Brecon Rd	30
-	Merthyr Tydfil, High St, Cefn-coed-y-cymmer	30
-	Merthyr Tydfil, Vaynor Rd, Cefn-coed-y-cymmer	30
-	Merthyr Tydfil, High St, Dowlais	30
-	Merthyr Tydfil, Goetre La	30
-	Merthyr Tydfil, Gurnos Rd	30
-	Merthyr Tydfil, Heol-Tai-Mawr, Gellideg	30
-	Merthyr Tydfil, Swansea Rd, Gellideg	30
-	Merthyr Tydfil, Heolgerrig Rd	30
-	Merthyr Tydfil, Pant Rd	30
-	Merthyr Tydfil, High St, Pen-y-Darren	30
-	Merthyr Tydfil, Plymouth St	30
-	Merthyr Tydfil, The Walk	30
-	Merthyr Tydfil, Rocky Rd	30
-	Milford Haven, Priory Rd	30
-	Milford Haven, St Lawrence Hill	30
-	Mountain Ash, Llanwonno Rd	30
-	Nant-y-caws (from Heol Login along Nant-y-caws Hill) (east of Carmarthen)	60
-	Nash, West Nash Rd	30
-	Neath, Crymlyn Rd, Skewen	30
-	Newport, Allt-Yr-Yn Ave	30
-	Newport, Corporation Rd	30
-	Newport, Rowan Way, Malpas	30
-	New Quay (central)	30
-	New Tredegar, White Rose Way	30
-	Newbridge, Park Rd	30
-	Pencoed, Felindre Rd	30
-	Pendine (outside school)	30
-	South of Pentrecagel (near Newcastle Emlyn)	40
-	Pontypool, Greenhill/Sunnybank Rd, Griffithstown	30
-	Pontypool, Station Rd, Griffithstown	30
-	Pontypool, Plas y Coed Rd, Pontnewynydd	30
-	Pontypool, Riverside	30
-	Pontypool, Usk Rd	30
-	Porthcawl, Fulmar Rd	30
-	Port Talbot, Village Rd, Sandfields	30
-	Pyle, Fairfield, North Cornelly	30
-	Rhymney, Llys Joseph Parry (near Farmers Arms)	30
-	Risca, Holly Rd	30
-	Risca, Waun Fawr Park Rd	30
-	Rogerstone, Pontymason La	30
-	Sarn, Heol-Yr, Ysgol, Ynyswdre	30
-	St Athan, Cowbridge Rd	30
-	St Mellons, Willowbrook Dr	30
-	Steynton, Thornton Rd	40
-	Sully (near Barry), Hayes Rd	30
-	Swansea, Llethri Rd, Felinfoel	30
-	Swansea, Pentregethin Rd Farm Shop	30
-	Swansea, Mynydd Garnllwyd Rd/Caemawr Rd/Parry Rd/ Vicarage Rd (Heol Ddu to Clasemont Rd) Morriston	30
-	Swansea, Rhyd-y-Dafaid Dr, Derwen Fawr	30
-	Tiers Cross	60
-	Tredegar, Vale Terrace	30
-	Upper Boat, (near Pontypridd), Tonteg Rd	30
-	Usk Bridge to Llanbadoc	30
-	Usk, Usk to Raglan road (at Coldharbour)	60
-	Whitland, Market St	30
-	Whitland, North Rd	30
-	Whitland (east), Spring Gardens	30
-	Whitland (west)	30

North Wales

Road number	Location	Speed limit (mph)
A5	Bangor to Llandygai	30/40
A5	Froncysyllte to Betws-y-Coed (seasonal)	30/40/60
A5	London Rd, Holyhead	30
A5	Menai Bridge to Gwalchmai	30/40/60
A5/A5025	Holyhead to Llanfachraeth	20/30/40/60
A458	Cwm-Cewydd east to county boundary (seasonal)	60
A470	Dolgellau (A496 to east of A494)	40/60
A470	Llansanffraid Glan Conwy to Betws-y-Coed	30/60
A470	Llandudno to A55, jct 19	30/40/60
A470	Mallwyd to A487 (seasonal)	30/40/60
A470	North of Rhiwbrifdir to Congl-y-wal, Blaenau Ffestiniog	30/40/60
A483/A5	Ruabon to Chirk	60
A487	Caernarfon to Dolbenmaen	30/40/50/60
A487	Pantperthog to A470 (seasonal)	30/40/60
A487	Penmorfa to Gellilydan	30/40/60
A494	Bala to Glan-yr-afon	40/60
A494	Llyn Tegid (Bala Lake)	30
A494	Ruthin to Corwen (seasonal)	30/40/60
A494	Ruthin to Llanferres	40/60
A496	Harlech to Llanbedr	30/40/60
A499	Pwllheli to Penrhos	30/40/60
A525	Llanfair Dyffryn Clwyd to Llandegla (near B5430)	30/40/60
A525	Ruthin to Denbigh	40/60
A525	St Asaph to Trefnant	30/40/60
A525	Vale Rd/Rhuddlan Rd, Rhyl	30
A525	Wrexham to Minera	30/60
A525	Wrexham to Redbrook	30/40/60
A534	Holt Rd, Wrexham	30
A539	Mill St, Llangollen	30/60
A539	Trevor to Erbistock (A528 jct)	30/40/60
A541	Caergwrle to Wrexham	30/40/60/70
A541	Mold to Caergwrle	30/40/60/70
A541	Mold Rd, Wrexham	30
A541	Trefnant to Bodfari	30/40/60
A542	Horseshoe Pass (seasonal)	60
A543	Denbigh to Pentrefoelas (seasonal)	30/60
A545	Menai Bridge to Beaumaris	30/40/60
A547	Colwyn Bay to Old Colwyn	30/40/50
A547	Prestatyn to Rhuddlan	30/40/60
A548	Dundonald Ave, Abergele	30
A548	Gronant to Flint (Oakenholt)	30/40/50/60/70
A548	Rhyl to Prestatyn	30/40
A548	Abergele to Kinmel Bay	30/40
A549	Mynydd Isa to Buckley	30/60
A550	Hawarden	30
A4080	Brynsiencyn to Rhosneigr (seasonal)	30/40/60
A4086	Cwm-y-Glo to Llanrug	30/40/60
A4086	Llanberis (seasonal)	30/40/60
A4212	Bala	30/60
A4212	Trawsfynydd to Llyn Celyn	60
A4244	Cwm-y-Glo to B4547	60
A5025	Amlwch to Menai Bridge	30/40/50/60
A5025/A5	Llanfachraeth to Holyhead	20/30/40/60
A5104	Coed-Talon to Leeswood (A541 to B5101)	30
A5104	Coed-Talon to A494 (seasonal)	30
A5119	Flint to Mold	30/50/60
A5152	Chester Rd, Wrexham	30
A5152	Rhostyllen	30/40
A5154	Victoria Rd, Holyhead	30
B4501	Denbigh to Cerrigydrudion (seasonal)	30/40/60
B4545	Kingsland to Valley (via Trearddur Bay)	30/40
B5105	Ruthin to Cerrigydrudion (seasonal)	30/40/60
B5108	Brynteg to Benllech	30/60
B5109	Llangefni towards Bodffordd	30
B5113	Kings Rd/Kings Dr, Colwyn Bay	30
B5115	Llandudno Promenade to Penrhyn Bay	30/40
B5115	Llandudno Rd, Llandrillo-yn-Rhos	30
B5118	Rhyl Promenade, Rhyl	30
B5120	Pendyffryn Rd, Prestatyn	30
B5125	Hawarden	30
B5129	Kelsterton to Saltney Ferry	30/60
B5420	Menai Bridge (Four Crosses to Menai Bridge Sq)	30
B5425	Wrexham to Llay	30/60
B5445	Rossett	30
B5605	Johnstown to Ruabon	30/40/60
-	Holyhead, Prince of Wales Rd	30
-	Penrhyn Bay to Rhos Point (coast road)	30
-	Kinmel Bay, St Asaph Ave	30/60

Key to listing

- Motorway
- Primary route
- Other A road
- B road
- Minor road

Avoiding congestion trouble spots

These 'jam-busting' maps pinpoint locations where traffic jams regularly occur and help you plan a route to avoid them. Only motorways and major A-roads are included but you can use the main-map pages in this atlas to plot a detailed route around potential trouble spots.

AA mobile phone SMS traffic alerts
Set up SMS text message traffic alerts for single journeys or for your daily commute and the AA will monitor your route and text you about delays before you leave. For each traffic alert SMS you will be reverse-billed 50p.
For further information see
www.aatrafficalerts.co.uk

Acknowledgements

The Route planning section of this atlas was edited, designed and produced by AA Publishing.
© Automobile Association Developments Limited 2006
Crown copyright material (road signs) is reproduced under licence from the Controller of HMSO and the Driving Standards Agency. Crown copyright material (mobile speed cameras) is reproduced with the permission of the Controller of HMSO and the Queen's Printer for Scotland (licence number C02W0005858).

The publishers wish to acknowledge and thank the following for their contribution to the 'Route planning' section of this atlas.
AA Motoring Trust, ITIS, Safety Camera Partnerships.

Traffic congestion 12 © ITIS Holdings

Severn Bridges: Westbound holiday traffic may find queues at the tolls.

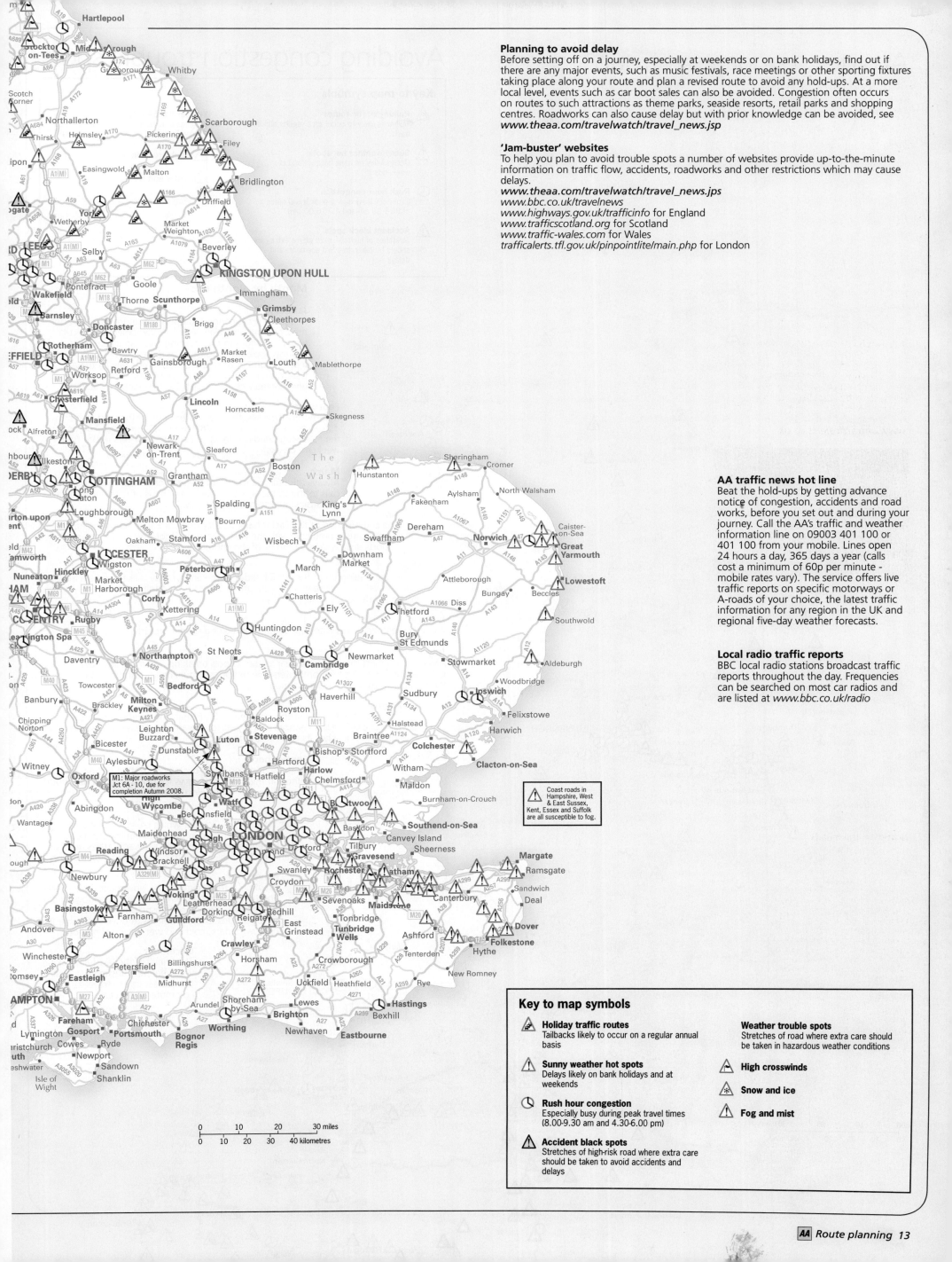

Planning to avoid delay

Before setting off on a journey, especially at weekends or on bank holidays, find out if there are any major events, such as music festivals, race meetings or other sporting fixtures taking place along your route and plan a revised route to avoid any hold-ups. At a more local level, events such as car boot sales can also be avoided. Congestion often occurs on routes to such attractions as theme parks, seaside resorts, retail parks and shopping centres. Roadworks can also cause delay but with prior knowledge can be avoided, see *www.theaa.com/travelwatch/travel_news.jsp*

'Jam-buster' websites

To help you plan to avoid trouble spots a number of websites provide up-to-the-minute information on traffic flow, accidents, roadworks and other restrictions which may cause delays.

www.theaa.com/travelwatch/travel_news.jps
www.bbc.co.uk/travelnews
www.highways.gov.uk/trafficinfo for England
www.trafficscotland.org for Scotland
www.traffic-wales.com for Wales
trafficalerts.tfl.gov.uk/pinpointlite/main.php for London

AA traffic news hot line

Beat the hold-ups by getting advance notice of congestion, accidents and road works, before you set out and during your journey. Call the AA's traffic and weather information line on 09003 401 100 or 401 100 from your mobile. Lines open 24 hours a day, 365 days a year (calls cost a minimum of 60p per minute - mobile rates vary). The service offers live traffic reports on specific motorways or A-roads of your choice, the latest traffic information for any region in the UK and regional five-day weather forecasts.

Local radio traffic reports

BBC local radio stations broadcast traffic reports throughout the day. Frequencies can be searched on most car radios and are listed at *www.bbc.co.uk/radio*

M1: Major roadworks Jct 6A - 10, due for completion Autumn 2008.

Coast roads in Hampshire, West & East Sussex, Kent, Essex and Suffolk are all susceptible to fog.

0   10   20   30 miles
0   10   20   30   40 kilometres

Key to map symbols

Holiday traffic routes
Tailbacks likely to occur on a regular annual basis

Sunny weather hot spots
Delays likely on bank holidays and at weekends

Rush hour congestion
Especially busy during peak travel times (8.00-9.30 am and 4.30-6.00 pm)

Accident black spots
Stretches of high-risk road where extra care should be taken to avoid accidents and delays

Weather trouble spots
Stretches of road where extra care should be taken in hazardous weather conditions

High crosswinds

Snow and ice

Fog and mist

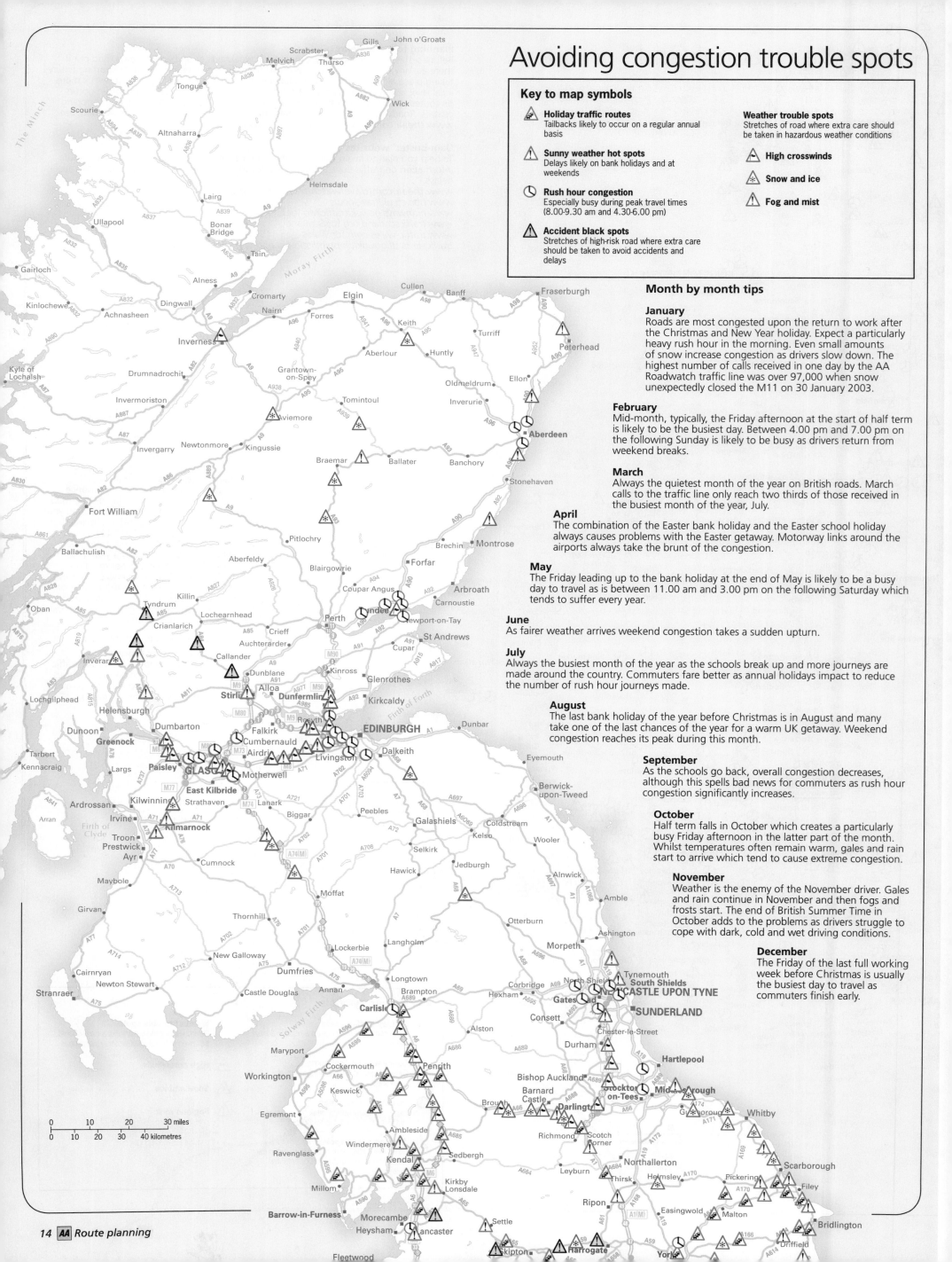

Avoiding congestion trouble spots

Key to map symbols

Holiday traffic routes
Tailbacks likely to occur on a regular annual basis

Sunny weather hot spots
Delays likely on bank holidays and at weekends

Rush hour congestion
Especially busy during peak travel times (8.00-9.30 am and 4.30-6.00 pm)

Accident black spots
Stretches of high-risk road where extra care should be taken to avoid accidents and delays

Weather trouble spots
Stretches of road where extra care should be taken in hazardous weather conditions

High crosswinds

Snow and ice

Fog and mist

Month by month tips

January
Roads are most congested upon the return to work after the Christmas and New Year holiday. Expect a particularly heavy rush hour in the morning. Even small amounts of snow increase congestion as drivers slow down. The highest number of calls received in one day by the AA Roadwatch traffic line was over 97,000 when snow unexpectedly closed the M11 on 30 January 2003.

February
Mid-month, typically, the Friday afternoon at the start of half term is likely to be the busiest day. Between 4.00 pm and 7.00 pm on the following Sunday is likely to be busy as drivers return from weekend breaks.

March
Always the quietest month of the year on British roads. March calls to the traffic line only reach two thirds of those received in the busiest month of the year, July.

April
The combination of the Easter bank holiday and the Easter school holiday always causes problems with the Easter getaway. Motorway links around the airports always take the brunt of the congestion.

May
The Friday leading up to the bank holiday at the end of May is likely to be a busy day to travel as is between 11.00 am and 3.00 pm on the following Saturday which tends to suffer every year.

June
As fairer weather arrives weekend congestion takes a sudden upturn.

July
Always the busiest month of the year as the schools break up and more journeys are made around the country. Commuters fare better as annual holidays impact to reduce the number of rush hour journeys made.

August
The last bank holiday of the year before Christmas is in August and many take one of the last chances of the year for a warm UK getaway. Weekend congestion reaches its peak during this month.

September
As the schools go back, overall congestion decreases, although this spells bad news for commuters as rush hour congestion significantly increases.

October
Half term falls in October which creates a particularly busy Friday afternoon in the latter part of the month. Whilst temperatures often remain warm, gales and rain start to arrive which tend to cause extreme congestion.

November
Weather is the enemy of the November driver. Gales and rain continue in November and then fogs and frosts start. The end of British Summer Time in October adds to the problems as drivers struggle to cope with dark, cold and wet driving conditions.

December
The Friday of the last full working week before Christmas is usually the busiest day to travel as commuters finish early.

Using the National Grid

With an Ordnance Survey National Grid reference you can pinpoint anywhere in the country using this atlas. The blue grid lines which divide the main-map pages into 5km squares for ease of indexing also match the National Grid. A National Grid reference gives two letters and some figures. This example shows how to find the summit of mount Snowdon using its 4-figure grid reference of **SH6154**.

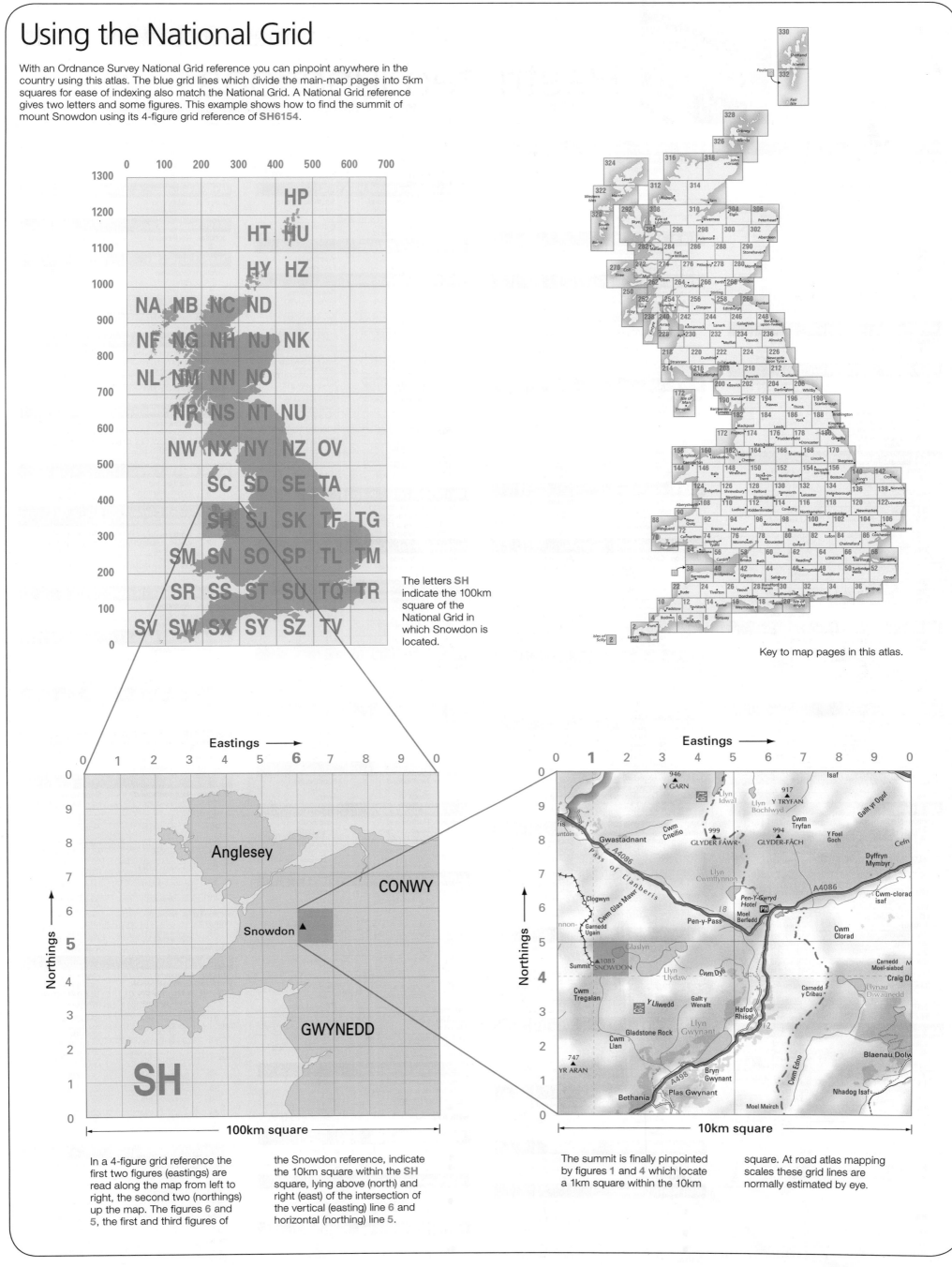

The letters **SH** indicate the 100km square of the National Grid in which Snowdon is located.

Key to map pages in this atlas.

In a 4-figure grid reference the first two figures (eastings) are read along the map from left to right, the second two (northings) up the map. The figures **6** and **5**, the first and third figures of the Snowdon reference, indicate the 10km square within the **SH** square, lying above (north) and right (east) of the intersection of the vertical (easting) line **6** and horizontal (northing) line **5**.

The summit is finally pinpointed by figures **1** and **4** which locate a 1km square within the 10km square. At road atlas mapping scales these grid lines are normally estimated by eye.

Restricted junctions

Numbered motorway and primary route junctions which have access or exit restrictions are shown thus ③ , ⑯ on the map pages.

M1 London - Leeds

Junction	Northbound	Southbound
2	Access only from A1 (*northbound*)	Exit only to A1 (*southbound*)
4	Access only from A41 (*northbound*)	Exit only to A41 (*southbound*)
6A	Access only from M25 (no link from A405)	Exit only to M25 (no link from A405)
7	Access only from M10	Exit only to M10
17	Exit only to M45	Access only from M45
19	Exit only to northbound M6	Access only from M6
21A	Exit only to A46	Access only from A46
23A	Access only from A42	Exit only to A42
24A	Access only from A50	Exit only to A50
35A	Exit only to A616	Access only from A616
43	Exit only to M621	Access only from M621
48	Exit only to A1(M) (*northbound*)	Access only from A1(M) (*southbound*)

M2 Rochester - Faversham

Junction	Westbound	Eastbound
1	Exit only to A289 (*eastbound*)	Access only from A289 (*westbound*)

M3 Sunbury - Southampton

Junction	Southwestbound	Northeastbound
8	Exit only to A303	Access only from A303
10	Access only from Winchester & A31	Exit only to Winchester & A31
13	Access only to M27 (westbound) & A33	No restriction
14	Exit only to M27 (eastbound) & A33	Access only

M4 London - South Wales

Junction	Westbound	Eastbound
1	Access only from A4 (*westbound*)	Exit only to A4 (*eastbound*)
4A	No exit to A4 (*westbound*)	No restriction
21	Exit only to M48	Access only from M48
23	Access only from M48	Exit only to M48
25	Exit only to B4596	Access only from B4596
25A	Exit only to A4042	Access only from A4042
29	Exit only to A48(M)	Access only from A48(M)
38	Exit only to A48	No restriction
39	Access only from A48	No access/exit
42	Staggered junction; follow signs - exit only to A483	Staggered junction; follow signs - access only from A483

M5 Birmingham - Exeter

Junction	Southwestbound	Northeastbound
10	Exit only to A4019	Access only from A4019
11A	Exit only to A417 (*eastbound*)	Access only from A417 (*westbound*)
18A	Access only from M49	Exit only to M49
29	Access only from A30 (*westbound*)	No restriction

M6 Toll Motorway

Junction	Northbound	Southbound
T1	Access only	No access or exit
T2	No access or exit	Exit only
T3	Staggered junction; follow signs - access only from A38	Staggered junction; follow signs - no restriction
T5	Access only from A5127 (*southbound*)	Exit only to A5148 (*northbound*)
T7	Exit only	Access only
T8	Exit only	Access only

M6 Rugby - Carlisle

Junction	Northbound	Southbound
3A	Exit only	Access only
4	No access from M42 (*southbound*). No exit to M42 (*northbound*)	No access from M42 (*southbound*). No exit to M42
4A	Access only from M42 (*southbound*)	Exit only to M42
5	Exit only to A452	Access only from A452
10A	Exit only to M54	Access only from M54
11A	Access only	Exit only
20A (with M56)	No restriction	No access from M56 (*westbound*)
20	Access only from A50	No restriction
24	Access only from A58	Exit only to A58
25	Exit only	Access only
29	No direct access, use adjacent slip road to jct 29A	No direct exit, use adjacent slip road from jct 29A
29A	No direct exit, use adjacent slip road from jct 29	No direct access, use adjacent slip road to jct 29
30	Access only from M61	Exit only to M61
31A	Exit only	Access only

M8 Edinburgh - Bishopton

Junction	Westbound	Eastbound
8	No access from M73 (*southbound*) or from A8 (*eastbound*) & A89	No exit to M73 (*northbound*) or to A8 (*westbound*) & A89
9	Access only	Exit only
13	Access only from M80 (*southbound*)	Exit only to M80 (*northbound*)
14	Access only	Exit only
16	Exit only to A804	Access only from A879
17	Exit only to A82	No restriction
18	Access only from A82 (*eastbound*)	Exit only to A814
19	No access from A814 (westbound)	Exit only to A814 (*westbound*)
20	Exit only	Access only
21	Access only	Exit only to A8
22	Exit only to M77 (*southbound*)	Access only from M77 (*northbound*)
23	Exit only to B768	Access only from B768
25	No access or exit from or to A8	No access or exit from or to A8
25A	Exit only	Access only
28	Exit only	Access only
28A	Exit only to A737	Access only from A737

M9 Edinburgh - Dunblane

Junction	Northwestbound	Southeastbound
1A	Exit only to A8000	Access only from A8000
2	Access only	Exit only
3	Exit only	Access only
6	Access only from A904	Exit only to A905
8	Exit only to M876 (*southwestbound*)	Access only from M876 (*northeastbound*)

M10 St Albans - M1

Junction	Northwestbound	Southeastbound
with M1 (jct 7)	Exit only to M1 (*northbound*)	Access only from M1 (*southbound*)

M11 London - Cambridge

Junction	Northbound	Southbound
4	Access only from A406	Exit only to A406
5	Exit only to A1168	Access only from A1168
9	Exit only to A11	Access only from A11
13	Exit only to A1303	Access only from A1303
14	Exit only to A14 (*eastbound*)	Access only from A14

M20 Swanley - Folkestone

Junction	Southeastbound	Northwestbound
2	Staggered junction; follow signs - exit only to A227	Staggered junction; follow signs - access only from A227
3	Access only from M26 (*eastbound*)	Exit only to M26 (*westbound*)
5	For access follow signs - exit only to A20	Access only from A20
6	For exit follow signs	No restriction
11A	Exit only	Access only

M23 Hooley - Crawley

Junction	Southbound	Northbound
7	Access only from A23 (*southbound*)	Exit only to A23 (*northbound*)
10A	Exit only to B2036	Access only from B2036

M25 London Orbital Motorway

Junction	Clockwise	Anticlockwise
1B	No direct access, use slip road to Jct 2. Exit only to A296	Access only from A296. No exit - use jct 2
5	No exit to M26	No access from M26
19	Exit only to A41	Access only from A41
21	Access only from M1 (*southbound*). Exit only to M1 (*northbound*)	Access only from M1 (*southbound*). Exit only to M1 (*northbound*)
31	No exit (use slip road via jct 30)	For access follow signs

M26 Sevenoaks - Wrotham

Junction	Eastbound	Westbound
with M25 (jct 5)	Access only from anticlockwise M25 (*eastbound*)	Exit only to clockwise M25 (*westbound*)
with M20 (jct 3)	Exit only to M20 (*southeastbound*)	Access only from M20 (*northwestbound*)

M27 Cadnam - Portsmouth

Junction	Eastbound	Westbound
4	Staggered junction; follow signs - access only from M3 (*southbound*). Exit only to M3 (*northbound*)	Staggered junction; follow signs - access only from M3 (*southbound*). Exit only to M3 (*northbound*)
10	Access only from A32	Exit only to A32
12	Staggered junction; follow signs - access only from M275 (*northbound*)	Staggered junction; follow signs - exit only to M275 (*southbound*)

M40 London - Birmingham

Junction	Northwestbound	Southeastbound
3	Exit only to A40	Access only from A40
7	Exit only to A329	Access only from A329
8	Exit only to A40	Access only from A40
13	Exit only to A452	Access only from A452
14	Access only from A452	Exit only to A452
16	Access only from A3400	Exit only to A3400

M42 Bromsgrove - Measham

Junction	Northeastbound	Southwestbound
1	Access only from A38	Exit only to A38
7	Exit only to M6 (*northwestbound*)	Access only from M6 (*northwestbound*)
7A	Exit only to M6 (*southeastbound*)	No access or exit
8	Access only from M6 (*southeastbound*)	Exit only to M6 (*northwestbound*)

M45 Coventry - M1

Junction	Eastbound	Westbound
unnumbered (Dunchurch)	Access only from A45 & B4429	Exit only to A45 & B4429
with M1 (jct 17)	Exit only to M1 (*southbound*)	Access only from M1 (*northbound*)

M53 Mersey Tunnel - Chester

Junction	Southeastbound	Northwestbound
11	Access only from M56 (*westbound*). Exit only to M56 (*eastbound*)	Access only from M56 (*westbound*). Exit only to M56 (*eastbound*)

M54 Telford

Junction	Westbound	Eastbound
with M6 (jct 10A)	Access only from M6 (*northbound*)	Exit only to M6 (*soutbound*)

M56 North Cheshire

Junction	Westbound	Eastbound
1	Access only from M60 (*westbound*)	Exit only to M60 (*eastbound*) & A34 (*northbound*)
2	Exit only to A560	Access only from A560
3	Access only from A5103	Exit only to A5103 & A560
4	Exit only	Access only
9	Exit to M6 (*southbound*) via A50 interchange	Access from M6 (*northbound*) via A50 interchange
15	Exit only to M53	Access only from M53

M57 Liverpool Outer Ring Road

Junction	Northwestbound	Southeastbound
3	Access only from A526	Exit only to A526
5	Access only from A580 (*westbound*)	Exit only to A580

M58 Liverpool - Wigan

Junction	Eastbound	Westbound
1	Access only	Exit Only

M60 Manchester Orbital

Junction	Clockwise	Anticlockwise
2	Access only from A560	Exit only to A560
3	No access from M56	Access only from A34 (*northbound*)
4	Access only from A34 (*northbound*). Exit only to M56	Access only from M56 (*eastbound*). Exit only to A34 (*southbound*)
5	Access and exit only from and to A5103 (*northbound*)	Access and exit only from and to A5103 (*southbound*)
7	No direct access, use slip road to jct 8. Exit only to A56	Access only from A56. No exit - use jct 8
14	Access from A580 (*eastbound*)	Exit only to A580 (*westbound*)
16	Access only from A666	Exit only to A666
20	Exit only to A664	Access only from A664
22	No restriction	Exit only to A62
25	Exit only to A6017	No restriction
26	No restriction	No access or exit
27	Access only from A626	Exit only to A626

M61 Manchester - Preston

Junction	Northwestbound	Southeastbound
3	No access or exit	Exit only to A666
with M6 (jct 30)	Exit only to M6 (*northbound*)	Access only from M6 (*southbound*)

M62 Liverpool - Kingston upon Hull

Junction	Eastbound	Westbound
23	Exit only to A640	Access only from A640

M65 Preston - Colne

Junction	Northeastbound	Southwestbound
1	Access and exit to M6 only	Access and exit to M6 only
9	Exit only to A679	Access only from A679
11	Access only	Exit only

M66 Bury

Junction	Southbound	Northbound
with A56	Access only from A56 (*southbound*)	Exit only to A56 (*northbound*)
1	Access only from A56	Exit only to A56

M67 Hyde Bypass

Junction	Eastbound	Westbound
1	Exit only to A6017	Access only from A6017
2	Access only	Exit only to A57
3	No restriction	Exit only to A627

M69 Coventry - Leicester

Junction	Northbound	Southbound
2	Access only from B4669	Exit only to B4669

M73 East of Glasgow

Junction	Northbound	Southbound
2	No access from or exit to A89. No access from M8 (*eastbound*).	No access from or exit to A89. No exit to M8 (*westbound*)
3	Exit only to A80 (*northeastbound*)	Access only from A80 (*southwestbound*)

M74 and A74(M) Glasgow - Gretna

Junction	Southbound	Northbound
2	Access only from A763	Exit only to A763
3	Exit only	Access only
7	Exit only to A72	Access only from A72
9	Exit only to B7078	No access or exit
10	Access only from B7078	No restrictions
11	Exit only to B7078	Access only from B7078
12	Access only from A70	Exit only to A70
18	Access only from B723	Exit only to B723
21	Exit only to B6357	Access only from B6357
with B7076	Access only	Exit only
Gretna Green	Exit only	Access only
with A75	Access only from A75	Exit only to A75
with A6071	Exit only to A74 (*southbound*)	Access only from A74 (*northbound*)

M77 South of Glasgow

Junction	Southbound	Northbound
with M8 (jct 22)	No access from M8 (*eastbound*)	No exit to M8 (*westbound*)
4	Exit only	Access only
with A77	Exit only to A77 (*southbound*)	Access only from A77 (*northbound*)

M80 Stepps Bypass

Junction	Northeastbound	Southwestbound
1	Access only	No restriction
3	Exit only	Access only

M80 Bonnybridge - Stirling

Junction	Northbound	Southbound
5	Exit only to M876 (*northeastbound*)	Access only from M876 (*southwestbound*)

M90 Forth Road Bridge - Perth

Junction	Northbound	Southbound
2A	Exit only to A92 (*eastbound*)	Access only from A92 (*westbound*)
7	Access only from A91	Exit only to A91
8	Exit only to A91	Access only from A91
10	No access from A912. No exit to A912 (*southbound*)	No access from A912 (*northbound*). No exit to A912

M180 Doncaster - Grimsby

Junction	Eastbound	Westbound
1	Exit only A18	Access only from A18

M606 Bradford Spur

Junction	Northbound	Southbound
2	Exit only	No restriction

M621 Leeds - M1

Junction	Clockwise	Anticlockwise
2A	Access only	Exit only
4	Exit only	No restriction
5	Access only	Exit only
6	Exit only	Access only
with M1 (jct 43)	Exit only to M1 (*southbound*)	Access only from M1 (*northbound*)

M876 Bonnybridge - Kincardine Bridge

Junction	Northeastbound	Southwestbound
with M80 (jct 5)	Access only from M80 (*northbound*)	Exit only to M80 (*southbound*)
2	Exit only to A9	Access only from A9
with M9 (jct 8)	Exit only to M9 (*eastbound*)	Access only from M9 (*westbound*)

A1(M) South Mimms - Baldock

Junction	Northbound	Southbound
2	Exit only to A1001	Access only from A1001
3	No restriction	Exit only to A414
5	Access only	No access or exit

A1(M) East of Leeds

Junction	Northbound	Southbound
44	Access only from M1 (*northbound*)	Exit only to M1 (*southbound*)

A1(M) Scotch Corner - Newcastle upon Tyne

Junction	Northbound	Southbound
57	Exit only to A66(M) (*eastbound*)	Access only from A66(M) (*westbound*)
65	No access Exit only to A194(M) & A1 (*northbound*)	No exit Access only from A194(M) and A1 (*southbound*)

A3(M) Horndean - Havant

Junction	Southbound	Northbound
1	Exit only to A3	Access only from A3
4	Access only	Exit only

A48(M) Cardiff Spur

Junction	Westbound	Eastbound
29	Access only from M4 (*westbound*)	Exit only to M4 (*eastbound*)
29A	Exit only to A48 (*westbound*)	Access only from A48 (*eastbound*)

A66(M) Darlington Spur

Junction	Eastbound	Westbound
with A1(M) (jct 57)	Access only from A1(M) (*northbound*)	Exit only to A1(M) (*southbound*)

A194(M) Newcastle upon Tyne

Junction	Northbound	Southbound
with A1(M) (jct 65)	Access only from A1(M) (*northbound*)	Exit only to A1(M) (*southbound*)

A12 M25 - Ipswich

Junction	Northeastbound	Southwestbound
13	Access only from B1002	No restriction
14	Exit only	Access only
20A	Exit only to B1137 B1137	Access only from
20B	Access only B1137	Exit only to B1137
21	No restriction	Access only from B1389
23	Exit only to B1024	Access only from B1024
24	Access only from B1024	Exit only from B1024
27	Exit only to A113	Access only from A113
unnumbered (with A120)	Exit only A120	Access only from A120
29	Access only from A120 and A1232	Exit only to A120 and A1232
unnumbered	Exit only	Access only

A14 M1 - Felixstowe

Junction	Eastbound	Westbound
With M1/M6 (jct19)	Access only from M6 and M1 (*southbound*)	Exit only to M6 and M1 (*northbound*)
4	Access only from B669	Exit only to B669
31	Access only from A428 & M11. Exit only to A1307	Exit only to A428 & M11. Access only from A1307
34	Exit only to B1047	Access only from B1047
unnumbered	No access from or exit to A1303	Access only from A1303
36	Access only from A11	Exit only to A11
38	Exit only to A11	Access only from A11
39	Access only from B1506	Exit only to B1506
49	Exit only to A1308	Access only from A1308
61	Exit only to A154	Access only from A154

A55 Holyhead - Chester

Junction	Eastbound	Westbound
8A	Access only from A5	Exit only to A5
23A	Exit only	Access only
24A	No access or exit	Exit only
33A	No access from or exit to B5126	Exit only to B5126
33B	Access only from A494	Exit only to A494
35A (west)	Exit only A5104	Access only from A5104
35B (east)	Access only from A5104	Exit only to A5104

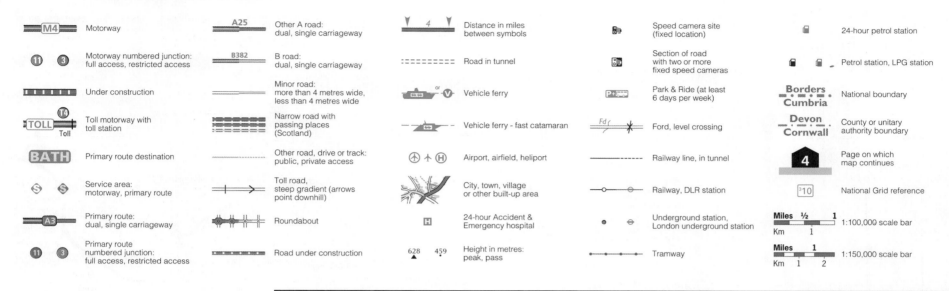

Atlas symbols

Motoring information

M4	Motorway	A25	Other A road: dual, single carriageway
11 3	Motorway numbered junction: full access, restricted access	B382	B road: dual, single carriageway
	Under construction		Minor road: more than 4 metres wide, less than 4 metres wide
TOLL T4 Toll	Toll motorway with toll station		Narrow road with passing places (Scotland)
BATH	Primary route destination		Other road, drive or track: public, private access
S S	Service area: motorway, primary route		Toll road, steep gradient (arrows point downhill)
A3	Primary route: dual, single carriageway		Roundabout
11 3	Primary route numbered junction: full access, restricted access		Road under construction

4	Distance in miles between symbols
:======:	Road in tunnel
or V	Vehicle ferry
	Vehicle ferry - fast catamaran
Airport, airfield, heliport
City, town, village or other built-up area
H	24-hour Accident & Emergency hospital
628 459	Height in metres: peak, pass

	Speed camera site (fixed location)
	Section of road with two or more fixed speed cameras
P+R	Park & Ride (at least 6 days per week)
Fd	Ford, level crossing
	Railway line, in tunnel
	Railway, DLR station
	Underground station, London underground station
	Tramway

	24-hour petrol station
	Petrol station, LPG station
Borders Cumbria	National boundary
Devon Cornwall	County or unitary authority boundary
4	Page on which map continues
²10	National Grid reference
Miles ½ 1 / Km 1	1:100,000 scale bar
Miles 1 / Km 1 2	1:150,000 scale bar

Recreation and leisure
Before visiting check opening times, to avoid disappointment.

	Sandy beach, heritage coast		Abbey, cathedral or priory
	National Park boundary		Abbey, cathedral or priory in ruins
	Scenic area		Agricultural showground
	Woodland		Air show venue
	Heritage railway		Ancient monument
Tarka Trail	National Cycle Network (Sustrans)		Aquarium
Pennine Way	Selection of national trails		Aqueduct or viaduct
Hadrian's Wall	Ancient wall		Arboretum
A	AA approved campsite	X	Battle site
	AA approved caravan site		Bird collection
	AA approved caravan & campsite		Bird reserve (RSPB)
C&CC site	Camping & Caravanning Club site (AA approved)		Castle
Sun Inn PH	AA recommended pub (selected for good food, character & comfort)		Cave

	Country park
	Farm or animal centre
	Garden
	Hill-fort
	Historic house
	Industrial attraction
	Marina
	Monument
	Museum or gallery
	National Nature Reserve: England, Scotland, Wales
	Local nature reserve
NTS	National Trust for Scotland property
NT	National Trust property

	Picnic site
	Roman remains
	Steam railway
	Theme park
	Tourist Information Centre all year, seasonal
	Viewpoint
	Vineyard
	Visitor or heritage centre
	Windmill
★	World Heritage Site (UNESCO)
	Zoo or wildlife collection
★	Other place of interest
	Boxed symbols indicate in-town attractions

	AA golf course
	Athletics
	County cricket
	Football
	Horse racing
	Ice hockey
	Motorsport
	Rugby Union
	Rugby League
	Ski slope: natural, artificial
	Speedway
	Tennis
	Arena (indoor), stadium

Town and airport plans

M8	Motorway		Minor road: dual, single carriageway
	Primary route: dual, single carriageway	or	Other road, drive or track: (access may be restricted)
	Other A road: dual, single carriageway		Road under construction
	B road: dual, single carriageway	)====(	Road in tunnel

:======:	Track or footpath
	Pedestrians only road
←	One-way street
P	Car park

P+R	Park & Ride (at least 6 days per week)
	Building of interest
H	24-hour Accident & Emergency hospital
6 3	Junction numbers

†	Church/chapel
	Public toilet
	Toilet with facilities for the less able
	Refer to the recreation and leisure legend, above, for a complete list of symbols.

Central London plan (see pages 334 - 336)

	Central London Congestion Charging Zone boundary, including the western extension (operational from February 2007)		Charge-free routes through the Charging Zone		Theatre, Cinema
			AA inspected restaurant		Public Library

Central London Congestion Charging Zone

Introduced in 2003 and extended westwards to include most of Chelsea, Kensington and Westminster (due operational February 2007), the charge for driving or parking in the Central London area is £8 per vehicle per day. The zone operates between 7.00 am and 6.30 pm (6.00 pm from February 2007) Monday to Friday only. There are two charge free routes through the charging zone: the A40 (Westway) and the A5/A4202/A302/A202 (Edgware Road - Park Lane - Grosvenor Place - Vauxhall Bridge Road). There is currently no charge on weekends and public holidays.

For up-to-date information on the status of the zone, exemptions, discounts and how to pay, telephone 0845 900 1234 (020 7649 9121 for minicom users), visit www.cclondon.com or write to Congestion Charging London, P.O. Box 2985, Coventry, CV7 8ZR.

Royal Parks (opening and closing times for traffic)

Green Park	Constitution Hill: closed Sundays, 8.00 am–dusk
Hyde Park	Open 5.00 am–midnight
Regent's Park	Open 5.00 am–midnight
St James's Park	The Mall: closed Sundays, 8.00 am–dusk

Traffic regulations in the City of London include security checkpoints and restrict the number of entry and exit points.

Note: Oxford Street is closed to through-traffic (except buses & taxis) 7.00 am–7.00 pm, Monday–Saturday. Restricted parts of Frith Street/Old Compton Street are closed to vehicles 12.00 noon–1.00 am daily.

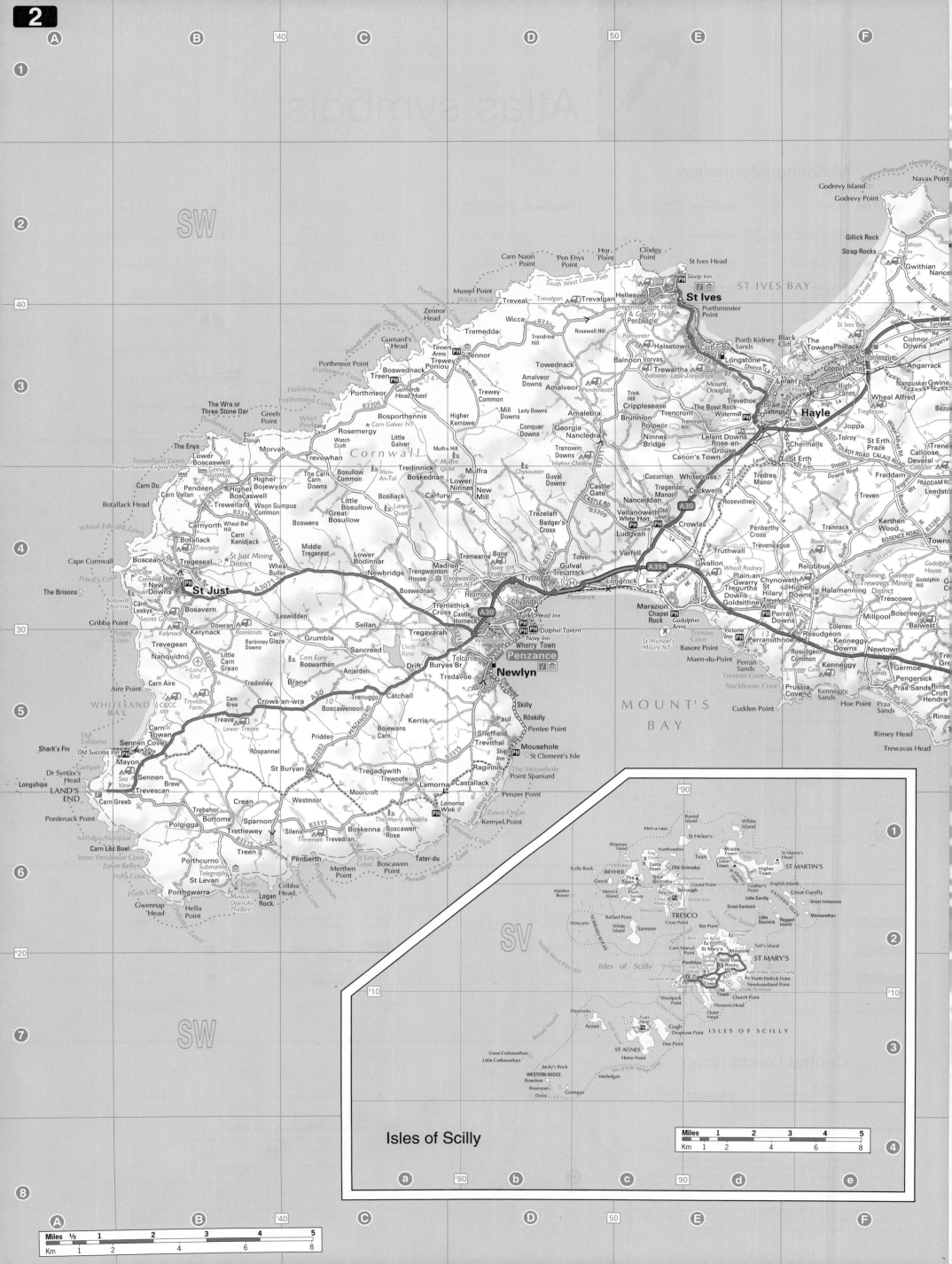

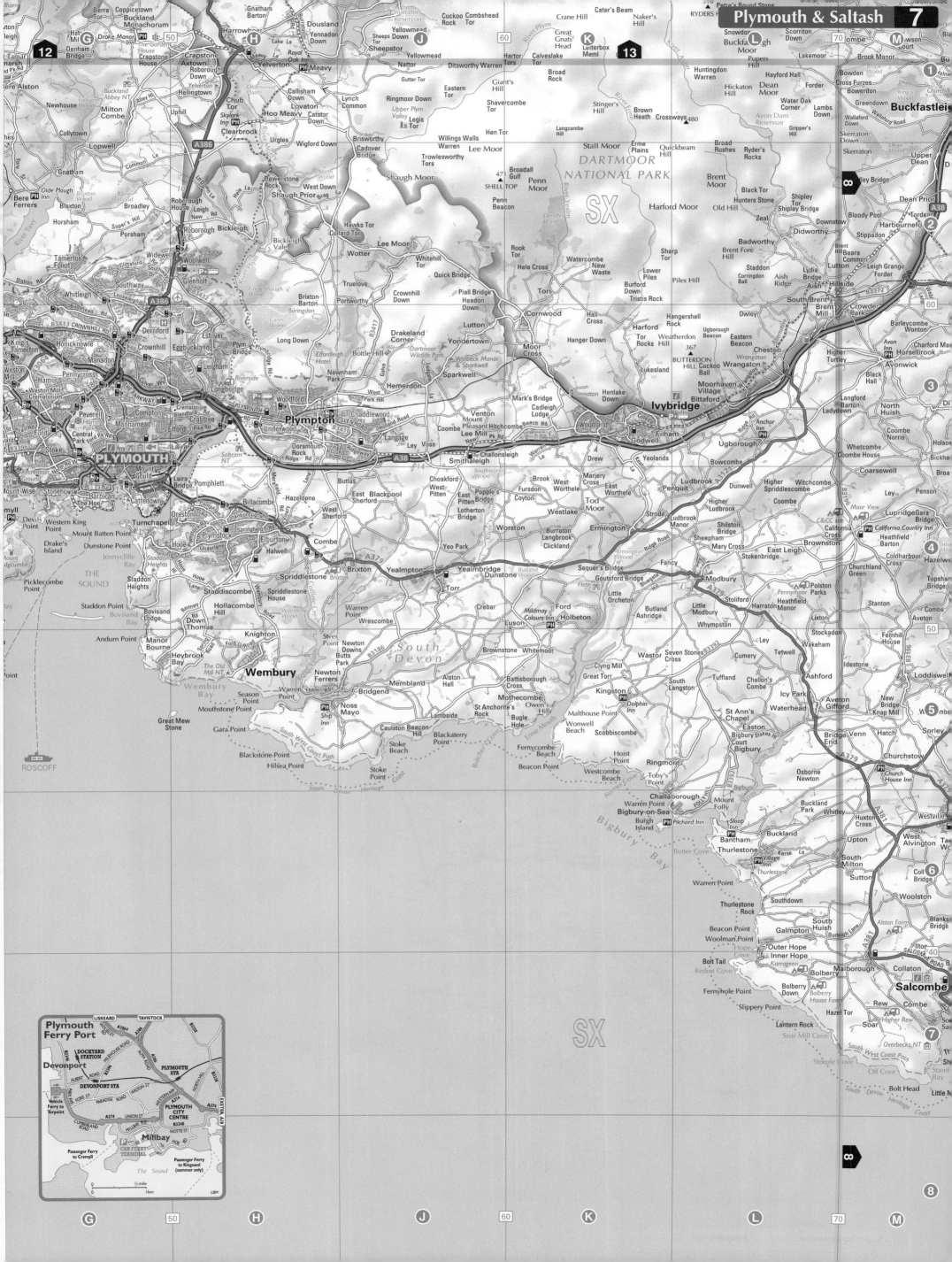

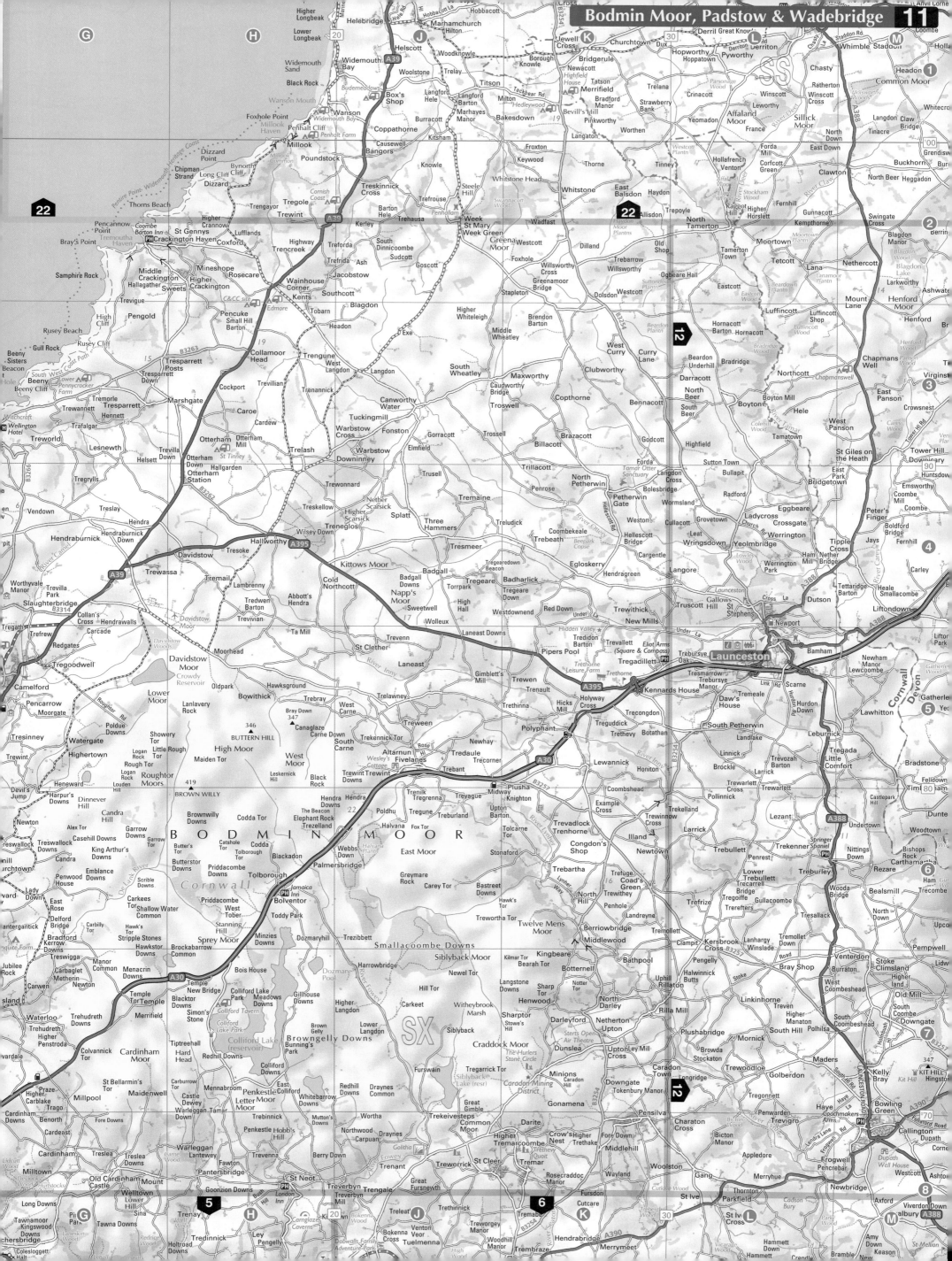

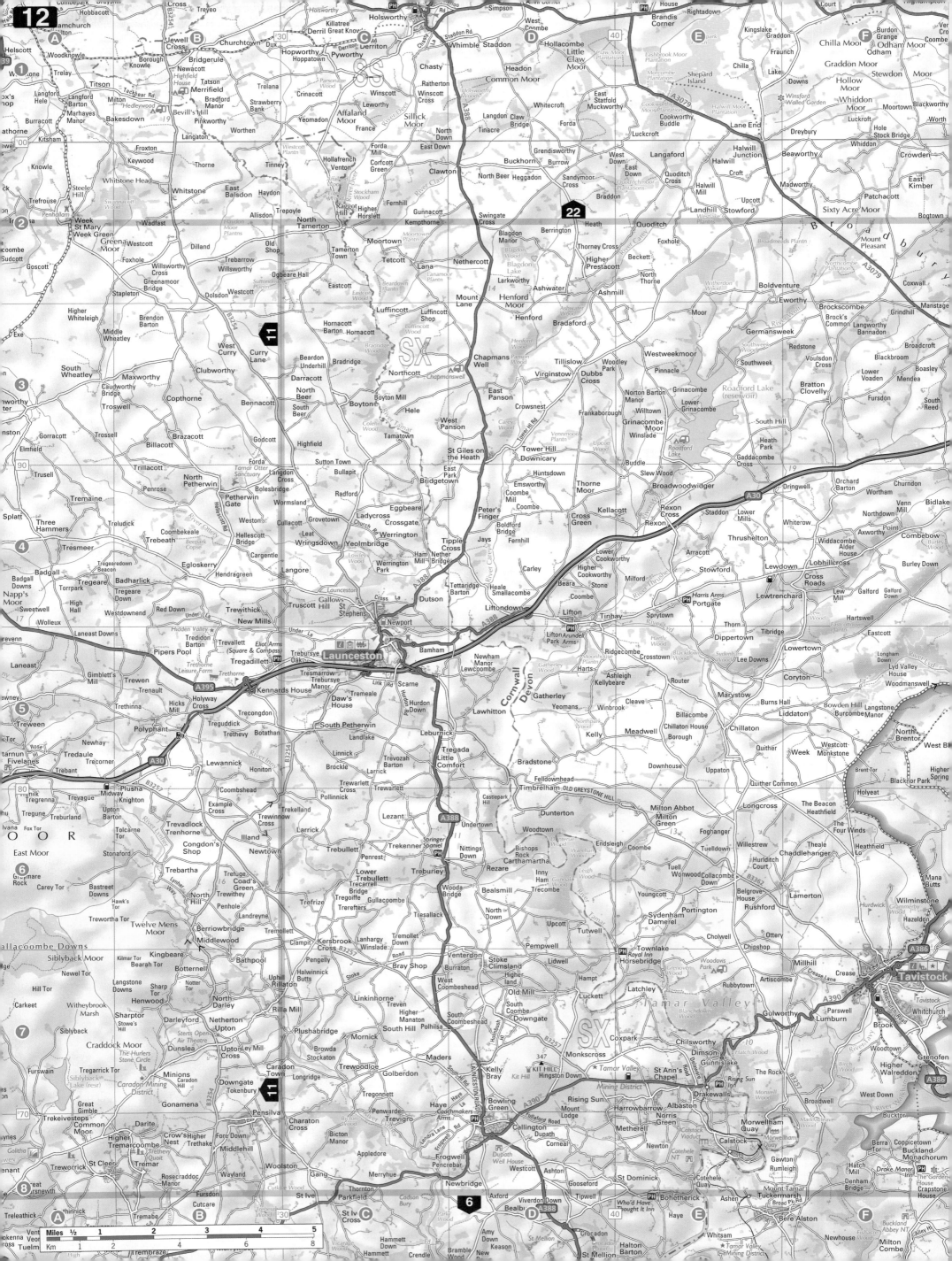

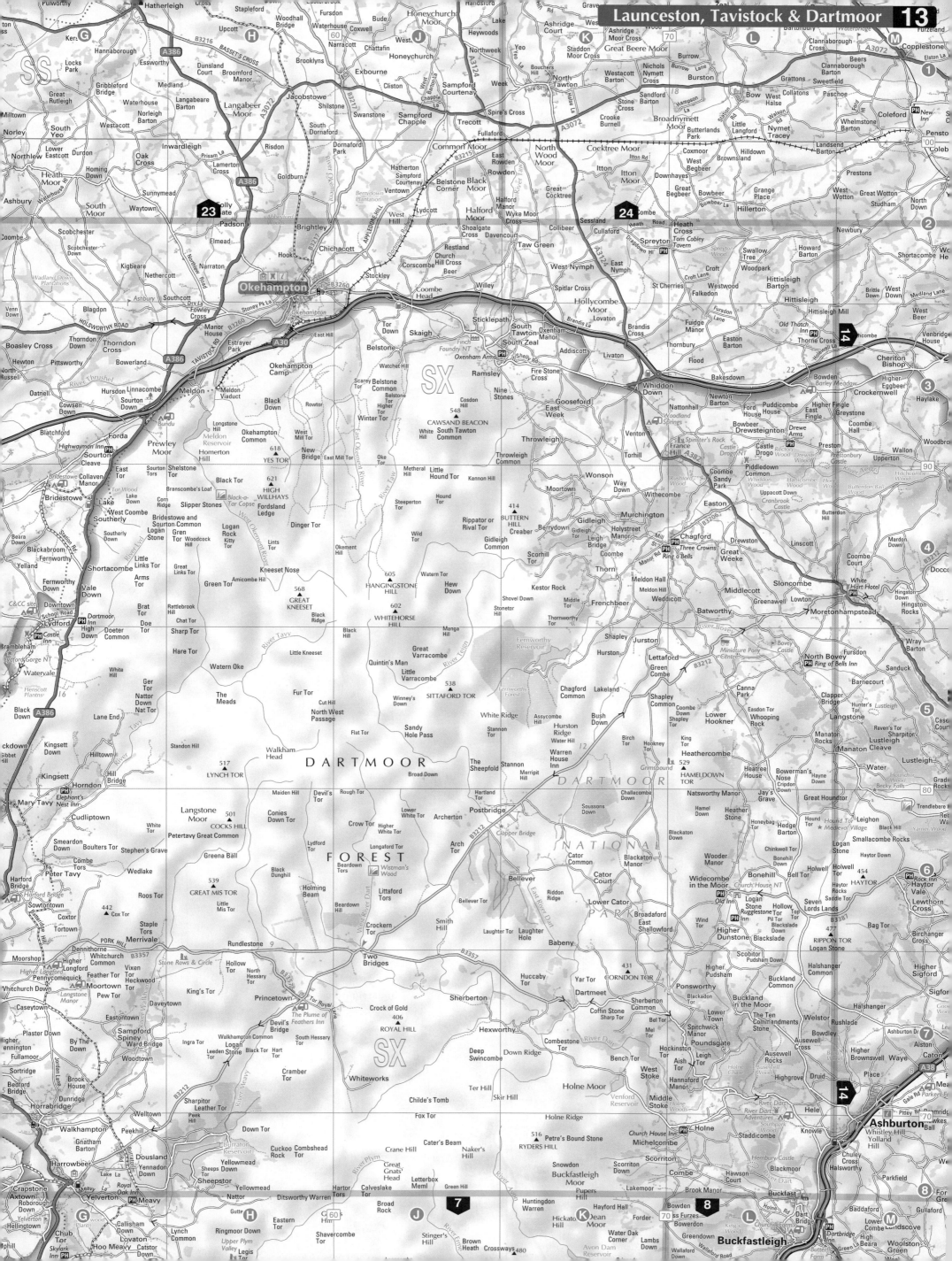

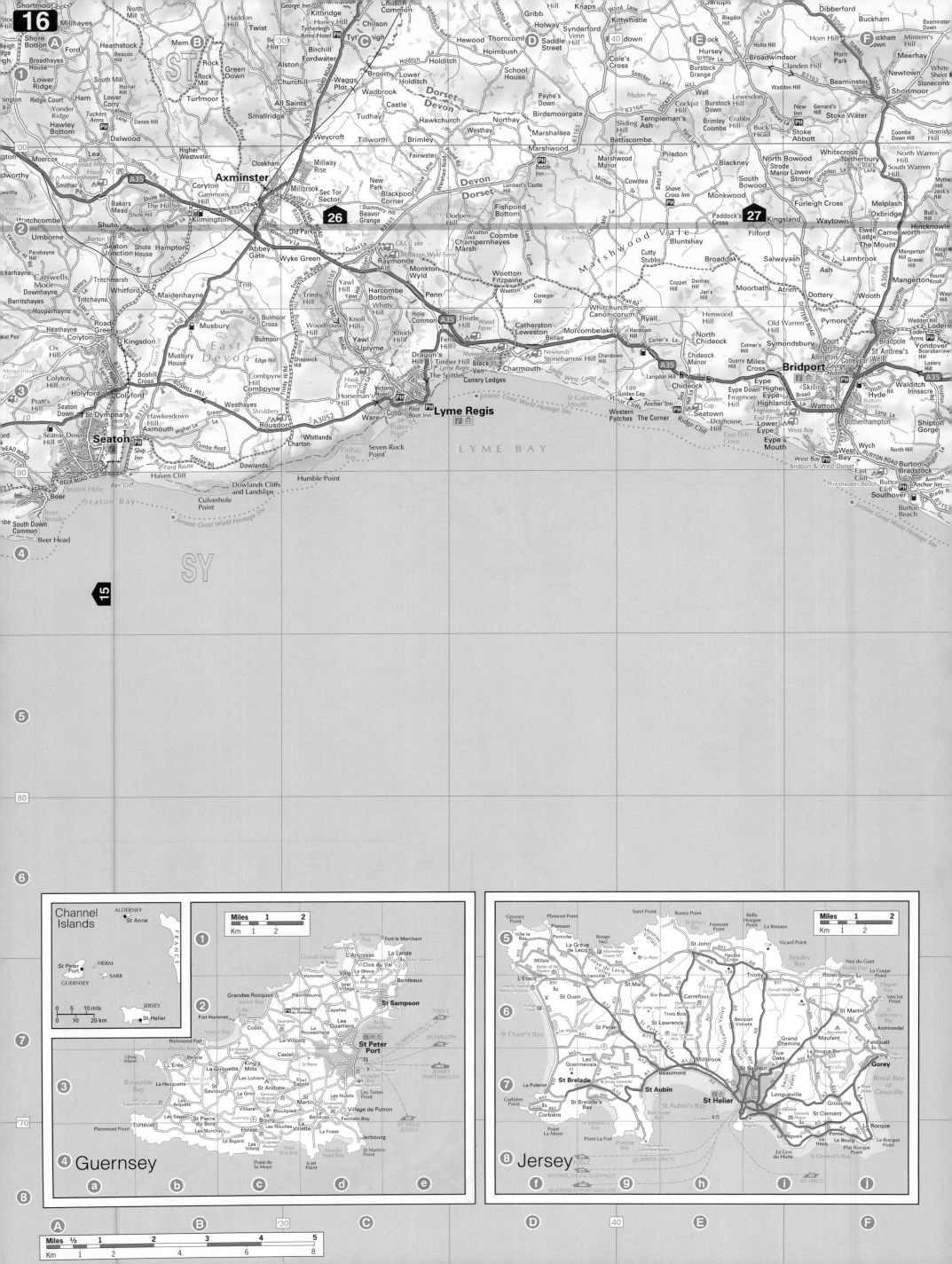

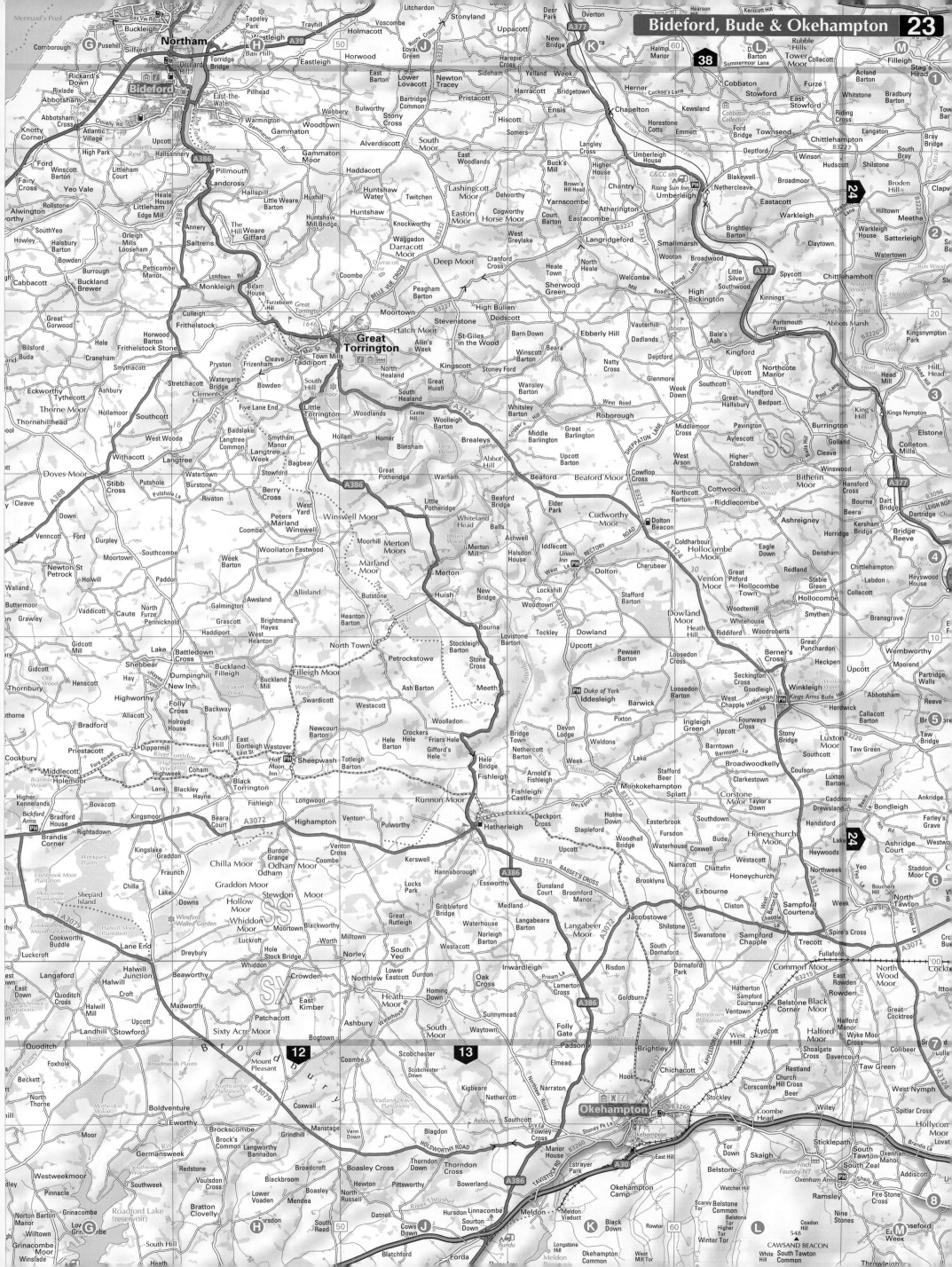

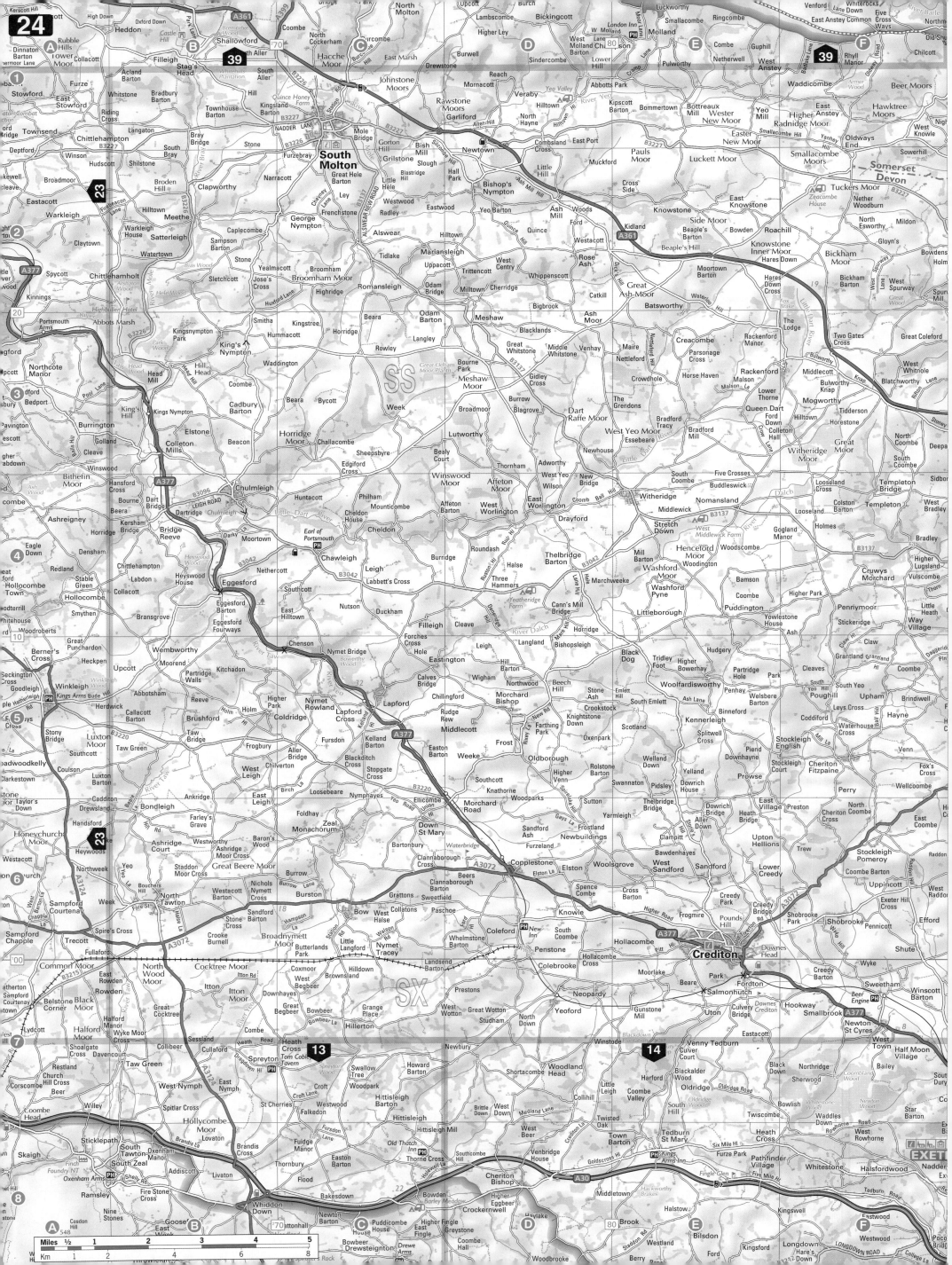

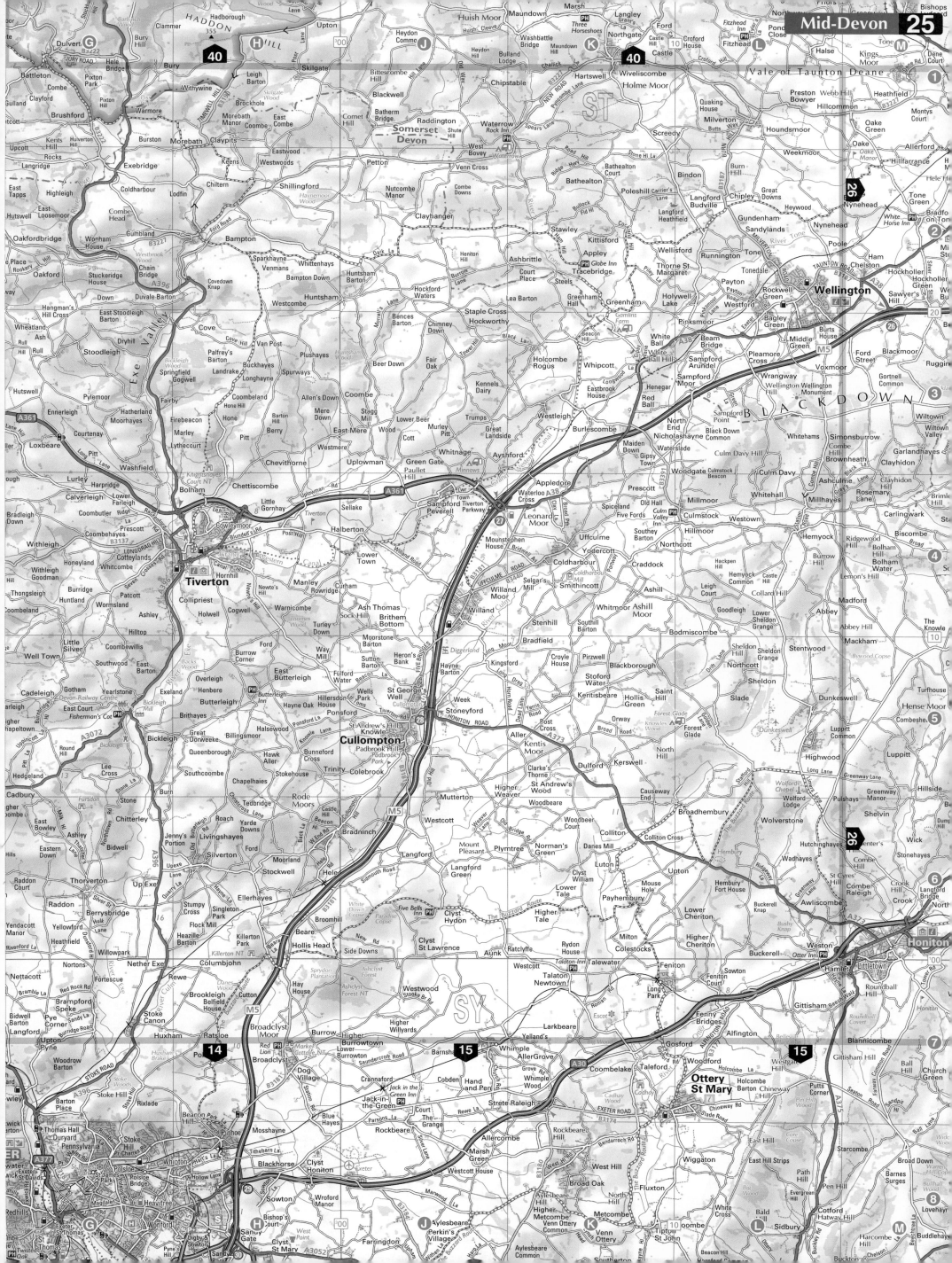

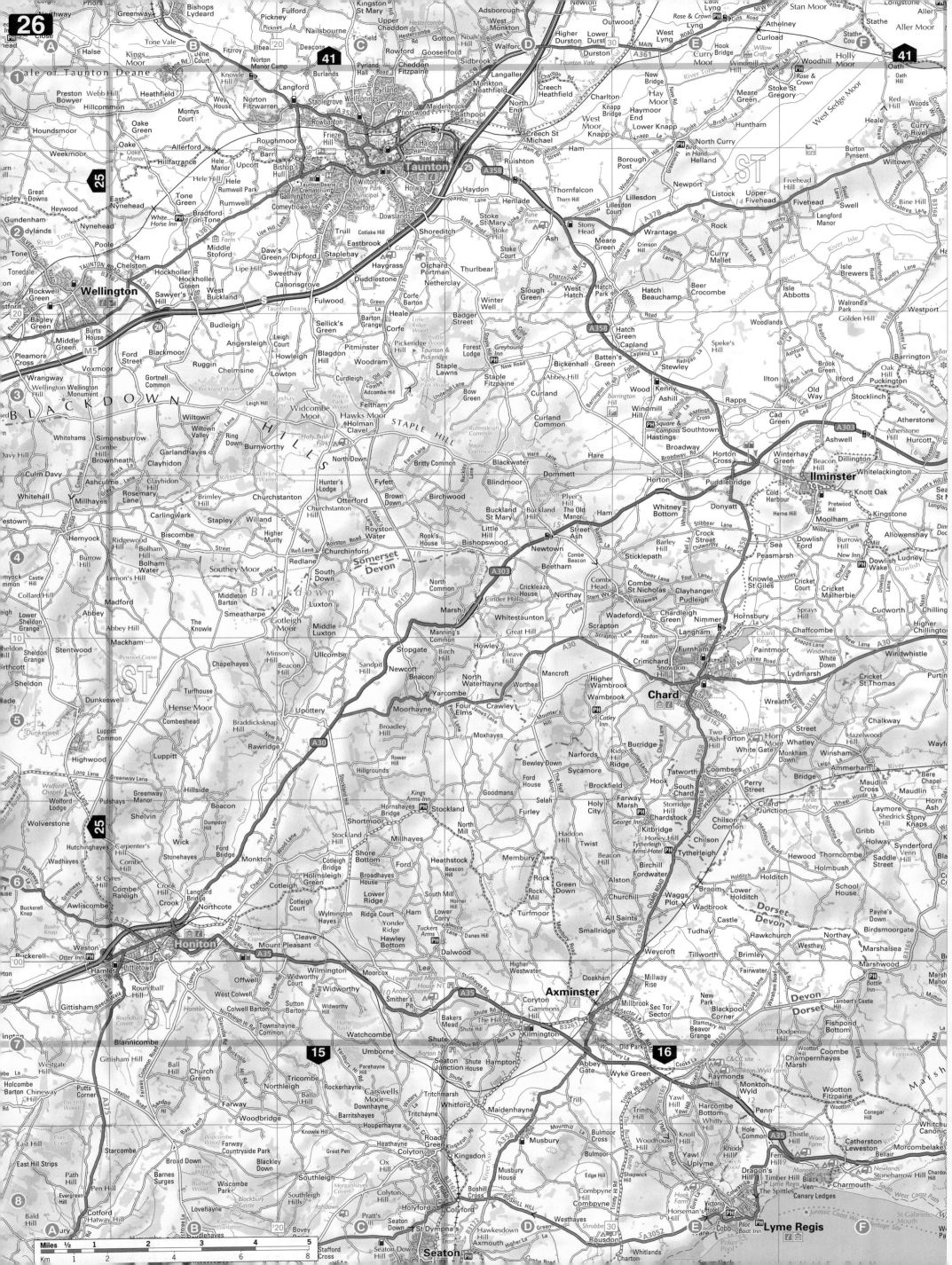

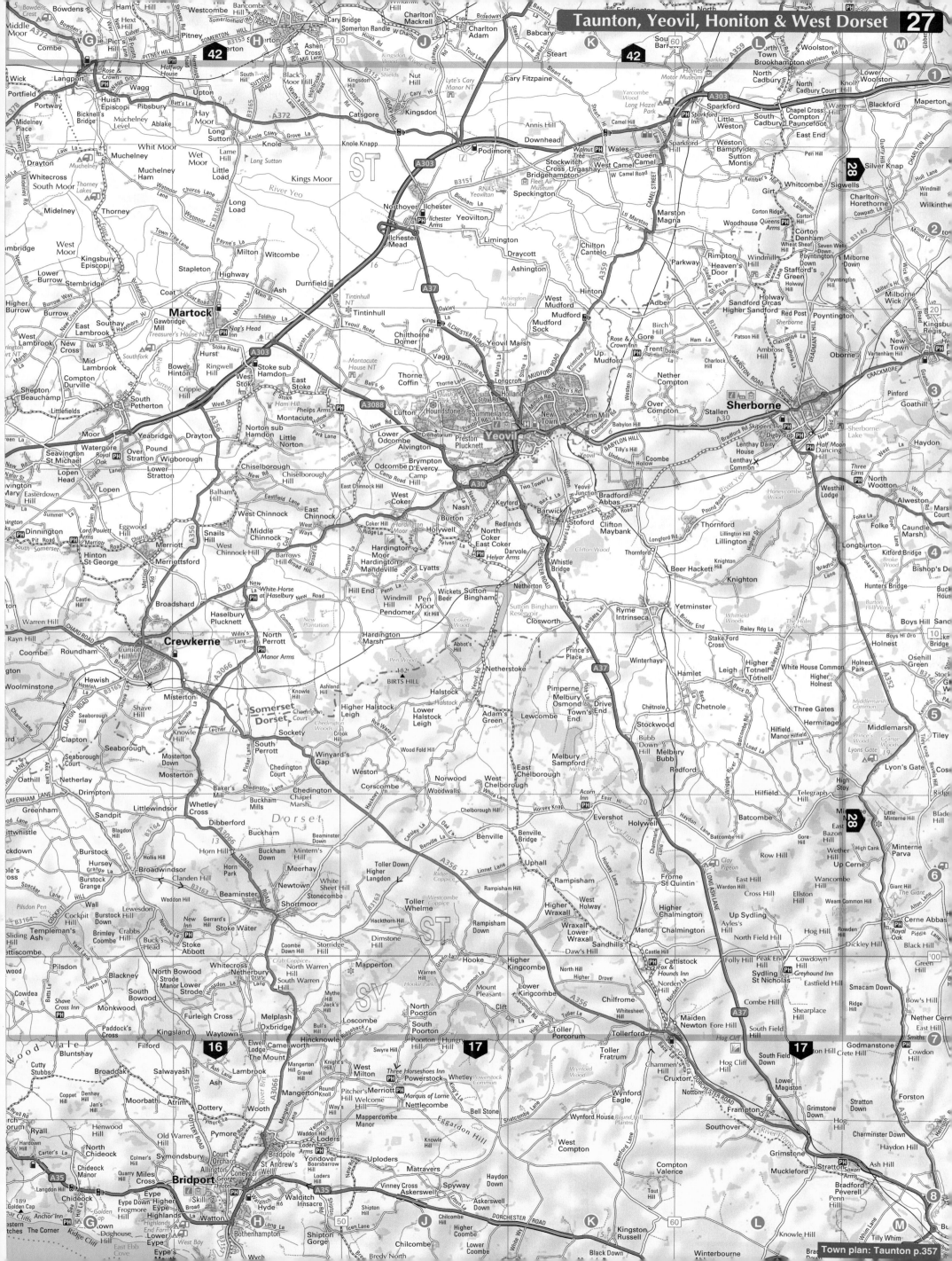

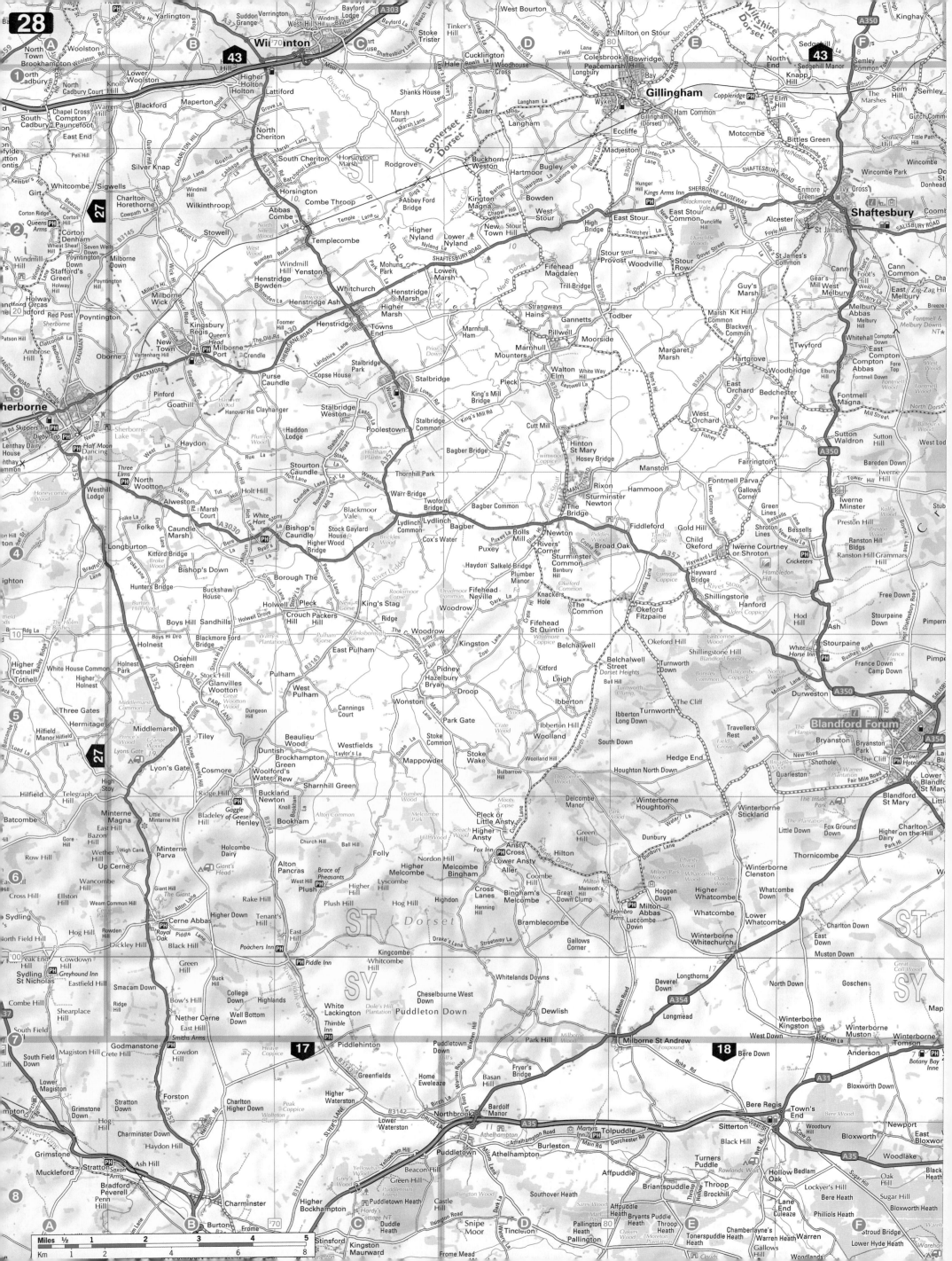

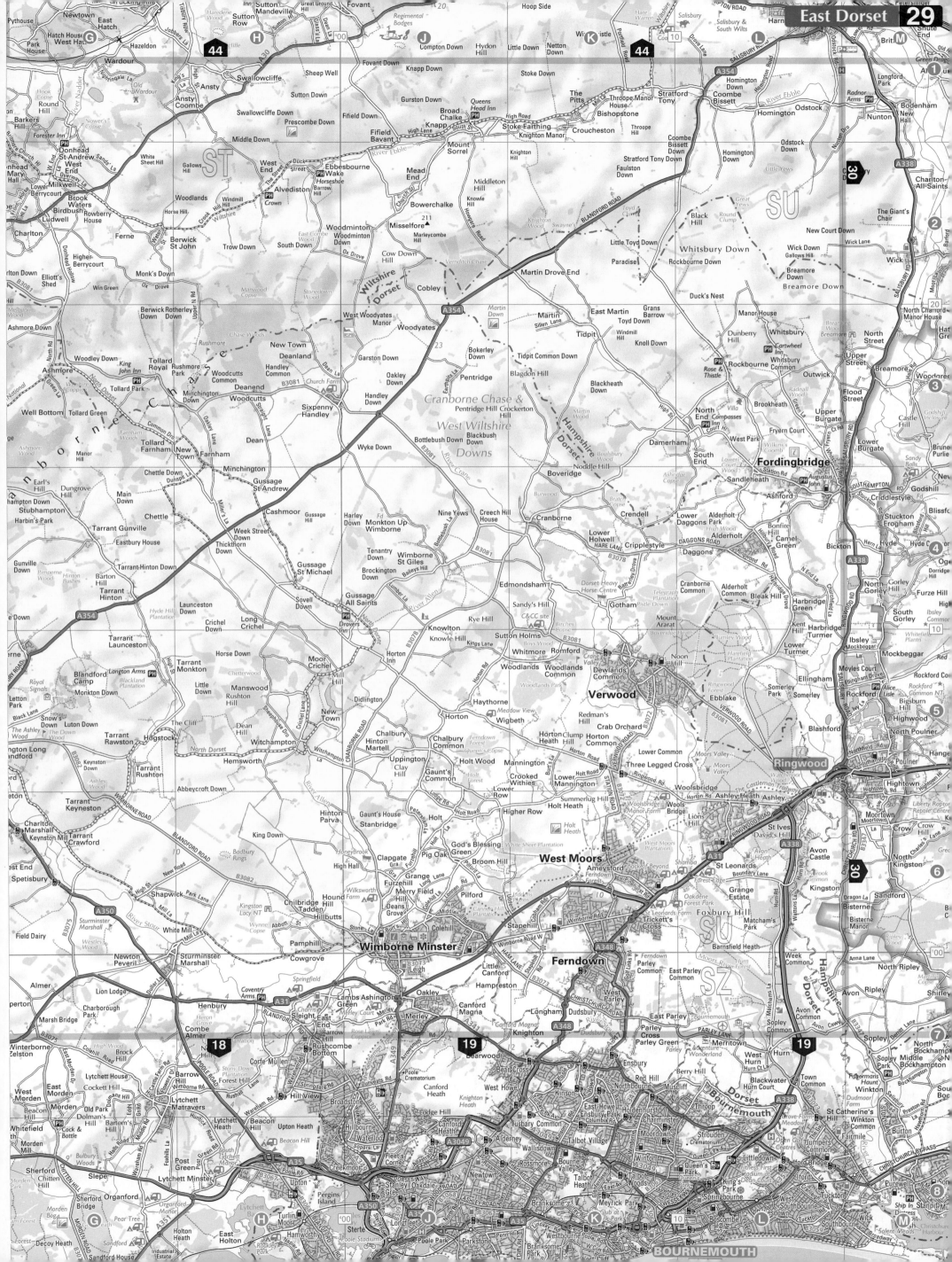

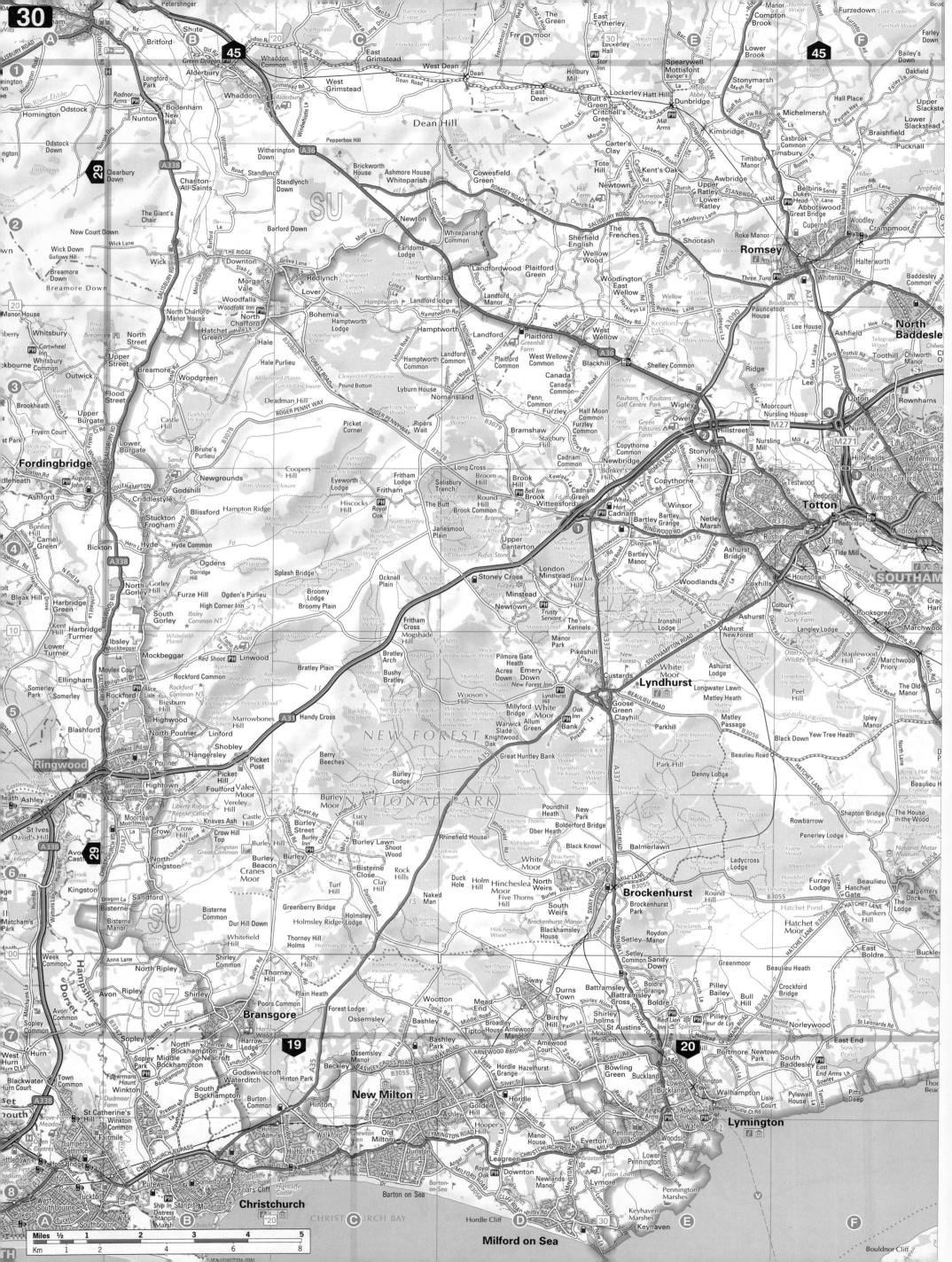

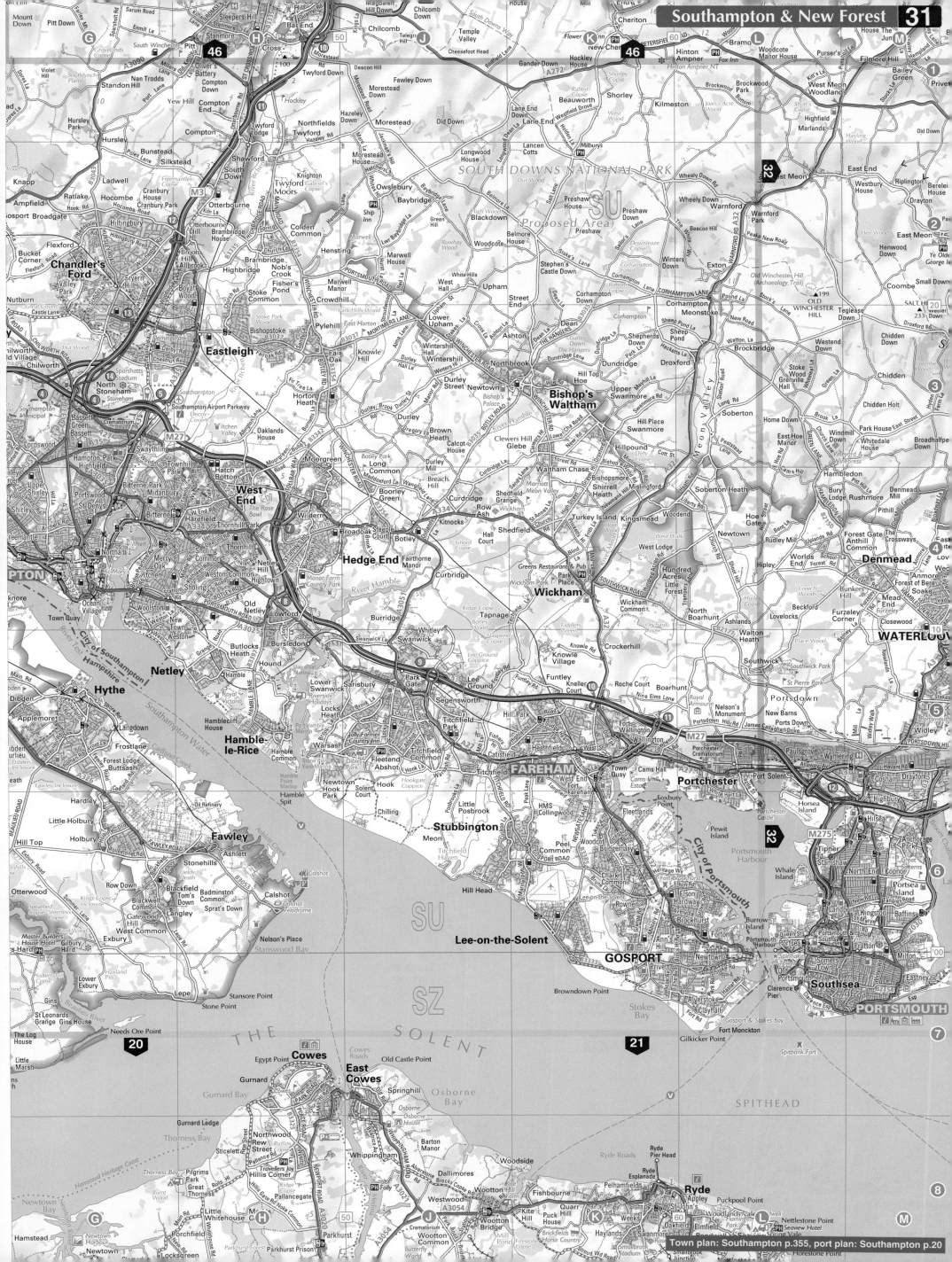

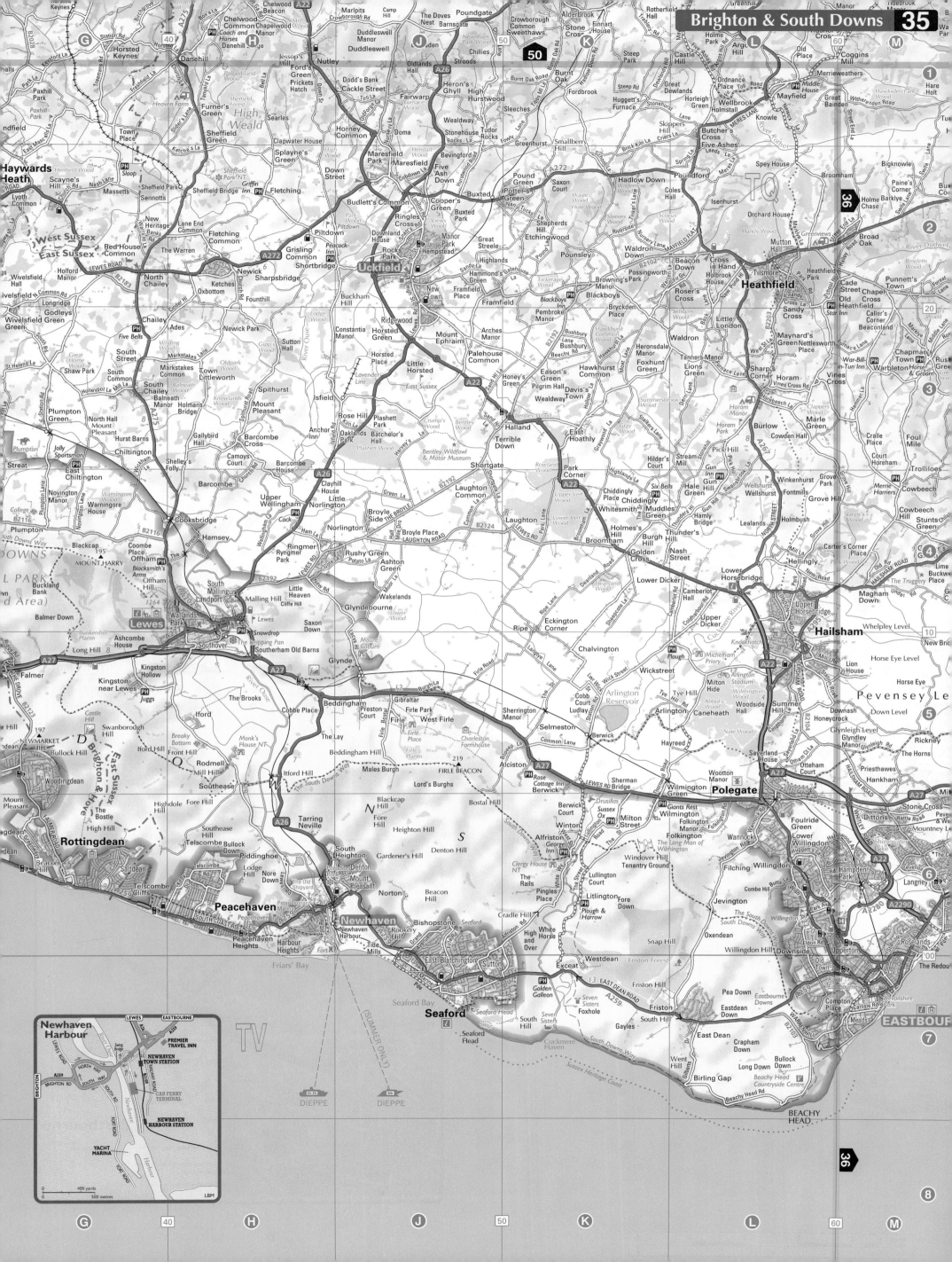

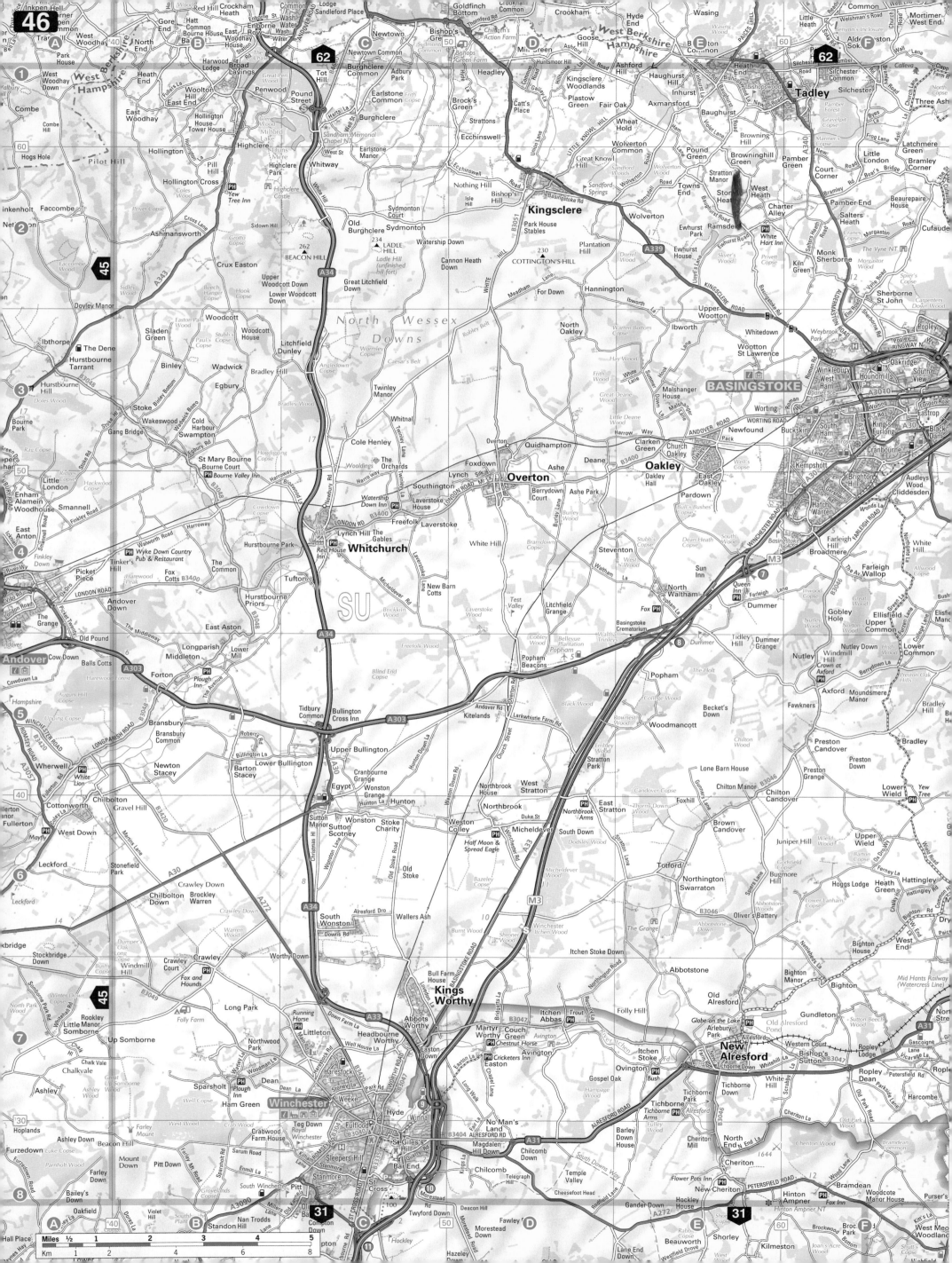

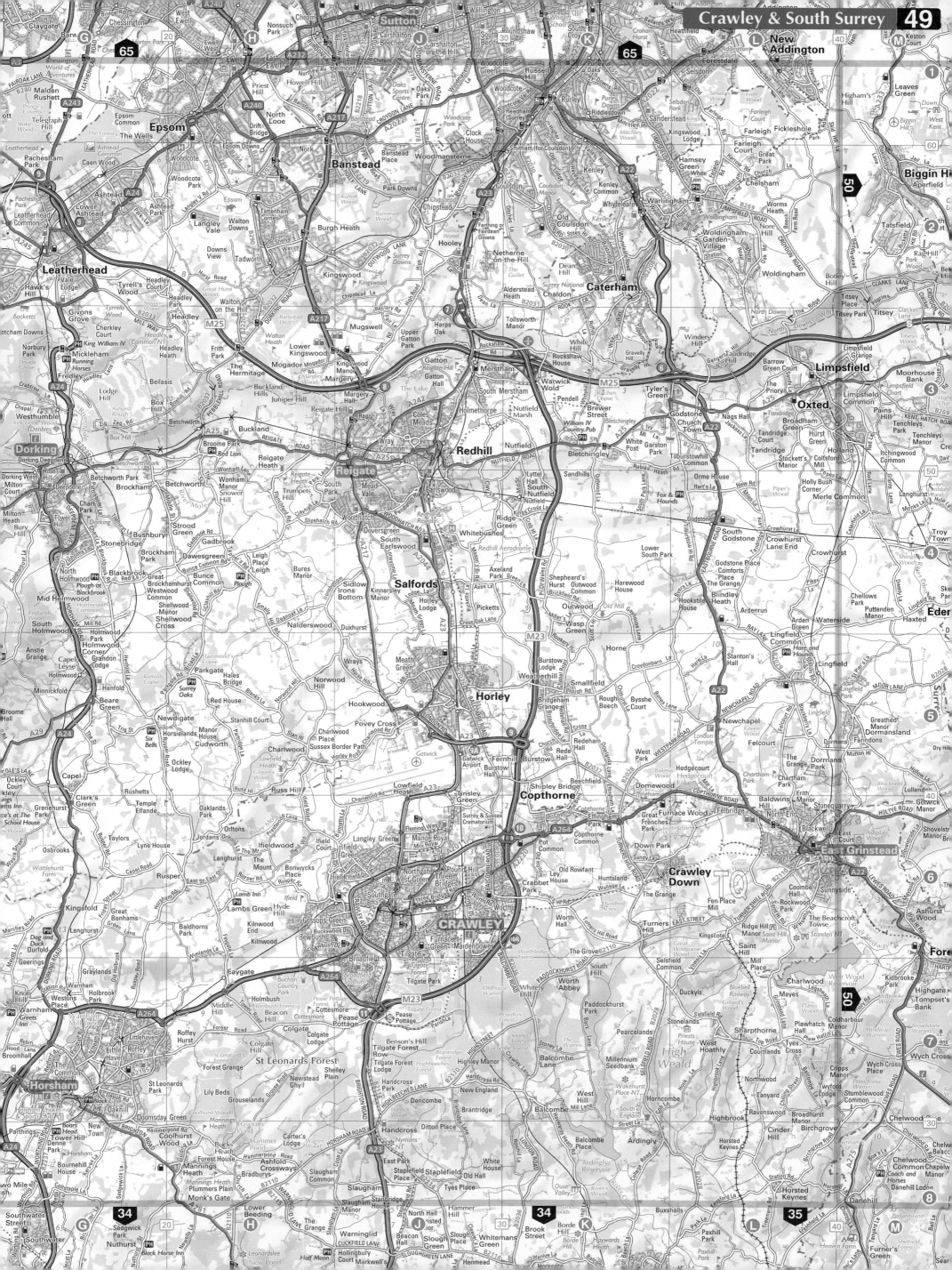

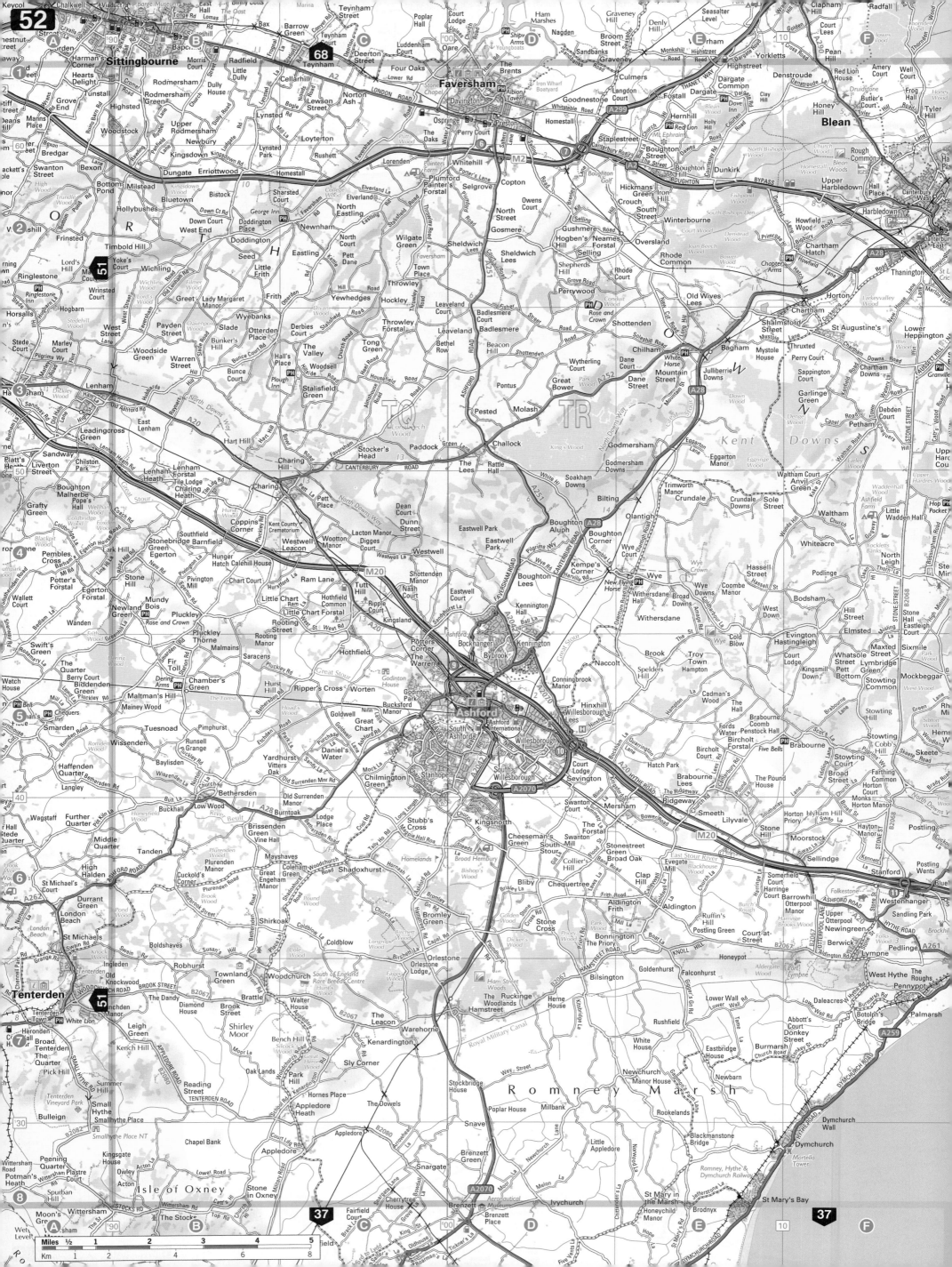

STRAIT OF DOVER

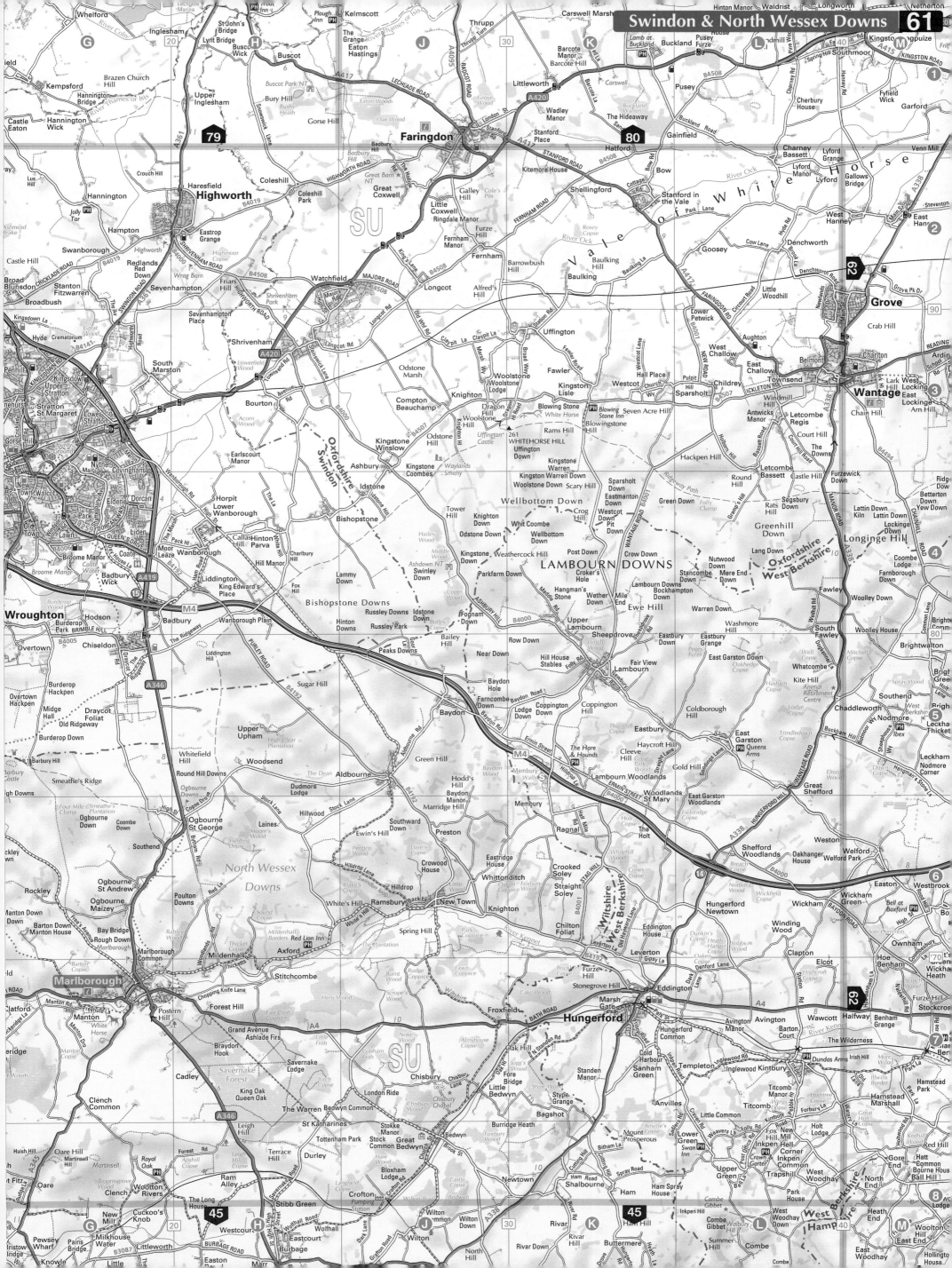

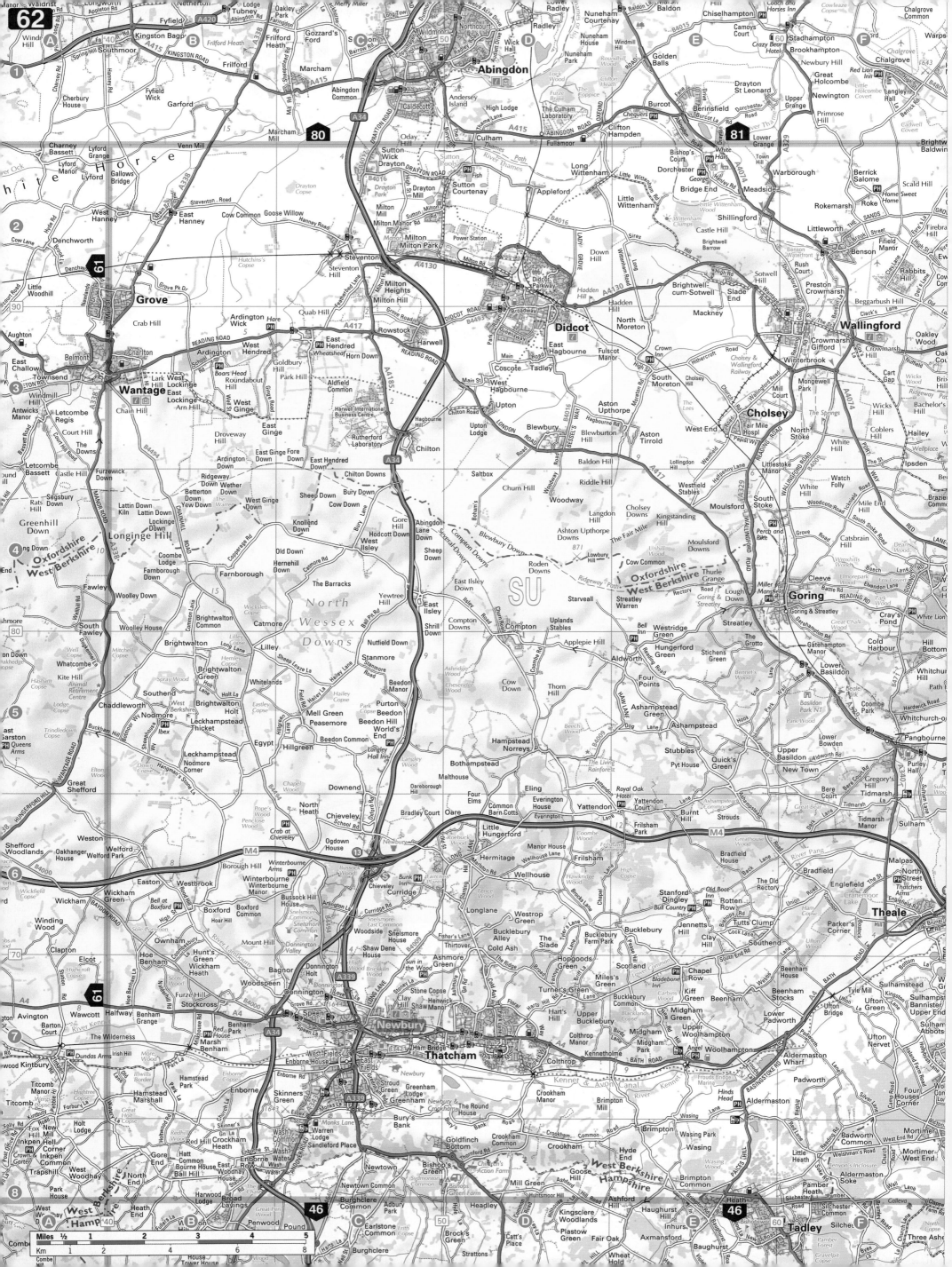

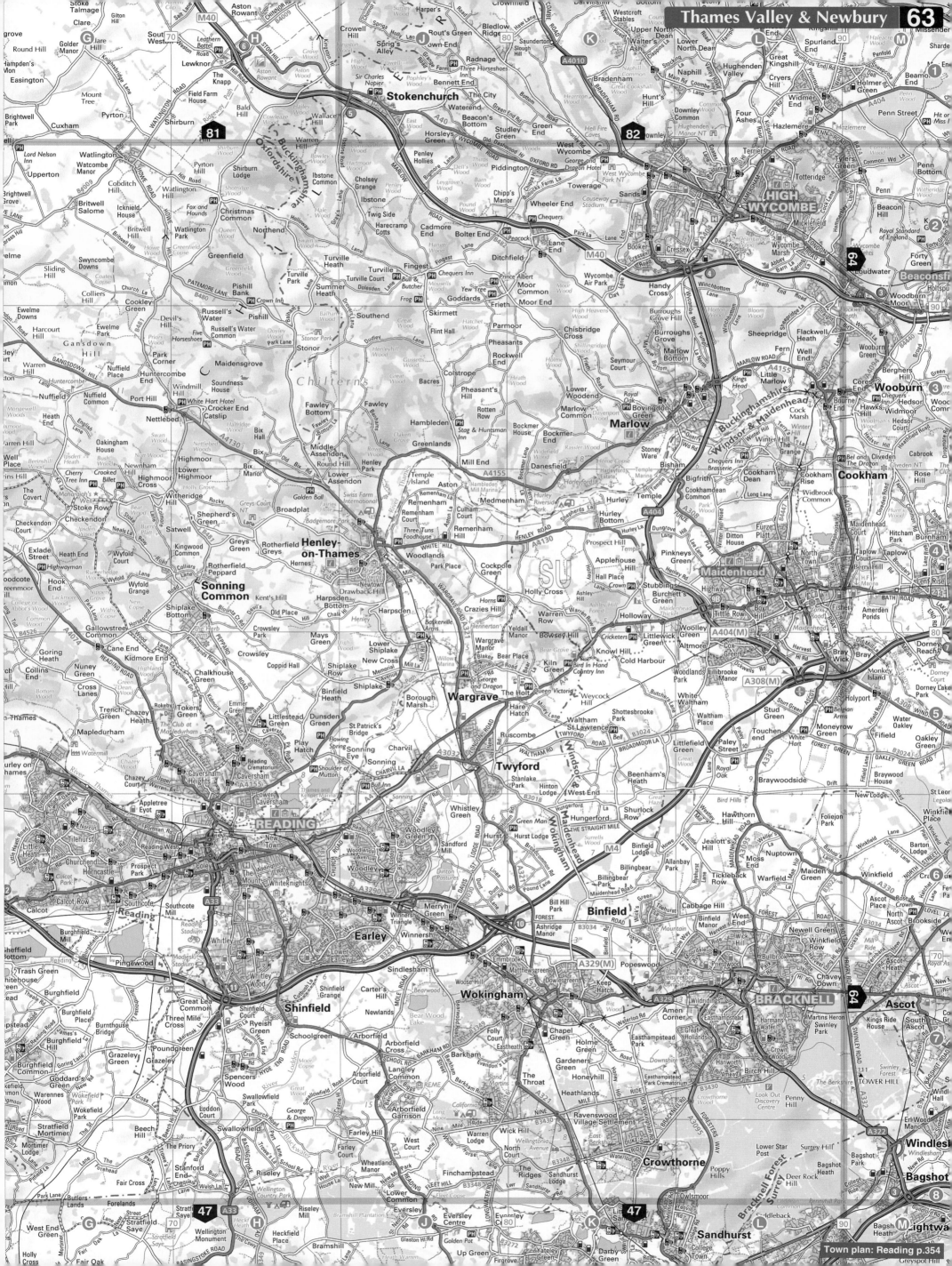

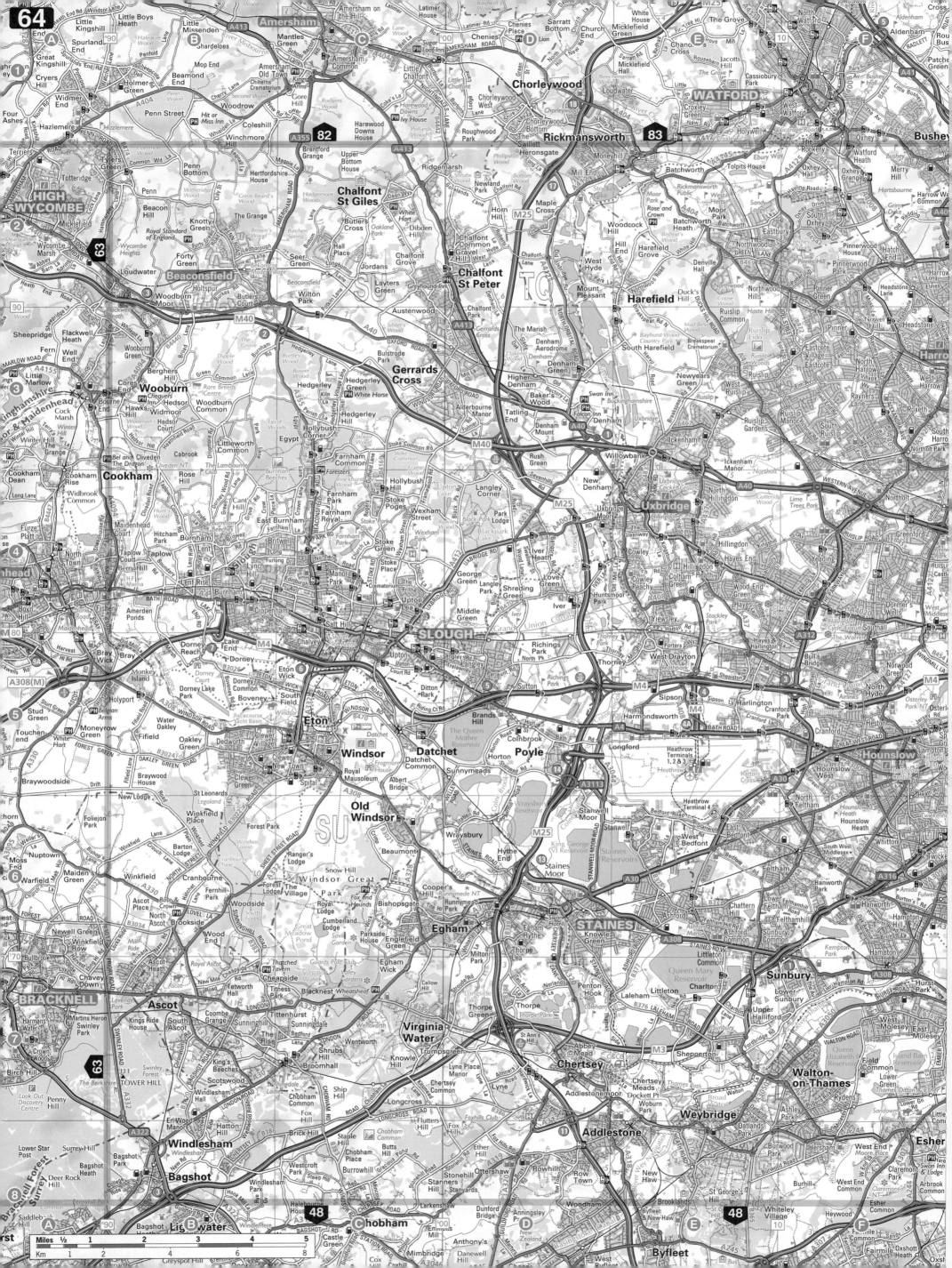

Margate

0   200 metres

QUEENS HALL & WINTER GARDENS
LIFEBOAT STATION
DROIT HOUSE
B2051
FORT CRESCENT
TRINITY SQUARE
CASINO
LIGHTHOUSE
MARGATE PIER
POLICE STATION
WAR MEM
• WM
MARGATE CAVES
• WM
TRINITY SQ
Northdown Road
TUDOR HOUSE
MUS
COLLEGE SQ SHOPPING CENTRE
AMF BOWLING
SALVATION ARMY
THE SHOPPING CENTRE
ADULT EDUCATION CENTRE
THEATRE ROYAL
SCHOOL
MAG COURT
CLOCK TOWER
MARINE TERRACE
BELGRAVE ROAD
DREAMLAND CINEMA/BINGO
ARLINGTON SQUARE SHOPPING CENTRE
DREAMLAND AMUSEMENT PARK (Summer only)
FIRE STA
P.O.
ST JOHNS BUSINESS CENTRE
ROYAL SCHOOL FOR DEAF CHILDREN
MARGATE STATION
A28
LONDON, CANTERBURY
Thanet Coastal Path
Nayland Rock
The Bay
MILL LANE
ALL SAINTS INDUSTRIAL ESTATE
TIVOLI INDUSTRIAL ESTATE
HARTSDOWN PARK APPROACH GOLF COURSE
Games Centre
HARTSDOWN LEISURE CENTRE
MARGATE FOOTBALL CLUB
Playing Fields
Recreation Ground
MARGATE LAWN TENNIS CLUB
ALEXANDRA ROAD
BUCKINGHAM ROAD
MARLBOROUGH ROAD
CONNAUGHT ROAD
CONNAUGHT GDNS
A254
RAMSGATE ROAD
ST PETER'S RD
BROADSTAIRS
RAMSGATE
LBM

Ramsgate

0   200 metres

BROADSTAIRS
ST LUKE'S AVENUE
ANNE ROAD
HERESON RD A255
PO
ALBERT
B2054
VICTORIA ROAD
GRANVILLE THEATRE & CINEMA
MARGATE
CANTERBURY DOVER
B2054
MARGATE RD
CHATHAM STREET
A254
CHATHAM HOUSE GRAMMAR SCHOOL
BOUNDARY ROAD
PARK ROAD
BRUNSWICK STREET
ARTILLERY ROAD
HIGH STREET
BROAD ST
BANDSTAND
LIFT
DC OFFICES
OBELISK
GROSVENOR CASINO
RAMSGATE SPORTS CENTRE
LIBRARY
SCHOOL
FIRE STA
LEOPOLD
ARGYLE SHOPPING CENTRE
MARITIME MUSEUM
STEAM TUG 'CERVIA'
ALMSHOUSES
DSS
MASTHEAD
Inner Harbour
Marina
N
PO
TENNIS COURTS
MOTOR MUSEUM
RAMSGATE NEW PORT FREIGHT FERRY TERMINAL
MEDICAL CENTRE
SCHOOL
ST AUGUSTINE'S ABBEY
B2054
GRANGE ROAD
RAMSGATE MODEL VILLAGE
PO
To A253 (Terminal Access Road)
RAMSGATE
LBM

TR

North Kent Coast coastal map area:

Herne Bay
Western Esp
Central Parade
Studd's Hill
Hampton
Eddington
Beltinge
Hawthorn Corner
Bishopstone
Reculver
The Viking Coastal Trail
Plumpudding Island
Wade Marsh
Brooks End
Birchington
Quex Park
Quex
Two Chimneys
Spitfire & Hurricane Memorial Museum
St Mildred's Bay
Westgate on Sea
Grenham Bay
Epple Bay
Minnis Bay
Westbrook
Garlinge
MARGATE
Royal Esplanade
Cliftonville
Fulsham Rock
Walpole Rocks
Palm Bay
Long Nose Spit
Forness Point
Botany Bay
White Ness
Kingsgate
Kingsgate Bay
Northdown
Joss Bay
North Foreland
Reading Street
St Peter's
East Cliff
Broomfield
Hunters Forstal
Lower Herne
Herne
Millbank
Ford
Gate Inn
Shelvingford
Boyden Gate
Gilling Drove
Chitty
Chislet
Sarre
Gore Street
Monkton
Highstead
Under the Wood
Marshside
St Nicholas at Wade
Potten Street
Potten Street Road
Hale
Acol
ISLE OF THANET
Shottendane
Thanet Creamatorium
Nash Court
Lydden
Westwood
Updown House
North Foreland Lighthouse
Upton
Bromstone
Broomfield
Creamatorium
Haine
Newington
Northwood
Dumpton
South Cliff
Dumpton Park
East Cliff
Dumpton Gap
West End
Herne Common
Maypole
Old Tree
Hoath
Knave's Ash
Hicks Forstal
Rushbourne Manor
Chislet Forstal
Chislet Park
Hollow Street
Wall End
Upstreet
Hersden
Calcott
Chislet Marshes
St Nicholas
Monkton Marshes
Sheriffs Court
Plucks Gutter
Docker Hill
Minster
Minster Marshes
Cleve Court
Alland Grange
Mount Pleasant
Manston
Manston Kent International
Way Hill
Ospringe
St Lawrence
Cliffs End
Chilton
Pegwell
Richborough Port
St Augustine's Cross
Cottington Hill
Viking Ship 'Hugin'
Sandwich & Pegwell Bay
Pegwell Bay
Shell Ness
Ramsgate
Broadstairs
A299
A28
A253
A256
A299
A2990
B2050
B2190
West Bean Wood
Wildwood
Wealden Forest Park
Broad Oak
Den Grove Wood
Langton Lodge
Allcroft
Westbere
Stodmarsh
Grove Ferry
West Stourmouth
East Stourmouth
Stodmarsh
Westmarsh
Paramour Street
Ware
Marshborough
Preston
OOSTENDE
53
53
River Stour
Great Stour
Sandwich Flats

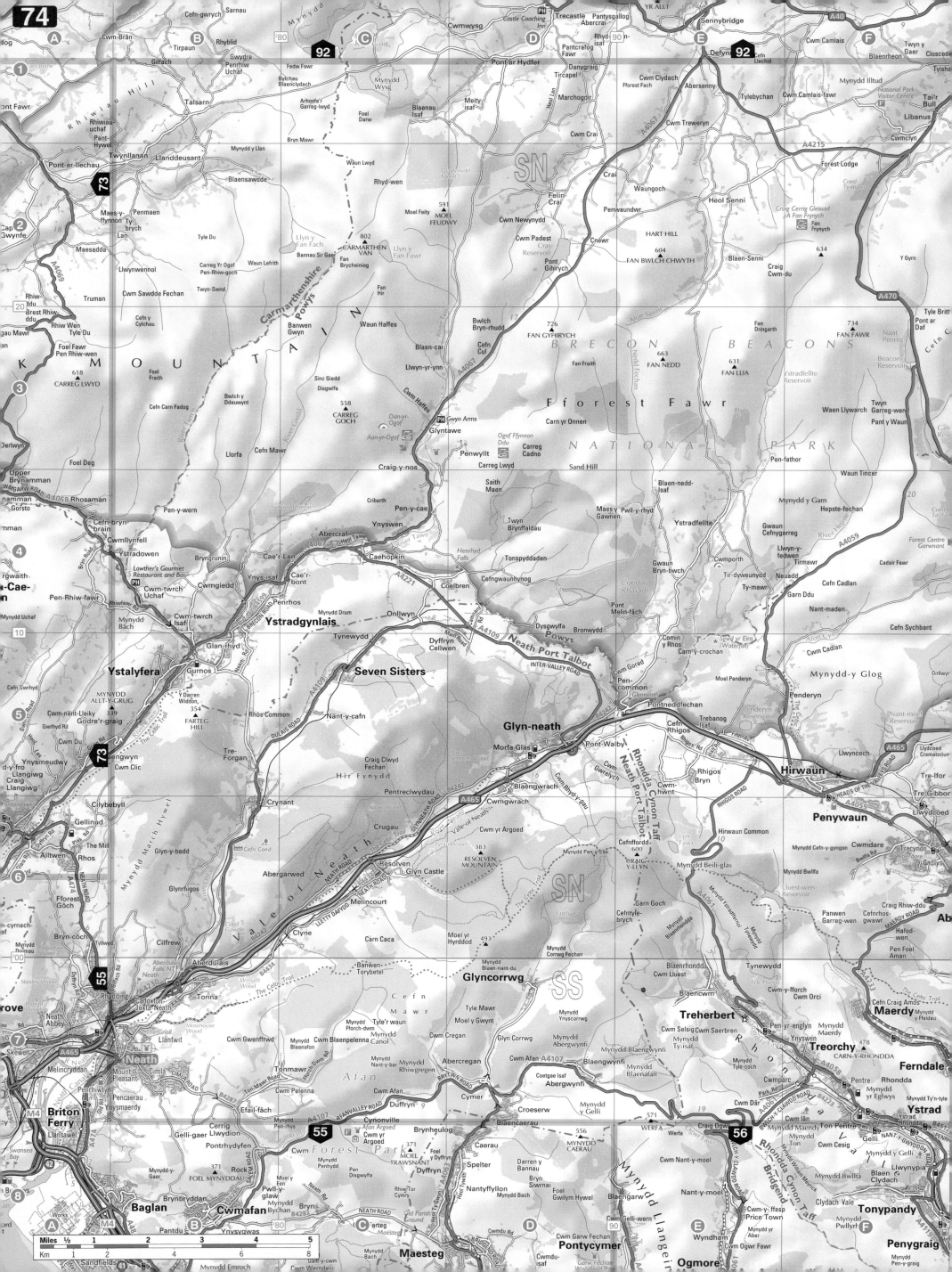

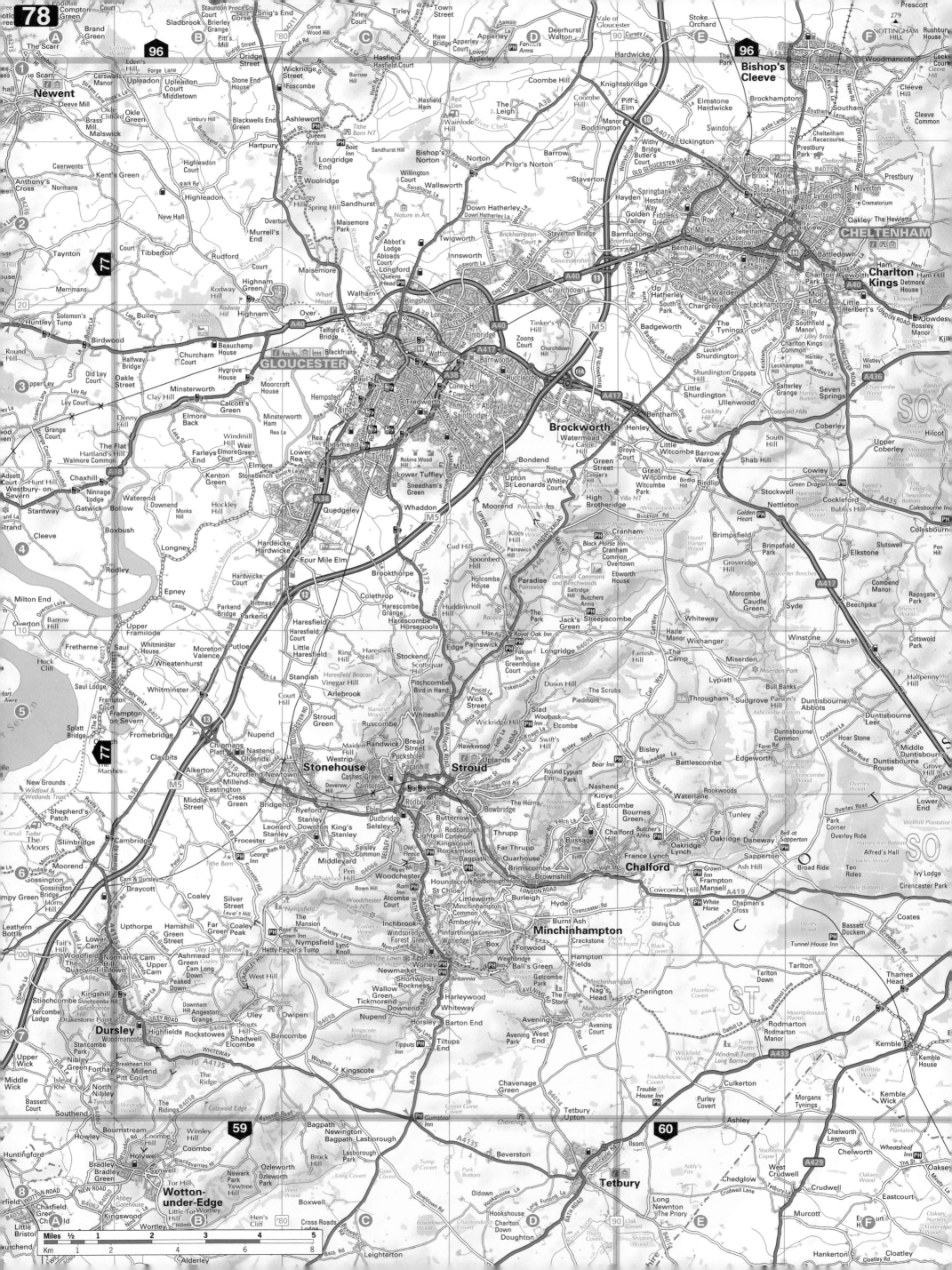

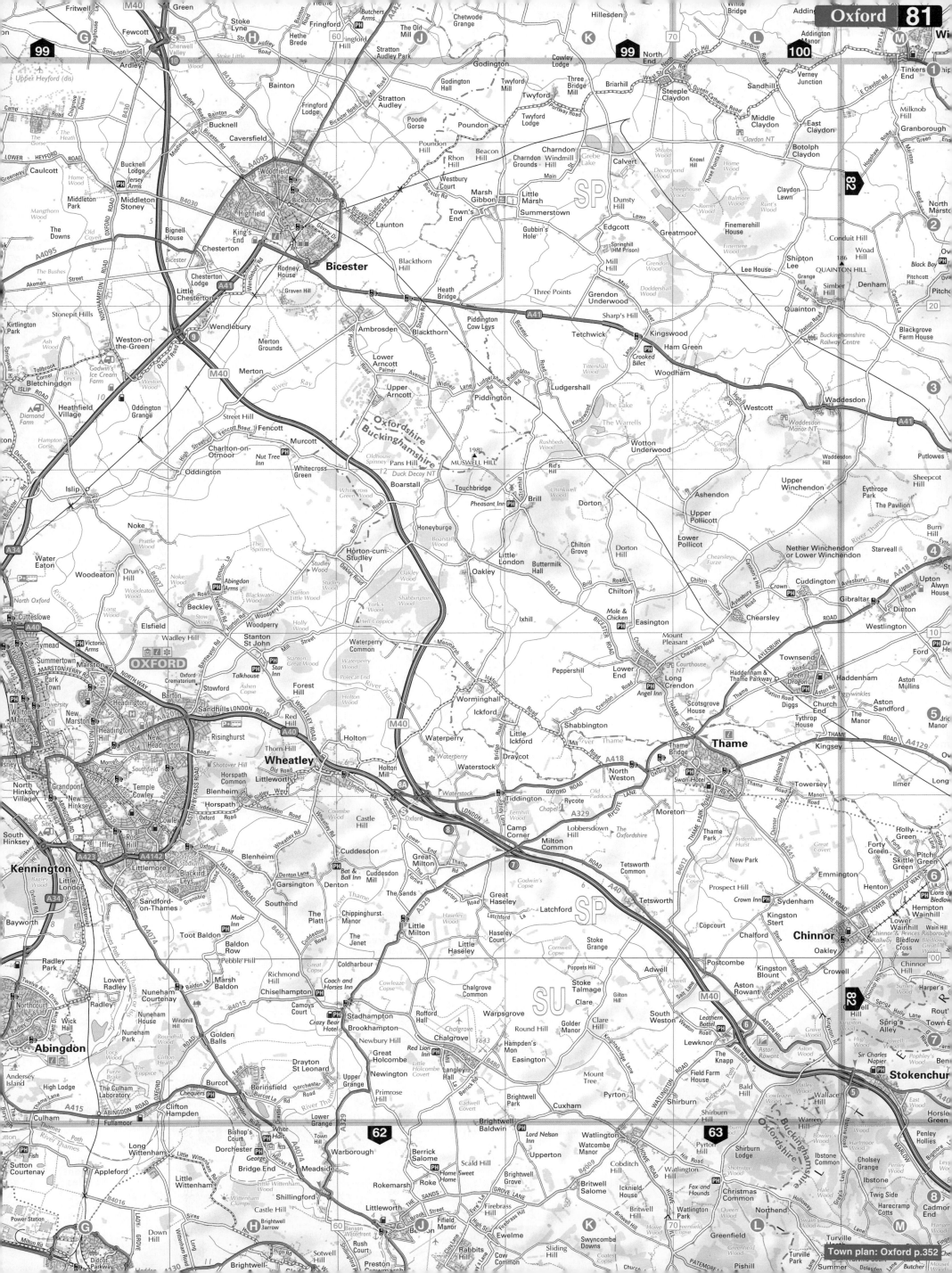

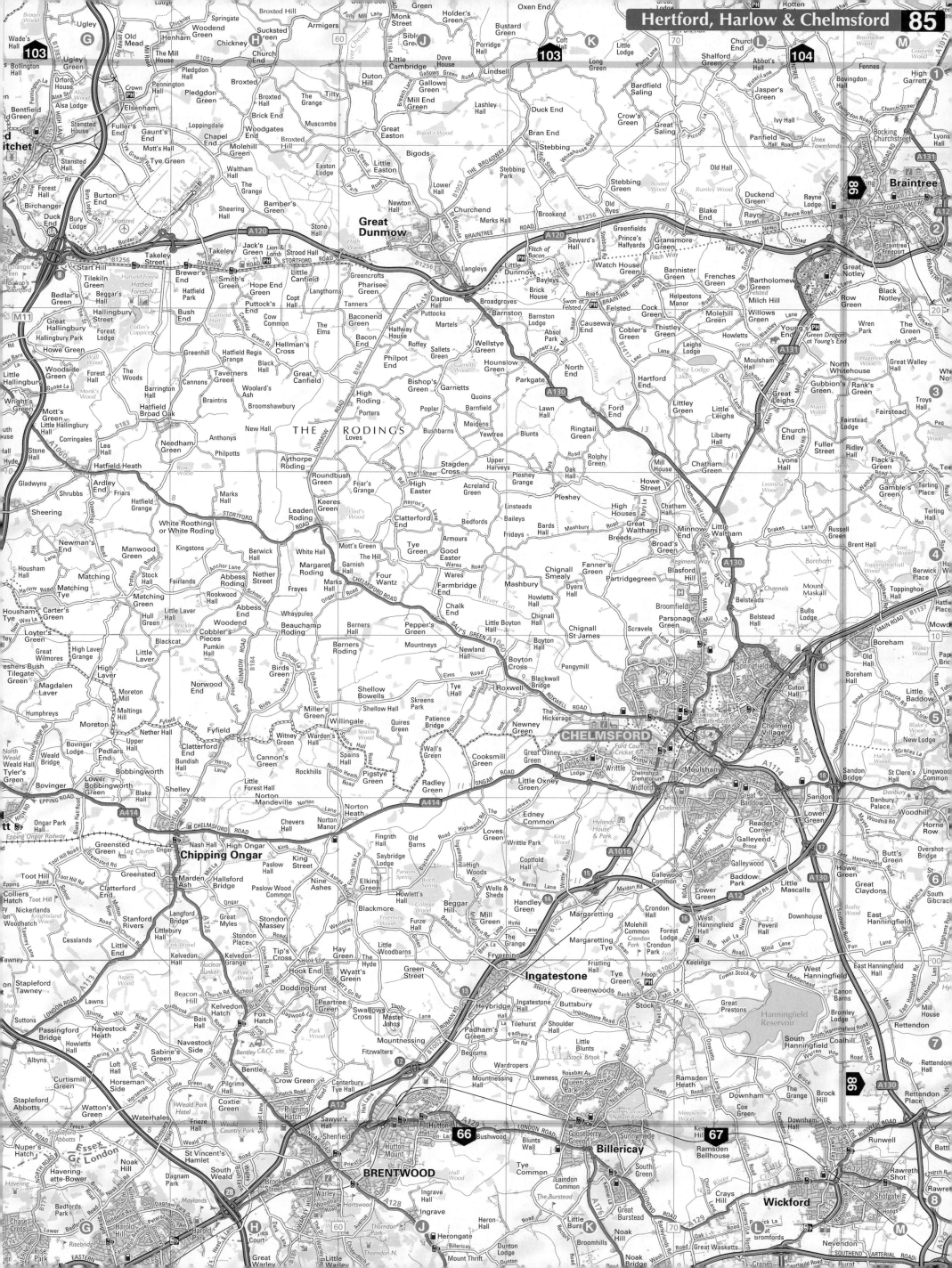

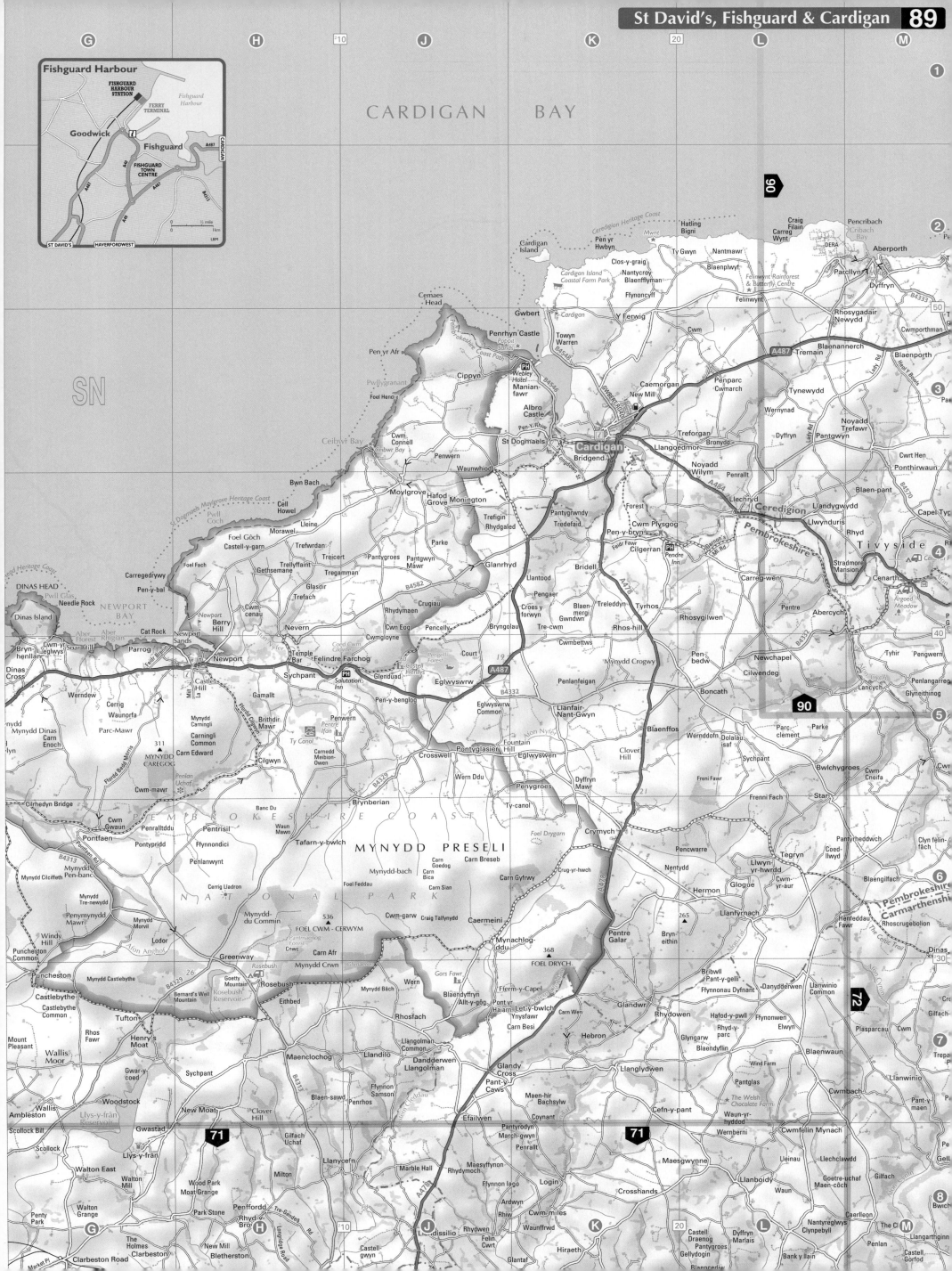

Fishguard Harbour

FISHGUARD HARBOUR STATION
FERRY TERMINAL
Fishguard Harbour
Goodwick
Fishguard
FISHGUARD TOWN CENTRE
A487 CARDIGAN
A40
ST DAVID'S   HAVERFORDWEST

CARDIGAN BAY

SN

Ceredigion Heritage Coast

Cardigan Island   Hatling Bigni   Craig Filain Carreg Wynt   Pencribach Cribach Bay
Pen yr Hwbyn   Mwnt   Ty Gwyn   Nantmawr   DERA   Aberporth
Cardigan Island Coastal Farm Park   Clos-y-graig   Blaenplwyf   Parcllyn   Dyffryn
Cemaes Head   Nantycroy Blaenfflyman   Felinwynt Rainforest & Butterfly Centre
Penrhyn Castle   Ffynnoncyff   Felinwynt   Rhosygadair Newydd   Cwmporthman
Pen yr Afr   Poppit Sands   Gwbert   Cardigan   Y Ferwig   Cwm   B4333
Webley Hotel   Towyn Warren   A487 Tremain   Blaenannerch   Blaenporth
Foel Hendre   Manianfawr   Caemorgan New Mill   Penparc Cwmarch   Tynewydd   Llechryd   Ladd Rd
Cippyn   Albro Castle   Pen-Y-Rhiw   St Dogmaels   Wernynad   Noyadd Trefawr
Cwm Connell   Penwern   Cardigan   Bridgend   Llangoedmor   Treforgan   Bronydd   Dyffryn   Pantgwyn
Ceibwr Bay   Waunwhiod   Noyadd Wilym   Penrallt   Cwrt Hen   Ponthirwaun
Bwn Bach   Moylgrove   Hafod Grove   Monington   Pantygrwndy   Tredefaid   Forest   Cwm Plysgog   Llandygwydd   Blaen-pant
Cell Howel   Lleine   Trefigin Rhydgaled   Pen-y-bryn   Cilgerran   Pendre Inn   Carreg-wen   Llwynduris   Rhyd   Capel Tyg
Morawel   Parke   Glanrhyd   Llantood   Bridell   Pentre   Stradmore Mansion   Tivyside
Foel Gôch   Castell-y-garn   Pantygroes   Crugiau   Pengaer   Bryngolau   Treleddyn   Tyrhos   Rhosygilwen   Abercych   Cenarth   Argoed Meadow
Trefwrdan   Treicert   Tregamman   Cwn Eog   Pencelly   Croes y forwyn   Blaenmergi Gwndwn   Tre-cwm   Rhos-hill   Newchapel   Tyhir   Pengwern
Trellyffaint   Glasdir   Rhydymaen   Cwmgloyne   Court   Cwmbettws   Cilwendeg   Lancych   Glyneithinog   Penlangarreg
Pengelli Forest   Penbedw   Blaenffos   Wernddofn Dolalau isaf   Parc-clement   Sychpant   Bwlchygroes   Cwm Cneifa
Newport Bay   NEWPORT   Felindre Farchog   Eglwyswrw   Penlanfeigan   Llanfair-Nant-Gwyn   Blaenffos   Clover Hill   Freni Fawr   Star
Bryn-henllan   Parrog   Newport Sands   Temple Bar   Glenduad   Eglwyswrw Common   Fountain Hill   Eglwyswen   Dyffryn Mawr   Frenni Fach   Pantyrheddwch
Dinas Island   Cat Rock   Berry Hill   Sychpant   Salutation Inn   Pen-y-benglog   Crosswell   Pontyglasien   Penygroes   Crymych   Pencwarre   Tegryn   Clyn felin fâch
Pwll Glas   Needle Rock   Cwm-yr-eglwys   Soar Hill   Gamallt   Brithdir Mawr   Ty-canol   Hermon   Llwyn-yr-hwrddd   Cwm-yr-aur   Coed llwyd
Dinas Cross   Werndew   Carningli Common   Penwern   Wern Ddu   Glogue   Blaengilfach
Mynydd Dinas Carn Enoch   Cerrig Waunorfa   Mynydd Carningli   Carn Edward   Penlan Uchaf   Brynberian   Ty-canol   Pembrokeshire   Carmarthenshire
Parc-Mawr   Mynydd Caregog   311   Cilgwyn   Banc Du   Waun Mawn   Nentydd   Llanfyrnach   Henfeddau Fawr   Rhoscrugebolion
Cilrhedyn Bridge   Cwm-mawr   PEMBROKESHIRE COAST   Crug-yr-hwch   Bryn-eithin   Dinas
Pontfaen   Cwm Gwaun   Penralltddu   Pentrisil   Tafarn-y-bwlch   MYNYDD PRESELI   Carn Goedog   Carn Breseb   Carn Gyfrwy   Hermon   Pentre Galar   Glangarw
Mynydd Cilciffeth Pen-banc   Ffynnondici   Mynydd-bach   Carn Bica   Carn Sian   Caermeini   Mynachlog-ddu   Bribwll Pant-y-gelli   Ffynnonau Dyfnant   Danydderwen
NATIONAL PARK   Cerrig Lladron   Penlanwynt   Carn Afr   Cwm-garw   Craig Talfynydd   365   Brybreith   Llanwinio Common
Windy Hill   Mynydd Tre-newydd   Mynydd Morvil   536   Cwm-garw   368   FOEL DRYCH   Blaendyflin   72
Puncheston Common   Mynydd Mawr   FOEL CWM-CERWYM   Greenway   Gors Fawr   Foel Feddau   Caermeini   Pentre Galar   Glyngarw   Ffynnonwen   Elwyn
Puncheston   Lodor   Rosebush   Mynydd Crwn   Wern   Blaendyffryn   Fferm-y-Capel   Gland wr   Rhydowen   Hafod-y-pwll   Plasparcau   Cwm
Castlebythe   Mynydd Castlebythe   Goetty Mountain   Rosebush Reservoir   Allt-y-gôg   Pont yr Haiarn-Let'y-bwlch   Rhyd-y-parc   Blaenwaun
Castlebythe Common   Bernard's Well Mountain   Eithbed   Ynysfawr   Carn Wen   Llanglydwen   Wind Farm
Mount Pleasant   Tufton   Rhos Fawr   Henry's Moat   Rhosfach   Llangolman Common   Carn Besi   Hebron   Blaendyflin   Wernberni   7
Wallis Moor   Gwar-y-coed   Sychpant   Maenclochog   Llandilo   Dandderwen   Glandy Cross   Llanglydwen   Pantglas   The Welsh Chocolate Farm   Trepa
Scollock Bill   Llys-y-frân Reservoir   Llangolman   Pant-Caws   Maen-hir Bachsylw   Cefn-y-pant   Waun-yr-hyddod   Cwmfelin Mynach   Pant-y-maen
Wallis Ambleston   71   Woodstock   New Moat   Clover Hill   Ffynnon Samson   Penrhos   Pantyrodyn   March-gwyn   Coynant   Penrallt   Maesgwynne   Llanboidy   Gilfach   Gell
Mount Pleasant   Gwastad   Gilfach Uchaf   Llanycefn   Blaen-sawd   Efailwen   Maesyffynon   Rhydymoch   Login   Crosshands   Lleinau   Llechclawdd
Scollock   Llys-y-frân   Marble Hall   Rhydwen   Ffynnon Iago   Ardwyn   Rhiw   Cwm-miles   Waun   Llanboidy   Goetre-uchaf Maen-côch   Gilfach
Walton East   Walton Mill   Moat Grange   Penffordd Rhyd-y-Bro   New Mill Bletherston   Castellgwyn   Llandissilio   Felin Cwrt   Waunffrwd   Hiraeth   Castell Draenog Pantygroes Gellydogin   Penlan   Castell Gorfod
Penty Park   Walton Grange   Wood Park   Park Stone   Tre-Gendeg   Longdown Rd   Glantaf   Dyffryn Marlais   Bank y llain   Llangarthmun   The Cle
The Holmes Clarbeston   Clarbeston Road   71   Llangatheryn

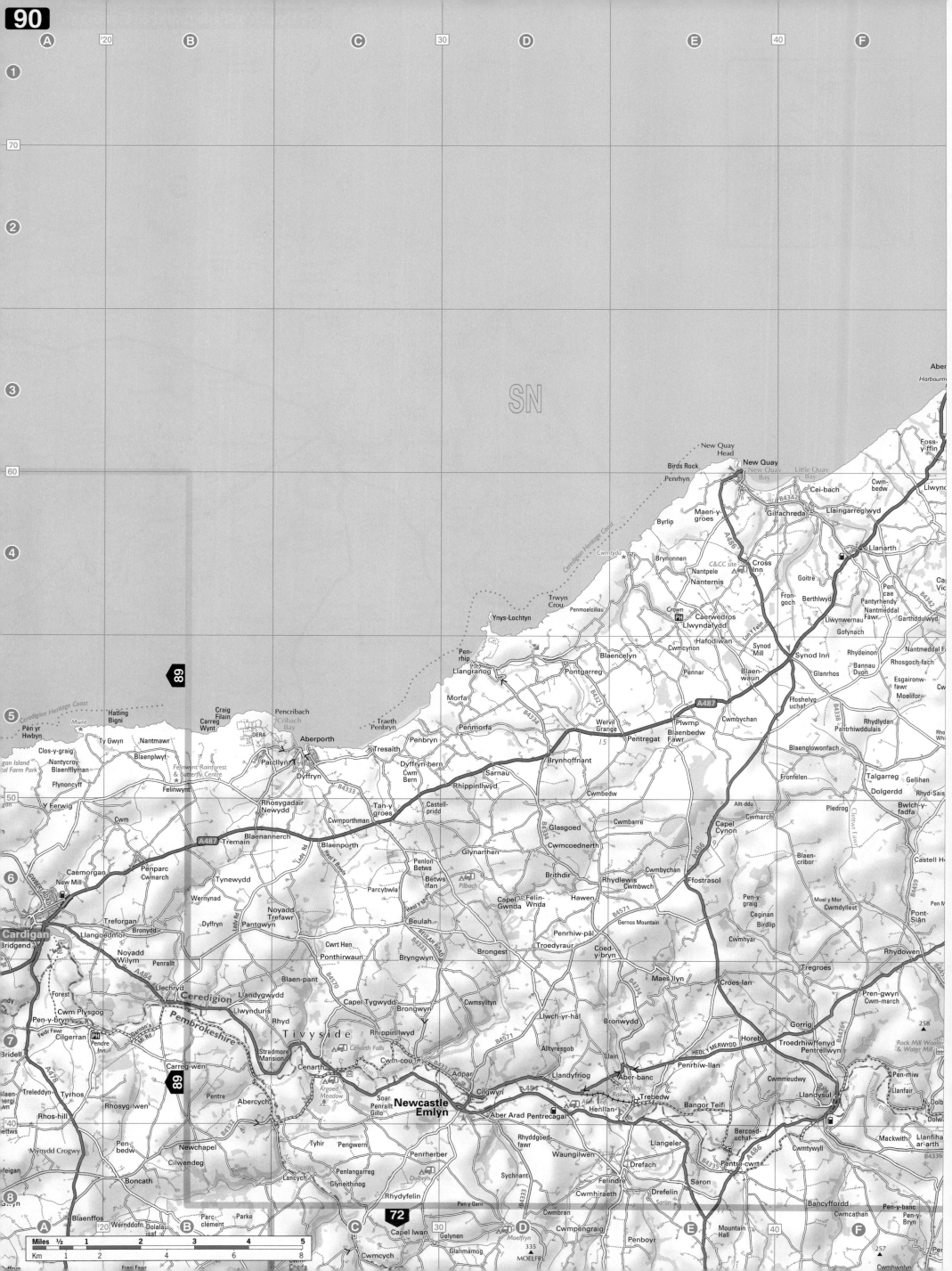

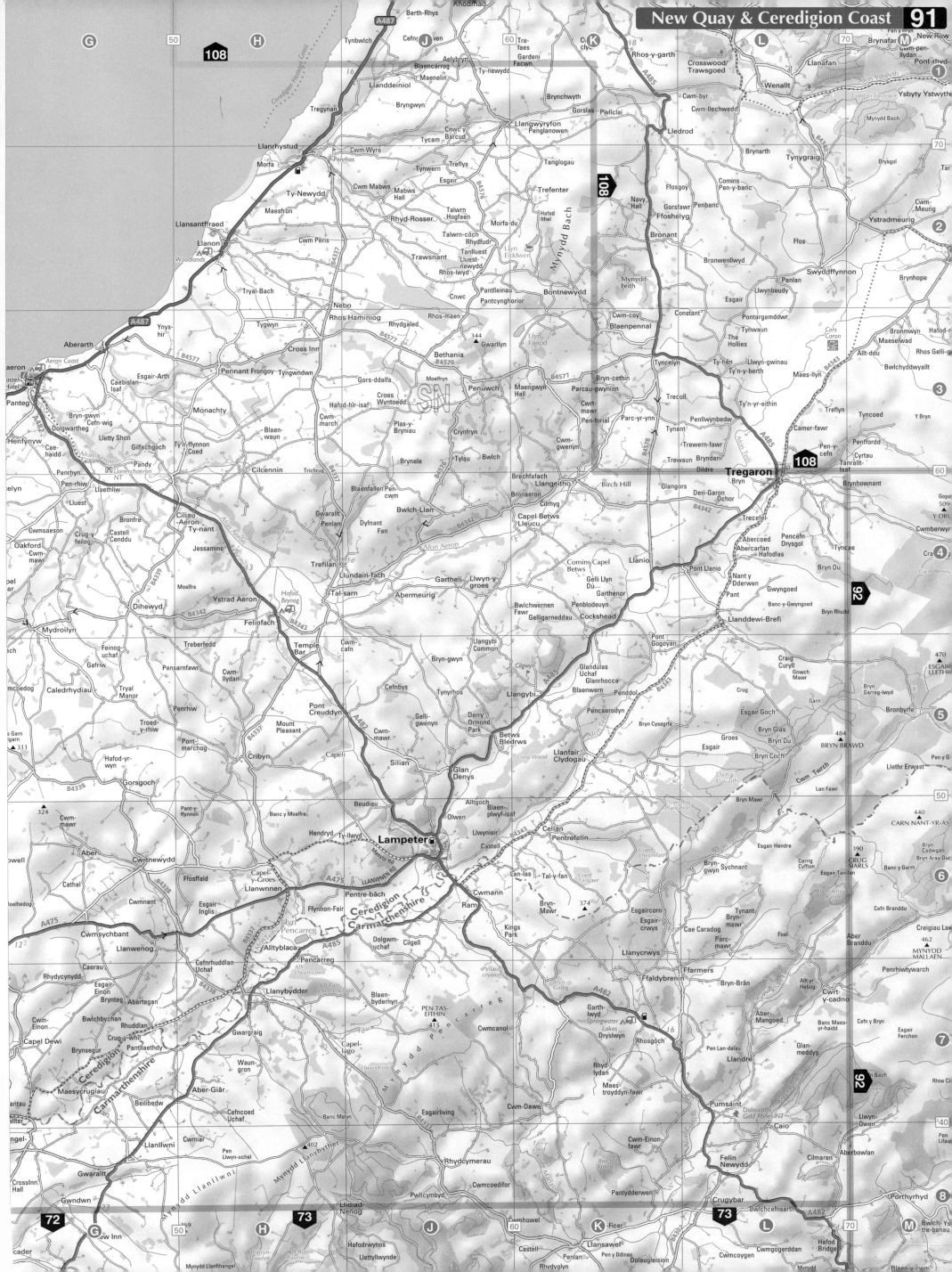

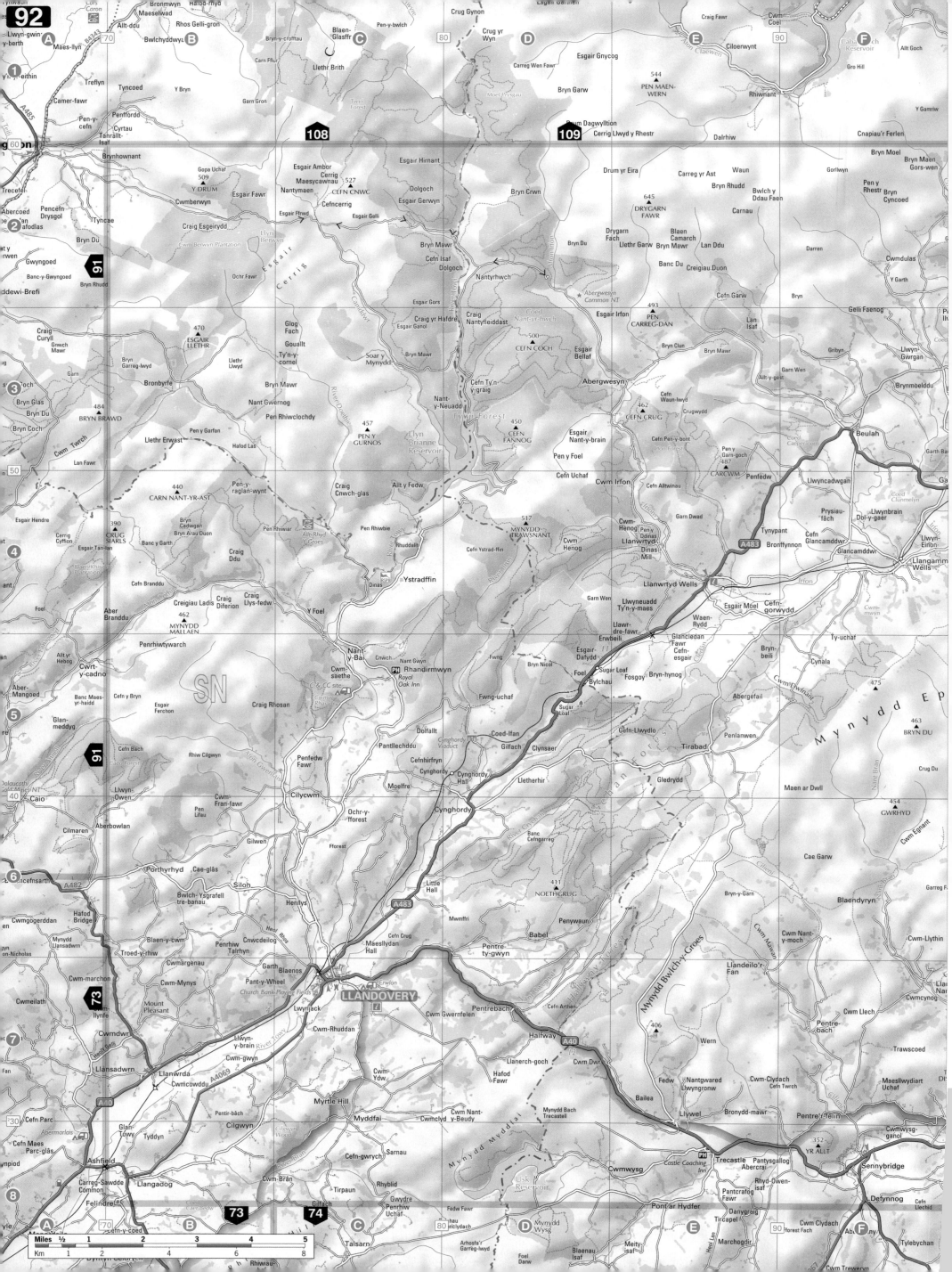

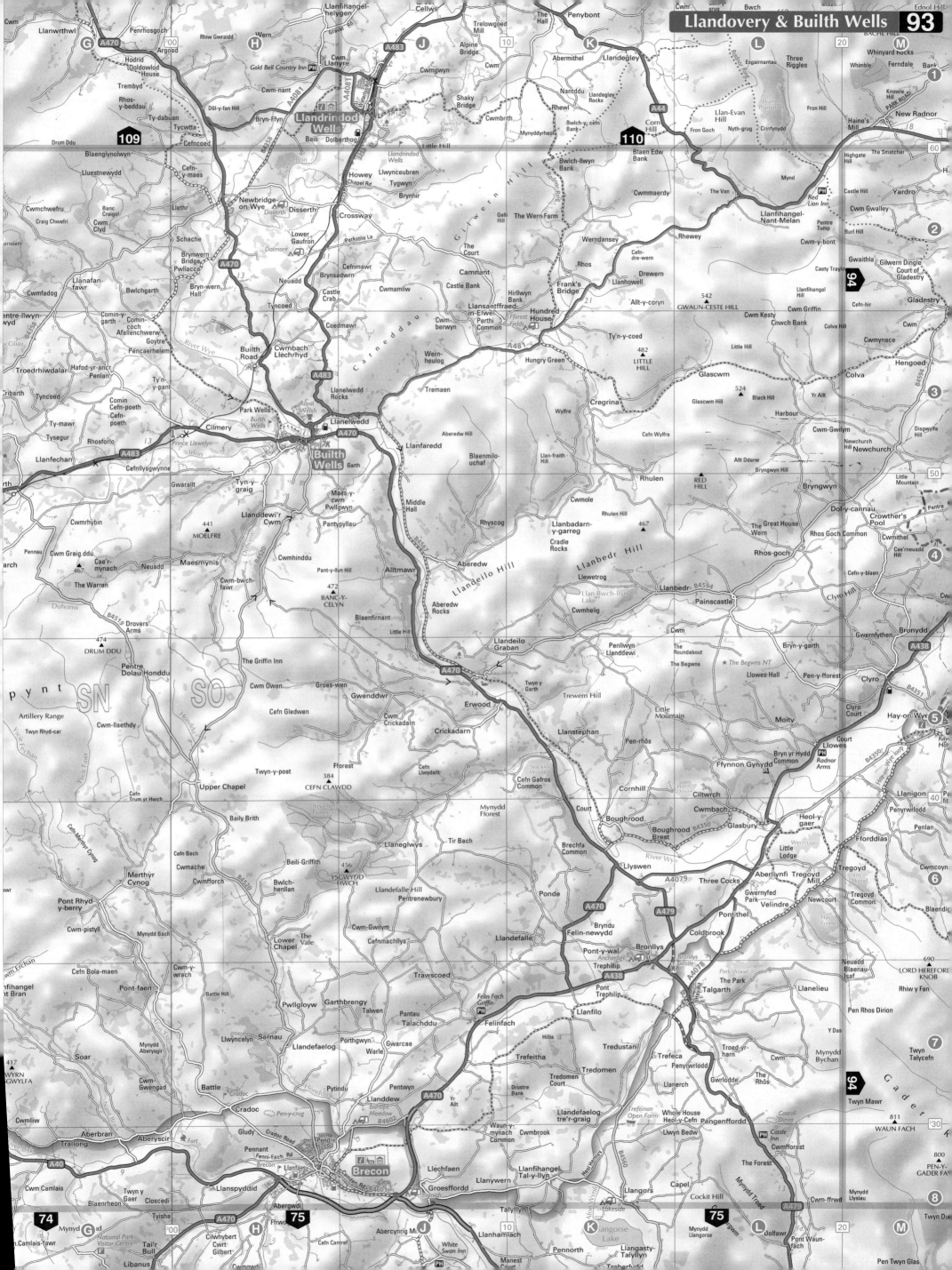

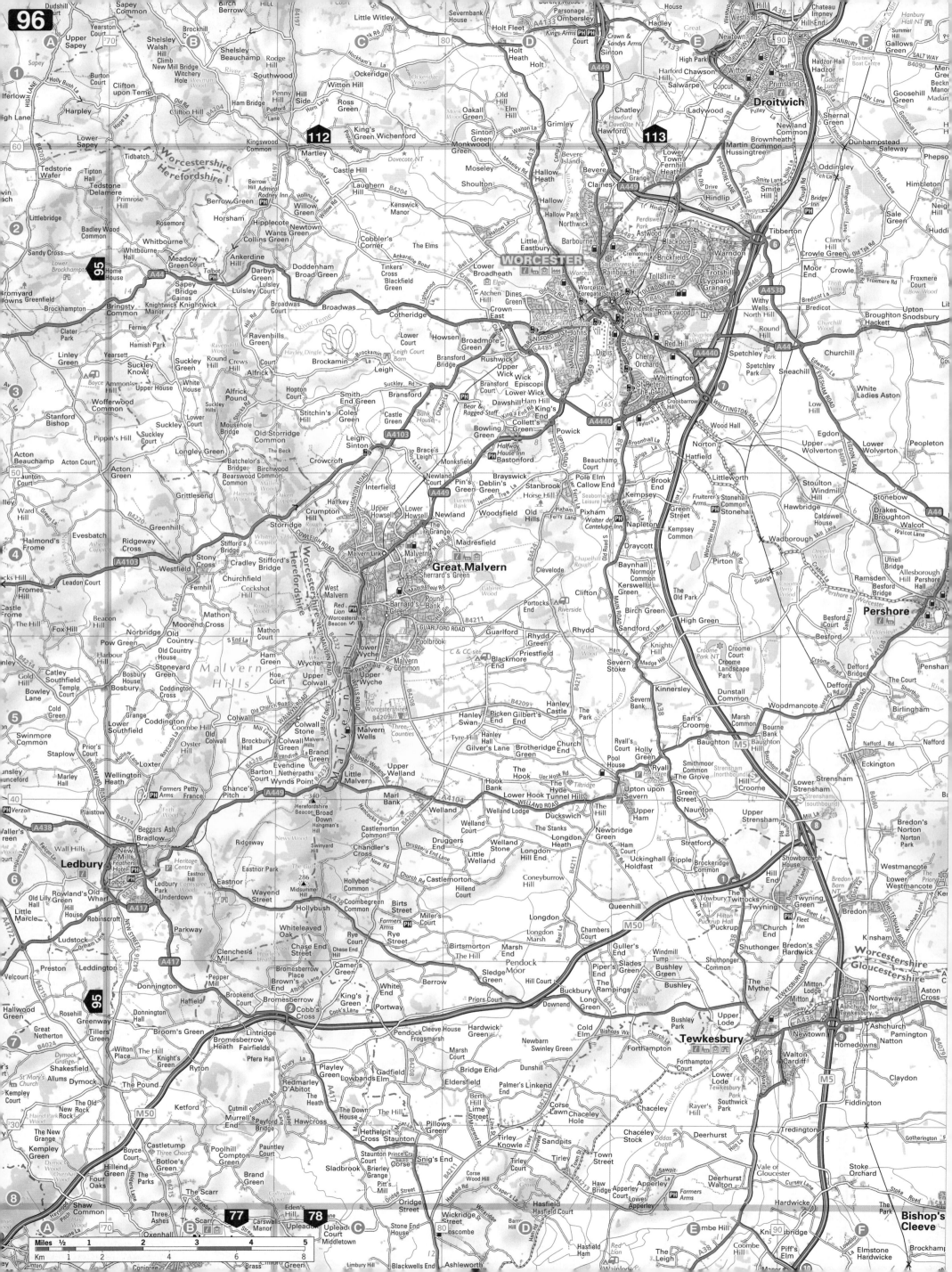

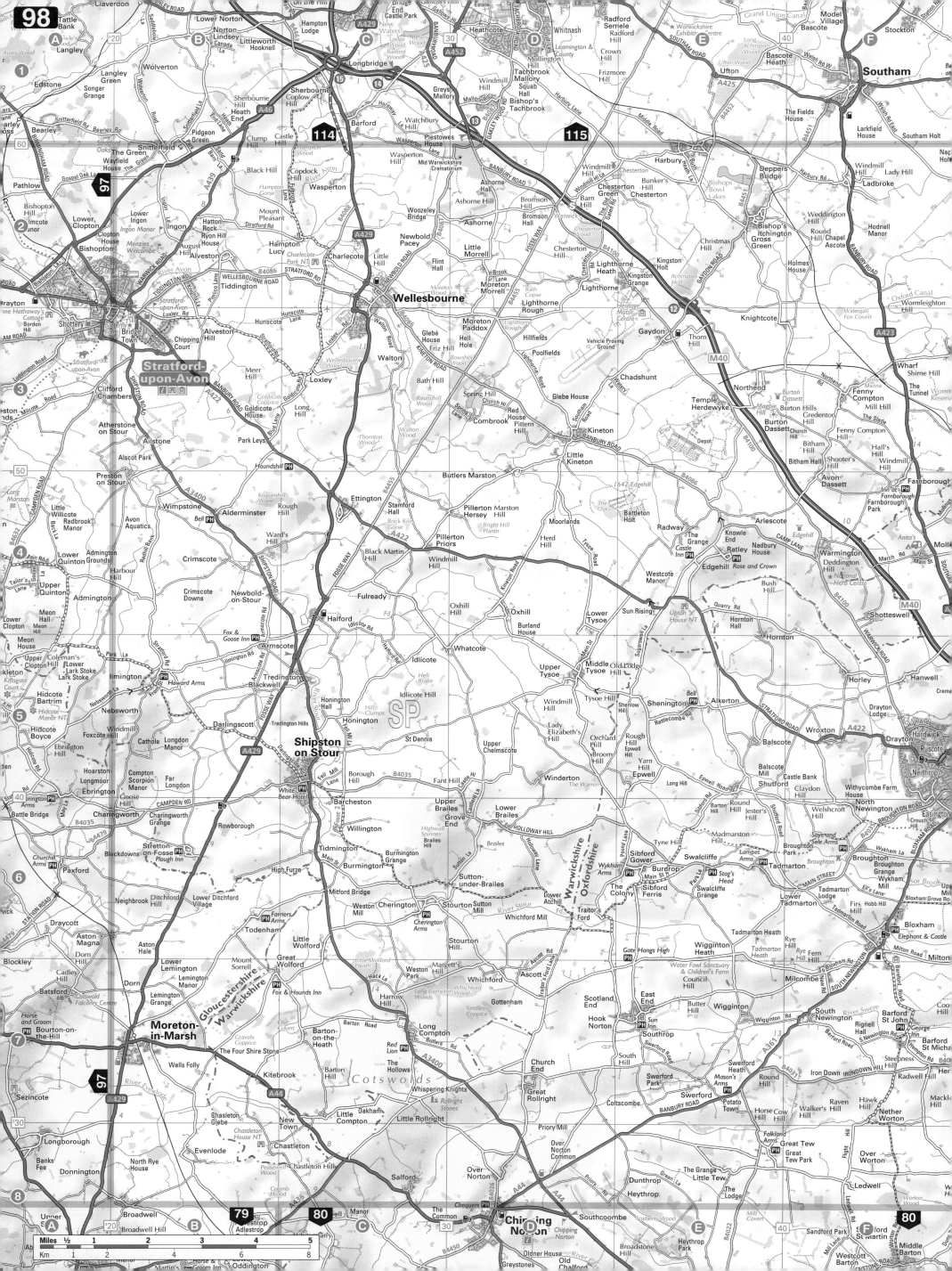

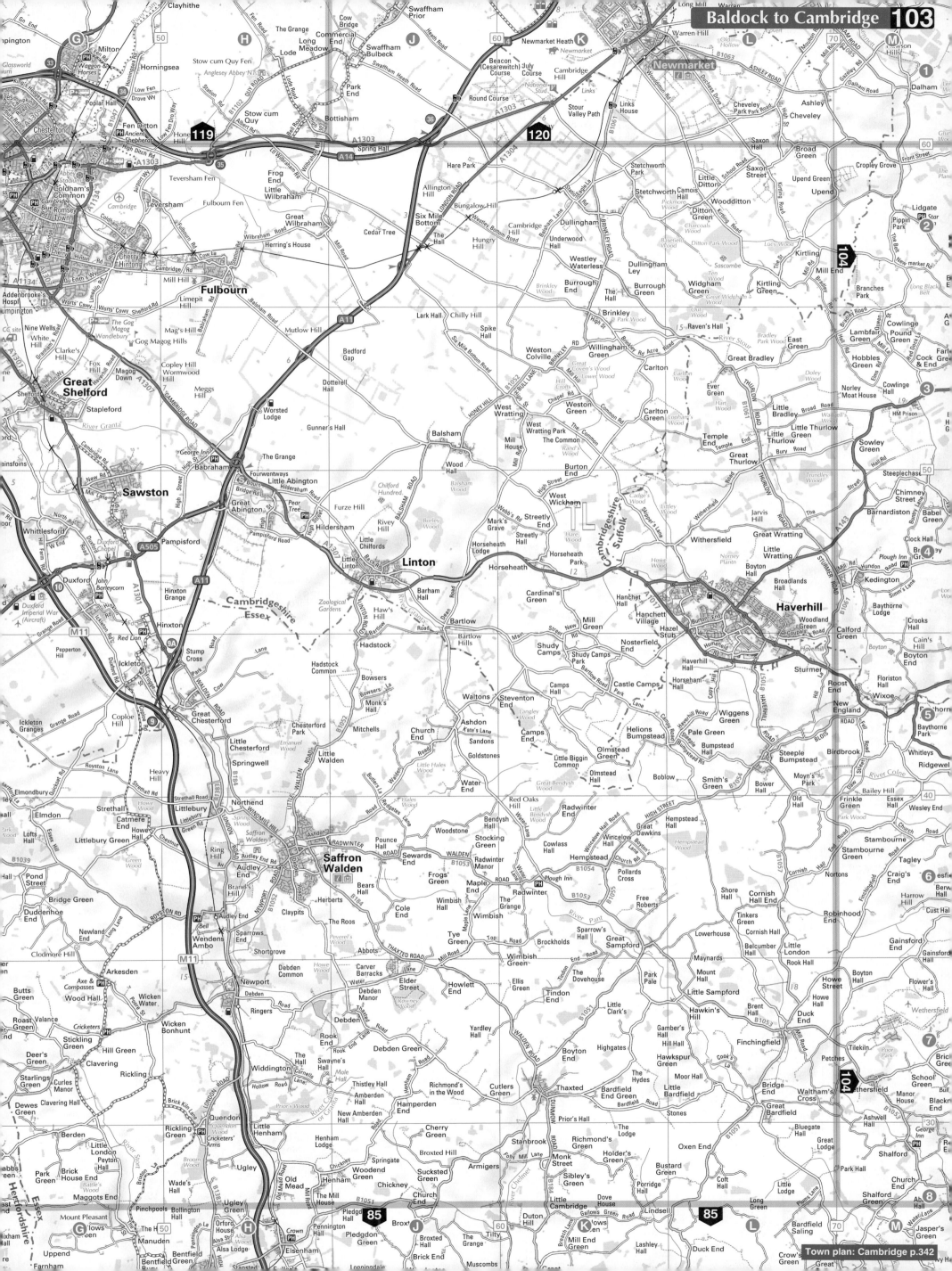

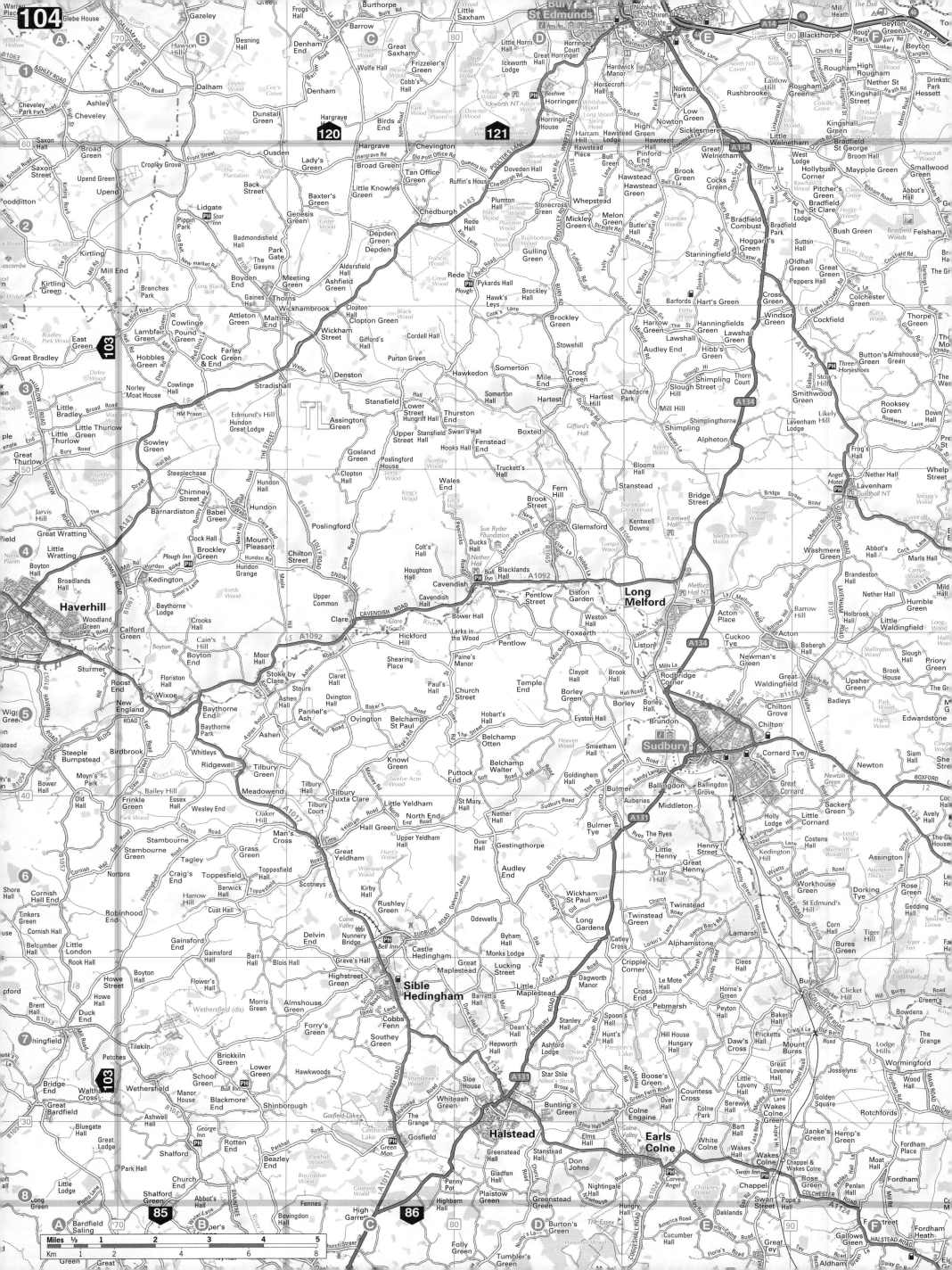

G   H   J   K   L   M

1
2
3
4
5
6
7
8

Leiston
Sizewell

123

Knodishall
Coldfair
Green
Aldringham
Thorpe Ness

Saxmundham
Knodishall Green
Bull's
Hall
Billeaford
Hall
Dolphin
Inn
Thorpeness

Swefling
Clay Hills
Lover's
Hills
Power
Stat

Great Glemham
North
Green
Benhall
Green
Sternfield
Friston
Hazlewood
Hall
South Warren
Red
House
The Haven
The Meare

Mill
Green
Parham
Silverlace
Green
Benhall
Street
Benhall
Place
Crown Inn
Whitearch
Friday
Street
Marsh
Snape
Watering
The Priory
A 1094
Hazelwood
Common
Black Heath
Black Heath Wood
Round
Hill
North
Warren
Thorpe Ness

Marlesford
Stratford
St Andrew
Farnham
FARNHAM ROAD
Gromford
Golden Key
Crown Inn
Snape
Snape
Warren
The Maltings
Barber's
Point
Aldeburgh Marshes
Mill
Inn
Aldeburgh
Fort Green

Little
Glemham
Langham
Bridge
Blaxhall
Dunningworth
Hall
Plough
& Sail
Iken
Wood
Long Reach
Iken
Marshes
Yarn
Hill
Slaughden
ALDEBURGH
BAY

Lower
Hacheston
Campsea
Ashe
Blaxhall
Stone
Common
Blaxhall
Blaxhall Common
or Blaxhall Heath
Cliff Reach
Iken
Iken Heath
High Street
Cowton

Wickham Market
Tunstall
Tunstall
Common
Fazeboons
Sudbourne
Great
Wood
Captain's
Wood
Lambert's La
Sudbourne
Marshes
TM

Eyke
Friday Street
Rendlesham
Watersfield
Park
Wantisden
Hall
Froize
Inn
Chillesford
Butley Mills
Butley
Sudbourne Park
Chillesford
Lodge
Sudbourne
The Firs
Ferry Road
Hospital
Rd
Town
Marshes
Raydon Hall
Sudbourne
Beach
Lantern
Marshes
Radio Station

Suffolk Coast
& Heaths
Carmen's
Wood
Oak
Wood
Gedgrave
Hall
King's
Marshes
ORFORD
NESS

Bromeswell
Heath
Sutton Heath
Estate
Folly
House
Capel
Green
Butley Low
Corner
Butley High
Corner
The Clumps
Orford
Crown and
Castle
Jolly
Sailor Inn
Gedgrave
Marshes
Orfordness-
Havergate

Sutton
Common
Tangham House
Scotland
Fens
Capel St
Andrew
Burrow
Hill
The Cliff
The
Rods
Havergate Island
RSPB
Beach

Rendlesham Forest
Oak Hill
World's
End Plantn
Red
Lodge
Boyton
Boyton
Marshes
Flybury Point
Dove Point

Sutton
Street
St Margaret's
House
Lower
Hollesley
Common
Hollesley
Heath
Woodbridge Walk
Grove House
Hollesley Bay
Colony
North Weir Point

Shottisham
The Lodge
Hollesley
Duck
Corner
Oak Hill
HM Young
Offender
Institution
Oxley
Marshes
HOLLESLEY   BAY

Shottisham
Hall
Box Hall
Bushy
Lane
Shingle
Street

Ramsholt
Peyton
Hall
Alderton
The
Grove
Alderton
House

Bawdsey
Bawdsey
Hall
East La

Felixstowe
Ferry
Bawdsey Manor
Suffolk Heritage Coast

TM

Felixstowe
Woodbridge
Haven
Old
Felixstowe

HOEK VAN HOLLAND

HOEK VAN HOLLAND
ESBJERG

Harwich International Port
River Stour
HARWICH
INTERNATIONAL PORT STATION
(PASSENGER/FERRY TERMINAL)
CAR FERRY
TERMINAL
EAST DOCK RD
INTERNATIONAL
FREIGHT
ENTRANCE
WEST DOCK RD
PETROL
STATION
Parkeston
PARKESTON
ROUNDABOUT
ST NICHOLAS
ROUNDABOUT
Premier
Travel Inn
PATRICKS
JUNCTION
IPSWICH/COLCHESTER
A120
DOVERCOURT B/PASS
MAIN ROAD
HARWICH

Town plan: Ipswich p.346

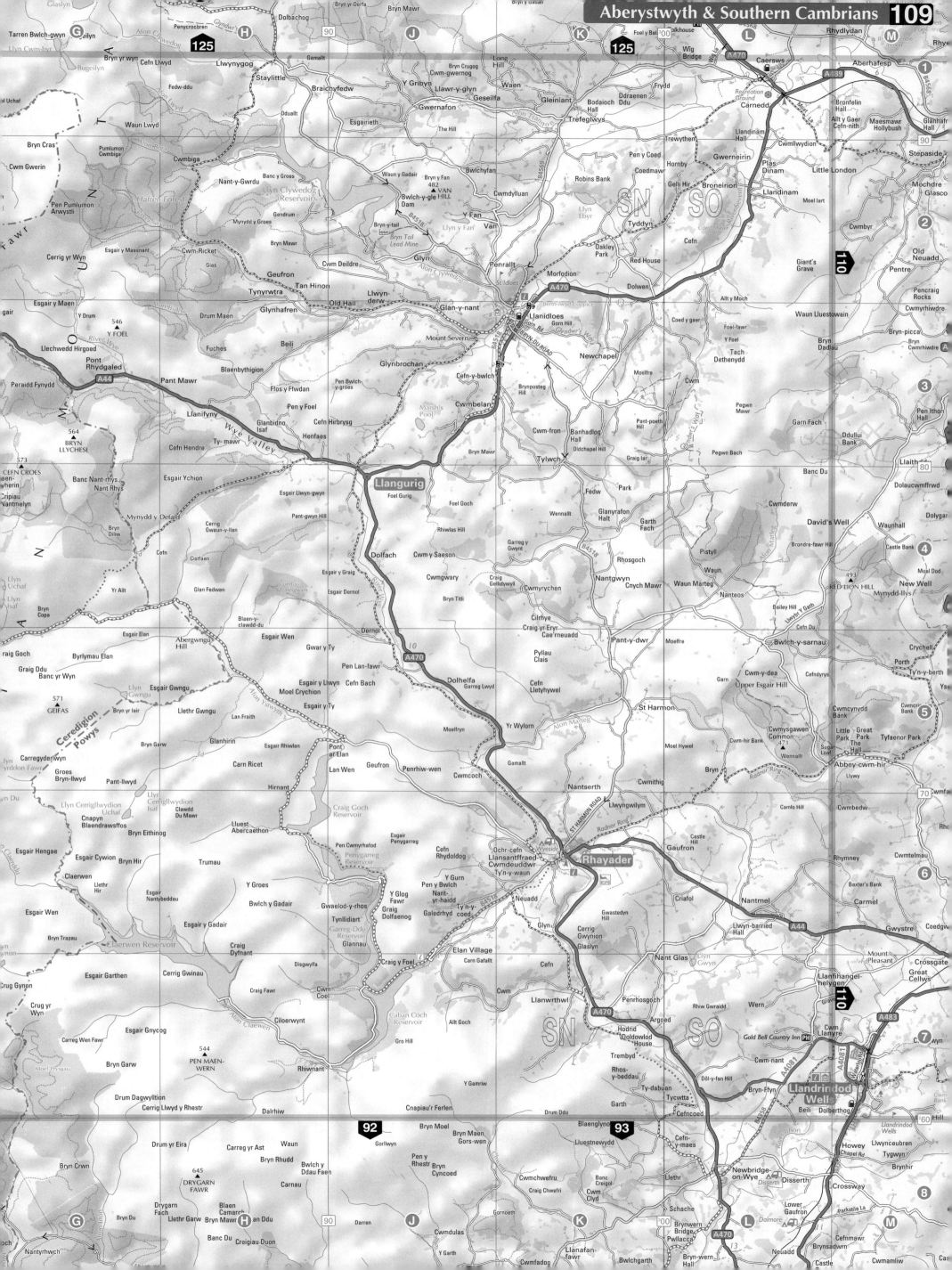

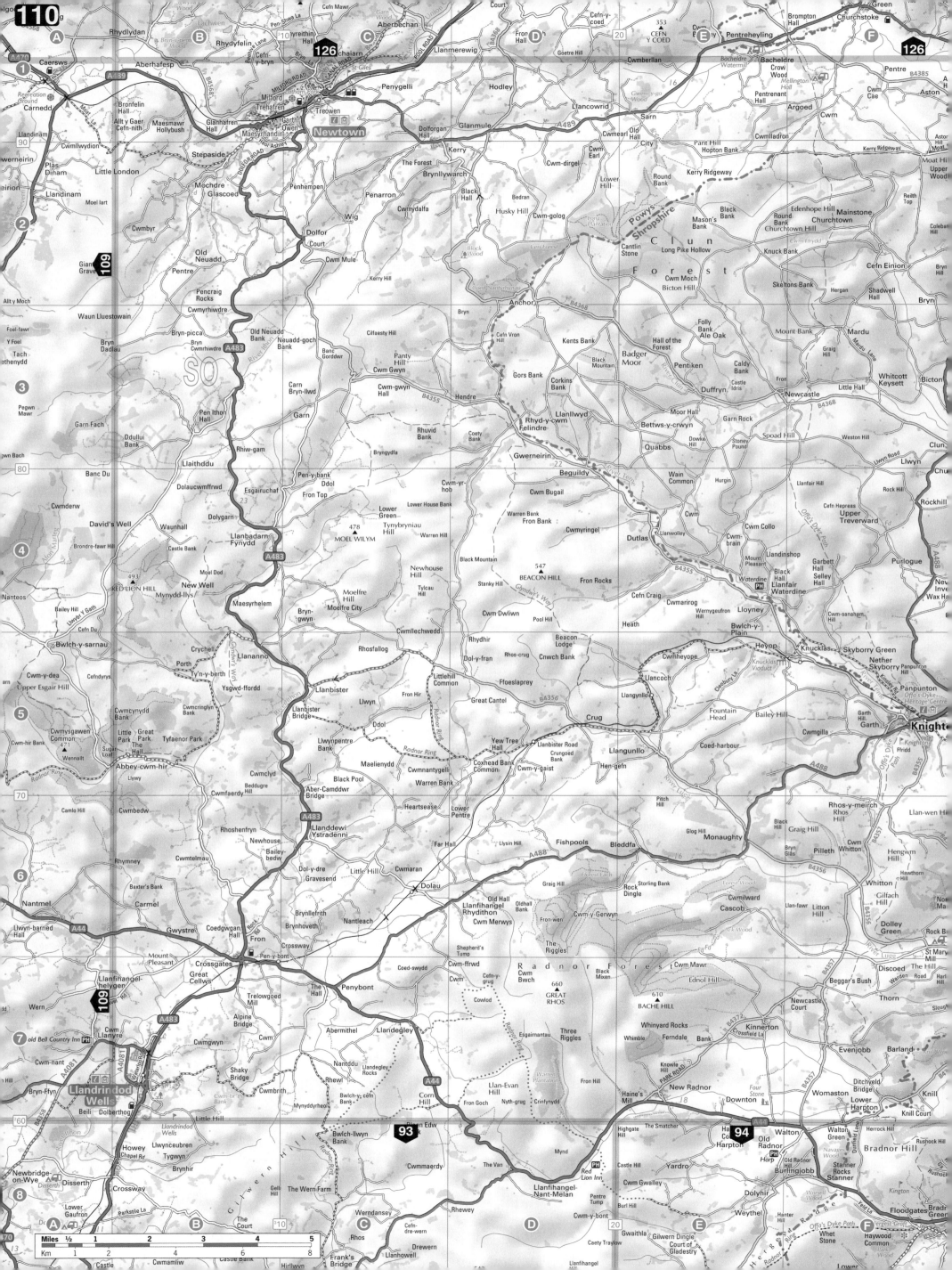

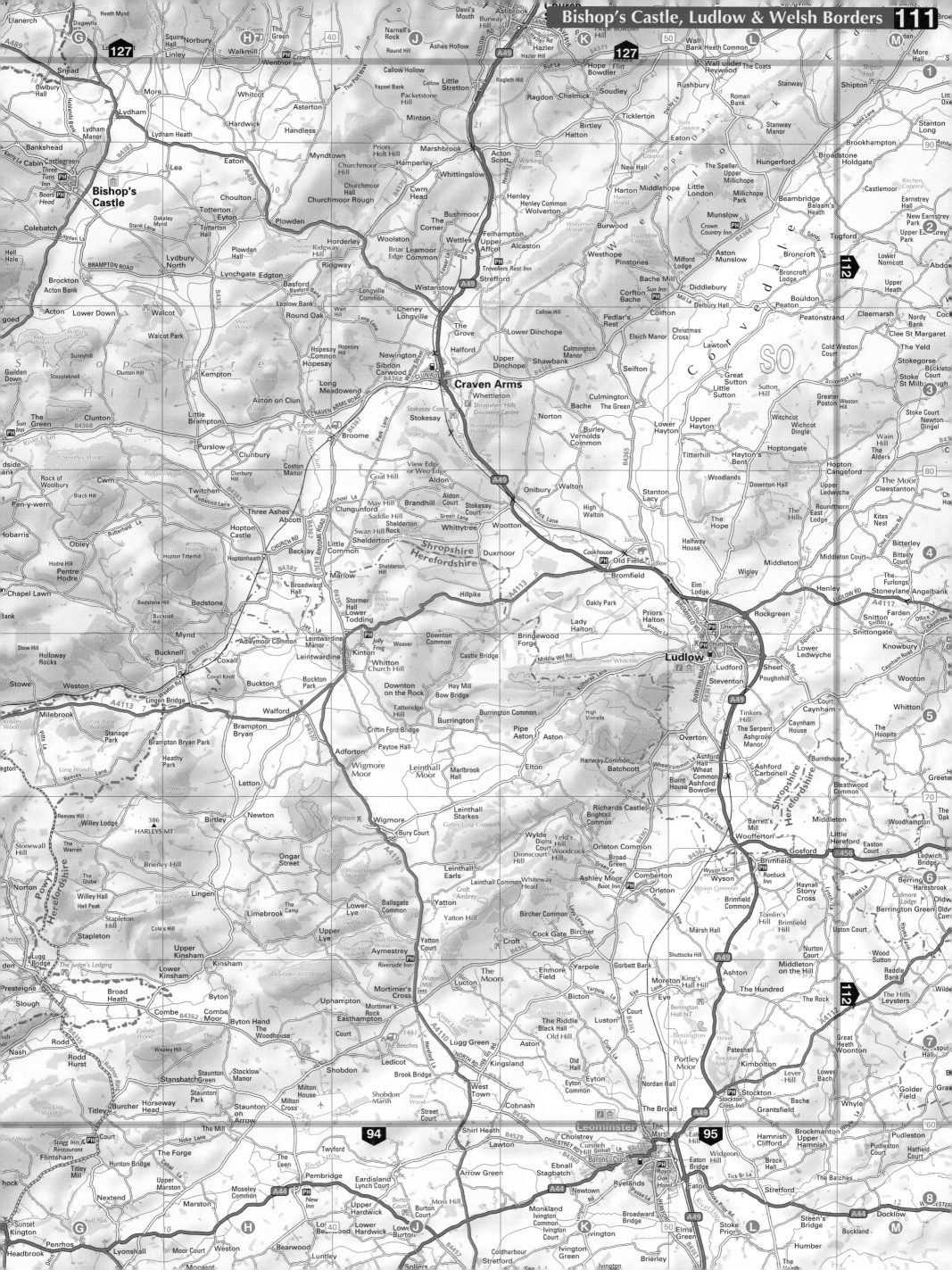

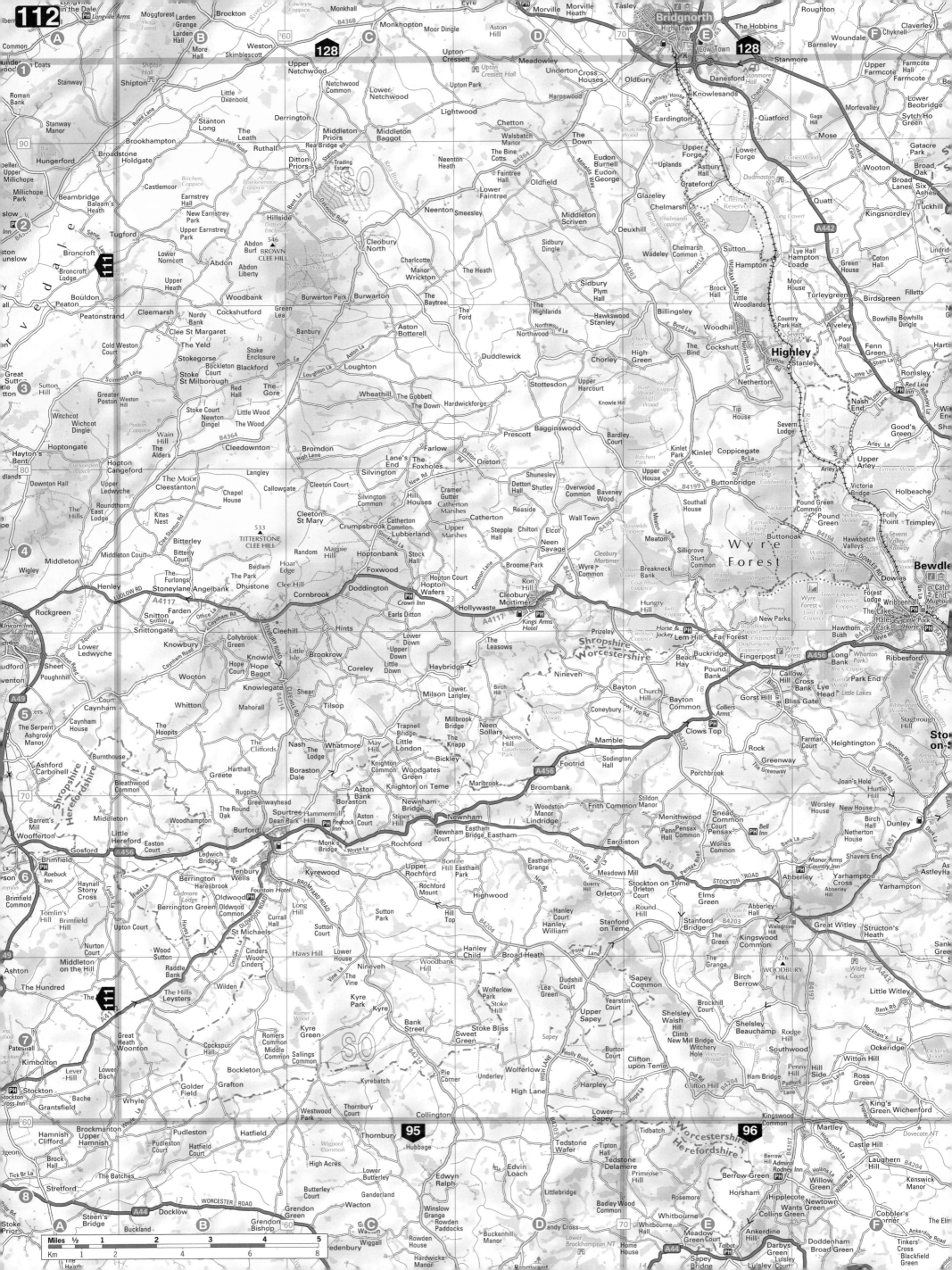

Town plan: Cambridge p.342

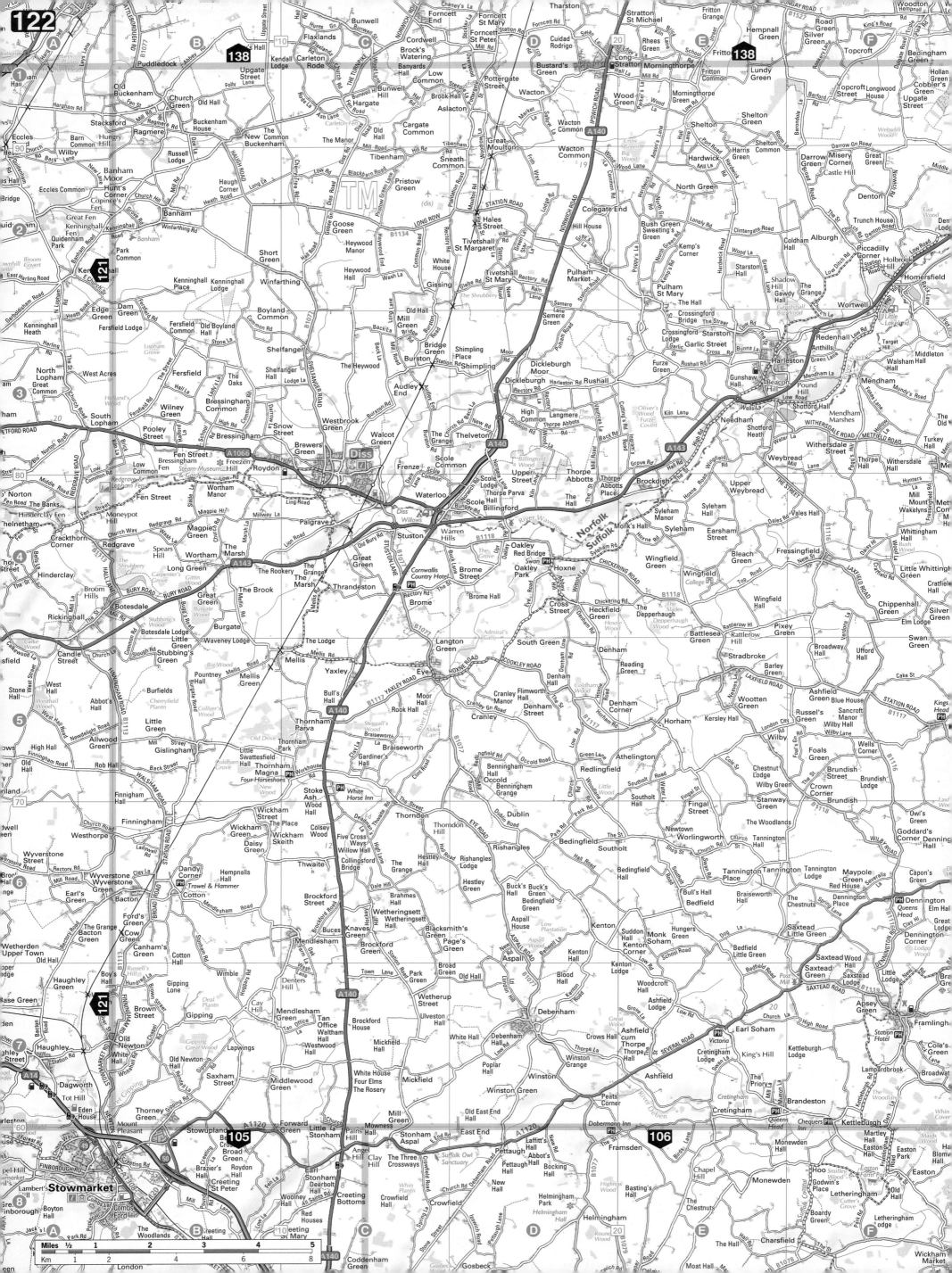

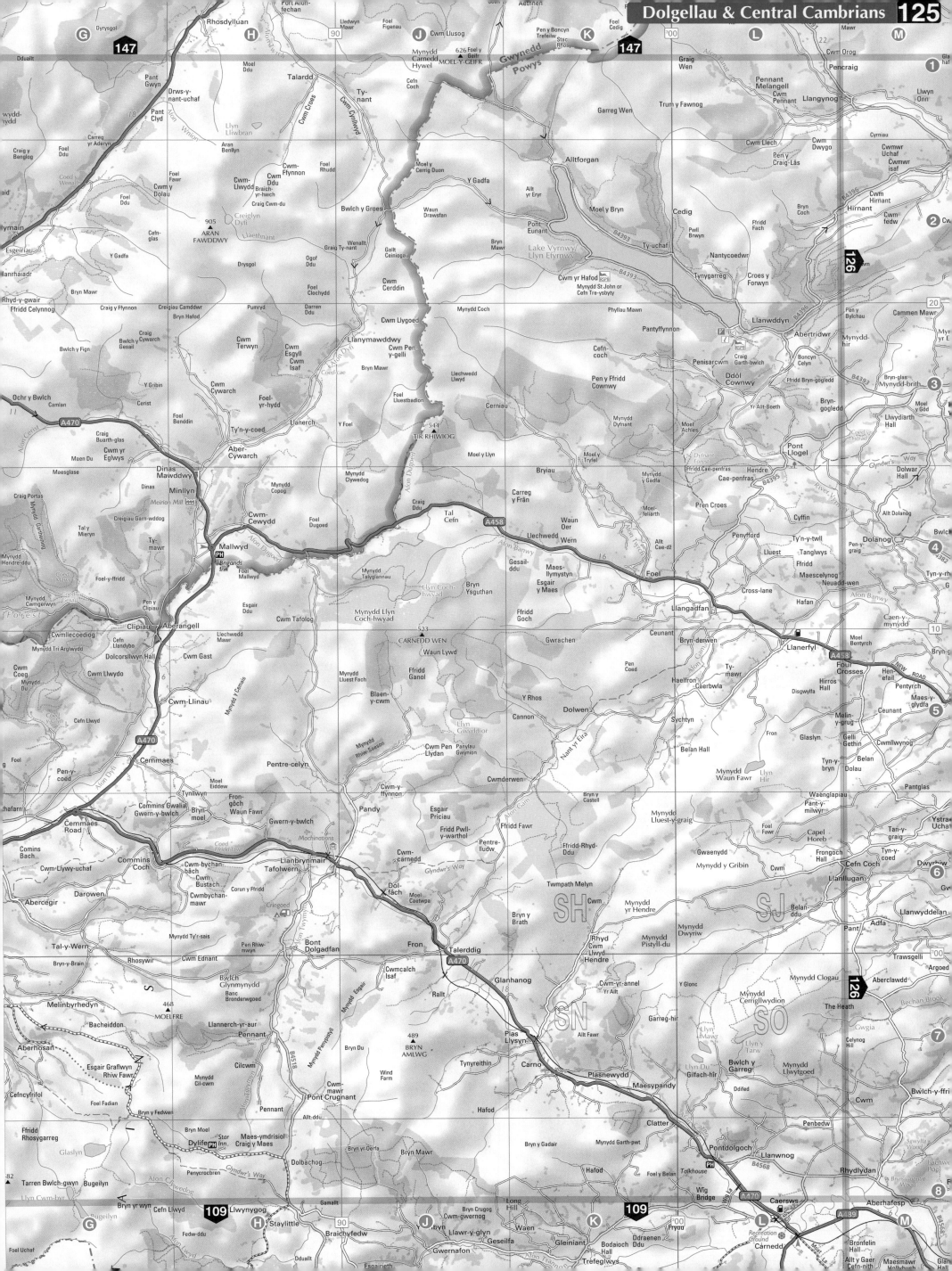

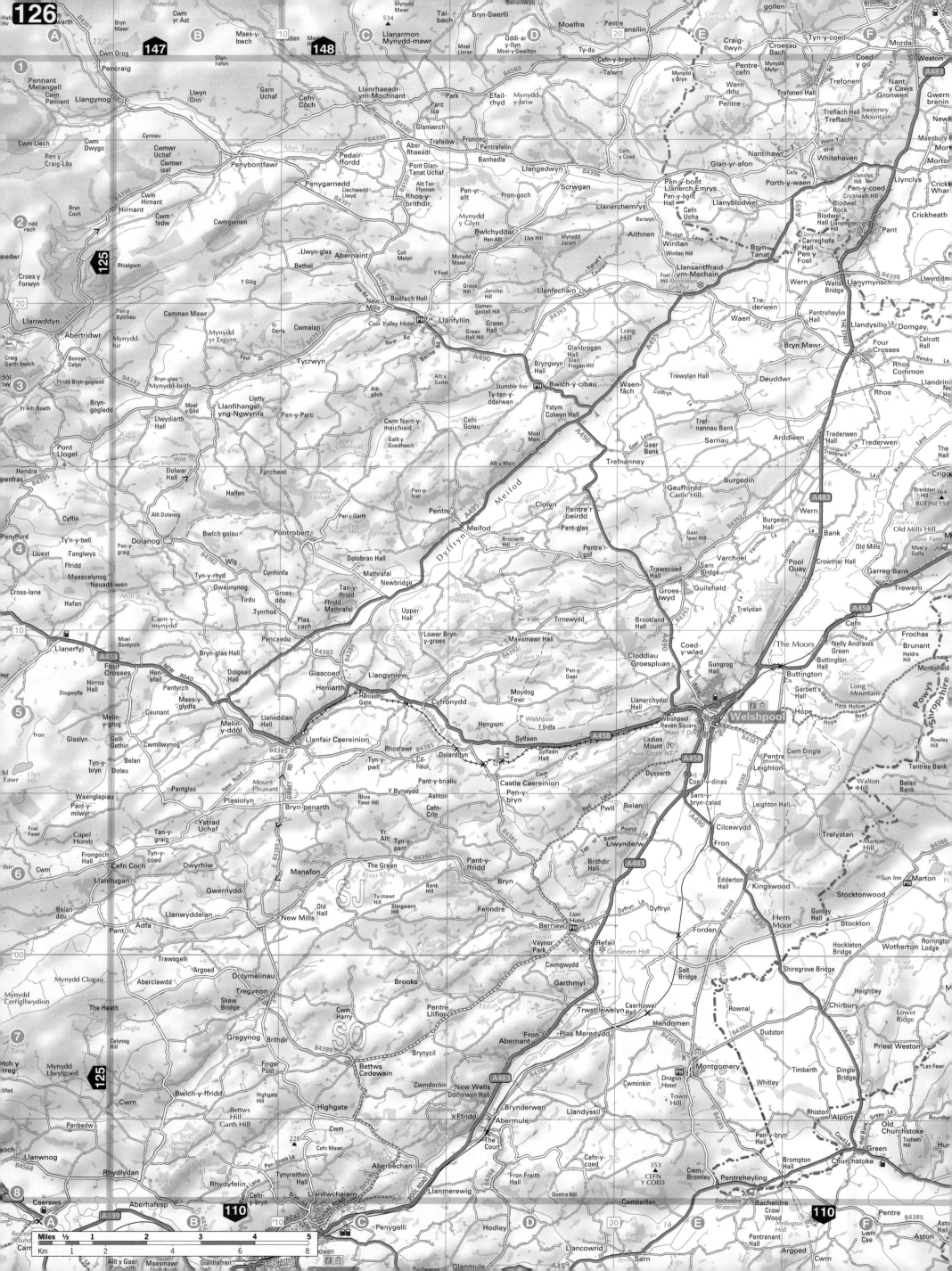

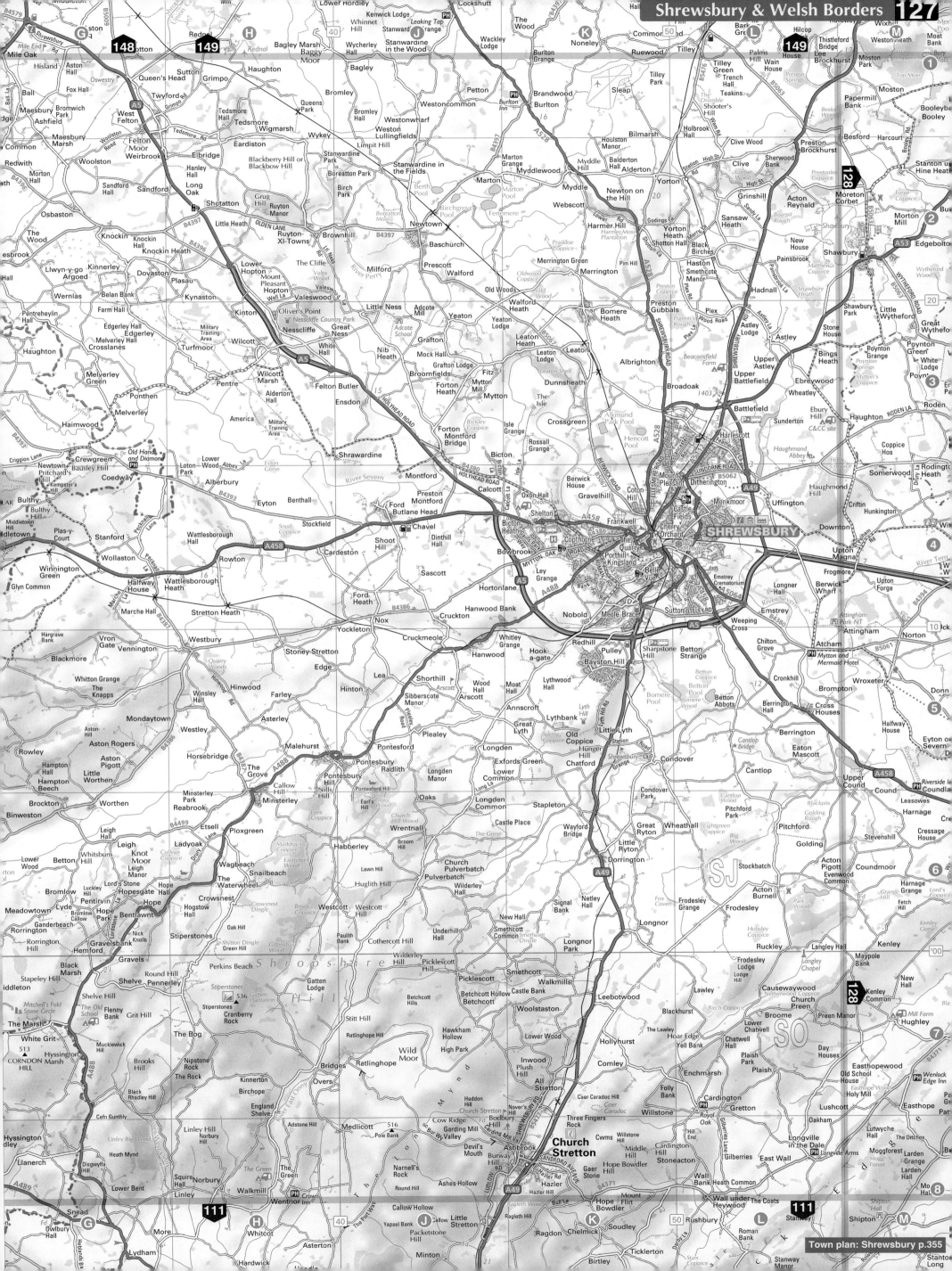

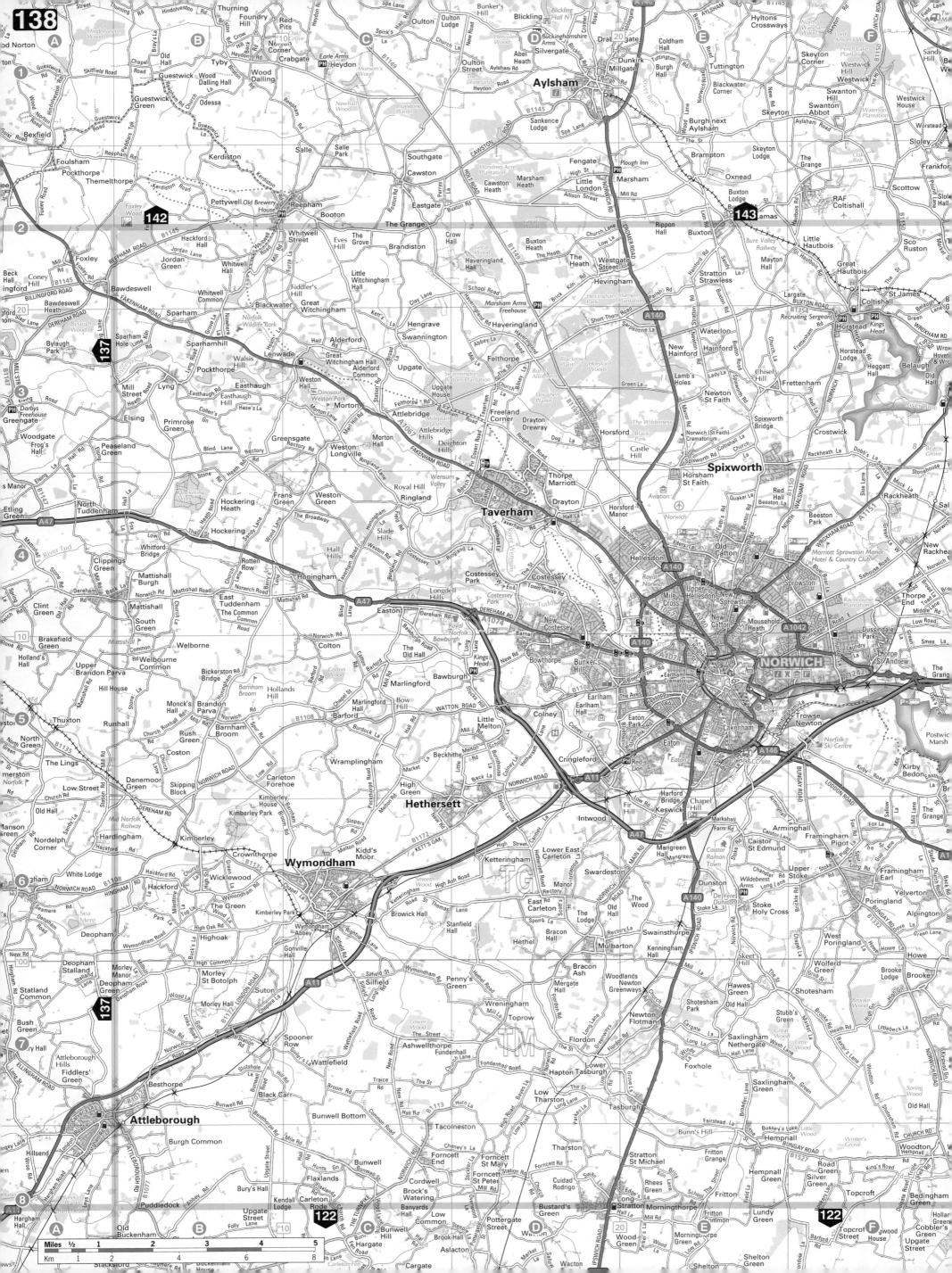

NORTH SEA

TG

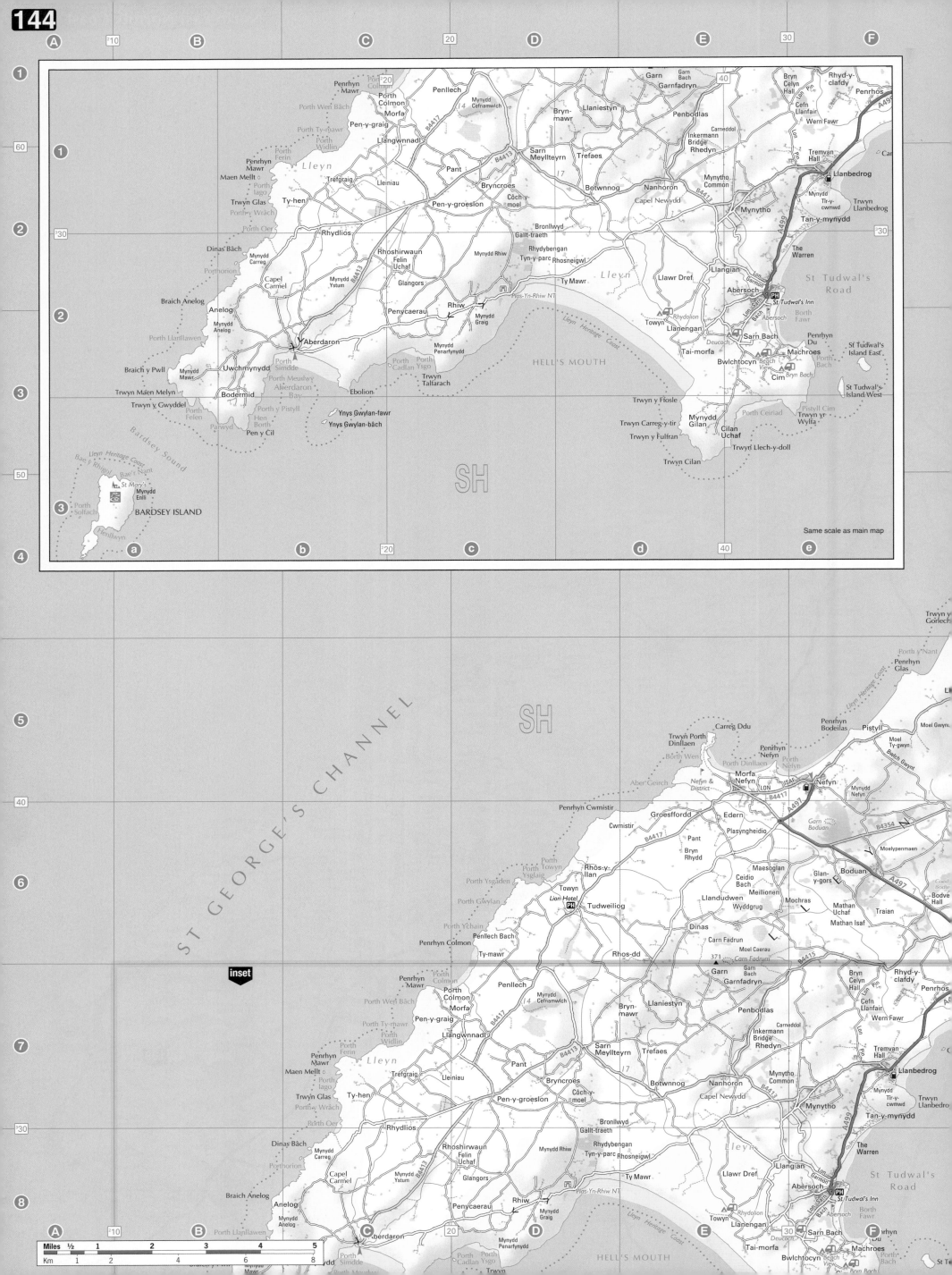

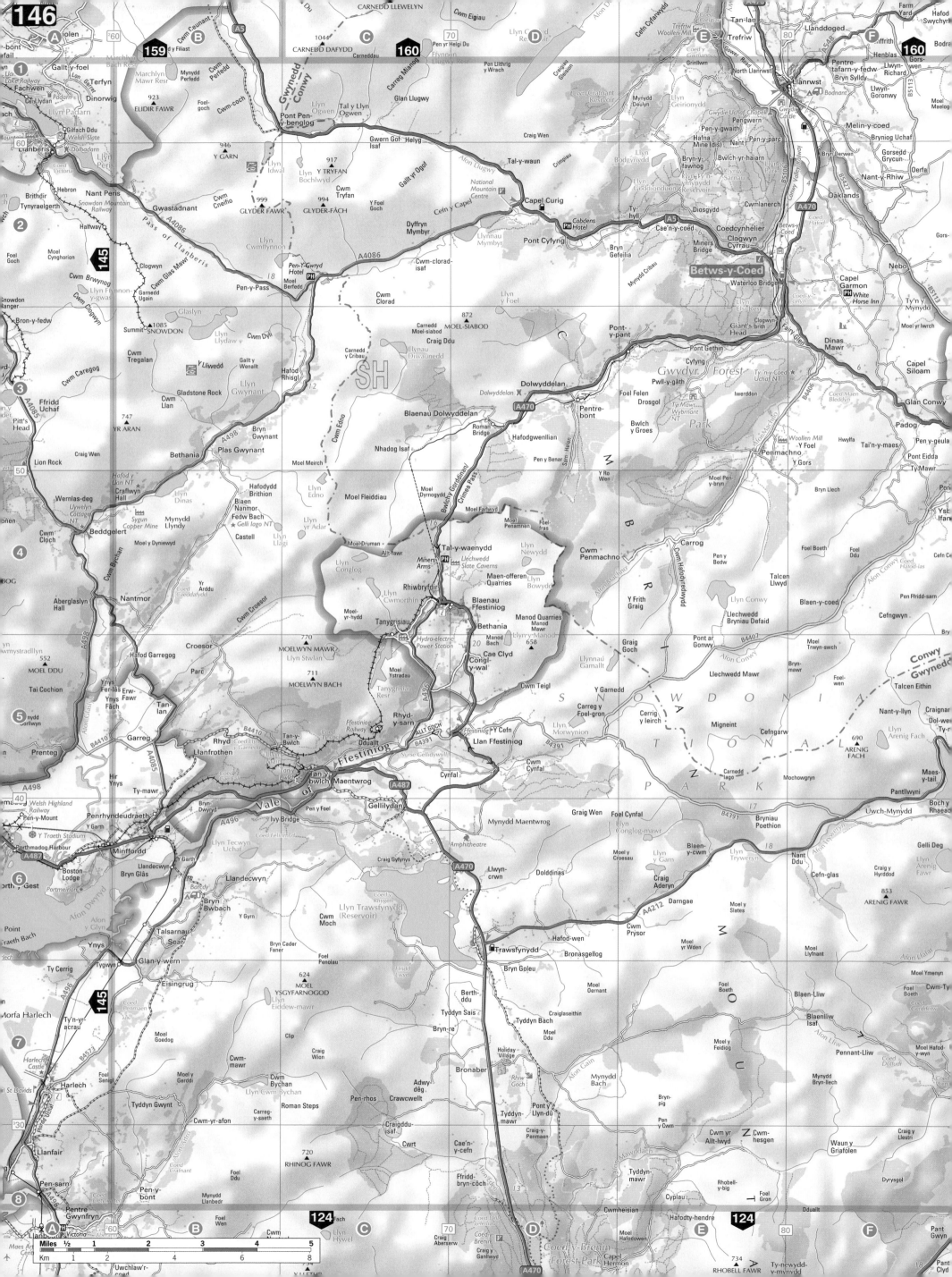

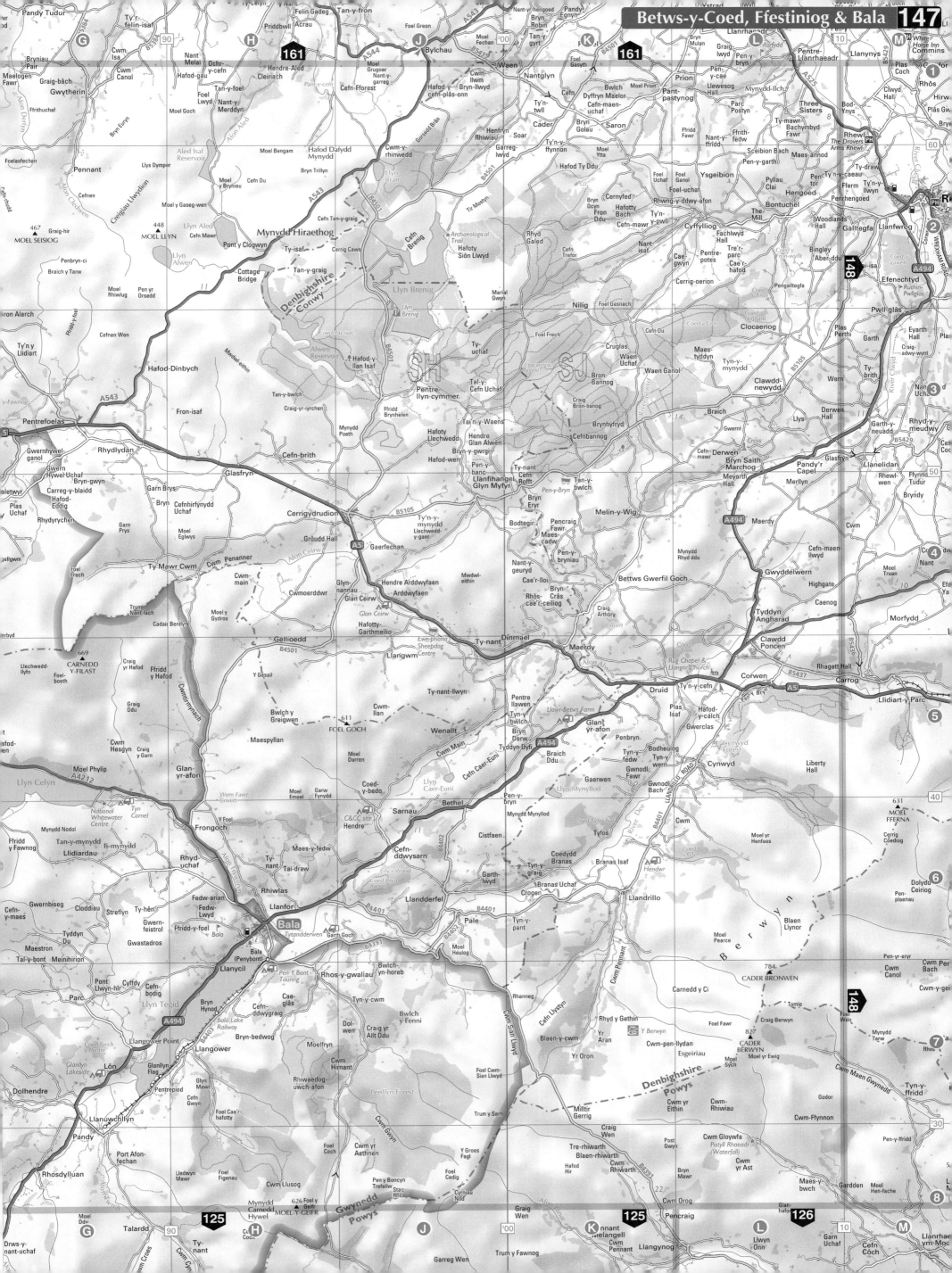

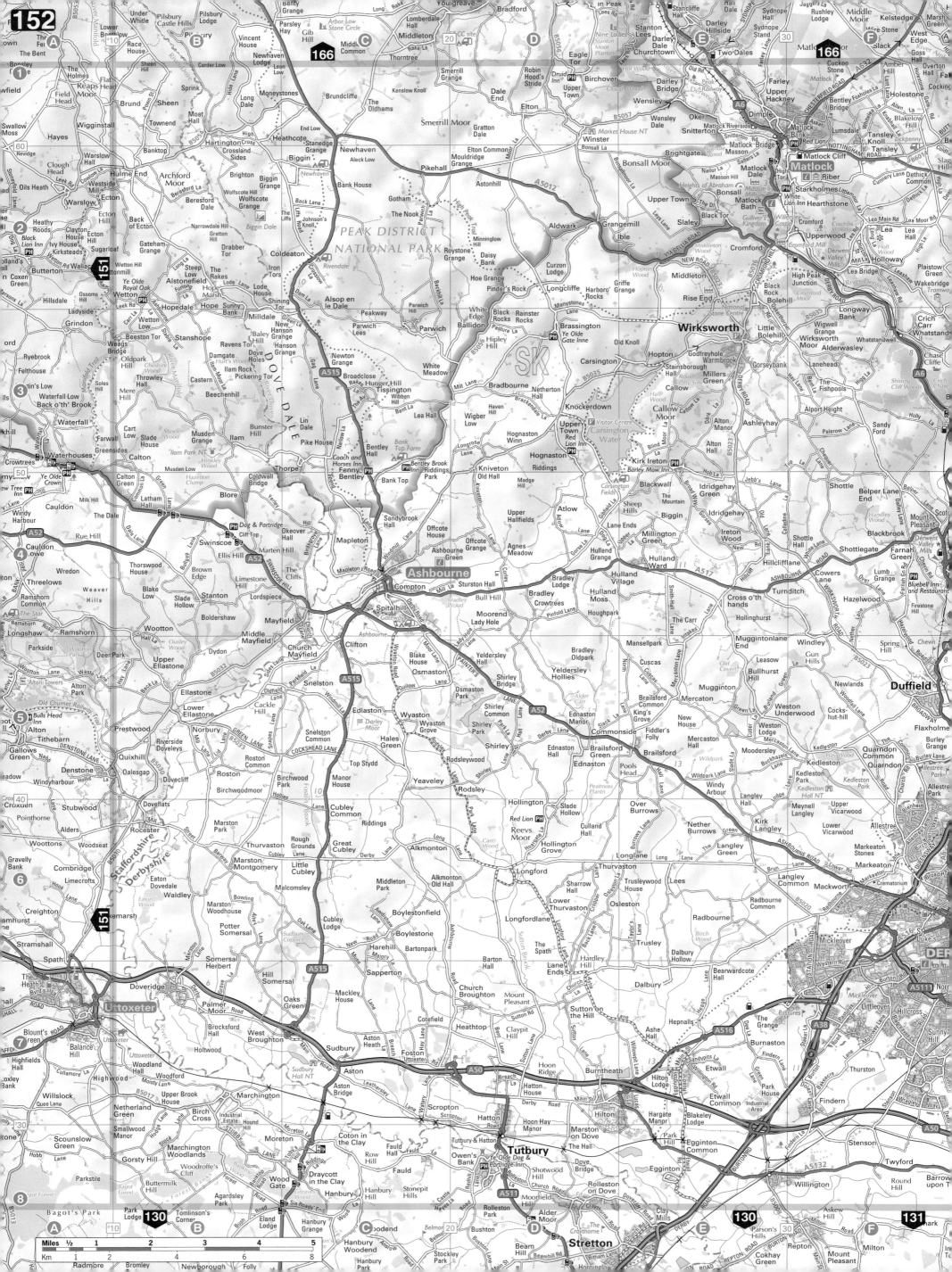

A · B · C · D · E · F

Holyhead Harbour

New Harbour
SALT ISLAND TERMINAL
Outer Harbour
BEACH ROAD
NORTH · FELIN ROAD
WALTHEW AVENUE
VICTORIA RD
SOUTH
STACK RD
Admiralty Pier
New Fish Quay
P
HOLYHEAD STATION
FERRY TERMINAL
PLAS ROAD
PORTHDAFARCH
LLANFAWR ROAD
LONDON ROAD
A5
A5153
BANGOR
A5 A5
LBM
800 yards
500 metres

The Skerries/
Ynysoedd y Moelrhoniaid

North Anglesey Heritage Coast
Trwyn Cemlyn
Porth-y-pistyll
Power Station
Wylfa Head
Cemaes
Tregele
Hell's Mouth
Llanbadrig
Betws
Nant-y-frân
Criw
Cemaes Bay
Porth Llugwy

CARMEL HEAD
Porth y Dyfn
Hen Borth
NT
Mynachdy
Taldrwst
Hen-dy
Llanfairynghornwy
Mynydd y Garn
Pen-yr-orsedd
Cefn-coch
Bwlch
Foel-bâch
Llanfechell
Bodwyryd

Anglesey

Church Bay
Rhydwyn
Llanrhyddlad
Llanfflewyn
Llyn Llygeirian
Mynydd Mechell
Carreglefn
Tyddyn-y-pand
Llyn Hafodol
Yny

Porth Trwyn
A5025
Llanfaethlu
Gaerwen
Llanbabo
Penbo Uchaf
Llyn Alaw

HOLYHEAD BAY
Porth Trefadog
Porth Tywyn-mawr
Llanddeusant
Llynnon Mill
Elim
Fferam-uchaf
Bod Deiniol
Meini-
Chwaen-gôch
W

Porth Penrhyn-mawr
Bodfardden-ddu
Llanfwrog
Llynon Hall
Stryd y Facsen
Llantrisant

North Stack
Ynys Wellt
Soldiers' Point
New Harbour
Bodlasan Fawr
Llanfachraeth
Mynydd-yr-eithin
Llanfigael
Chwaen-wen
Pen-llyn
Carmel
Breakwater Quarry
Mountain
Llaingoch
Porth-y-felin
Salt Island
Holyhead
Bodlasan Groes
Llanynghenedl
Llechcynfarwy
Gogarth Bay
Holyhead Mountain
Mountain
Pont Hwfa
Stryd
Môrawelon
Gorsedd-y-penrhyn
Clwch
South Stack
Goferydd
Holyhead Mountain Hut Group
Twr
Kingsland
Penrhos Works
Penrhos
Bodedern
Tre Iorwerth
Trefor
Penyrorsedd
Gwyndy
Pen-las Rock
Penrhos-Feilw
Plas
London Road
A5
Newlands Park
Bodowyr
Tre Hwfa
Rhydyfelin
Glan-yr-afon
A N G
Abraham's Bosom
Penrhosfeilw
Trefignath
A55
Valley
Ysbyllir
B5109
B5112
Bodfeillion
Penrhyn Mawr
Anglesey
Holyhead
Isallt Bach
Trearddur
Cae Hywel
Bryngwran
Clegir Mawr
Bryn Ala
Porth Dafarch NT
Four Mile Bridge
Llanfihangel yn Nhowyn
Traffwll
A5
Gwalch
Holyhead Mountain Heritage Coast
Treaddur Bay
Cae'r-Sais
Llyn Dinam
Minffordd Rd
Tai-croeson
A55
Engedi
Gwal Ucha
Porth Diana
Bodior
Llyn Penrhyn
Cae Hywel
Capel Gwyn
A5
Raven's Point
Porth-y-garan
Llanfairyneubwll
Llyn Traffwll
Cefnysgwydd Bach
Dyfrie
Ty Newydd
Dothan
Cefn Du
Rhoscolyn
Dowyn
Tywyn Trewan Common
Valley
Ty Newydd
Pencarnisiog
Cerrig-myna
Grugor-bach
Soar
Rhoscolyn Head
Eilian House
Dryfol
HOLY ISLAND
Silver Bay
Cymyran Bay
Ynys Feirig
Anglesey
Llanfaelog
Bryn Du
Llyn Padrig
Rhoscolyn Beacon
Ty Hen
Llyn Maelog
Rhosneigr
Llyn Coron
Bethel
Bodorgan
Traeth Llydan
Ty Croes
Penhenllys
Ty-mawr
Graig
Porth Nobla
Barclodiad y Gawres
Bodelwa
Merddyn-y-bit
Llangadwaladr
Porth Trecastell
Aberffraw
A4080
Hermon
Mynydd Esgair-Eebrill
Caethle
Tywyn Aberffraw
Anglesey
Ynys Meibion
Braich-lwyd
Porth China
Porth Cwyfan
Traeth Mawr
Cwningâr Trefri
Mai
Bonc Twni
Bodorgan
SH
IRISH SEA
DUBLIN
DUBLIN DÚN LAOGHAIRE
Aberffraw Bay Heritage Coast
Pen-y-parc
Dinas Bâch
Porth Tywyn-mawr
Dinas-lwyd
Malltraeth Bay
Llanddwy
Island

Miles ½ 1 2 3 4 5
Km 1 2 4 6 8

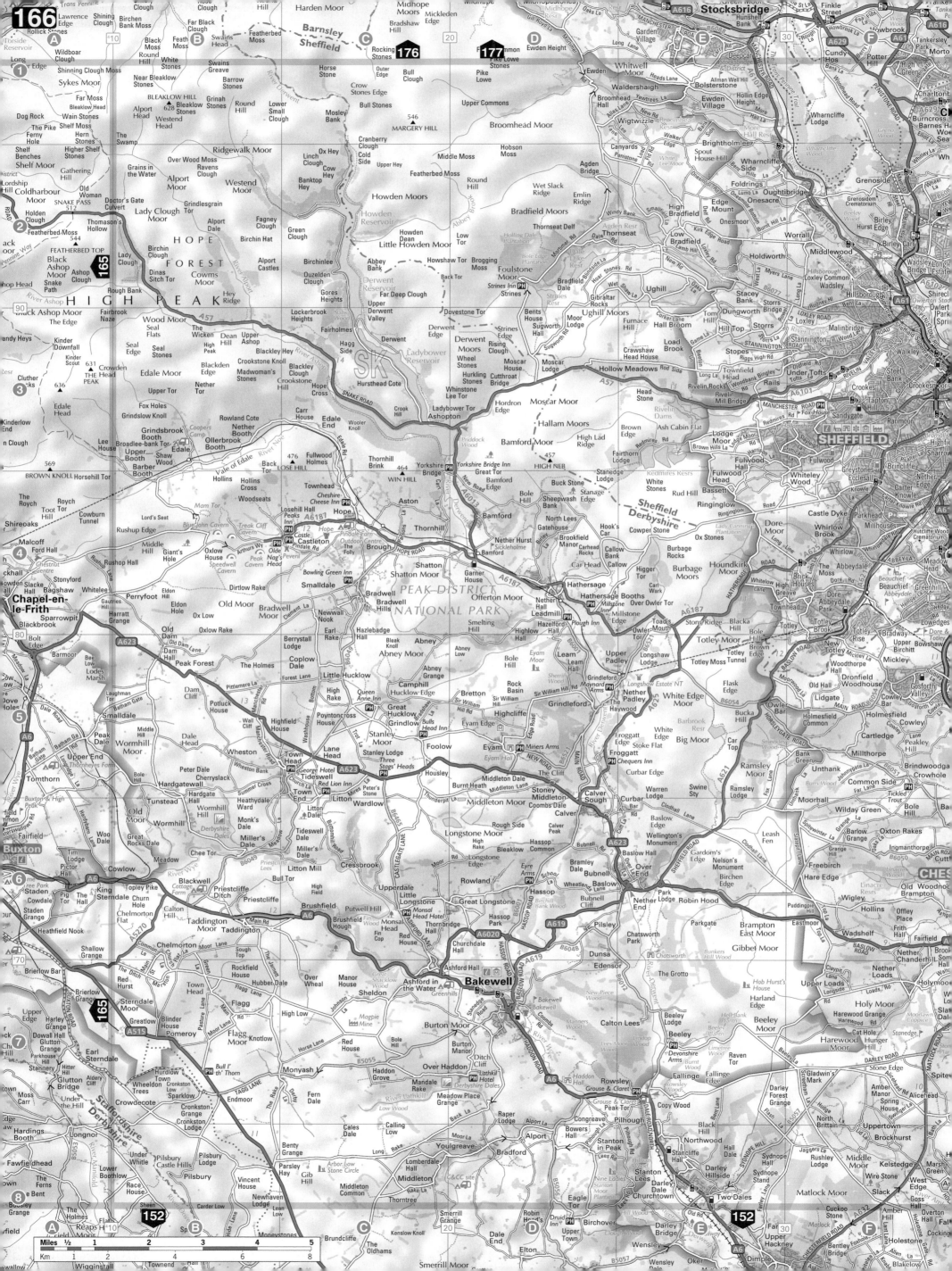

Hull Port

YORK
SUTTON ROAD
BRIDLINGTON
B1237
SALTHOUSE ROAD
B1238
YORK
A1165
CLOUGH RD
A1079
HEDON ROAD
INGS ROAD
PAYBURY ROAD
MARKET LANE
KINGSTON UPON HULL CITY CENTRE
LEEDS
A63 GARRISON
HEDON ROAD
A1033
CAR FERRY TERMINAL
River Humber

GRIMSBY

Cleethorpes

Humberston

Waltham

Withernsea

Patrington

SPURN HEAD

Humber Estuary

Mouth of the Humber

ROTTERDAM (EUROPOORT) ZEEBRUGGE

River Humber

Town plan: Kingston upon Hull p.347

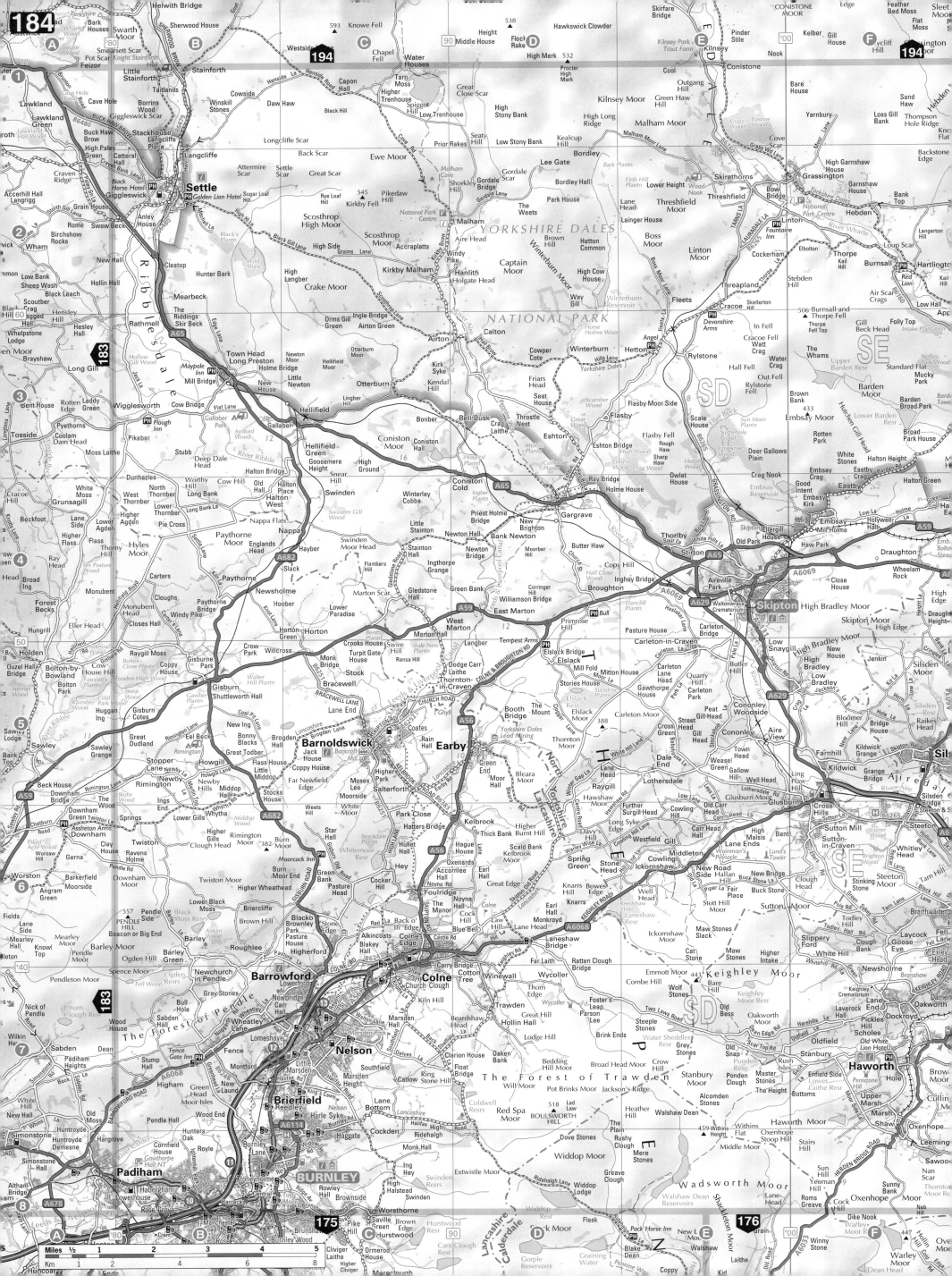

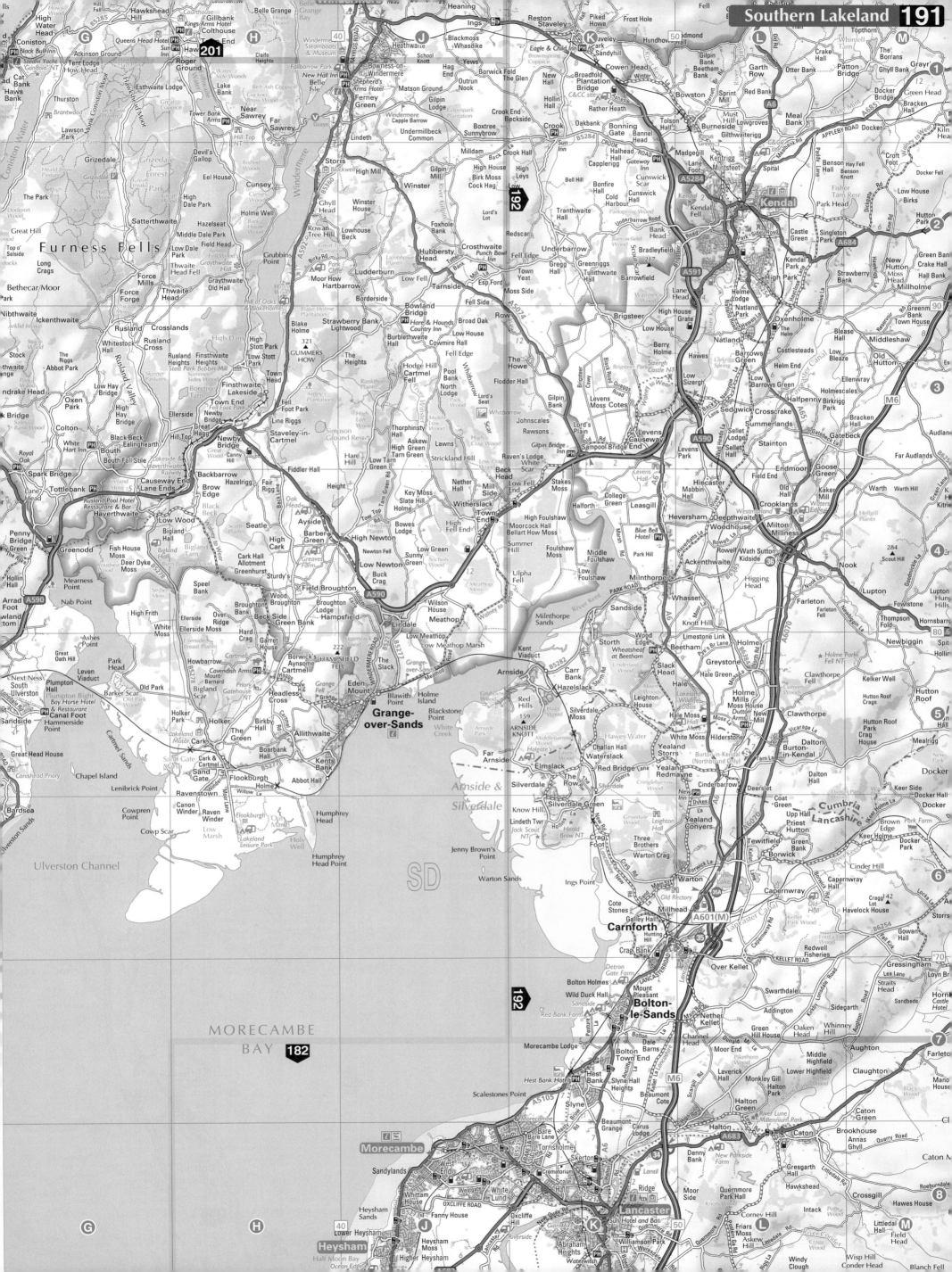

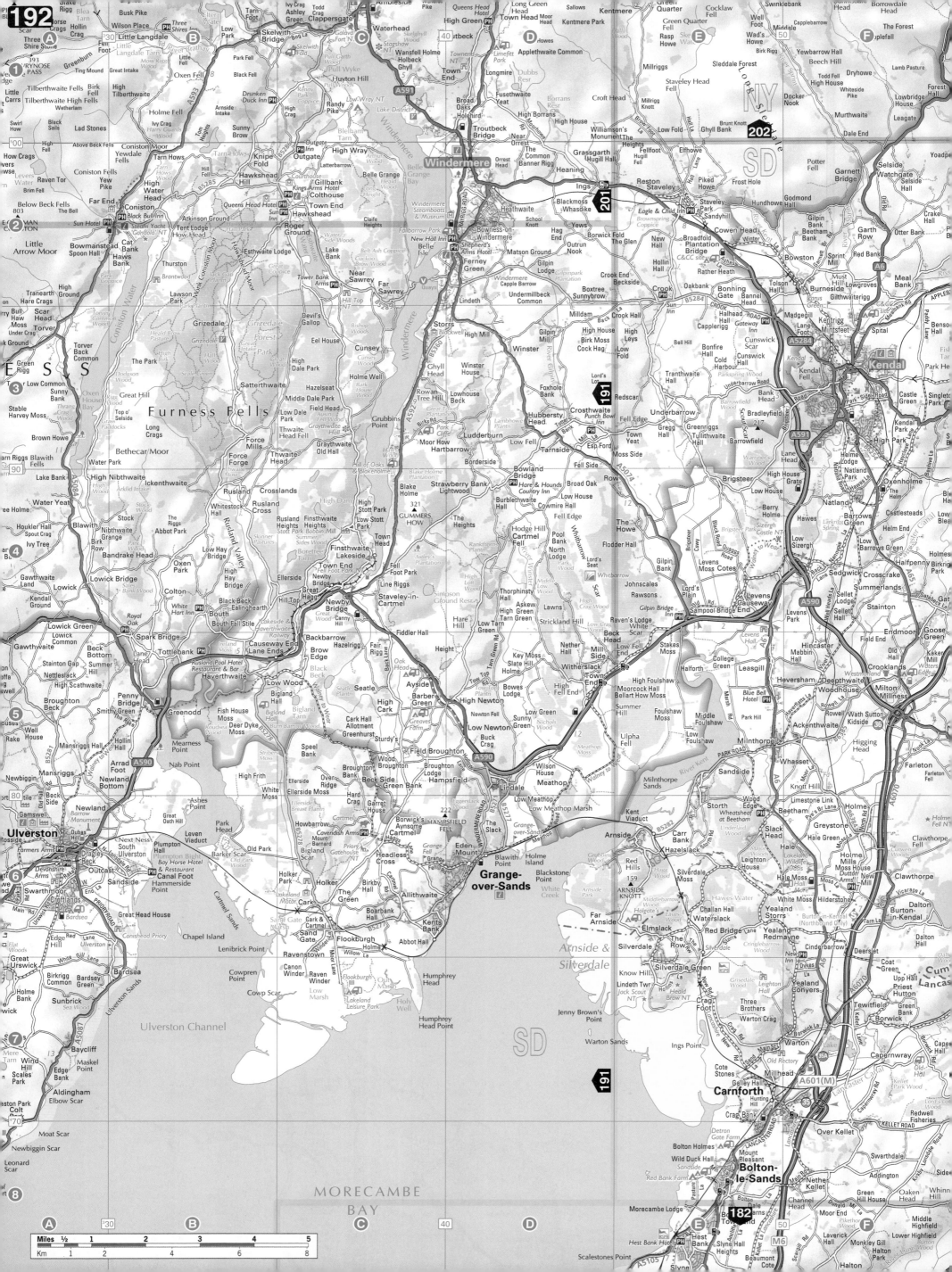

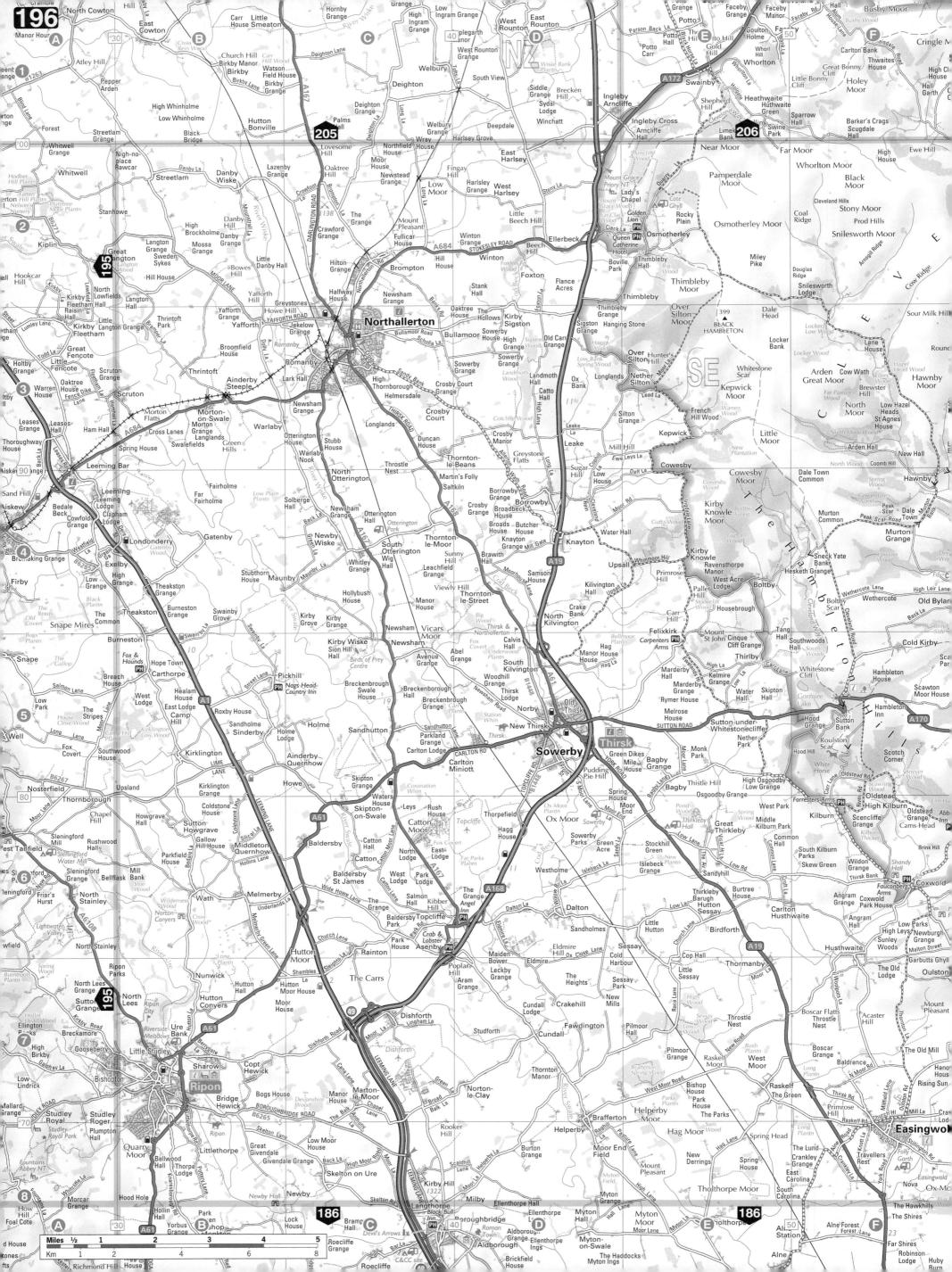

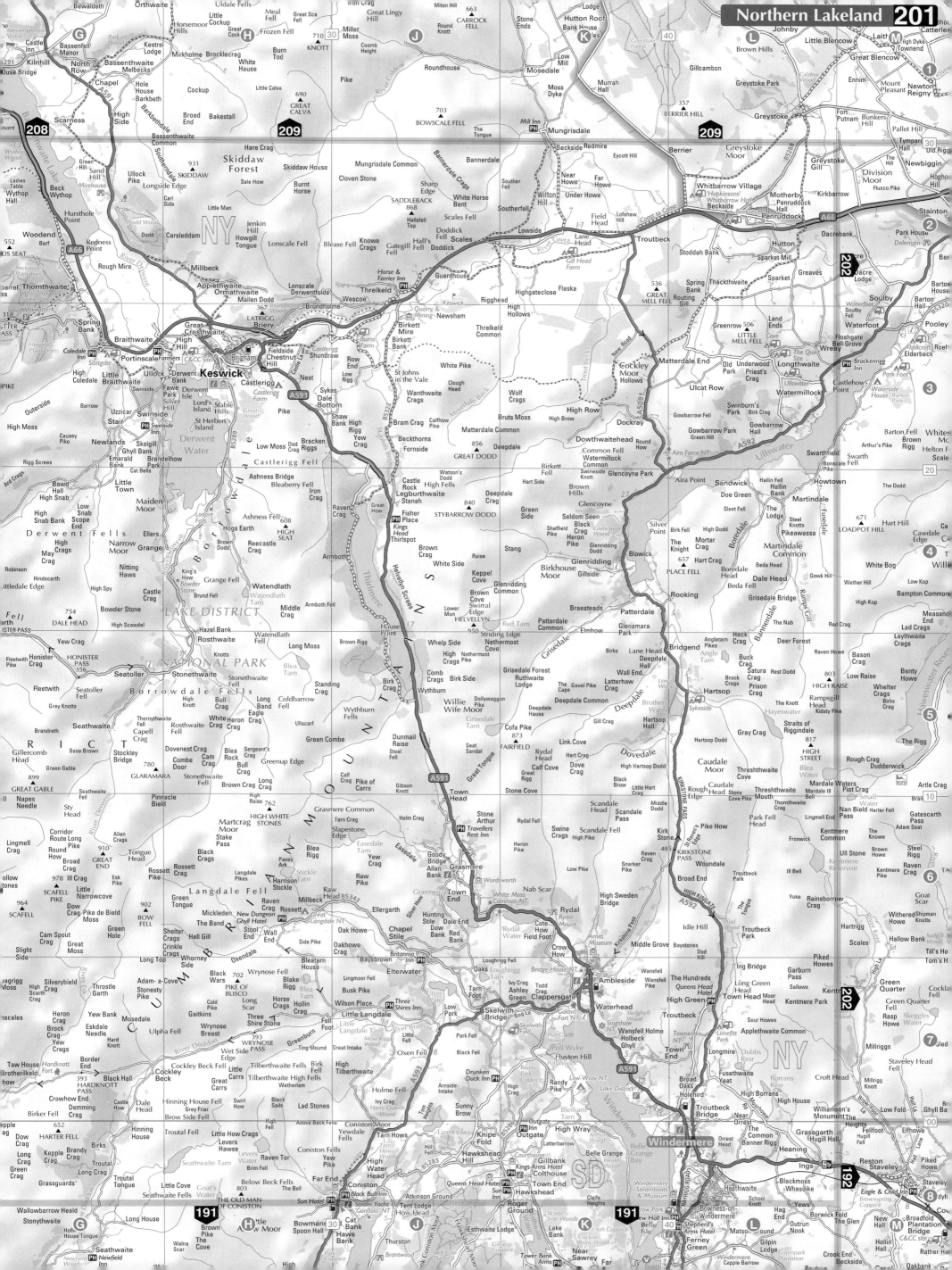

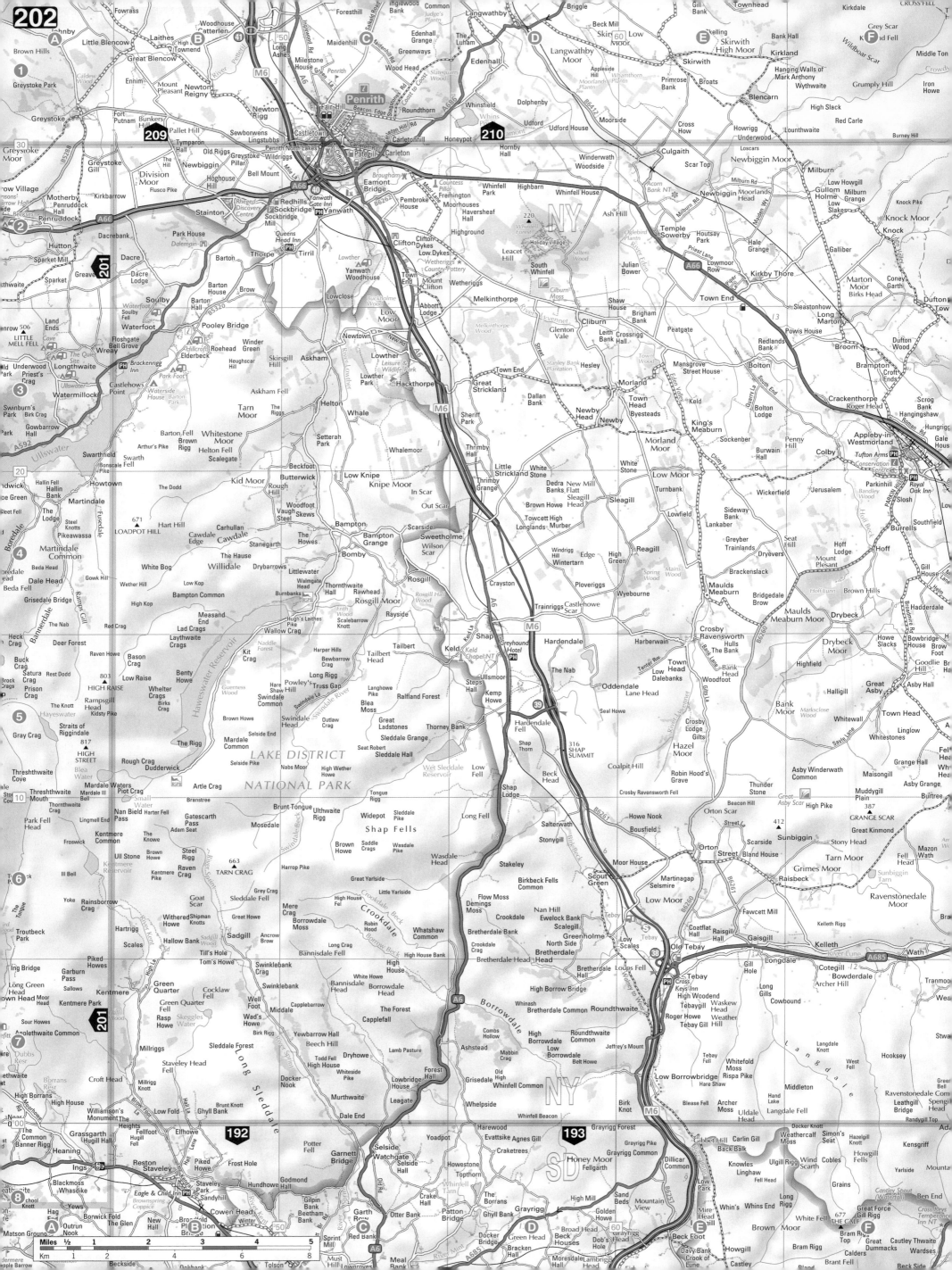

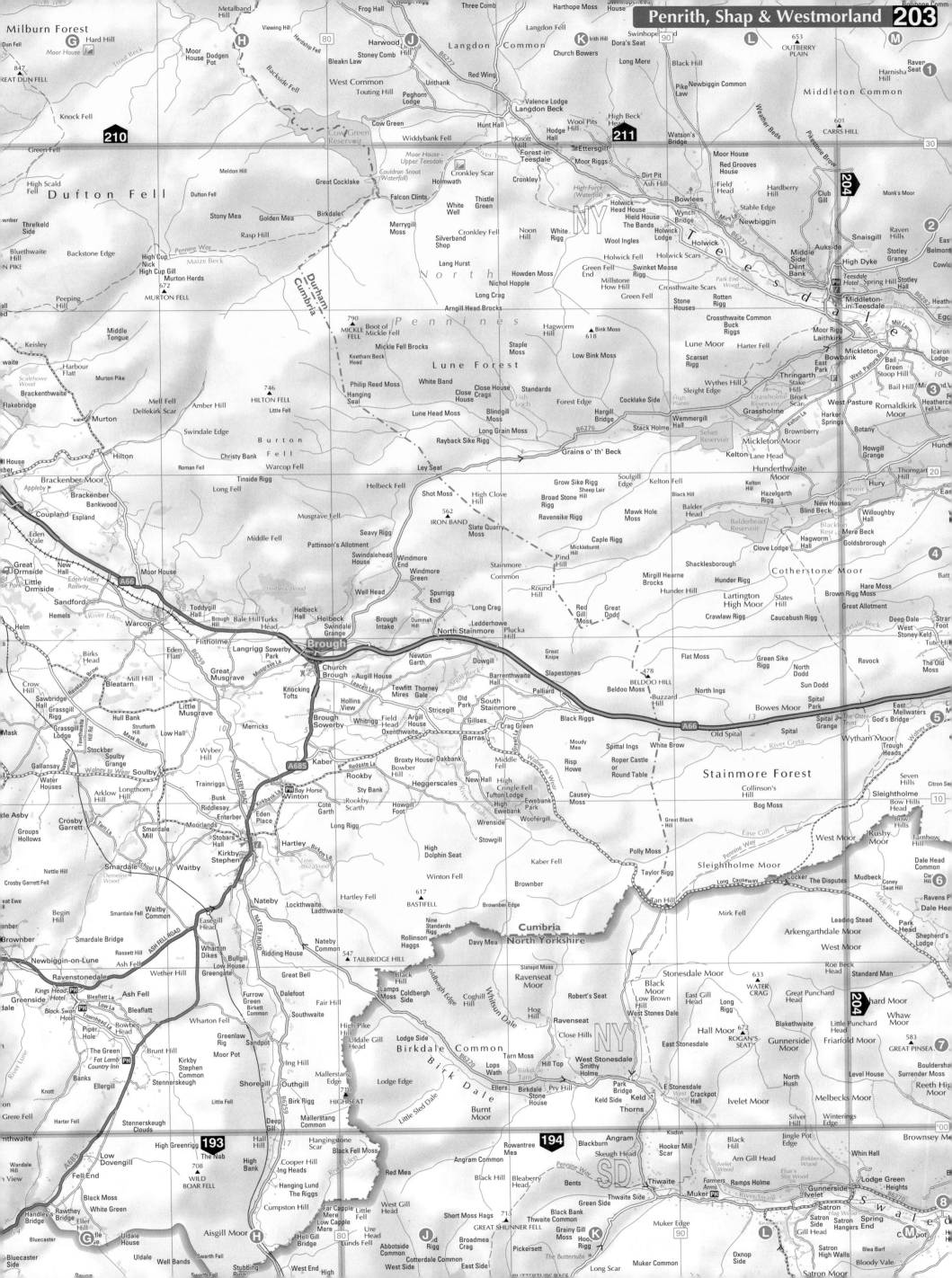

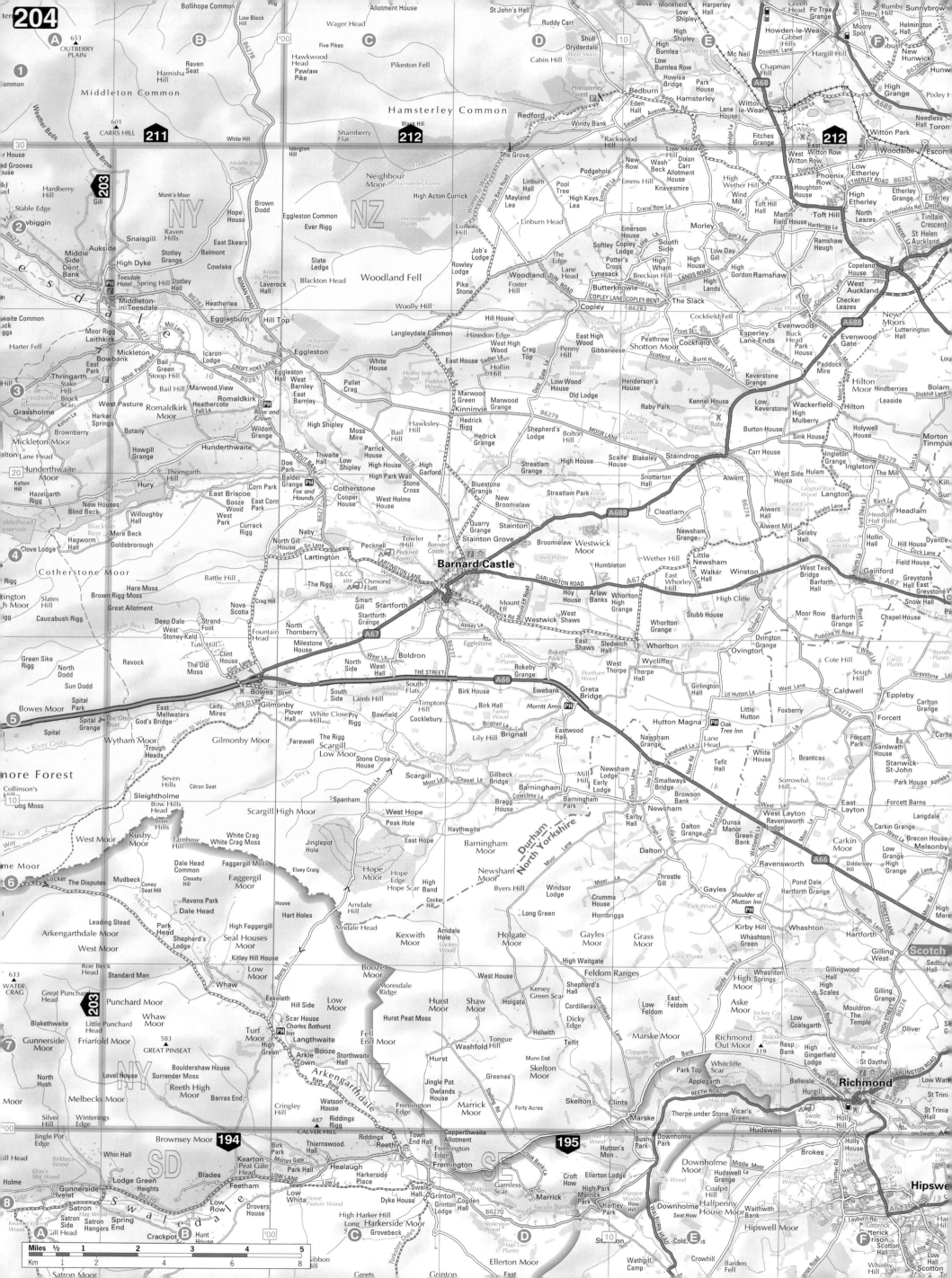

NORTH

SEA

NZ

NORTH YORK MOORS NATIONAL PARK

Loftus

Whitby

SE

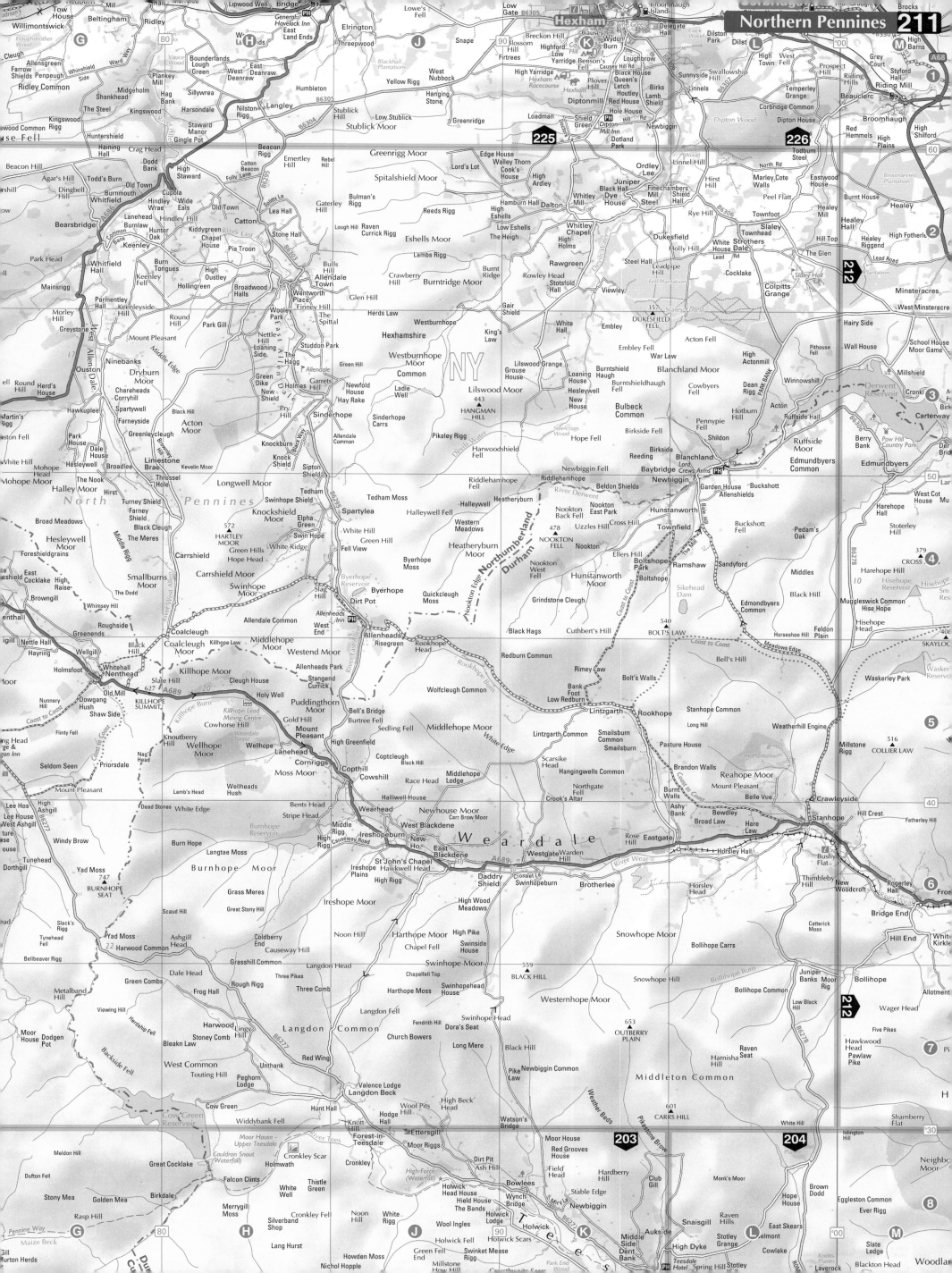

Town plans: Durham p.344, Sunderland p.356

Castle Douglas

Dalbeattie

Chapmanton
Halket Leathes
Upper Torrs
Guffogland
Barskeoch Hill
Buittle Hill
Allan Bank
Cuil
Gelston
Torglass Hill
Flock Hill
Galgrie Hill
Caigton Hill
Barchain Hill
Marnoch Hill
Barlochan Hill
Barlae Hill
Blackbellie
Barlochan
Palnackie
Dunguile Hill
Croach Hill
Potterland Hill
Green Hill
Airieland Moor
Tun Hill
Ingleston Moor
Screel Hill
Isle
North Glen
South Glen
Park Hill
Linkins Glen
SCREEL HILL
BENGAIRN
Bengairn
Forest Hill
Court Hill
The Holm
Castle Hill
Glen Isle
Chapel Croft Plantn
Bentudor
Mid Hill
Dungarry
Orchardton Tower
Orchardton Bay
Barhill Wood
Barcloy Hill
Blackbreast
Collin Hill
Girvellan Point
Torr Hill
Moyl
White Port
Almorness Point
Loch Moss
Suie Hill
Icroft Loch
Auchencairn
Auchencairn Moss
Auchencairn Bay
Balcary Fishery
Hestan Island
Kirkcarswell
Over Hazelfield
Cairn Hill
Airds Cott
Balcary Bay
Nether Hazelfield
Balcary Hill
Balcary Point
Rascarrel
Big Airds Hill
Airds
Airds Point
Fagra Hill
Knockmult
Rascarrel Bay
Orroland
Barlocco Bay
Castle Muir Point
Port Mary

Blackerne
Dalmoney Hill
Firthhead
Glenearly
Dalbeattie
Edingham Moss
Drumfern Moss
Nether Hill
Buittle Bridge
Moss Rd
Blantain Loch
Aucheninnes Moss
Aucheninnes Plantn
Richorn Plantn
Cloak Moss
Cloak Hill
Dalbeattie Forest
Moyle Hill
Barscraigh Hill
Ironhash Hill
Clonyards Loch
Barean Loch
North Glen
South Glen
Kippford
Mark Hill
Mote of Mark
Rockcliffe
Port Donnel
Rough Firth
Rough Island
Gibbs Hole Wood
Horse Isles Bay
Castle Point
Barcloy Hill
Castlehill Point
Urr Waterfoot

Meikle Firthhead
Plascow
Barclosh Hill
Loch Fern Isles
Land Hill
Clawbelly Hill
Blood Moss
Drumstinchall
B793
Banks Hill
Smithland Hill
Barcloy Hill
Barend
Sandyhills
Sandyhills Bay
Shiel Hill
White Loch
Grennan Hill
The Torrs
Colvend
Portling
White Hill
Portling Bay
Gillis Craig
Gutcher's Isle
Port O' Warren Bay
Moyl

Torkirra
Plascow
Maidenpap
Round Fell
Nether Hill
Auchenlosh
Auchenskeoch Lodge
Bennel Hill
Bainloch Hill
Fairgirth Hill
Laggan
Nether Clifton
Clifton Craig
Craigneuk Point
Saltpan Rocks
Mersehead Sands

Long Fell
CUIL HILL
430
Ryes Hill
Blood Moss
Millbank Hill
Caulkerbush
Nether Clifton
RSPB

Thorter Fell
Tannock Hill
Hard Hill
Meikle Hard Hill
Abbey Fell
Boreland Hill
Airdrie Hill
Redbank Hill
Drumbuie
Prestonmill
Mainsriddle
East Preston
Preston Merse

Kinharvie Hill
Craig Moss
Criffel
569
CRIFFELL
Drumburn Wood
Kirkbean
Kirkbean Glen
Arbigland
Carsethorn
Gillfoot Bay
Southerness
Southerness Point
Black Craigs
Thirl Stane

Overton
Knockendoch
Drum Bay
Midtown
Earn's Craig
Carse Bay
Hogus Point
Borron Point

SOLWAY FIRTH

NX

Maryport
Fothergill
Flimby
St Helens
Wind Farm
Siddick
Seaton
North Hawk Side
Salmon Hall
Borough Park
Barepot
Stainburn
Workington
Steel Works
Mossbay
Moorclose
Westfield
Salterbeck
Moss Bay
Hunday
Winscales

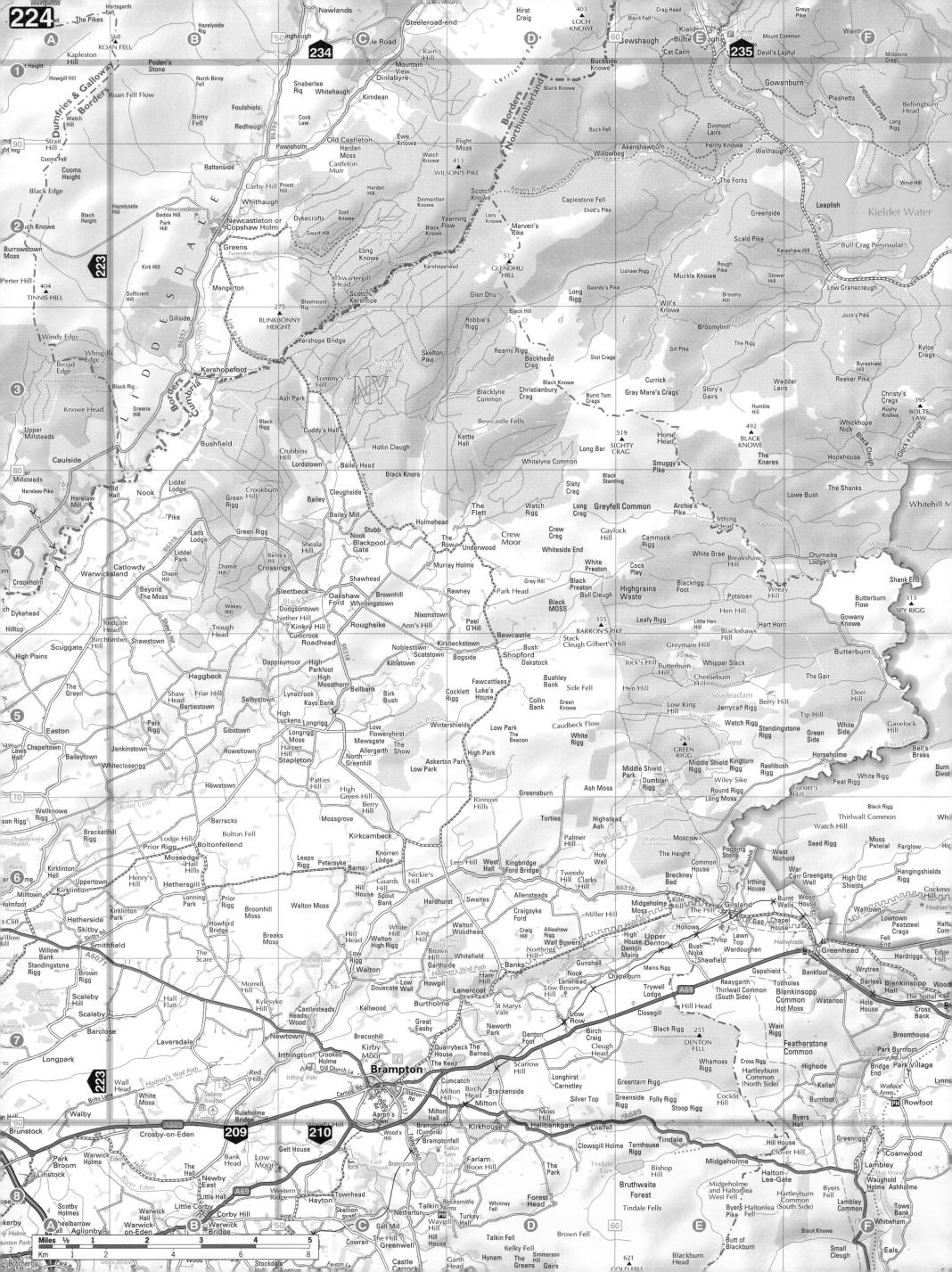

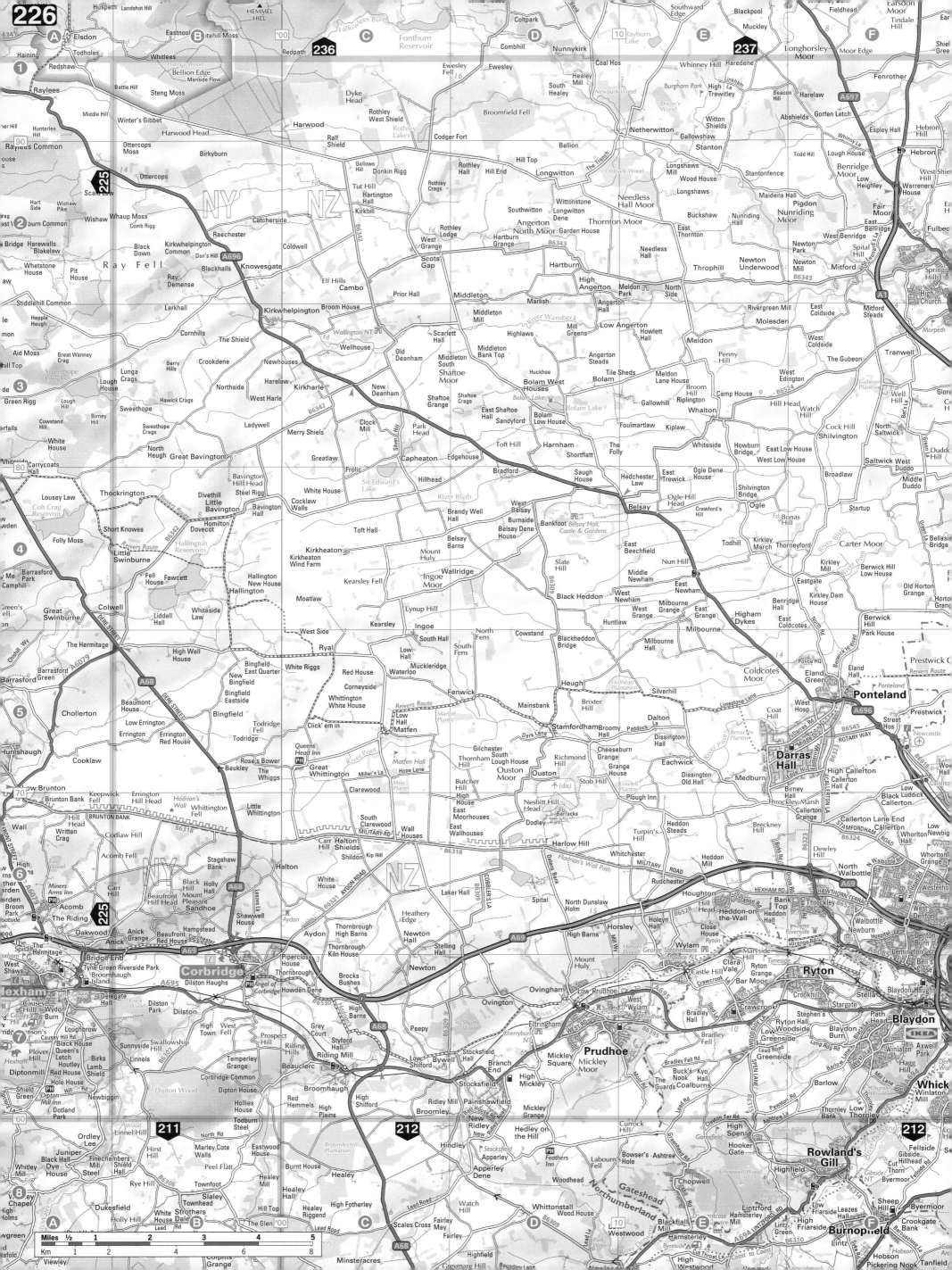

240 · 241

Drumadoon Point · Shiskine

Blackwaterfoot · North Feorline · Cnoc Ballygown · Loch Cnoc an Loch · Corriehiam Hill · Urie · The · Urie Loch · Lag an Daer · Kingscross · Pillar Rock Point

South Feorline · Beinn Tarsuinn · Cnoc an t-Seabhaig · Cnoc Dubh · Sloc Ruaridh · Auchencairn · Kingscross Point

Drumadoon Bay · Cnocan Chrannchuir

Kilpatrick · Lean a' Chneamh · Buican Hill · Cnocan na Caillich · Tighvein · Glas Choirein · Glenashdale Burn · Knockenkelly · North Kiscadale · Whiting Bay

Kilpatrick Point · Rubha Garbhard · Kilpatrick Dun · Corn Ban · Cnoc Lean na Meine · Whiting Bay · South Kiscadale · Whiting Bay

Brown Head · The Torr · Cnoc Clauchog · Cnoc Donn · Cnoc an Fheidh · Cnoc Mòr · Largymore

Cnocan Donn · Corriecravie Moor · Glen Ashdale

Àird nan Ron · Cnoc Reamhar · Largymeanoch · Cnoc na Comhairle

Rinn a' Chrubain · Corriecravie · Meall Buidhe · Cnoc Craobhach · Cnoc na Garbad · Largybeg · Largybeg Point · Port na Gallin

Torr a Chaisteal Fort · Bennecarrigan · Torr Dubh Mòr · Auchenhew Hill · Dippen

Port na Feannaiche · Sliddery · Torr a' Bheannain · Levencorroch Hill · Dippin Lodge · Dippin Head

Port Mòr · Kilbride Hill · Levencorroch · Auchenhew · Porta Leacach

Lagg · Kilmory · A841 · East Bennan · Kildonan

Torrylinn · Shannochie · Porta Buidhe · Port Dearg

Torrylin Cairn · West Bennan · Port a'Ghillie Ghlais

Bennan Head · Sound of Pladda

Pladda

NR · NS

NR · NS

Swine Holes

338 · THE CAIRN · Foreland Point

Stranny Point · Ailsa Craig

NX

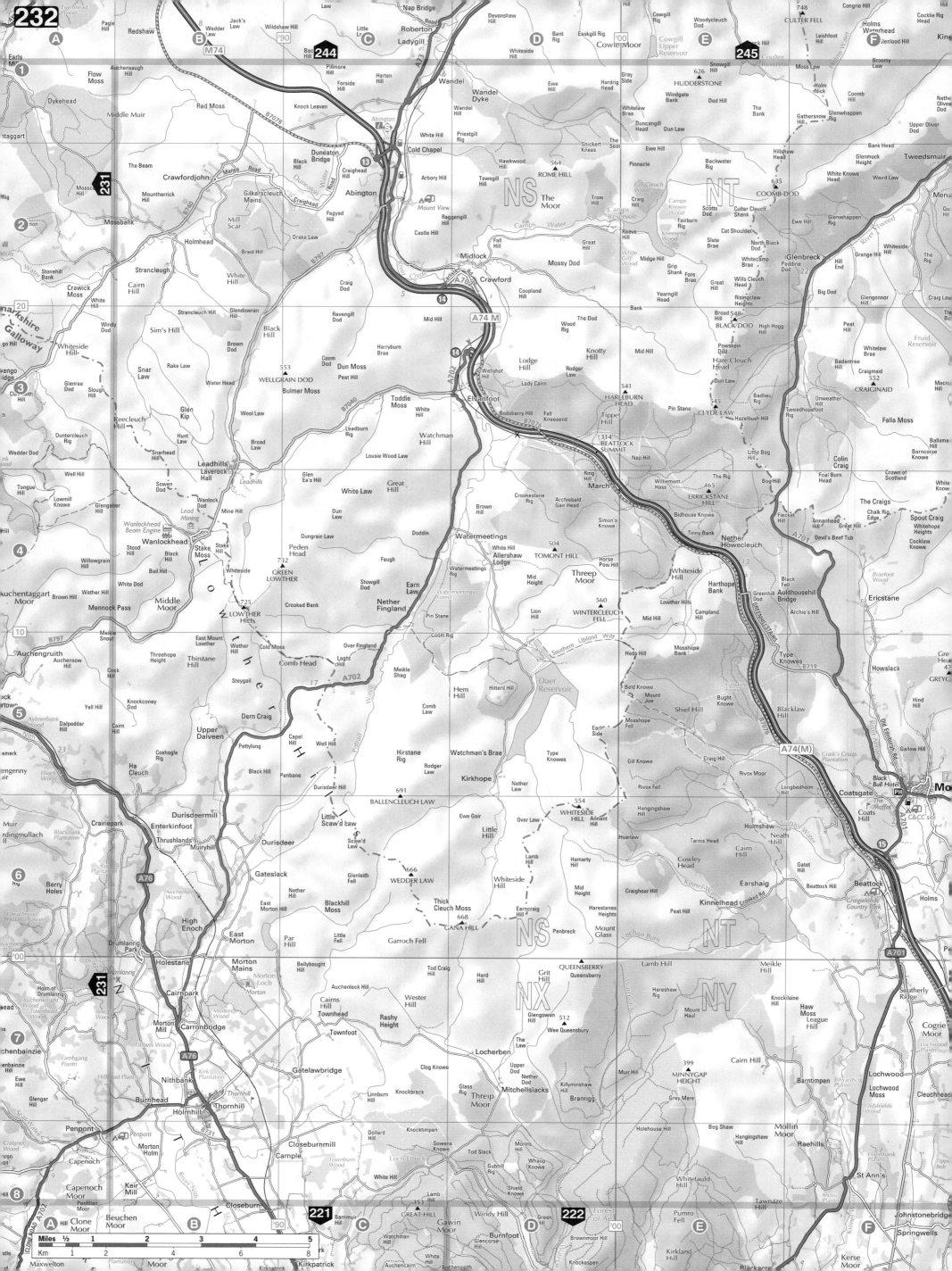

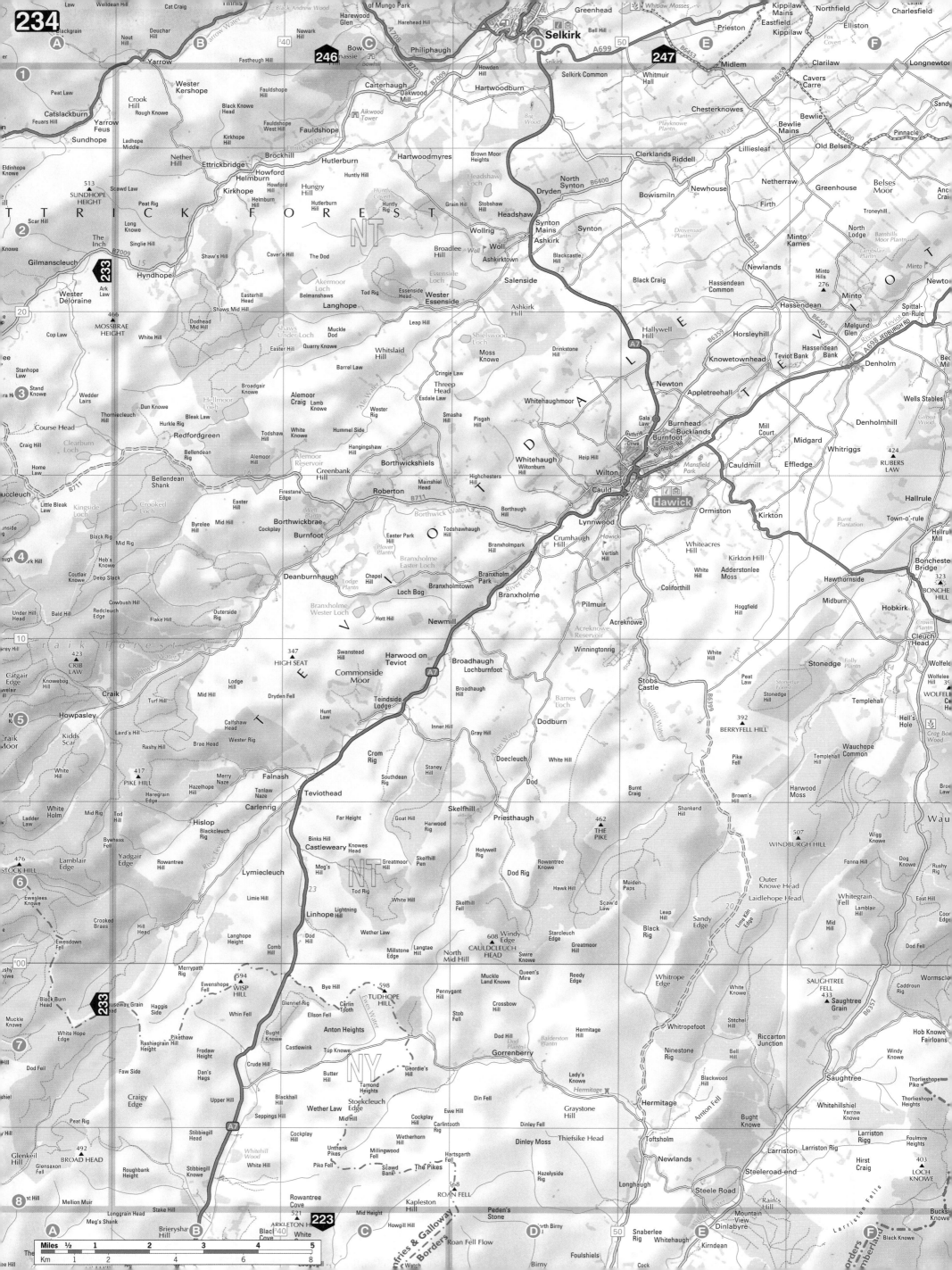

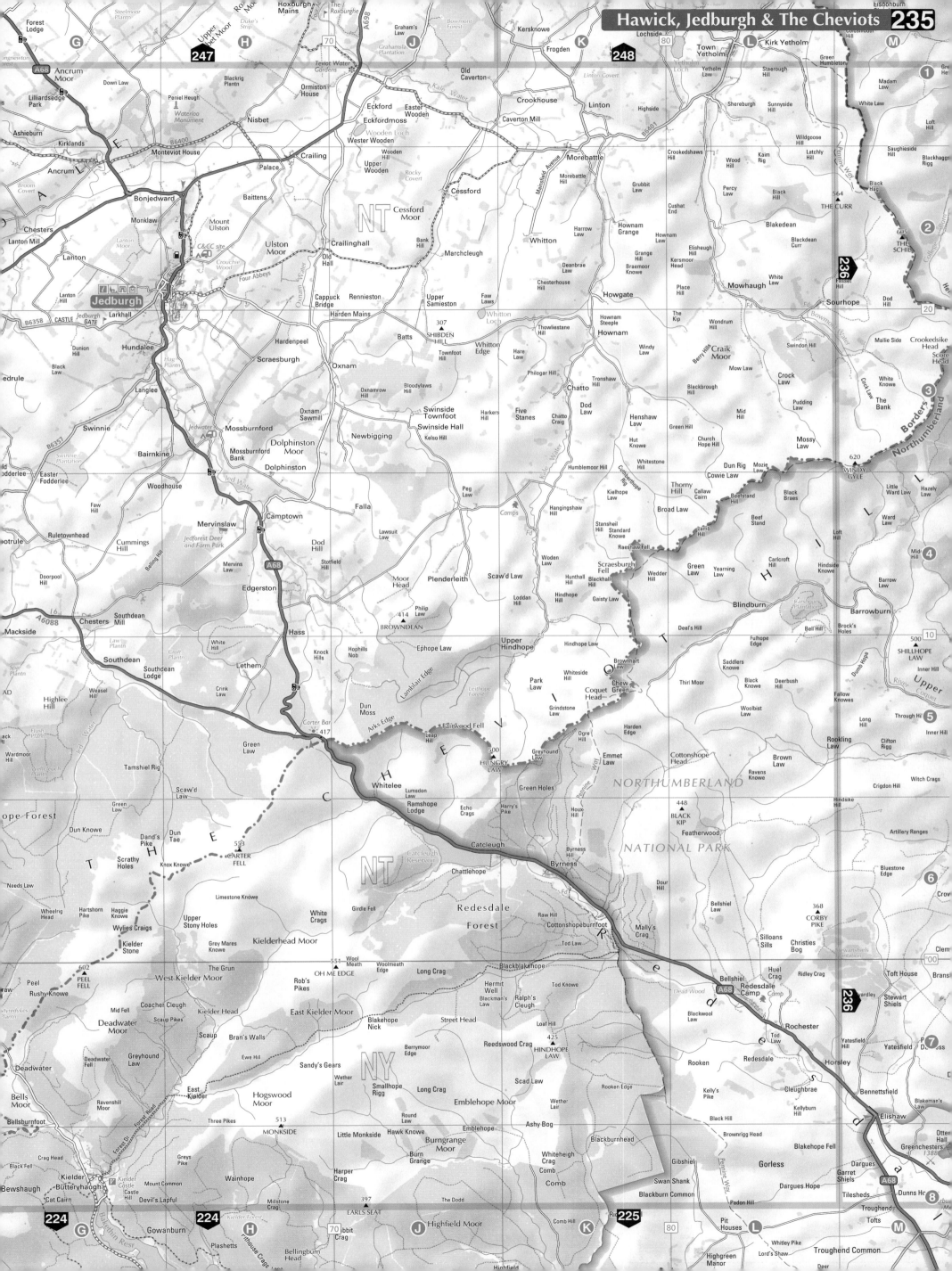

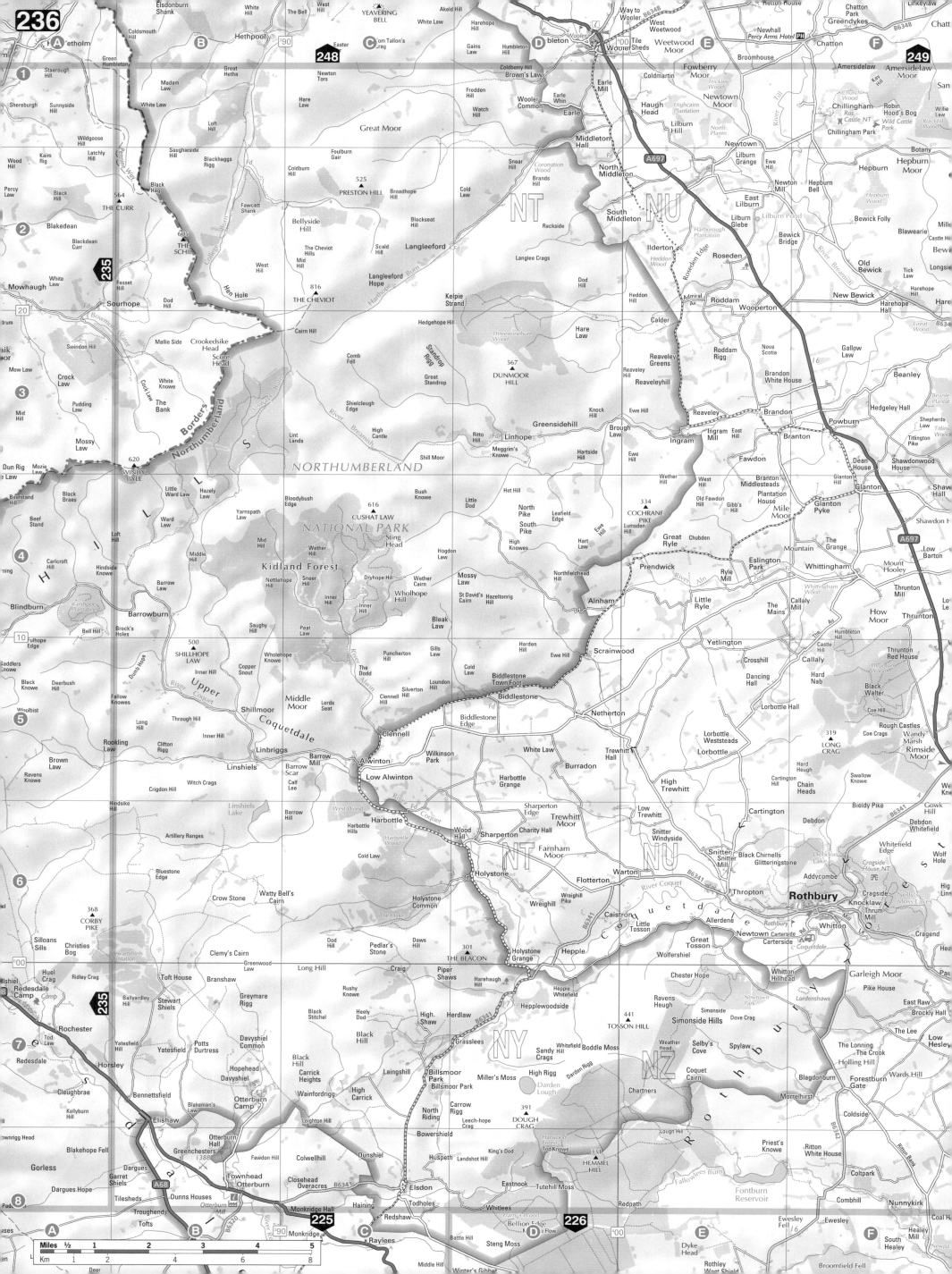

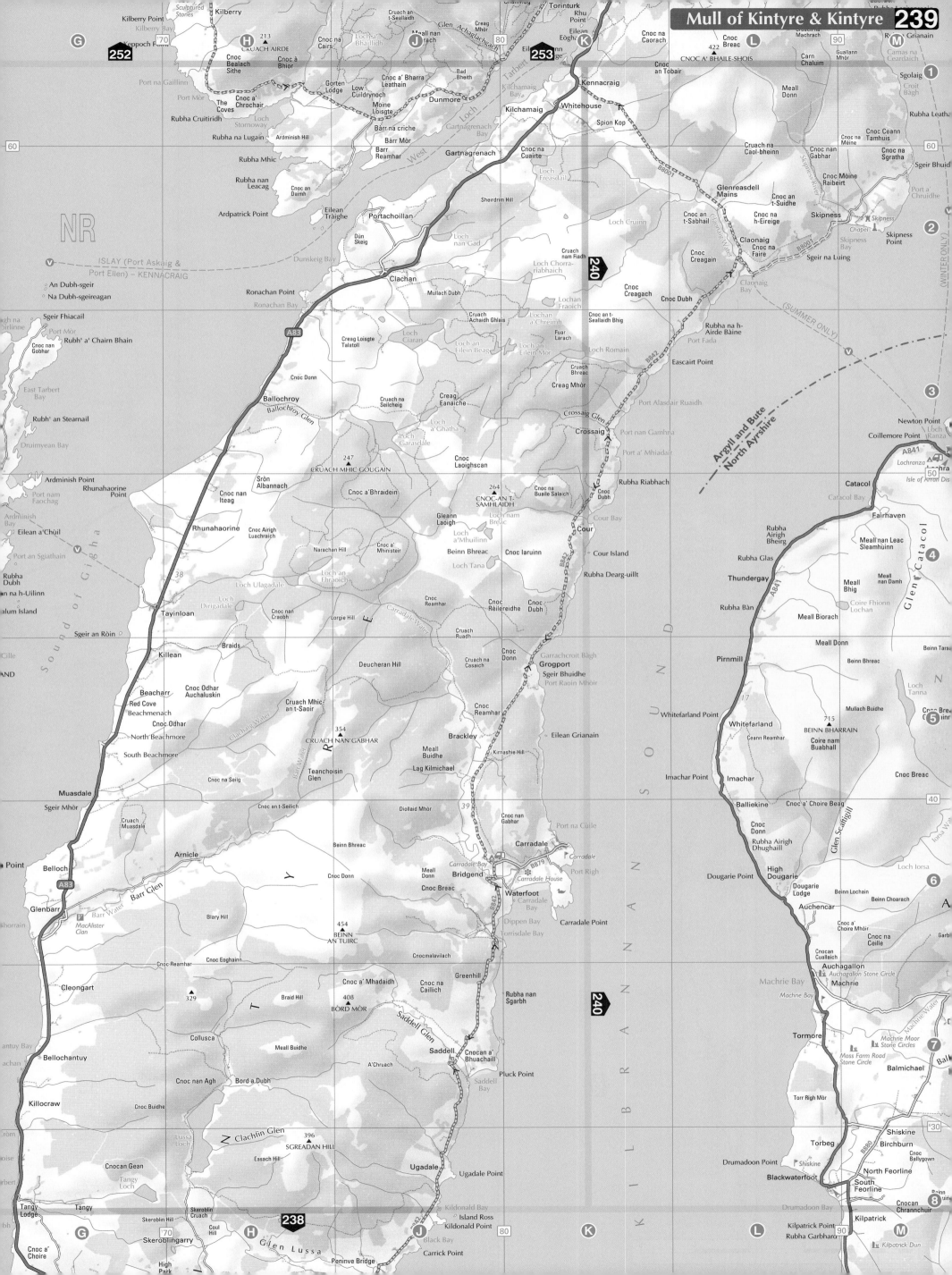

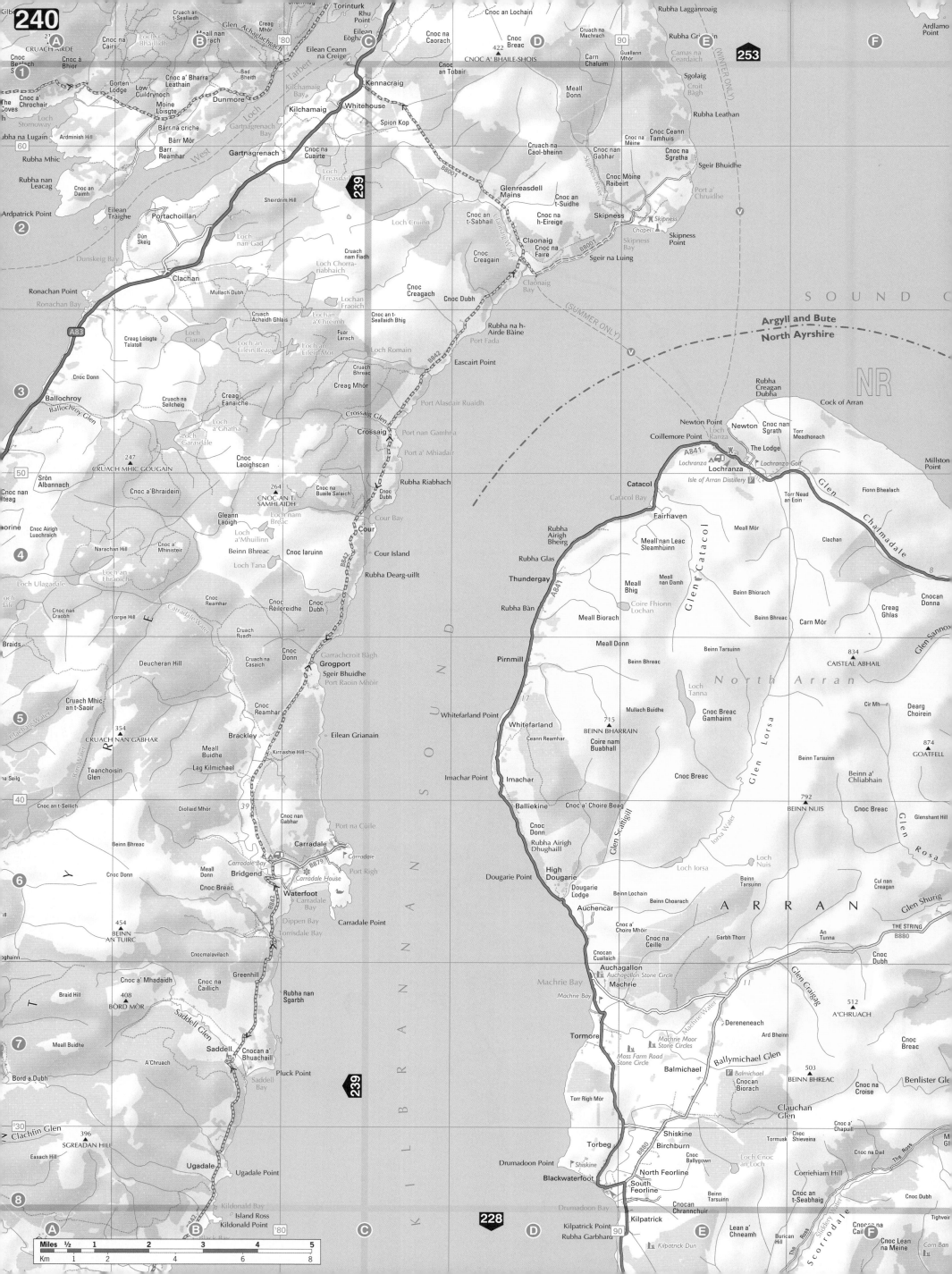

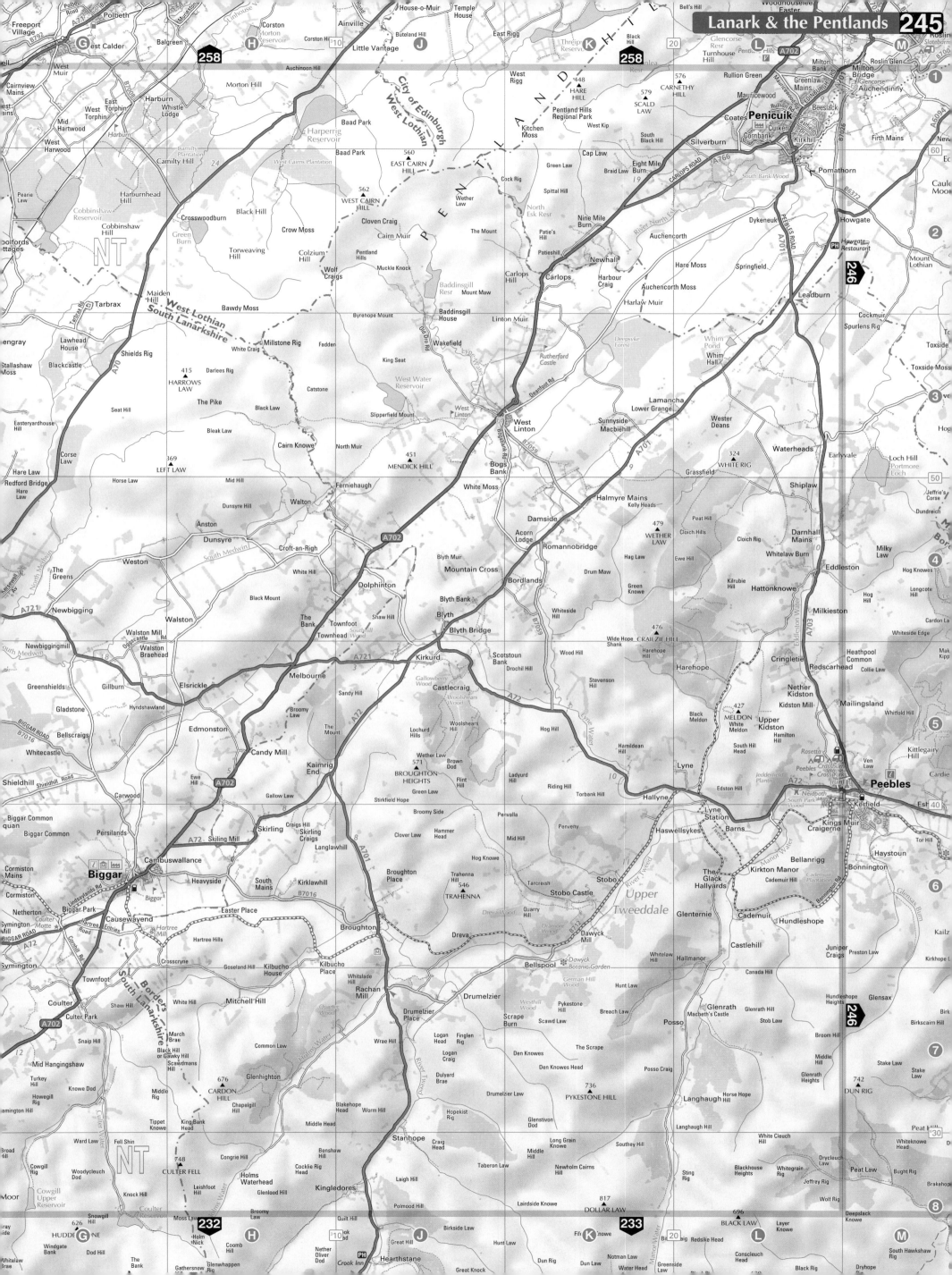

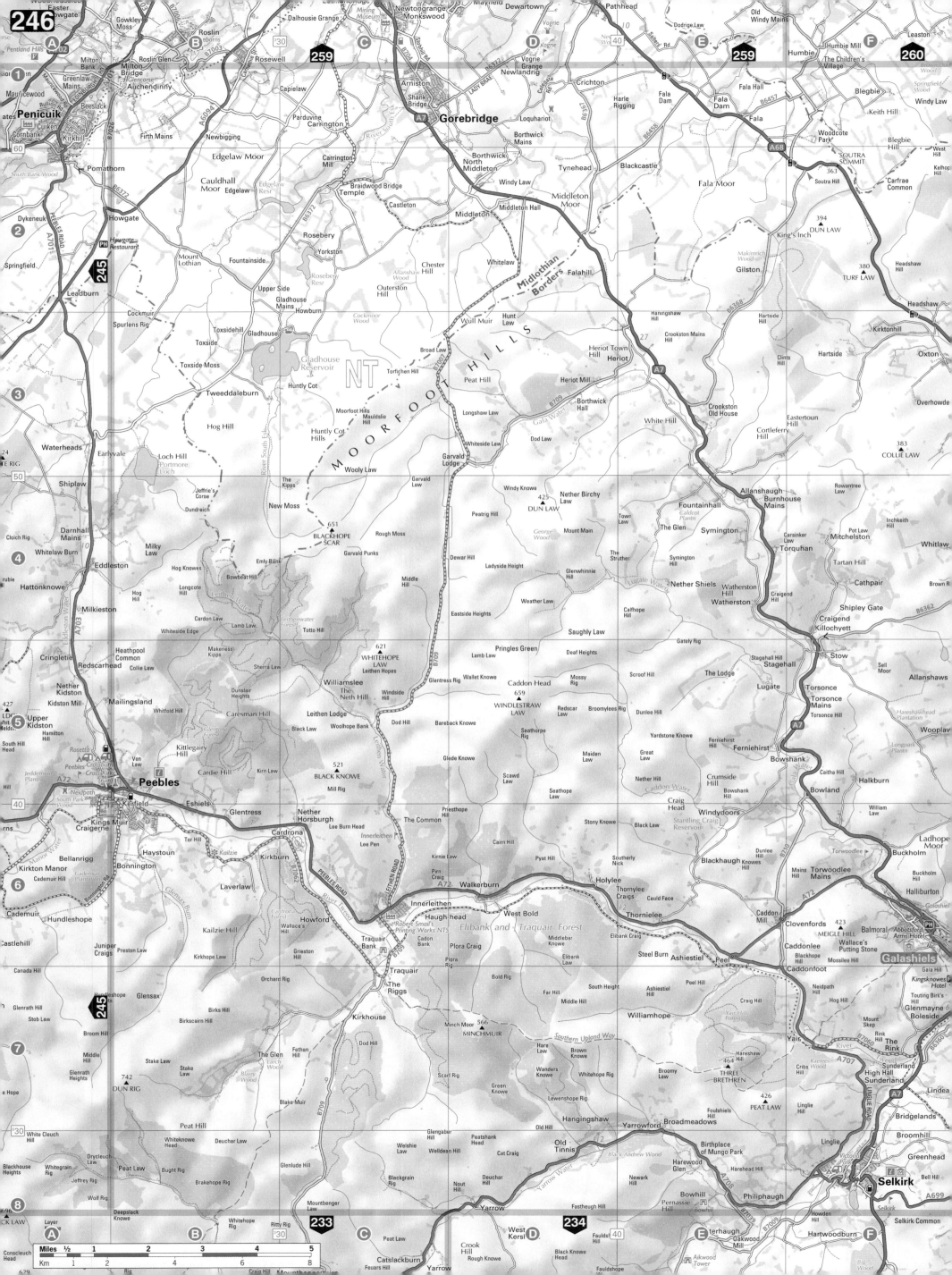

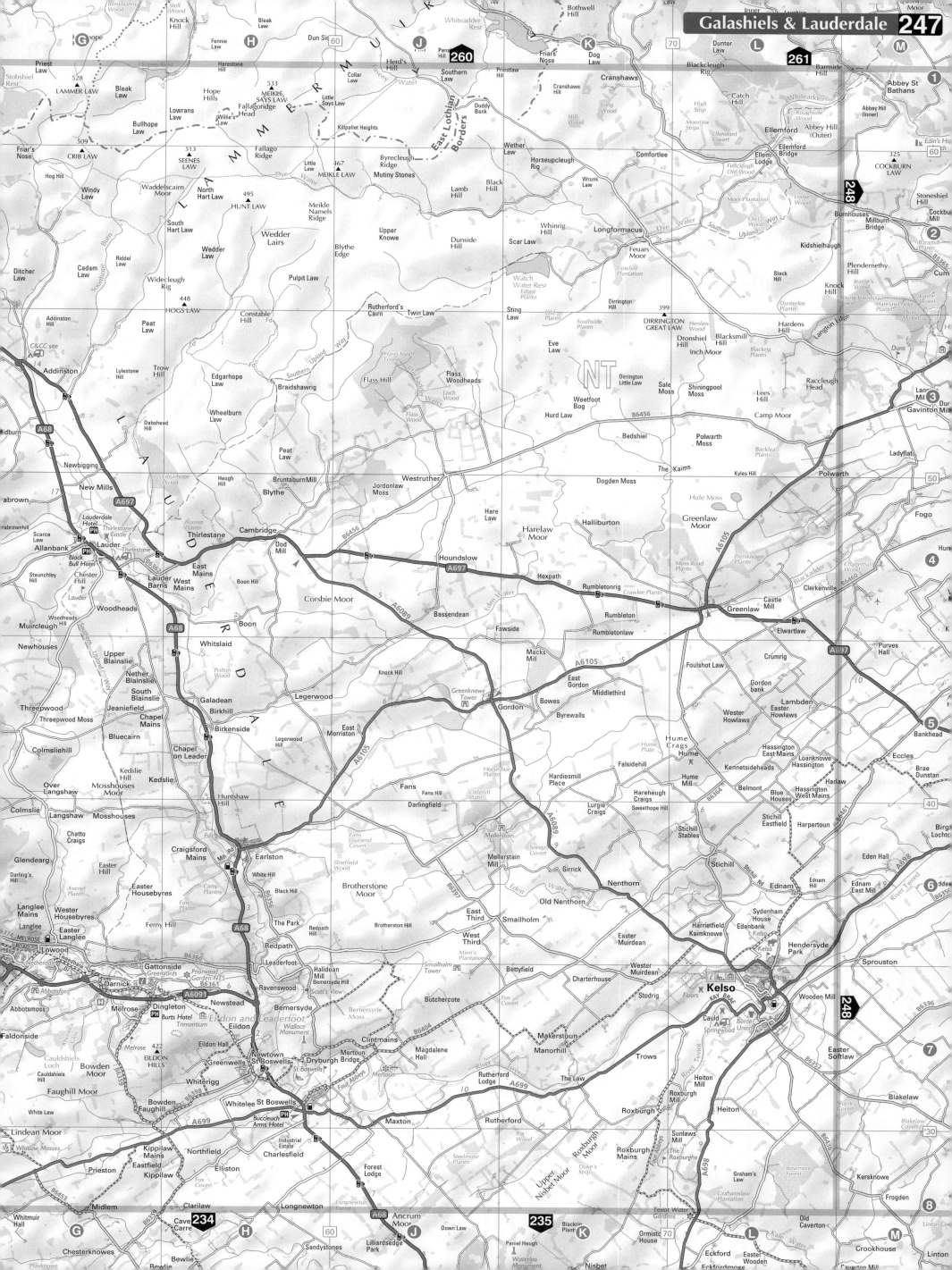

North Northumberland Heritage Coast

Brotherston's Hole
Magdalene Fields
Sharper's Head

Ladies Skerrs
Carrocks
Berwick-upon-Tweed
Town Ramparts
Meadow Haven
Sandstell Pt
Spittal

Bear's Head
Huds Head
Redshin Cove

Scremerston

Chesterston Hill

A1
Nabhill
East Ancroft
Ancroft
Cheswick
Cheswick Buildings
Windmill Hill
Cheswick Sands
Berwick-upon-Tweed (Goswick)

North Northumberland Heritage Coast

Ancroft Mill
Bridge Mill
Berrington
New Haggerston
Haggerston Castle
Haggerston
Goswick
Goswick Sands

Snipe Pt
Coves Haven
Keel Head
Emmanuel Head
HOLY ISLAND

Lickar
Dean
Lickar Lea
Eelwell
Lowick Mill
Hunting Hall
West Mains
Mount Hooley
Fenhamhill
Beal Point
Beal Burn
Beal Sands
Lindisfarne Cswy
Beal
Snook Point
Primrose Bank
Holy Island Sands
Causeway flooded at High Tide
Lindisfarne NNR
Sheldrake Pool
Chare Ends
Lindisfarne NT
Lindisfarne Priory
The Harbour
Castle Point
Hole Mouth

B6353
West Kyloe
Black Heddon
Fenwick
East Kyloe
Old Mill
Granary Point
Lowmoor Point
Guile Point
Burrows Hole

Lowick
Lowick Low Steads
Kyloe Hills
Bogle Hos
Kyloe Wood
Shepherdskirk Hill
Buckton
Fenham le Moor
Tealhole Point
Ross Point
Ross Back Sands
Skate Road
Longstone Lighthouse
Longstone
Brada
Little Harcar
Roddam and Green
Staple Island

Barmore Red House
Moorhouse
Buckton Moor
Rabbit Hill
Shiellow Wood
Detchant Wood
Detchant Park
Lowmoor Crossing
Heather Law
Smeafield
White Hill
Northumberland Coast
Ross Links
Ross
Megstone
FARNE ISLANDS
Staple Sound
Inner Farne
Little Scarcar
The Kettles

Laverock Law
Holburn
Holburn Moss
St Cuthbert's Cave NT
Ivy House
Detchant
Detchant Lodge
Elwick
Budle Point
Inner Sound

Doddington North Moor
Holburn Mill
Holburn Grange
Greensheen Hill
Swinhoe Lakes
Easington Grange
Middleton
Easington
Budle Bay
Budle
Bamburgh Castle
Newtown
Bamburgh

Bill Law
Hetton Law
White Law
North Hazelrigg
Hazelrigg Mill
Dancing Green Hill
Cockenheugh
Tilesheds Wood
Craggyhall
Blue Bell Hotel
The Belford
Waren Mill
Waren
Glororum
Victoria Hotel
LINKS

NU
Hetton Hall
Old Hazelrigg
Belford Moor
Early Knowe
Sionside
Belford
Spindlestone
Glororum
Burton
Fowberry
Shoreston Hall
Seahouses
NU

Doddington Moor and Law
Town Law
West Horton
East Horton
Hazelrigg
Spylaw
North Lyham
Old Lyham
Lyham Moor
Newlands North Moor
Belford Mains
Mousen
Bradford
Humbleton Hill
Snook or North Point
North Sunderland

Weetwood Hill
Weetwood Hall
Chimney Hill
West Lyham
South Lyham
Lyham Hill
Redheugh Knowe
Warenton
Bellshill
Adderstone Mains
Adderstone Lowmill
Adderstone Grange
Adderstone
Lucker
Hoppen Law
Elford
Burnhouse
Linkhouse
C&CC site
Beadnell
Collith Hole
Beadnell Haven

Tile Sheds
West Weetwood
Weetwood Moor
Hetton House
Chattonpark Hill
Linkeylaw
North Wood
Hemphole Plantn
Embleton's Bog
Hill Crest
East Fleetham
Newham Hall
Nacker Hole
Lady's Hole

Coldmartin
Fowberry Moor
Newhall
Percy Arms Hotel
Chatton
Chatton Park
Greendykes
Chatton Moor
Brownridge
Cocklaw Dean
Twizell
Warenford
Warenford Lodge
Birchwood Plantn
High Hagg Dean
Newham
Newham Bog
West Fleetham
Swinhoe
Tuggall Grange
Tughall Mill
Beadnell Bay

Haugh Head
Newtown Moor
Lilburn
Highcairn Plantation
Chillingham
Ros Castle NT
Wild Cattle Park
Amersidelaw
Amersidelaw Moor
Whitehill Head
Sandford Moor
Robin Hood's Bog
Willie Law
Chatton Sandyfords
Rayheugh
Rayheugh Moor
Rosebrough
Rosebrough Moor
March Plantation
Crutch Bog
Chathill
Broad Wood
The Nest
Tughall
Newton Links
Snook Point
Football Hole

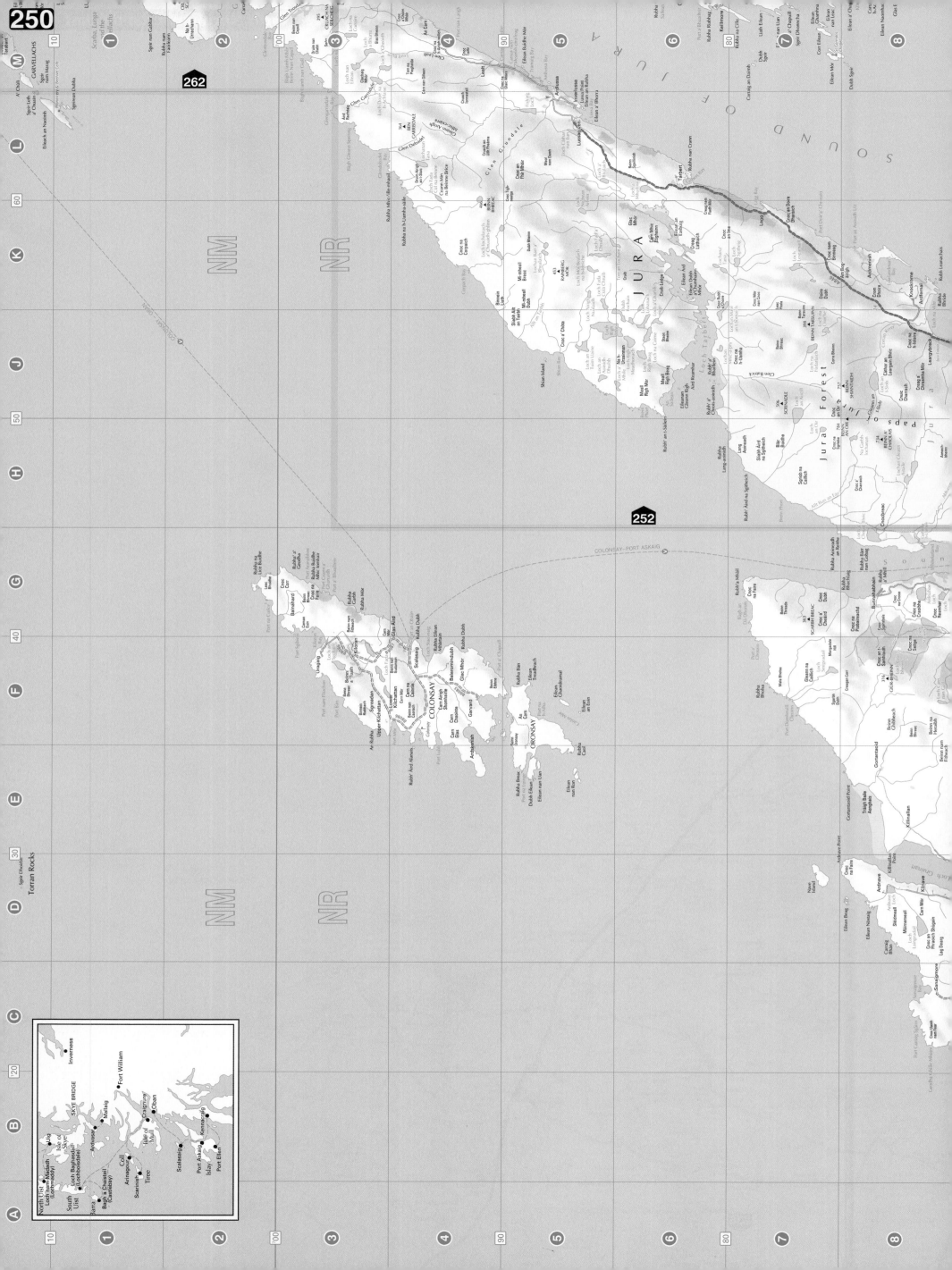

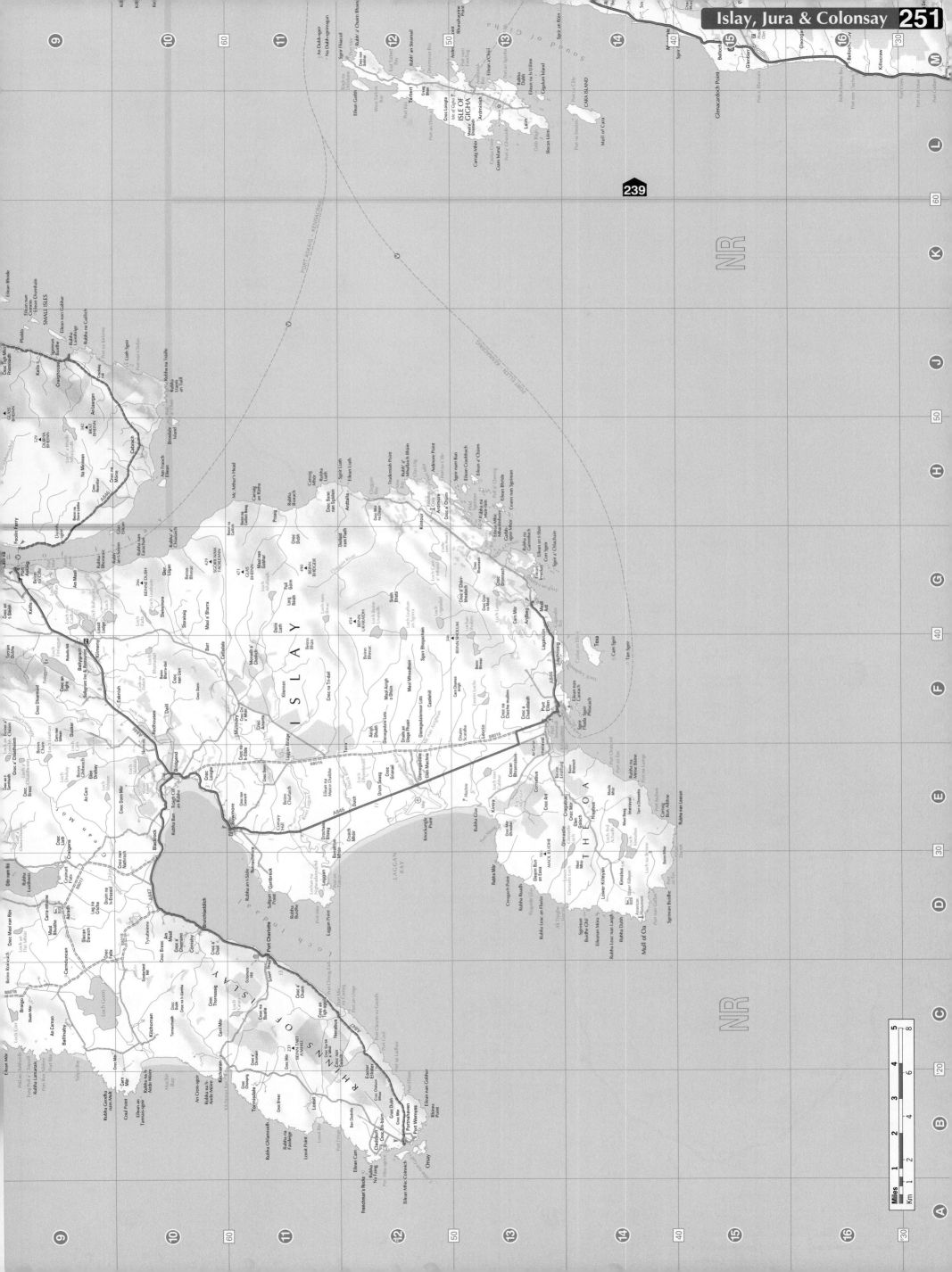

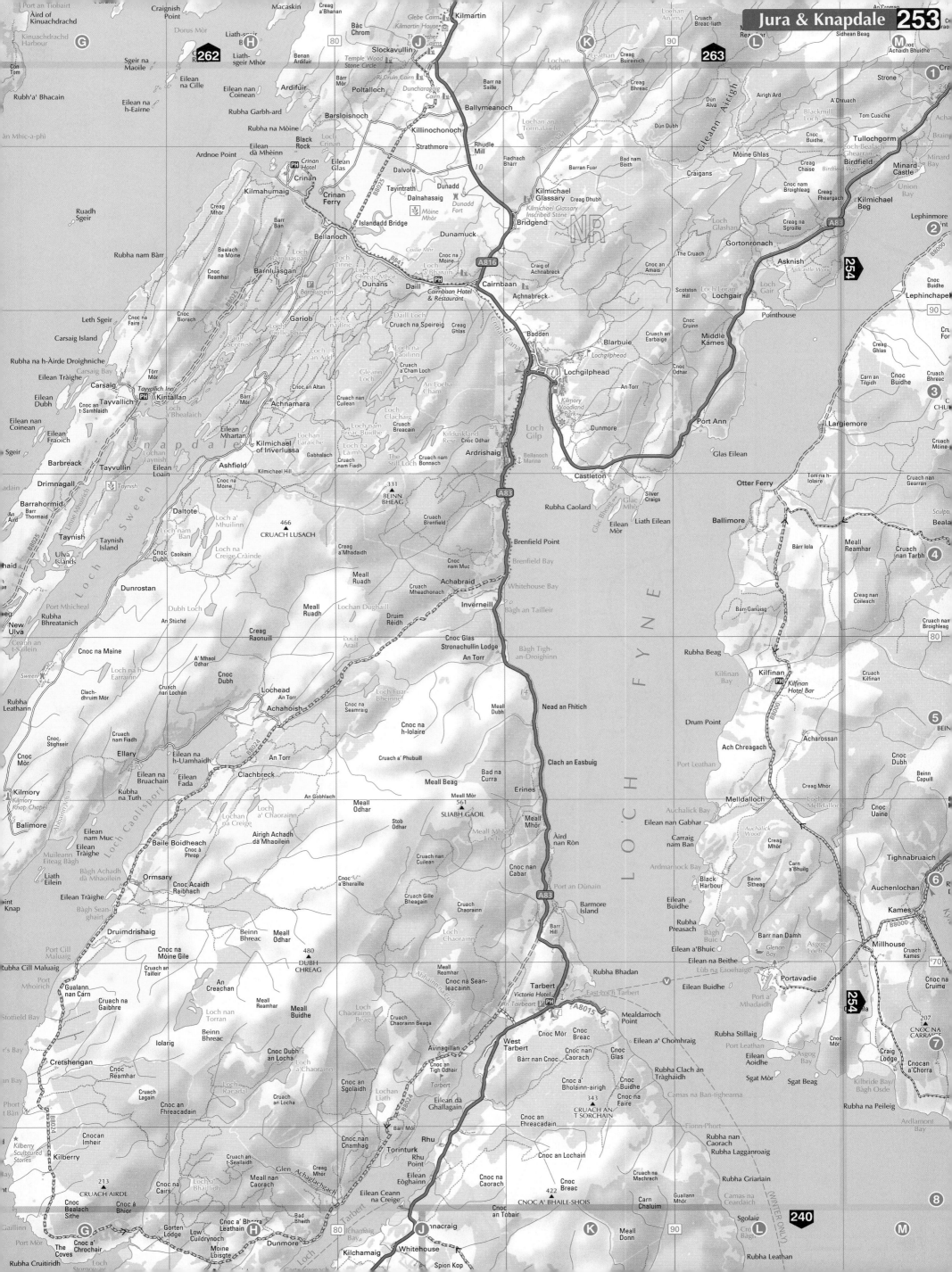

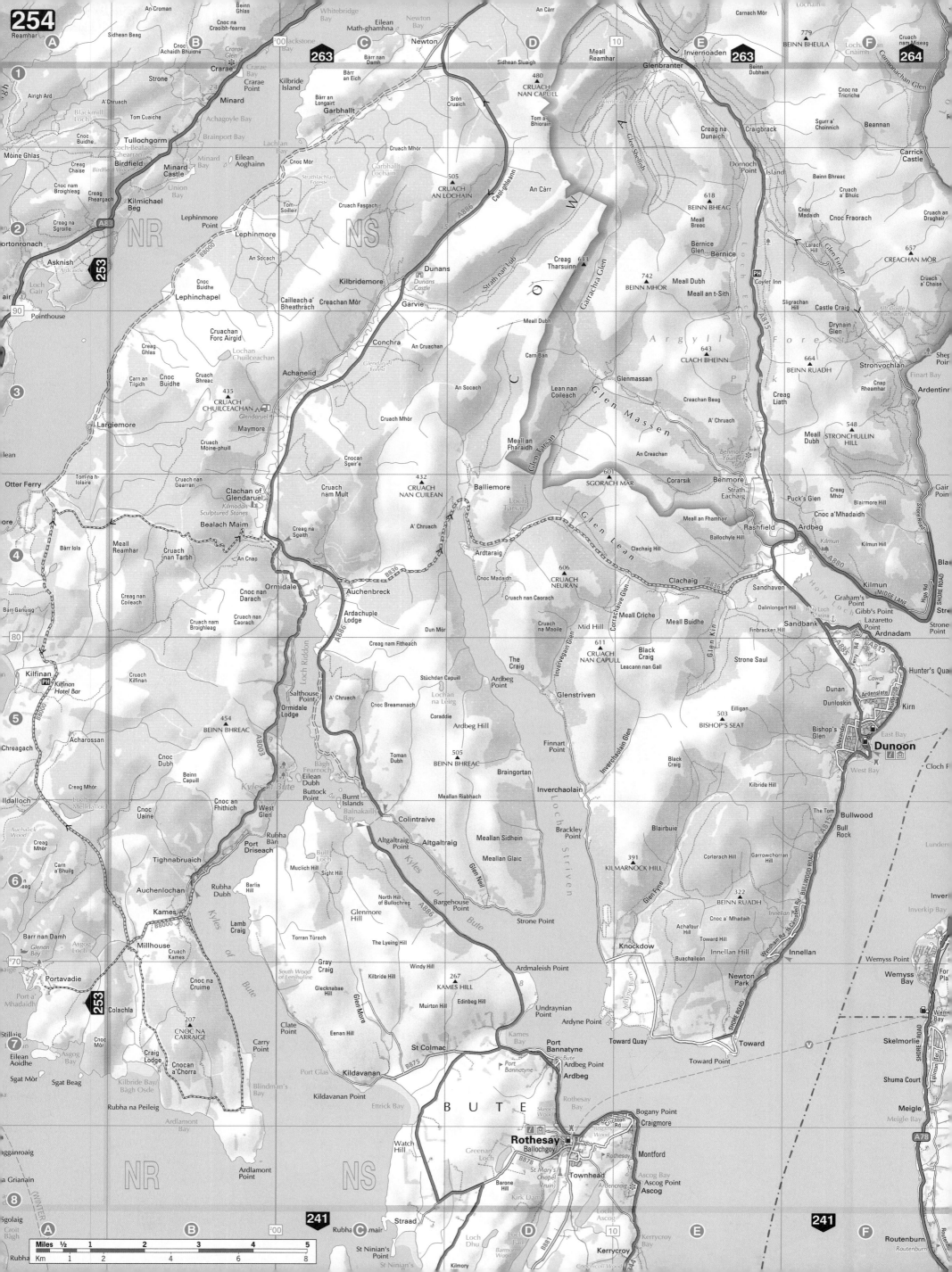

G   H   J   K   L   M

1

N O R T H   S E A

2

NT

3

4

5

Mill
Stone Neuk
White
Sands   Barns Ness
          C&CC
          site
          Chapel Point
          Skateraw
          Harbour   Torness Point
          Skateraw   Long Craig
          Power
          Station
Innerwick   Thorntonloch
Barns Ness Ter

6

Old
Branxton   Branxton   Bilsdean
                    Creek
                    Reed
                    Point
Blackcastle   Cove Harbour
Hill   Belvidere   Cove
319   Wood   Pease Bay
COCKLAW   Collegiate   Red Rock
HILL   Church   Greenheugh   Fast Castle
Weather   Cockburnspath   Point   Siccar Point   Head   Wheat Stack
Law   Dovecot   Meikle   Telegraph
Oldhamstocks   Hall   Poo Craig   Hill   Fast
                              Castle

7

                    Old Cambus
Wightman   Townhead   Old Cambus   A1107   Dowlaw   Road
Hill   Old   Oatlee
          Townhead   Hill   St Abb's Head
Ecclaw   Ewieside   Greenside   196   Lumsdaine
Dod Hill   Hill   Hill   Meikle   BROWN RIG   Coldingham   Mire   Kirk
                    Black Law   Coldingham   Lumsdaine   Loch   Loch   Hill   Horsecastle Bay
Paits   Ecclaw   Penmanshiel   Common   Moor   Cross   St Abbs   Starney Bay
Hill   Hill   Moor   Laverlock   Law   West Loch   Northfield
                    Gowel   Law   Coldingham   Bell Hill
Corse   Dunglass   Blackburn   Hill   Moor   St Abb's
Law   Common   Hopsdale   Bell   Moorside   Haven   Coldingham
HEART   Blackburn   Hill   Drone   School   Road   Temple   Scoutscroft   Bay
391   LAW   Mill   Hill   Hall   Coldingham   Yellow Craig
Ewelairs   Blackburning   Three Burn   Abbey   Callercove
Hill   Wood   Grantshouse   Brockholes   Grange   Park   A1107   22   Point   Hairy
Black   Roadside   Wood   Dalks   Grange   Bee   Hallydown   Ness
Law   Woods   Brockholes   Law   Plantn   Edge   Eyemouth
Inner   Quixwood   Hill   Gallows   **Eyemouth**
Hill   Laughing   Moor   Landsend   A1   Houndwood   Law   Cairncross   Eyemouth
Law   Wood   Scout Point
Dunter   Blakerstone   Mount   Heugh   Linthill   Horse
Law   Moor   Alban   Head   Head
Blackcleugh   Barnside   Drakemyre   Fancove Head
          Hill   262   MAIN STREET   Millbank   Breeches
247   **248**   HORSELEY HILL   Reston   East   **248**   Rock
G   H   80   J   K   90   Reston   L   M
High   Catch   Abbey St   Auchencrow   Ayton   Burnmouth Hill
Strip   Hill   Bathans   Ayton   Castle
Ellemford   Abbey Hill   Abbey Hill   Gallows   B6355   Burnmouth
          (Inner)   Drakemire

8

70

80

90

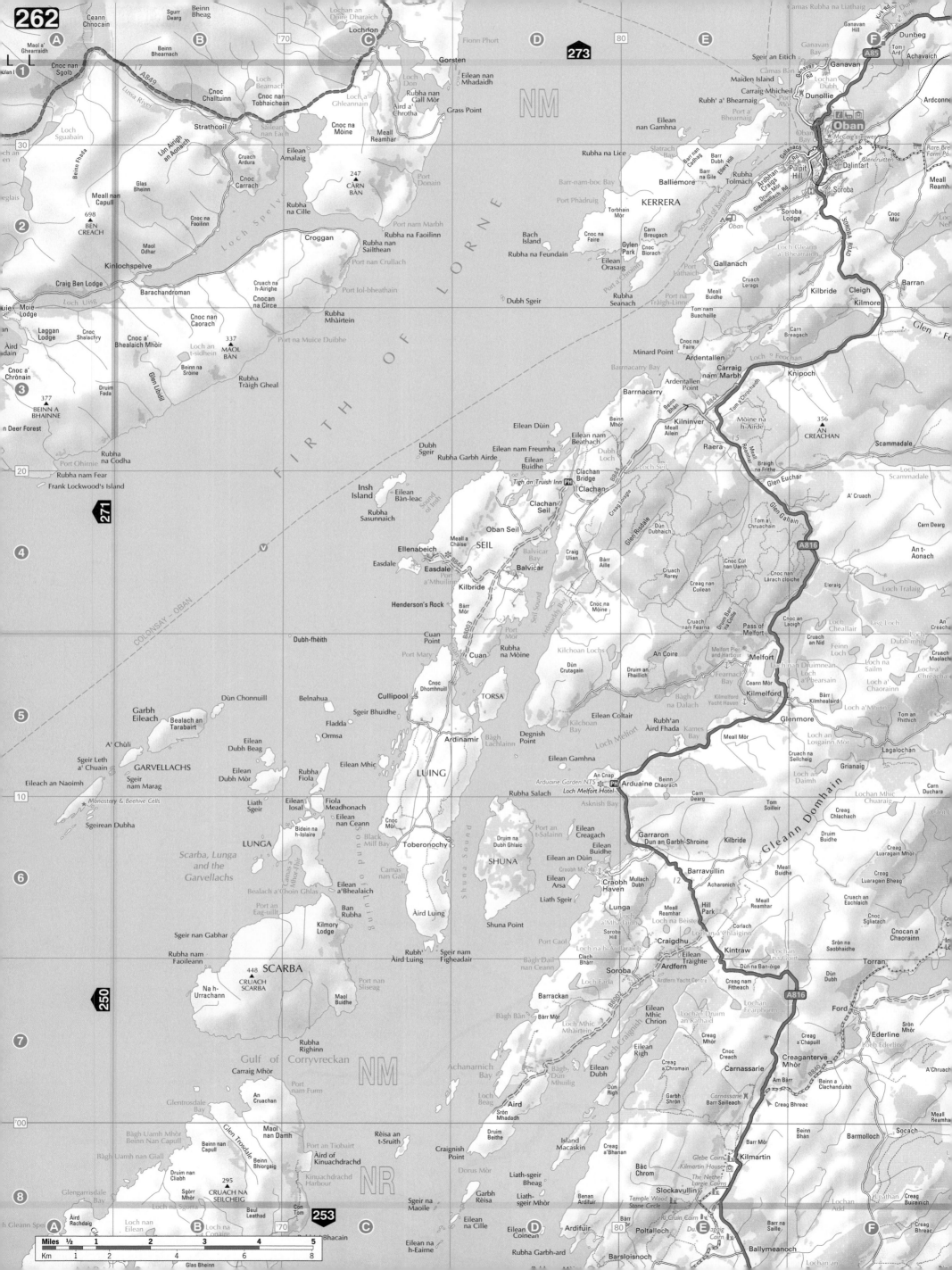

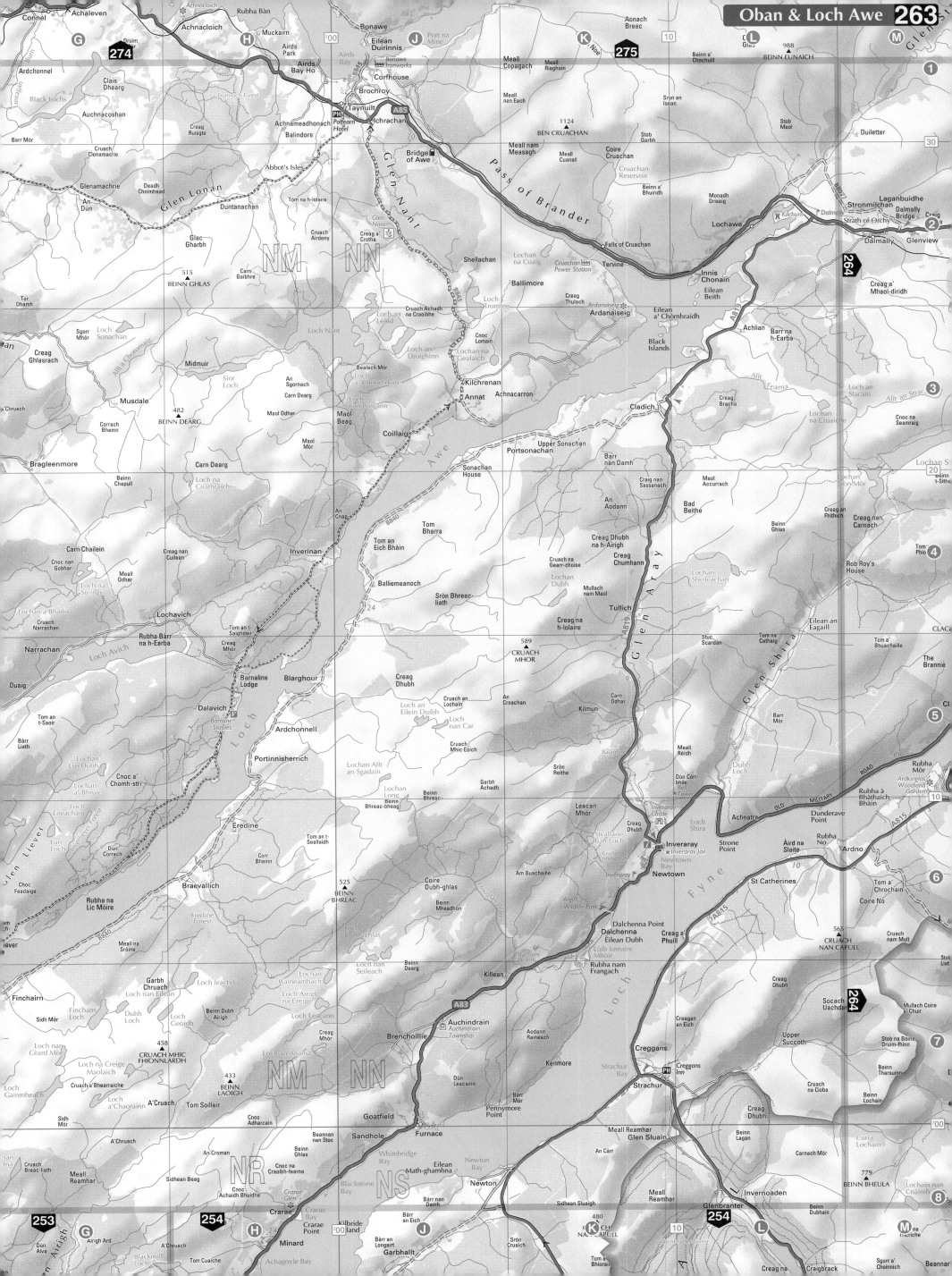

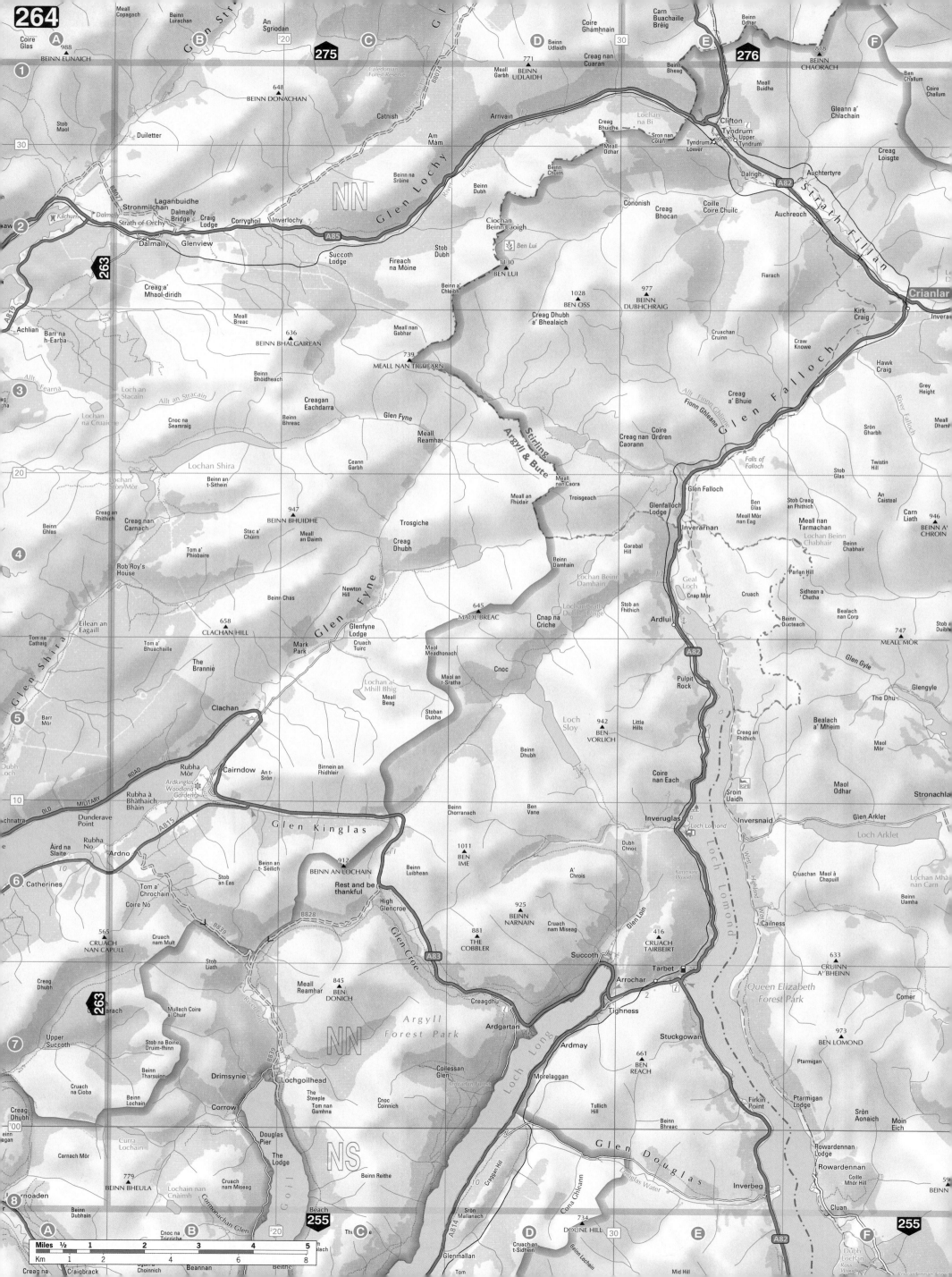

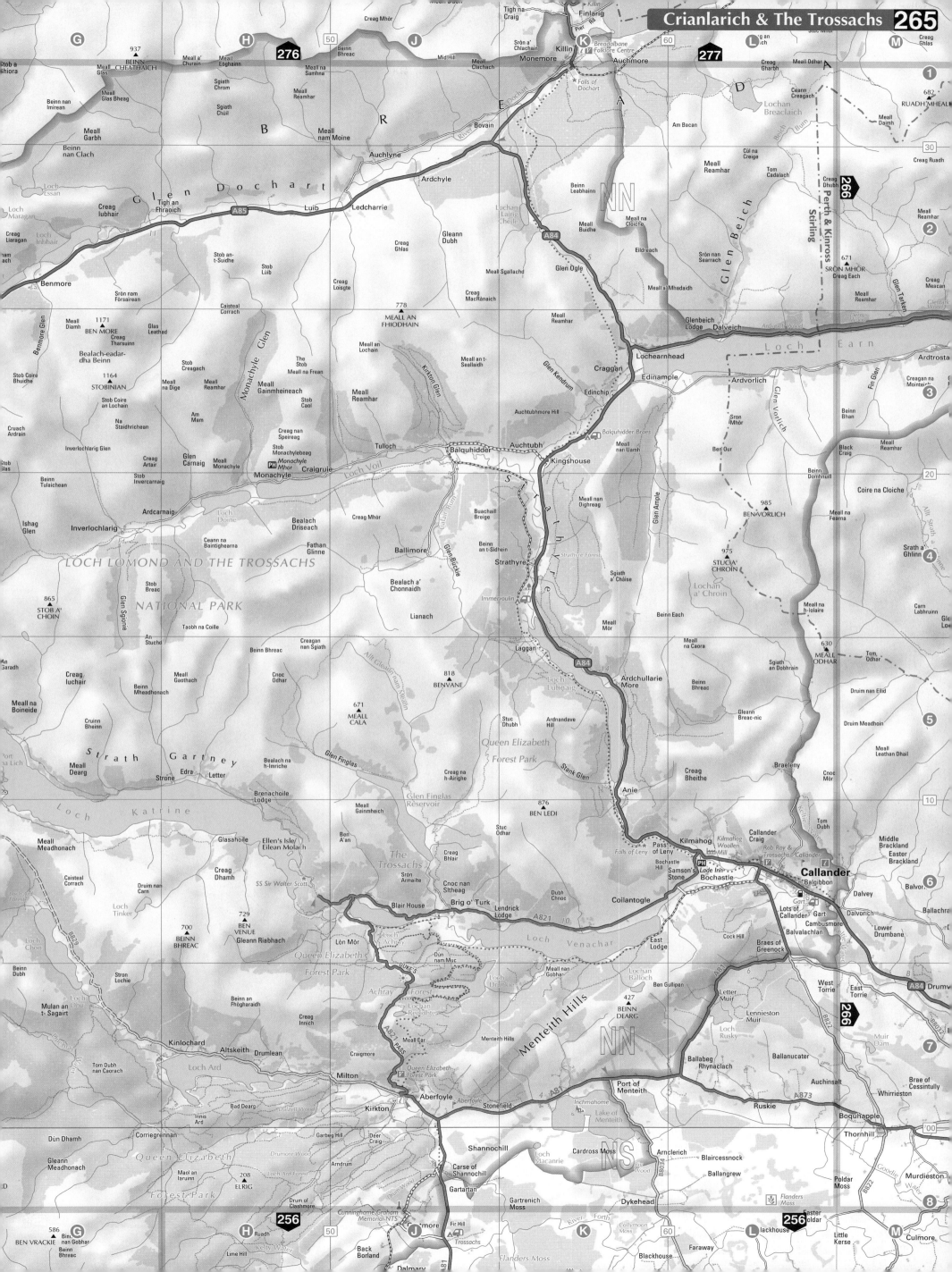

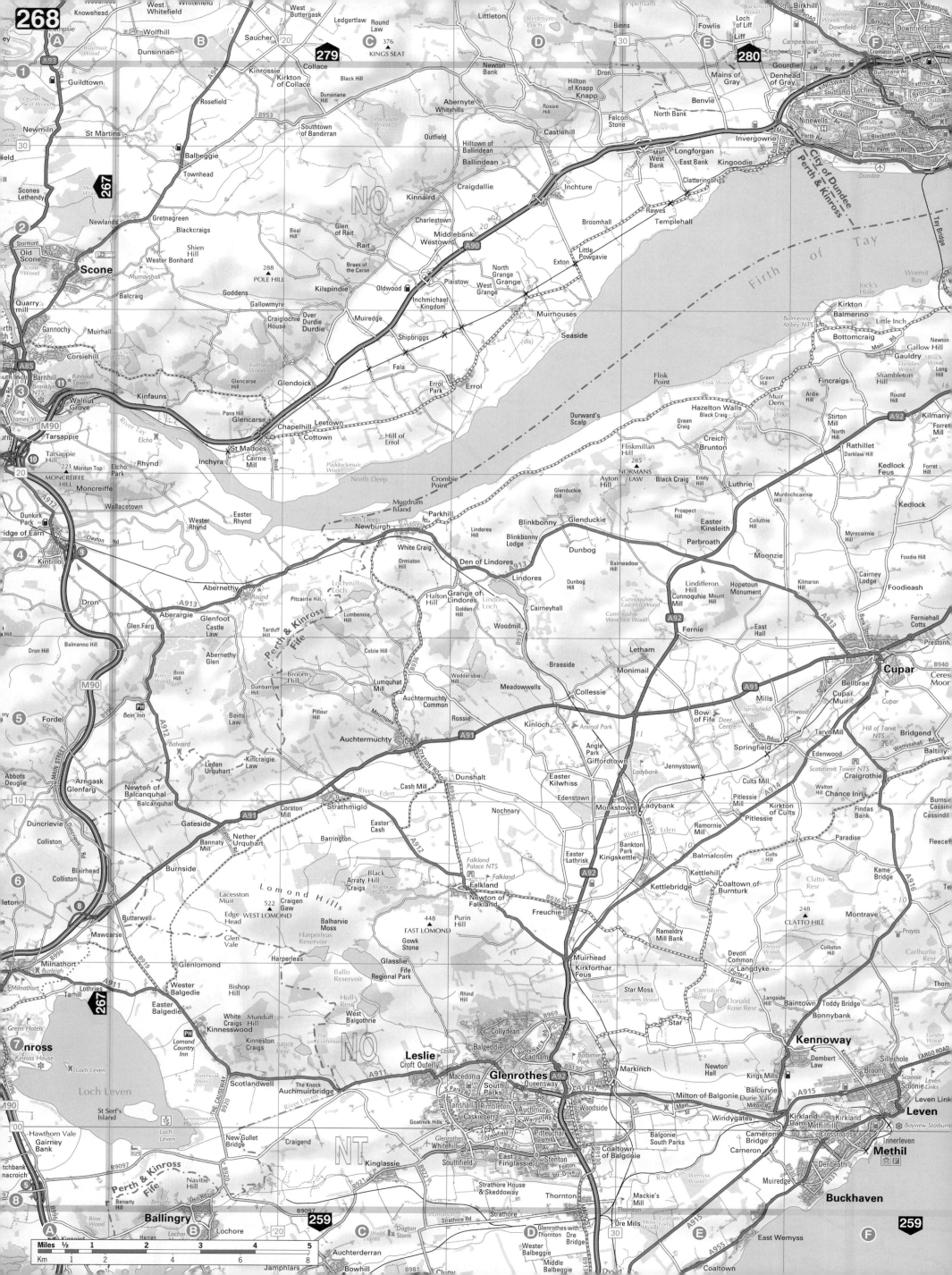

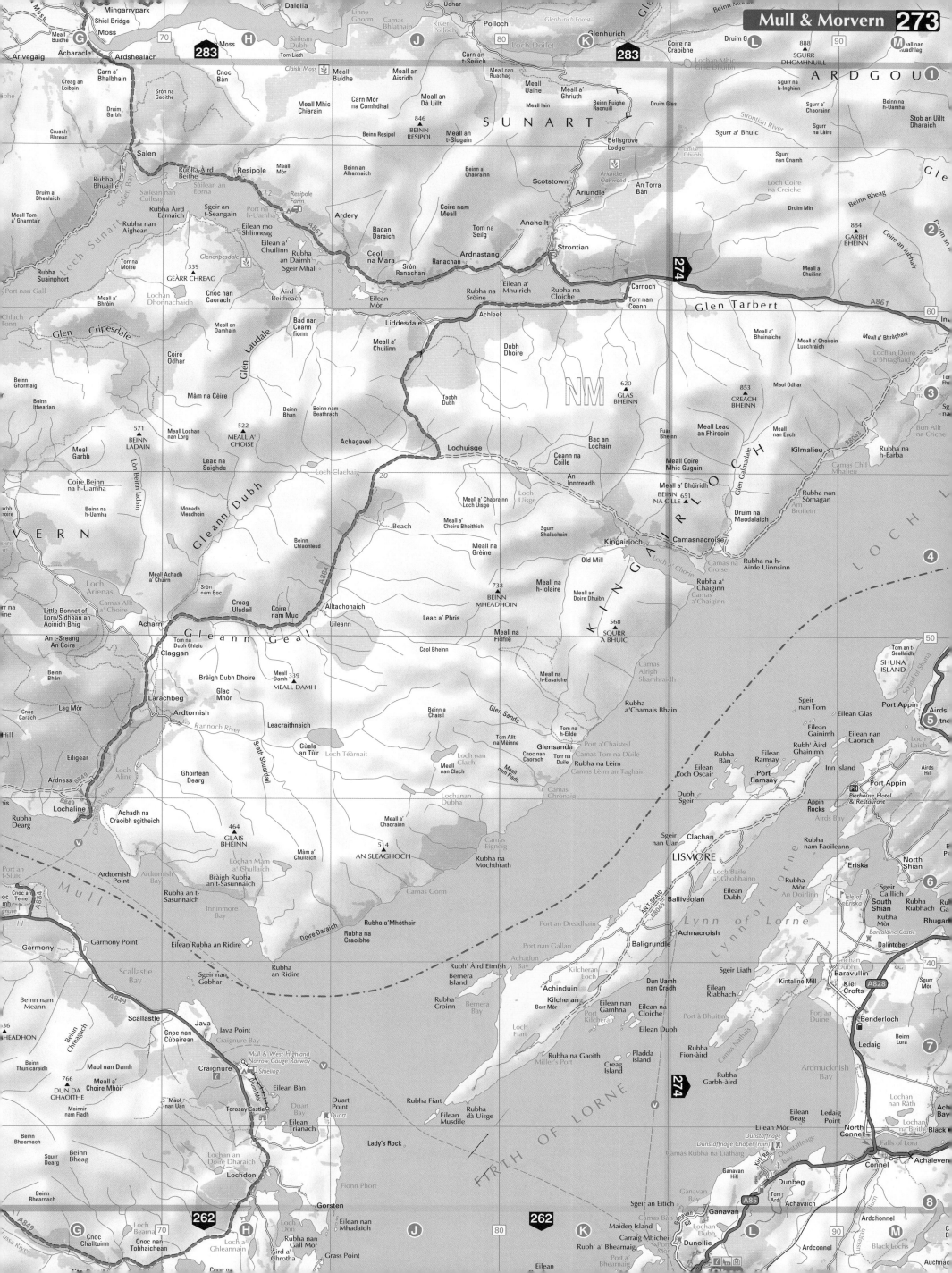

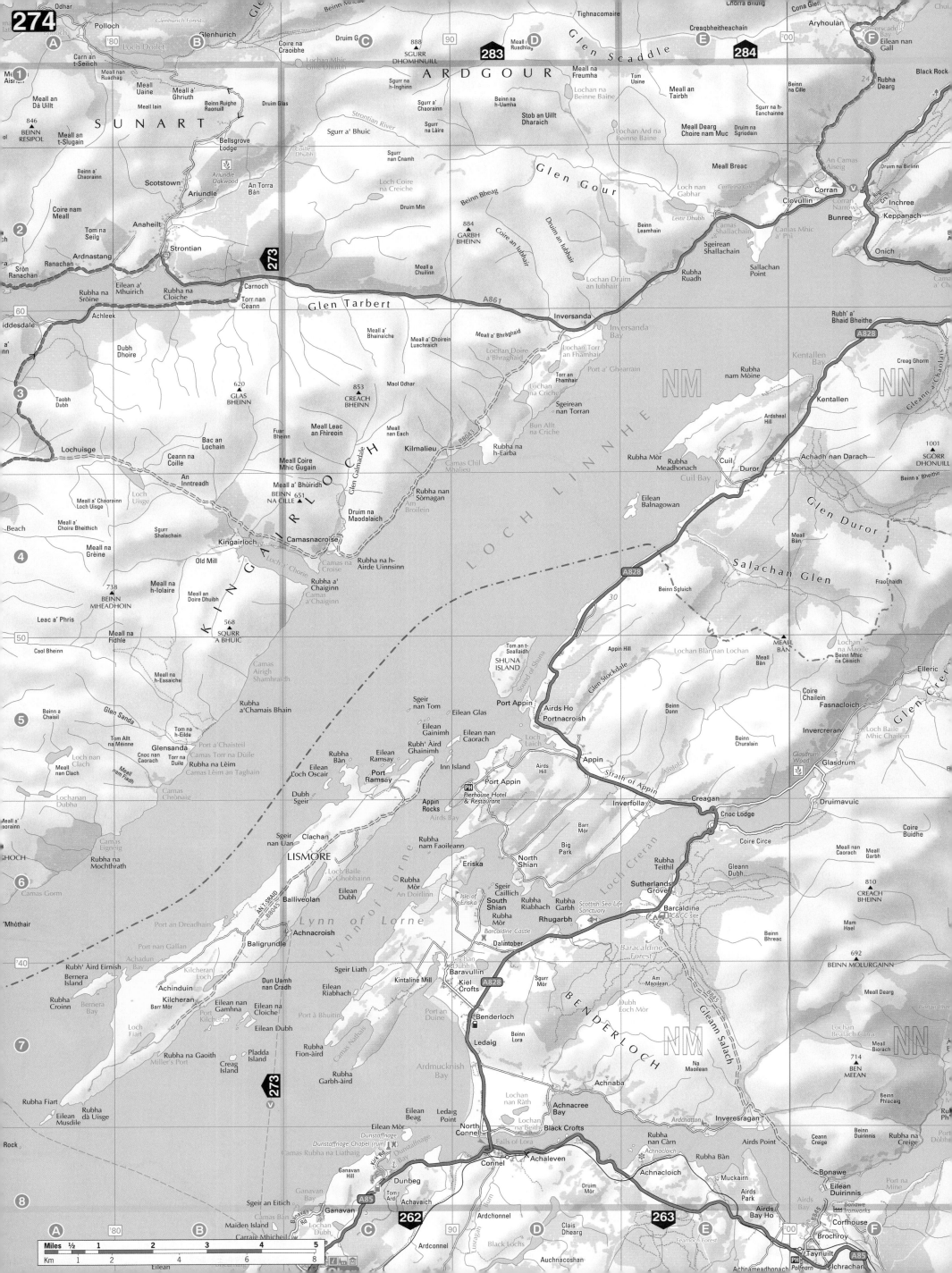

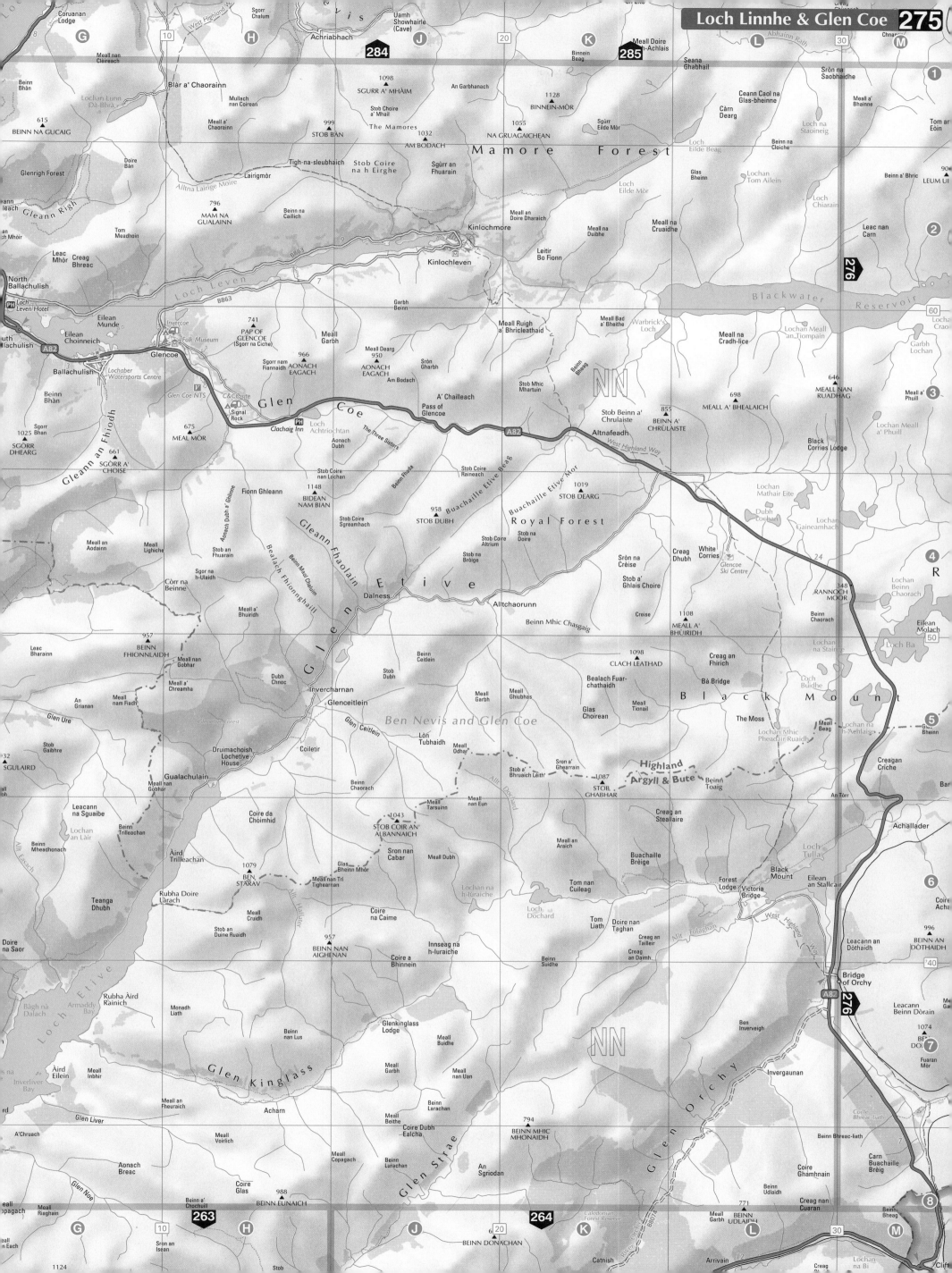

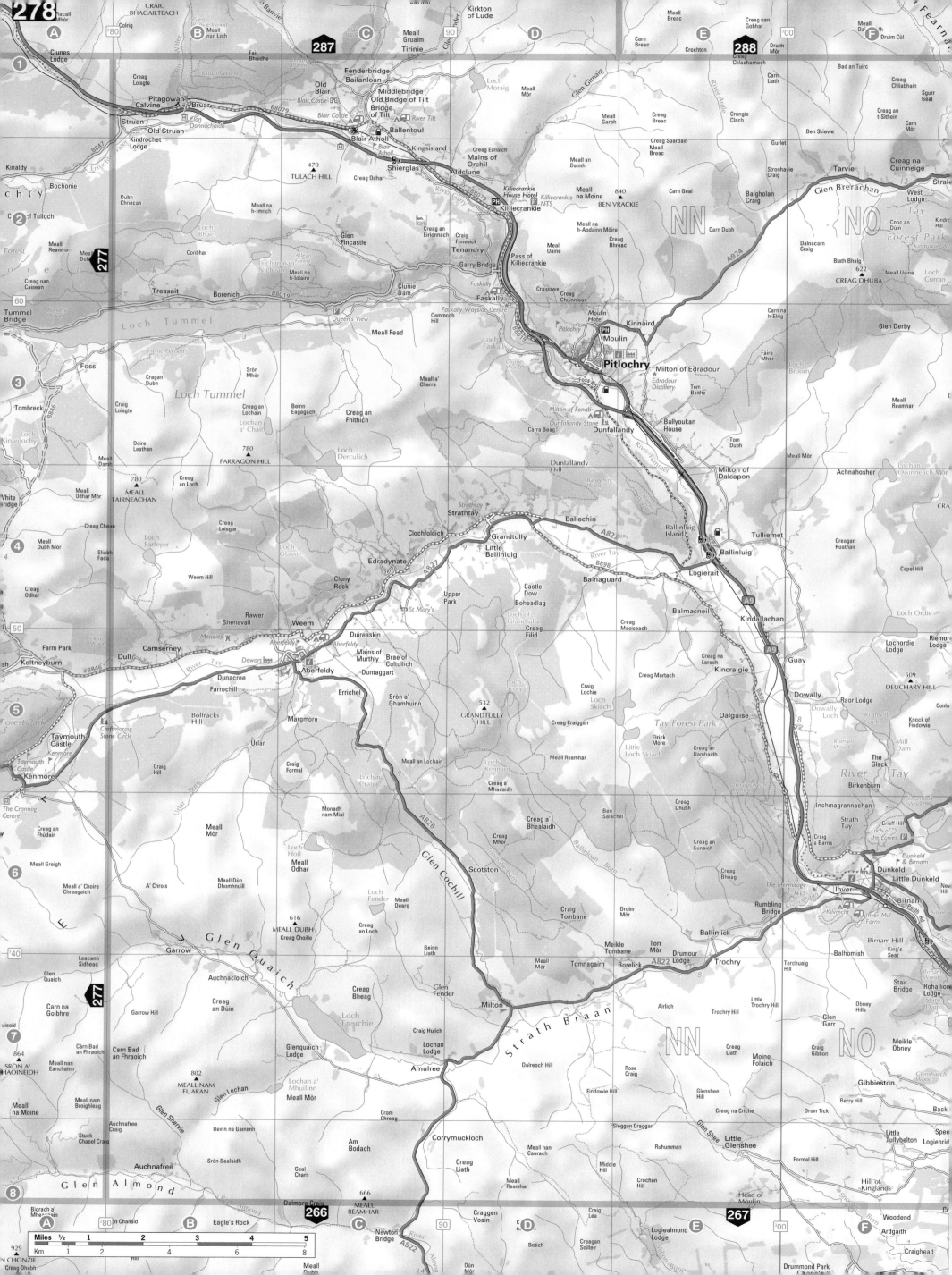

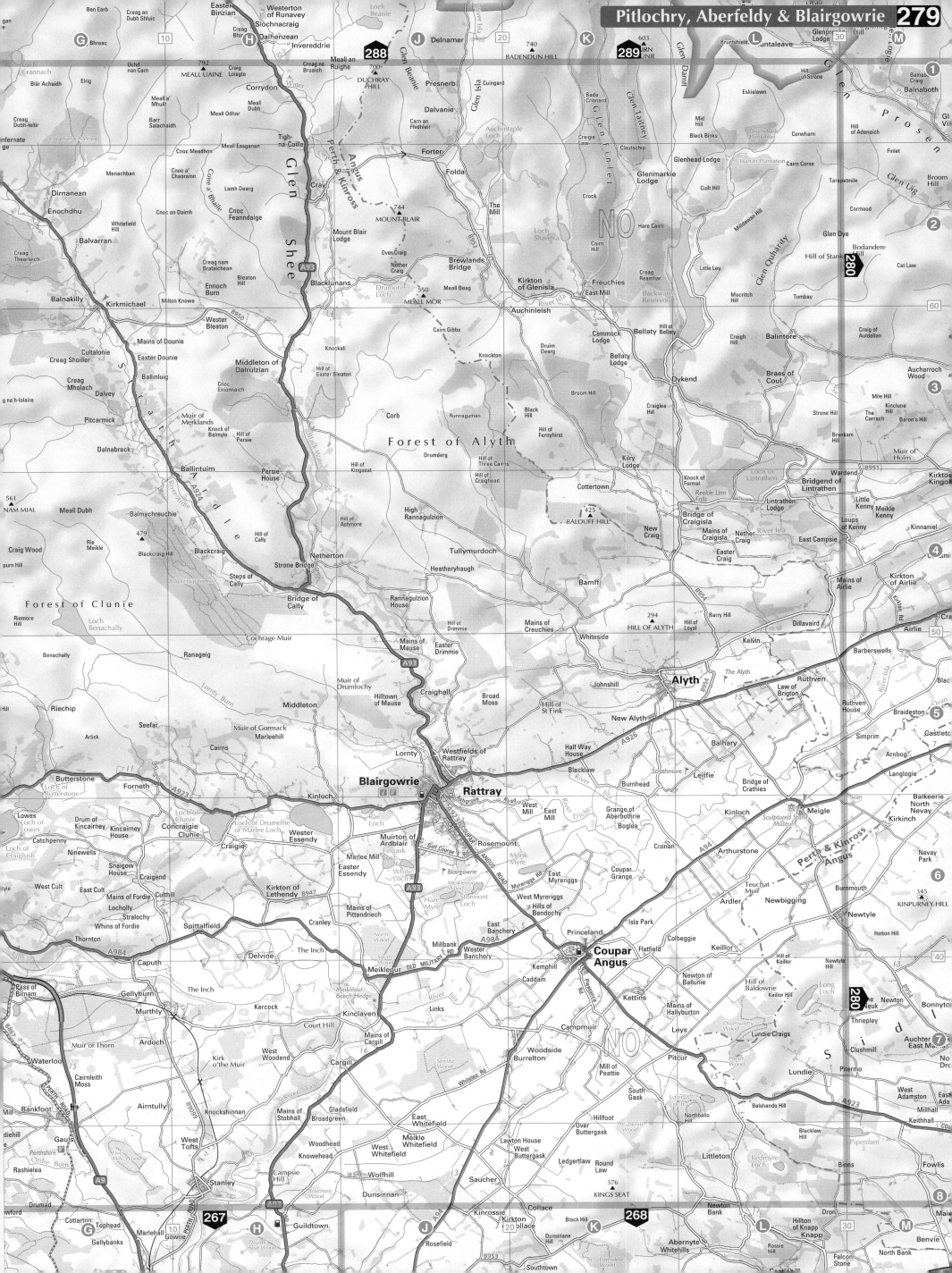

Dundee

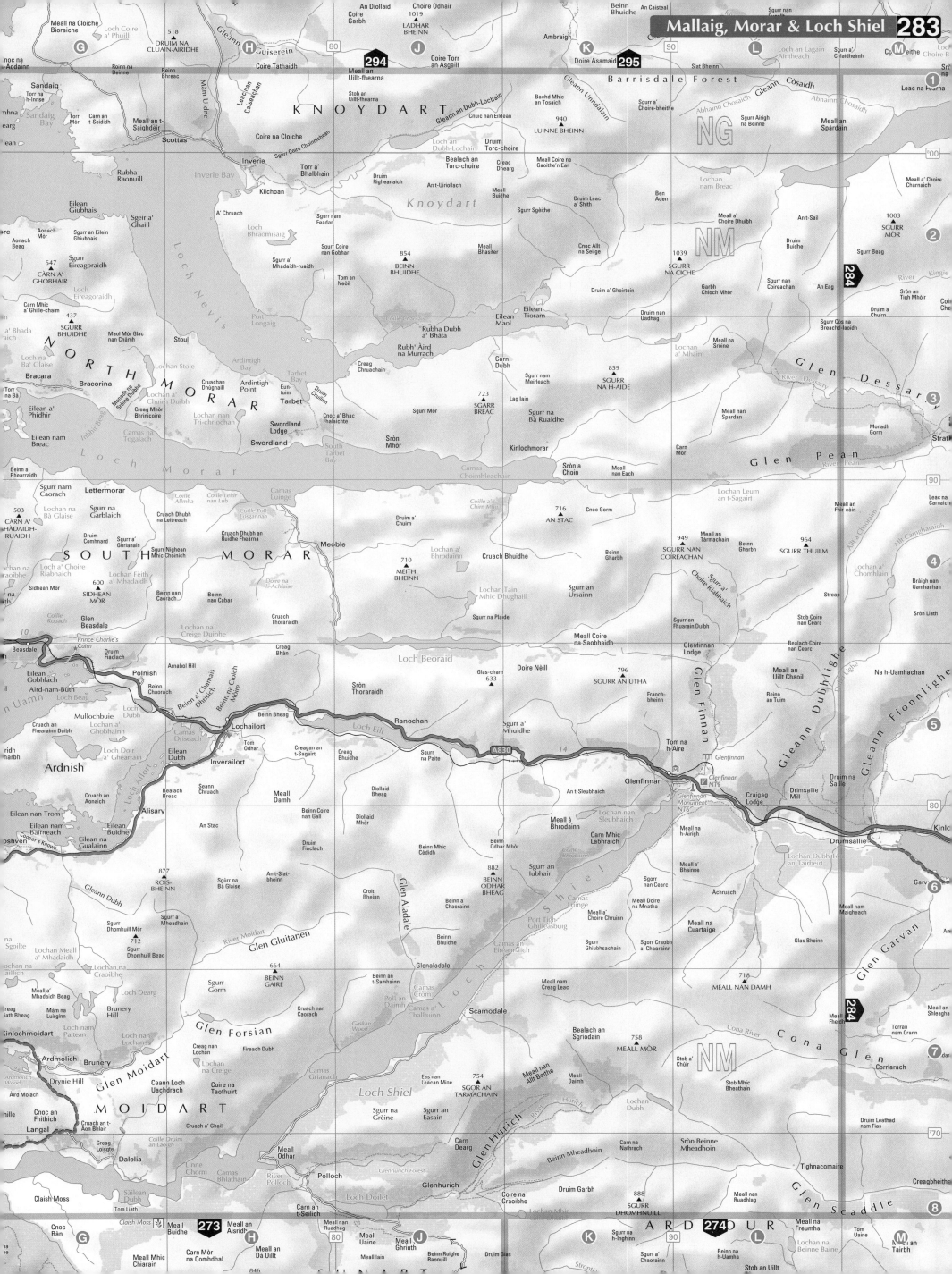

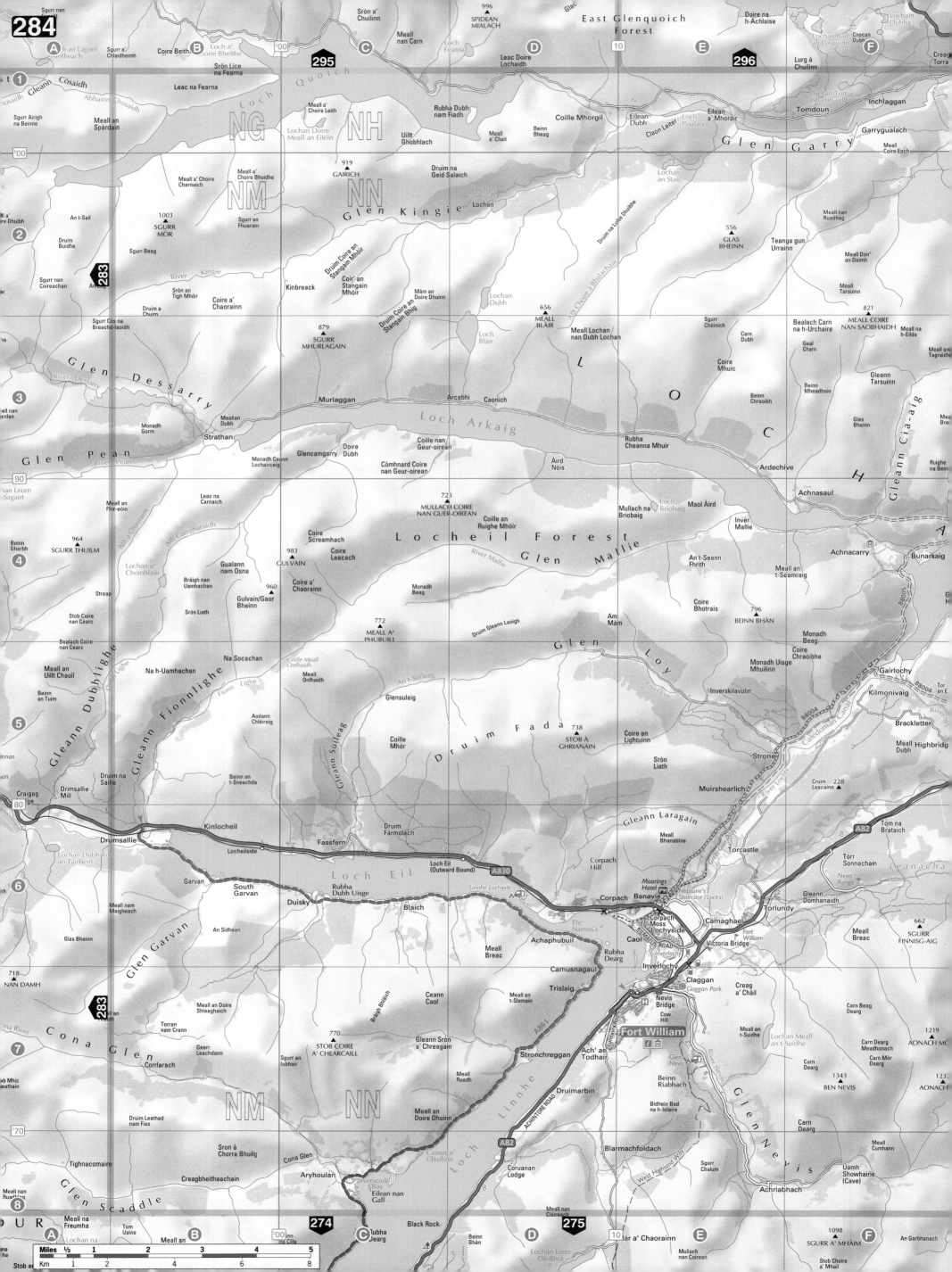

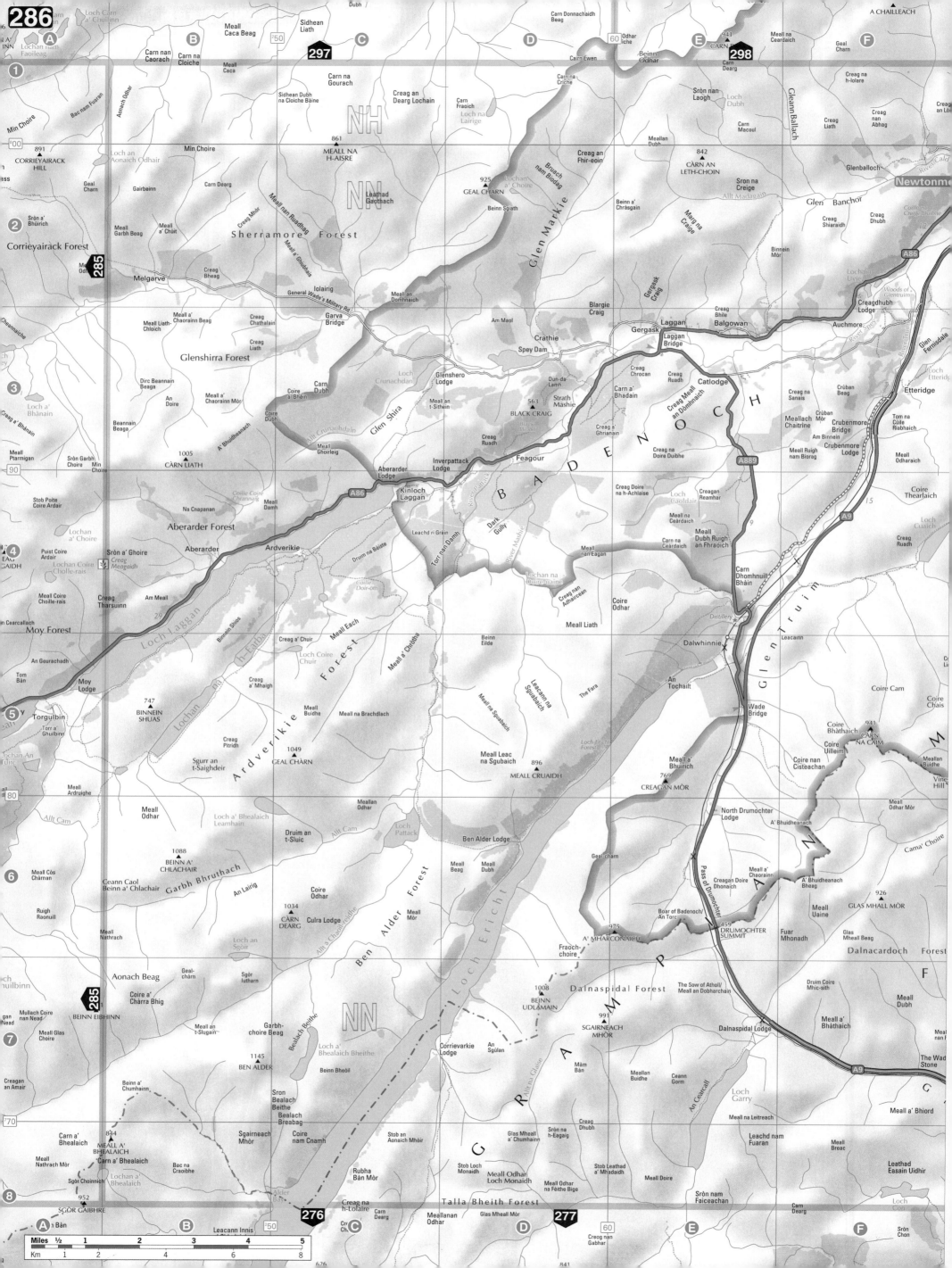

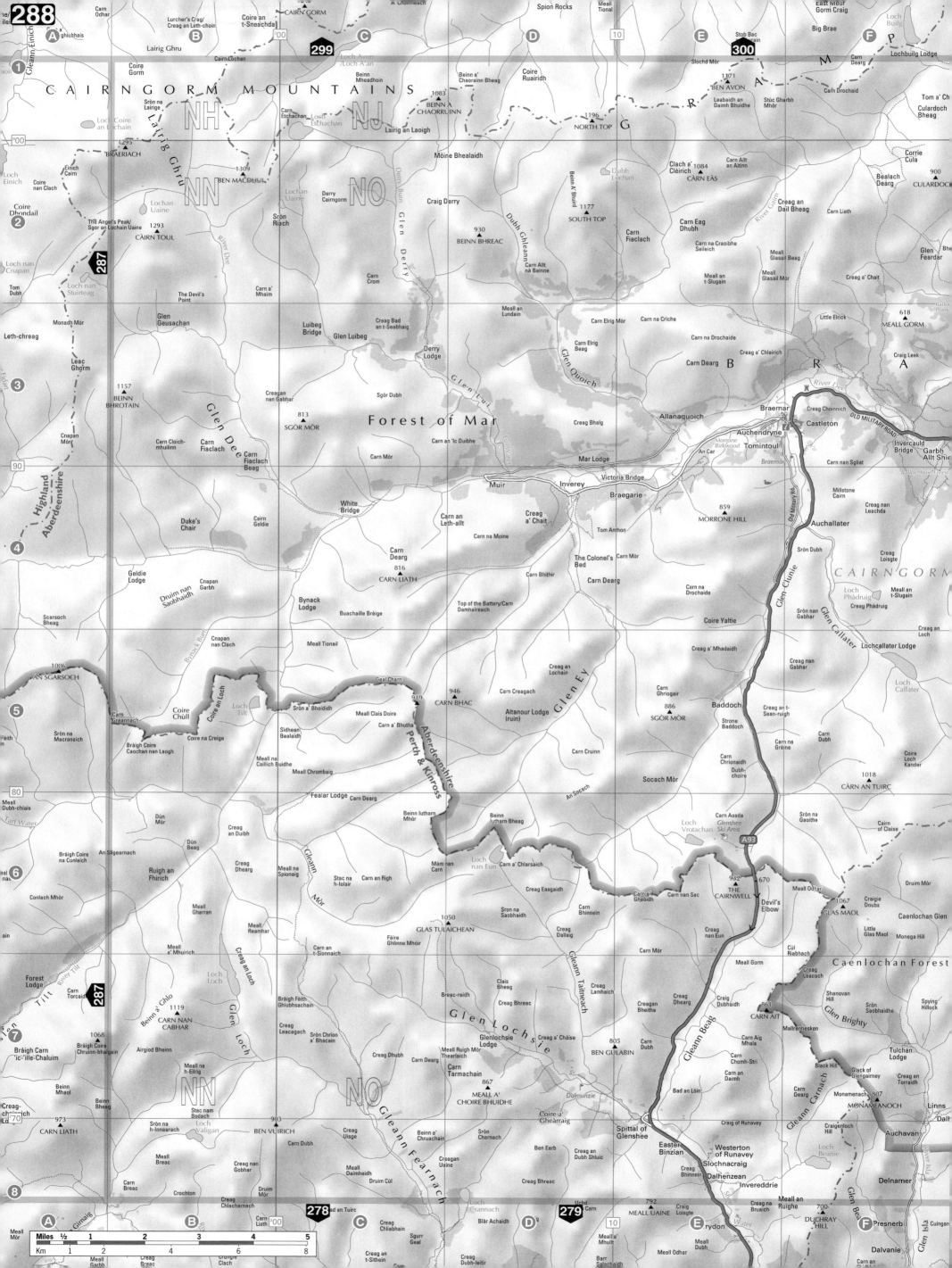

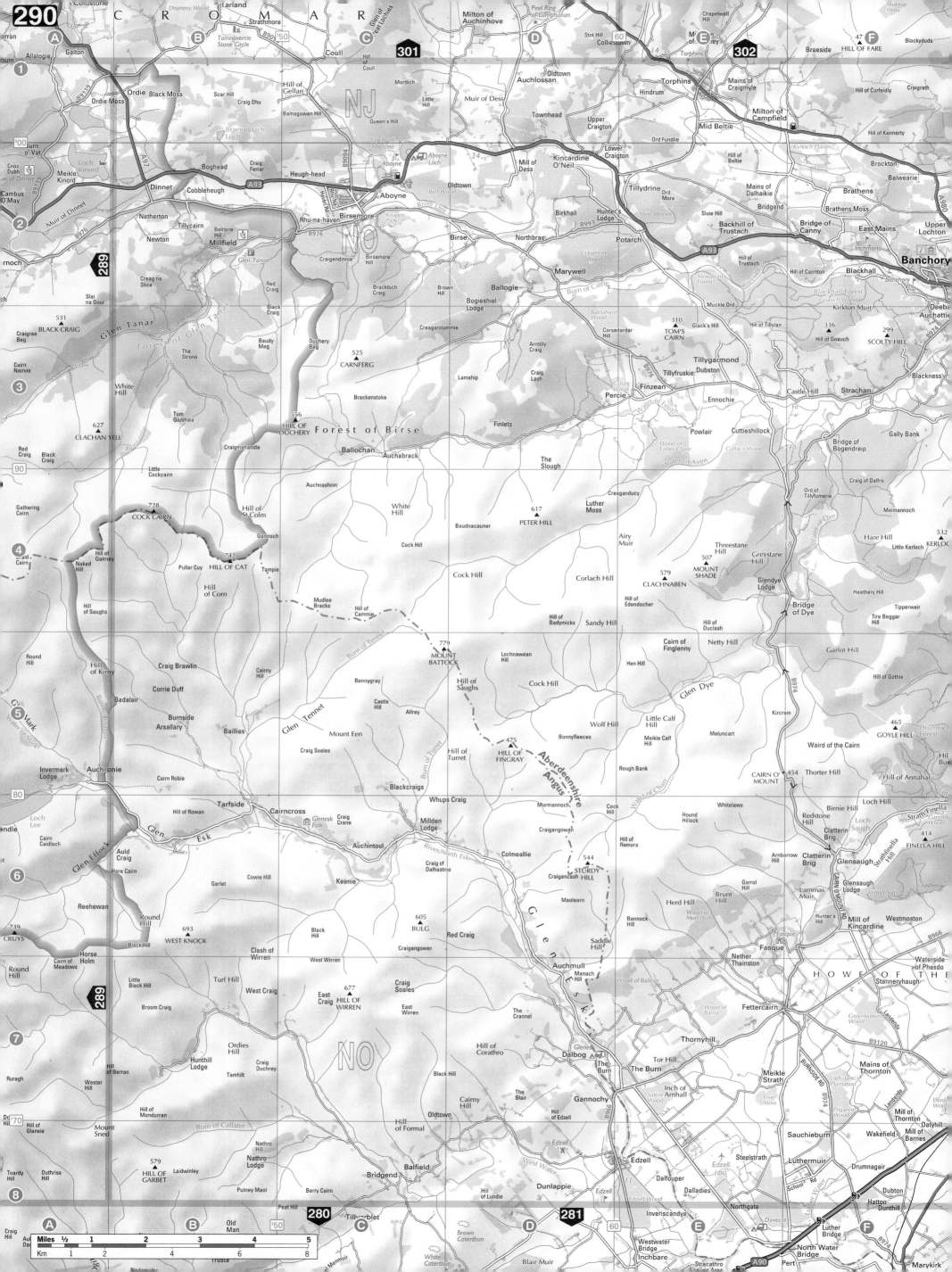

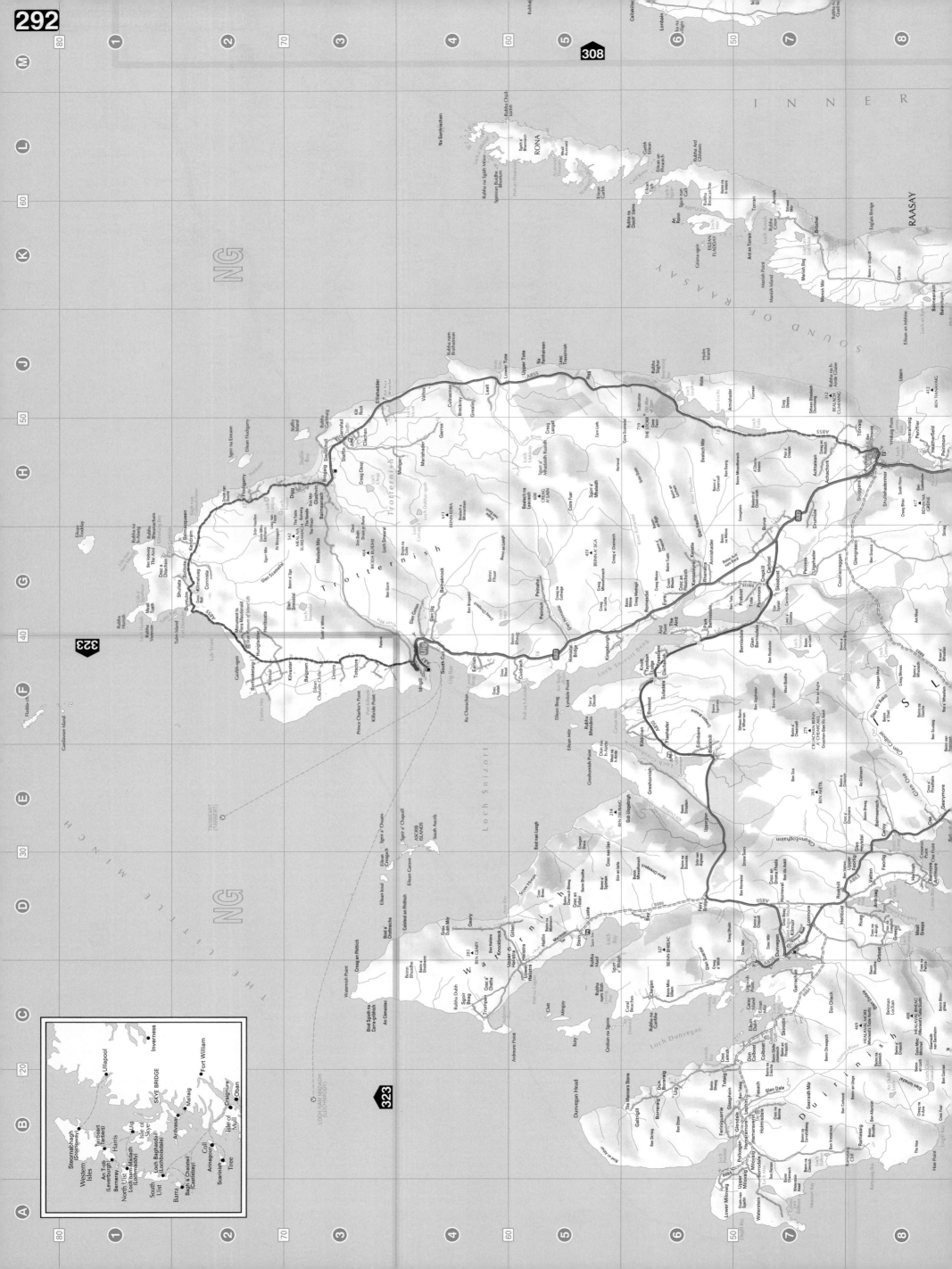

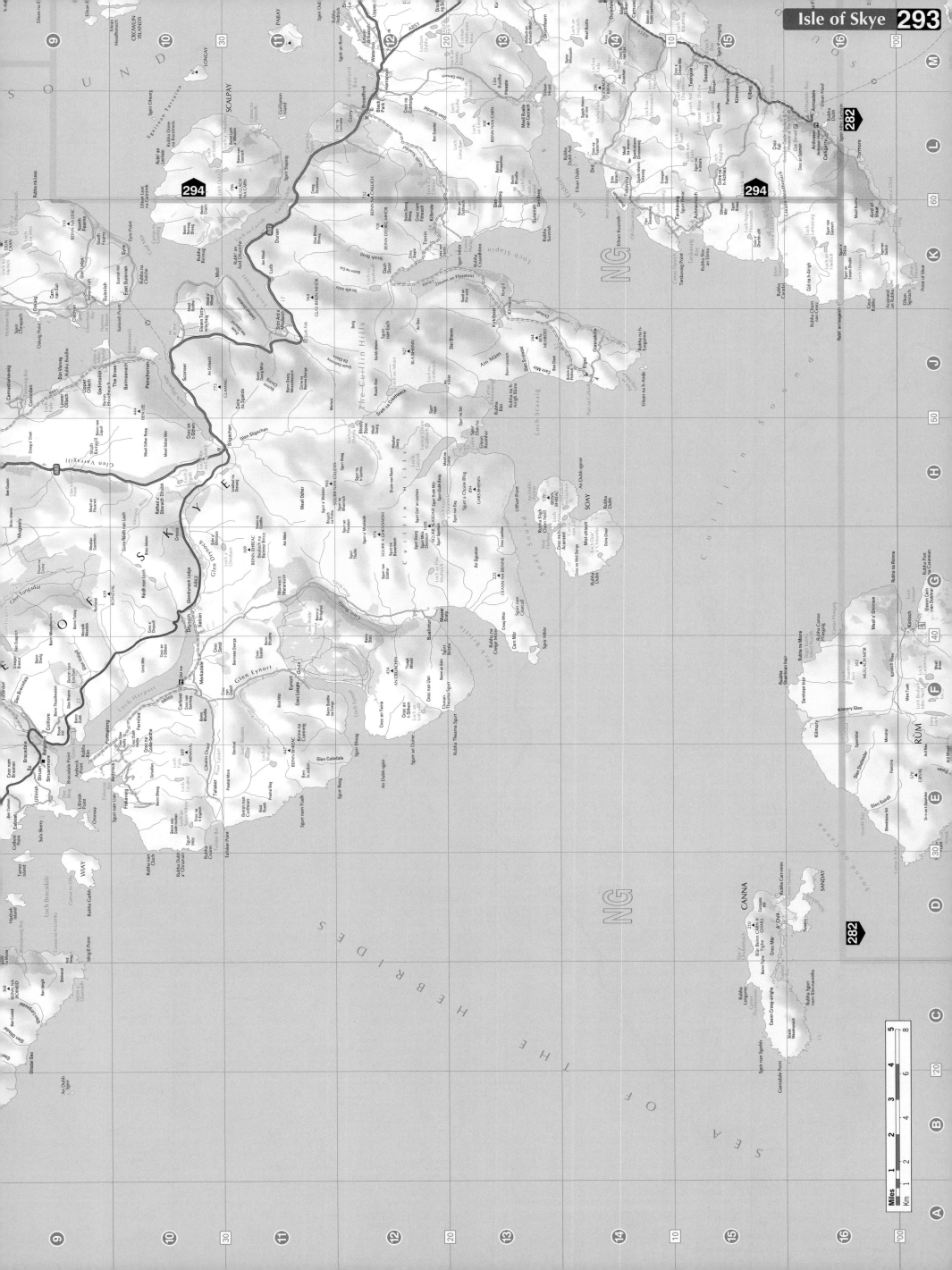

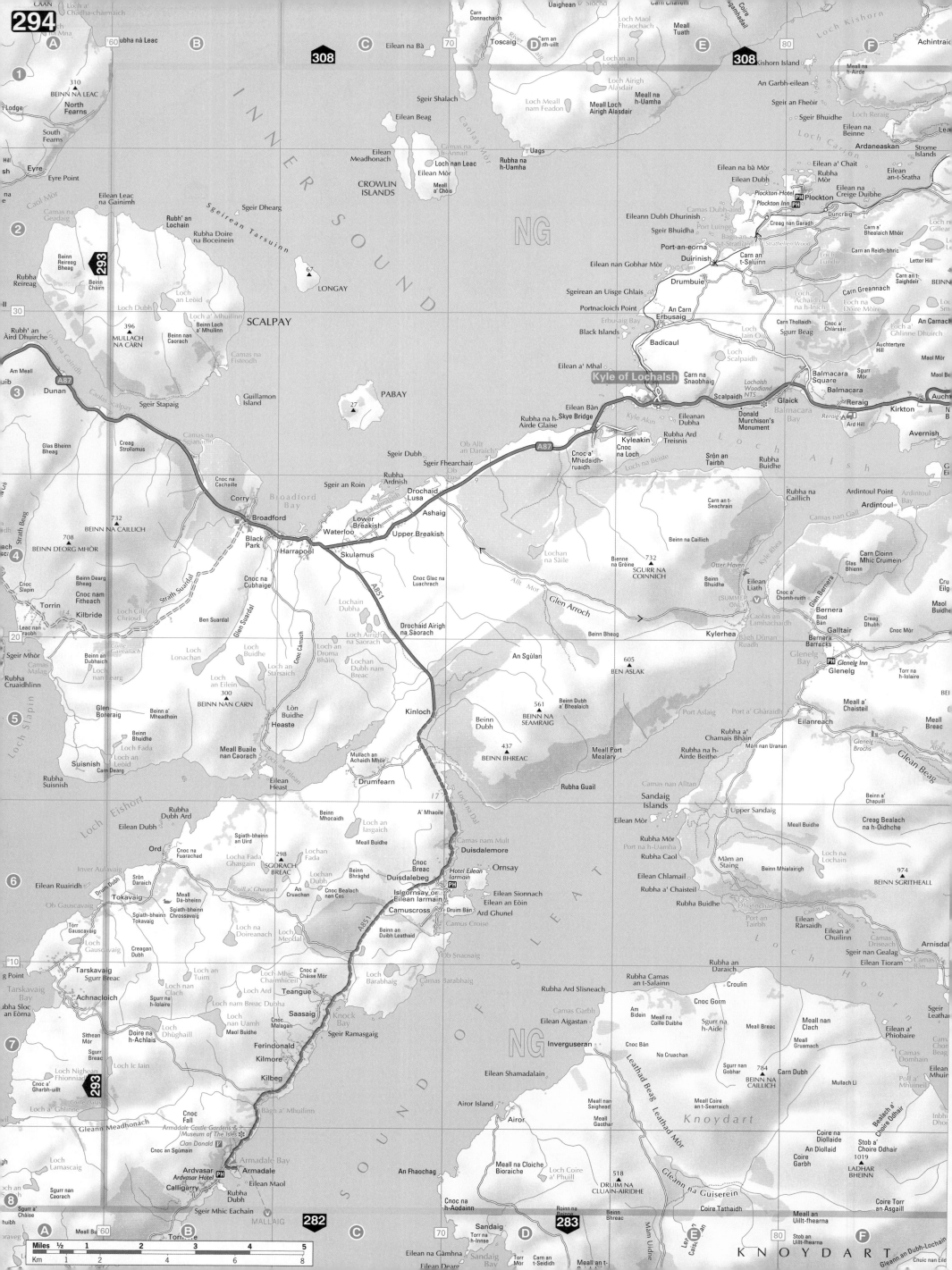

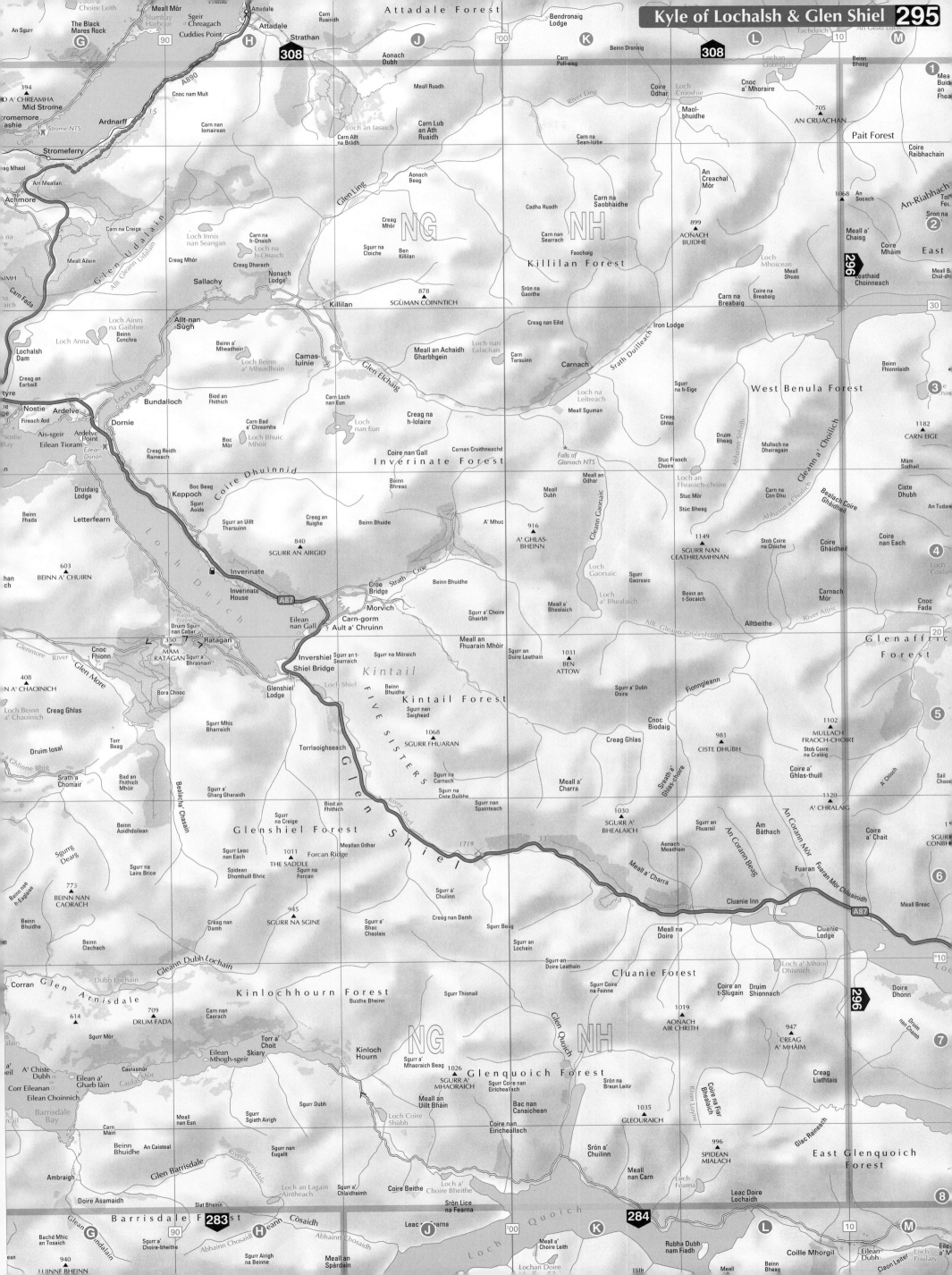

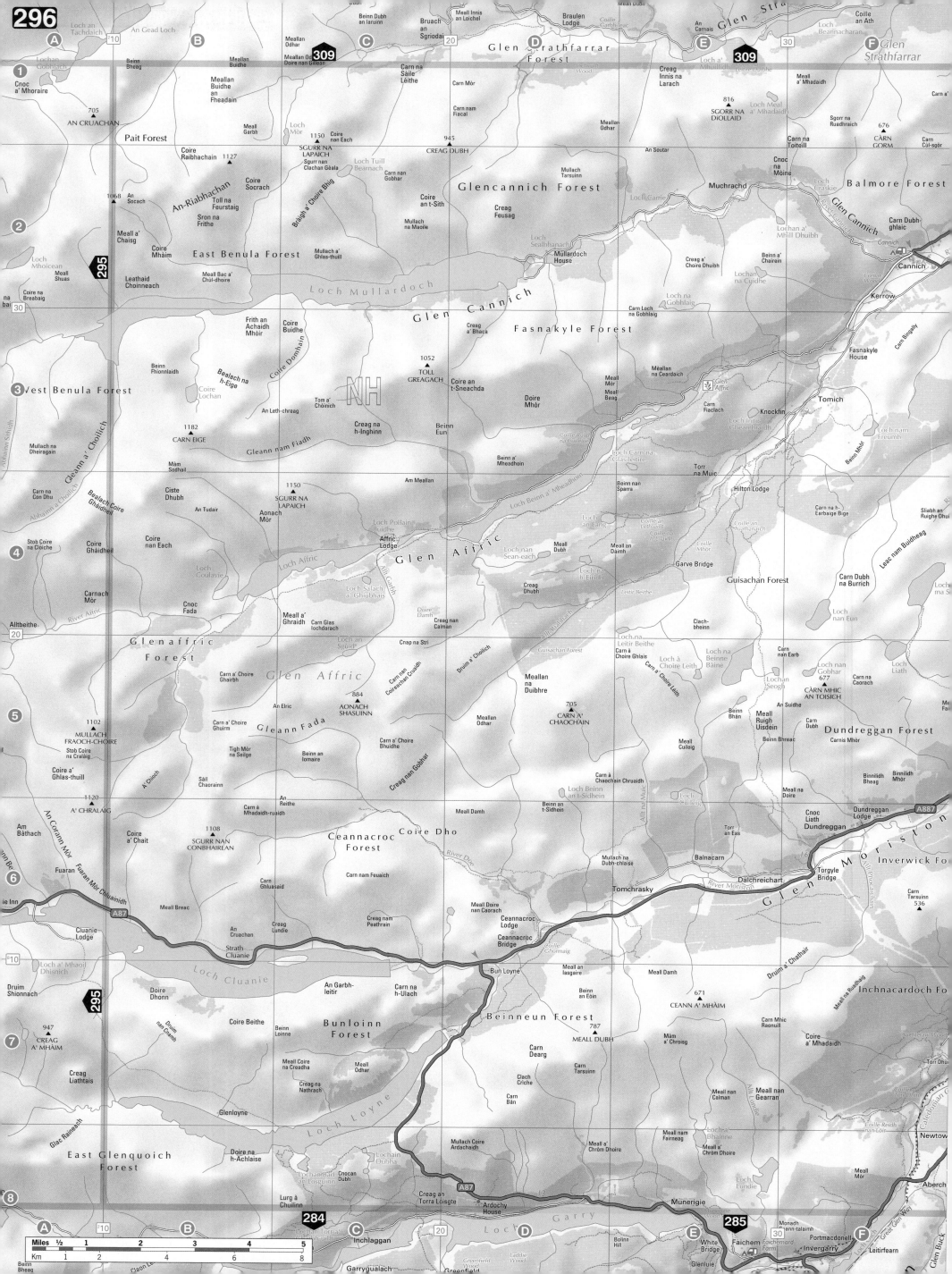

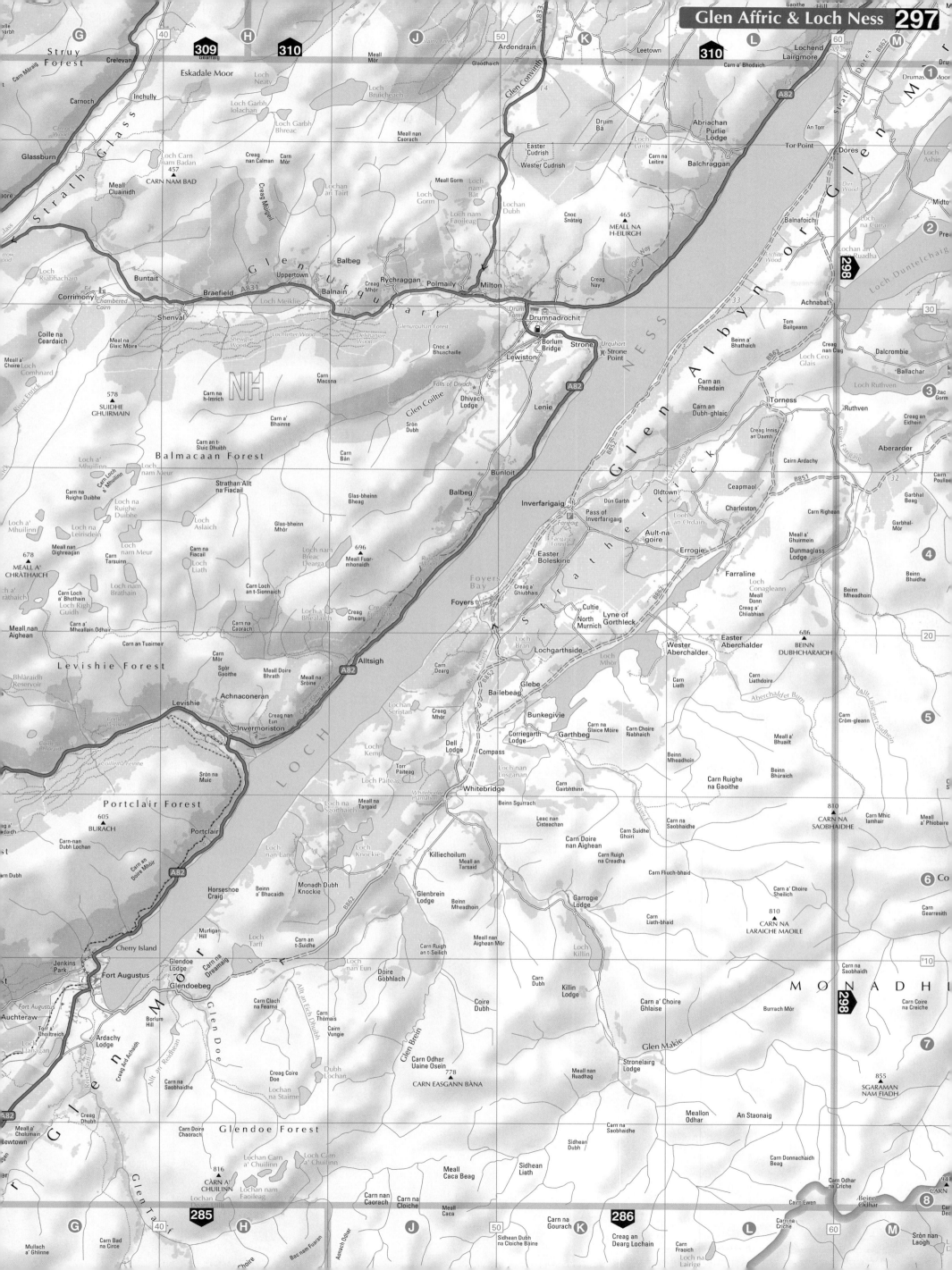

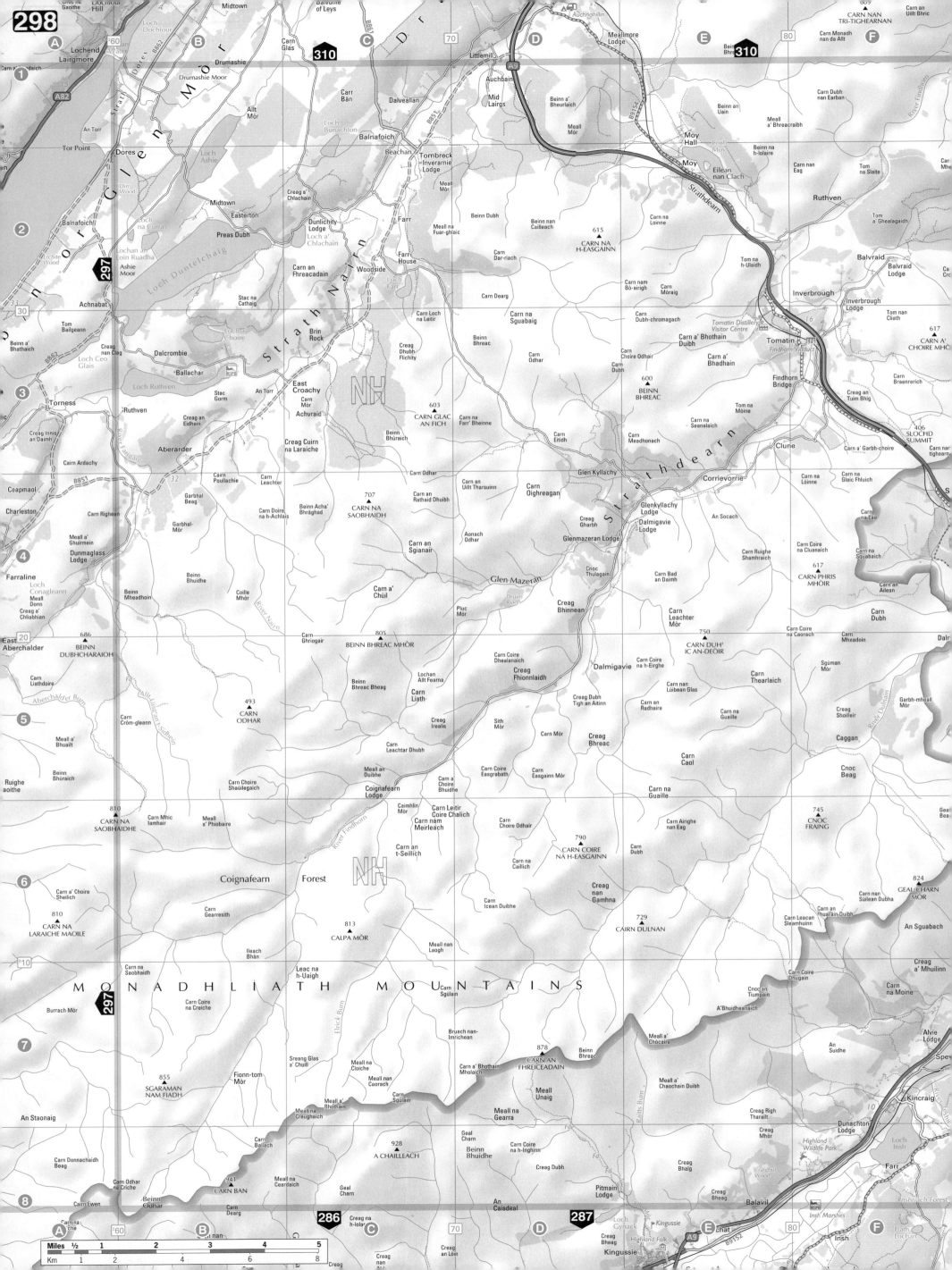

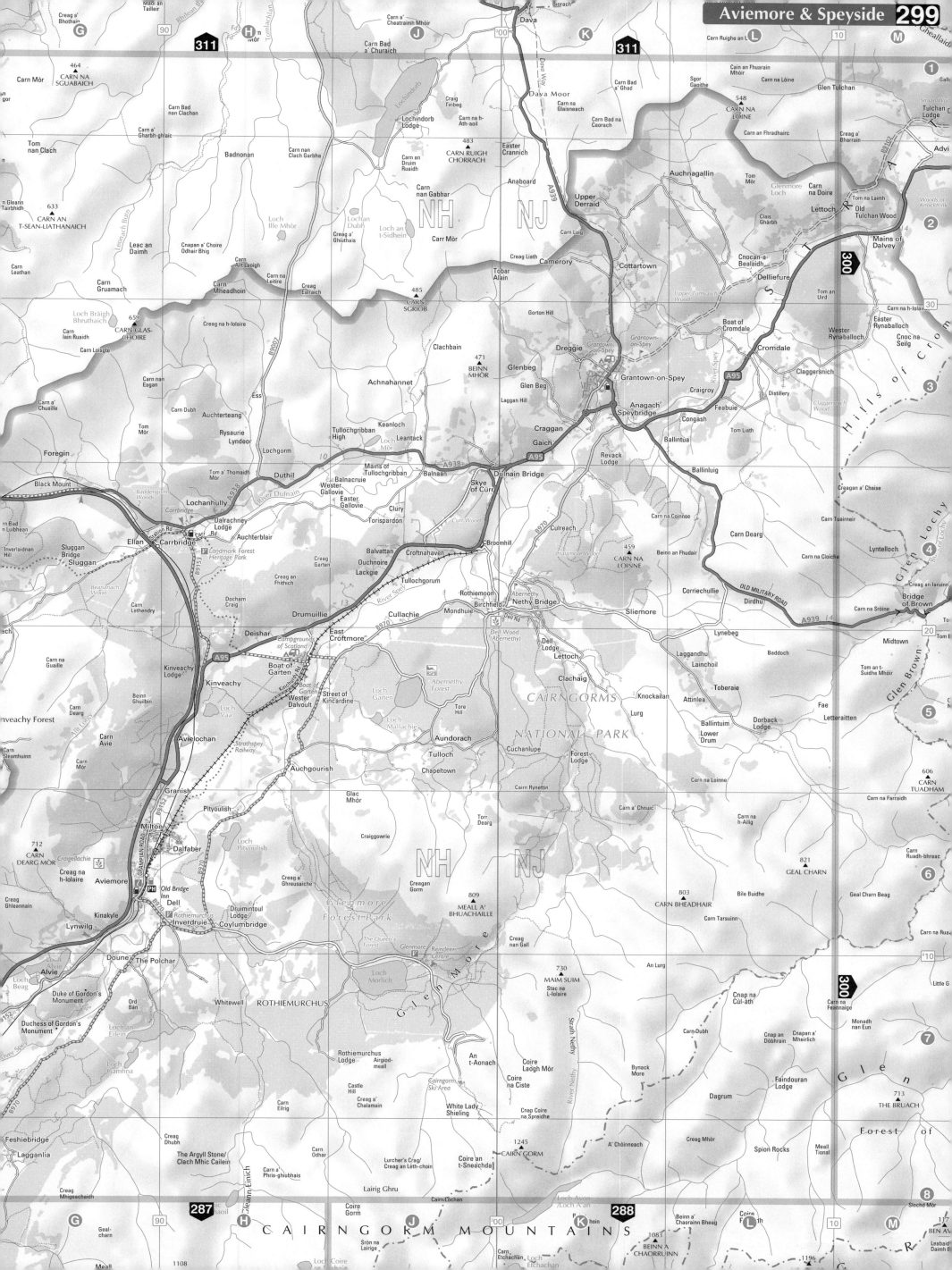

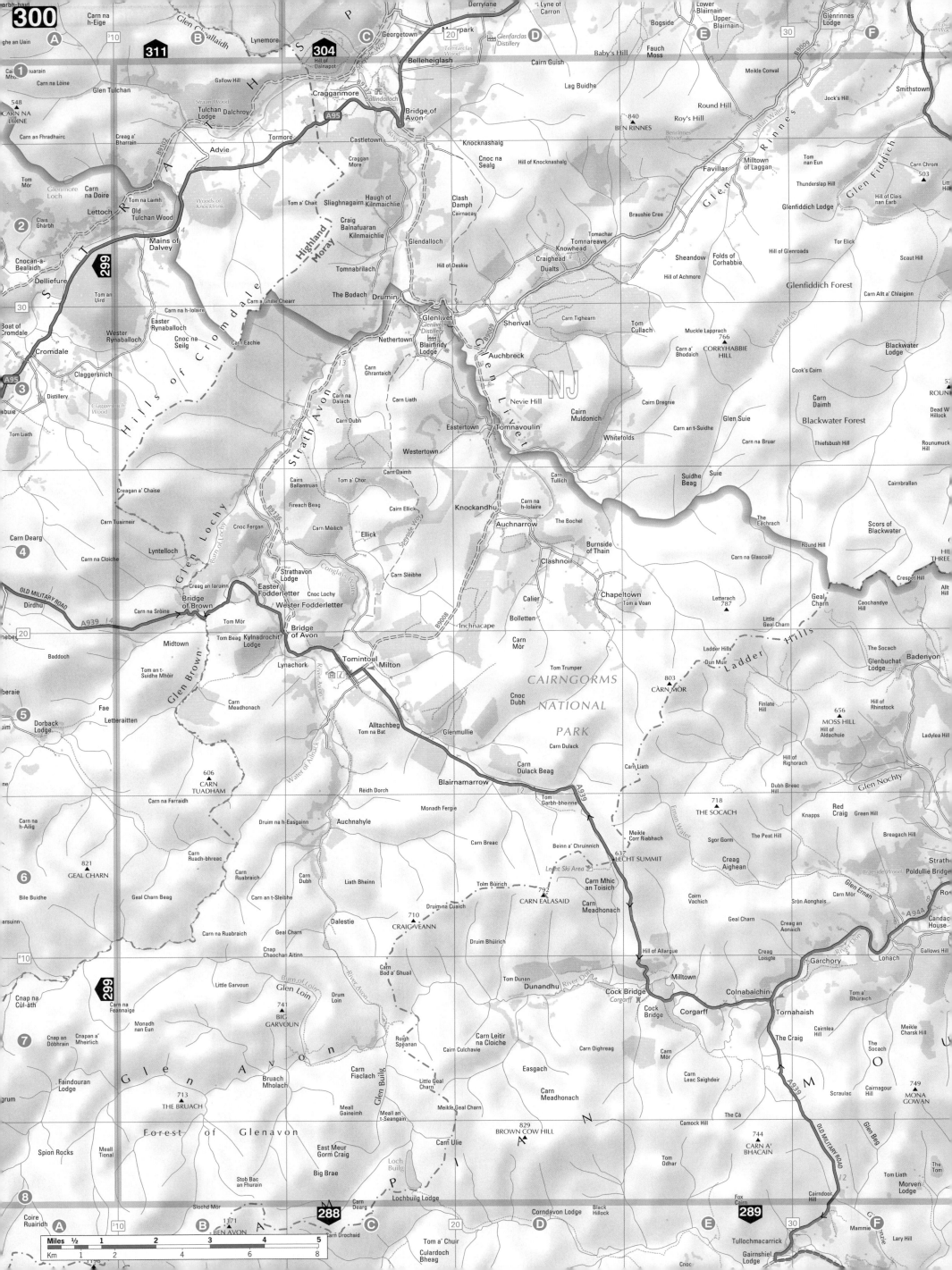

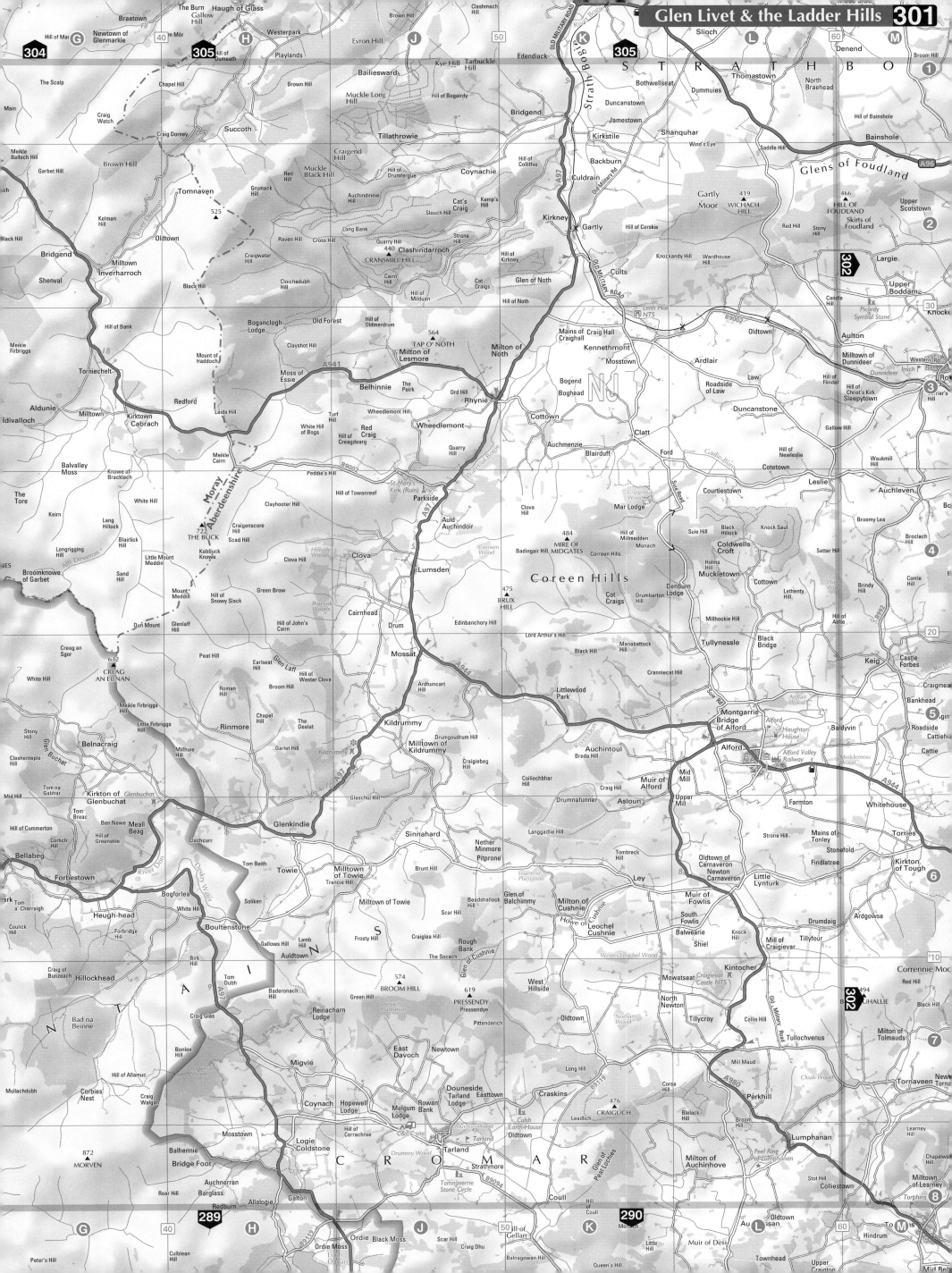

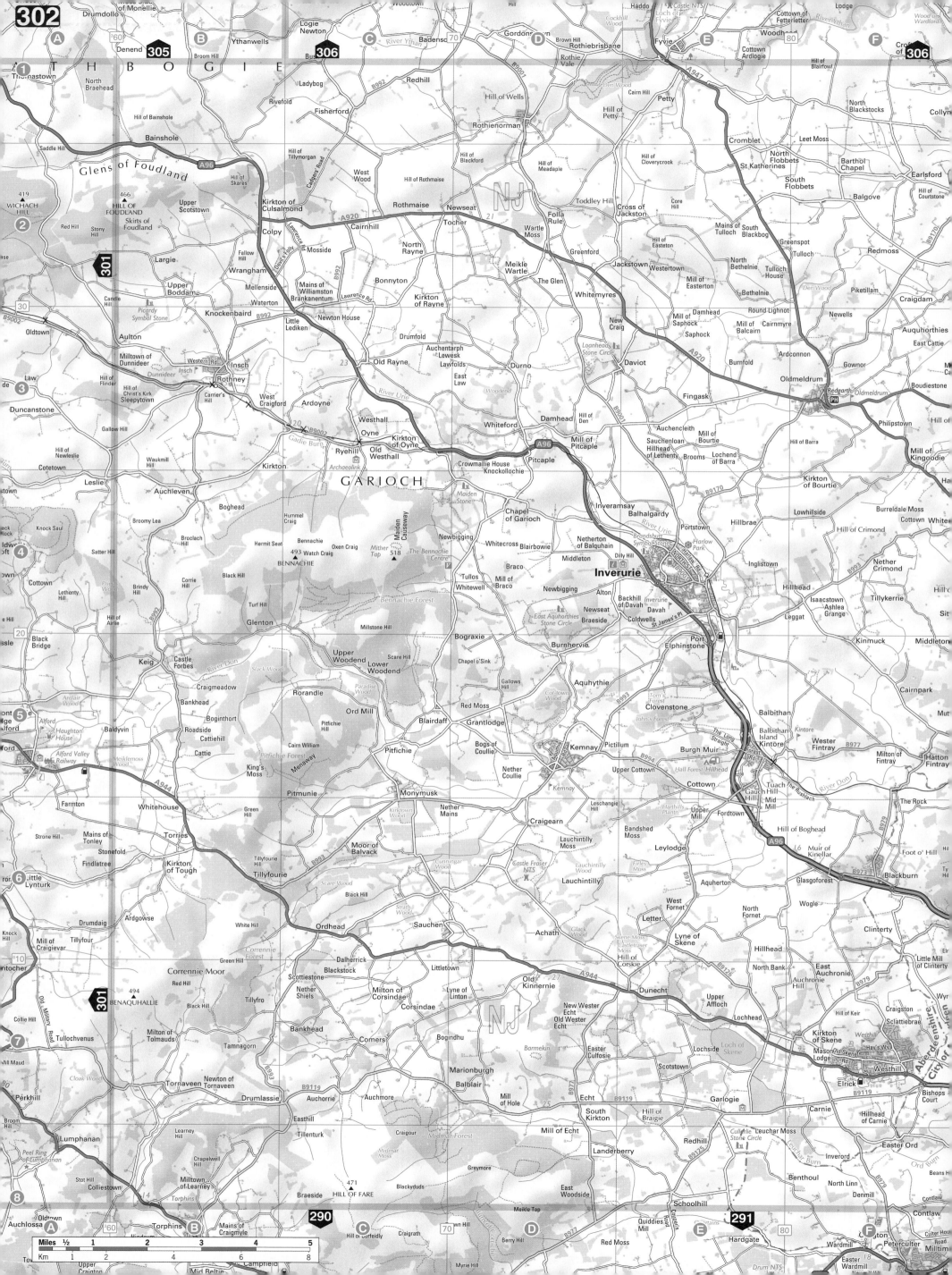

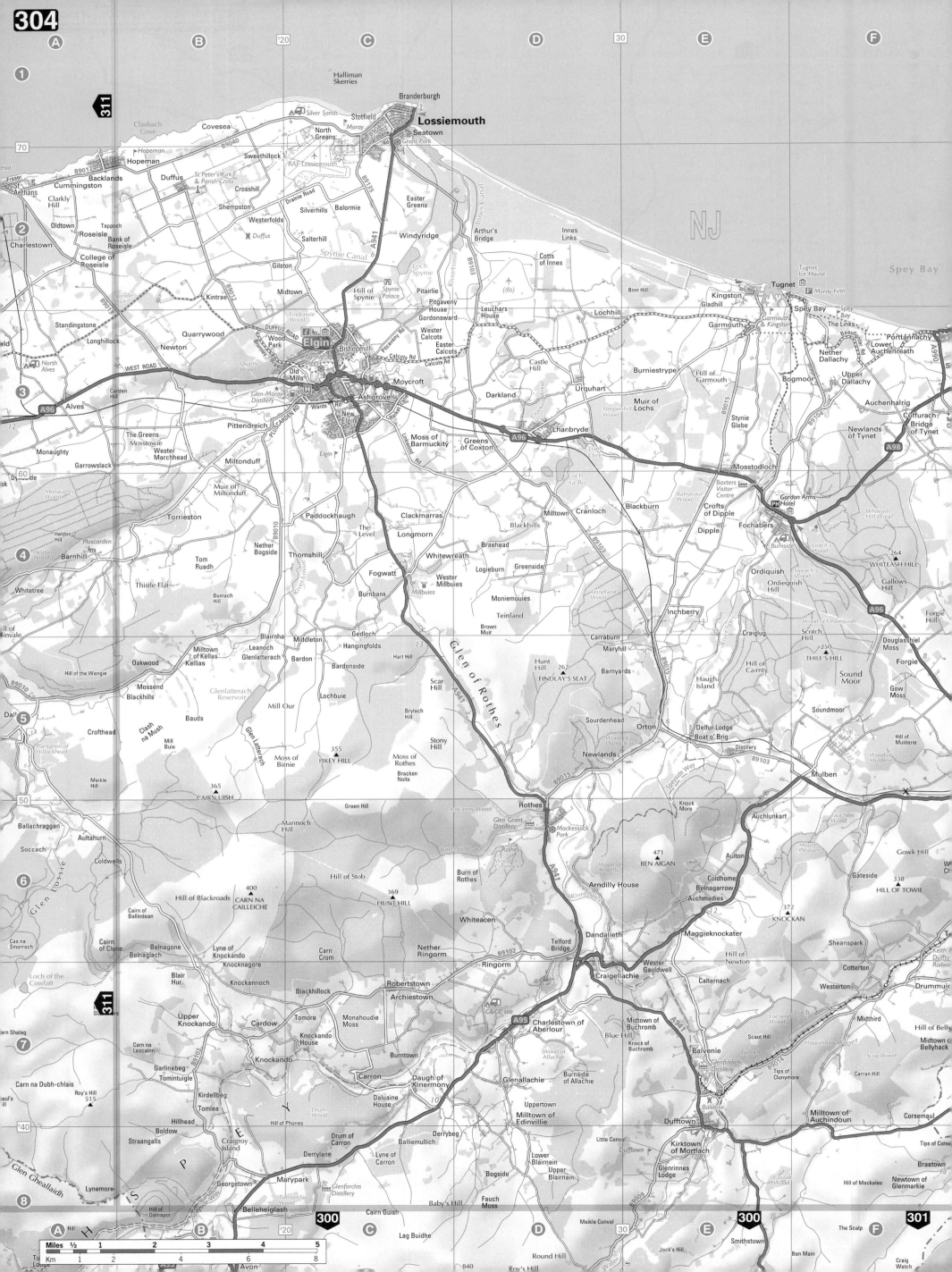

303

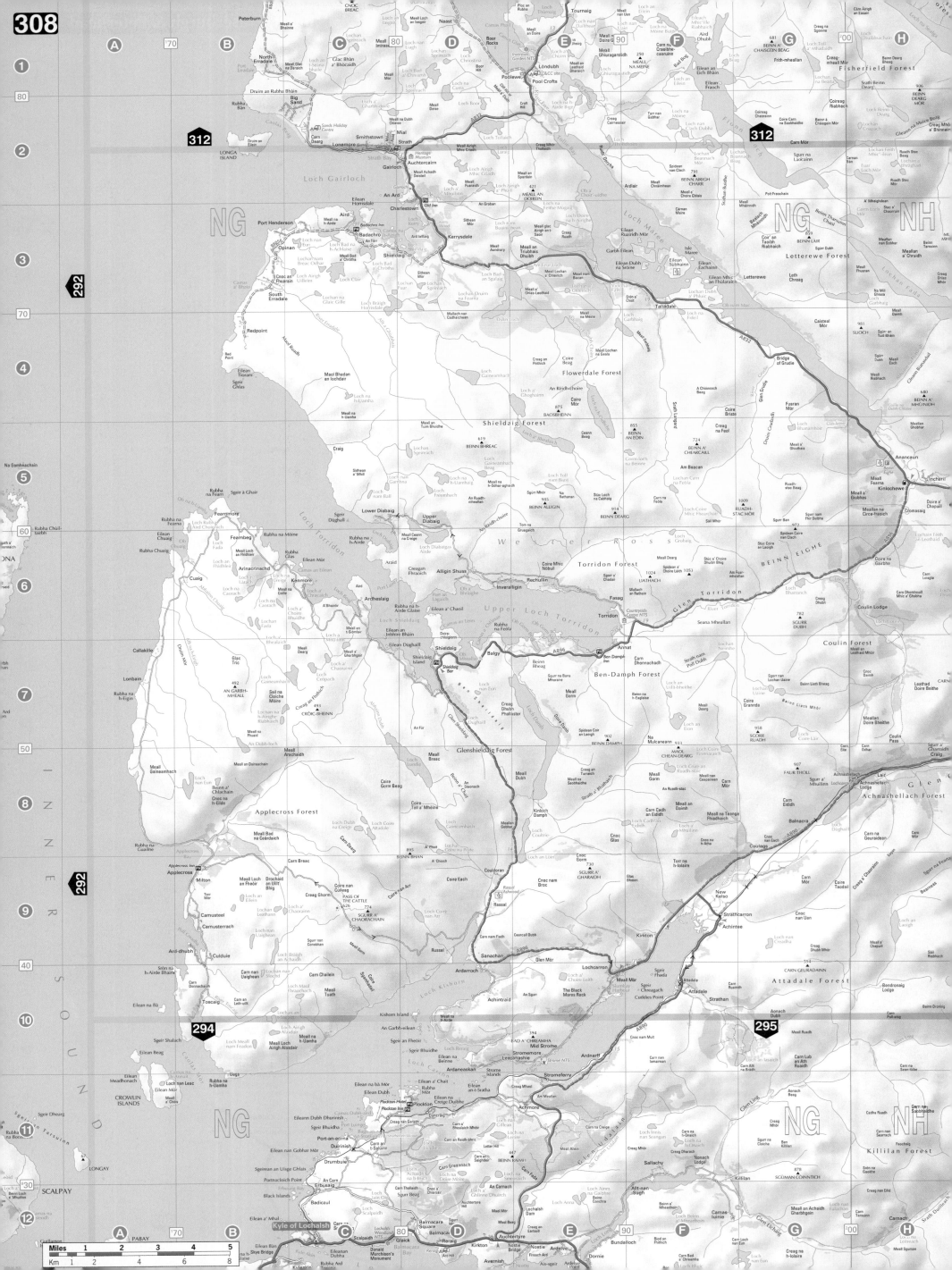

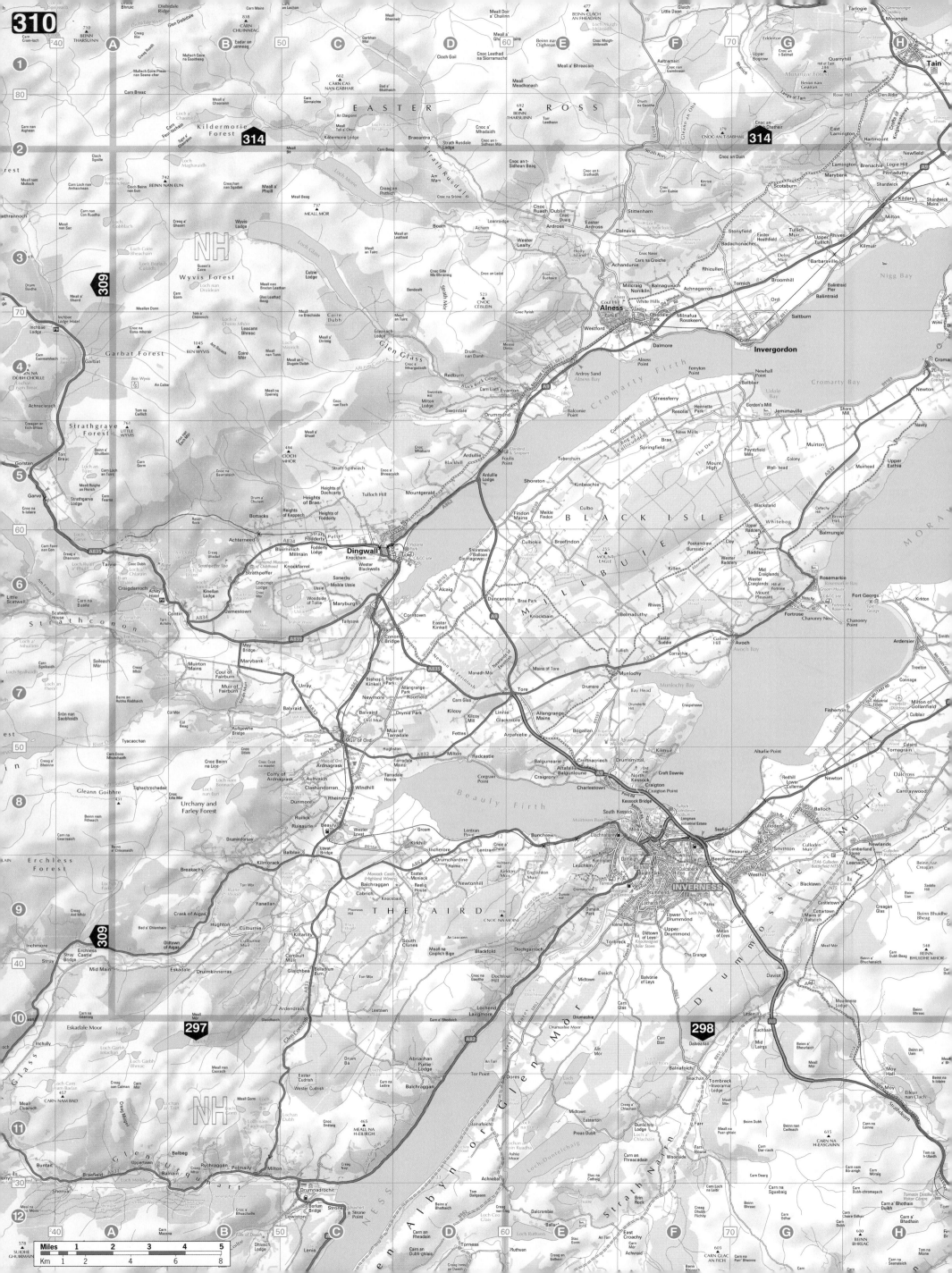

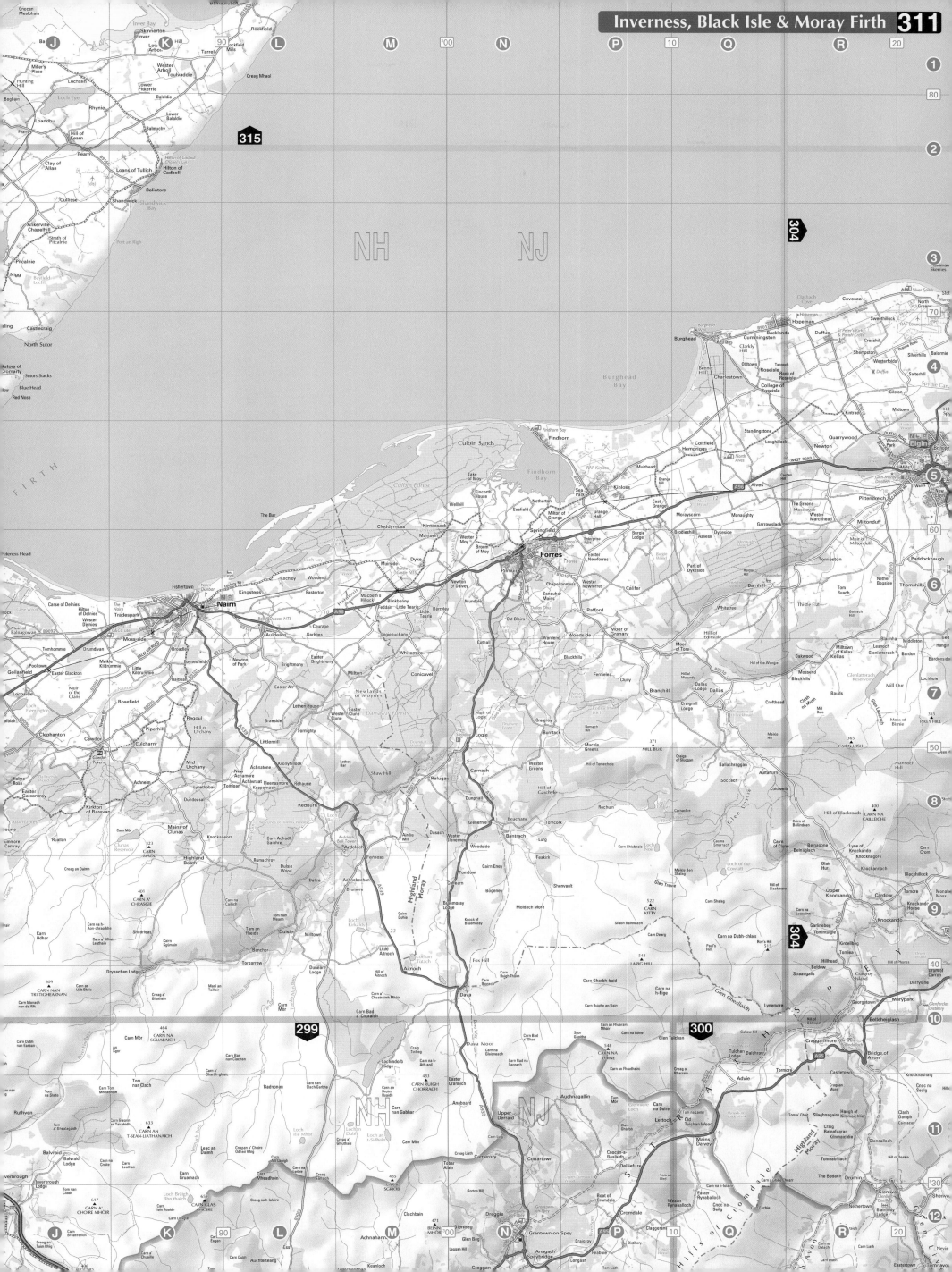

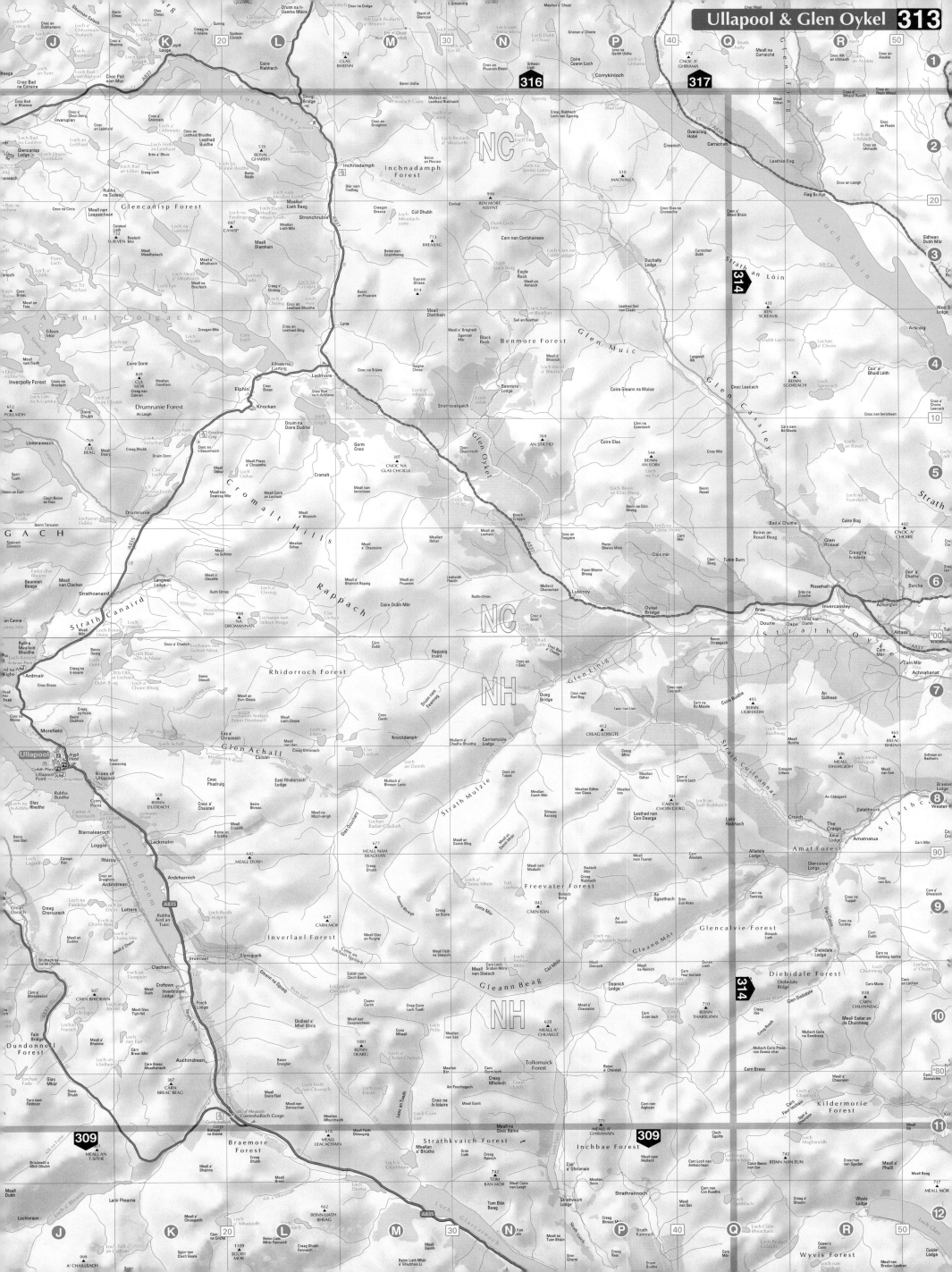

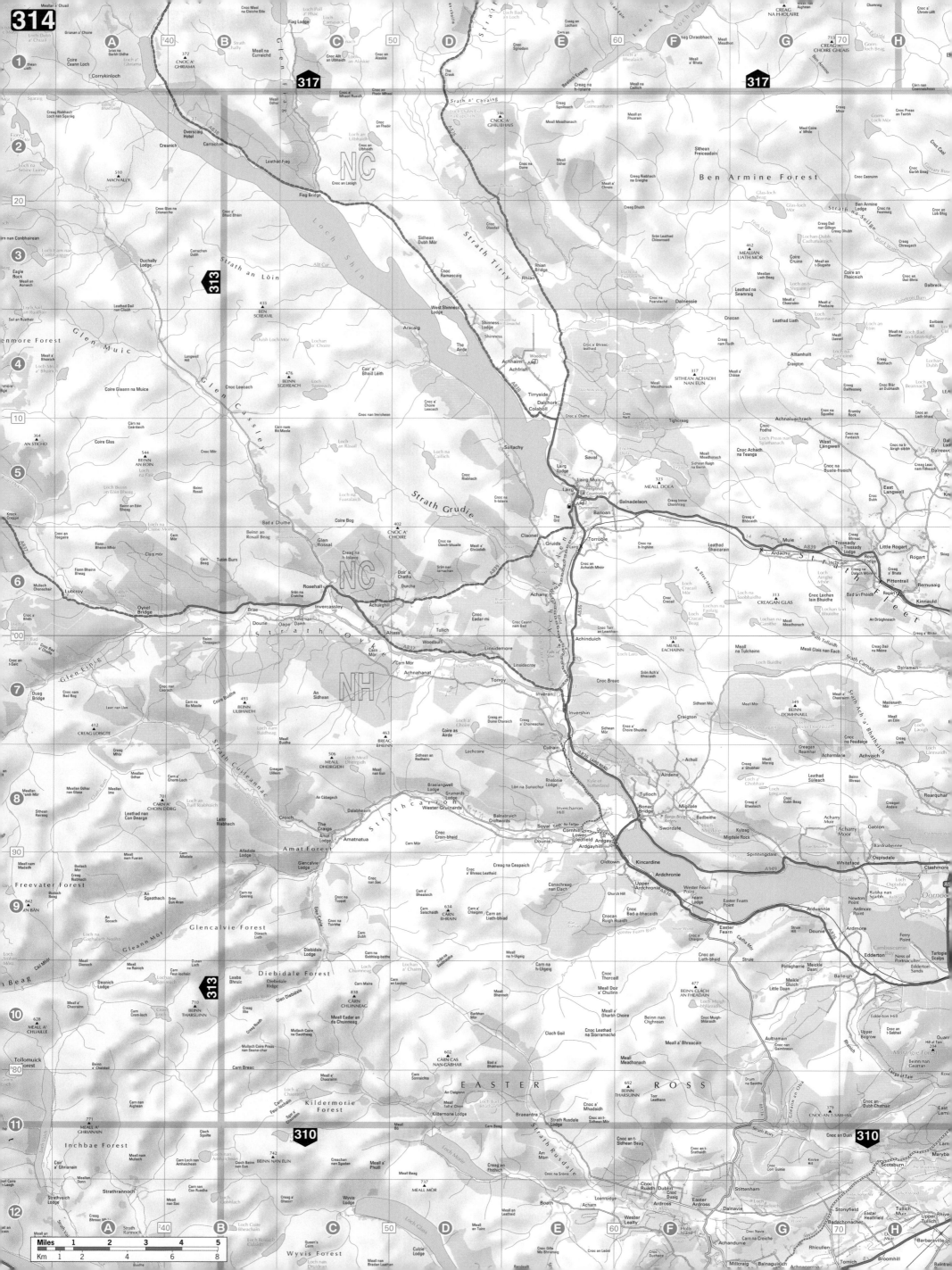

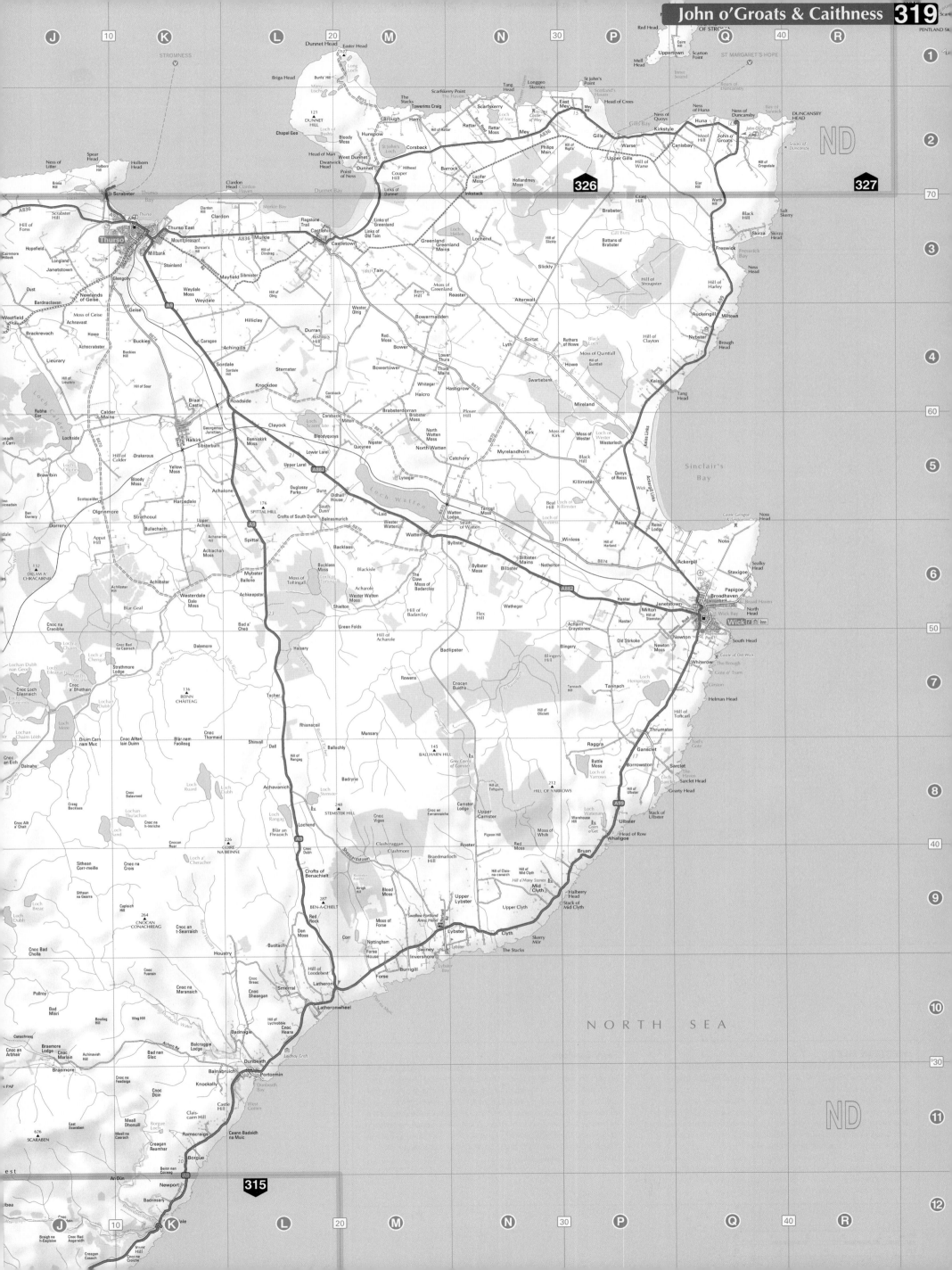

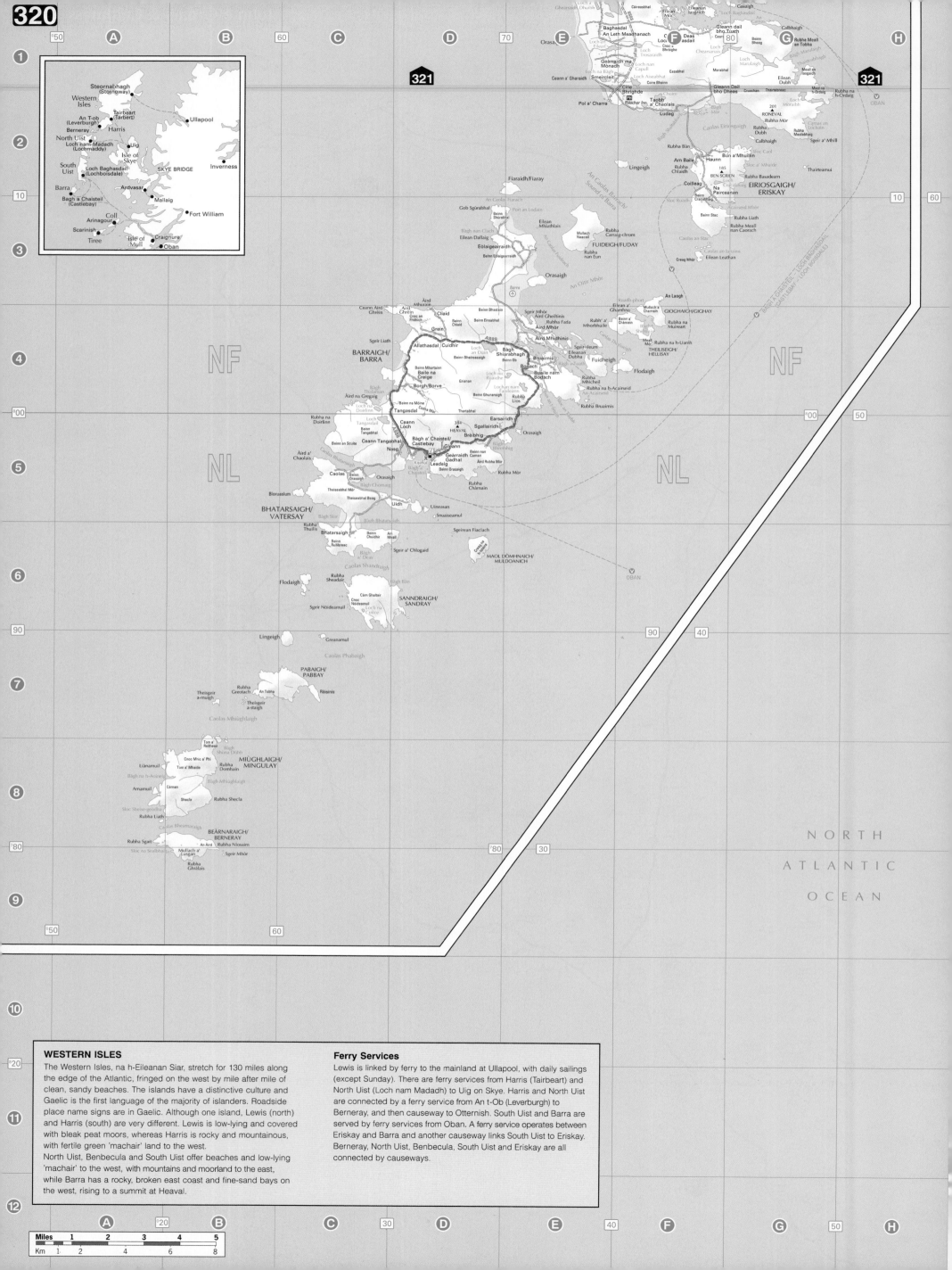

WESTERN ISLES

The Western Isles, na h-Eileanan Siar, stretch for 130 miles along the edge of the Atlantic, fringed on the west by mile after mile of clean, sandy beaches. The islands have a distinctive culture and Gaelic is the first language of the majority of islanders. Roadside place name signs are in Gaelic. Although one island, Lewis (north) and Harris (south) are very different. Lewis is low-lying and covered with bleak peat moors, whereas Harris is rocky and mountainous, with fertile green 'machair' land to the west.

North Uist, Benbecula and South Uist offer beaches and low-lying 'machair' to the west, with mountains and moorland to the east, while Barra has a rocky, broken east coast and fine-sand bays on the west, rising to a summit at Heaval.

Ferry Services

Lewis is linked by ferry to the mainland at Ullapool, with daily sailings (except Sunday). There are ferry services from Harris (Tairbeart) and North Uist (Loch nam Madadh) to Uig on Skye. Harris and North Uist are connected by a ferry service from An t-Ob (Leverburgh) to Berneray, and then causeway to Otternish. South Uist and Barra are served by ferry services from Oban. A ferry service operates between Eriskay and Barra and another causeway links South Uist to Eriskay. Berneray, North Uist, Benbecula, South Uist and Eriskay are all connected by causeways.

WESTERN ISLES

The Western Isles, na h-Eileanan Siar, stretch for 130 miles along the edge of the Atlantic, fringed on the west by mile after mile of clean, sandy beaches. The islands have a distinctive culture and Gaelic is the first language of the majority of islanders. Roadside place name signs are in Gaelic. Although one island, Lewis (north) and Harris (south) are very different. Lewis is low-lying and covered with bleak peat moors, whereas Harris is rocky and mountainous, with fertile green 'machair' land to the west.
North Uist, Benbecula and South Uist offer beaches and low-lying 'machair' to the west, with mountains and moorland to the east, while Barra has a rocky, broken east coast and fine-sand bays on the west, rising to a summit at Heaval.

Ferry Services

Lewis is linked by ferry to the mainland at Ullapool, with daily sailings (except Sunday). There are ferry services from Harris (Tairbeart) and North Uist (Loch nam Madadh) to Uig on Skye. Harris and North Uist are connected by a ferry service from An t-Ob (Leverburgh) to Berneray, and then causeway to Otternish. South Uist and Barra are served by ferry services from Oban. A ferry service operates between Eriskay and Barra and another causeway links South Uist to Eriskay. Berneray, North Uist, Benbecula, South Uist and Eriskay are all connected by causeways.

WESTERN ISLES

The Western Isles, na h-Eileanan Siar, stretch for 130 miles along the edge of the Atlantic, fringed on the west by mile after mile of clean, sandy beaches. The islands have a distinctive culture and Gaelic is the first language of the majority of islanders. Roadside place name signs are in Gaelic. Although one island, Lewis (north) and Harris (south) are very different. Lewis is low-lying and covered with bleak peat moors, whereas Harris is rocky and mountainous, with fertile green 'machair' land to the west.
North Uist, Benbecula and South Uist offer beaches and low-lying 'machair' to the west, with mountains and moorland to the east, while Barra has a rocky, broken east coast and fine-sand bays on the west, rising to a summit at Heaval.

Ferry Services

Lewis is linked by ferry to the mainland at Ullapool, with daily sailings (except Sunday). There are ferry services from Harris (Tairbeart) and North Uist (Loch nam Madadh) to Uig on Skye. Harris and North Uist are connected by a ferry service from An t-Ob (Leverburgh) to Berneray, and then causeway to Otternish. South Uist and Barra are served by ferry services from Oban. A ferry service operates between Eriskay and Barra and another causeway links South Uist to Eriskay. Berneray, North Uist, Benbecula, South Uist and Eriskay are all connected by causeways.

329

319

ORKNEY ISLANDS

Lying 20 miles north of the Scottish mainland, Orkney comprises 70 islands, 18 of which are inhabited, Mainland being the largest. Apart from Hoy, Orkney is generally green and flat, with few trees. The islands abound with prehistoric antiquities and rare birds. The climate is one of even temperatures and 'twilight' summer nights, but with violent winds at times.

Ferry Services

The main service is from Scrabster on the Caithness coast to Stromness and there is a further service from Gills to St Margaret's Hope on South Ronaldsay. A service from Aberdeen to Kirkwall provides a link to Shetland at Lerwick. Inter-island car ferry services are also operated (advance reservations recommended).

327

ORKNEY ISLANDS
Lying 20 miles north of the Scottish mainland, Orkney comprises
70 islands, 18 of which are inhabited, Mainland being the largest.
Apart from Hoy, Orkney is generally green and flat, with few trees.
The islands abound with prehistoric antiquities and rare birds. The
climate is one of even temperatures and 'twilight' summer nights,
but with violent winds at times.

Ferry Services
The main service is from Scrabster on the Caithness coast to
Stromness and there is a further service from Gills to St Margaret's
Hope on South Ronaldsay. A service from Aberdeen to Kirkwall
provides a link to Shetland at Lerwick. Inter-island car ferry services
are also operated (advance reservations recommended).

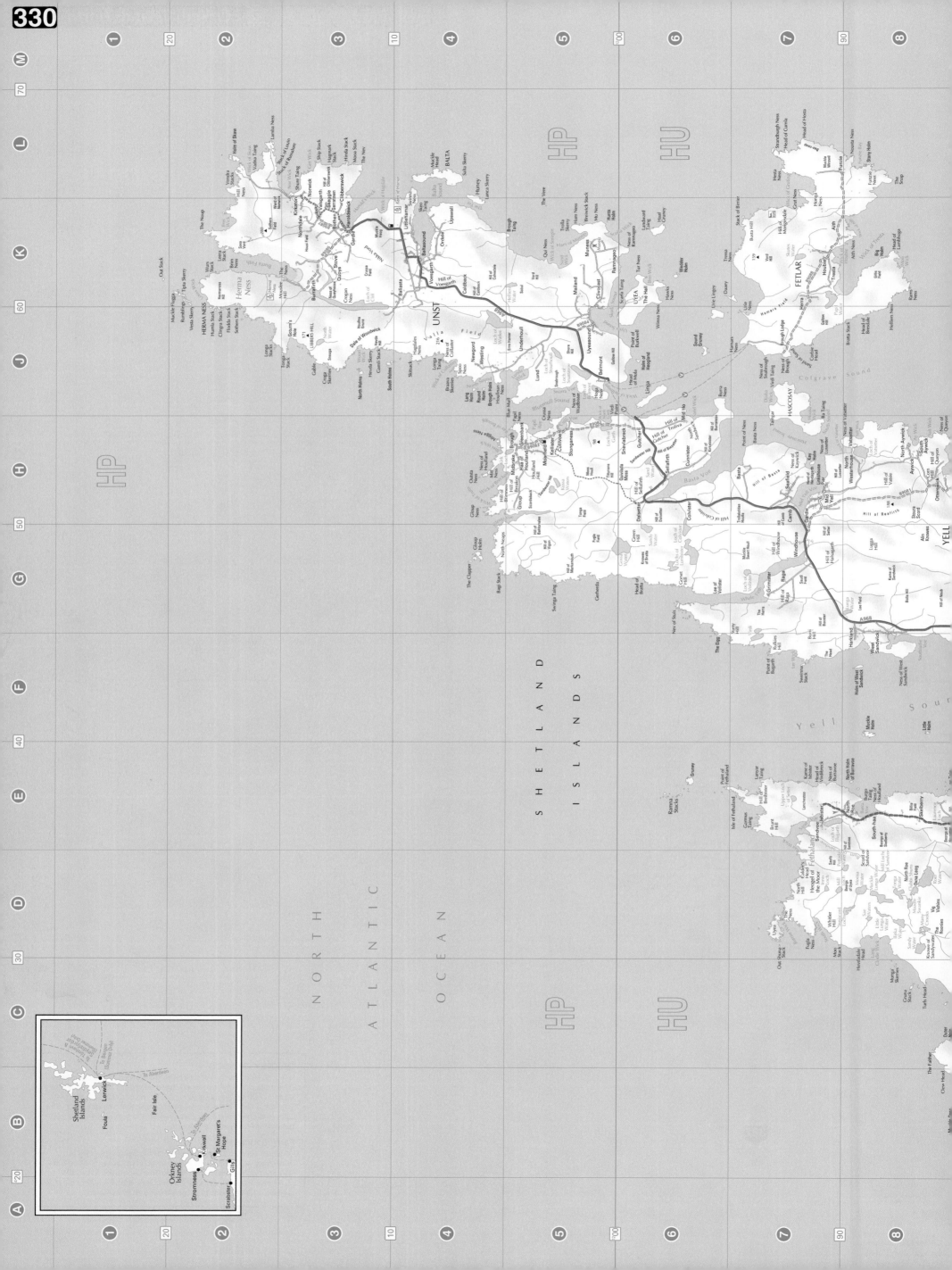

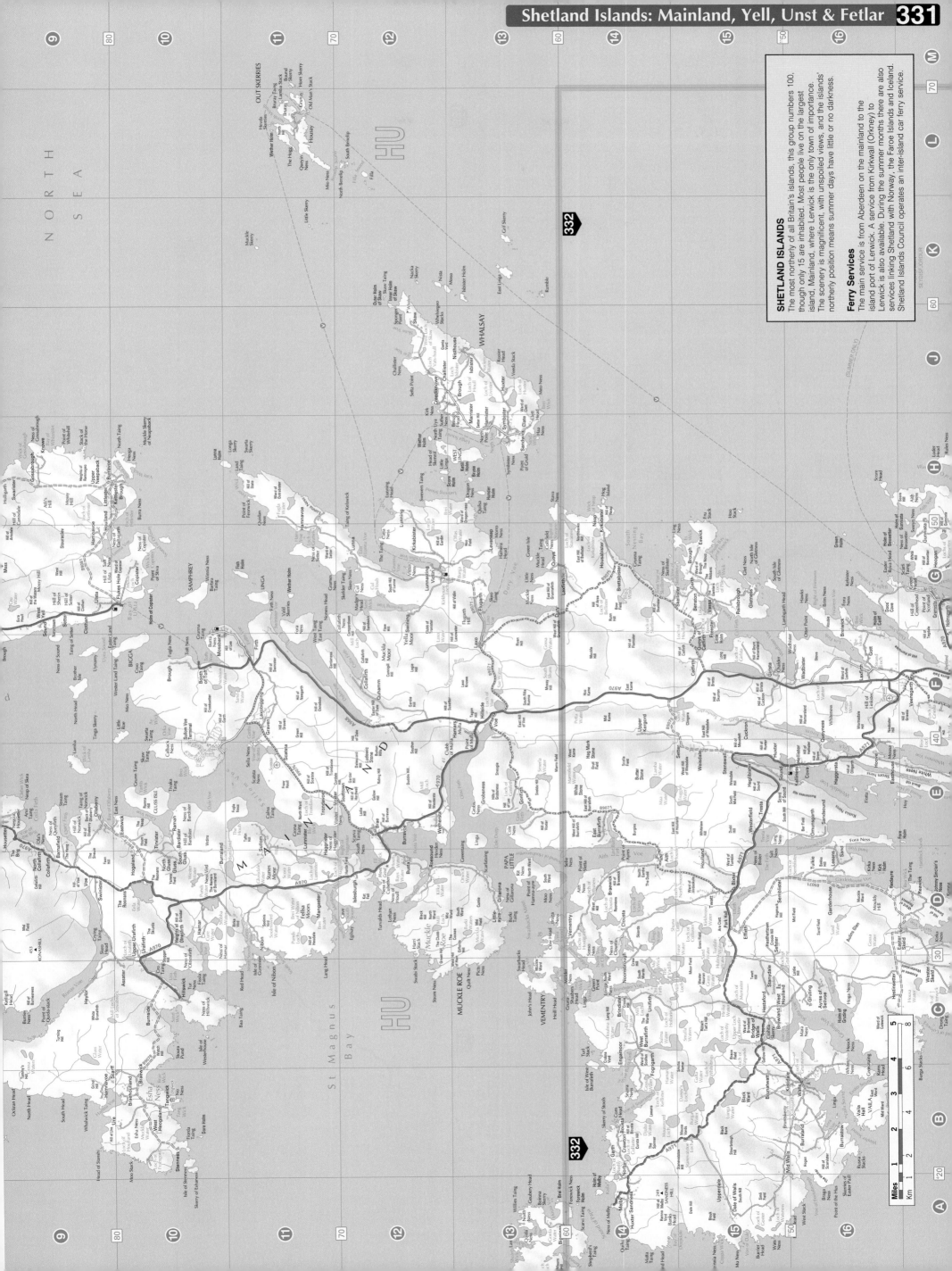

SHETLAND ISLANDS

The most northerly of all Britain's islands, this group numbers 100, though only 15 are inhabited. Most people live on the largest island, Mainland, where Lerwick is the only town of importance. The scenery is magnificent, with unspoiled views, and the islands' northerly position means summer days have little or no darkness.

Ferry Services

The main service is from Aberdeen on the mainland to the island port of Lerwick. A service from Kirkwall (Orkney) to Lerwick is also available. During the summer months there are also services linking Shetland with Norway, the Faroe Islands and Iceland. Shetland Islands Council operates an inter-island car ferry service.

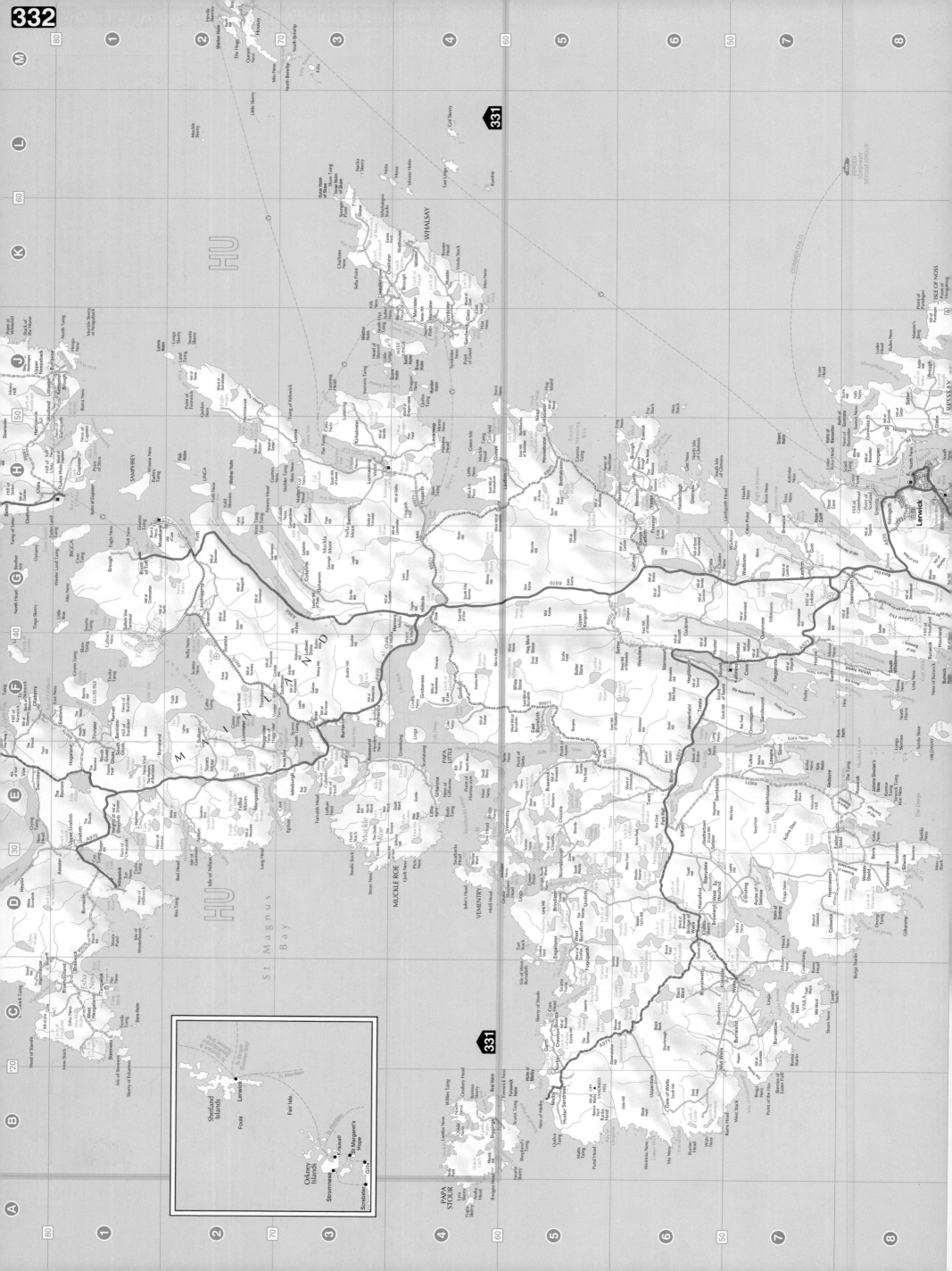

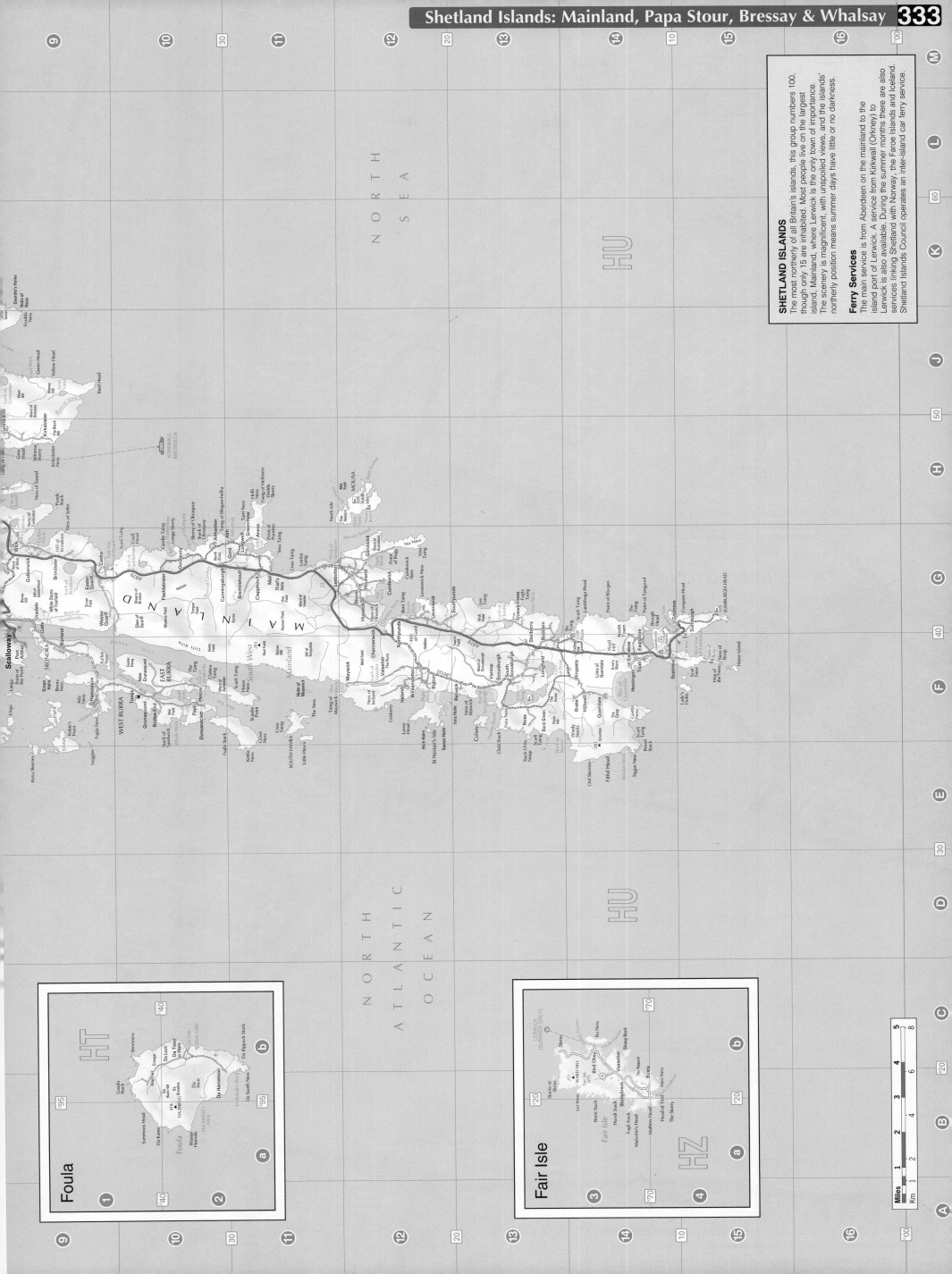

SHETLAND ISLANDS

The most northerly of all Britain's islands, this group numbers 100, though only 15 are inhabited. Most people live on the largest island, Mainland, where Lerwick is the only town of importance. The scenery is magnificent, with unspoiled views, and the islands' northerly position means summer days have little or no darkness.

Ferry Services

The main service is from Aberdeen on the mainland to the island port of Lerwick. A service from Kirkwall (Orkney) to Lerwick is also available. During the summer months there are also services linking Shetland with Norway, the Faroe Islands and Iceland. Shetland Islands Council operates an inter-island car ferry service.

Central London street index

In the index, street names are listed in alphabetical order and written in full, but may be abbreviated on the map. Each entry is followed by its Postcode District and each street name is preceded by the page number and the grid reference to the square in which the name is found.
Names are asterisked (*) in the index where there is insufficient space to show them on the map.

A

336 H13 Abbots Lane SE1
336 F10 Abchurch Lane EC4N
334 B5 Aberdeen Place NW8
335 R15 Abingdon Street SW1P
335 T3 Acton Street WC1X
334 A3 Ada Court NW8
334 J11 Adam's Row W1K
335 S11 Adam Street WC2R
336 B10 Addle Hill EC4V
336 D8 Addle Street EC2V
335 R11 Adelaide Street WC2N
335 Q7 Adeline Place WC1B
335 S11 Adelphi Terrace WC2N
336 L8 Adler Street E1
334 B6 Adpar Street W2
335 U1 Affleck Street N1
335 R11 Agar Street WC2N
336 A4 Agdon Street EC1V
335 V13 Alaska Street SE1
335 N11 Albany Courtyard W1J
334 L2 Albany Street NW1
335 M11 Albemarle Street W1S
336 A5 Albemarle Way EC1M
334 G14 Albert Gate SW1X
334 E10 Albion Close W2
334 E10 Albion Gate W2
334 E9 Albion Mews W2
336 A6 Albion Place EC1M
334 E9 Albion Street W2
335 S1 Albion Walk N1
336 C7 Albion Way EC1A
335 S1 Albion Yard N1
334 J8 Aldburgh Mews W1U
335 N1 Aldenham Street NW1
336 D8 Aldermanbury EC2V
336 D8 Aldermanbury Square EC2V
336 C6 Aldersgate Street EC1A
334 H12 Aldford Street W1K
336 H9 Aldgate EC3M
336 K8 Aldgate Barrs * E1
336 J9 Aldgate High Street EC3N
335 T9 Aldwych WC2B
334 B14 Alexandra Gate SW7
335 P6 Alford Place N1
335 P6 Alfred Mews W1T
335 P6 Alfred Place W1T
336 K9 Alie Street E1
336 K1 Allgood Street E2
336 E11 Allhallows Lane EC4R
334 D1 Allitsen Road NW8
334 D1 Allitson Road NW8
334 G5 Allsop Place NW1
334 L7 All Souls' Place W1B
334 A2 Alma Square NW8
336 E4 Alpha Close NW1
336 B9 Amen Corner EC4M
336 B9 Amen Court EC4M
336 J10 America Square EC3N
336 C13 America Street SE1
335 M1 Ampthill Estate NW1
335 N1 Ampthill Square NW1
335 T3 Ampton Street WC1X
335 V2 Amwell Street EC1R
336 D4 Anchor Yard EC1V
335 Q8 Andrew Borde Street WC2H
336 K7 Angel Alley E1
336 F8 Angel Court EC2R
336 E11 Angel Passage EC4R
335 X1 Angel Square * EC1V
336 C8 Angel Street EC1A
336 H4 Anning Street EC2A
334 G15 Ann's Close SW1X
336 L12 Anthony's Close E1W
335 X9 Apothecary Street EC4V
335 N12 Apple Tree Yard SW1Y
336 G6 Appold Street EC2A
334 K13 Apsley Way * W1J
335 W13 Aquinas Street SE1
335 P10 Archer Street W1D
334 E9 Archery Close W2
334 J11 Archibald Mews W1J
336 G1 Arden Estate N1
335 S2 Argyle Square WC1H
335 R2 Argyle Street NW1
335 R3 Argyle Walk WC1H
335 M9 Argyll Street W1B
336 H15 Arhchie Street SE1
335 M12 Arlington Street W1J
335 W2 Arlington Way EC1R
335 S9 Arne Street WC2H
336 J3 Arnold Circus E2
336 K15 Arnold Estate SE1
336 F11 Arthur Street EC4R
336 H7 Artillery Lane EC2M
336 H7 Artillery Passage E1
336 H8 Artizan Street E1
335 U10 Arundel Street WC2R
334 D5 Ashbridge Street NW8
336 B3 Ashby Street EC1V
336 G2 Ashford Street N1
334 H6 Ashland Place W1U
334 D6 Ashmill Street NW8
336 G2 Aske Street N1
336 L8 Assam Street E1
335 V4 Attneave Street WC1X
334 J12 Audley Square W1K
334 L1 Augustus Street NW1
336 F8 Austin Friars EC2N
336 F8 Austin Friars Square EC2N
336 J3 Austin Street E2
336 B9 Ave Marie Lane EC4M
334 K10 Avery Row W1K
334 H7 Aybrook Street W1U
335 X5 Aylesbury Street EC1R
336 D14 Ayres Street SE1

B

335 P12 Babmaes Street SW1Y
336 F3 Bache's Street N1
336 L9 Back Church Lane E1
335 W5 Back Hill EC1R
336 K4 Bacon Street E2
336 E14 Baden Place SE1
335 Q8 Bainbridge Street WC1A
336 D4 Baird Street EC1Y
334 H8 Baker's Mews W1U
336 J2 Bakers Rents E2
335 X5 Baker's Row EC1R
334 G5 Baker Street NW1
335 V5 Baker's Yard EC1R
334 F2 Balcombe Street NW1
334 J9 Balderton Street W1K
335 V6 Baldwin's Gardens WC1X
336 E3 Baldwin Street EC1V
335 S1 Balfe Street N1
334 J12 Balfour Mews W1K
334 J11 Balfour Place W1K
336 C5 Baltic Street East EC1Y
336 C5 Baltic Street West EC1Y
335 R10 Banbury Court WC2E
336 D12 Bank End SE1
336 C11 Bankside SE1
336 D5 Banner Street EC1Y
335 S6 Barbon Close WC1N
335 W12 Barge House Street SE1
334 L11 Barlow Place W1J
335 N1 Barnby Street NW1
336 L2 Barnet Grove E2
336 H14 Barnham Street SE1
336 K2 Baroness Road E2
335 W15 Baron's Place SE1
335 W1 Baron Street N1
334 J9 Barrett Street W1H
334 D1 Barrow Hill Estate NW8
334 D1 Barrow Hill Road NW8
335 W7 Barter Street WC1A
336 C7 Bartholomew Close EC1A
336 F8 Bartholomew Lane EC2R
336 D4 Bartholomew Square EC1V
335 W8 Bartlett Court EC4A
334 F15 Basil Street SW3
336 E8 Basinghall Avenue EC2V
336 E8 Basinghall Street EC2V
336 H2 Basing Place E2
336 B4 Bastwick Street EC1V
336 H4 Bateman's Row EC2A
335 P9 Bateman Street W1D
336 L1 Bath Grove E2
336 G3 Bath Place N1
336 D3 Bath Street EC1V
334 C10 Bathurst Mews W2
334 C10 Bathurst Street W2
336 G13 Battle Bridge Lane SE1
335 R1 Battle Bridge Road NW1
336 L2 Baxendale Street E2
335 P7 Bayley Street W1T
334 D10 Bayswater Road W2
335 M10 Beak Street W1B
336 C12 Bear Gardens SE1
336 B12 Bear Lane SE1
335 Q10 Bear Street WC2H
335 V7 Beauchamp Street EC1N
334 J6 Beaumont Mews W1U
335 N4 Beaumont Place W1T
334 J6 Beaumont Street W1U
336 E13 Bedale Street SE1
335 Q7 Bedford Avenue WC1B
335 R10 Bedfordbury WC2N
335 R11 Bedford Court WC2N
335 R8 Bedford Place WC1B
335 U6 Bedford Row WC1X
335 Q7 Bedford Square WC1B
335 R10 Bedford Street WC2E
335 Q5 Bedford Way WC1H
334 C5 Bedlow Close NW8
336 C6 Beech Street (Below) EC2Y
335 R2 Belgrove Street NW1
336 J7 Bell Lane E1
334 D6 Bell Street NW1
336 D11 Bell Wharf Lane EC4R
335 V9 Bell Yard WC2A
336 H15 Bell Yard Mews SE1
336 B15 Belvedere Buildings SE1
335 T14 Belvedere Road SE1
334 E5 Bendall Mews NW1
335 X6 Benjamin Street EC1M
336 B10 Bennet's Hill EC4V
335 M12 Bennett Street SW1A
334 J8 Bentinck Mews W1U
334 J8 Bentinck Street W1U
334 G8 Berkeley Mews W1H
334 L11 Berkeley Square W1J
334 L11 Berkeley Street W1J
336 G13 Bermondsey Street SE1
336 L14 Bermondsey Wall West SE16
335 R5 Bernard Street WC1N
335 N7 Berners Mews W1T
335 N8 Berners Place W1T
335 N7 Berners Street W1T
336 L9 Berner Terrace * E1
334 D4 Bernhardt Crescent NW8
336 B3 Berry Place EC1V
336 B5 Berry Street EC1V
335 N9 Berwick Street W1F
336 K4 Bethnal Green Road E2
335 R9 Betterton Street WC2H
336 F2 Bevenden Street N1
334 F7 Beverston Mews W1H
335 V1 Bevin Way N1
336 H8 Bevis Marks EC3A
334 G6 Bickenhall Street W1U
336 H15 Bickles Yard SE1
335 R3 Bidborough Street WC1H
336 H9 Billiter Square EC3M
336 H9 Billiter Street EC3M
334 H5 Bingham Place W1U
334 J10 Binney Street W1K
336 F9 Birchen Lane EC3V
335 N15 Birdcage Walk SW1H
334 J9 Bird Street W1U
335 S2 Birkenhead Street N1
334 A8 Bishop's Bridge Road W2
336 B8 Bishop's Court EC4M
336 H7 Bishopsgate EC2M
336 H6 Bishopsgate Arcade EC2M
336 C15 Bittern Street SE1
336 G4 Blackall Street EC2A
336 K2 Blackbird Yard E2
334 H10 Blackburne's Mews W1K
335 X11 Blackfriars Bridge SE1
336 A9 Black Friars Lane EC4V
336 A10 Blackfriars Passage EC4V
336 A12 Blackfriars Road SE1
336 B10 Blackfriars Underpass EC4V
336 K4 Blackmans Yard * E2
336 G14 Black Swan Yard SE1
334 E5 Blandford Square NW1
334 G8 Blandford Street W1U
335 W7 Bleeding Heart Yard EC1N
334 K9 Blenheim Street W1K
336 D1 Bletchley Street N1
334 A5 Blomfield Road W9
336 F7 Blomfield Street EC2M
334 L10 Bloomfield Place W1K
335 S7 Bloomsbury Place WC1A
335 S7 Bloomsbury Square WC1A
335 Q6 Bloomsbury Street WC1E
335 R7 Bloomsbury Way WC1A
336 H5 Blossom Street E1
336 L10 Blue Anchor Yard E1
335 M13 Blue Ball Yard SW1A
334 D5 Boldero Place NW8
334 D15 Bolney Gate SW7
334 L5 Bolsover Street W1W
335 W9 Bolt Court EC4A
334 L12 Bolton Street W1J
336 F5 Bonhill Street EC2A
336 C10 Booth Lane EC4V
336 G3 Boot Street N1
336 B1 Boreas Walk N1
336 D15 Borough High Street SE1
336 C15 Borough Square SE1
334 C6 Boscobel Street W2
336 J14 Boss Street SE1
334 F5 Boston Place NW1
335 S6 Boswell Court WC1N
335 S6 Boswell Street WC1N
336 G11 Botolph Alley EC3R
336 G11 Botolph Lane EC3R
335 X14 Boundary Row SE1
336 J3 Boundary Street E2
335 P10 Bourchier Street W1F
334 L10 Bourdon Place W1K
334 L10 Bourdon Street W1K
335 M7 Bourlet Close W1T
335 V6 Bourne Estate * EC1N
334 C8 Bouverie Place W2
335 W9 Bouverie Street EC4Y
336 D9 Bow Churchyard EC4M
334 G15 Bowland Yard SW1X
336 D9 Bow Lane EC4M
335 W5 Bowling Green Lane EC1R
336 E14 Bowling Green Place SE1
336 G2 Bowling Green Walk N1
336 L10 Bowmans Mews E1
335 S9 Bow Street WC2E
336 L9 Boyd Street E1
336 B15 Boyfield Street SE1
336 D6 Brackley Street EC2Y
335 W13 Brad Street SE1
336 K9 Braham Street E1
336 E6 Brandon Mews * EC2Y
336 L5 Bratley Street E1
335 S1 Bravingtons Walk N1
336 D10 Bread Street EC4V
335 V8 Bream's Buildings EC4A
334 E8 Brendon Street W1H
335 N10 Brewer Street W1B
336 B5 Brewery Square EC1V
336 J13 Brewery Square SE1
336 A4 Brewhouse Yard EC1V
335 V9 Brick Court * EC4Y
336 K5 Brick Lane E1
334 K13 Brick Street W1J
335 X9 Bride Court EC4V
335 X9 Bride Lane EC4Y
335 X1 Bridel Mews EC1V
335 X9 Bridewell Place EC4V
334 L6 Bridford Mews W1B
334 D1 Bridgeman Street NW8
335 R15 Bridge Street SW1P
336 C6 Bridgewater Square EC2Y
336 C6 Bridgewater Street EC2Y
335 N1 Bridgeway Street NW1
335 N10 Bridle Lane W1F
335 Q1 Brill Place NW1
336 A13 Brinton Walk SE1
336 A6 Briset Street EC1M
335 T2 Britannia Street WC1X
336 E1 Britannia Walk N1
335 X5 Britton Street EC1M
334 K10 Broadbent Street W1K
335 S9 Broad Court WC2E
334 D6 Broadley Street NW8
334 E5 Broadley Terrace NW8
334 H7 Broadstone Place W1U
336 G7 Broad Street Avenue EC2M
336 F7 Broad Street Place EC2M
335 W12 Broadwall SE1
335 P15 Broadway SW1H
335 N10 Broadwick Street W1F
335 X5 Broad Yard EC1M
336 C10 Broken Wharf EC4V
334 F15 Brompton Arcade SW1X
335 V6 Brooke's Market EC1N
335 V7 Brooke Street EC1N
334 G11 Brook Gate W2
334 A10 Brook Mews North W2
334 K10 Brook's Mews W1K
334 J10 Brook Street W1K
334 C10 Brook Street W2
334 J10 Brown Hart Gardens W1K
334 A5 Browning Close W9
334 J7 Browning Mews W1G
335 U4 Brownlow Mews WC1X
335 U7 Brownlow Street WC1R
334 F8 Brown Street W1H
336 J7 Brune Street E1
336 H15 Brunswick Court SE1
334 G8 Brunswick Mews W1H
336 F3 Brunswick Place N1
334 J5 Brunswick Place NW1
335 S4 Brunswick Square WC1N
336 H6 Brushfield Street E1
334 L11 Bruton Lane W1J
334 L11 Bruton Place W1J
334 L11 Bruton Street W1J
334 F7 Bryanston Mews East W1H
334 F7 Bryanston Mews West W1H
334 F7 Bryanston Place W1H
334 F8 Bryanston Square W1H
334 F9 Bryanston Street W1H
335 R11 Brydges Place WC2N
335 S11 Buckingham Street WC2N
336 F1 Buckland Street N1
336 E9 Bucklersbury EC4N
336 K8 Buckle Street E1
335 R8 Bucknall Street WC1A
336 E10 Budge Row EC4N
334 J7 Bulstrode Place W1U
334 J8 Bulstrode Street W1U
336 E4 Bunhill Row EC1Y
336 B9 Burgon Street EC4V
336 B9 Burgon Street Hill EC4V
335 S10 Burleigh Street WC2E
335 M11 Burlington Arcade W1S
335 M11 Burlington Gardens W1S
334 D6 Burne Street NW1
336 L12 Burr Close E1W
336 A12 Burrell Street SE1
335 X14 Burrows Mews SE1
336 G13 Bursar Street SE1
335 Q4 Burton Place WC1H
335 Q4 Burton Street WC1H
334 E8 Burwood Place W2
336 H8 Bury Court EC3A
335 R7 Bury Place WC1A
336 H9 Bury Street EC3A
335 M12 Bury Street SW1Y
336 E10 Bush Lane EC4R
336 K14 Butlers & Colonial Wharf SE1
336 F2 Buttesland Street N1
336 L5 Buxton Street E1
335 Q5 Byng Place WC1E
336 H11 Byward Street EC3R
335 M7 Bywell Place W1W

C

334 D7 Cabbell Street NW1
336 K1 Cadell Close E2
336 D5 Cahill Street EC1Y
335 S1 Caledonia Street N1
335 U4 Calthorpe Street WC1X
336 H3 Calvert Avenue E2
336 J5 Calvin Street E1
335 Q9 Cambridge Circus W1D
334 K3 Cambridge Gate NW1
334 L3 Cambridge Gate Mews NW1
334 D8 Cambridge Square W2
334 K3 Cambridge Terrace NW1
334 L3 Cambridge Terrace Mews NW1
336 J4 Camlet Street E2
336 H8 Camomile Street EC3A
336 K9 Camperdown Street E1
335 M7 Candover Street W1W
336 C9 Cannon Street EC4M
335 R15 Canon Row SW1A
336 C12 Canvey Street SE1
334 H15 Capener's Close SW1X
334 C4 Capland Street NW8
334 L6 Carburton Street W1W
335 N2 Cardington Street NW1
336 C8 Carey Lane EC2V
335 U9 Carey Street WC2A
336 H9 Carlisle Avenue EC3N
335 P9 Carlisle Street W1F
334 J11 Carlos Place W1K
335 P13 Carlton Gardens SW1Y
335 P13 Carlton House Terrace SW1Y
335 P11 Carlton Street SW1Y
335 W10 Carmelite Street EC4Y
335 M10 Carnaby Street W1B
336 H2 Caroline Gardens E2
334 K11 Carpenter Street W1K
334 K13 Carrington Street W1J
335 P15 Carteret Street SW1H
336 B9 Carter Lane EC4V
336 C6 Carthusian Street EC1M
335 S11 Carting Lane WC2R
335 R3 Cartwright Gardens WC1H
336 K10 Cartwright Street EC3N
334 D3 Casey Close NW8
334 E5 Casey Close NW8
336 L7 Casson Street E1
336 B10 Castle Baynard Street EC4V
336 F9 Castle Court EC3V
334 F8 Castlereagh Street W1H
336 B12 Castle Yard SE1
336 E12 Cathedral Street SE1
335 W4 Catherine Griffiths Court EC1R
335 T10 Catherine Street WC2B
336 H7 Catherine Wheel Alley EC2M
335 M13 Catherine Wheel Yard SW1A
334 E7 Cato Street W1H
335 T7 Catton Street WC1B
334 C1 Cavendish Avenue NW8
334 C2 Cavendish Close NW8
334 L6 Cavendish Mews North W1B
334 L7 Cavendish Mews South W1W
334 L8 Cavendish Place W1G
334 L8 Cavendish Square W1G
336 E1 Cavendish Street N1
336 H14 Cayenne Court SE1
336 E3 Cayton Street EC1V
335 R10 Cecil Court WC2H
336 C2 Central Street EC1V
335 W2 Chadwell Street EC1R
334 F5 Chagford Street NW1
335 Q2 Chalton Street NW1
336 L14 Chambers Street SE16
336 K10 Chamber Street E1
336 K3 Chambord Street E2
336 A12 Chancel Street SE1
335 U7 Chancery Lane WC2A
336 J4 Chance Street E2
335 R11 Chandos Place WC2N
334 L7 Chandos Street W1G
336 E14 Chapel Court SE1
334 K8 Chapel Place W1G
334 D7 Chapel Street NW1
335 W14 Chaplin Close SE1
335 R12 Charing Cross WC2N
335 Q8 Charing Cross Road W1D
335 P12 Charles II Street SW1Y
334 D1 Charles Lane NW8
335 N3 Charles Place NW1
336 F3 Charles Square N1
336 F3 Charles Square Estate N1
334 K12 Charles Street W1J
335 N6 Charlotte Mews W1T
335 N7 Charlotte Place W1T
336 G3 Charlotte Road EC2A
335 N6 Charlotte Street W1T
336 C5 Charterhouse Buildings EC1M
336 B6 Charterhouse Mews EC1M
335 W7 Charterhouse Street EC1N
336 F2 Chart Street N1
336 D9 Cheapside EC2V
335 P5 Chenies Mews WC1E
335 P6 Chenies Street W1T
336 E5 Chequer Street EC1Y
336 F1 Cherbury Street N1
336 D5 Cherry Tree Walk EC1Y
336 L4 Cheshire Street E2
334 J15 Chester Close SW1X
334 L2 Chester Close North NW1
334 L3 Chester Close South NW1
334 K12 Chesterfield Gardens W1J
334 K11 Chesterfield Hill W1J
334 K12 Chesterfield Street W1J
334 K3 Chester Gate NW1
334 K2 Chester Place NW1
334 J3 Chester Road NW1
334 K2 Chester Terrace NW1
335 U14 Chicheley Street SE1
336 L6 Chicksand Estate E1
336 K7 Chicksand Street E1
334 H6 Chiltern Street W1U
336 K4 Chilton Street E2
334 A9 Chilworth Mews W2
334 A9 Chilworth Street W2
336 E6 Chiswell Street EC1Y
335 N6 Chitty Street W1T
336 G4 Christina Street EC2A
335 Q2 Christopher Place NW1
336 F5 Christopher Street EC2A
334 C6 Church Street W2
334 C5 Church Street Estate NW8
335 Q2 Churchway NW1
334 F6 Circus Mews W1H
336 F7 Circus Place EC2M
334 B2 Circus Road NW8
336 B1 City Garden Row N1
335 X1 City Road EC1V
336 F6 City Road EC2A
335 W1 Claremont Close N1
335 V1 Claremont Square N1
334 L3 Clarence Gardens NW1
334 G4 Clarence Gate NW1
335 R1 Clarence Passage NW1
334 G4 Clarence Terrace NW1
334 D10 Clarendon Close W2
334 A5 Clarendon Gardens W9
334 D10 Clarendon Gate W2
334 D10 Clarendon Mews W2
334 D10 Clarendon Place W2
334 A4 Clarendon Terrace W9
334 K12 Clarges Mews W1J
334 L12 Clarges Street W1J
334 J6 Clarkes Mews W1G
335 M1 Clarkson Row NW1
334 G7 Clay Street W1U
335 U9 Clements Inn WC2A
336 F10 Clement's Lane EC4N
336 D14 Clennam Street SE1
334 F8 Clenston Mews W1H
336 F4 Clere Place EC2A
336 F4 Clere Street EC2A
335 W5 Clerkenwell Close EC1R
335 X5 Clerkenwell Green EC1R
335 V5 Clerkenwell Road EC1R
335 M6 Cleveland Mews W1T
335 N12 Cleveland Place SW1Y
335 N13 Cleveland Row SW1A
334 L5 Cleveland Street NW1
334 A8 Cleveland Terrace W2
335 M11 Clifford Street W1S
334 C10 Clifton Place W2
334 A4 Clifton Road W9
336 G6 Clifton Street EC2A
336 E12 Clink Street SE1
335 M5 Clipstone Mews W1W
334 L6 Clipstone Street W1W
336 D10 Cloak Lane EC4R
336 B7 Cloth Court EC1A
336 B7 Cloth Fair EC1A
336 H8 Clothier Street EC3A
336 C6 Cloth Street EC1A
336 J4 Club Row E2
336 F1 Clunbury Street N1
334 L10 Coach & Horses Yard W1S
336 J8 Cobb Street E1
335 N3 Cobourg Street NW1
334 C1 Cochrane Mews NW8
334 C1 Cochrane Street NW8
336 A7 Cock Lane EC1A
335 Q12 Cockspur Court SW1Y
335 Q12 Cockspur Street SW1Y
336 K5 Code Street E1
335 W13 Coin Street SE1
336 L8 Coke Street E1
336 K8 Colchester Street E1
335 V5 Coldbath Square EC1R
335 X1 Colebrooke Row N1
336 E8 Coleman Street EC2R
336 D15 Cole Street SE1
335 U5 Coley Street WC1X
336 K7 College East * E1
336 D10 College Hill EC4R
336 D10 College Street EC4R
335 T1 Collier Street N1
336 C15 Collinson Street SE1
336 C15 Collinson Walk SE1
335 X13 Colombo Street SE1
335 R5 Colonnade WC1N
334 L4 Colosseum Terrace NW1
336 J2 Columbia Road E2
335 N7 Colville Place W1T
336 L8 Commercial Road E1
336 J5 Commercial Street E1
334 L3 Compton Close NW1
336 B4 Compton Passage EC1V
335 R4 Compton Place WC1H
336 A4 Compton Street EC1V
336 L10 Conant Mews E1
335 U13 Concert Hall Approach SE1
335 R10 Conduit Court WC2E
334 B9 Conduit Mews W2
334 B9 Conduit Passage W2
334 B9 Conduit Place W2
334 L10 Conduit Street W1S
334 E9 Coniston Court W2
334 D9 Connaught Close W2
334 F10 Connaught Place W2
334 E9 Connaught Square W2
334 E9 Connaught Street W2
335 W14 Cons Street SE1
334 K14 Constitution Hill SW1A
335 M6 Conway Mews W1T
335 M5 Conway Street W1T
336 B1 Coombs Street N1
335 W15 Cooper Close SE1
335 Q1 Coopers Lane NW1
336 J10 Cooper's Row EC3N
336 B14 Copperfield Street SE1
336 J13 Copper Row SE1
336 F8 Copthall Avenue EC2R
335 R7 Coptic Street WC1A
335 W15 Coral Street SE1
335 R5 Coram Street WC1H
336 J6 Corbet Place E1
335 M11 Cork St Mews W1S
335 M11 Cork Street W1S
334 D6 Corlett Street W2
336 F9 Cornhill EC3V
335 V13 Cornwall Road SE1
334 G5 Cornwall Terrace NW1
334 G5 Cornwall Terrace Mews NW1
336 G3 Coronet Street N1
335 W4 Corporation Row EC1R
336 F3 Corsham Street N1
335 S6 Cosmo Place WC1B
334 E6 Cosway Street NW1
336 H2 Cotton's Gardens E2
336 G12 Counter Street SE1
336 E11 Cousin Lane EC4R
335 S10 Covent Garden WC2E
335 S10 Covent Garden Piazza WC2E
335 P11 Coventry Street W1J
335 X6 Cowcross Street EC1M
336 F4 Cowper Street EC1Y
336 J15 Coxson Way SE1
336 J1 Crabtree Close E2
335 R12 Craig's Court SW1A
334 J7 Cramer Street W1U
335 Q10 Cranbourn Street WC2H
335 W9 Crane Court EC4A
335 N1 Cranleigh Street NW1
336 F3 Cranwood Street EC1V
334 A10 Craven Hill W2
334 A10 Craven Hill Mews W2
334 A10 Craven Road W2
335 R12 Craven Street WC2N
334 A10 Craven Terrace W2
335 V5 Crawford Passage EC1R
334 E8 Crawford Place W2
334 F7 Crawford Street W1H
336 H9 Creechurch Lane EC3A
336 H9 Creechurch Place EC3A
336 B9 Creed Lane EC4V
336 J1 Cremer Street E2
336 J10 Crescent EC3N
336 C5 Crescent Row EC1Y
335 S2 Crestfield Street NW1
336 C6 Cripplegate Street EC2Y
336 J7 Crispin Street E1
336 L11 Crofts Street E1
336 L11 Croft Street E1
335 S3 Cromer Street WC1H
334 B5 Crompton Street W2
336 F1 Crondall Street N1
334 A3 Cropthorne Court NW8
336 E15 Crosby Row SE1
334 J7 Cross Keys Close W1U
336 J10 Crosswall EC3N
335 S9 Crown Court WC2B
335 V10 Crown Office Row EC4Y
335 N13 Crown Passage SW1Y
336 G5 Crown Place EC2A
336 G14 Crucifix Lane SE1
335 V2 Cruickshank Street WC1X
336 H10 Crutched Friars EC3R
335 U3 Cubitt Street WC1X
336 G10 Cullum Street EC3M
334 H11 Culross Street W1K
334 D1 Culworth Street NW8
335 U2 Cumberland Gardens WC1X
334 F10 Cumberland Gate W2
334 K2 Cumberland Gate NW1
334 L2 Cumberland Market NW1
334 K2 Cumberland Place NW1
334 K1 Cumberland Terrace NW1
334 K1 Cumberland Terrace Mews NW1
335 U1 Cumming Street N1
334 B4 Cunningham Place NW8
336 J14 Curlew Street SE1
335 V8 Cursitor Street EC4A
336 H4 Curtain Place EC2A
336 H3 Curtain Road N1
334 J13 Curzon Place W1K
334 J13 Curzon Street W1K
334 B6 Cuthbert Street W2
336 H8 Cutlers Gardens Arcade E1
336 H8 Cutler Street EC3A
336 K4 Cygnet Street E1
335 U1 Cynthia Street N1
336 B4 Cyrus Street EC1V

D

336 B4 Dallington Square EC1V
336 B5 Dallington Street EC1V
335 T7 Dane Street WC1R
335 P10 Dansey Place W1D
336 L6 Daplyn Street E1
335 N9 D'Arblay Street W1F
335 P15 Dartmouth Street SW1H
334 D6 Daventry Street NW1
336 A15 Davidge Street SE1
334 G6 David Mews W1U
334 K10 Davies Mews W1K
334 K10 Davies Street W1K
336 K1 Dawson Street E2
336 L6 Deal Street E1
334 J12 Deanery Mews W1K
334 J12 Deanery Street W1K
336 B9 Dean's Court EC4V
334 L8 Dean's Mews W1G
335 P8 Dean Street W1F
336 L2 Delta Estate * E2
336 L2 Delta Street E2
335 N11 Denman Street W1B
335 Q9 Denmark Street WC2H
334 A2 Denning Close NW8
335 R14 Derby Gate SW1A
334 J13 Derby Street W1J
336 H4 Dereham Place EC2A
334 K9 Dering Street W1S
335 V9 Devereux Court WC2R
334 K6 Devonshire Close W1G
334 K6 Devonshire Mews South W1G
334 J5 Devonshire Mews West W1G
334 J5 Devonshire Place W1G
334 J5 Devonshire Place Mews W1U
336 H7 Devonshire Row EC2M
336 H8 Devonshire Square EC2M
334 J6 Devonshire Street W1G
334 A9 Devonshire Terrace W2
334 J7 De Walden Street W1G
335 P8 Diadem Court W1D
334 L4 Diana Place NW1
336 L15 Dickens Estate SE1
335 X5 Dickens Mews * EC1M
336 D3 Dingley Place EC1V
336 C3 Dingley Road EC1V
336 D14 Disney Place SE1
336 D14 Disney Street SE1
336 J2 Diss Street E2
336 C10 Distaff Lane EC4V
336 K15 Dockhead SE1
336 L10 Dock Street E1
335 W15 Dodson Street SE1
336 B13 Dolben Street SE1
335 T6 Dombey Street WC1N
336 C4 Domingo Street EC1V
336 F6 Dominion Street EC2M
335 U1 Donegal Street N1
335 V12 Doon Street SE1
335 P2 Doric Way NW1
335 V6 Dorrington Street EC1N
336 D14 Dorrit Street SE1
335 X9 Dorset Buildings EC4Y
334 F6 Dorset Close NW1
335 X9 Dorset Rise EC4Y
334 F6 Dorset Square NW1
334 H7 Dorset Street W1U
335 T5 Doughty Mews WC1N
335 U5 Doughty Street WC1N
336 E9 Dove Court EC2R
335 M12 Dover Street W1J
336 E10 Dowgate Hill EC4R
335 R14 Downing Street SW1A
334 K13 Down Street W1J
334 K14 Down Street Mews W1J
336 C14 Doyce Street SE1
335 T7 Drake Street WC1N
336 J14 Druid Street SE1
335 P2 Drummond Crescent NW1
335 M4 Drummond Street NW1
336 K8 Drum Street E1
335 S8 Drury Lane WC1V
335 S9 Dryden Street WC2E
336 H2 Drysdale Place E2
336 H3 Drysdale Street N1
336 K3 Ducal Street E2
334 L7 Duchess Mews W1G
334 L7 Duchess Street W1B
335 W12 Duchy Street SE1
335 P9 Duck Lane W1F
334 B7 Dudley Street W2
336 E5 Dufferin Avenue EC1Y
336 D5 Dufferin Street EC1Y
335 N9 Dufour's Place W1F
334 J14 Duke of Wellington Place W1J
335 N12 Duke of York Street SW1Y
334 J8 Duke's Mews W1U
336 J9 Duke's Place EC3A
335 Q3 Duke's Road NW1
334 J8 Duke Street W1H
336 F12 Duke Street Hill SE1
335 N12 Duke Street St James's W1J
334 J10 Duke's Yard W1K
335 R11 Duncannon Street WC2N
335 X1 Duncan Terrace N1
336 J1 Dunloe Street E2
334 G10 Dunraven Street W1K
334 J6 Dunstable Mews W1G
336 G10 Dunster Court EC3M
336 F15 Dunsterville Way SE1
334 G15 Duplex Ride SW1X
336 L2 Durant Street E2
335 S11 Durham House Street WC2N
334 G6 Durweston Mews W1U
335 V7 Dyer's Buildings EC4A
335 Q7 Dyott Street WC1B
336 F5 Dysart Street EC2A

E

336 A6 Eagle Court EC1M
335 T7 Eagle Street WC1R
335 Q9 Earlham Street WC2H
336 A2 Earlstoke Estate EC1V
336 A2 Earlstoke Street EC1V
336 G6 Earl Street EC2A
335 Q8 Earnshaw Street WC1A
334 A8 Eastbourne Mews W2
334 A8 Eastbourne Terrace W2
335 M8 Eastcastle Street W1W
336 F10 Eastcheap EC3M
335 W8 East Harding Street EC4A
335 V4 Easton Street WC1X
336 C6 East Passage EC1A
336 A7 East Poultry Avenue EC1M
336 F2 East Road N1
336 K11 East Smithfield E1W
336 K9 East Tenter Street E1
336 E2 Ebenezer Street N1
336 J4 Ebor Street E2
334 B5 Edgware Road W2
334 F14 Edinburgh Gate W2
334 L2 Edward Mews NW1
334 H9 Edwards Mews W1H
336 J6 Elder Street E1
336 F7 Eldon Street EC2M
336 A1 Elia Mews N1
336 A1 Elia Street N1
334 A5 Elizabeth Close W9
334 B10 Elms Mews W2
335 U5 Elm Street WC1X
334 B2 Elm Tree Close NW8
334 B3 Elm Tree Road NW8
336 L2 Elwin Street E2
335 W7 Ely Place EC1N
335 S12 Embankment Place WC2N
335 T6 Emerald Street WC1N
336 C12 Emerson Street SE1
336 E15 Empire Square SE1
336 B4 Enclave Court EC1V
335 R8 Endell Street WC2H
335 P4 Endsleigh Gardens WC1H
335 Q4 Endsleigh Place WC1H
335 Q4 Endsleigh Street WC1H
334 F6 Enford Street W1H
334 D15 Ennismore Mews SW7
336 L10 Ensign Street E1
336 F5 Epworth Street EC2A
336 K3 Equity Square E2
336 D5 Errol Street EC1Y
335 V9 Essex Court * WC2R
335 V9 Essex Street WC2R
336 C3 Europa Place EC1V
335 M4 Euston Centre NW1
335 M4 Euston Road NW1
335 P3 Euston Square NW1
335 N4 Euston Street NW1
336 E1 Evelyn Walk N1
335 N1 Eversholt Street NW1
335 M3 Everton Buildings NW1
336 C13 Ewer Street SE1
335 Q11 Excel Court WC2H
336 G7 Exchange Arcade EC2M
335 S11 Exchange Court WC2E
336 H6 Exchange Square * EC2A
335 S10 Exeter Street WC2E
334 C15 Exhibition Road SW7
335 V4 Exmouth Market EC1R
335 N3 Exmouth Mews NW1
335 V13 Exton Street SE1
335 V5 Eyre Street Hill EC1R
336 K2 Ezra Street E2

F

336 E1 Fairbank Estate N1
336 H5 Fairchild Place EC2A
336 H5 Fairchild Street EC2A
336 H14 Fair Street SE1
335 P8 Falconberg Court W1D
336 B12 Falcon Close SE1
336 B1 Falcon Court N1
336 H1 Falkirk Street N1
336 C5 Fann Street EC1M
336 G2 Fanshaw Street N1
335 P8 Fareham Street W1F
334 K11 Farm Street W1J
336 B13 Farnham Place SE1
335 W5 Farringdon Lane EC1R
335 V4 Farringdon Road WC1X
335 X8 Farringdon Street EC1A
336 L15 Farthing Alley SE1
336 J7 Fashion Street E1
336 E4 Featherstone Street EC1Y
336 G9 Fenchurch Avenue EC3M
336 H9 Fenchurch Buildings EC3M
336 H10 Fenchurch Place EC3M
336 G10 Fenchurch Street EC3M
336 G14 Fenning Street SE1
335 V3 Fernsbury Street WC1X
335 W9 Fetter Lane EC4A
335 U7 Field Court WC1R
335 T2 Field Street WC1X
336 F9 Finch Lane EC3V
336 F7 Finsbury Avenue EC2M
336 F7 Finsbury Circus EC2M
335 W3 Finsbury Estate EC1R
336 G6 Finsbury Market EC2A
336 F6 Finsbury Pavement EC2A
336 F6 Finsbury Square EC2A

338 Central London index: Finsbury Street - Pall Mall East

336 E6 Finsbury Street EC1Y
335 T7 Fisher Street WC1B
334 B5 Fisherton Street NW8
336 F11 Fish Street Hill EC3R
334 H8 Fitzhardinge Street W1H
334 L12 Fitzmaurice Place W1J
335 M5 Fitzroy Mews W1W
335 M5 Fitzroy Square W1T
335 M5 Fitzroy Street NW1
336 L10 Flank Street E1
335 Q3 Flaxman Terrace WC1H
335 X8 Fleet Place EC4M
335 T3 Fleet Square WC1X
335 W9 Fleet Street EC4A
336 L5 Fleet Street Hill E2
335 H5 Fleur de Lis Street E1
335 Q9 Flitcroft Street WC2H
336 L14 Flockton Street SE16
335 S10 Floral Street WC2E
336 K7 Flower & Dean Walk E1
335 M7 Foley Street W1W
336 H6 Folgate Street E1
336 E7 Fore Street EC2Y
334 E8 Forset Street W1H
336 H7 Fort Street E1
336 D5 Fortune Street EC1Y
335 T14 Forum Magnum Square SE1
336 C8 Foster Lane EC2V
335 M9 Fouberts Place W1B
335 N4 Foundry Mews NW1
336 J6 Fournier Street E1
336 B6 Fox & Knot Street EC1M
334 C5 Frampton Street NW8
335 V15 Frazier Street SE1
334 E10 Frederick Close W2
336 E9 Frederick's Place EC2R
336 A2 Frederick's Row EC1V
335 T3 Frederick Street WC1X
334 H15 Frederic Mews SW1X
336 H3 French Place EC2A
336 B12 Friars Close * SE1
336 C10 Friday Street EC4V
335 X2 Friend Street EC1V
335 P9 Frith Street W1D
336 D6 Frobisher Crescent * EC2Y
336 K7 Frostic Walk E1
336 H7 Frying Pan Alley E1
336 L4 Fuller Close E2
336 F2 Fullwood's Mews N1
335 U7 Fulwood Place WC1R
335 V8 Furnival Street EC4A
336 C10 Fye Foot Lane EC4V

G

335 V12 Gabriel's Wharf SE1
336 J13 Gainsford Street SE1
336 C14 Gaitskell Way SE1
335 R7 Galen Place WC1A
336 D3 Galway Street EC1V
336 B13 Gambia Street SE1
335 M10 Ganton Street W1B
334 J6 Garbutt Place W1U
335 V10 Garden Court * WC2R
334 A2 Garden Road NW8
336 G4 Garden Walk EC2A
336 C10 Gardners Lane EC4V
336 B2 Gard Street EC1V
336 D10 Garlick Hill EC4V
335 W3 Garnault Mews EC1R
335 W3 Garnault Place EC1R
336 C6 Garrett Street EC1Y
335 R10 Garrick Street WC2E
335 R10 Garrick Yard WC2N
336 J2 Gascoigne Place E2
334 D5 Gateforth Street NW8
336 D12 Gatehouse Square SE1
334 E15 Gate Mews SW7
335 T8 Gate Street WC1V
334 J9 Gees Court W1U
336 C4 Gee Street EC1V
336 H1 Geffrye Estate N1
335 M3 George Mews NW1
336 L15 George Row SE16
334 F8 George Street W1H
336 F9 George Yard EC3V
334 J10 George Yard W1K
336 K2 Georgina Gardens * E2
335 Q10 Gerrard Place W1D
335 P10 Gerrard Street W1D
335 W15 Gerridge Street SE1
336 K3 Gibraltar Walk E2
335 R7 Gilbert Place WC1A
334 J9 Gilbert Street W1K
334 L7 Gildea Street W1B
334 A7 Gilpin Close W2
336 B8 Giltspur Street EC1A
336 B14 Glasshill Street SE1
335 N11 Glasshouse Street W1B
336 C5 Glasshouse Yard EC1A
334 G5 Glentworth Street NW1
336 E15 Globe Street SE1
336 H11 Gloucester Court EC3R
334 A9 Gloucester Mews W2
334 F4 Gloucester Place NW1
334 G7 Gloucester Place Mews W1H
334 C9 Gloucester Square W2
334 A9 Gloucester Terrace W2
335 W3 Gloucester Way EC1R
336 B9 Godliman Street EC4V
335 T12 Golden Jubilee Bridge SE1
336 C4 Golden Lane EC1Y
336 C5 Golden Lane Estate EC1Y
335 N10 Golden Square W1F
336 L4 Goldman Close E2
336 D8 Goldsmith Street EC2V
335 N7 Goodge Place W1T
335 N7 Goodge Street W1T
336 L8 Goodman's Stile E1
336 J10 Goodman's Yard EC3N
335 R10 Goodwins Court WC2N
336 E10 Gophir Lane EC4R
335 Q4 Gordon Square WC1H
335 P4 Gordon Street WC1H
336 H8 Goring Street EC3A
336 J2 Gorsuch Place E2
336 J2 Gorsuch Street E2
334 L6 Gosfield Street W1W
335 Q8 Goslett Yard W1D
336 L3 Gosset Street E2
336 B3 Goswell Place EC1V
336 B2 Goswell Road EC1V
335 W8 Gough Square EC4A
335 U4 Gough Street WC1X
336 J8 Goulston Street E1
335 Q7 Gower Mews WC1E
335 N4 Gower Place WC1H
335 P5 Gower Street WC1E
336 L8 Gower's Walk E1
336 F10 Gracechurch Street EC3V
336 L10 Grace's Alley E1
334 A1 Graces Mews * NW8
335 M5 Grafton Mews W1T
335 P3 Grafton Place NW1
334 L11 Grafton Street W1J
335 M5 Grafton Way W1T
336 B1 Graham Street N1
336 L4 Granby Street E2
335 M1 Granby Terrace NW1
336 B6 Grand Avenue EC1M
336 C1 Grand Junction Wharf * N1
334 K13 Grantham Place W1J
334 H9 Granville Place W1H
335 U3 Granville Square WC1X
335 R8 Grape Street WC2H
336 J8 Gravel Lane E1
335 S2 Gray's Inn Road N1
335 V6 Gray's Inn Square WC1R
335 X14 Gray Street SE1
334 J9 Gray's Yard W1U
335 M8 Great Castle Street W1B
334 F6 Great Central Street NW1
335 P8 Great Chapel Street W1F
334 F9 Great Cumberland Mews W1H
334 F8 Great Cumberland Place W1H
336 G3 Great Eastern Street EC2A
335 Q15 Great George Street SW1H
336 C13 Great Guildford Street SE1
335 T6 Great James Street WC1N
335 M9 Great Marlborough Street W1F
336 F13 Great Maze Pond SE1
335 W8 Great New Street EC4A
336 L6 Greatorex Street E1
335 S6 Great Ormond Street WC1N
335 U2 Great Percy Street WC1X
334 L6 Great Portland Street W1W
335 N10 Great Pulteney Street W1F
335 S8 Great Queen Street WC2B
335 Q8 Great Russell Street W1T
336 G9 Great St Helen's EC3A
336 D10 Great St Thomas Apostle EC4V
335 R13 Great Scotland Yard SW1A
336 B13 Great Suffolk Street SE1
336 B5 Great Sutton Street EC1V
336 E8 Great Swan Alley EC2R
334 L6 Great Titchfield Street W1W
336 G10 Great Tower Street EC3R
336 D10 Great Trinity Lane EC4V
335 U7 Great Turnstile WC1V
336 F8 Great Winchester Street EC2N
335 P10 Great Windmill Street W1F
335 Q9 Greek Street W1D
336 A8 Green Arbour Court EC4M
334 D1 Greenberry Street NW8
336 L7 Green Dragon Yard E1
335 V15 Greenham Close SE1
336 A6 Greenhill's Rents EC1M
335 P10 Green's Court W1F
334 G10 Green Street W1K
335 W3 Green Terrace EC1R
334 L5 Greenwell Street W1W
335 U4 Green Yard WC1X
335 W13 Greet Street SE1
334 D4 Grendon Street NW8
335 S5 Grenville Street WC1N
336 C8 Gresham Street EC2V
335 P7 Gresse Street W1T
335 W7 Greville Street EC1N
336 K6 Grey Eagle Street E1
336 K5 Grimsby Street E2
335 V15 Grindal Street SE1
336 E9 Grocers' Hall Court EC2R
334 J15 Grosvenor Crescent SW1X
334 H15 Grosvenor Crescent Mews SW1X
334 G11 Grosvenor Gate W2
334 K10 Grosvenor Hill W1K
334 J14 Grosvenor Place SW1X
334 J10 Grosvenor Square W1K
334 J10 Grosvenor Street W1K
336 C14 Grotto Court SE1
334 H6 Grotto Passage W1U
334 B2 Grove End Road NW8
334 E3 Grove Gardens NW8
336 D9 Groveland Court EC4M
336 D8 Guildhall Buildings EC2V
336 D8 Guildhall Yard EC2V
335 T5 Guilford Place WC1N
335 T5 Guilford Street WC1N
336 J7 Gun Street E1
336 K7 Gunthorpe Street E1
336 C8 Gutter Lane EC2V
336 F14 Guy Street SE1

H

336 F2 Haberdasher Place N1
336 F2 Haberdasher Street N1
336 J2 Hackney Road E2
336 K9 Half Moon Passage E1
336 K9 Halfmoon Passage E1
334 L12 Half Moon Street W1J
334 J15 Halkin Street SW1X
334 L6 Hallam Mews W1B
334 L6 Hallam Street W1W
334 A3 Hall Gate NW8
334 B5 Hall Place W2
334 A3 Hall Road NW8
336 B2 Hall Street EC1V
334 B3 Hamilton Close NW8
334 A2 Hamilton Gardens NW8
334 J13 Hamilton Place W1K
334 A3 Hamilton Terrace NW8
336 F15 Hamlet Way SE1
336 J10 Hammett Street EC3N
335 Q1 Hampden Close NW1
334 F9 Hampden Gurney Street W1H
335 M1 Hampstead Road NW1
335 P10 Ham Yard W1D
336 L6 Hanbury Street E1
335 U7 Hand Court WC1V
335 S4 Handel Street WC1N
336 F15 Hankey Place SE1
335 S9 Hanover Place WC2E
334 L9 Hanover Square W1S
334 E9 Hanover Steps * W2
334 L9 Hanover Street W1S
334 F3 Hanover Terrace NW1
334 E3 Hanover Terrace Mews NW1
335 M6 Hanson Street W1W
335 P8 Hanway Place W1T
335 P8 Hanway Street W1T
334 C7 Harbet Road W2
334 E7 Harcourt Street NW1
335 U3 Hardwick Mews WC1X
335 W3 Hardwick Street EC1R
336 G14 Hardwidge Street SE1
335 V9 Hare Court * EC4Y
336 L4 Hare Marsh E2
336 H1 Hare Walk N1
334 E4 Harewood Avenue NW1
334 L9 Harewood Place W1S
334 E6 Harewood Row NW1
334 K7 Harley Place W1G
334 K6 Harley Street W1G
336 G11 Harp Cross Lane EC3R
335 T6 Harpur Street WC1N
334 G15 Harriet Street SW1X
334 G15 Harriet Walk SW1X
335 M1 Harrington Street NW1
335 S3 Harrison Street WC1H
334 E8 Harrowby Street W1H
336 H8 Harrow Place E1
334 C7 Harrow Road Flyover W2
334 E6 Harrow Street NW1
336 H10 Hart Street EC3R
336 K1 Hassard Street E2
335 R3 Hastings Street WC1H
336 H15 Hatchers Mews SE1
335 W12 Hatfields SE1
336 B5 Hat & Mitre Court EC1M
335 W6 Hatton Garden EC1R
335 W5 Hatton Place EC1N
334 C5 Hatton Row NW8
334 C5 Hatton Street NW8
335 V6 Hatton Wall EC1N
334 K9 Haunch of Venison Yard W1K
335 W1 Haverstock Place N1
336 B1 Haverstock Street N1
336 J10 Haydon Street EC3N
336 J9 Haydon Walk E1
334 E5 Hayes Place NW1
334 L11 Hay Hill W1J
335 P11 Haymarket SW1Y
336 B6 Hayne Street EC1A
336 G12 Hays Lane SE1
334 K12 Hay's Mews W1J
335 X5 Hayward's Place EC1R
334 J15 Headfort Place SW1X
336 H5 Hearn Street EC2A
335 T4 Heathcote Street WC1N
335 M11 Heddon Street W1S
336 D4 Helmet Row EC1V
334 B4 Henderson Drive NW8
336 H9 Heneage Lane EC3A
336 K6 Heneage Street E1
335 S4 Henrietta Mews WC1N
334 K8 Henrietta Place W1G
335 S10 Henrietta Street WC2E
335 W5 Herbal Hill EC1R
335 R5 Herbrand Street WC1N
336 L4 Hereford Street E2
335 V1 Hermes Street N1
334 B7 Hermitage Street W2
335 X2 Hermit Street EC1V
334 K12 Hertford Street W1J
336 H5 Hewett Street EC2A
335 S8 High Holborn WC1V
336 C10 High Timber Street EC4V
334 E6 Highworth Street NW1
334 A1 Hill Road NW8
335 M9 Hills Place W1F
334 K12 Hill Street W1J
335 W9 Hind Court EC4A
334 J8 Hinde Mews W1U
334 J8 Hinde Street W1U
336 L6 Hobsons Place E1
336 J3 Hocker Street E2
336 F2 Hoffman Square * N1
334 B6 Hogan Mews W2
335 V7 Holborn EC1N
335 W7 Holborn Circus EC1N
335 T7 Holborn Place WC1V
335 X7 Holborn Viaduct EC1N
335 T2 Holford Mews * WC1X
335 V2 Holford Street WC1X
335 V1 Holford Yard * N1
336 B12 Holland Street SE1
335 N9 Hollen Street W1F
334 L8 Holles Street W1G
335 V14 Holmes Terrace SE1
335 U5 Holsworthy Square WC1X
336 G13 Holyrood Street SE1
336 H4 Holywell Lane EC2A
336 G5 Holywell Row EC2A
336 G1 Homefield Street N1
334 E7 Homer Row NW1
334 E7 Homer Street NW1
336 C4 Honduras Street EC1V
336 L9 Hooper Street E1
336 K7 Hopetown Street E1
335 R11 Hop Gardens WC2N
335 N9 Hopkins Street W1F
336 B12 Hoptons Gardens * SE1
336 B12 Hopton Street SE1
336 K1 Horatio Street E2
335 R13 Horse Guards Avenue SW1A
335 Q13 Horse Guards Road SW1A
336 J14 Horselydown Lane SE1
336 A7 Hosier Lane EC1A
335 U9 Houghton Street WC2B
336 H8 Houndsditch EC3A
335 N6 Howland Mews East W1T
335 N6 Howland Street W1T
334 A6 Howley Place W2
336 G3 Hoxton Market N1
336 G3 Hoxton Square N1
336 H2 Hoxton Street E2
336 D10 Huggin Hill EC4V
336 K6 Huguenot Place E1
336 C3 Hull Street EC1V
336 D15 Hulme Place SE1
335 S4 Hunter Street WC1N
335 N5 Huntley Street WC1E
336 L6 Hunton Street E1
334 F4 Huntsworth Mews NW1
335 W9 Hutton Street EC4Y
334 J14 Hyde Park Corner W1J
334 D9 Hyde Park Crescent W2
334 C10 Hyde Park Gardens W2
334 C10 Hyde Park Gardens Mews W2
334 A15 Hyde Park Gate SW7
334 A15 Hyde Park Gate Mews SW7
334 E10 Hyde Park Place W2
334 D9 Hyde Park Square W2
334 D10 Hyde Park Street W2

I

336 G11 Idol Lane EC3R
336 J9 India Street EC3N
335 N9 Ingestre Place W1F
335 V2 Inglebert Street EC1R
334 H3 Inner Circle NW1
336 A12 Invicta Plaza SE1
336 L1 Ion Square E2
336 E9 Ironmonger Lane EC2V
336 D3 Ironmonger Row EC1V
335 Q11 Irving Street WC2H
336 D14 Isaac Way SE1
335 X13 Isabella Street SE1
334 F5 Ivor Place NW1

J

336 K14 Jacob Street SE1
334 J8 Jacob's Well Mews W1U
336 K15 Jamaica Road SE1
335 S10 James Street WC2E
334 J9 James Street W1U
334 A15 Jay Mews SW7
335 M12 Jermyn Street SW1Y
334 D4 Jerome Crescent NW8
336 J6 Jerome Street E1
336 H1 Jerrold Street N1
335 X5 Jerusalem Passage EC1R
336 J9 Jewry Street EC3N
335 X13 Joan Street SE1
335 U6 Jockey's Fields WC1X
335 V15 Johanna Street SE1
335 S12 John Adam Street WC2N
334 A6 John Aird Court W2
335 X10 John Carpenter Street EC4Y
336 L15 John Felton Road SE16
336 L10 John Fisher Street E1
334 K7 John Prince's Street W1G
335 U5 John's Mews WC1N
335 W9 Johnson's Court EC4A
335 U5 John Street WC1N
336 C6 John Trundle Highwalk * EC2Y
336 F13 Joiner Street SE1
335 W3 Joseph Trotter Close EC1R
335 U13 Jubilee Gardens * SE1
335 R3 Judd Street WC1H
334 D8 Junction Mews W2
334 C8 Junction Place W2

K

335 T9 Kean Street WC2B
335 T9 Keeley Street WC2B
335 T9 Kemble Street WC2B
334 H7 Kendall Place W1U
334 E9 Kendal Steps * W2
334 E9 Kendal Street W2
336 D10 Kennett Wharf Lane EC4V
334 H6 Kenrick Place W1U
334 A15 Kensington Gore SW7
334 D15 Kensington Road SW7
335 R4 Kenton Street WC1H
335 P4 Kent Passage NW1
334 E3 Kent Terrace NW1
334 E15 Kent Yard SW7
335 Q6 Keppel Street WC1E
336 L4 Kerbela Street E2
335 S1 Keystone Crescent N1
335 R12 King Charles I Island WC2N
335 Q14 King Charles Street SW1A
336 C8 King Edward Street EC1A
336 C7 Kinghorn Street EC1A
336 B15 King James Street SE1
336 H4 King John Court EC2A
335 N10 Kingly Court * W1B
335 M9 Kingly Street W1B
336 E8 King's Arms Yard EC2R
336 B14 King's Bench Street SE1
335 W10 King's Bench Walk * EC4Y
335 X10 Kingscote Street EC4V
336 B14 King's Court SE1
335 S2 King's Cross Bridge WC1X
335 T2 King's Cross Road WC1X
336 H1 Kingsland Road E2
335 U5 King's Mews WC1N
336 C15 King's Place SE1
336 C3 King Square EC1V
335 W10 Kings Reach SE1
335 S13 Kings Reach SW1A
336 D9 King Street EC2V
335 N13 King Street SW1Y
335 R10 King Street WC2E
335 T9 Kingsway WC2B
335 W4 Kingsway Place EC1R
336 F11 King William Street EC4R
334 G15 Kinnerton Place North SW1X
334 G15 Kinnerton Place South SW1X
334 H15 Kinnerton Street SW1X
334 H15 Kinnerton Yard SW1X
336 F15 Kipling Estate SE1
336 F15 Kipling Street SE1
336 G14 Kirby Grove SE1
335 W6 Kirby Street EC1N
336 K3 Kirton Gardens E2
336 B9 Knightrider Court EC4V
336 C10 Knightrider Street EC4V
334 E15 Knightsbridge SW7
334 F15 Knightsbridge Green SW1X
334 F6 Knox Street W1H

L

336 F6 Lackington Street EC2A
336 J14 Lafone Street SE1
336 C6 Lambert Jones Mews * EC2Y
336 C10 Lambeth Hill EC4V
335 T6 Lamb's Conduit Passage WC1X
335 T5 Lamb's Conduit Street WC1N
336 E5 Lamb's Passage EC1Y
336 J6 Lamb Street E1
336 G15 Lamb Walk SE1
334 A4 Lanark Place W9
334 K10 Lancashire Court W1K
334 A10 Lancaster Court W2
334 A11 Lancaster Gate W2
334 A10 Lancaster Mews W2
335 T10 Lancaster Place WC2E
336 A15 Lancaster Street SE1
334 B10 Lancaster Terrace W2
334 F15 Lancelot Place SW7
335 P3 Lancing Street NW1
334 A1 Langford Place NW8
334 L7 Langham Place W1G
334 L7 Langham Street W1B
335 R10 Langley Court WC2E
335 R9 Langley Street WC2H
336 F8 Langthorn Court EC2R
335 U3 Langton Close WC1X
335 S5 Lansdowne Terrace WC1N
336 C14 Lant Street SE1
336 D7 Lauderdale Place * EC2Y
335 V15 Launcelot Street SE1
336 E10 Laurence Pountney Hill EC4R
336 E10 Laurence Pountney Lane EC4R
336 B13 Lavington Street SE1
336 D9 Lawrence Lane EC2V
334 L4 Laxton Place NW1
335 V5 Laystall Street WC1X
335 R10 Lazenby Court WC2E
336 G9 Leadenhall Place EC3M
336 G9 Leadenhall Street EC3V
335 U14 Leake Street SE1
335 V5 Leather Lane EC1R
336 G15 Leathermarket Court SE1
336 G15 Leathermarket Street SE1
335 T2 Leeke Street WC1X
334 H10 Lees Place W1K
335 Q10 Leicester Place WC2H
335 Q11 Leicester Square WC2H
335 Q10 Leicester Street W1D
335 R4 Leigh Street WC1H
336 K9 Leman Street E1
336 F4 Leonard Street EC2A
336 C3 Lever Street EC1V
335 N9 Lexington Street W1F
336 J7 Leyden Street E1
336 B15 Library Street SE1
335 M1 Lidlington Place NW1
336 J4 Ligonier Street E2
334 D4 Lilestone Street NW8
335 W6 Lily Place EC1N
336 A8 Limeburner Lane EC4M
336 G10 Lime Street EC3M
336 G9 Lime Street Passage EC3V
335 T8 Lincoln's Inn Fields WC2A
336 B6 Lindsey Street EC1M
334 F4 Linhope Street NW1
336 K6 Links Yard E1
335 Q10 Lisle Street W1D
334 C4 Lisson Grove NW8
334 D6 Lisson Street NW8
335 Q10 Litchfield Street WC2H
334 L4 Little Albany Street NW1
335 M9 Little Argyll Street W1S
336 B7 Little Britain EC1A
336 D14 Little Dorrit Court SE1
334 L2 Little Edward Street NW1
335 V10 Little Essex Street WC2R
335 R15 Little George Street SW1P
335 M9 Little Marlborough Street W1B
335 Q10 Little Newport Street WC2H
335 W8 Little New Street EC4A
334 L8 Little Portland Street W1B
335 R7 Little Russell Street WC1A
335 M13 Little St James's Street SW1A
335 M7 Little Titchfield Street W1W
336 D10 Little Trinity Lane EC4V
335 T7 Little Turnstile WC1V
336 G7 Liverpool Street EC2M
336 D3 Lizard Street EC1V
335 V3 Lloyd Baker Street WC1X
336 H9 Lloyd's Avenue EC3M
335 V2 Lloyd Square WC1X
335 W3 Lloyd's Row EC1R
335 V2 Lloyd Street WC1X
336 F15 Lockyer Street SE1
334 C3 Lodge Road NW8
336 K7 Lolesworth Close E1
336 B14 Loman Street SE1
335 W9 Lombard Lane EC4Y
336 F9 Lombard Street EC3V
336 F11 London Bridge EC4R
336 F13 London Bridge Street SE1
336 F12 London Bridge Walk SE1
334 C9 London Mews W2
336 H10 London Street EC3M
334 B9 London Street W2
336 L1 London Terrace * E2
336 D7 London Wall EC2Y
336 F7 London Wall Buildings EC2M
335 R9 Long Acre WC2E
334 L4 Longford Street NW1
336 B6 Long Lane EC1A
336 F15 Long Lane SE1
336 J1 Long Street E2
336 J2 Long Street E2
335 T5 Long Yard WC1N
336 L3 Lorden Walk E2
334 D3 Lords View NW8
335 T2 Lorenzo Street WC1X
334 E3 Lorne Close NW8
336 E8 Lothbury EC2R
336 G10 Lovat Lane EC3M
336 D8 Love Lane EC2V
335 N10 Lower James Street W1F
335 N10 Lower John Street W1F
335 U15 Lower Marsh SE1
336 H11 Lower Thames Street EC3R
335 M9 Lowndes Court W1B
334 G15 Lowndes Square SW1X
335 S3 Loxham Street WC1H
336 B9 Ludgate Broadway EC4V
336 A9 Ludgate Circus EC4M
336 A9 Ludgate Hill EC4M
336 B9 Ludgate Square EC4V
336 C4 Ludlow Street EC1V
336 G4 Luke Street EC2A
334 J9 Lumley Street W1K
334 C5 Luton Street NW8
334 H5 Luxborough Street W1U
334 B5 Lyons Place NW8

M

335 Q3 Mabledon Place NW1
336 C2 Macclesfield Road EC1V
335 Q10 Macclesfield Street W1D
334 J5 MacFarren Place NW1
334 E1 Mackennal Street NW8
335 S8 Macklin Street WC2B
335 M2 Mackworth Street NW1
334 L10 Maddox Street W1K
334 E12 Magazine Gate * W2
336 G13 Magdalen Street SE1
336 K14 Maguire Street SE1
334 A6 Maida Avenue W2
334 A4 Maida Vale W9
336 D13 Maiden Lane SE1
335 S11 Maiden Lane WC2E
336 D13 Maidstone Buildings Mews SE1
335 P5 Malet Street WC1E
334 E5 Mallory Street NW8
336 E4 Mallow Street EC1V
336 A4 Malta Street EC1V
336 J15 Maltby Street SE1
336 H14 Maltings Place SE1
335 U10 Maltravers Street WC2R
334 H7 Manchester Mews W1U
334 H8 Manchester Square W1H
334 H7 Manchester Street W1U
336 F15 Manciple Street SE1
334 J8 Mandeville Place W1U
335 Q9 Manette Street W1D
336 A2 Manningford Close EC1V
336 L8 Manningtree Street E1
336 K9 Mansell Street E1
334 K7 Mansfield Mews W1G
334 K7 Mansfield Street W1G
336 E9 Mansion House Place EC4N
335 N6 Maple Place W1T
335 M6 Maple Street W1T
336 K12 Marble Quay E1W
335 R4 Marchmont Street WC1N
335 M8 Margaret Street W1W
335 V3 Margery Street WC1X
335 X11 Marigold Alley SE1
334 K13 Market Mews W1J
335 M8 Market Place W1D
336 H10 Mark Lane EC3R
336 G4 Mark Street EC2A
335 M10 Marlborough Court W1B
334 B11 Marlborough Gate W2
335 N13 Marlborough Road SW1A
335 N9 Marshall Street W1F
336 D14 Marshalsea Road SE1
336 E4 Martha's Buildings EC1V
336 F10 Martin Lane EC4R
335 S9 Martlett Court WC2B
334 J7 Marylebone High Street W1U
334 J8 Marylebone Lane W1U
334 J7 Marylebone Mews W1G
335 N8 Marylebone Passage W1W
334 E6 Marylebone Road NW1
334 J7 Marylebone Street W1U
334 L9 Mason's Arms Mews W1S
336 E8 Mason's Avenue EC2V
336 B2 Mason's Place EC1V
336 C4 Masons Yard EC1V
335 N12 Masons Yard SW1Y
335 R9 Mathews Yard WC2H
336 B15 Mathieson Court SE1
336 D13 Mayall Close SE1
334 L12 Mayfair Place W1J
335 R11 Mays Court WC2N
336 C15 McCold Way SE1
335 P9 Meard Street W1F
335 T4 Mecklenburgh Place WC1N
335 T4 Mecklenburgh Square WC1N
335 T4 Mecklenburgh Street WC1N
335 U9 Melbourne Place WC2B
334 E5 Melbury Terrace NW1
334 F6 Melcombe Place NW1
334 G5 Melcombe Street NW1
334 B3 Melina Place NW8
336 G14 Melior Place SE1
336 F14 Melior Street SE1
335 N3 Melton Street NW1
336 C5 Memel Street EC1Y
335 V14 Mepham Street SE1
335 R9 Mercer Street WC2H
335 X3 Meredith Street EC1R
335 V3 Merlin Street WC1X
336 E14 Mermaid Court SE1
334 F8 Mertoun Terrace * W1H
336 K12 Mews Street E1W
335 X13 Meymott Street SE1
336 C2 Micawber Street N1
336 H7 Middlesex Street E1
336 C6 Middle Street EC1A
335 V9 Middle Temple Lane WC2R
335 M7 Middleton Buildings W1W
335 M7 Middleton Place W1W
336 F12 Middle Yard SE1
335 N5 Midford Place W1T
335 S3 Midhope Street WC1H
335 R2 Midland Road NW1
336 A15 Milcote Street SE1
335 V10 Milford Lane WC2R
336 D8 Milk Street EC2V
336 C11 Millennium Bridge SE1
336 J14 Millennium Square SE1
335 W13 Miller Walk SE1
335 T5 Millman Mews WC1N
335 T5 Millman Place WC1N
335 T5 Millman Street WC1N
335 Q12 Millshott Close SW1Y
336 J15 Millstream Road SE1
336 K15 Mill Street SE1
334 L10 Mill Street W1S
335 W12 Milroy Walk SE1
336 E6 Milton Court EC2Y
336 E6 Milton Street EC2Y
336 G10 Mincing Lane EC3R
336 J9 Minories EC3N
336 G10 Minster Court EC3R
336 C14 Mint Street SE1
336 L9 Mitali Passage E1
336 C4 Mitchell Street EC1V
335 W14 Mitre Road SE1
336 H9 Mitre Square EC3A
336 H9 Mitre Street EC3A
334 E7 Molyneux Street W1H
334 D15 Moncorvo Close SW7
336 D7 Monkwell Square EC2Y
335 R9 Monmouth Street WC2H
336 E12 Montague Close SE1
335 Q6 Montague Place WC1E
335 R6 Montague Street WC1B
336 C7 Montague Street EC1A
334 G7 Montagu Mansions W1U
334 G7 Montagu Mews North W1H
334 G8 Montagu Mews South W1H
334 G8 Montagu Mews West W1H
334 F7 Montagu Place W1H
334 G7 Montagu Row W1U
334 G7 Montagu Square W1H
334 G8 Montagu Street W1H
336 J3 Montclare Street E2
336 L7 Monthope Road E1
334 E15 Montpelier Street SW7
334 E15 Montpelier Terrace SW7
334 E15 Montpelier Walk SW7
335 T10 Montreal Place WC2B
334 J15 Montrose Place SW1X
336 F11 Monument Street EC3R
336 E7 Moorfields EC2M
336 E7 Moorfields Highwalk EC2Y
336 E8 Moorgate EC2R
336 E8 Moorgate Place EC2R
336 E7 Moor Lane EC2Y
335 Q9 Moor Street W1D
336 D3 Mora Street EC1V
336 B2 Moreland Street EC1V
336 G13 More London Place SE1
336 H13 More London Riverside SE1
336 G13 Morgans Lane SE1
335 W15 Morley Street SE1
336 G15 Morocco Street SE1
334 L8 Mortimer Street W1B
335 P7 Morwell Street W1T
336 L8 Mountfort Street E1
336 B3 Mount Mills EC1V
335 V5 Mount Pleasant WC1X
334 K11 Mount Row W1K
334 H11 Mount Street W1K
334 H7 Moxon Street W1U
336 L8 Mulberry Street E1
334 D5 Mulready Street NW8
336 D8 Mumford Court EC2V
336 G2 Mundy Street N1
334 L3 Munster Square NW1
335 V15 Murphy Street SE1
336 E1 Murray Grove N1
336 H11 Muscovy Street EC3N
335 R8 Museum Street WC1A
335 W2 Myddelton Passage EC1R
335 W2 Myddelton Square EC1R
335 W3 Myddelton Street EC1R
335 V1 Mylne Street EC1R
336 G1 Myrtle Street N1
336 G1 Myrtle Walk N1

N

335 V3 Naoroji Street WC1X
336 D1 Napier Grove N1
334 L2 Nash Street NW1
335 M7 Nassau Street W1W
336 K7 Nathaniel Close E1
336 J4 Navarre Street E2
336 J2 Nazrul Street E2
335 R9 Neal Street WC2H
335 R9 Neal's Yard WC2H
336 K15 Neckinger Street SE1
336 B1 Nelson Place N1
336 A14 Nelson Square SE1
336 B1 Nelson Terrace EC1V
336 L12 Nesham Street E1W
335 M3 Netley Street NW1
334 L9 New Bond Street W1K
336 A9 New Bridge Street EC4M
336 F7 New Broad Street EC2M
335 M9 Newburgh Street W1F
335 M10 New Burlington Mews W1S
335 M10 New Burlington Place W1S
335 M10 New Burlington Street W1S
336 C7 Newbury Street EC1A
335 X8 Newcastle Close EC4M
334 C7 Newcastle Place W2
335 W5 Newcastle Row EC1R
334 J7 New Cavendish Street W1U
336 C9 New Change EC4M
336 B2 New Charles Street EC1V
336 E14 Newcomen Street SE1
335 Q9 New Compton Street WC2H
335 V10 New Court * WC2R
334 D1 Newcourt Street NW8
335 W8 New Fetter Lane EC4A
336 B8 Newgate Street EC1A
336 C12 New Globe Walk SE1
336 J8 New Goulston Street E1
336 H15 Newham's Row SE1
336 H4 New Inn Broadway EC2A
336 H4 New Inn Square EC2A
336 H4 New Inn Street EC2A
336 H4 New Inn Yard EC2A
336 K3 Newling Estate E2
336 H10 New London Street EC3R
335 U7 Newman's Row WC2A
335 N7 Newman Street W1T
336 G4 New North Place EC2A
336 F1 New North Road N1
335 T6 New North Street WC1N
335 R8 New Oxford Street WC1A
335 Q10 Newport Court WC2H
335 Q10 Newport Place W1D
334 G9 New Quebec Street W1H
335 R10 New Row WC2N
335 U8 New Square WC2A
335 W8 New Street EC1A
336 H7 New Street EC2M
335 W8 New Street Square EC4A
335 S8 Newton Street WC2B
336 E7 New Union Street EC2Y
336 F10 Nicholas Lane EC4N
336 A13 Nicholson Street SE1
336 E2 Nile Street N1
336 C8 Noble Street EC2V
335 N9 Noel Street W1F
334 D8 Norfolk Crescent W2
334 C8 Norfolk Place W2
334 C9 Norfolk Square W2
334 C9 Norfolk Square Mews W2
336 C3 Norman Street EC1V
335 P11 Norris Street SW1Y
335 W4 Northampton Road EC1R
335 W4 Northampton Row EC1R
336 A3 Northampton Square EC1V
334 H10 North Audley Street W1K
334 D3 North Bank NW8
336 B5 Northburgh Street EC1V
334 E10 North Carriage Drive W2
335 P6 North Crescent W1T
335 T1 Northdown Street N1
335 M3 North Gower Street NW1
335 T6 Northington Street WC1N
335 U5 North Mews WC1N
334 E9 North Rise * W2
334 G10 North Row W1K
336 K9 North Tenter Street E1
336 H9 Northumberland Alley EC3N
335 R12 Northumberland Avenue WC2N
335 R12 Northumberland Street WC2N
334 B7 North Wharf Road W2
334 B4 Northwick Close NW8
334 B4 Northwick Terrace NW8
336 H5 Norton Folgate E1
335 V8 Norwich Street EC4A
335 R9 Nottingham Court WC2H
334 H5 Nottingham Place W1U
334 H6 Nottingham Street W1U
334 H5 Nottingham Terrace NW1
334 A1 Nugent Terrace NW8
334 E8 Nutford Place W2

O

336 B1 Oakley Crescent EC1V
336 K4 Oakley Yard * E2
334 C3 Oak Tree Road NW8
336 C8 Oat Lane EC2V
336 G7 Octagon Arcade EC2M
335 R9 Odhams Walk WC2H
335 M6 Ogle Street W1W
336 B9 Old Bailey EC4M
334 H14 Old Barrack Yard SW1X
335 M11 Old Bond Street W1S
336 G8 Old Broad Street EC2M
335 V8 Old Buildings WC2A
335 M10 Old Burlington Street W1S
334 J6 Oldbury Place W1U
336 J8 Old Castle Street E1
334 K8 Old Cavendish Street W1G
335 P10 Old Compton Street W1D
336 C10 Old Fish Street Hill EC4V
335 X8 Old Fleet Lane EC4M
335 S6 Old Gloucester Street WC1N
336 E9 Old Jewry EC2R
336 J2 Old Market Square E2
334 E7 Old Marylebone Road NW1
335 W9 Old Mitre Court EC4Y
336 L7 Old Montague Street E1
336 J4 Old Nichol Street E2
335 T6 Old North Street WC1X
334 J13 Old Park Lane W1J
334 G9 Old Quebec Street W1H
335 Q15 Old Queen Street SW1H
335 X9 Old Seacoal Lane EC4M
335 U8 Old Square WC2A
336 C4 Old Street EC1V
336 F4 Oliver's Yard EC1Y
336 D13 O'Meara Street SE1
335 S1 Omega Place N1
335 W5 Onslow Street EC1M
335 Q11 Orange Street WC2H
334 B5 Orchardson Street NW8
334 H9 Orchard Street W1H
335 T6 Orde Hall Street WC1N
335 S6 Ormond Close WC1N
335 N12 Ormond Yard SW1Y
336 L13 Orton Street E1W
336 K7 Osborn Street E1
334 L5 Osnaburgh Street NW1
334 L4 Osnaburgh Terrace NW1
334 H6 Ossington Buildings W1U
335 Q1 Ossulston Street NW1
334 F4 Outer Circle NW1
336 H8 Outwich Street EC3A
335 X2 Owen's Row EC1V
335 X1 Owen Street EC1V
335 P11 Oxendon Street W1D
336 E10 Oxford Court EC4N
334 E9 Oxford Square W2
334 H9 Oxford Street W1K

P

336 K3 Padbury Court E2
334 B7 Paddington Green W2
334 H6 Paddington Street W1U
336 A2 Paget Street EC1V
335 U3 Pakenham Street WC1X
334 E4 Palgrave Gardens NW1
336 J3 Palissy Street E2
335 P13 Pall Mall SW1Y
335 P12 Pall Mall East SW1Y

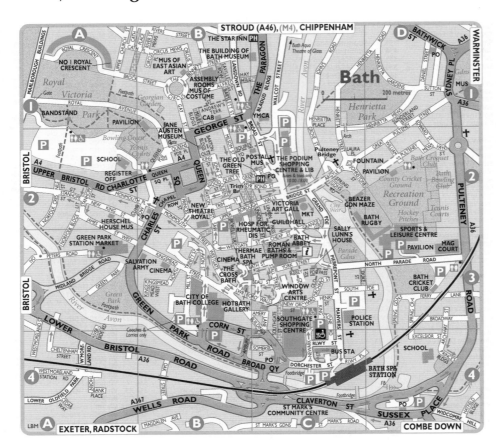

Bath

Bath is found on atlas page **59 H7**

C3	Abbey Square	A3	Lower Bristol Road
B1	Alfred Street	A4	Lower Oldfield Park
B4	Ambury	B2	Manvers Street
C2	Argyle Street	A3	Midland Bridge Road
B3	Avon Street	B3	Mill Street
B2	Barton Street	B2	Milsom Street
B3	Bath Street	A2	Monmouth Place
C3	Beau Street	B2	Monmouth Street
B1	Bennett Street	B2	New Bond Street
C1	Bladud Buildings	A2	New King Street
C3	Bridewell Lane	C3	New Orchard Street
C2	Bridge Street	D3	North Parade Road
D3	Broadway	B4	Oak Street
A1	Brock Street	C3	Old Orchard Street
B2	Chapel Row	C3	Pierrepont Street
B3	Charles Street	B2	Princes Street
A2	Charlotte Street	D2	Pulteney Road
C3	Cheap Street	B2	Queen Square
B1	Circus Mews	B2	Queen Square Place
C4	Claverton Street	B2	Queen Street
B3	Corn Street	B2	Queens Parade Place
C4	Dorchester Street	B2	Quiet Street
D2	Edward Street	C4	Railway Street
D3	Ferry Lane	A1	Royal Avenue
B1	Gay Street	A1	Royal Crescent
B1	George Street	B1	Russell Street
C2	Grand Parade	C1	St John's Road
C2	Grange Grove	B2	Saw Close
D2	Great Pulteney Street	C3	South Parade
A2	Great Stanhope Street	C4	Southgate Street
A3	Green Park	C3	Stall Street
B3	Green Park Road	D4	Sussex Place
B2	Green Street	D1	Sydney Place
C2	Grove Street	B1	The Circus
D1	Henrietta Gardens	C1	The Vineyards
D1	Henrietta Mews	B2	Trim Street
C1	Henrietta Road	C2	Union Passage
C1	Henrietta Street	C2	Union Street
C3	Henry Street	B2	Upper Borough Walls
A2	James Street West	A2	Upper Bristol Road
B2	John Street	A1	Upper Church Street
B3	Kingsmead North	C1	Walcot Street
B3	Kingsmead Street	B4	Wells Road
B1	Lansdown Road	B3	Westgate Buildings
A2	Little Stanhope Street	B3	Westgate Street
B3	Lower Borough Walls	A4	Westmoreland Road
		B2	Wood Street
		C3	York Street

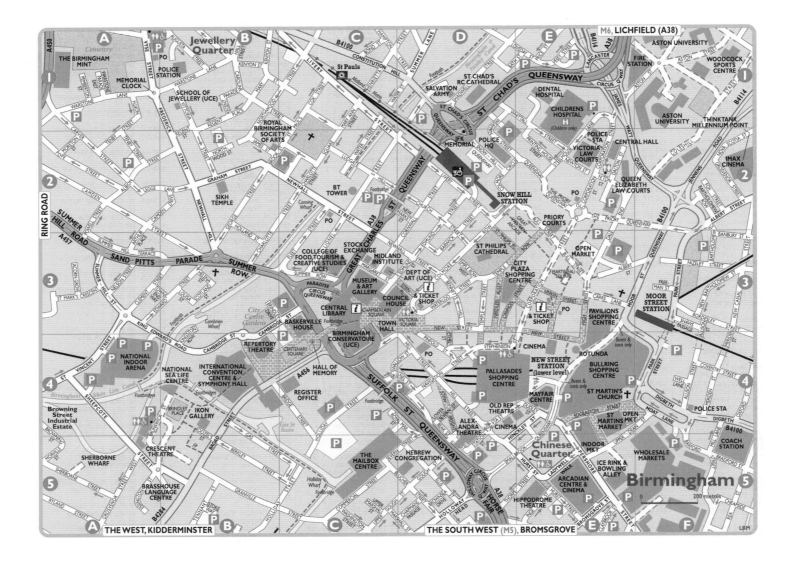

Birmingham

Birmingham is found on atlas page **114 B2**

A3	Acorn Grove	E3	Carrs Lane	B4	Gas Street	C3	Lionel Street	A1	Pemberton Street	A3	Summer Hill Terrace
E3	Albert Street	A2	Carver Street	B2	George Street	C1	Livery Street	E5	Pershore Street	D1	Summer Lane
A2	Albion Street	C4	Centenary Square	D5	Gough Street	B3	Louisa Street	D4	Pinfold Street	B3	Summer Row
F4	Allison Street	C3	Chamberlain Square	B2	Graham Street	E1	Loveday Street	A2	Pope Street	C4	Swallow Street
A3	Arthur Place	D5	Chapmans Passage	B5	Granville Street	D4	Lower Severn Street	A2	Powell Street	D3	Temple Row
F1	Aston Street	B3	Charlotte Street	C3	Great Charles Street	C2	Ludgate Hill	E2	Price Street	D3	Temple Row West
B1	Augusta Street	F5	Cheapside		Queensway	A2	Margaret Street	F2	Printing House Street	D3	Temple Street
F3	Banbury Street	D2	Church Street	E2	Great Western Arcade	C5	Marshall Street	F5	Rea Street	A2	Tenby Street
F5	Barford Street	E3	Claybrook Street	F2	Grosvenor Street	E3	Martineau Square	B1	Regent Parade	A2	Tenby Street North
F2	Bartholomew Row	F2	Clement Street	A5	Grosvenor Street West	C1	Mary Ann Street	B1	Regent Place	B5	Tennant Street
F3	Bartholomew Street	F2	Coleshill Street	B1	Hall Street	B1	Mary Street	B2	Regent Street	E2	The Priory Queensway
D3	Barwick Street	E2	Colmore Circus	C1	Hampton Street	F4	Meriden Street	C4	Royal Mail Street	D5	Thorpe Street
D1	Bath Street		Queensway	B3	Helena Street	F5	Mill Lane	A5	Ryland Street	A3	Townsend Way
D4	Beak Street	D3	Colmore Row	C1	Henrietta Street	F4	Moat Lane	D1	St Chad's Circus	E5	Union Street
D3	Bennetts Hill	C5	Commercial Street	E3	High Street	E3	Moor Street Queensway		Queensway	E5	Upper Dean Street
B5	Berkley Street	C1	Constitution Hill	D5	Hinckley Street	A2	Moreton Street	D1	St Chad's Queensway	E5	Upper Gough Street
D5	Blucher Street	D2	Cornwall Street	B2	Holland Street	A5	Morville Street	A3	St Mark's Crescent	C5	Upper Marshall Street
C1	Bond Street	E3	Corporation Street	B5	Holliday Street	D4	Navigation Street	C2	St Paul's Square	E1	Vesey Street
F3	Bordesley Street	F4	Coventry Street	D5	Holloway Circus	D3	Needless Alley	B3	St Philips Place	D3	Victoria Square
F5	Bradford Street	C1	Cox Street		Queensway	A3	Nelson Street	A4	St Vincent Street	B1	Vittoria Street
C4	Bridge Street	E3	Dale End	D5	Holloway Head	A3	New Bartholomew Street	A3	Sand Pits	E5	Vyse Street
B4	Brindley Drive	E2	Dalton Street	F4	Horse Fair	F3	New Canal Street	B3	Scotland Street	A1	Warstone Lane
F4	Brindley Place	E4	Dudley Street	E5	Hurst Street	D2	New Market Street	C5	Severn Street	A1	Warstone Parade East
B5	Broad Street	D3	Eden Place	E5	Inge Street	D3	New Street	D1	Shadwell Street	C5	Washington Street
C4	Brunel Street	E4	Edgbaston Street	E1	James Street	B2	Newhall Hill	F3	Shaws Passage	C2	Water Street
C4	Brunswick Street	D3	Edmund Street	E1	James Watt Queensway	C2	Newhall Street	A4	Sheepcote Street	D3	Waterloo Street
E2	Bull Street	A3	Edward Street	F2	Jennens Road	E2	Newton Street	A5	Sherborne Street	D1	Weaman Street
B4	Cambridge Street	E3	Ellis Street	D4	John Bright Street	B2	Northwood Street	D2	Snow Hill Queensway	F4	Well Lane
A2	Camden Drive	B3	Essington Street	B1	Kenyon Street	B2	Nova Scotia Street	D5	Station Street	E2	Whittall Street
A2	Camden Street	D4	Ethel Street	A3	King Edwards Road	E2	Old Square	E2	Steelhouse Lane		
D3	Cannon Street	F3	Fazeley Street	B4	Kingston Row	B4	Oozel's Street	E2	Stephenson Place		
B1	Caroline Street	F2	Fleet Street	E1	Ladywell Walk	F4	Oxford Street	D4	Stephenson Street		
		F2	Fox Street	E1	Lancaster Circus	B3	Parade	B5	Stoke Way		
		B1	Frederick Street		Queensway	C3	Paradise Circus	C4	Suffolk Street Queensway		
		E1	Freeman Street	A2	Legge Lane		Queensway	A2	Summer Hill Road		
				F4	Park Street			A3	Summer Hill Street		

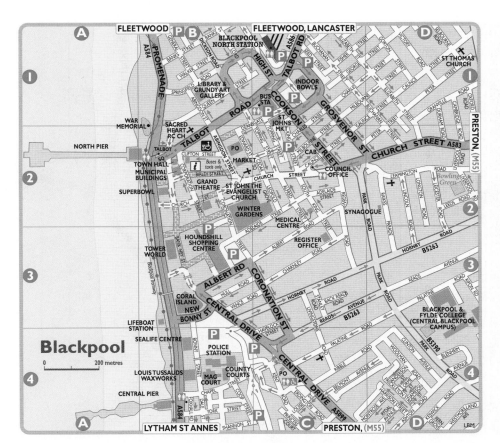

Blackpool

Blackpool is found on atlas page **182 B7**

B2	Abingdon Street	C3	Hornby Road
C2	Adelaide Street	B3	Hull Road
B3	Albert Road	D4	Jameson Street
C2	Alfred Street	C4	Kent Road
D4	Anderson Street	D4	Keswick Road
C3	Back Reads Road	C2	King Street
B3	Bank Hey Street	D2	Leamington Road
B1	Banks Street	D2	Leeds Road
C4	Belmont Avenue	D2	Leicester Road
B2	Birley Street	C2	Leopold Grove
D4	Blenheim Avenue	D2	Lincoln Road
B4	Bonny Street	D2	Liverpool Road
C1	Buchanan Street	C3	Livingstone Road
D1	Cambridge Road	D2	Longton Road
C2	Caunce Street	B1	Lord Street
C2	Cedar Square	C4	Louise Street
B3	Central Drive	C1	Milbourne Street
B4	Chapel Street	D4	Montrose Avenue
C1	Charles Street	B3	New Bonny Street
C3	Charnley Road	D4	Orme Street
C2	Church Street	D1	Oxford Road
B2	Clifton Street	C4	Palatine Road
D4	Clinton Avenue	D3	Park Road
C1	Cookson Street	D1	Peter Street
B4	Coop Street	D1	Princess Court
C3	Coronation Street	B1	Queen Street
B2	Corporation Street	D2	Raikes Parade
B4	Dale Street	C3	Reads Avenue
B2	Deansgate	C2	Regent Road
B1	Dickson Road	C4	Ribble Road
D1	Durham Road	D3	Ripon Road
C2	East Topping Street	D4	Rydal Avenue
B2	Edward Street	C1	Seed Street
C1	Elizabeth Street	D1	Selbourne Road
B4	Erdington Road	B4	Shannon Street
D4	Fern Grove	C2	South King Street
C1	Fisher Street	B1	Springfield Road
B4	Foxhall Road	C3	Stanley Road
D4	Freckleton Street	B2	Talbot Road
B1	General Street	B2	Talbot Square
C1	George Street	C2	Topping Street
C1	Gorton Street	B3	Vance Road
D1	Granville Road	D1	Victory Road
C4	Grosvenor Street	B1	Walker Street
D4	Harrison Street	D4	Westmoreland Avenue
C4	Havelock Street	D4	Woolman Road
C1	High Street	B4	York Street

Bradford

Bradford is found on atlas page **185 J8**

B2	Bank Street	A1	Lumb Lane
D2	Barkerend Road	B4	Manchester Road
B2	Barry Street	B1	Manningham Lane
C2	Bolton Road	A4	Mannville Terrace
B3	Bridge Street	B1	Manor Row
D2	Broadway	C3	Market Street
D2	Burnett Street	A4	Morley Street
C2	Canal Road	B4	Neal Street
D1	Captain Street	C4	Nelson Street
A3	Carlton Street	B3	Norfolk Gardens
B3	Channing Way	C1	North Brook Street
D3	Chapel Street	B1	North Parade
C2	Charles Street	B1	Northgate
C2	Cheapside	D1	Otley Road
A4	Chester Street	D2	Peckover Street
C2	Church Bank	C2	Petergate
A4	Claremont	B2	Piccadilly
C4	Croft Street	B3	Princes Way
C2	Currer Street	A2	Providence Street
B2	Dale Street	B3	Quebec Street
A1	Darfield Street	B2	Rawson Place
B2	Darley Street	A2	Rawson Road
C3	Diamond Street	B2	Rawson Square
C3	Drake Street	C1	St Blaise Way
A1	Drewton Road	A2	St Thomas Road
D4	Dryden Street	B1	Salem Street
B2	Duke Street	B4	Senior Way
D3	East Parade	B4	Sharpe Street
D3	Ebenezer Street	D3	Shipley Airedale Road
A4	Edmund Street	A2	Simes Street
C4	Edward Street	C2	Stott Hill
C2	Forster Square	A2	Sunbridge Road
B2	Godwin Street	A3	Tetley Street
A2	Grattan Road	A3	Thornton Road
A3	Great Horton Road	A3	Tumbling Hill Street
C4	Guy Street	B3	Tyrrel Street
C3	Hall Ings	D2	Upper Parkgate
B1	Hamm Strasse	B2	Upper Piccadilly
C1	Holdsworth Street	C1	Valley Road
A1	Houghton Place	C1	Vicar Lane
A4	Howard Street	D4	Wakefield Road
B3	Ivegate	C2	Well Street
B2	James Street	D2	Wellington Street
B2	John Street	A2	Westgate
B2	Kirkgate	C1	Wharf Street
D3	Leeds Road	A1	White Abbey Road
B4	Little Horton Lane	A2	Wigan Street
C2	Lower Kirkgate	A4	Wilton Street

Bristol

Bristol is found on atlas page **58 E6**

A3	Anchor Road	A2	Park Row
B3	Baldwin Street	C1	Penn Street
C1	Barton Street	A2	Perry Road
B1	Bond Street	A2	Pipe Lane
A3	Brandon Street	C4	Portwall Lane
B2	Bridewell Street	B4	Prince Street
C1	Broad Mead	D1	Pritchard Street
B2	Broad Quay	C4	Pump Lane
B2	Broad Street	C1	Quakers Friars
C2	Broad Weir	B2	Quay Street
B3	Canons Road	B3	Queen Charlotte Street
A4	Canons Way	B4	Queen Square
D2	Castle Street	C3	Redcliff Street
C1	Charles Street	C4	Redcliffe Hill
B2	Christmas Steps	C4	Redcliffe Mead Lane
A3	College Green	C4	Redcliffe Parade East
B2	Colston Avenue	C4	Redcliffe Way
B2	Colston Street	D1	River Street
B2	Corn Street	A1	Royal Fort Road
C3	Countership	B2	Rupert Street
D1	Dale Street	B3	St Augustine's Parade
A3	Deanery Road	A3	St George's Road
A3	Denmark Street	D1	St Matthias Park
B1	Earl Street	A1	St Michael's Hill
C2	Fairfax Street	B2	St Nicholas Street
B4	Farrs Lane	D1	St Paul's Street
A2	Frogmore Street	B2	St Stephen's Street
A3	Great George Street	C3	St Thomas Street
B4	Guinea Street	C1	Silver Street
C1	Haymarket	B2	Small Street
C2	High Street	A1	Southwell Street
A2	Hill Street	C3	Temple Back
B1	Horfield Road	C3	Temple Street
B3	King Street	D3	Temple Way
B1	Lewins Mead	B1	Terrell Street
A2	Lodge Street	B4	The Grove
D2	Lower Castle Street	C1	The Horsefair
B1	Lower Maudlin Street	D2	Tower Hill
B1	Lower Park Row	B2	Trenchard Street
B1	Marlborough Street	A1	Tyndall Avenue
B3	Marsh Street	A1	Union Street
C1	Merchant Street	B1	Upper Maudlin Street
B1	Montague Street	C3	Victoria Street
D2	Narrow Plain	B4	Wapping Road
B2	Nelson Street	C3	Welsh Back
D1	Newfoundland Street	C2	Wine Street
D2	Newgate	A1	Woodland Road
D2	Old Market Street	C1	York Street

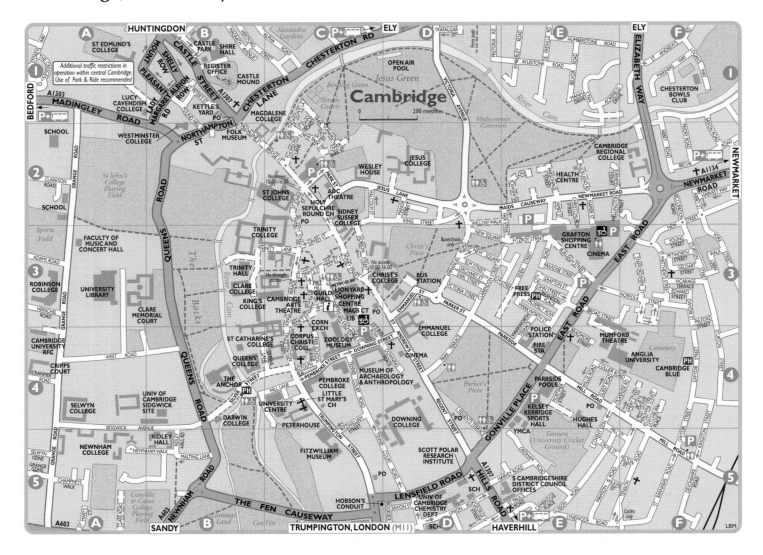

Cambridge

Cambridge is found on atlas page 102 **F2**

University
Colleges

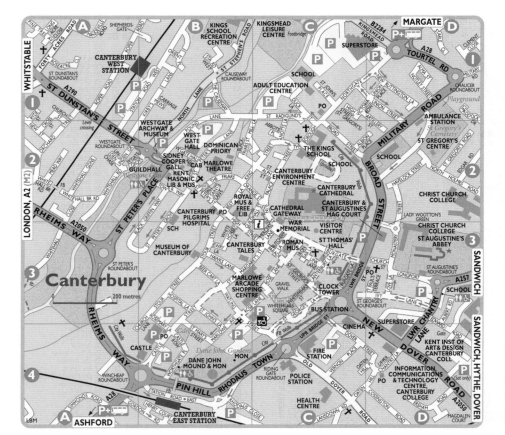

Canterbury

Canterbury is found on atlas page 53 **G2**

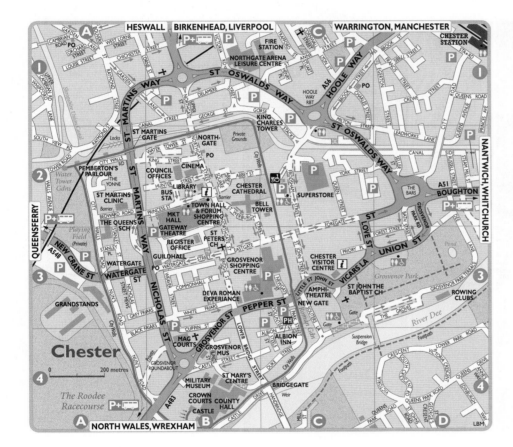

Cardiff

Cardiff is found on atlas page **57 G5**

D3	Adam Street	B4	Mill Lane
B3	Bakers Row	D2	Moira Place
B2	Barrack Lane	D2	Moira Terrace
B2	Boulevard de Nantes	B3	Morgan Arcade
C3	Bridge Street	B1	Museum Avenue
C4	Bute Street	B1	Museum Place
C3	Bute Terrace	D1	Newport Road
B4	Callaghan Square	C2	North Edward Street
B3	Caroline Street	A1	North Road
A3	Castle Street	D1	Oxford Lane
D4	Central Link	B1	Park Grove
B4	Central Square	B1	Park Lane
B2	Charles Street	B1	Park Place
B3	Church Street	B4	Penarth Road
C2	Churchill Way	A3	Quay Street
A1	City Hall Road	B2	Queen Street
D1	City Road	C1	Richmond Crescent
D1	College Road	C1	Richmond Road
B2	Crockherbtown Lane	B3	Royal Arcade
B4	Custom House Street	B1	St Andrew's Crescent
B2	Duke Street	C1	St Andrew's Lane
C2	Dumfries Place	B1	St Andrew's Place
C1	East Grove	B2	St John Street
D3	Ellen Street	B3	St Mary Street
D2	Fitzalan Place	C1	St Peter's Street
D2	Fitzalan Road	C1	Salisbury Road
A3	Fitzhamon Embankment	C3	Sandon Street
B3	Frederick Street	D4	Schooner Way
D1	Glossop Road	B1	Senghennydd Road
B3	Golate	C2	Station Terrace
B4	Great Western Lane	B2	Stuttgarter Strasse
B2	Greyfriars Place	C3	Taff Street
B2	Greyfriars Road	B2	The Friary
C3	Guildford Crescent	B3	The Hayes
C2	Guildford Street	C1	The Parade
B3	Hayes Bridge Road	B4	Tresillian Way
C4	Herbert Street	B3	Trinity Street
B3	High Street	B3	Tyndall Street
B3	Hill's Street	C1	West Grove
D2	Howard Gardens	A3	Westgate Street
D2	Howard Place	B3	Wharton Street
A1	King Edward VII Avenue	C2	Windsor Lane
B2	Kingsway	C2	Windsor Place
C2	Knox Road	D2	Windsor Road
C4	Lloyd George Avenue	A3	Womanby Street
D1	Longcross Street	B4	Wood Street
C3	Mary Ann Street	D1	Wordsworth Avenue
D2	Meteor Road	B3	Working Street

Chester

Chester is found on atlas page **163 H7**

B2	Abbey Square	C1	Milton Street
B2	Abbey Street	A3	New Crane Street
C4	Albion Street	C3	Newgate Street
D2	Bath Street	B3	Nicholas Street
A2	Bedward Road	A3	Nicholas Street Mews
A4	Black Friars	B2	Northgate Street
D2	Boughton	A3	Nun's Road
B3	Bridge Street	C3	Park Street
B4	Bunce Street	B3	Pepper Street
D2	Canal Side	B2	Princess Street
B1	Canal Street	C2	Queen Street
B4	Castle Drive	D2	Queens Avenue
B4	Castle Street	D4	Queens Drive
C1	Charles Street	D4	Queens Park Road
A1	Chichester Street	D1	Queens Road
D1	City Road	A1	Raymond Street
A2	City Walls Road	D2	Russell Street
B3	Commonhall Street	C1	St Anne Street
D1	Crewe Street	C3	St John Street
B3	Cuppin Street	A2	St Martins Way
D2	Dee Lane	B1	St Oswalds Way
B3	Delamere Street	B2	St Werburgh Street
C4	Duke Street	D2	Seller Street
B3	Eastgate Street	C3	Souters Lane
D1	Egerton Street	D4	South Crescent Road
C2	Foregate Street	A2	South View Road
D3	Forest Street	A3	Stanley Street
D1	Francis Street	D1	Station Road
D2	Frodsham Street	D2	Steam Mill Street
A1	Garden Lane	C4	Steele Street
B1	George Street	D2	The Bars
C1	Gorse Stacks	D3	The Groves
A3	Grey Friars	A2	Tower Road
D2	Grosvenor Park Road	C1	Trafford Street
D3	Grosvenor Park Terrace	D3	Union Street
B4	Grosvenor Street	B1	Upper Northgate Street
C4	Handbridge	C3	Vicars Lane
C1	Hoole Way	D4	Victoria Crescent
B2	Hunter Street	B1	Victoria Road
B2	King Street	C3	Volunteer Street
D2	Leadworks Lane	A2	Walls Avenue
C3	Little St John Street	B2	Water Tower Street
B1	Lorne Street	A2	Watergate Street
A1	Louise Street	B3	Weaver Street
C3	Love Street	A1	West Lorne Street
B4	Lower Bridge Street	A1	Whipcord Lane
D4	Lower Park Road	B3	White Friars
C1	Lyon Street	C2	York Street

Coventry

Coventry is found on atlas page **115 G4**

A1	Abbotts Lane	A2	Meriden Street
D4	Acacia Avenue	A1	Middleborough Road
D2	Alma Street	C4	Mile Lane
A2	Barras Lane	C3	Much Park Street
C2	Bayley Lane	C2	New Buildings
C1	Bird Street	B3	New Union Street
B1	Bishop Street	A2	Norfolk Street
B2	Bond Street	B4	Park Road
B2	Broadgate	C4	Parkside
B2	Burges	D1	Primrose Hill Street
A3	Butts Road	C2	Priory Row
D1	Canterbury Street	C2	Priory Street
C2	Chantry Place	C4	Puma Way
B2	Chapel Street	D4	Quarryfield Lane
D1	Charles Street	B3	Queen Victoria Road
D1	Colchester Street	A3	Queens Road
C1	Cook Street	C4	Quinton Road
B2	Corporation Street	B1	Radford Road
A1	Coundon Road	D2	Raglan Street
D1	Cox Street	A4	Regent Street
A3	Croft Road	A2	Ringway Hill Cross
B2	Cross Cheaping	A3	Ringway Queens
C3	Earl Street	A3	Ringway Rudge
B4	Eaton Road	C3	Ringway St Johns
C2	Fairfax Street	B1	Ringway St Nicholas
D2	Ford Street	B4	Ringway St Patrick
B4	Friars Road	B3	Ringway Swanswell
D3	Gosford Street	D3	Ringway Whitefriars
B3	Greyfriars Lane	C3	St John's Street
B3	Greyfriars Road	B1	St Nicholas Street
A4	Grosvenor Road	B4	St Patrick's Road
D3	Gulson Road	C3	Salt Lane
B2	Hales Street	B1	Silver Street
C3	Hay Lane	A2	Spon Street
B3	Hertford Street	B4	Stoney Road
C3	High Street	C1	Stoney Stanton Road
A2	Hill Street	D4	Strathmore Avenue
A2	Holyhead Road	C2	Swanswell Gate
D2	Hood Street	B1	Tower Street
C3	Jordan Well	C2	Trinity Street
D1	King William Street	B2	Upper Well Street
B1	Lamb Street	D1	Victoria Street
C3	Little Park Street	C1	Vine Street
B2	London Road	B3	Warwick Road
D2	Lower Ford Street	A4	Westminster Road
B3	Manor House Drive	C1	White Street
A3	Manor Road	C3	Whitefriars Street
A3	Meadow Street	D1	Yardley Street

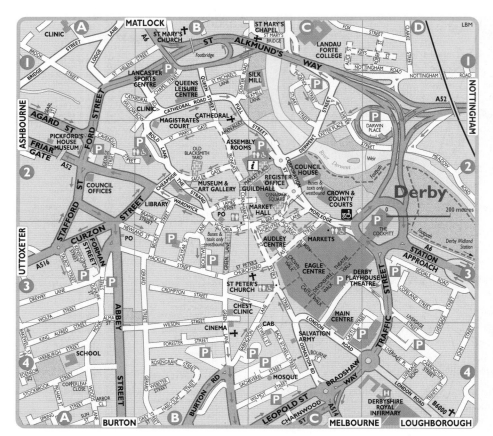

Derby

Derby is found on atlas page **153 G6**

A3	Abbey Street	C4	Leopold Street
A1	Agard Street	D4	Liversage Place
C2	Albert Street	D4	Liversage Road
C3	Albion Street	D3	Liversage Street
A3	Alma Street	A1	Lodge Lane
B2	Amen Alley	D4	London Road
B4	Babington Lane	B3	Macklin Street
C4	Back Sitwell Street	C2	Market Place
A4	Bakewell Street	D2	Meadow Road
B3	Becket Street	A4	Monk Street
B3	Becketwell Lane	C2	Morledge
B2	Bold Lane	D1	Newland Street
C4	Bradshaw Way	D1	Nottingham Road
B2	Bramble Street	B2	Old Blacksmith Yard
A1	Bridge Street	C4	Osmaston Road
A1	Brook Street	C2	Osnabrück Square
B4	Burton Road	C1	Phoenix Street
D4	Carrington Street	B1	Queen Street
C3	Castle Walk	B4	Sacheverel Street
B1	Cathedral Road	B1	Sadler Gate
A2	Cavendish Street	B1	St Alkmund's Way
B1	Chapel Street	A1	St Helens Street
C4	Charnwood Street	B2	St James Street
B2	Cheapside	C1	St Mary's Bridge
B3	Colyear Street	B2	St Mary's Gate
D3	Copeland Street	B1	St Michael's Lane
B2	Cornmarket	B2	St Peter's Churchyard
C2	Corporation Street	C3	St Peter's Street
C3	Crown Walk	D3	Siddals Road
A3	Curzon Street	C1	Silkmill Lane
D2	Darwin Place	C4	Sitwell Street
C2	Derwent Street	B1	Sowter Road
C3	Devonshire Walk	A3	Stafford Street
A3	Drewry Lane	D3	Station Approach
C3	East Street	A4	Stockbrook Street
C3	Exchange Street	C1	Stuart Street
C2	Exeter Place	A3	Talbot Street
C1	Exeter Street	D3	The Cockpitt
A2	Ford Street	B2	The Strand
B4	Forester Street	C3	Theatre Walk
A3	Forman Street	D4	Traffic Street
C1	Fox Street	D4	Trinity Street
A2	Friar Gate	B3	Victoria Street
B1	Full Street	B2	Wardwick
B3	Gerard Street	A4	Werburgh Street
B3	Green Lane	A1	Willow Row
B2	Irongate	C4	Wilmot Street
A4	King Alfred Street	B4	Wilson Street

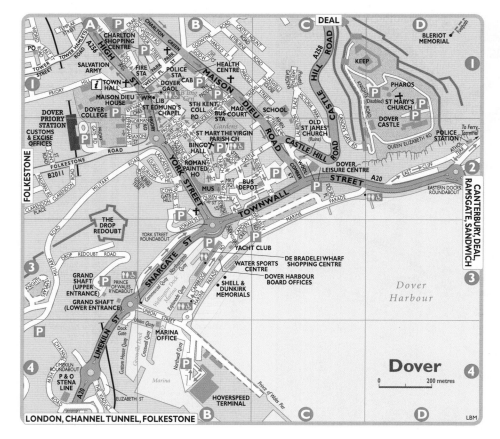

Dover

Dover is found on atlas page **53 K5**

B3	Adrian Street	B2	Market Square
C2	Ashen Tree Lane	A3	Military Road
D2	Athol Terrace	B2	Mill Lane
B2	Bench Street	B3	New Bridge
B2	Biggin Street	B2	New Street
B2	Bowling Green Terrace	A2	Norman Street
B3	Cambridge Road	B1	Park Place
B3	Camden Crescent	B1	Park Street
B2	Cannon Street	B1	Pencester Road
C2	Canon's Gate Road	B2	Princes Street
C2	Castle Hill Road	A2	Priory Gate Road
B1	Castle Mount Road	A1	Priory Hill
B2	Castle Street	B2	Priory Road
A4	Channel View Road	B2	Priory Street
B1	Charlton Green	D2	Queen Elizabeth Road
B2	Church Street	B2	Queen Street
A2	Clarendon Place	B2	Queens Gardens
A2	Clarendon Road	C2	Russell Street
B2	Cowgate Hill	A2	St John's Road
A1	Crafford Street	A2	Saxon Street
B1	Dour Street	B3	Snargate Street
C2	Douro Place	B2	Stem Brook
A3	Drop Redoubt Road	C1	Taswell Close
B2	Durham Close	C1	Taswell Street
B2	Durham Hill	A1	Templar Street
D2	East Cliff	B1	The Paddock
A1	East Street	A4	The Viaduct
A1	Effingham Crescent	A1	Tower Hamlets Road
A2	Effingham Street	A1	Tower Street
A4	Elizabeth Street	C2	Townwall Street
A2	Folkestone Road	B3	Union Street
B2	Godwyne Close	C1	Victoria Park
B1	Godwyne Road	C2	Wellesley Road
B1	Harold Street	A1	Widred Road
C1	Heritage Gardens	A1	Wood Street
B1	Hewitt Road	C2	Woolcomber Street
A1	High Street	B2	Worthington Street
B2	King Street	B2	York Street
C1	Knights Road		
A3	Knights Templars		
B1	Ladywell		
B2	Lancaster Road		
C2	Laureston Place		
B1	Leyburne Road		
A4	Limekiln Street		
B1	Maison Dieu Road		
A2	Malvern Road		
B3	Marine Parade		

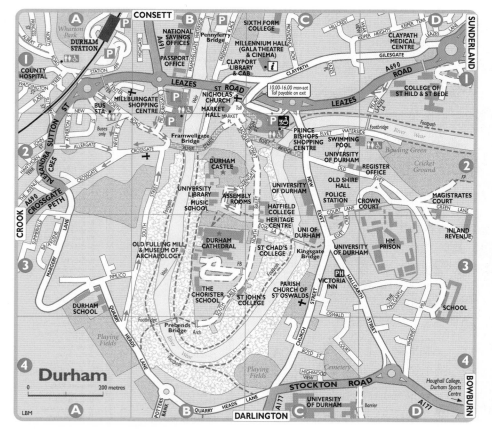

Durham

Durham is found on atlas page **213 G5**

A1	Albert Street	A3	Quarry Heads Lane
A2	Alexandra Crescent	B2	Saddler Street
A2	Allergate	B2	Silver Street
A2	Atherton Street	B3	South Bailey
C3	Bow Lane	B3	South Street
C4	Boyd Street	A1	Station Approach
A3	Briardene	C4	Stockton Road
C1	Church Street	A3	Summerville
A2	Claypath	A2	Sutton Street
A2	Court Lane	A1	Tenter Terrace
A2	Crossgate	A2	The Avenue
A2	Crossgate Peth	D3	The Hallgarth
C2	Elvet Bridge	A1	Waddington Street
C3	Elvet Crescent	D1	Wear View
C2	Elvet Waterside	D4	Whinney Hill
A1	Flass Street		
B1	Framwellgate Waterside		
B1	Freemans Place		
D1	Gilesgate		
D2	Green Lane		
C3	Hallgarth Street		
A2	Hawthorn Terrace		
B1	Highgate		
C2	High Street		
C2	Highwood View		
C1	Hillcrest		
A2	John Street		
D1	Keiper Heights		
C1	Keiper Terrace		
D1	Leazes Lane		
C1	Leazes Place		
B1	Leazes Road		
A3	Margery Lane		
B2	Market Place		
B1	Millburngate		
A2	Neville Street		
C2	New Elvet		
A1	New Street		
C3	North Bailey		
A1	North Road		
C2	Old Elvet		
C3	Oswald Court		
C2	Owengate		
A3	Pelaw Leazes Lane		
A3	Pimlico		
B4	Potters Bank		
C1	Princess Street		
C1	Providence Row		

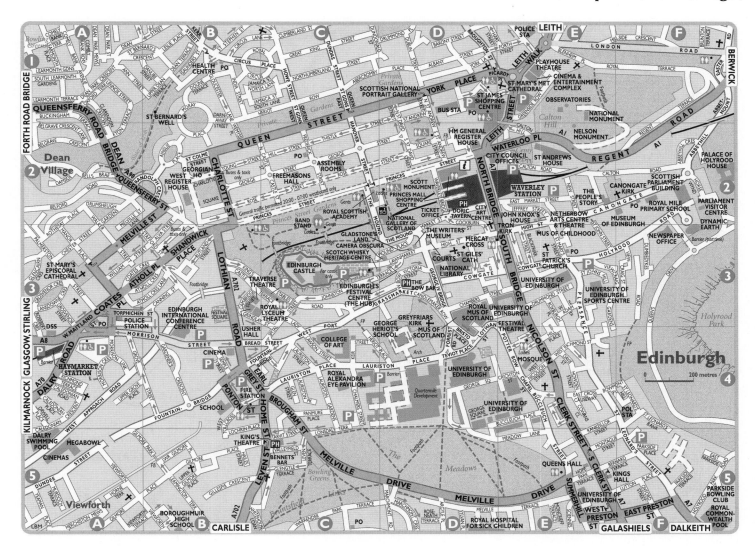

Edinburgh

Edinburgh is found on atlas page **259 H5**

F2	Abbeyhill	B3	Castle Terrace	
C4	Abbeyhill Crescent	C4	Chalmers Street	
F1	Abbeymount	D3	Chambers Street	
C1	Abercromby Place	E4	Chapel Street	
B2	Ainslie Place	B2	Charlotte Square	
D1	Albany Street	A3	Chester Street	
B3	Alva Street	C4	Chester Street Gardens	
A1	Ann Street	B1	Circus Lane	
D5	Argyle Place	B1	Circus Place	
B3	Atholl Crescent	A1	Clarendon Crescent	
B3	Atholl Crescent Lane	E4	Clerk Street	
A3	Atholl Place	A3	Coates Crescent	
D1	Barony Street	A3	Coates Place	
A2	Belford Road	D2	Cockburn Street	
A2	Belgrave Crescent	A1	Comely Bank Avenue	
A2	Belgrave Crescent Lane	D3	Cowgate	
A2	Bells Brae	E4	Crichton Street	
E5	Bernard Terrace	A4	Dalry Road	
E3	Blackfriar Street	A2	Damside	
E4	Bowmont Place	B1	Danube Street	
B4	Bread Street	B1	Darnaway Street	
D4	Bristo Place	A2	Davie Street	
C4	Brougham Street	A2	Dean Bridge	
D1	Broughton Street	A1	Dean Park Crescent	
E4	Buccleuch Place	A1	Dean Park Mews	
E4	Buccleuch Street	A1	Dean Park Street	
A1	Buckingham Terrace	A1	Dean Street	
A4	Caledonian Crescent	B1	Doune Terrace	
E2	Calton Hill	D1	Drummond Place	
E2	Calton Road	E3	Drummond Street	
B3	Cambridge Street	A2	Drumsheugh	
B3	Canning Street	D1	Dublin Street	
E2	Canongate	C1	Dundas Street	
C2	Castle Street	A5	Dundee Street	
		B4	Earl Grey Street	
E4	East Cross Causeway	B1	Jamaica Street North Lane	
E2	East Market Street	C1	Jamaica Street South Lane	
F5	East Preston Street	E2	Jeffrey Street	
A2	Eton Terrace	C3	Johnston Terrace	
B3	Festival Square	C4	Keir Street	
D4	Forrest Road	B1	Kerr Street	
E1	Forth Street	B3	King's Stables Road	
B4	Fountainbridge	C4	Lady Lawson Street	
C2	Frederick Street	A3	Lansdowne Crescent	
B4	Gardener's Crescent	C4	Lauriston Gardens	
D3	George IV Bridge	C4	Lauriston Park	
D4	George Square	C4	Lauriston Place	
B2	George Street	C4	Lauriston Street	
B5	Gillespie Crescent	D3	Lawnmarket	
B5	Gilmore Park	B5	Leamington Terrace	
B5	Gilmore Place	A1	Learmonth Terrace	
C4	Glen Street	E1	Leith Street	
C5	Glengyle Terrace	E1	Leith Walk	
B1	Gloucester Lane	A4	Lennox Street	
D3	Grassmarket	B1	Leslie Place	
C1	Great King Street	C5	Leven Street	
E1	Greenside Row	C5	Leven Terrace	
B3	Grindlay Street	B5	Lochrin Place	
A3	Grosvenor Crescent	E1	London Road	
A3	Grosvenor Street	C5	Lonsdale Terrace	
A4	Grove Street	B3	Lothian Road	
C2	Hanover Street	D4	Lothian Street	
C4	Heriot Place	A3	Manor Place	
C1	Heriot Row	D5	Marchmont Crescent	
D3	High Street	D5	Marchmont Road	
E4	Hill Place	D2	Market Street	
C2	Hill Street	B5	Meadow Lane	
F1	Hillside Crescent	C5	Melville Drive	
F5	Holyrood Park Road	A3	Melville Street	
E3	Holyrood Road	A2	Melville Street Lane	
C4	Home Street	D5	Melville Terrace	
E5	Hope Park Terrace	E5	Montague Street	
F2	Horse Wynd	A3	Moray Place	
E4	Howden Street	A4	Morrison Crescent	
C1	Howe Street	A4	Morrison Link	
B1	India Street	A4	Morrison Street	
		D3	Mound Place	
A5	Murdoch Terrace	F5	St Leonard's Street	
E2	New Street	E3	St Mary's Street	
E4	Nicholson Street	B1	St Stephen Street	
D2	North Bridge	B4	Semple Street	
C2	North Castle Street	B3	Shandwick Place	
D1	North St Andrew Street	E3	South Bridge	
D1	North St David Street	E5	South Clerk Street	
C1	Northumberland Street	A1	South Learmonth Gardens	
F5	Oxford Street	D2	South St Andrew Street	
A3	Palmerston Place	D2	South St David Street	
C4	Panmure Place	C4	Spital Street	
F5	Parkside Terrace	B3	Stafford Street	
E1	Picardy Place	E5	Summerhall	
E3	Pleasance	C5	Tarvit Street	
B4	Ponton Street	D4	Teviot Place	
E4	Potter Row	C2	The Mound	
C2	Princes Street	C2	Thistle Street	
B2	Queen Street	A3	Torphichen Street	
C1	Queen Street Gardens East / West	B1	Upper Dean Terrace	
F3	Queen's Drive	B5	Upper Gilmore Place	
A1	Queensferry Road	A4	Upper Grove Place	
A2	Queensferry Street	C5	Valleyfield Street	
B2	Randolph Crescent	D3	Victoria Street	
E4	Rankeillor Street	E3	Viewcraig Gardens	
E2	Regent Road	F3	Viewcraig Street	
F2	Regent Terrace	A5	Viewforth	
B2	Rose Street	A3	Walker Street	
A3	Rothesay Place	C5	Warrender Park Terrace	
E3	Roxburgh Place	E2	Waterloo Place	
B1	Royal Circus	D2	Waverley Bridge	
F1	Royal Terrace	A4	West Approach Road	
B3	Rutland Street	C2	West Bow	
D2	St Andrew Square	A4	West Maitland Street	
A1	St Bernard's Crescent	E4	West Nicholson Street	
B2	St Colme Street	C4	West Port	
E3	St John Street	E5	West Preston Street	
E3	St Johns Hill	E4	West Richmond Street	
F4	St Leonard's Bank	B4	West Tollcross	
		A3	William Street	
		D1	York Place	
		B2	Young Street	

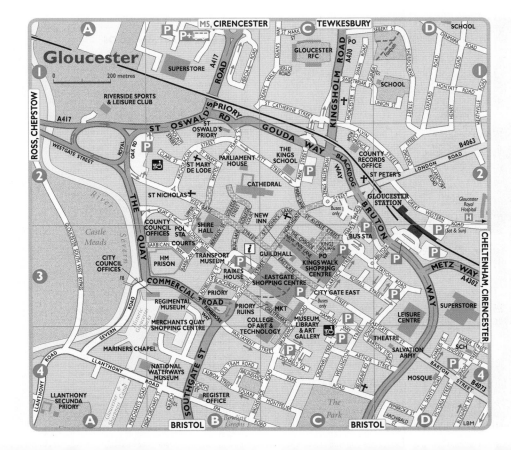

Gloucester

Gloucester is found on atlas page **78 C3**

B4	Albion Street	C2	Market Parade	
D4	All Saints Road	A4	Merchants Road	
C2	Alvin Street	B1	Mercia Road	
C2	Archdeacon Street	D3	Metz Way	
C4	Arthur Street	C4	Montpelier	
B3	Barbican Road	B2	Mount Street	
B3	Barbican Way	D4	Napier Street	
D4	Barton Street	C3	New Inn Lane	
C4	Belgrave Road	B4	North Street	
B3	Berkeley Street	C2	Northgate Street	
C2	Blackdog Way	B4	Old Tram Road	
B3	Blackfriars	D1	Oxford Road	
C4	Brunswick Road	D2	Oxford Street	
B4	Brunswick Square	C4	Park Road	
D3	Bruton Way	C2	Park Street	
B3	Bull Lane	B4	Parliament Street	
B2	Clare Street	C2	Pitt Street	
D2	Claremont Road	B1	Priory Road	
C2	Clarence Row	B2	Quay Street	
C2	Clarence Street	A2	Royal Oak Road	
B2	College Court	C3	Russell Street	
B2	College Street	C2	St Aldate Street	
B3	Commercial Road	C1	St Catherine Street	
C1	Cromwell Street	C2	St John's Lane	
C1	Dean's Walk	C1	St Mark Street	
C1	Dean's Way	B2	St Mary's Square	
D1	Denmark Road	B2	St Mary's Street	
D1	Eastgate Street	C4	St Michael's Square	
A2	Gloucester South West Bypass	B2	St Oswald's Road	
C2	Gouda Way	D1	Sebert Street	
D2	Great Western Road	C1	Serlo Road	
C3	Greyfriars	A4	Severn Road	
C1	Guinea Street	D4	Sherbourne Street	
C1	Hampden Way	D4	Sinope Street	
C1	Hare Lane	B3	Southgate Street	
D1	Heathville Road	B4	Spa Road	
D1	Henry Road	D3	Station Road	
B4	High Orchard Street	C1	Swan Road	
D1	Honyatt Road	C1	Sweetbriar Street	
B3	Kimbrose Way	A2	The Quay	
C4	Kings Barton Street	C3	The Oxbode	
C1	Kings Square	D1	Union Street	
C1	Kingsholm Road	B2	Upper Quay Street	
B3	Ladybellegate Street	D4	Victoria Street	
A4	Llanthony Road	C4	Wellington Street	
D2	London Road	B2	Westgate Street	
B3	Longsmith Street	C1	Worcester Street	

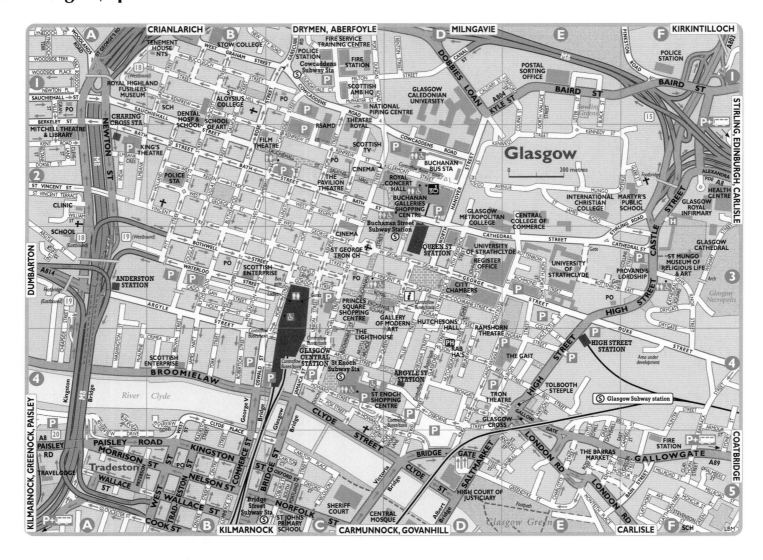

Glasgow

Glasgow is found on atlas page **256 D7**

E4	Albion Street	F5	Claythorn Avenue	A5	Gloucester Street	F5	Millroad Street	B2	Rose Street	B1	West Graham Street
F2	Alexandra Parade	F5	Claythorn Park	C3	Gordon Street	C1	Milton Street	E5	Ross Street	C3	West Nile Street
C4	Argyll Arcade	F5	Claythorn Street	A1	Granville Street	C3	Mitchell Street	E3	Rottenrow	B2	West Regent Street
B3	Argyle Street	A2	Cleveland Street	E5	Great Dovehill	E5	Moncur Street	E3	Rottenrow East	B4	West Street
F4	Armour Street	B4	Clyde Place	F5	Green Street	E5	Monteith Row	C3	Royal Exchange Square	A2	William Street
F5	Bain Street	D5	Clyde Street	E5	Greendyke Street	D3	Montrose Street	E5	St Andrews Street	D4	Wilson Street
E1	Baird Street	C5	Coburg Street	E4	High Street	A5	Morrison Street	A1	St Georges Road	F3	Wishart Street
F4	Barrack Street	D3	Cochrane Street	B1	Hill Street	B2	Nelson Street	E2	St James Road	A1	Woodlands Road
B2	Bath Street	E4	College Street	B2	Holland Street	B1	New City Road	E2	St Mungo Avenue	A1	Woodside Crescent
E4	Bell Street	F3	Collins Street	B5	Holm Street	A1	Newton Place	A3	St Vincent Place	A1	Woodside Place
A2	Beltane Street	B5	Commerce Street	C3	Hope Street	C5	Nicholson Street	A2	St Vincent Street	A1	Woodside Terrace
A1	Berkeley Street	B5	Cook Street	C4	Howard Street	C5	Norfolk Street	A2	St Vincent Terrace	B4	York Street
E1	Black Street	E1	Coupar Street	F4	Hunter Street	D3	North Frederick Street	D5	Saltmarket		
B3	Blythswood Street	C1	Cowcaddens Road	D4	Hutcheson Street	D3	North Hanover Street	A1	Sauchiehall Street		
B3	Bothwell Street	B4	Crimea Street	A2	India Street	E3	North Portland Street	B1	Scott Street		
D5	Bridgegate	B1	Dalhousie Street	D3	Ingram Street	E1	North Wallace Street	E4	Shuttle Street		
C5	Bridge Street	C4	Dixon Street	C4	Jamaica Street	D4	Osborne Street	D3	South Frederick Street		
B4	Broomielaw	D1	Dobbies Loan	B4	James Watt Street	B4	Oswald Street	C5	South Portland Street		
B4	Brown Street	A2	Dorset Street	F3	John Knox Street	C5	Oxford Street	E1	Stafford Street		
D4	Brunswick Street	B2	Douglas Street	D3	John Street	A5	Paisley Road	D5	Steel Street		
B1	Buccleuch Street	F3	Drygate	E2	Kennedy Street	A5	Parnie Street	F5	Stevenson Street		
C4	Buchanan Street	F4	Duke Street	A2	Kent Road	A5	Paterson Street	E3	Stirling Road		
B3	Cadogan Street	C1	Dundasvale Court	E5	Kent Street	F1	Pinkston Road	D5	Stockwell Street		
D1	Calgary Street	C5	Dunlop Street	D2	Killermont Street	B3	Pitt Street	F5	Sydney Street		
C2	Cambridge Street	F5	East Campbell Street	D5	King Street	C1	Port Dundas Road	C3	Turnbull Street		
D1	Canal Street	E1	Elmbank Crescent	B5	Kingston Street	C4	Queen Street	D4	Trongate		
E1	Candleriggs	A2	Elmbank Street	D1	Kyle Street	C3	Renfield Lane	E5	Turnbull Street		
C5	Carlton Court	C4	Fox Street	E1	Lister Street	C3	Renfield Street	C3	Union Street		
C5	Carlton Place	E4	Gallowgate	E4	Little Dovehill	B1	Renfrew Street	D4	Virginia Street		
F3	Castle Street	B1	Garnet Street	E5	London Road	D1	Renton Street	A5	Wallace Street		
F3	Cathedral Square	C1	Garscube Road	A1	Lynedoch Street	E3	Richmond Street	A4	Washington Street		
D3	Cathedral Street	D3	George Square	A1	Lynedoch Terrace	A5	Riverview Drive	B3	Waterloo Street		
B5	Centre Street	D3	George Street	A4	McAlpine Street	B4	Riverview Gardens	E4	Watson Street		
F5	Chambers Street	F5	Gibson Street	A3	McIntyre Street	A4	Riverview Place	B3	Wellington Street		
E5	Charlotte Street	D4	Glassford Street	C1	McPhater Street	B4	Robertson Street	B3	West Campbell Street		
A4	Cheapside Street	F2	Glebe Street	D4	Miller Street	D5	Ropework Lane	B2	West George Street		

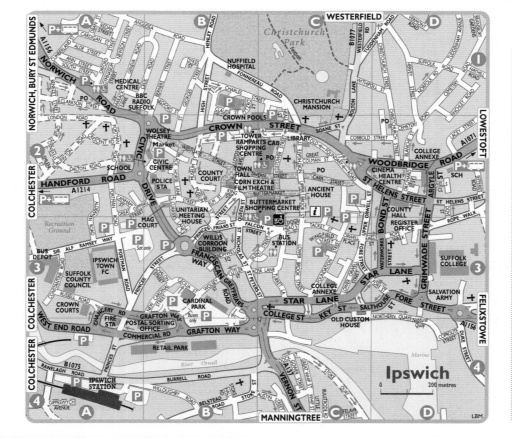

Ipswich

Ipswich is found on atlas page **106 D5**

A1	Anglesea Road	C3	Key Street
A1	Ann Street	B2	King Street
D2	Argyle Street	D2	Lacey Street
B4	Belstead Road	B2	Lloyds Avenue
B1	Berners Street	A2	London Road
B2	Black Horse Lane	C3	Lower Brook Street
C1	Bolton Lane	B2	Museum Street
D2	Bond Street	B3	New Cardinal Street
A2	Burlington Road	D3	Northern Quays
B4	Burrell Road	C2	Northgate Street
C2	Buttermarket	A1	Norwich Road
C2	Carr Street	C2	Old Foundary Road
B1	Cecil Road	A1	Orford Street
B3	Cecilia Street	C3	Orwell Place
D2	Cemetery Road	A2	Portman Road
A3	Chancery Road	A4	Princes Street
B1	Charles Street	B2	Queen Street
D1	Christchurch Street	A4	Ranelagh Road
A2	Civic Drive	D3	Rope Walk
A1	Clarkson Street	C3	Rose Lane
B1	Claude Street	A3	Russell Road
C3	Cobbold Street	B1	St Georges Street
C3	College Street	D2	St Helens Street
A4	Commercial Road	B3	St Nicholas Street
A3	Constantine Road	B3	St Peters Street
C2	Crown Street	C3	Salthouse Street
A1	Cumberland Street	B3	Silent Street
B3	Cutler Street	A3	Sir Alf Ramsey Way
A2	Dalton Road	C2	Soane Street
C4	Dock Street	C3	Star Lane
C3	Dogs Head Street	C4	Stoke Quay
D4	Duke Street	B4	Stoke Street
B2	Elm Street	D1	Suffolk Road
B3	Falcon Street	C3	Tacket Street
B1	Fonnereau Road	C2	Tavern Street
C3	Foundation Street	C2	Tower Street
B3	Franciscan Way	C1	Tuddenham Road
B3	Friars Street	C2	Turret Lane
A1	Geneva Road	C2	Upper Brook Street
B3	Grafton Way	C3	Upper Orwell Street
C2	Great Colman Street	C4	Vernon Street
B3	Greyfriars Road	D3	Waterworks Street
D3	Grimwade Street	A4	West End Road
A2	Handford Road	C1	Westerfield Road
B1	Henley Road	B2	Westgate Street
D1	Hervey Street	B4	Willoughby Road
B1	High Street	D2	Wolsey Street
		D2	Woodbridge Road

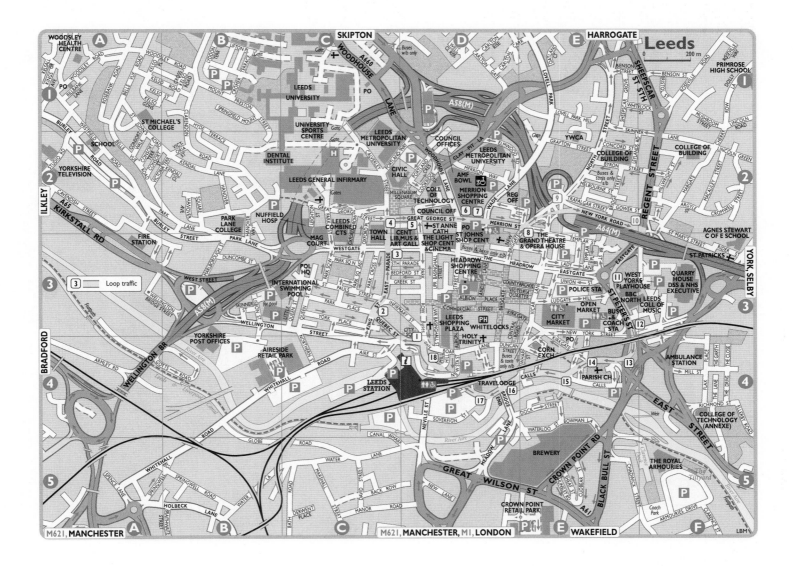

Kingston upon Hull

Kingston upon Hull is found on atlas page 180 D2

Leeds

Leeds is found on atlas page 177 J1

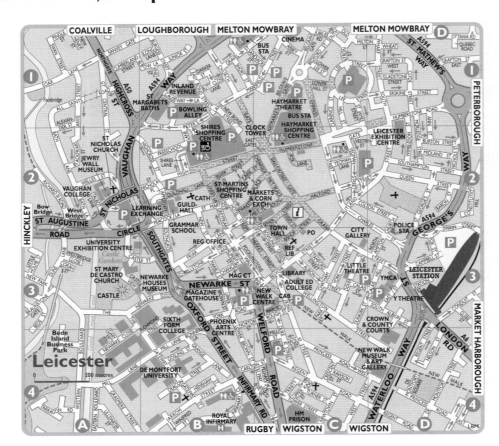

Leicester

Leicester is found on atlas page 132 B6

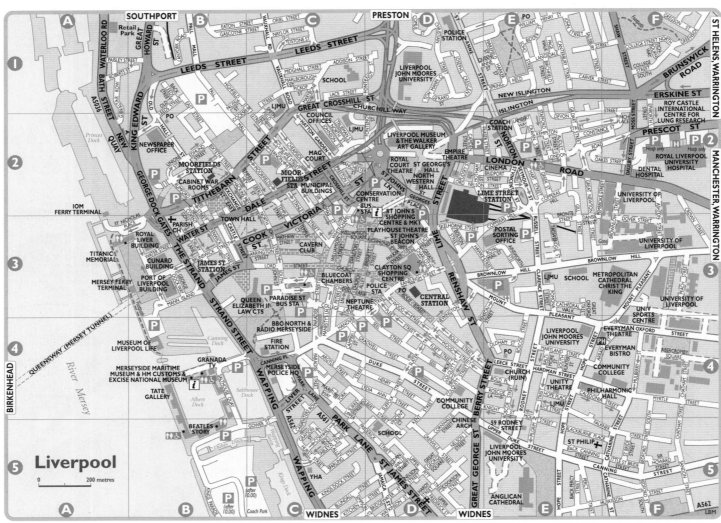

Liverpool

Liverpool is found on atlas page 162 F2

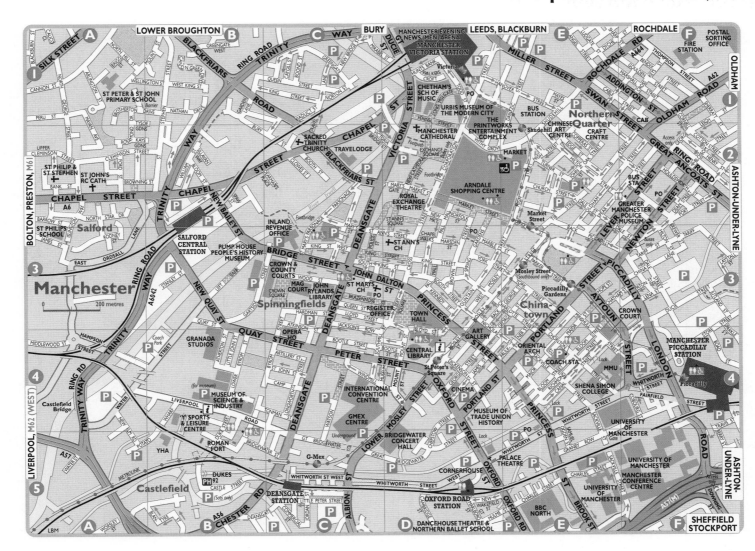

Manchester

Manchester is found on atlas page **164 F1**

E1	Addington Street	B2	Bury Street	F5	Downing Street	F3	Jutland Street	D5	New Wakefield Street	E5	Samuel Ogden Street
D3	Albert Square	C4	Byrom Street	F3	Ducie Street	A2	Kays Gardens	F3	Newton Street	E1	Sharp Street
C5	Albion Street	E1	Cable Street	B5	Duke Street	D3	Kennedy Street	D3	Nicholas Street	F1	Sherratt Street
E1	Angel Street	D5	Cambridge Street	E1	Dyche Street	C1	King Street	D2	Norfolk Street	E2	Shudehill
A1	Arlington Street	C4	Camp Street	A3	East Ordsall Lane	C3	King Street	A1	North George Street	A1	Silk Street
C4	Artillery Street	E4	Canal Street	E2	Edge Street	C3	King Street West	A1	North Hill Street	B2	Sillavan Way
B4	Atherton Street	A1	Cannon Street	D2	Exchange Square	F3	Laystall Street	A2	North Star Drive	C3	South King Street
C3	Atkinson Street	B1	Canon Green Drive	F4	Fairfield Street	B3	Left Bank	C1	Norton Street	C4	Southmill Street
E3	Aytoun Street	B5	Castle Street	E4	Faulkner Street	F3	Lena Street	E2	Oak Street	C4	Sparkle Street
E3	Back George Street	C1	Caygill Street	D1	Fennel Street	E3	Lever Street	F1	Oldham Road	B2	Spaw Street
E3	Back Piccadilly	A2	Chapel Street	F2	Ford Street	B4	Little John Street	E2	Oldham Street	E2	Spear Street
A2	Bank Street	D3	Chapel Walks	D3	Fountain Street	C5	Little Peter Street	E5	Oxford Road	D3	Spring Gardens
A2	Barrow Street	E5	Charles Street	B1	Garden Lane	B4	Liverpool Road	D4	Oxford Street	B3	Stanley Street
F1	Bendix Street	E3	Charlotte Street	B3	Gartside Street	C3	Lloyd Street	E3	Pall Mall	F4	Store Street
F5	Berry Street	E3	Chatham Street	F2	George Leigh Street	F4	London Road	E3	Parker Street	E1	Swan Street
A1	Blackburn Street	D5	Chepstow Street	D4	George Street	D1	Long Millgate	C2	Parsonage	F3	Tariff Street
B1	Blackfriars Road	B5	Chester Road	F1	Goulden Street	C4	Longworth Street	F3	Paton Street	F1	Thompson Street
C2	Blackfriars Street	F3	China Lane	E5	Granby Row	B4	Lower Byrom Street	A1	Peru Street	E2	Tib Street
B5	Blantyre Street	E4	Chorlton Street	C1	Gravel Lane	C5	Lower Mosley Street	C4	Peter Street	D1	Todd Street
B2	Bloom Street	E1	Church Street	F2	Great Ancoats Street	E1	Ludgate Street	E3	Piccadilly	C4	Tonman Street
E4	Bloom Street	A2	Clowes Street	C5	Great Bridgewater Street	E4	Major Street	C3	Police Street	F4	Travis Street
F2	Blossom Street	F4	Cobourg Street	D1	Great Ducie Street	D3	Marble Street	F2	Port Street	A4	Trinity Way
F4	Boad Street	C5	Commercial Street	D5	Great Marlborough Street	D2	Market Street	E4	Portland Street	E2	Turner Street
C1	Boond Street	E2	Copperas Street	C1	Greengate	D3	Marsden Street	A5	Potato Wharf	A1	Tysoe Gardens
C2	Booth Street	F1	Cornell Street	B1	Greengate West	F1	Marshall Street	D3	Princess Street	A2	Upper Cleminson Street
D3	Booth Street	D2	Corporation Street	A4	Hampson Street	A1	Mayan Avenue	B4	Quay Street	C1	Viaduct Street
C4	Bootle Street	F2	Cotton Street	E1	Hanover Street	E1	Mayes Street	C1	Queen Street	C2	Victoria Bridge Street
C3	Brazennose Street	F1	Cross Keys Street	C3	Hardman Street	A4	Middlewood Street	C3	Queen Street	D2	Victoria Street
F3	Brewer Street	D3	Cross Street	F2	Henry Street	E1	Miller Street	E4	Richmond Street	D1	Walkers Croft
C3	Bridge Street	E2	Dale Street	E2	High Street	C1	Minshull Street	E1	Rochdale Road	A4	Water Street
B5	Bridgewater Street	E1	Dantzic Street	E2	Hilton Street	A3	Mirabel Street	A3	Rodney Street	C4	Watson Street
A1	Briggs Street	F2	Dean Street	E3	Hope Street	D4	Mosley Street	A2	Rosamond Drive	B1	Wellington Street
E5	Brook Street	C4	Deansgate	D2	Houldsworth Street	B1	Mount Street	E4	Sackville Street	B1	West King Street
A1	Brotherton Drive	C2	Dearman's Place	D5	Hulme Street	D4	Mount Street	D2	St Ann's Square	D3	West Mosley Street
D3	Brown Street	D4	Dickenson Street	D1	Hunts Bank	D4	Museum Street	D4	St Ann's Street	E5	Whitworth Street
A2	Browning Street			A2	Islington Way	B1	Nathan Drive	D4	St James Street	C5	Whitworth Street West
				C3	Jackson's Row	B2	New Bailey Street	C4	St John Street	B2	William Street
				A3	James Street	C1	New Bridge Street	D2	St Mary's Gate	B4	Windmill Street
				D4	John Dalton Street	A4	New Elm Road	C3	St Mary's Parsonage	D2	Withy Grove
				E2	John Street	D2	New Market	C2	St Mary's Street	D4	Wood Street
				C5	Jordan Street	B3	New Quay Street	B2	St Stephen Street	D3	York Street

Middlesbrough

Middlesbrough is found on atlas page **206 B4**

D4	Abingdon Road	B2	Lees Road
C2	Albert Road	B4	Linthorpe Road
C1	Albert Street	A4	Longford Street
C4	Albert Terrace	D4	Lothian Road
B2	Alwent Road	B1	Marsh Road
A4	Ayresome Green Lane	A2	Marsh Street
A3	Ayresome Green Road	D2	Marton Road
A4	Ayresome Street	A3	Meath Street
C2	Baker Street	D2	Melrose Street
C2	Bedford Street	B1	Metz Bridge Road
C2	Borough Road	D3	Newlands Road
C2	Brentnall Street	A2	Newport Road
D1	Bridge Street	B1	North Road
D2	Bright Street	B3	Outram Street
D4	Byelands Street	B4	Oxford Road
B2	Cadogan Street	C4	Park Lane
B2	Cannon Park Road	B4	Park Road South
B2	Cannon Park Way	D4	Park Vale Road
A2	Cannon Street	A3	Parliament Road
A3	Carlow Street	C3	Pelham Street
B4	Chester Street	C3	Percy Street
D4	Clairville Road	C3	Portman Street
B3	Clarendon Road	B3	Princes Road
B3	Clifton Street	D1	Queens Square
B4	Clive Road	D3	Roscoe Street
C2	Corporation Road	D2	Russell Street
A3	Crescent Road	C2	St Aidens Drive
A2	Derwent Street	B2	St Pauls Road
B3	Diamond Road	C3	Southfield Road
D2	Emily Street	C3	Southfield Lane
A4	Essex Street	C3	Stamford Street
D1	Exchange Square	C3	Stephenson Street
C2	Fairbridge Street	C3	Stowe Street
D2	Fife Street	C3	Tennyson Street
B2	Fleetham Street	D2	The Boulevard
C2	Garnet Street	B3	Union Street
C2	Gilkes Street	C3	Victoria Road
B3	Glebe Road	A3	Waterloo Road
C2	Grange Road	D3	Wicklow Street
B3	Granville Road	C1	Wilson Street
B3	Gresham Road	C3	Wilton Street
A2	Greta Street	B2	Windsor Street
D2	Gurney Street	D1	Windward Way
A4	Harford Street	A3	Woodlands Road
B2	Hartington Road	C3	Worcester Street
B4	Kensington Road	B4	Wylam Street
A3	Lamport Street	B3	Zetland Road
C4	Laura Street	C1	

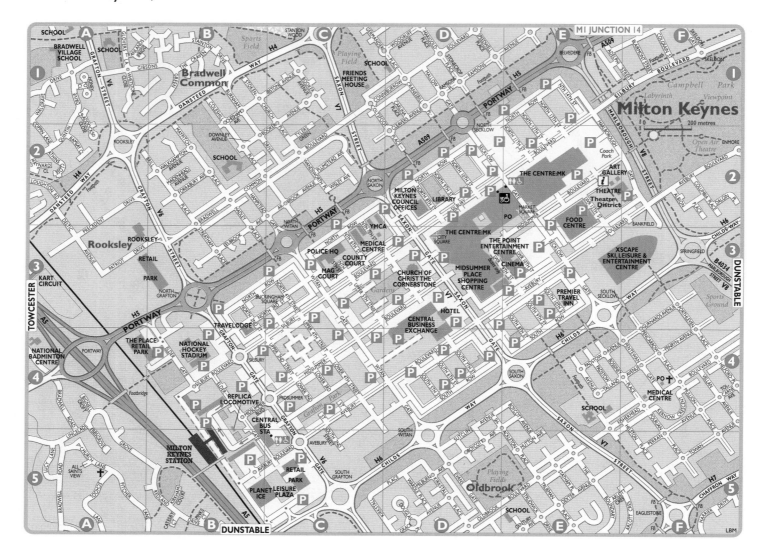

Milton Keynes

Milton Keynes is found on atlas page **100 D6**

E1	Adelphi Street	A2	Dansteed Way	E2	Lower 12th Street	C2	Plumstead Avenue	B1	The Craven
F2	Albion Place	A2	Deltic Avenue	A5	Lucy Lane	F4	Polruan Place	F4	Tolcarne Avenue
A5	All Saints View	E5	Dexter Avenue	B2	Maidenhead Avenue	F3	Porthleven Place	F5	Towan Avenue
C2	Arbrook Avenue	D5	Douglas Place	D1	Mallow Gate	A4	Portway	A1	Tranlands Brigg
E5	Arlott Crescent	B2	Downley Avenue	D1	Marigold Place	A3	Precedent Drive	E5	Trueman Place
A2	Athins Close	A5	Ebbsgrove	E2	Market Square	A2	Quintin Drive	C2	Tylers Green
C5	Avebury Boulevard	B3	Eelbrook Avenue	E2	Marlborough Street	A2	Ramsay Close	C4	Upper 2nd Street
A4	Bignell Croft	B4	Elder Gate	E1	Marlborough Gate	D1	Ramsons Avenue	C4	Upper 4th Street
F1	Blairmont Street	D5	Evans Gate	A2	Maynard Close	D1	Ramsons Place	C3	Upper 5th Street
B2	Booker Avenue	F4	Fishermead Boulevard	B2	Maypitch Place	B5	Redland Drive	F4	Vellan Avenue
E4	Bossiney Place	B2	Forrabury Avenue	B4	Midsummer Boulevard	D3	Saxon Gate	A1	Walgrave Drive
D5	Boycott Avenue	C1	Germander Place	D5	Milburn Avenue	C1	Saxon Street	B2	Walkhampton Avenue
B2	Bradwell Common	A1	Gibsons Green	F4	Mullion Place	E4	Saxon Street	C2	Wandsworth Place
	Boulevard	A1	Glovers Lane	B3	North 2nd Street	A5	School Lane	D5	Wardle Place
A5	Bradwell Road	D5	Grace Avenue	C3	North 3rd Street	D2	Secklow Gate	A1	Whetstone Close
B2	Brill Place	B4	Grafton Gate	C3	North 4th Street	D4	Shackleton Place	C2	Wisley Avenue
B3	Buckingham Square	A1	Grafton Street	C3	North 5th Street	B4	Silbury Boulevard	C3	Witan Gate
B1	Burnham Drive	F3	Gurnards Avenue	C3	North 6th Street	F1	Skeldon Gate	D1	Woodruff Avenue
D1	Caruna Place	B2	Hadley Place	C2	North 7th Street	C5	South 2nd Street		
B5	Catesby Court	B2	Hampstead Gate	D2	North 8th Street	D4	South 5th Street		
E5	Century Avenue	F5	Harrier Drive	D2	North 9th Street	D4	South 6th Street		
F5	Chaffron Way	F4	Helford Place	D2	North 10th Street	D4	South 7th Street		
B1	Chesham Avenue	F5	Helston Place	E2	North 11th Street	E3	South 8th Street		
D5	Childs Way	A1	Honey Pot Close	E1	North 12th Street	E3	South 9th Street		
A5	Church Lane	E5	Hutton Avenue	E1	North 13th Street	E3	South 10th Street		
D3	City Square	C1	Ibstone Avenue	E1	North 14th Street	D4	South Row		
D1	Cleavers Avenue	F4	Kernow Crescent	B3	North Row	D1	Speedwell Place		
B1	Coleshill Place	B5	Kirkham Court	D5	Oldbrook Boulevard	B1	Stainton Drive		
F1	Colgrain Street	C5	Kirkstall Place	E4	Padstow Avenue	B1	Statham Place		
C1	Coltsfoot Place	A5	Lincelade Grove	A3	Patriot Drive	B1	Stokenchurch Place		
F2	Columbia Place	A2	Loughton Road	A2	Pencarrow Place	D1	Stonecrop Place		
C1	Conniburrow Boulevard	C4	Lower 2nd Street	F4	Penryn Avenue	B3	Streatham Place		
A2	Coppin Lane	C4	Lower 3rd Street	F4	Pentewan Gate	E5	Strudwick Drive		
A1	Craddocks Close	C4	Lower 4th Street	F5	Perran Avenue	D5	Sutcliffe Avenue		
D1	Cranesbill Place	D3	Lower 9th Street	B5	Pinks Court	E4	Talland Avenue		
F2	Dalgin Place	E3	Lower 10th Street	A5	Pitcher Lane	E5	The Boundary		

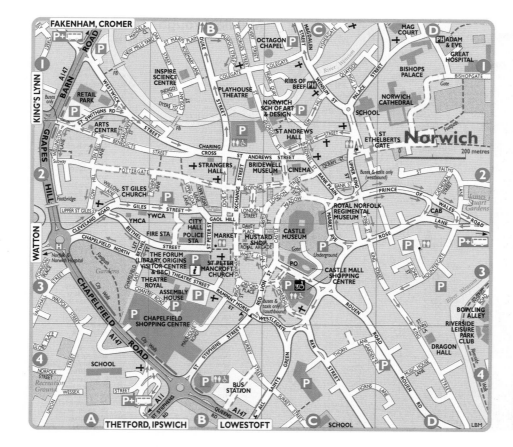

Norwich

Norwich is found on atlas page **138 E5**

C4	All Saints Green	C2	Opie Street
C2	Bank Plain	B3	Orford Place
C2	Bank Street	B1	Palace Street
A1	Barn Road	C1	Pigg Lane
B2	Bedford Street	A2	Pottergate
C4	Ber Street	D2	Prince of Wales Road
A3	Bethel Street	C2	Princes Street
D1	Bishopgate	C1	Quayside
B3	Brigg Street	C2	Queen Street
B1	Calvert Street	B4	Queens Road
C3	Castle Meadow	B3	Rampant Horse Street
C2	Castle Street	B3	Red Lion Street
D2	Cathedral Street	C2	Redwell Street
B3	Chantry Road	D3	Rose Lane
A3	Chapelfield East	B1	Rosemary Lane
A3	Chapelfield North	C3	Rouen Road
A3	Chapelfield Road	B3	Royal Arcade
B2	Charing Cross	B2	St Andrews Street
A3	Cleveland Road	D3	St Ann Lane
B1	Colegate	A2	St Benedicts Street
B1	Coslany Street	D2	St Faiths Lane
A2	Cow Hill	B1	St Georges Street
B3	Davey Place	D3	St John Street
B1	Dove Street	A2	St Margarets Street
B1	Duke Street	A2	St Marys Plain
C1	Elm Hill	B3	St Peter Street
B2	Exchange Street	B4	St Stephens Road
C1	Fishergate	B4	St Stephens Street
C1	Friars Quay	A1	St Swithins Road
B2	Gaol Hill	B4	Surrey Street
C4	Garden Street	A2	Ten Bell Lane
A2	Giles Street	B3	Theatre Street
A2	Grapes Hill	B3	Thorn Lane
B3	Haymarket	C4	Thorn Lane
C4	Horns Lane	C3	Timberhill
C2	King Street	A4	Union Street
A3	Little Bethel Street	B2	Unthank Street
B2	London Street	B2	Upper Goat Lane
C2	Lower Goat Lane	C2	Upper King Street
C1	Magdalen Street	C2	Upper St Giles Street
B4	Malthouse Road	A3	Vauxhall St reet
C2	Market Avenue	A3	Walpole Street
D3	Mountergate	A2	Wellington Lane
D4	Music House Lane	C1	Wensum Street
B1	Muspole Street	A4	Wessex Street
B1	New Mills Yard	A1	Westlegate
A4	Norfolk Street	C3	Westlegate
B1	Oak Street	B3	White Lion Street
		A2	Willow Lane

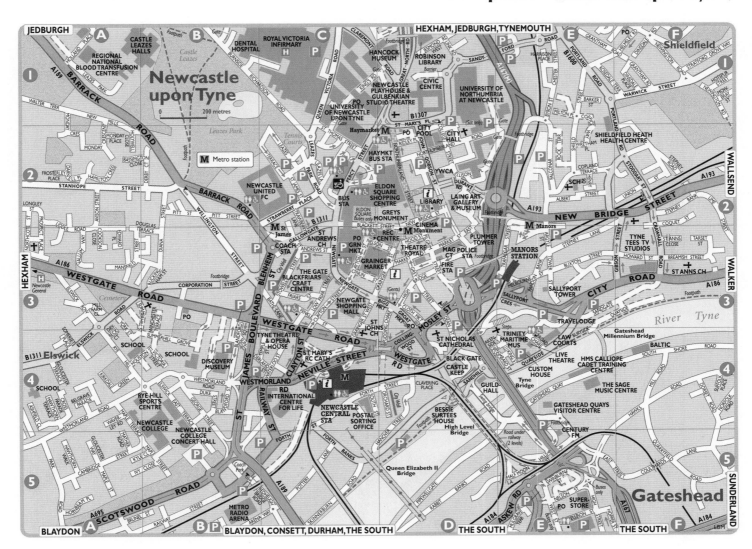

Newcastle upon Tyne

Newcastle upon Tyne is found on atlas page **227 G7**

D4	Akenside Hill	E1	Coppice Way	A5	Gloucester Way	C2	Leazes Park Road	D4	Orchard Street	A4	Somerset Place
E2	Albert Street	F2	Coquet Street	D3	Grainger Street	C2	Leazes Terrace	E3	Pandon Bank	F4	South Shore Road
B5	Arena Way	B3	Corporation Street	C3	Grainger Street West	A3	Liddle Road	A5	Park Road	C4	South Street
E3	Argyle Street	F5	Coulthards Lane	E1	Grantham Road	F2	Lime Street	C4	Peel Lane	A2	Stanhope Street
A4	Ashfield Close	F3	Crawhall Road	D1	Great North Road	D1	Link Road	C2	Percy Street	F2	Stepney Bank
E5	Askew Road	A4	Cross Parade	D3	Grey Street	E4	Lombard Street	D3	Pilgrim Street	E3	Stepney Lane
A2	Avison Street	A2	Darnell Place	D3	Groat Market	A2	Longley Street	D5	Pipewellgate	F2	Stepney Road
E1	Barker Street	D3	Dean Street	E5	Half Moon Lane	C3	Low Friar Street	B2	Pitt Street	F2	Stoddart Street
A1	Barrack Road	B2	Derby Court	A2	Hamilton Crescent	A3	Mansfield Street	E1	Portland Road	C3	Stowell Street
A2	Bassington Close	B3	Diana Street	D5	Hanover Street	B5	Maple Street	C5	Pottery Lane	F1	Stratford Grove Way
C3	Bath Lane	F1	Dinsdale Place	E1	Harrison Place	A4	Maple Terrace	A2	Prospect Place	C2	Strawberry Lane
A4	Belgrave Parade	F1	Dinsdale Road	F4	Hawks Road	D3	Market Street	D4	Pudding Chare	C2	Strawberry Place
D3	Bigg Market	F4	Dorset Road	A4	Hawthorn Terrace	D3	Market Street East	D3	Quarryfield Road	C2	Suffolk Place
C2	Blackett Street	B3	Douglas Terrace	A5	Hawthorn Walk	A5	Mather Road	E4	Quayside	B4	Summerhill Grove
B4	Blandford Square	A4	Drybeck Court	A1	Helmsley Road	E3	Melbourne Street	C1	Queen Victoria Road	B3	Summerhill Street
B4	Blandford Street	B4	Duke Street	E2	Henry Square	A3	Mill Farm Close	D5	Rabbit Banks Road	B4	Sunderland Street
C3	Blenheim Street	D2	Durant Road	D3	High Bridge	F4	Mill Road	B5	Railway Street	E5	Swinburne Street
F3	Breamish Street	E5	East Street	E5	High Street	E1	Milton Place	C5	Redheugh Bridge Road	F3	Tarset Street
E4	Broad Chare	A3	Edward Place	E5	Hills Street	A2	Monday Crescent	B1	Richardson Road	C4	Temple Street
A5	Brunel Street	C2	Eldon Square	A1	Holland Place	A2	Monday Place	E2	Ridley Place	D4	The Close
B3	Buckingham Street	D2	Ellison Place	A2	Holywell Close	D3	Mosley Street	E2	Rock Terrace	E3	Tower Street
B1	Burnside	E5	Ellison Street	D3	Hood Street	F1	Mowbray Street	E1	Rosedale Terrace	E3	Trafalgar Street
E4	Buryside	B4	Elswick East Terrace	E5	Hopper Street	E5	Mulgrave Terrace	A4	Rye Hill	F2	Union Street
E3	Buxton Street	A4	Elswick Road	A5	Hornbeam Place	C3	Nelson Street	C3	St Andrews Street	A3	Vallum Way
E1	Byron Street	A3	Elswick Row	F1	Hotspur Street	E5	Nelson Street (Gateshead)	F3	St Anns Close	B4	Victoria Street
A5	Cambridge Street	E2	Falconar Street	A4	Houston Street	C4	Neville Street	B4	St James Boulevard	F1	Walter Terrace
E1	Chester Street	C3	Fenckle Street	F3	Howard Street	D2	New Bridge Street	C2	St James Street	F1	Warwick Street
E3	Forth Banks	C5	Forth Banks	A5	Ivy Close	E2	New Bridge Street	B1	St Mary's Place	C4	Waterloo Street
C1	Claremont Road	C4	Forth Street	D1	Jesmond Road West	A1	New Mills	C2	St Thomas Street	A4	Waverley Road
D4	Clavering Place	C3	Friars Street	D2	John Dobson Street	C3	Newgate	E3	Sallyport Crescent	B2	Wellington Street
C4	Clayton Street	A2	Frosterley Place	C1	King's Road	F1	Newington Road	E3	Sandgate	E5	West Street
D3	Cloth Market	C3	Gallowgate	E4	King Street	F4	Norfolk Road	D4	Sandhill	C4	Westgate Road
D2	College Street	E4	Gateshead Quay	A4	Kirkdale Green	A3	Northcote Street	A5	Scotswood Road	A4	Westmorland Road
D4	Collingwood Street	B4	George Street	A5	Kyle Close	D2	Northumberland Road	C2	Shield Street	B3	Winchester Terrace
A3	Cookson Close	F3	Gibson Street	A5	Leazes Lane	D2	Northumberland Street	C5	Skinnerburn Road	E2	Wretham Place
E2	Copland Terrace	A4	Gloucester Terrace	A1	Leazes Park	C3	Nun Street			A3	York Street

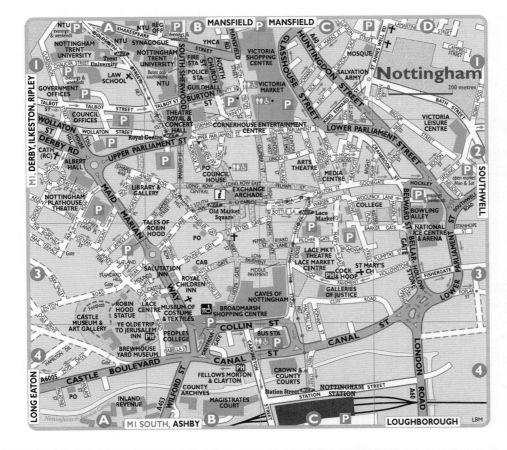

Nottingham

Nottingham is found on atlas page **153 L6**

B3	Albert Street	C1	Huntingdon Street
B2	Angel Row	C1	King Edward Street
C3	Barker Gate	B2	King Street
D1	Bath Street	D2	Lennox Street
B2	Beastmarket Hill	C2	Lincoln Street
C1	Beck Street	B3	Lister Gate
D3	Bellargate	D4	London Road
D2	Belward Street	B2	Long Row Central
C2	Bridlesmith Gate	B2	Long Row East
C2	Broad Street	B3	Low Pavement
A2	Bromley Place	C2	Lower Parliament Street
D1	Brook Street	A2	Maid Marion Way
B1	Burton Street	B1	Mansfield Road
B4	Canal Street	B2	Market Street
C2	Carlton Street	C3	Middle Hill
B4	Carrington Street	B1	Milton Street
A4	Castle Boulevard	A3	Mount Street
B3	Castle Gate	C2	Old Lenton Street
A3	Castle Road	A3	Park Row
A1	Chaucer Street	C2	Pelham Street
B2	Cheapside	D3	Pemberton Street
C3	Cliff Road	C3	Pilcher Gate
C2	Clinton Street East	C2	Plumptre Street
A1	Clarendon Street	B2	Queen Street
C2	Clumber Street	D1	St Annes Well Road
B4	Collin Street	A3	St James's Street
C1	Conuent Street	C1	St Marks Street
D2	Cranbrook Street	C2	St Mary's Gate
A2	Cumberland Place	B3	St Peters Gate
C1	Curzon Place	A1	Shakespeare Street
A2	Derby Road	B2	South Parade
C1	East Circus Street	B1	South Sherwood Street
C2	East Street	C4	Station Street
D3	Fishergate	C2	Stoney Street
C3	Fletcher Gate	A1	Talbot Street
B2	Forman Street	A2	Thurland Street
A3	Friar Lane	A2	Toll House Hill
D2	Gedling Street	B1	Trent Street
C2	Glasshouse Street	C3	Trinity Square
C1	Goldsmith Street	A2	Upper Parliament Street
A1	Goosegate	C2	Victoria Street
C2	Greyfriar Gate	C2	Warser Gate
B4	Heathcote Street	C3	Weekday Cross
C2	High Cross Street	A2	Wellington Circus
C3	High Pavement	B2	Wheeler Gate
D2	High Street	B4	Wilford Street
D2	Hockley	A2	Wollaton Street
D3	Hollowstone	C2	Woolpack Lane

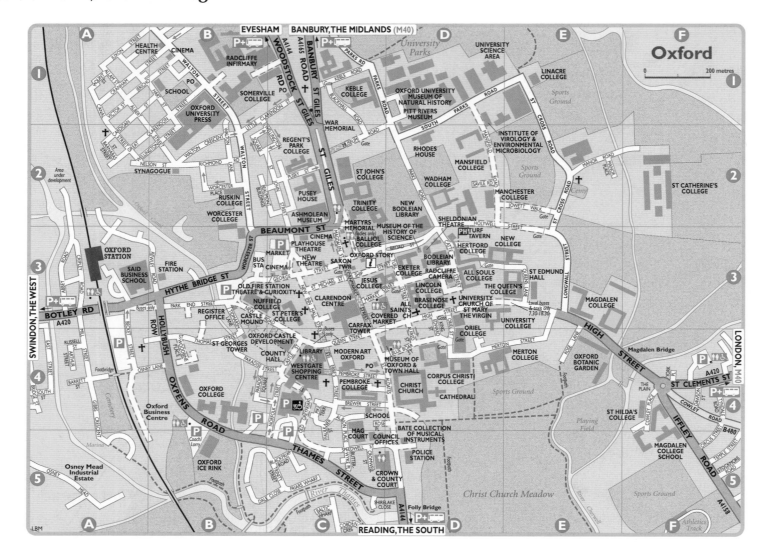

Oxford

Oxford is found on atlas page **81 G5**

A3	Abbey Road	C5	Faulkner Street
A1	Albert Street	C5	Friars Wharf
C4	Albion Place	C3	George Street
D4	Alfred Street	A4	Gibbs Crescent
A4	Allam Street	A2	Great Clarendon Street
A4	Arthur Street	B1	Hart Street
C5	Baltic Wharf	D3	High Street
C1	Banbury Road	B3	Hollybush Row
A4	Barrett Street	D2	Holywell Street
B2	Beaumont Buildings	B3	Hythe Bridge Street
C3	Beaumont Street	F4	Iffley Road
A3	Becket Street	A1	Jericho Street
C5	Blackfriars Road	E2	Jowett Walk
C1	Blackhall Road	A1	Juxon Street
D4	Blue Boar Street	C1	Keble Road
A3	Botley Road	D3	King Edward Street
F4	Boulter Street	B2	Little Clarendon Street
C4	Brewer Street	E3	Longwall Street
A4	Bridge Street	C3	Magdalen Street
D3	Broad Street	E2	Manor Place
C5	Butterwyke Place	E2	Manor Road
A1	Canal Street	D2	Mansfield Road
A2	Cardigan Street	C3	Market Street
C4	Castle Street	D4	Merton Street
D3	Catte Street	A4	Mill Street
F5	Circus Street	A1	Mount Street
C5	Cobden Crescent	C2	Museum Road
C3	Cornmarket Street	A2	Nelson Street
F4	Cowley Place	C3	New Inn Hall Street
F4	Cowley Road	B3	New Road
A1	Cranham Street	C4	Norfolk Street
A3	Cripley Road	C4	Old Greyfriars Street
C5	Cromwell Street	D3	Oriel Street
C5	Dale Close	A4	Osney Lane
F4	Dawson Street	A5	Osney Mead
A4	East Street	B4	Oxpens Road

B4	Paradise Square	F4	Tyndale Road
B4	Paradise Street	A1	Victor Street
B3	Park End Street	B2	Walton Crescent
C1	Parks Road	B2	Walton Lane
C4	Pembroke Street	B1	Walton Street
C4	Pike Terrace	C2	Wellington Square
C2	Pusey Street	A2	Wellington Street
C4	Queen Street	B4	Woodbine Place
E3	Queens Lane	C1	Woodstock Road
B3	Rewley Road	B2	Worcester Place
B2	Richmond Road	B3	Worcester Street
E4	Rose Lane	F4	York Place
C4	Rose Place		
A4	Russell Street		
D4	St Aldates		
A2	St Barnabas Street		
F4	St Clements Street		
E1	St Cross Road		
C4	St Ebbe's Street		
C1	St Giles		
C2	St John Street		
C3	St Michael Street		
B4	St Thomas Street		
D2	Savile Road		
C3	Ship Street		
C5	Shirelake Close		
D1	South Parks Road		
A4	South Street		
C5	Speedwell Street		
F5	Stockmore Road		
F5	Temple Street		
C5	Thames Street		
F4	The Plain		
B3	Tidmarsh Lane		
C5	Trinity Street		
D3	Turl Street		

University Colleges

D3	All Souls College
C3	Balliol College
D3	Brasenose College
D4	Christ Church College
D4	Corpus Christi College
D3	Exeter College
D2	Hertford College
C1	Jesus College
C1	Keble College
E1	Linacre College
D3	Lincoln College
E3	Magdalen College
D2	Manchester College
D2	Mansfield College
E4	Merton College
D3	New College
B3	Nuffield College
D4	Oriel College
C4	Pembroke College
E3	Queen's College
B2	Regent's Park College
B2	Ruskin College
F2	St Catherine's College
E3	St Edmund Hall
F4	St Hilda's College
C2	St John's College
C3	St Peter's College
B1	Somerville College
C2	Trinity College
D3	University College
D2	Wadham College
B2	Worcester College

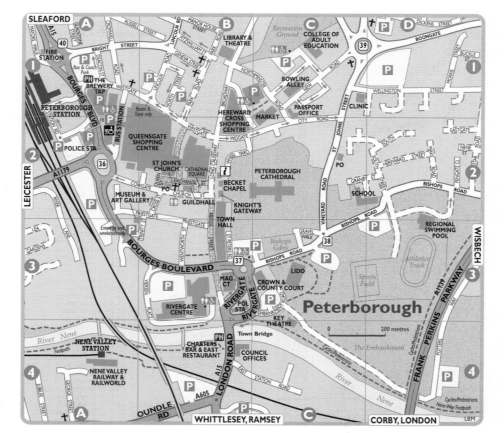

Peterborough

Peterborough is found on atlas page **134 D6**

C3	Bishops Road	A1	Russell Street
D1	Boongate	C2	St Johns Street
A1	Bourges Boulevard	B3	St Peters Road
B3	Bridge Street	D2	South Street
A1	Bright Street	D2	Star Road
B1	Broadway	A2	Station Road
D1	Buckle Street	B3	Trinity Street
B2	Cathedral Square	B3	Versen Platz
B2	Church Street	C2	Vineyard Road
C2	City Road	D1	Wake Road
A2	Cowgate	D1	Wellington Street
A1	Cromwell Road	B3	Wentworth Street
B2	Cross Street	A1	Westgate
A1	Deacon Street	B2	Wheel Yard
D1	Dickens Street		
B4	East Station Road		
D2	Eastgate		
C3	Embankment Road		
B2	Exchange Street		
D2	Fengate Close		
B1	Fitzwilliam Street		
D4	Frank Perkins Parkway		
B1	Geneva Street		
A4	George Street		
A1	Gladstone Street		
C2	Granby Street		
C3	Gravel Walk		
D2	Hereward Street		
A4	Jubilee Street		
A3	Lea Gardens		
B1	Lincoln Road		
B1	London Road		
B2	Long Causeway		
B1	Manor House Street		
A1	Mayors Walk		
B2	Midgate		
D1	Morris Street		
D2	Nene Street		
C1	New Road		
B1	North Street		
B1	Northminster Road		
B4	Oundle Road		
B1	Park Road		
D4	Potters Way		
B2	Priestgate		
B2	Queen Street		
A2	Rivergate		
B3	Rivergate		

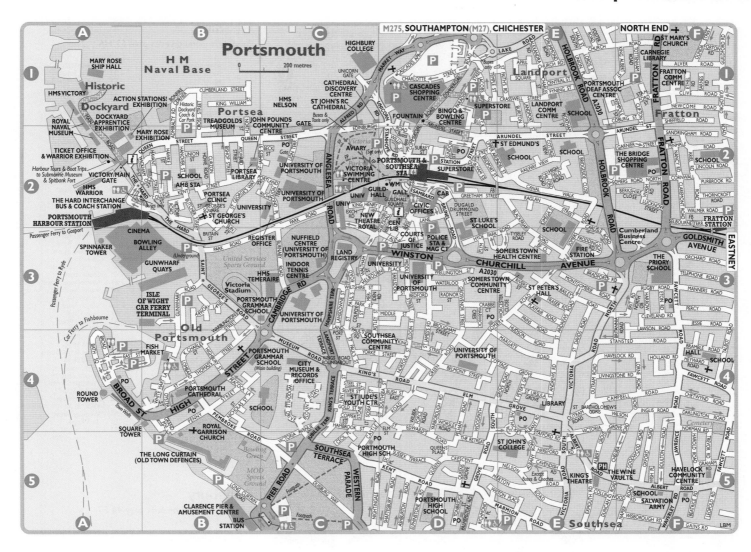

Portsmouth

Portsmouth is found on atlas page 32 **B6**

B2	Admiralty Road	F4	Campbell Road	E5	Exmouth Road	C2	King Henry I Street	B4	Oyster Street	C5	Southsea Terrace
E5	Albany Road	E2	Canal Walk	F3	Fawcett Road	D4	King Street	E3	Pains Road	E5	Stafford Road
E5	Albert Grove	E3	Carlisle Road	C4	Flint Street	D5	Palmerston Road	D2	Stanhope Road
E5	Albert Road	D1	Cascades Approach	E3	Fraser Road	B1	King William Street	D1	Paradise Street	F4	Stansted Road
D3	Alec Rose Lane	C4	Castle Road	F1	Fratton Road	C4	King's Road	B3	Park Road	D2	Station Street
E1	Alexandra Road	E5	Cavendish Road	F2	Garnier Street	C4	King's Terrace	C4	Park Street	C4	Stone Street
C1	Alfred Road	E1	Charles Street	C4	Gold Street	E1	Lake Road	B4	Peacock Lane	D2	Surrey Street
F1	Alver Road	D1	Charlotte Street	F3	Goldsmith Avenue	C3	Landport Street	D4	Pelham Road	D5	Sussex Terrace
C2	Anglesea Road	D3	Grosvenor Street	F5	Goodwood Road	C4	Landport Terrace	B4	Pembroke Road	F3	Telephone Road
E1	April Square	E5	Chelsea Road	D4	Great Southsea Street	C4	Lansdowne Street	F2	Penhale Road	D1	Temple Street
F2	Ariel Road	F4	Chetwynd Road	D4	Green Road	F3	Lawrence Road	B4	Penny Street	A2	The Hard
B3	Armory Lane	E1	Church Road	D2	Greetham Street	F3	Lawson Road	C5	Pier Road	D5	The Retreat
E2	Arundel Street	F2	Claremont Road	D3	Grosvenor Street	C2	Lion Terrace	E3	Playfair Road	E4	The Thicket
D5	Ashburton Road	F3	Cleveland Road	E4	Grove Road North	E4	Little Southsea Street	B2	Queen Street	D1	Unicorn Road
C3	Astley Street	F1	Clifton Street	D5	Grove Road South	E4	Livingstone Road	D5	Queens Crescent	E1	Union Place
B2	Aylward Street	F1	Clive Road	D2	Guildhall Square	B5	Long Curtain Road	D5	Queens Grove	D2	Upper Arundel Street
E3	Baileys Road	E5	Coburg Street	D2	Guildhall Walk	E1	Lords Street	D5	Queens Place	C5	Victoria Avenue
A4	Bath Square	D2	Collingwood Road	B3	Gunwharf Road	F4	Lorne Road	E2	Raglan Street	E4	Victoria Grove
D4	Belmont Street	F2	Commercial Road	C4	Hambrook Street	F2	Lucknow Street	E2	Railway View	E4	Victoria Road North
B2	Bishop Street	E2	Cottage Grove	C3	Hampshire Terrace	A1	Main Road	E4	Rugby Road	E5	Victoria Road South
E2	Blackfriars Road	E2	Cottage View	B2	Hanover Street	D1	Market Way	E4	St Andrews Road	B2	Victory Road
C4	Blount Road	E1	Crasswell Street	F5	Harold Road	C3	Marmion Road	E4	St Davids Road	F2	Vivash Road
B1	Bonfire Corner	B1	Cross Street	B2	Havant Street	D1	Melbourne Place	D4	St Edward's Road	F2	Walmer Road
F5	Boulton Road	B1	Cumberland Street	E4	Havelock Road	E5	Merton Road	E1	St Faith's Road	C3	Waltham Street
F4	Bramble Road	B2	Curzon Howe Road	E5	Hawke Street	C3	Middle Street	B3	Saint George's Road	B3	Warblington Street
E2	Bridgeside Close	F4	Darlington Road	E5	Hereford Road	C4	Montgomerie Road	B2	St George's Way	D3	Warwick Crescent
D2	Bridport Street	D2	Dugald Drummond Street	E1	Heyward Road	C4	Museum Road	D4	St James's Road	C3	Waterloo Street
F3	Britannia Road	C5	Duisburg Way	B4	High Street	F2	Nancy Road	C2	St James's Street	F5	Waverley Road
F3	Britannia Road North	B5	Duncan Road	B4	Highbury Street	F5	Napier Road	B4	St Nicholas Street	D3	Wellington Street
A4	Broad Street	D2	Durham Street	E1	Holbrook Road	E5	Nelson Road	C3	St Paul's Road	C5	Western Parade
D3	Brougham Street	D3	Earlsdon Street	E4	Hudson Road	E4	Newcome Road	C4	St Paul's Street	B4	White Hart Lane
D1	Buck Street	A4	East Street	D3	Hyde Park Road	C5	Nightingale Road	E4	St Peter's Grove	B2	Wickham Street
E1	Buriton Street	C2	Edinburgh Road	F4	Inglis Road	D4	Norfolk Street	B4	St Thomas's Street	D2	Willis Street
C3	Burnaby Road	D4	Eldon Street	B4	Isambard Brunel Road	E4	Norman Road	E2	Sandringham Road	F4	Wilson Grove
B2	Butcher Street	D4	Elm Grove	D1	Jacobs Street	F3	Orchard Road	F2	Selbourne Terrace	C3	Wiltshire Street
C3	Cambridge Road	D5	Elphinstone Road	F3	Jessie Road	E4	Outram Road	D5	Shaftesbury Road	D3	Winston Churchill Avenue
				C4	Jubilee Terrace	F5	Oxford Road	F1	Sheffield Road	F5	Wisborough Road
				D5	Kent Road			C4	Silver Street	D4	Woodpath
				B2	Kent Street			B2	North Street	C4	Woodville Drive
				F1	King Albert Street			E3	Somers Road	D4	Yarborough Road
				B4	King Charles Street			F2	Somers Road North	C4	Yorke Street

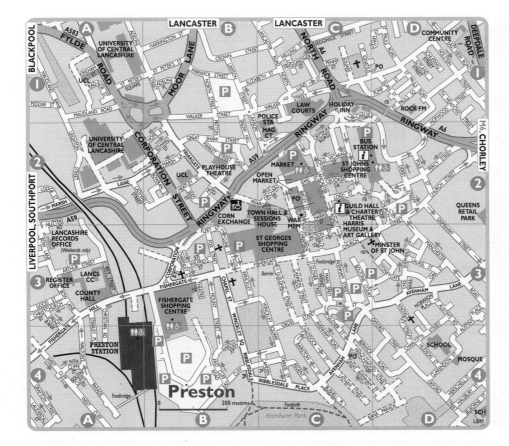

Preston

Preston is found on atlas page 174 **B2**

A1	Adelphi Street	D3	Knowsley Street
A3	Arthur Street	A2	Ladywell Street
C4	Avenham Lane	C2	Lancaster Road
C4	Avenham Road	C1	Lancaster Road North
C3	Avenham Street	D3	Laurel Street
C4	Bairstow Street	B1	Lawson Street
C4	Berwick Road	A2	Leighton Street
C2	Birley Street	C2	Lord Street
A3	Bow Lane	C1	Lund Street
B2	Bowran Street	B3	Lune Street
C1	Cannon Street	D3	Manchester Road
C1	Carlisle Street	B2	Market Street West
C4	Chaddock Street	A2	Marsh Lane
B3	Chapel Street	A1	Maudland Bank
D2	Charlotte Street	A1	Maudland Road
C3	Cheapside	C1	Melling Street
D2	Church Row	B1	Moor Lane
C3	Church Street	B3	Mount Street
D4	Clarendon Street	C1	North Road
B2	Corporation Street	B1	North Street
C2	Crooked Lane	D3	Oak Street
C3	Cross Street	C2	Old Vicarage Street
B1	Crown Street	C2	Orchard Street
D2	Derby Street	D4	Ormskirk Road
B2	Earl Street	D2	Oxford Street
B4	East Cliff	D2	Percy Street
B4	East Cliff Road	A3	Pitt Street
D1	Egan Street	D2	Pole Street
B1	Elizabeth Street	D1	Pump Street
B3	Fishergate	C4	Ribblesdale Place
A4	Fishergate Hill	B2	Ringway
B3	Fleet Street	D4	St Austin's Place
B3	Fox Street	D3	St Austin's Road
C4	Frenchwood Street	C1	St Ignatius Square
B2	Friargate	D1	St Pauls Road
A1	Fylde Road	D1	St Pauls Square
C3	Glover Street	A1	St Peter's Square
C4	Great Avenham Street	B1	St Peter's Street
C4	Great Shaw Street	B2	Seed Street
D3	Grimshaw Street	D3	Shepherd Street
C3	Guildhall Street	C2	Starkie Street
B1	Harrington Street	C3	Syke Street
C2	Harris Street	B1	Walker Street
B2	Heatley Street	A4	Walton's Parade
B2	Hill Street	B1	Warwick Street
D1	Holstein Street	A4	West Cliff
D1	Hopwood Street	B3	Winckley Square
C3	Jacson Street	B3	Winckley Street

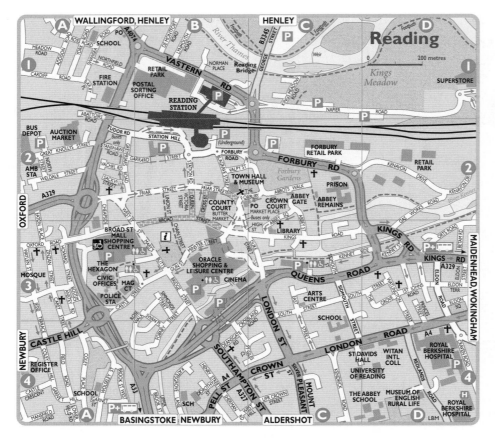

Reading

Reading is found on atlas page **63 H6**

A1	Abattoirs Road	C3	Kennet Side
C2	Abbey Square	D1	Kennet Street
C2	Abbey Street	C1	Kings Meadow Road
C2	Abbots Walk	D3	Kings Road
A1	Addison Road	C4	London Road
A3	Anstey Road	C3	London Street
A1	Barry Place	A1	Meadow Road
D3	Betam Road	B3	Minster Street
B2	Blagrave Street	C4	Mount Pleasant
B3	Bridge Street	C1	Napier Road
B3	Broad Street	A1	Northfield Road
A4	Brook Street West	D3	Orts Road
A1	Cardiff Road	A3	Oxford Road
A3	Carey Street	B4	Pell Street
A4	Castle Hill	B2	Queen Victoria Street
A3	Castle Street	C3	Queens Road
B3	Chain Street	D4	Redlands Road
A2	Cheapside	B3	Rose Walk
A4	Coley Hill	A1	Ross Road
A4	Coley Place	A2	Sackville Street
D4	Craven Road	C4	St Giles Close
B2	Cross Street	D3	St Johns Road
B4	Crossland Road	B3	St Mary's Butts
C4	Crown Street	B3	Sherman Road
B4	Deansgate Road	C3	Sidmouth Street
C3	Duke Street	C4	Silver Street
C3	East Street	B3	Simmonds Street
A2	Eaton Place	C3	South Street
D3	Eldon Road	B4	Southampton Street
D3	Eldon Terrace	A2	Stanshawe Road
A4	Field Road	A2	Station Hill
B4	Fobney Street	B2	Station Road
B2	Forbury Road	B3	Swan Place
B2	Friar Street	A1	Swansea Road
A4	Garnet Hill	D3	The Grove
A4	Garnet Street	A2	Tudor Road
B2	Garrard Street	B2	Union Street
D2	Gas Works Road	B4	Upper Brook Street
C1	George Street	A2	Vachel Road
A2	Great Knollys Street	B2	Valpy Street
A2	Greyfriars Road	B1	Vastern Road
B3	Gun Street	D3	Watlington Street
B4	Henry Street	A3	Waylen Street
A3	Howard Street	A2	Weldale Street
A3	Jesse Terrace	A4	West Street
B4	Katesgrove Lane	A4	Wolseley Street
D2	Kenavon Drive	A1	York Road
C4	Kendrick Road	A3	Zinzan Street

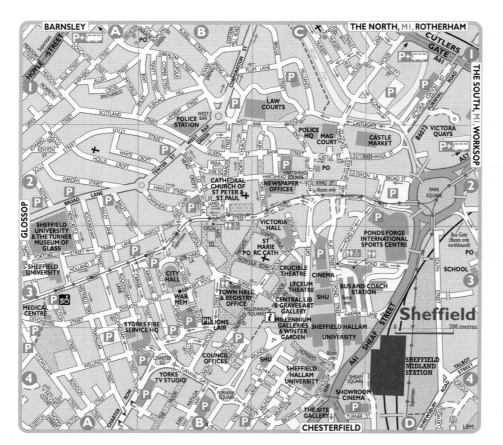

Salisbury

Salisbury is found on atlas page **44 F7**

C1	Albany Road	A1	Kingsland Road
A1	Ashley Road	D3	Laverstock Road
B2	Avon Approach	D1	London Road
C3	Barnard Street	D2	Manor Road
C2	Bedwin Street	C3	Market Place
C2	Belle Vue Road	A1	Marsh Lane
C4	Bishops Walk	A1	Meadow Road
C3	Blue Boar Row	D3	Milford Hill
D1	Bourne Avenue	C3	Milford Street
C2	Bourne Hill	A3	Mill Road
B3	Bridge Street	B2	Millstream Approach
C3	Brown Street	C3	Minster Street
C3	Butchers Row	C3	New Canal
D1	Campbell Road	C3	New Street
B1	Castle Street	B3	North Street
C3	Catherine Street	B4	North Walk
C2	Chipper Lane	C1	Park Street
A2	Churchfields Road	C3	Pennyfarthing Street
D3	Churchill Way East	C1	Queens Road
C1	Churchill Way North	D2	Rampart Road
C4	Churchill Way South	C2	Rollestone Street
B2	Churchill Way West	C4	St Ann Street
A1	Clifton Road	C2	St Edmunds Church Street
A1	Coldharbour Lane	C3	St John's Street
C1	College Street	D1	St Mark's Avenue
B3	Crane Street	C1	St Mark's Road
B3	Cranebridge Road	A2	St Pauls Road
A1	Devizes Road	C2	Salt Lane
A3	Dews Street	C2	Scots Lane
D3	Dolphin Street	D3	Shady Bower
D2	Elm Grove Road	B3	Silver Street
C2	Endless Street	B3	South Street
D2	Estcourt Road	A2	South Western Road
C4	Exeter Street	D4	Southampton Road
B2	Fisherton Street	C1	Swaynes Close
D3	Fowlers Hill	D3	The Avenue
D3	Fowlers Road	D4	Tollgate Road
C4	Friary Lane	C3	Trinity Street
A1	Gas Lane	D1	Wain-A-Long Road
C3	Gigant Street	A3	West Street
C2	Greencroft Street	A3	West Walk
C3	Guilder Street	A2	Wilton Road
B1	Hamilton Road	A2	Winchester Street
B3	Harcourt Terrace	A2	Windsor Road
B3	High Street	A2	Windsor Street
A1	Ivy Street	C1	Wyndham Road
D2	Kelsey Road	C1	Wyndham Terrace
C1	Kings Road	A2	York Road

Sheffield

Sheffield is found on atlas page **167 G3**

A1	Allen Street	C2	King Street
C2	Angel Street	B1	Lambert Street
C4	Arundel Gate	B3	Leopold Street
C4	Arundel Street	A1	Meadow Street
A2	Bailey Lane	A4	Milton Street
B3	Balm Green	C2	New Street
C2	Bank Street	A2	Newcastle Street
B3	Barker's Pool	B3	Norfolk Row
D1	Blonk Street	C3	Norfolk Street
B1	Bower Spring	B2	North Church Street
C1	Bridge Street	C1	Nursery Street
A2	Broad Lane	B3	Orchard Square
D2	Broad Street	B2	Paradise Square
C4	Brown Street	B2	Paradise Street
B3	Burgess Street	D2	Park Square
B3	Cambridge Street	C4	Paternoster Row
B3	Campo Lane	B3	Pinfold Street
B3	Carver Street	B4	Pinstone Street
C2	Castle Street	B1	Plum Lane
C1	Castlegate	C3	Pond Street
C3	Chapel Walk	A3	Portobello Street
B4	Charles Street	B2	Queen Street
B4	Charter Square	A2	Rockingham Street
B2	Church Street	B1	Russell Street
C2	Commercial Street	B2	St James Street
B1	Corporation Street	A4	Scotland Street
A3	Devonshire Street	C4	Sheaf Square
A3	Division Street	A1	Shepherd Street
A3	Doncaster Street	C2	Snig Hill
A3	Eldon Street	B1	Snow Lane
D2	Exchange Street	A2	Solly Street
B4	Eyre Lane	D3	South Street
B3	Fargate	C2	Spring Street
A4	Fitzwilliam Street	B1	Stanley Street
C3	Flat Street	B3	Surrey Street
B1	Furnace Hill	B2	Townhead Street
D1	Furnival Road	A4	Trafalgar Street
B4	Furnival Street	A3	Trippet Lane
A2	Garden Street	C3	Tudor Square
C2	George Street	B4	Union Street
B1	Gibraltar Street	C2	Waingate
C3	Harmer Lane	A4	Wellington Street
B2	Hawley Street	B1	West Bar
B2	Haymarket	B1	West Bar Green
C2	High Street	A3	West Street
A2	Hollis Croft	D1	Wicker
B3	Holly Street	C1	Wicker Lane
A1	Hoyle Road	C2	York Street

Shrewsbury

Shrewsbury is found on atlas page **127 K4**

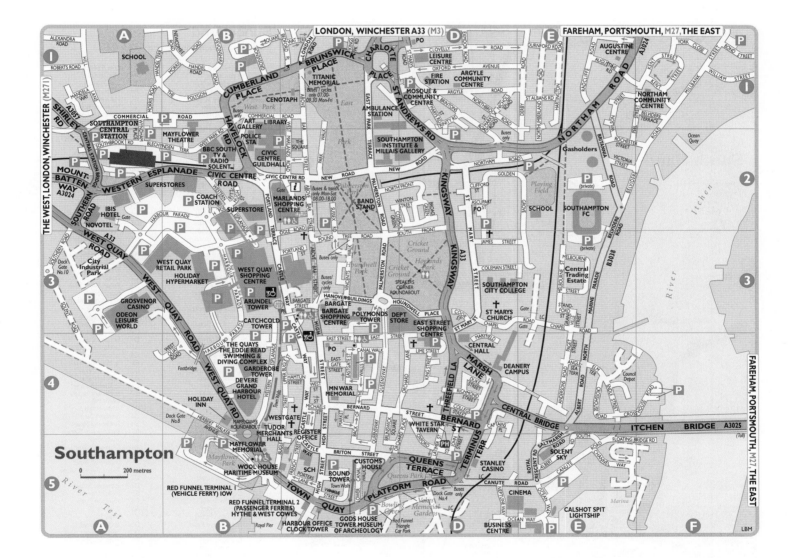

Southampton

Southampton is found on atlas page **31 G4**

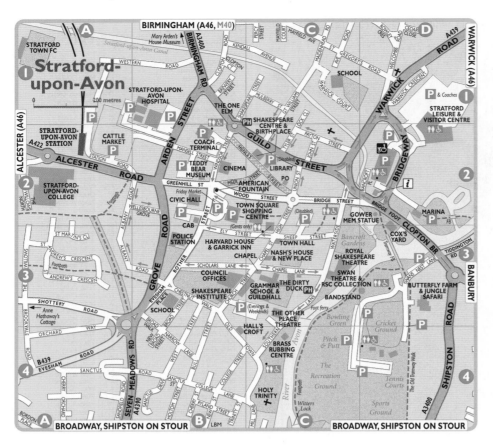

Stratford-upon-Avon

Stratford-upon-Avon is found on atlas page **98 B3**

A3	Albany Road	B4	New Broad Street
A2	Alcester Road	B4	New Street
A2	Arden Street	B3	Old Town
C1	Avenue Road	A4	Orchard Way
D2	Bancroft Place	C2	Payton Street
B1	Birmingham Road	C1	Percy Street
A4	Bordon Place	B3	Rother Street
B1	Brewery Street	D1	Rowley Crescent
D2	Bridge Foot	B4	Ryland Street
D2	Bridge Street	A3	St Andrew's Crescent
D2	Bridgeway	C1	St Gregory's Road
B3	Broad Street	A3	St Martin's Close
B3	Broad Walk	A4	Sanctus Drive
A3	Brookvale Road	A4	Sanctus Road
B4	Bull Street	A4	Sanctus Street
D1	Cedar Close	A4	Sandfield Road
C2	Chapel Lane	B3	Scholars Lane
C3	Chapel Street	A4	Seven Meadows Road
A4	Cherry Orchard	B1	Shakespeare Street
B4	Cherry Street	C3	Sheep Street
B3	Chestnut Walk	D4	Shipston Road
B3	Church Street	A3	Shottery Road
D3	Clopton Bridge	C4	Southern Lane
B1	Clopton Court	A2	Station Road
B1	Clopton Road	D3	Swans Nest Lane
B4	College Lane	A3	The Willows
B4	College Street	A2	The Willows North
B3	Ely Street	D3	Tiddington Road
B3	Evesham Place	B3	Trinity Street
A4	Evesham Road	C2	Tyler Street
B2	Great Williams Street	C2	Union Street
B3	Greenhill Street	C1	Warwick Court
B3	Grove Road	D1	Warwick Crescent
C2	Guild Street	D1	Warwick Road
B2	Henley Street	C3	Waterside
C2	High Street	D1	Welcombe Road
B4	Holtom Street	B2	Wellesbourne Grove
C2	John Street	B4	West Street
B1	Kendall Avenue	A1	Western Road
C1	Lock Close	B2	Windsor Street
C1	Maidenhead Road	B2	Wood Street
B2	Mansell Street		
C1	Mayfield Avenue		
C1	Mayfield Court		
B2	Meer Street		
C4	Mill Lane		
C1	Mulberry Street		
B4	Narrow Lane		

Sunderland

Sunderland is found on atlas page **213 K2**

B7	Abbotsford Grove	D4	Low Street
C2	Abbs Street	A4	May Street
C6	Alice Street	A8	Meadowside
A4	Alliance Street	A4	Millburn Street
D6	Amberley Street	B2	Millennium Way
C6	Argyle Square	D7	Mowbray Road
B6	Argyle Street	D5	Murton Street
C1	Ashberry Grove	B6	New Durham Road
C8	Ashbrooke Road	C1	Newcastle Road
A6	Ashwood Street	B1	Newington Street
A7	Ashwood Terrace	D4	Nile Street
C5	Athenaeum Street	D5	Norfolk Street
B6	Azalea Terrace North	C3	North Bridge Street
C7	Azalea Terrace South	D6	Northcote Avenue
A3	Beach Street	A7	Oakwood Street
C4	Bedford Street	A7	Otto Terrace
A6	Beechwood Street	C4	Pann Lane
A7	Beechwood Terrace	C5	Park Lane
B8	Belle Vue Park	D7	Park Place East
B7	Belvedere Road	D7	Park Place West
A7	Beresford Park	D6	Park Road
A8	Birchfield Road	D6	Peel Street
C5	Blandford Street	C1	Portobello Lane
B1	Bond Close	B6	Princess Street
C3	Bonner's Field	A4	Ravensworth Street
C5	Borough Road	B3	Richmond Street
C4	Bridge Street	D1	Ripon Street
B7	Briery Vale Road	C2	Roker Avenue
D1	Bright Street	D1	Roker Baths Road
A7	Broad Meadows	A4	Rose Street
B3	Brooke Street	A5	Rosedale Street
C5	Brougham Street	B1	Ross Street
C6	Burdon Road	D4	Russell Street
A6	Burn Park Road	D8	Ryhope Road
A1	Byrom Street	C7	St Bedes Terrace
D1	Cardwell Street	D7	St Lucia Close
C7	Carlton Street	A5	St Mark's Crescent
D3	Charles Street	C4	St Marys Way
A6	Chester Road	B5	St Michaels Way
A5	Chester Terrace	D3	St Peters View
B1	Chilton Street	D3	St Peters Way
D2	Church Street	C5	St Thomas Street
D6	Churchill Street	D7	St Vincent Street
A5	Clanny Street	D7	Salem Hill
C8	Corby Gate	D7	Salem Street
C8	Corby Hall Drive	D6	Salisbury Street
D4	Cork Street	D1	Selbourne Street
C6	Cowan Terrace	B6	Shakespeare Terrace
B1	Crozier Street	A8	Shallcross
C3	Dame Dorothy Street	A4	Silksworth Row
A4	Deptford Road	D7	South Hill Crescent
A2	Deptford Terrace	B1	Southwick Road
B6	Derby Street	D5	Spring Garden Close
B5	Derwent Street	C2	Stadium Way
C1	Devonshire Street	D1	Stansfield Street
D2	Dock Street	B3	Stobart Street
C3	Dundas Street	C6	Stockton Road
A7	Durham Road	A6	Summerhill
B3	Easington Street	B1	Swan Street
A7	Eden House Road	D5	Tatham Street
B6	Edwin Terrace	D5	Tatham Street Back
D6	Egerton Street	D5	Tavistock Place
B1	Eglinton Street	C7	The Avenue
A4	Elmwood Street	C7	The Cloisters
A3	Farringdon Row	C7	The Elms
C5	Fawcett Street	A5	The Leazes
B1	Finsbury Street	D7	The Oaks West
D1	Forster Street	A6	The Royalty
A7	Fox Street	C2	Thomas Street North
D5	Foyle Street	B7	Thornhill Gardens
D5	Frederick Street	B7	Thornhill Park
D1	Fulwell Road	B6	Thornhill Terrace
A4	Gilhurst Grange	A7	Thornholme Road
D1	Gladstone Street	D6	Toward Road
C7	Gorse Road	A4	Trimdon Street
C6	Grange Terrace	B6	Tunstall Road
D7	Gray Road	B6	Tunstall Terrace
B5	Green Terrace	B8	Tunstall Vale
A3	Hanover Place	B7	Valerbrooke Avenue
A5	Harlow Street	D8	Villette Road
D7	Harold Square	D4	Villiers Street
D1	Hartington Street	D5	Villiers Street South
A6	Havelock Terrace	B5	Vine Place
C4	Hay Street	A4	Violet Street
D4	High Street East	C1	Warwick Street
B5	High Street West	B1	Wayman Street
C4	High Street West	A8	Wayside
B8	Holmlands Park North	A5	Wentworth Terrace
C5	Holmeside	C8	West Lawn
C3	Howick Park	C5	West Street
D5	Hudson Street	D5	West Sunniside
A5	Hylton Road	D4	West Wear Street
C4	John Street	A5	Westbourne Road
A1	Keir Hardie Way	A6	Western Hill
C1	Kenton Grove	A5	Wharncliffe Street
C4	Lambton Street	D2	Whickham Street
D6	Laura Street	D4	William Street
A4	Lily Street	B3	Wilson Street North
B4	Livingstone Road	B6	Worcester Street
C7	Lorne Terrace	B6	Worcester Terrace
B5	Low Row	C4	York Street

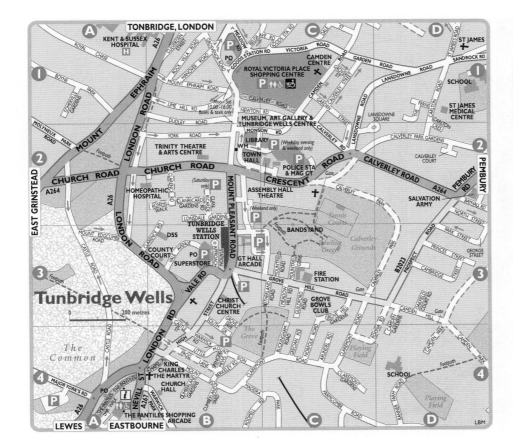

Taunton

Taunton is found on atlas page **26 C2**

B2	Albermarle Road	B4	Mary Street
D3	Alfred Street	A1	Maxwell Street
C4	Alma Street	B3	Middle Street
B2	Belvedere Road	B3	North Street
C4	Billetfield	A2	Northfield Road
A2	Birch Grove	C1	Obridge Road
B3	Bridge Street	D2	Obridge Viaduct
B2	Canal Road	B4	Old Pig Market
A4	Cann Street	A4	Park Street
C3	Canon Street	B4	Paul Street
B3	Castle Green	A3	Portland Street
A3	Castle Street	B1	Priorswood Road
D4	Church Street	C3	Priory Avenue
A3	Clarence Street	C2	Priory Bridge Road
A3	Cleveland Street	C2	Priory Park
B1	Clifton Terrace	D4	Queen Street
A4	Compass Hill	B1	Railway Street
B4	Corporation Street	B1	Raymond Street
C4	Cranmer Road	A1	Rupert Street
D2	Critchard Way	C3	St Augustine Street
A1	Cyril Street	B3	St James Street
A1	Cyril Street West	A4	St Johns Road
B2	Dellers Wharf	A4	Shuttern
C3	Duke Street	C4	Silver Street
D3	East Reach	C4	South Road
C3	Eastbourne Road	D4	South Street
D4	Eastleigh Road	A1	Staplegrove Road
C1	Eaton Crescent	B2	Station Road
A2	Elm Grove	C3	Stephen Street
B4	Fore Street	C3	Tancred Street
A1	Fowler Street	A2	The Avenue
A2	French Weir Avenue	B3	The Bridge
D4	Grays Road	B4	The Crescent
B3	Greenbrook Terrace	B1	Thomas Street
B1	Greenway Avenue	D2	Toneway
B3	Hammet Street	B4	Tower Street
C3	Haydon Road	D4	Trinity Road
C1	Heavitree Way	D4	Trinity Street
B1	Herbert Street	A3	Upper High Street
C4	Hurdle Way	A3	Upper Wood Street
B1	Kingston Road	D3	Victoria Gate
C3	Laburnum Street	D4	Victoria Street
A2	Linden Grove	D4	Viney Street
B3	Lower Middle Street	B1	William Street
C3	Magdalene Street	C3	Winchester Street
C1	Malvern Terrace	C2	Winters Field
C4	Mansfield Road	B3	Wood Street
		B3	Yarde Place

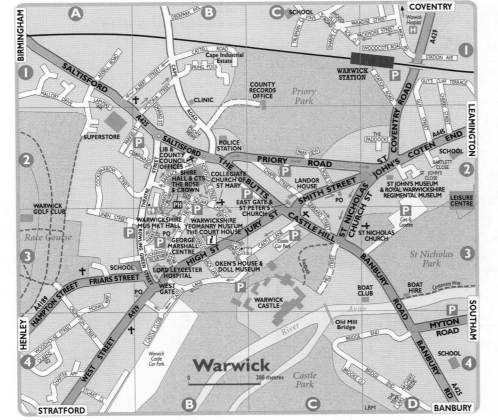

Tunbridge Wells

Tunbridge Wells is found on atlas page **50 E6**

C4	Arundel Road	B1	Lime Hill Road
D4	Banner Farm Road	B4	Little Mount Sion
D2	Bayhall Road	A2	London Road
B1	Belgrave Road	B2	Lonsdale Gardens
B4	Berkeley Road	B4	Madeira Park
A1	Boyne Park	A4	Major York's Road
C4	Buckingham Road	C3	Meadow Hill Road
C2	Calverley Park	B1	Meadow Road
D2	Calverley Park Gardens	A2	Molyneux Park Road
B1	Calverley Road	B2	Monson Road
C1	Calverley Street	A3	Mount Edgcumbe Road
D3	Cambridge Street	A2	Mount Ephraim
D3	Camden Gardens	B1	Mount Ephraim Road
D3	Camden Hill	B2	Mount Pleasant Road
D4	Camden Park	B4	Mount Sion
C1	Camden Road	C3	Mountfield Gardens
D2	Carlton Crescent	C3	Mountfield Road
D1	Carlton Road	A4	Nevill Street
A4	Castle Road	B1	Newton Road
B3	Castle Street	C4	Norfolk Road
B4	Chapel Place	D2	North Street
A2	Church Road	D3	Oakfield Court Road
B2	Clanricarde Gardens	D2	Park Street
B1	Clanricarde Road	D2	Pembury Road
C4	Claremont Gardens	C4	Poona Road
B4	Claremont Road	D3	Princes Street
B2	Clarence Road	D3	Prospect Road
C2	Crescent Road	B1	Rock Villa Road
B1	Culverden Street	B4	Rodmell Road
B4	Cumberland Gardens	B2	Rosehill Walk
B4	Cumberland Yard	A1	Royal Chase
B1	Dudley Road	D1	St James's Road
C4	Farmcombe Road	D1	Sandrock Road
B4	Frog Lane	A1	Somerville Gardens
C1	Garden Road	B3	South Grove
C1	Garden Street	B4	Spencer Mews
B1	Goods Station Road	B3	Station Approach
C4	Grecian Road	D1	Stone Street
B1	Grosvenor Road	B3	Sutherland Road
B3	Grove Avenue	D1	The Ferns
C3	Grove Hill Gardens	A4	The Pantiles Lower
C3	Grove Hill Road		Walk
C1	Grover Street	A4	The Pantiles
C3	Guildford Road	B3	Vale Avenue
B1	Hanover Road	B3	Vale Road
B4	High Street	C1	Victoria Road
C1	Lansdowne Road	B4	Warwick Road
C2	Lansdowne Square	B2	York Road

Warwick

Warwick is found on atlas page **114 F6**

B1	Albert Street	B2	Old Square
A1	Ansell Road	D1	Packmore Street
D4	Archery Fields	D1	Paradise Street
B3	Back Lane	A2	Parkes Street
D4	Banbury Road	C2	Parkview
B2	Barrack Street	B2	Priory Mews
D2	Bartlett Close	C2	Priory Road
B3	Bowling Green Street	B3	Puckerings Lane
D4	Bridge End	A4	Queens Square
B3	Brook Street	C1	Roe Close
C4	Brooke Close	D2	St John's
B1	Cape Road	D2	St John's Close
B4	Castle Close	C3	St Nicholas Church Street
C3	Castle Hill	B2	Saltisford
B3	Castle Lane	C1	Sharpe Close
B3	Castle Street	C2	Smith Street
B1	Cattell Road	B1	Spring Pool
D3	Centenary Way	D1	Station Avenue
C2	Chapel Street	D1	Station Road
A4	Charter Approach	A4	Stuart Close
D1	Cherry Street	B3	Swan Street
B3	Church Street	C2	The Butts
A2	Cocksparrow Street	D2	The Paddocks
B2	Commainge Close	D4	The Templars
D2	Coten End	B2	Theatre Street
D2	Coventry Road	C1	Trueman Close
A3	Crompton Street	B1	Victoria Street
C2	Cross Street	C1	Vine Lane
B2	Deerpark Avenue	A4	West Street
B2	Edward Street	A4	Woodcote Road
A3	Friars Street	D1	Woodhouse Street
C3	Gerrard Street	A4	Woodville Road
D1	Guy Street	C1	
D1	Guy's Cliff Terrace		
A4	Hampton Street		
B3	High Street		
B2	Jury Street		
D1	Lakin Road		
A1	Lammas Walk		
A3	Linen Street		
A1	Mallory Drive		
B2	Market Place		
B3	Market Street		
C3	Mill Street		
A3	Monks Way		
D4	Myton Road		
B3	New Street		
B2	Northgate Street		

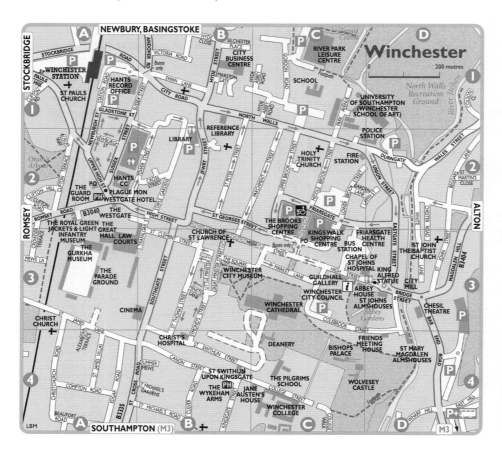

Winchester

Winchester is found on atlas page **46 C8**

A4	Alexandra Terrace	A2	Newburgh Street
A2	Alison Way	B1	North Walls
B1	Andover Road	C2	Parchment Street
D3	Bar End Road	C1	Park Avenue
A4	Beaufort Road	A2	Romsey Road
D2	Beggars Lane	B3	St Clement Street
D3	Bridge Street	A4	St Cross Road
B4	Canon Street	B2	St Georges Street
D2	Chester Road	A3	St James Lane
A4	Christchurch Road	A4	St James Villas
B1	City Road	D3	St John Street
A2	Clifton Hill	D2	St Martin's Close
A2	Clifton Road	B4	St Michael's Gardens
A1	Clifton Road	B4	St Michael's Road
A2	Clifton Terrace	A1	St Pauls Hill
C3	Colebrook Street	B2	St Peter Street
C4	College Street	B4	St Swithun Street
C4	College Walk	B3	St Thomas Street
D1	Colson Close	B3	Southgate Street
A4	Compton Road	B2	Staple Gardens
B2	Cross Street	A1	Station Road
A3	Crowder Terrace	A1	Stockbridge Road
B4	Culver Road	A2	Sussex Street
B4	Dummer Mews	B1	Swan Lane
D2	Durngate	B3	Symond's Street
D4	East Hill	B3	The Square
D3	Eastgate Street	B2	Tower Street
A4	Edgar Road	B3	Trafalgar Street
C2	Friarsgate	D2	Union Street
C2	Garden Lane	C2	Upper Brook Street
A1	Gladstone Street	A2	Upper High Street
C1	Gordon Road	B1	Victoria Road
B3	Great Minster Street	D2	Wales Street
B2	High Street	D4	Wharf Hill
C1	Hyde Abbey Road	D2	White Lane
B1	Hyde Close		
B1	Hyde Street		
B2	Jewry Street		
B4	Kingsgate Street		
D2	Lawn Street		
B3	Little Minster Street		
C2	Lower Brook Street		
D3	Magdalen Hill		
C3	Market Lane		
B1	Marston Gate		
A3	Mews Lane		
C2	Middle Brook Street		
B3	Minster Lane		

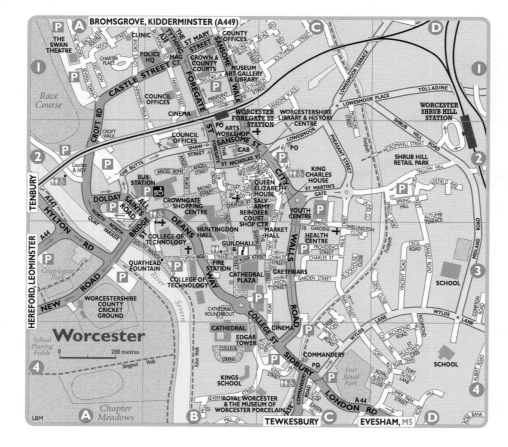

Worcester

Worcester is found on atlas page **96 D2**

A2	All Saints Road	A3	New Road
B2	Angel Place	C3	New Street
B2	Angel Row	A3	North Parade
B2	Angel Street	A2	North Quay
B1	Arboretum Road	C3	Park Street
C4	Bath Road	C2	Pheasant Street
A3	Bridge Street	B1	Pierpoint Street
B1	Britannia Road	C3	Providence Street
B2	Broad Street	B3	Pump Street
D2	Byefield Rise	C2	Queen Street
A1	Castle Street	D4	Richmond Hill
D3	Cecil Road	D4	Richmond Road
C3	Charles Street	D4	Rose Terrace
A1	Charter Place	C2	St James Close
B2	Church Street	C2	St Martin's Gate
C2	City Walls Road	B1	St Mary Street
D4	Cole Hill	B2	St Nicholas Street
B4	College Green	C3	St Paul's Street
B3	College Street	B2	St Swithuns Street
C4	Commandery Road	D4	St Wulstan's Crescent
B3	Copenhagen Street	C1	Sansome Place
A2	Croft Road	B2	Sansome Street
D2	Cromwell Street	B1	Sansome Walk
B3	Deans Way	B4	Severn Street
D3	Dent Close	A1	Severn Terrace
A2	Dolday	B2	Shaw Street
A1	Easy Row	D2	Shrub Hill Road
B1	Farrier Street	C4	Sidbury
B1	Foregate Street	A3	South Parade
D4	Fort Royal Hill	C1	Southfield Street
C3	Friar Street	C3	Spring Gardens
C3	Garden Street	D2	Spring Hill
C4	Green Hill	D3	Spring Lane
C4	Hamilton Road	D3	Stanley Road
B3	High Street	D2	Tallow Hill
D2	Hill Street	B1	Taylors Lane
A2	Hylton Road	A2	The Butts
A1	Infirmary Walk	B2	The Cross
C4	King Street	B2	The Foregate
B1	Little Southfield Street	C3	The Shambles
C4	London Road	B1	The Tything
A1	Love's Grove	D1	Tolladine
C2	Lowesmoor	B2	Trinity Street
C1	Lowesmoor Place	C3	Union Street
C1	Lowesmoor Terrace	D4	Upper Park Street
B1	Middle Street	D3	Vincent Road
D3	Midland Road	C3	Wellington Close
A1	Moor Street	C4	Wylds Lane

York

York is found on atlas page **187 H4**

C1	Aldwark	B3	Low Ousegate
B4	Baile Hill Terrace	C1	Low Petergate
A3	Barker Lane	D3	Margaret Street
C2	Bartle Garth	C2	Market Street
A3	Bishophill Junior	B1	Marygate
B3	Bishophill Senior	A3	Micklegate
B4	Bishopgate Street	D4	Mill Street
B2	Blake Street	C1	Minster Yard
A4	Blossom Street	C1	Monkgate
B1	Bootham	B2	Museum Street
B1	Bootham Row	D3	Navigation Road
C3	Castlegate	B4	Newton Terrace
B4	Clementhorpe	B2	North Street
C3	Clifford Street	A3	Nunnery Lane
C1	College Street	A4	Nunthorpe Road
C2	Colliergate	C1	Ogleforth
B2	Coney Street	D4	Paragon Street
C3	Coppergate	C2	Parliament Street
B4	Cromwell Road	C2	Pavement
A4	Dale Street	D2	Peasholme Green
C1	Davygate	D3	Peel Street
B1	Deangate	C3	Percy's Lane
D4	Fawcett Street	C3	Piccadilly
C2	Feasegate	B4	Price's Lane
B3	Fetter Lane	A3	Priory Street
D4	Fishergate	A3	Queen Street
C3	Foss Bank	B2	Rougier Street
D2	Foss Islands Road	C2	St Andrewgate
C3	Fossgate	C3	St Denys Road
A1	Frederic Street	B2	St Helens Square
C2	Garden Place	B1	St Leonards Place
B2	George Hudson Street	B3	St Martins Lane
D3	George Street	C1	St Maurice's Road
B1	Gillygate	C2	St Saviourgate
C2	Goodramgate	C2	Shambles
C2	Grape Lane	B3	Skeldergate
C3	High Ousegate	A3	Spen Lane
B1	High Petergate	A3	Station Road
D4	Hope Street	B2	Stonegate
D4	Kent Street	A4	Swann Street
C2	Kings Square	C2	Swinegate
B3	Kings Staith	A3	Tanner Row
D4	Leadmill Lane	C2	The Stonebow
A2	Leeman Road	C3	Toft Green
B3	Lendal	C3	Tower Street
C1	Lord Mayor's Walk	A3	Trinity Lane
		B4	Victor Street
		C4	Walmgate

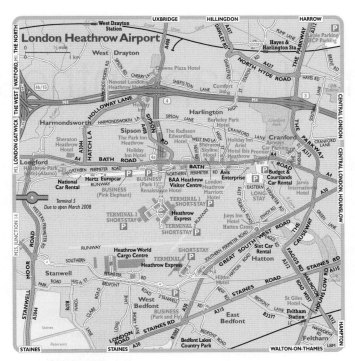

London Heathrow Airport – 16 miles west of London

Telephone: 0870 000 0123 or visit *www.heathrowairport.com*
Parking: short-stay, long-stay and business parking is available.
For charge details tel: 0870 000 1000
Public Transport: coach, bus, rail and London Underground.
There are several 4-star and 3-star hotels within easy reach of the airport.
Car hire facilities are available.

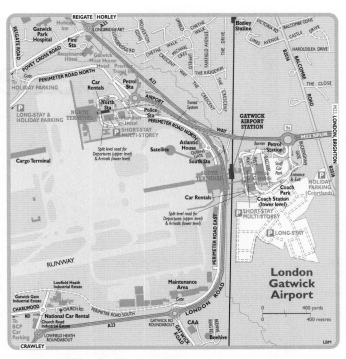

London Gatwick Airport – 35 miles south of London

Telephone: 0870 000 2468 or visit *www.gatwickairport.com*
Parking: short and long-stay parking is available at both the North and South terminals.
Public Transport: coach, bus and rail.
There are several 4-star and 3-star hotels within easy reach of the airport.
Car hire facilities are available.

London Stansted Airport – 36 miles north east of London

Telephone: 0870 000 0303 or visit *www.stanstedairport.com*
Parking: short, mid and long-stay open-air parking is available.
For charge details tel: 0870 000 1000
Public Transport: coach, bus and direct rail link to London on the Stansted Express.
There are several hotels within easy reach of the airport.
Car hire facilities are available.

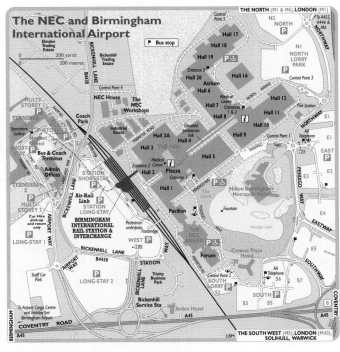

Birmingham International Airport – 8 miles east of Birmingham

Telephone: 0870 733 5511 or visit *www.bhx.co.uk*
Parking: short and long-stay parking is available. For charge details tel: 0870 733 5511
Public Transport: Air-Rail Link service operates every 2 minutes to and from Birmingham International Railway Station & Interchange.
There is one 3-star hotel adjacent to the airport and several 4 and 3-star hotels within easy reach of the airport. Car hire facilities are available.

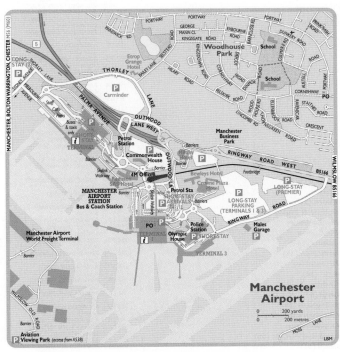

Manchester Airport – 10 miles south of Manchester

Telephone: 0161 489 3000 or visit *www.manchesterairport.co.uk*
Parking: short and long-stay parking is available.
For charge details tel: 0161 489 3723
Public Transport: bus, coach and rail.
There are several 4-star and 3-star hotels within easy reach of the airport.
Car hire facilities are available.

Glasgow Airport – 8 miles west of Glasgow

Telephone: 0870 040 0008 or visit *www.glasgowairport.com*
Parking: short and long-stay parking is available.
For charge details tel: 0870 000 1000
Public Transport: regular coach services operate direct to central Glasgow and Edinburgh.
There are several 3-star hotels within easy reach of the airport.
Car hire facilities are available.

Gazetteer of map entries

Both sections of this gazetteer list entries appearing in the main-map section of the atlas in alphabetical order. The reference before each name gives the atlas page number and grid reference of the square in which the place appears. The map shows counties, unitary authorities and administrative areas, together with a list of the abbreviated name forms used in the gazetteer. The recreation and leisure index lists places of tourist interest including airports and airfields (shown in blue type), National Parks, main physical features, campsites, golf courses and cycle routes. The city, town and village index lists settlements.

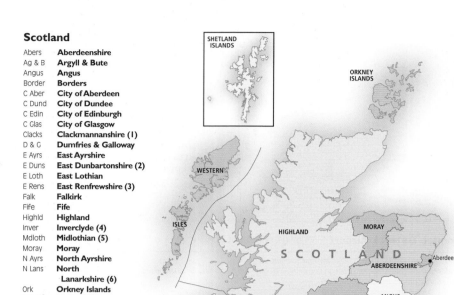

Recreation and leisure index

City, town and village index

A

48 C5 Aaron's Hill Surrey
28 B2 Abbas Combe Somset
112 E6 Abberley Worcs
87 G3 Abberton Essex
97 G3 Abberton Worcs
237 G4 Abberwick Nthumb
85 H4 Abbess End Essex
85 H4 Abbess Roding Essex
25 L4 Abbey Devon
110 B5 Abbey-cwm-hir Powys
78 D3 Abbeydale Gloucs
166 F4 Abbeydale Sheff
166 F4 Abbeydale Park Sheff
94 E7 Abbey Dore Herefs
86 F2 Abbey Field Essex
16 B2 Abbey Gate Devon
51 J2 Abbey Gate Kent
149 K7 Abbey Green Shrops
151 J2 Abbey Green Staffs
165 G1 Abbey Hey Manch
259 H6 Abbeyhill C Edin
26 D3 Abbey Hill Somset
151 H4 Abbey Hulton C Stke
64 D7 Abbey Mead Surrey
248 B1 Abbey St Bathans Border
183 G4 Abbeystead Lancs
208 E3 Abbey Town Cumb
174 D3 Abbey Village Lancs
66 C5 Abbey Wood Gt Lon
221 G7 Abbey Yard D & G
234 F4 Abbotrule Border
22 F4 Abbots Bickington Devon
130 B2 Abbots Bromley Staffs
17 H4 Abbotsbury Dorset
34 E2 Abbotsford W Susx
23 G1 Abbotsham Devon
14 C8 Abbotskerswell Devon
83 H6 Abbots Langley Herts
8 C5 Abbotsleigh Devon
58 D6 Abbots Leigh N Som
102 B2 Abbotsley Cambs
163 G7 Abbot's Meads Ches
97 H3 Abbots Morton Worcs
118 E4 Abbots Ripton Cambs
97 J3 Abbot's Salford Warwks
46 E7 Abbotstone Hants
30 F2 Abbotswood Hants
46 C7 Abbots Worthy Hants
45 K5 Abbotts Ann Hants
111 H4 Abcott Shrops
112 B2 Abdon Shrops
177 L8 Abdy Rothm
91 G6 Aber Cerdgn
90 F3 Aberaeron Cerdgn
75 G6 Aberaman Rhondd
125 G4 Aberangell Gwynd
90 D7 Aber Arad Carmth
286 B4 Aberarder Highld
298 B3 Aberarder Highld
268 B4 Aberargie P & K
91 G3 Aberarth Cerdgn
55 J3 Aberavon Neath
90 E7 Aber-banc Cerdgn
75 K6 Aberbargoed Caerph
126 C8 Aberbechan Powys
75 K6 Aberbeeg Caerph
93 G8 Aberbran Powys
75 G6 Abercanaid Myr Td
57 G2 Abercarn Caerph
88 D6 Abercastle Pembks
125 G6 Abercegir Powys
296 F8 Aberchalder Highld
305 L5 Aberchirder Abers
258 D5 Abercorn W Loth
74 C4 Abercraf Powys
74 C7 Abercregan Neath
269 J7 Abercrombie Fife
75 G7 Abercwmboi Rhondd
90 B7 Abercych Pembks
75 H7 Abercynon Rhondd
125 H3 Aber-Cywarch Gwynd
267 K4 Aberdalgie P & K
74 F6 Aberdare Rhondd
144 b2 Aberdaron Gwynd
303 H7 Aberdeen C Aber
145 H3 Aberdesach Gwynd
258 F4 Aberdour Fife
74 B7 Aberdulais Neath
124 C7 Aberdyfi Gwynd
93 J4 Aberedw Powys
88 B6 Abereiddy Pembks
145 H6 Abererch Gwynd
75 H6 Aberfan Myr Td
278 C5 Aberfeldy P & K
158 E7 Aberffraw IoA
108 D4 Aberffrwd Cerdgn
76 C5 Aberffrwd Mons
186 D7 Aberford Leeds
265 J7 Aberfoyle Stirlg
56 B4 Abergarw Brdgnd
74 B6 Abergarwed Neath
76 C4 Abergavenny Mons
161 G5 Abergele Conwy
91 H7 Aber-Giâr Carmth
73 H2 Abergorlech Carmth
92 D3 Abergwesyn Powys
72 E4 Abergwili Carmth
124 D3 Abergwynant Gwynd
74 D7 Abergwynfi Neath
159 L6 Abergwyngregyn Gwynd
124 D5 Abergynolwyn Gwynd
110 B1 Aberhafesp Powys
125 G7 Aberhosan Powys
55 L5 Aberkenfig Brdgnd
260 B5 Aberlady E Loth
280 F3 Aberlemno Angus
108 C1 Aberlerry Cerdgn
124 F5 Aberllefenni Gwynd
93 L6 Aberllynfi Powys
108 D5 Abermagwr Cerdgn
91 J4 Abermeurig Cerdgn
148 E2 Abermorddu Flints
126 D8 Abermule Powys
126 C2 Abernaint Powys
72 C4 Abernant Carmth
126 D7 Abernant Powys
75 G6 Abernant Rhondd
268 B4 Abernethy P & K
268 C1 Abernyte P & K
148 E4 Aber-oer Wrexhm
90 C5 Aberporth Cerdgn
144 F8 Abersoch Gwynd
76 B6 Abersychan Torfn
124 C7 Aber-Tafol Gwynd
56 D5 Aberthin V Glam
75 L6 Abertillery Blae G
56 F3 Abertridwr Caerph
125 L3 Abertridwr Powys
124 C5 Abertrinant Gwynd
75 J5 Abertysswg Caerph
267 H4 Aberuthven P & K
75 H2 Aber Village Powys
93 G8 Aberyscir Powys
108 B3 Aberystwyth Cerdgn
322 H3 Abhainn Suidhe W Isls
81 G7 Abingdon Oxon
48 F4 Abinger Common Surrey
48 E4 Abinger Hammer Surrey
116 F7 Abington Nhants
232 C2 Abington S Lans
102 D5 Abington Pigotts Cambs
116 F7 Abington Vale Nhants
34 B3 Abingworth W Susx
132 E2 Ab Kettleby Leics
97 H3 Ab Lench Worcs
79 J5 Ablington Gloucs
45 G4 Ablington Wilts
166 C5 Abney Derbys
290 C2 Aboyne Abers
182 E2 Abraham Heights Lancs
174 D7 Abram Wigan
297 L1 Abriachan Highld
84 F7 Abridge Essex
257 H5 Abronhill N Lans
31 J5 Abshot Hants
59 H6 Abson S Glos
99 K4 Abthorpe Nhants
328 C8 Abune-the-Hill Ork
171 H5 Aby Lincs
282 D7 Acarsaid Highld
187 G5 Acaster Malbis York
187 G6 Acaster Selby N York
175 G2 Accrington Lancs
270 F4 Acha Ag & B
253 J4 Achabraid Ag & B
292 H7 Achachork Highld
274 F3 Achadh nan Darach Highld
253 H5 Achahoish Ag & B
274 D8 Achaleven Ag & B
276 B6 Achallader Ag & B
319 K5 Achalone Highld
325 K9 Acha Mòr W Isls
309 N5 Achanalt Highld
310 E3 Achandunie Highld
254 C3 Achanelid Ag & B
284 D7 Ach' an Todhair Highld
314 E6 Achany Highld
284 D6 Achaphubuil Highld
282 F8 Acharacle Highld
317 Q6 Achargary Highld
289 H6 Acharn Angus
273 G4 Acharn Highld
277 K6 Acharn P & K
302 D6 Achath Abers
315 J8 Achavandra Muir Highld
319 L8 Achavanich Highld
54 B1 Achddu Carmth
312 H6 Achduart Highld
312 G5 Acheninver Highld
318 E10 Achentoul Highld
316 F9 Achfary Highld
314 E4 Achfrish Highld
312 D8 Achgarve Highld
316 G3 Achiemore Highld
318 E5 Achiemore Highld
282 a1 A' Chill Highld
312 G5 Achiltibuie Highld
317 Q4 Achina Highld
317 M4 Achinahuagh Highld
314 E7 Achinduich Highld
273 K7 Achinduin Ag & B
319 L4 Achingills Highld
317 M4 Achininver Highld
308 F9 Achintee Highld
308 D10 Achintraid Highld
272 B5 Achleck Ag & B
285 J5 Achluachrach Highld
316 E6 Achlyness Highld
312 H2 Achmelvich Highld
295 G2 Achmore Highld
312 G7 Achmore Highld
325 K9 Achmore W Isls
274 D7 Achnaba Ag & B
316 A10 Achnacarnin Highld
284 F4 Achnacarry Highld
274 E8 Achnacloich Ag & B
293 K15 Achnacloich Highld
297 H5 Achnaconeran Highld
274 D7 Achnacree Bay Ag & B
274 C6 Achnacroish Ag & B
272 B4 Achnadrish Ag & B
310 F3 Achnagarron Highld
282 B8 Achnaha Highld
314 D7 Achnahanat Highld
299 J3 Achnahannet Highld
271 K10 Achnahard Ag & B
314 D4 Achnairn Highld
314 G5 Achnaluachrach Highld
253 H3 Achnamara Ag & B
284 F4 Achnasaul Highld
309 K6 Achnasheen Highld
272 B1 Achosnich Highld
318 H3 Achreamie Highld
284 E8 Achriabhach Highld
316 F6 Achriesgill Highld
315 L5 Achrimsdale Highld
292 H7 Achtalean Highld
310 B6 Achterneed Highld
317 P4 Achtoty Highld
314 C6 Achuirghill Highld
117 L3 Achurch Nhants
317 M5 Achuvoldrach Highld
314 H8 Achvaich Highld
318 G4 Achvarasdal Highld
192 F5 Ackenthwaite Cumb
319 Q6 Ackergill Highld
206 B4 Acklam Middsb
187 L2 Acklam N York
128 F7 Ackleton Shrops
237 J6 Acklington Nthumb
177 L3 Ackton Wakefd
177 L4 Ackworth Moor Top Wakefd
139 J4 Acle Norfk
114 C3 Acock's Green Birm
69 K7 Acol Kent
225 L6 Acomb Nthumb
187 G4 Acomb York
95 H7 Aconbury Herefs
175 G3 Acre Lancs
175 K6 Acre Oldham
148 E5 Acrefair Wrexhm
85 J4 Acreland Green Essex
150 F3 Acres Nook Staffs
150 B3 Acton Ches
18 F6 Acton Dorset
65 H4 Acton Gt Lon
111 G3 Acton Shrops
150 F5 Acton Staffs
104 E5 Acton Suffk
113 G6 Acton Worcs
148 F3 Acton Wrexhm
95 L3 Acton Beauchamp Herefs
163 L5 Acton Bridge Ches
127 L6 Acton Burnell Shrops
96 B3 Acton Green Herefs
127 L6 Acton Pigott Shrops
104 E4 Acton Place Suffk
127 L2 Acton Reynald Shrops
128 C7 Acton Round Shrops
111 J2 Acton Scott Shrops
129 J3 Acton Trussell Staffs
59 K4 Acton Turville S Glos
325 P2 Adabroc W Isls
258 C7 Adambrae W Loth
27 J5 Adam's Green Dorset
193 J2 Adamthwaite Cumb
150 E8 Adbaston Staffs
27 K2 Adber Dorset
154 B6 Adbolton Notts
99 G6 Adderbury Oxon
150 C6 Adderley Shrops
151 H4 Adderley Green C Stke
249 J7 Adderstone Nthumb
258 B8 Addiewell W Loth
185 G4 Addingham Brad
185 G5 Addingham Moorside Brad
100 B8 Addington Bucks
6 C1 Addington Cnwll
65 L8 Addington Gt Lon
51 G2 Addington Kent
247 G3 Addinston Border
65 K7 Addiscombe Gt Lon
13 K3 Addiscott Devon
64 D8 Addlestone Surrey
64 D7 Addlestonemoor Surrey
171 K7 Addlethorpe Lincs
185 L7 Adel Leeds
128 D3 Adeney Wrekin
83 H5 Adeyfield Herts
126 B6 Adfa Powys
111 J5 Adforton Herefs
21 J4 Adgestone IoW
53 H3 Adisham Kent
79 L1 Adlestrop Gloucs
179 J3 Adlingfleet E R Yk
165 H4 Adlington Ches
174 D5 Adlington Lancs
174 C5 Adlington Park Lancs
129 L2 Admaston Staffs
128 C4 Admaston Wrekin
97 L4 Admington Warwks
90 D7 Adpar Cerdgn
41 J8 Adsborough Somset
41 G6 Adscombe Somset
100 B8 Adstock Bucks
99 J3 Adstone Nhants
165 G3 Adswood Stockp
33 L2 Adversane W Susx
300 B2 Advie Highld
177 G2 Adwalton Leeds
81 K7 Adwell Oxon
178 C6 Adwick Le Street Donc
178 B7 Adwick upon Dearne Donc
307 G5 Adziel Abers
222 B2 Ae D & G
175 G5 Affetside Bury
303 G4 Affleck Abers
18 B3 Affpuddle Dorset
148 E4 Afon Eitha Wrexhm
162 B6 Afon-wen Flints
145 H6 Afon Wen Gwynd
20 E4 Afton IoW
131 J4 Agar Nook Leics
113 G4 Aggborough Worcs
195 G4 Agglethorpe N York
209 K2 Aglionby Cumb
161 L7 Aifft Denbgs
163 G3 Aigburth Lpool
325 N8 Aiginis W Isls
188 F5 Aike E R Yk
328 F3 Aikerness Ork
327 L6 Aikers Ork
209 L4 Aiketgate Cumb
209 G3 Aikton Cumb
171 H5 Ailby Lincs
94 D4 Ailey Herefs
98 B3 Ailstone Warwks
134 C7 Ailsworth C Pete
84 D6 Aimes Green Essex
196 C5 Ainderby Quernhow N York
196 B3 Ainderby Steeple N York
87 J2 Aingers Green Essex
173 H5 Ainsdale Lancs
173 G5 Ainsdale-on-Sea Sefton
210 B4 Ainstable Cumb
175 G6 Ainsworth Bury
207 G6 Ainthorpe N York
173 J8 Aintree Sefton
258 E8 Ainville W Loth
262 D7 Aird Ag & B
218 D7 Aird D & G
308 C3 Aird Highld
321 N4 Aird W Isls
325 Q7 Aird W Isls
323 M6 Àird Adhanais W Isls
321 M5 Aird a' Mhachair W Isls
323 L2 Àird a' Mhulaidh W Isls
323 K4 Aird Asaig W Isls
321 N5 Àird Choinnich W Isls
325 N2 Àird Dhail W Isls
314 F8 Airdens Highld
320 E4 Àird Mhidhinis W Isls
323 J7 Àird Mhìghe W Isls
320 E4 Àird Mhòr W Isls
321 N5 Àird Mhòr W Isls
321 N5 Àird na Monadh W Isls
321 P3 Àird nan Srùban W Isls
271 N9 Aird of Kinloch Ag & B
282 D1 Aird of Sleat Highld
257 H7 Airdrie N Lans
257 H7 Airdriehill N Lans
321 M10 Àird Ruairidh W Isls
263 H1 Airds Bay Ho Ag & B
323 K7 Àird Shleibhe W Isls
274 D5 Airdsito Ag & B
325 N7 Aird Thunga W Isls
317 P4 Airdtorrisdale Highld
324 E7 Aird Uig W Isls
178 B2 Airedale Wakefd
184 E5 Aire View N York
324 H11 Airidh a Bhruaich W Isls
280 B4 Airlie Angus
179 G2 Airmyn E R Yk
279 G7 Airntully P & K
294 D7 Airor Highld
257 K3 Airth Falk
257 J1 Airthrey Castle Stirlg
184 C3 Airton N York
215 J4 Airyhassen D & G
207 K6 Airy Hill N York
215 H4 Airylick D & G
215 H4 Airyolland D & G
155 K6 Aisby Lincs
169 G2 Aisby Lincs
321 M10 Aisgernis W Isls
7 L2 Aish Devon
8 D3 Aish Devon
41 G6 Aisholt Somset
195 L4 Aiskew N York
197 L4 Aislaby N York
207 K6 Aislaby N York
205 K5 Aislaby S on T
169 H4 Aisthorpe Lincs
328 B10 Aith Ork
329 K8 Aith Ork
330 K7 Aith Shet
332 E5 Aith Shet
333 G11 Aith Shet
126 E2 Aithnen Powys
333 G10 Aithsetter Shet
311 M10 Aitnoch Highld
248 E8 Akeld Nthumb
100 B6 Akeley Bucks
106 C4 Akenham Suffk
213 G2 Albany Sundld
12 E7 Albaston Cnwll
127 H4 Alberbury Shrops
70 E3 Albert Town Pembks
131 G3 Albert Village Leics
34 E3 Albourne W Susx
34 E3 Albourne Green W Susx
127 K3 Albrighton Shrops
129 G6 Albrighton Shrops
89 K3 Albro Castle Cerdgn
122 F2 Alburgh Norfk
84 E2 Albury Herts
48 E4 Albury Surrey
84 E2 Albury End Herts
48 E4 Albury Heath Surrey
210 B3 Albyfield Cumb
142 F5 Alby Hill Norfk
85 G7 Albyns Essex
310 D6 Alcaig Highld
111 K2 Alcaston Shrops
28 E2 Alcester Dorset
97 J2 Alcester Warwks
114 B3 Alcester Lane's End Birm
35 J5 Alciston E Susx
59 J7 Alcombe Wilts
40 C4 Alcombe Somset
118 D4 Alconbury Cambs
118 D4 Alconbury Weston Cambs
142 F5 Aldborough Norfk
186 D1 Aldborough N York
66 C3 Aldborough Hatch Gt Lon
61 H5 Aldbourne Wilts
189 K7 Aldbrough E R Yk
205 G5 Aldbrough St John N York
82 F4 Aldbury Herts
182 E2 Aldcliffe Lancs
278 D2 Aldclune P & K
107 K2 Aldeburgh Suffk
139 K8 Aldeby Norfk
83 J7 Aldenham Herts
50 D8 Alderbrook E Susx
30 B1 Alderbury Wilts
153 H4 Aldercar Derbys
138 C3 Alderford Norfk
175 G7 Alder Forest Salfd
29 L4 Alderholt Dorset
59 J2 Alderley Gloucs
164 F5 Alderley Edge Ches
115 H3 Alderman's Green Covtry
62 E7 Aldermaston W Berk
62 F8 Aldermaston Soke W Berk
62 F7 Aldermaston Wharf W Berk
98 B4 Alderminster Warwks
30 F3 Aldermoor C Sotn
130 E1 Alder Moor Staffs
19 G3 Alderney Poole
43 J5 Alder Row Somset
66 B3 Aldersbrook Gt Lon
95 K6 Alder's End Herefs
149 J2 Aldersey Green Ches
130 C5 Aldershawe Staffs
47 K3 Aldershot Hants
97 H7 Alderton Gloucs
100 B4 Alderton Nhants
127 K2 Alderton Shrops
107 G5 Alderton Suffk
59 K4 Alderton Wilts
97 H7 Alderton Fields Gloucs
152 F3 Alderwasley Derbys
195 L8 Aldfield N York
149 H2 Aldford Ches
133 K6 Aldgate Rutlnd
86 E1 Aldham Essex
105 H5 Aldham Suffk
307 K7 Aldie Abers
33 H5 Aldingbourne W Susx
190 F6 Aldingham Cumb
52 E6 Aldington Kent
97 J5 Aldington Worcs
52 D6 Aldington Frith Kent
301 G3 Aldivalloch Moray
255 J2 Aldochlay Ag & B
111 J4 Aldon Shrops
208 D4 Aldoth Cumb
119 J5 Aldreth Cambs
130 B6 Aldridge Wsall
123 J7 Aldringham Suffk
34 E5 Aldrington Br & H
79 K4 Aldsworth Gloucs
301 G3 Aldunie Moray
152 D2 Aldwark Derbys
186 E2 Aldwark N York
167 H1 Aldwarke Rothm
33 H7 Aldwick W Susx
117 L3 Aldwincle Nhants
62 E5 Aldworth W Berk
110 E3 Ale Oak Shrops
255 K4 Alexandria Ag & B
41 G6 Aley Somset
83 H3 Aley Green Beds
22 D4 Alfardisworthy Devon
25 L7 Alfington Devon
48 D7 Alfold Surrey
48 D7 Alfold Bars W Susx
48 D6 Alfold Crossways Surrey
301 L5 Alford Abers
171 J5 Alford Lincs
42 F7 Alford Somset
113 J5 Alfred's Well Worcs
153 H2 Alfreton Derbys
96 B3 Alfrick Worcs
96 B3 Alfrick Pound Worcs
35 K6 Alfriston E Susx
156 E6 Algakirk Lincs
42 F7 Alhampton Somset
283 G6 Alisary Highld
179 K3 Alkborough N Linc
78 B5 Alkerton Gloucs
98 E5 Alkerton Oxon
53 J5 Alkham Kent
149 K6 Alkington Shrops
152 C6 Alkmonton Derbys
175 J7 Alkrington Garden Village Rochdl
8 D4 Allaleigh Devon
288 E3 Allanaquoich Abers
247 G4 Allanbank Border
244 C2 Allanbank N Lans
310 E7 Allangrange Mains Highld
246 E4 Allanshaugh Border
246 F5 Allanshaws Border
248 D3 Allanton Border
244 D2 Allanton S Lans
243 L3 Allanton S Lans
291 J7 Allardice Abers
77 J6 Allaston Gloucs
320 D4 Allathasdal W Isls
31 H2 Allbrook Hants
44 E1 All Cannings Wilts
211 H2 Allendale Town Nthumb
130 D7 Allen End Warwks
211 J4 Allenheads Nthumb
212 C3 Allensford Dur
84 F3 Allen's Green Herts
95 G6 Allensmore Herefs
153 G7 Allenton C Derb
209 L2 Allenwood Cumb
14 D8 Aller Devon
25 K5 Aller Devon
28 D6 Aller Dorset
41 L8 Aller Somset
208 C6 Allerby Cumb
15 G3 Allercombe Devon
26 B1 Allerford Somset
40 B4 Allerford Somset
15 H2 Aller Grove Devon
14 D8 Aller Park Devon
198 C5 Allerston N York
187 L5 Allerthorpe E R Yk
185 H8 Allerton Brad
8 C2 Allerton Devon
163 H3 Allerton Lpool
177 L2 Allerton Bywater Leeds
186 D3 Allerton Mauleverer N York
114 F3 Allesley Covtry
152 F6 Allestree C Derb
4 C5 Allet Cnwll
133 G6 Allexton Leics
165 J7 Allgreave Ches
67 K5 Allhallows Medway
67 K5 Allhallows-on-Sea Medway
308 D6 Alligin Shuas Highld
129 H3 Allimore Green Staffs
16 F3 Allington Dorset
51 H2 Allington Kent
155 G5 Allington Lincs
45 G6 Allington Wilts
59 L5 Allington Wilts
60 E8 Allington Wilts
59 L6 Allington Bar Wilts
191 H5 Allithwaite Cumb
317 K8 Allnabad Highld
257 K2 Alloa Clacks
208 C5 Allonby Cumb
164 D6 Allostock Ches
229 L3 Alloway S Ayrs
26 F4 Allowenshay Somset
26 D6 All Saints Devon
123 G3 All Saints South Elmham Suffk
128 E7 Allscot Shrops
128 C4 Allscott Wrekin
127 K7 All Stretton Shrops
54 E1 Allt Carmth
162 E7 Alltami Flints
275 J4 Alltchaorunn Highld
125 K2 Alltforgan Powys
93 J4 Alltmawr Powys
317 J7 Alltnacaillich Highld
295 H3 Allt-nan-Sùgh Highld
285 G5 Alltour Highld
297 J5 Alltsigh Highld
72 E2 Alltwalis Carmth
73 L8 Alltwen Neath
91 H6 Alltyblaca Cerdgn
57 J3 Allt-yr-yn Newpt
121 L5 Allwood Green Suffk
153 J3 Alma Notts
222 D4 Almagill D & G
94 D3 Almeley Herefs
94 D3 Almeley Wooton Herefs
29 G7 Almer Dorset
178 D6 Almholme Donc
150 D7 Almington Staffs
22 E2 Alminstone Cross Devon
267 K2 Almondbank P & K
176 F4 Almondbury Kirk
58 E4 Almondsbury S Glos
258 C7 Almondvale W Loth
104 B7 Almshouse Green Essex
186 E1 Alne N York
97 K2 Alne End Warwks
114 C7 Alne Hills Warwks
310 E3 Alness Highld
310 F4 Alnessferry Highld
186 E1 Alne Station N York
236 D4 Alnham Nthumb
237 J4 Alnmouth Nthumb
237 H4 Alnwick Nthumb
65 G4 Alperton Gt Lon
104 E6 Alphamstone Essex
104 E3 Alpheton Suffk
14 E4 Alphington Devon
138 F6 Alpington Norfk
166 D8 Alport Derbys
126 F7 Alport Powys
149 L2 Alpraham Ches
87 H2 Alresford Essex
130 D4 Alrewas Staffs
150 E2 Alsager Ches
150 E4 Alsagers Bank Staffs
82 B6 Alscot Bucks
152 C2 Alsop en le Dale Derbys
210 F4 Alston Cumb
26 D6 Alston Devon
78 E2 Alstone Gloucs
97 G7 Alstone Gloucs
41 K4 Alstone Somset
152 B2 Alstonefield Staffs
42 B3 Alston Sutton Somset
24 C2 Alswear Devon
175 K7 Alt Oldham
312 F4 Altandhu Highld
318 D11 Altanduin Highld
11 J5 Altarnun Cnwll
314 C6 Altass Highld
95 J8 Altbough Herefs
291 M1 Altens C Aber
319 N3 Alterwall Highld
254 C6 Altgaltraig Ag & B
183 L8 Altham Lancs
175 K7 Alt Hill Tamesd
86 E7 Althorne Essex
179 J6 Althorpe N Linc
63 L5 Altmore W & M
275 K3 Altnafeadh Highld
317 M9 Altnaharra Highld
177 K3 Altofts Wakefd
167 G8 Alton Derbys
47 H6 Alton Hants
151 L5 Alton Staffs
44 F4 Alton Wilts
44 E1 Alton Barnes Wilts
242 E6 Altonhill E Ayrs
28 C6 Alton Pancras Dorset
44 F1 Alton Priors Wilts
164 E3 Altrincham Traffd
285 G3 Altrua Highld
265 H7 Altskeith Stirlg
114 C2 Alum Rock Birm
257 K1 Alva Clacks
163 J6 Alvanley Ches
153 G7 Alvaston C Derb
113 L5 Alvechurch Worcs
130 E6 Alvecote Warwks
29 H2 Alvediston Wilts
112 F3 Alveley Shrops
23 J1 Alverdiscott Devon
31 L7 Alverstoke Hants
21 J4 Alverstone IoW
177 J3 Alverthorpe Wakefd
154 E5 Alverton Notts
311 Q5 Alves Moray
80 B6 Alvescot Oxon
58 F3 Alveston S Glos
98 B2 Alveston Warwks
58 F3 Alveston Down S Glos
98 B3 Alveston Hill Warwks
299 G7 Alvie Highld
170 F2 Alvingham Lincs
77 J6 Alvington Gloucs
27 J3 Alvington Somset
134 C7 Alwalton Cambs
57 K3 Alway Newpt
28 B4 Alweston Dorset
23 G2 Alwington Devon
236 C5 Alwinton Nthumb
185 L7 Alwoodley Leeds
186 B6 Alwoodley Gates Leeds
279 K5 Alyth P & K
2 D3 Amalebra Cnwll
2 D3 Amalveor Cnwll
314 C8 Amatnatua Highld
320 F2 Am Baile W Isls
153 H7 Ambaston Derbys
152 F3 Ambergate Derbys
78 C6 Amberley Gloucs
95 H4 Amberley Herefs
33 K4 Amberley W Susx
237 K6 Amble Nthumb
113 H2 Amblecote Dudley
201 K7 Ambleside Cumb
89 G7 Ambleston Pembks
81 J3 Ambrosden Oxon
179 J5 Amcotts N Linc
63 K7 Amen Corner Br For
82 E7 Amersham Bucks
82 F7 Amersham Common Bucks
82 E7 Amersham Old Town Bucks
82 F7 Amersham on the Hill Bucks
129 K1 Amerton Staffs
42 F2 Amesbury BaNES
45 G5 Amesbury Wilts
29 K6 Ameysford Dorset
130 E6 Amington Staffs
222 C3 Amisfield D & G
159 G2 Amlwch IoA
159 H2 Amlwch Port IoA
73 J6 Ammanford Carmth
26 F5 Ammerham Somset
197 L7 Amotherby N York
31 G2 Ampfield Hants
197 G6 Ampleforth N York
79 H6 Ampney Crucis Gloucs
79 H6 Ampney St Mary Gloucs
79 H6 Ampney St Peter Gloucs
45 J5 Amport Hants
101 H6 Ampthill Beds
121 H5 Ampton Suffk
71 K5 Amroth Pembks
278 C7 Amulree P & K
83 K4 Amwell Herts
299 K3 Anagach Highld
273 K2 Anaheilt Highld
308 H5 Anancaun Highld
308 C2 An Ard Highld
155 J5 Ancaster Lincs
110 D3 Anchor Shrops
32 C6 Anchorage Park C Port
137 L7 Anchor Corner Norfk
182 B6 Anchorsholme Lancs
143 J7 Anchor Street Norfk
325 N8 An Cnoc W Isls
325 P2 An Cnoc Ard W Isls
175 H8 Ancoats Manch
249 G4 Ancroft Nthumb
248 F4 Ancroft Northmoor Nthumb
235 G2 Ancrum Border
33 J6 Ancton W Susx
329 N2 Ancumtoun Ork
171 K5 Anderby Lincs
171 L5 Anderby Creek Lincs
41 K7 Andersea Somset
41 H7 Andersfield Somset
18 D2 Anderson Dorset
164 B5 Anderton Ches
6 F4 Anderton Cnwll
174 D5 Anderton Lancs
174 B5 Andertons Mill Lancs
45 L5 Andover Hants
45 L4 Andover Down Hants
79 G3 Andoversford Gloucs
172 g3 Andreas IoM
47 G3 Andwell Hants
144 B8 Anelog Gwynd
65 K7 Anerley Gt Lon
333 G11 Aness Shet
163 G2 Anfield Lpool
2 F3 Angarrack Cnwll
3 K3 Angarrick Cnwll
112 B4 Angelbank Shrops
26 B3 Angersleigh Somset
208 F2 Angerton Cumb
70 D6 Angle Pembks
325 M8 An Gleann Ur W Isls
33 L6 Angmering W Susx
186 F5 Angram N York
194 C2 Angram N York
225 L6 Anick Nthumb
265 K5 Anie Stirlg
96 B2 Ankerdine Hill Worcs
311 J3 Ankerville Highld
180 C2 Anlaby E R Yk
180 C2 Anlaby Park C KuH
321 M11 An Leth Meadhanach W Isls
140 E6 Anmer Norfk
32 C4 Anmore Hants
222 F6 Annan D & G
190 B3 Annaside Cumb
263 J3 Annat Ag & B
308 E7 Annat Highld
45 K5 Anna Valley Hants
230 B2 Annbank S Ayrs
153 K3 Annesley Notts
153 J3 Annesley Woodhouse Notts
212 E3 Annfield Plain Dur
256 C7 Anniesland C Glas
292 G6 Annishader Highld
123 H2 Annis Hill Suffk
227 H5 Annitsford N Tyne
307 G7 Annochie Abers
127 K5 Annscroft Shrops
31 K6 Ann's Hill Hants
131 G3 Annwell Place Derbys
173 H2 Ansdell Lancs
83 K3 Ansells End Herts
42 F7 Ansford Somset
115 G1 Ansley Warwks
131 G8 Ansley Common Warwks
130 E2 Anslow Staffs
130 D1 Anslow Gate Staffs
48 B7 Ansteadbrook Surrey
102 F7 Anstey Herts
131 L5 Anstey Leics
167 K4 Anston Rothm
269 K7 Anstruther Easter Fife
269 J7 Anstruther Wester Fife
115 H3 Ansty Warwks
29 H1 Ansty Wilts
34 E2 Ansty W Susx
29 H1 Ansty Coombe Wilts
28 D6 Ansty Cross Dorset
32 C4 Anthill Common Hants
48 D1 Anthony's Surrey
77 L2 Anthony's Cross Gloucs
208 E2 Anthorn Cumb
143 G5 Antingham Norfk
322 H7 An t-Ob W Isls
156 E4 Anton's Gowt Lincs
257 K4 Antonshill Falk
6 F4 Antony Cnwll
6 F3 Antony Passage Cnwll
164 B5 Antrobus Ches
52 F4 Anvil Green Kent
61 K7 Anvilles W Berk
156 B3 Anwick Lincs
216 C2 Anwoth D & G
285 G5 Aonachan Highld
150 F4 Apedale Staffs
50 B2 Aperfield Gt Lon
113 K5 Apes Dale Worcs
133 L7 Apethorpe Nhants
129 H3 Apeton Staffs
170 B5 Apley Lincs
128 E7 Apley Forge Shrops
167 G5 Apperknowle Derbys
96 E8 Apperley Gloucs
212 C2 Apperley Dene Nthumb
194 C3 Appersett N York
274 D5 Appin Ag & B
215 K5 Appleby D & G
180 B5 Appleby N Linc
202 F3 Appleby-in-Westmorland Cumb
131 G5 Appleby Magna Leics
131 G5 Appleby Parva Leics
308 A9 Applecross Highld
25 K4 Appledore Devon
38 B7 Appledore Devon
52 B8 Appledore Kent
52 C7 Appledore Heath Kent
62 D2 Appleford Oxon
222 E3 Applegarthtown D & G
63 K4 Applehouse Hill W & M
31 G5 Applemore Hants
45 J4 Appleshaw Hants
201 H2 Applethwaite Cumb
163 K3 Appleton Halton
80 E6 Appleton Oxon
197 K4 Appleton-le-Moors N York
197 K7 Appleton-le-Street N York
164 B4 Appleton Park Warrtn
187 G6 Appleton Roebuck N York
164 B4 Appleton Thorn Warrtn
205 K7 Appleton Wiske N York
234 E3 Appletreehall Border
184 F3 Appletreewick N York
21 K3 Appley IoW
25 K2 Appley Somset
174 B6 Appley Bridge Lancs
21 J5 Apse Heath IoW
122 F7 Apsey Green Suffk
101 K7 Apsley End Beds
32 F6 Apuldram W Susx
128 D5 Aqueduct Wrekin
302 D5 Aquhythie Abers
310 H2 Arabella Highld
281 H6 Arbirlot Angus
63 J7 Arborfield Wokham
63 J7 Arborfield Cross Wokham
63 J7 Arborfield Garrison Wokham
167 G3 Arbourthorne Sheff
281 H6 Arbroath Angus
119 J7 Arbury Cambs
291 H6 Arbuthnott Abers
205 G4 Archdeacon Newton Darltn
94 C5 Archenfield Herefs
304 C7 Archiestown Moray
16 j6 Archirondel Jersey
150 E1 Arclid Ches
150 E1 Arclid Green Ches
314 G6 Ardachu Highld
271 K11 Ardalanish Ag & B
307 J8 Ardallie Abers
263 K3 Ardanaiseig Ag & B
294 F1 Ardaneaskan Highld
308 D10 Ardarroch Highld
251 G13 Ardbeg Ag & B
254 D7 Ardbeg Ag & B
254 F4 Ardbeg Ag & B
313 K9 Ardcharnich Highld
271 K11 Ardchiavaig Ag & B
263 H5 Ardchonnell Ag & B
314 F9 Ardchronie Highld
265 K5 Ardchullarie More Stirlg
265 J2 Ardchyle Stirlg
311 M8 Ardclach Highld
255 G2 Arddarroch Ag & B
308 A9 Ard-dhubh Highld
126 E3 Arddleen Powys
284 E3 Ardechive Highld
84 C1 Ardeley Herts
295 G3 Ardelve Highld
255 K4 Arden Ag & B
243 G2 Arden C Glas
310 B10 Ardendrain Highld
165 H2 Arden Park Stockp
97 K3 Ardens Grafton Warwks
262 E3 Ardentallen Ag & B
254 F3 Ardentinny Ag & B
277 J7 Ardeonaig Stirlg
310 H7 Ardersier Highld
273 J2 Ardery Highld
312 G9 Ardessie Highld
262 E7 Ardfern Ag & B
252 D6 Ardfernal Ag & B
264 D7 Ardgartan Ag & B
314 E8 Ardgay Highld
314 E8 Ardgayhill Highld
255 G6 Ardgowan Inver
322 C11 Ardheisker W Isls
308 C6 Ardheslaig Highld
253 H1 Ardifuir Ag & B
262 C5 Ardinamir Ag & B
313 J9 Ardindrean Highld
49 K8 Ardingly W Susx
62 B3 Ardington Oxon
62 B3 Ardington Wick Oxon
294 F4 Ardintoul Highld
301 L3 Ardlair Abers
306 F3 Ardlawhill Abers
105 H8 Ardleigh Essex
66 D3 Ardleigh Green Gt Lon
105 J7 Ardleigh Heath Essex
87 H1 Ardleigh Park Essex
279 L6 Ardler P & K
81 G1 Ardley Oxon
85 G4 Ardley End Essex
264 E4 Ardlui Ag & B
252 E3 Ardlussa Ag & B
313 J7 Ardmair Highld
264 D7 Ardmay Ag & B
252 D6 Ardmenish Ag & B
238 F4 Ardminish Ag & B
283 G7 Ardmolich Highld
251 H12 Ardmore Ag & B
255 J5 Ardmore Ag & B
292 D8 Ardmore Highld
314 H9 Ardmore Highld
272 D5 Ardnacross Ag & B
254 F4 Ardnadam Ag & B
312 F5 Ardnagoine Highld
310 C8 Ardnagrask Highld
295 G1 Ardnarff Highld
273 J2 Ardnastang Highld
250 D8 Ardnave Ag & B
263 L6 Ardno Ag & B
306 F8 Ardo Abers
255 K5 Ardoch Ag & B
279 G7 Ardoch P & K
305 H7 Ardonald Abers
302 C3 Ardoyne Abers
255 G3 Ardpeaton Ag & B
253 J3 Ardrishaig Ag & B
292 D8 Ardroag Highld
310 E3 Ardross Highld
241 L5 Ardrossan N Ayrs
282 F8 Ardshealach Highld
250 E4 Ardskenish Ag & B
177 K6 Ardsley Barns
272 E2 Ardslignish Highld
251 H12 Ardtalla Ag & B
277 K7 Ardtalnaig P & K
282 E7 Ardtoe Highld
273 H5 Ardtornish Highld
293 E10 Ardtreck Highld
266 B3 Ardtrostan P & K
271 K10 Ardtun Ag & B
262 E5 Arduaine Ag & B
310 D5 Ardullie Highld
314 G9 Ardvannie Highld
294 B8 Ardvasar Highld
286 B4 Ardverikie Highld
265 L3 Ardvorlich P & K
323 L2 Ardvourlie W Isls
214 D4 Ardwell D & G
165 G1 Ardwick Manch
282 E7 Arean Highld
112 F5 Areley Kings Worcs
47 K6 Arford Hants
75 K6 Argoed Caerph
111 G3 Argoed Shrops
110 F1 Argoed Powys
127 G2 Argoed Shrops
50 E8 Argos Hill E Susx
324 H11 Aribruach W Isls
271 J10 Aridhglas Ag & B
270 F4 Arileod Ag & B
308 B6 Arinacrinachd Highld
270 G3 Arinagour Ag & B
328 C11 Arion Ork
282 F4 Arisaig Highld
273 K2 Ariundle Highld
282 F8 Arivegaig Highld
186 C2 Arkendale N York
103 G7 Arkesden Essex
193 G7 Arkholme Lancs
208 D6 Arkleby Cumb
223 K1 Arkleton D & G
204 C7 Arkle Town N York
83 L7 Arkley Gt Lon
178 D6 Arksey Donc
167 H6 Arkwright Town Derbys
78 E2 Arle Gloucs
78 C5 Arlebrook Gloucs
200 C4 Arlecdon Cumb
98 E4 Arlescote Warwks
101 L6 Arlesey Beds
128 D4 Arleston Wrekin
164 C4 Arley Ches
164 C4 Arley Green Ches
77 L4 Arlingham Gloucs
38 F5 Arlington Devon
35 K5 Arlington E Susx
79 J5 Arlington Gloucs
38 F5 Arlington Beccott Devon
294 B8 Armadale Highld
318 C4 Armadale Highld
257 L7 Armadale W Loth
209 L4 Armathwaite Cumb
103 J8 Armigers Essex
138 E6 Arminghall Norfk
130 B3 Armitage Staffs
176 E5 Armitage Bridge Kirk
185 L8 Armley Leeds
98 B5 Armscote Warwks
150 E7 Armsdale Staffs
151 H4 Armshead Staffs
118 B2 Armston Nhants
178 E7 Armthorpe Donc
270 F2 Arnabost Ag & B
190 D4 Arnaby Cumb
194 D7 Arncliffe N York
269 J6 Arncroach Fife
304 D6 Arndilly House Moray
18 F4 Arne Dorset
116 C1 Arnesby Leics
267 L5 Arngask P & K
239 H6 Arnicle Ag & B
294 F6 Arnisdale Highld
292 K7 Arnish Highld
246 C1 Arniston Mdloth
325 K5 Arnol W Isls
189 H6 Arnold E R Yk
153 L4 Arnold Notts
58 F6 Arno's Vale Bristl
256 E2 Arnprior Stirlg
191 J5 Arnside Cumb
272 E6 Aros Cott Ag & B
272 E5 Aros Mains Ag & B
149 J6 Arowry Wrexhm
310 D7 Arpafeelie Highld
53 G6 Arpinge Kent
191 G4 Arrad Foot Cumb
188 F6 Arram E R Yk
195 J3 Arrathorne N York
21 H4 Arreton IoW
264 E7 Arrochar Ag & B
97 J2 Arrow Warwks
162 E3 Arrowe Hill Wirral
113 L5 Arrowfield Top Worcs
94 F2 Arrow Green Herefs
176 E6 Arrunden Kirk
314 D4 Arscaig Highld
127 J5 Arscott Shrops
310 E8 Artafallie Highld
164 D3 Arthill Ches
185 L6 Arthington Leeds
116 F3 Arthingworth Nhants
124 C4 Arthog Gwynd
303 J1 Arthrath Abers
186 C7 Arthursdale Leeds
279 L6 Arthurstone P & K
48 C4 Artington Surrey
303 K2 Artrochie Abers
33 K5 Arundel W Susx
284 C8 Aryhoulan Highld
200 D3 Asby Cumb
254 E8 Ascog Ag & B
64 B7 Ascot W & M
98 D7 Ascott Warwks
80 C3 Ascott d' Oyley Oxon
80 B3 Ascott Earl Oxon
80 B3 Ascott-under-Wychwood Oxon
280 B3 Ascreavie Angus
196 C6 Asenby N York
132 E3 Asfordby Leics
132 E3 Asfordby Hill Leics
156 B4 Asgarby Lincs
170 F7 Asgarby Lincs
8 D5 Ash Devon
16 F2 Ash Dorset
28 F4 Ash Dorset
53 J2 Ash Kent
66 E8 Ash Kent
26 D2 Ash Somset
27 H2 Ash Somset
47 L4 Ash Surrey
294 C4 Ashaig Highld
62 E5 Ashampstead W Berk
62 E5 Ashampstead Green W Berk
51 K3 Ashbank Kent
151 H4 Ash Bank Staffs
40 E6 Ashbeer Somset
106 D3 Ashbocking Suffk
152 C4 Ashbourne Derbys
25 K2 Ashbrittle Somset
127 J8 Ashbrook Shrops
36 C3 Ashburnham Forge E Susx
14 B8 Ashburton Devon
23 J7 Ashbury Devon
61 J3 Ashbury Oxon
179 K6 Ashby N Linc
171 H7 Ashby by Partney Lincs
181 H7 Ashby cum Fenby NE Lin
155 L2 Ashby de la Launde Lincs
131 G3 Ashby-de-la-Zouch Leics
132 E4 Ashby Folville Leics
181 G7 Ashby Hill NE Lin
116 B1 Ashby Magna Leics
115 L2 Ashby Parva Leics
170 F6 Ashby Puerorum Lincs
116 B6 Ashby St Ledgers Nhants
139 G6 Ashby St Mary Norfk
96 F7 Ashchurch Gloucs
14 E6 Ashcombe Devon
41 K1 Ashcombe Park N Som
42 B6 Ashcott Somset
42 C5 Ashcott Corner Somset
25 L4 Ashculme Devon
103 J5 Ashdon Essex
46 D3 Ashe Hants
86 F6 Asheldham Essex
104 B5 Ashen Essex
81 L4 Ashendon Bucks
82 E6 Asheridge Bucks
21 J4 Ashey IoW
203 G7 Ash Fell Cumb
253 H3 Ashfield Ag & B
73 K3 Ashfield Carmth
30 F3 Ashfield Hants
77 H2 Ashfield Herefs
127 G1 Ashfield Shrops
266 D7 Ashfield Stirlg
122 E7 Ashfield Suffk
122 E7 Ashfield cum Thorpe Suffk
104 C2 Ashfield Green Suffk
122 F5 Ashfield Green Suffk
128 E1 Ashfields Shrops
49 H8 Ashfold Crossways W Susx
185 H1 Ashfold Side N York
7 L5 Ashford Devon
38 D6 Ashford Devon
29 L4 Ashford Hants
52 D5 Ashford Kent
64 E6 Ashford Surrey
111 L5 Ashford Bowdler Shrops
111 L5 Ashford Carbonell Shrops
64 E6 Ashford Common Surrey
46 D1 Ashford Hill Hants
166 C7 Ashford in the Water Derbys
167 G6 Ashgate Derbys
244 B4 Ashgill S Lans
48 B4 Ash Green Surrey
115 G3 Ash Green Warwks
43 G2 Ashgrove BaNES
304 C3 Ashgrove Moray
149 G5 Ash Grove Wrexhm
14 E7 Ash Hill Devon
246 E6 Ashiestiel Border
25 K4 Ashill Devon
26 E3 Ashill Somset
137 H6 Ashill Norfk
67 L2 Ashingdon Essex
227 G2 Ashington Nthumb
29 J7 Ashington Poole
27 K2 Ashington Somset
34 B3 Ashington W Susx
171 K7 Ashington End Lincs
234 D2 Ashkirk Border
31 H6 Ashlett Hants
78 C1 Ashleworth Gloucs
120 D7 Ashley Cambs
164 E4 Ashley Ches
29 L6 Ashley Dorset
60 B2 Ashley Wilts
20 C2 Ashley Hants
45 L7 Ashley Hants
53 K4 Ashley Kent
116 F1 Ashley Nhants
150 E6 Ashley Staffs
59 K7 Ashley Wilts
150 E6 Ashley Dale Staffs
58 E5 Ashley Down Bristl
82 F5 Ashley Green Bucks
152 E3 Ashleyhay Derbys
164 E3 Ashley Heath Traffd
29 L6 Ashley Heath Dorset
150 D6 Ashley Heath Staffs
111 K6 Ashley Moor Herefs
64 F7 Ashley Park Surrey
149 L6 Ash Magna Shrops
139 G2 Ashmanhaugh Norfk
46 B2 Ashmansworth Hants
22 E3 Ashmansworthy Devon
78 B7 Ashmead Green Gloucs
12 D2 Ashmill Devon
24 D2 Ash Mill Devon
24 D3 Ash Moor Devon
29 G3 Ashmore Dorset
62 C7 Ashmore Green W Berk
129 K7 Ashmore Lake Wsall
129 K6 Ashmore Park Wolves
166 C3 Ashopton Derbys
98 D2 Ashorne Warwks
166 F8 Ashover Derbys
153 G1 Ashover Hay Derbys
115 G5 Ashow Warwks
149 L6 Ash Parva Shrops
95 K5 Ashperton Herefs
8 D3 Ashprington Devon
40 F8 Ash Priors Somset
23 L4 Ashreigney Devon
24 B6 Ashridge Court Devon
105 H4 Ash Street Suffk
49 G2 Ashtead Surrey
25 J4 Ash Thomas Devon
163 K7 Ashton Ches
3 G5 Ashton Cnwll
134 C5 Ashton C Pete
31 J3 Ashton Hants
111 L7 Ashton Herefs
255 G5 Ashton Inver
100 C4 Ashton Nhants
118 B2 Ashton Nhants
42 B4 Ashton Somset
43 L2 Ashton Common Wilts
58 E6 Ashton Gate Bristl
35 J4 Ashton Green E Susx
163 L5 Ashton Heath Ches
174 C8 Ashton-in-Makerfield Wigan
60 E2 Ashton Keynes Wilts
97 G6 Ashton under Hill Worcs
175 K8 Ashton-under-Lyne Tamesd
164 E2 Ashton Upon Mersey Traffd
58 E6 Ashton Vale Bristl
30 E4 Ashurst Hants
50 D6 Ashurst Kent
173 L6 Ashurst Lancs
34 C3 Ashurst W Susx
30 E4 Ashurst Bridge Hants
50 B6 Ashurst Wood W Susx
75 J4 Ashvale Blae G
47 L3 Ash Vale Surrey
12 D2 Ashwater Devon
14 D7 Ashwell Devon
102 C6 Ashwell Herts
133 H4 Ashwell Rutlnd
26 F3 Ashwell Somset
102 C5 Ashwell End Herts
138 C7 Ashwellthorpe Norfk
42 F4 Ashwick Somset
136 E3 Ashwicken Norfk
113 H2 Ashwood Staffs
190 D5 Askam in Furness Cumb
178 D5 Askern Donc
17 G3 Askerswell Dorset
154 F4 Askerton Hill Notts
82 C5 Askett Bucks
202 C3 Askham Cumb
168 D6 Askham Notts
187 G5 Askham Bryan York
186 F5 Askham Richard York
253 L2 Asknish Ag & B
238 D4 Askomill Ag & B
194 D3 Askrigg N York
185 J5 Askwith N York
155 L7 Aslackby Lincs
122 C1 Aslacton Norfk
154 D5 Aslockton Notts
301 K6 Asloun Abers
42 C6 Asney Somset
122 D6 Aspall Suffk
208 D5 Aspatria Cumb
102 E8 Aspenden Herts
156 E6 Asperton Lincs
153 K5 Aspley C Nott
150 F7 Aspley Staffs
100 F6 Aspley Guise Beds
100 F6 Aspley Heath Beds
114 B5 Aspley Heath Warwks
174 D6 Aspull Wigan
174 D8 Aspult Common Wigan
331 C10 Assater Shet
179 G2 Asselby E R Yk
171 J5 Asserby Lincs
171 J5 Asserby Turn Lincs
104 F6 Assington Suffk
104 C3 Assington Green Suffk
150 F1 Astbury Ches
99 L3 Astcote Nhants
170 E5 Asterby Lincs
127 H5 Asterley Shrops
111 H1 Asterton Shrops
80 B4 Asthall Oxon
80 C4 Asthall Leigh Oxon
164 F6 Astle Ches
127 L3 Astley Shrops
115 G2 Astley Warwks
174 F7 Astley Wigan
112 F6 Astley Worcs
128 E7 Astley Abbotts Shrops
174 F5 Astley Bridge Bolton
113 G6 Astley Cross Worcs
174 F8 Astley Green Wigan
163 K4 Astmoor Halton
114 B2 Aston Birm
150 B4 Aston Ches
163 L5 Aston Ches
152 C7 Aston Derbys
166 C4 Aston Derbys
162 F7 Aston Flints
111 K5 Aston Powys
111 K7 Aston Herefs
84 B2 Aston Herts
80 C6 Aston Oxon
110 F1 Aston Powys
167 J4 Aston Rothm
129 G8 Aston Shrops
149 K8 Aston Shrops
129 H2 Aston Staffs
150 E5 Aston Staffs
63 J4 Aston Wokham
128 C5 Aston Wrekin
82 C2 Aston Abbotts Bucks
112 C5 Aston Bank Worcs
112 C3 Aston Botterell Shrops
151 H7 Aston-By-Stone Staffs
97 K2 Aston Cantlow Warwks
82 D4 Aston Clinton Bucks
77 K2 Aston Crews Herefs
96 F7 Aston Cross Gloucs
128 D8 Aston Eyre Shrops
113 K6 Aston Fields Worcs
115 K1 Aston Flamville Leics
77 K2 Aston Ingham Herefs
150 B2 Aston juxta Mondrum Ches
99 G3 Aston le Walls Nhants
97 L6 Aston Magna Gloucs
111 L2 Aston Munslow Shrops
96 F7 Aston on Carrant Gloucs
111 H3 Aston on Clun Shrops
153 H8 Aston-on-Trent Derbys
127 G5 Aston Pigott Shrops
127 G5 Aston Rogers Shrops
81 L7 Aston Rowant Oxon
82 B5 Aston Sandford Bucks
97 H6 Aston Somerville Worcs
148 F8 Aston Sq Shrops
97 K5 Aston Subedge Gloucs
62 E3 Aston Tirrold Oxon
62 D3 Aston Upthorpe Oxon
99 H6 Astrop Nhants
82 D3 Astrope Herts
102 B6 Astwick Beds
167 H8 Astwith Derbys
101 G4 Astwood M Keyn

96 E2 **Astwood** Worcs
113 J7 **Astwood** Worcs
113 L7 **Astwood Bank** Worcs
155 L6 **Aswarby** Lincs
171 G6 **Aswardby** Lincs
127 L5 **Atcham** Shrops
97 H3 **Atch Lench** Worcs
18 B3 **Athelhampton** Dorset
122 D5 **Athelington** Suffk
41 K8 **Athelney** Somset
260 C5 **Athelstaneford** E Loth
21 G6 **Atherfield Green** IoW
23 K2 **Atherington** Devon
33 K6 **Atherington** W Susx
177 K6 **Athersley South** Barns
26 F3 **Atherstone** Somset
131 G7 **Atherstone** Warwks
97 L3 **Atherstone on Stour** Warwks
174 E7 **Atherton** Wigan
152 D4 **Atlow** Derbys
16 E2 **Atrim** Dorset
308 F10 **Attadale** Highld
153 K7 **Attenborough** Notts
100 E6 **Atterbury** M Keyn
169 J2 **Atterby** Lincs
167 G3 **Attercliffe** Sheff
128 C7 **Atterley** Shrops
131 G7 **Atterton** Leics
128 B5 **Attingham** Shrops
138 B7 **Attleborough** Norfk
115 H1 **Attleborough** Warwks
138 C3 **Attlebridge** Norfk
104 B3 **Attleton Green** Suffk
189 J4 **Atwick** E R Yk
59 L7 **Atworth** Wilts
95 G4 **Auberrow** Herefs
155 H1 **Aubourn** Lincs
240 D7 **Auchagallon** N Ayrs
288 F4 **Auchallater** Abers
305 L7 **Aucharnie** Abers
290 F3 **Auchattie** Abers
288 F8 **Auchavan** Angus
300 D3 **Auchbreck** Moray
242 F2 **Auchenback** E Rens
231 L7 **Auchenbainzie** D & G
291 G6 **Auchenblae** Abers
231 K7 **Auchenbrack** D & G
254 C4 **Auchenbreck** Ag & B
217 G3 **Auchencairn** D & G
222 B3 **Auchencairn** D & G
241 G8 **Auchencairn** N Ayrs
240 D6 **Auchencar** N Ayrs
255 L4 **Auchencarroch** W Duns
248 D1 **Auchencrow** Border
246 B1 **Auchendinny** Mdloth
288 E3 **Auchendryne** Abers
244 F3 **Auchengray** S Lans
231 L5 **Auchengruith** D & G
304 F3 **Auchenhalrig** Moray
242 B5 **Auchenharvie** N Ayrs
244 C5 **Auchenheath** S Lans
231 K7 **Auchenhessnane** D & G
228 E2 **Auchenhew** N Ayrs
254 B6 **Auchenlochan** Ag & B
214 F3 **Auchenmalg** D & G
229 J8 **Auchensoul** S Ayrs
243 K3 **Auchentibber** S Lans
242 D4 **Auchentiber** N Ayrs
299 H5 **Auchgourish** Highld
256 E7 **Auchinairn** C Glas
305 G5 **Auchinderran** Moray
263 J7 **Auchindrain** Ag & B
313 K10 **Auchindrean** Highld
305 L6 **Auchininna** Abers
219 L5 **Auchinleck** D & G
230 F2 **Auchinleck** E Ayrs
279 K3 **Auchinleish** Angus
256 F6 **Auchinloch** N Lans
243 K2 **Auchinraith** S Lans
256 F5 **Auchinreoch** E Duns
257 G5 **Auchinstarry** N Lans
301 K5 **Auchintoul** Abers
287 K2 **Auchlean** Highld
291 K2 **Auchlee** Abers
303 K1 **Auchleuchries** Abers
302 B4 **Auchleven** Abers
244 B6 **Auchlochan** S Lans
290 D1 **Auchlossan** Abers
291 K2 **Auchlunies** Abers
265 J2 **Auchlyne** Stirlg
303 J2 **Auchmacoy** Abers
243 G8 **Auchmillan** E Ayrs
281 J6 **Auchmithie** Angus
277 G8 **Auchmore** Stirlg
268 C7 **Auchmuirbridge** Fife
290 D7 **Auchmull** Angus
268 D7 **Auchmuty** Fife
280 E2 **Auchnacree** Angus
278 B8 **Auchnafree** P & K
299 L2 **Auchnagallin** Highld
307 G7 **Auchnagatt** Abers
300 D4 **Auchnarrow** Moray
289 J3 **Aucholzie** Abers
289 L5 **Auchronie** Angus
267 G5 **Auchterarder** P & K
297 G7 **Auchteraw** Highld
308 D2 **Auchtercairn** Highld
259 G1 **Auchterderran** Fife
280 B7 **Auchterhouse** Angus
268 C5 **Auchtermuchty** Fife
259 G2 **Auchtertool** Fife
294 F3 **Auchtertyre** Highld
265 K3 **Auchtubh** Stirlg
319 Q4 **Auckengill** Highld
178 E7 **Auckley** Donc
165 H1 **Audenshaw** Tamesd
150 C5 **Audlem** Ches
150 E3 **Audley** Staffs
103 H6 **Audley End** Essex
104 D6 **Audley End** Essex
122 C3 **Audley End** Norfk
104 E3 **Audley End** Suffk
305 L3 **Auds** Abers
208 F6 **Aughertree** Cumb
187 K7 **Aughton** E R Yk
173 J7 **Aughton** Lancs
183 G1 **Aughton** Lancs
167 J3 **Aughton** Rothm
45 H2 **Aughton** Wilts
173 K6 **Aughton Park** Lancs
203 L2 **Aukside** Dur
215 L5 **Auldbreck** D & G
311 L6 **Auldearn** Highld
95 G3 **Aulden** Herefs
221 L2 **Auldgirth** D & G
260 D4 **Auldhame** E Loth
243 J3 **Auldhouse** S Lans
306 B7 **Auldyoch** Abers
295 H4 **Ault a' Chruinn** Highld
316 G9 **Aultanrynie** Highld
312 D9 **Aultbea** Highld
309 N4 **Aultdearg** Highld
312 A9 **Aultgrishan** Highld
167 J7 **Ault Hucknall** Derbys
315 P2 **Aultibea** Highld
318 D3 **Aultiphurst** Highld
318 D3 **Aultivullin** Highld
305 G5 **Aultmore** Moray
297 K4 **Ault-na-goire** Highld
302 B3 **Aulton** Abers
310 C8 **Aultvaich** Highld
133 L4 **Aunby** Lincs
299 J5 **Aundorach** Highld
25 J6 **Aunk** Devon
155 K6 **Aunsby** Lincs
302 F3 **Auquhorthies** Abers
58 E3 **Aust** S Glos
134 F2 **Austendike** Lincs
171 G2 **Austen Fen** Lincs
64 C3 **Austenwood** Bucks
168 C2 **Austerfield** Donc
175 L6 **Austerlands** Oldham
130 F5 **Austrey** Warwks
193 L8 **Austwick** N York
171 H4 **Authorpe** Lincs
171 K6 **Authorpe Row** Lincs
60 F7 **Avebury** Wilts
60 E7 **Avebury Trusloe** Wilts
66 E5 **Aveley** Thurr
78 D7 **Avening** Gloucs
59 H2 **Avening Green** S Glos
154 E3 **Averham** Notts
294 F3 **Avernish** Highld
66 B6 **Avery Hill** Gt Lon
7 L5 **Aveton Gifford** Devon
299 H5 **Avielochan** Highld
299 G6 **Aviemore** Highld
46 D7 **Avington** Hants
61 L7 **Avington** W Berk
310 G7 **Avoch** Highld
29 L7 **Avon** Hants
60 C5 **Avon** Wilts
257 K6 **Avonbridge** Falk
29 L6 **Avon Castle** Hants
43 J2 **Avoncliff** Wilts
98 F4 **Avon Dassett** Warwks
58 D5 **Avonmouth** Bristl
8 B3 **Avonwick** Devon
30 E2 **Awbridge** Hants
58 E3 **Awkley** S Glos
25 L6 **Awliscombe** Devon
77 L5 **Awre** Gloucs
153 J5 **Awsworth** Notts
42 B3 **Axbridge** Somset
46 F5 **Axford** Hants
61 H6 **Axford** Wilts
46 E1 **Axmansford** Hants
26 D7 **Axminster** Devon
16 B3 **Axmouth** Devon
161 K5 **Axton** Flints
7 H1 **Axtown** Devon
226 F7 **Axwell Park** Gatesd
53 K5 **Aycliff** Kent
205 H3 **Aycliffe Village** Dur
226 C6 **Aydon** Nthumb
213 G5 **Aykley Heads** Dur
77 J6 **Aylburton** Gloucs
77 J6 **Aylburton Common** Gloucs
210 F4 **Ayle** Nthumb
15 G3 **Aylesbeare** Devon
82 B4 **Aylesbury** Bucks
181 G6 **Aylesby** NE Lin
51 H2 **Aylesford** Kent
53 H3 **Aylesham** Kent
132 B6 **Aylestone** C Leic
95 H5 **Aylestone Hill** Herefs
132 B6 **Aylestone Park** C Leic
142 F4 **Aylmerton** Norfk
142 F6 **Aylsham** Norfk
95 L6 **Aylton** Herefs
79 H2 **Aylworth** Gloucs
111 J6 **Aymestrey** Herefs
99 H7 **Aynho** Nhants
83 L4 **Ayot Green** Herts
83 K3 **Ayot St Lawrence** Herts
83 L3 **Ayot St Peter** Herts
229 L2 **Ayr** S Ayrs
83 K4 **Ayres End** Herts
332 D7 **Ayres of Selivoe** Shet
213 J2 **Ayres Quay** Sundld
194 F4 **Aysgarth** N York
25 J3 **Ayshford** Devon
191 H4 **Ayside** Cumb
133 H6 **Ayston** Rutlnd
85 H3 **Aythorpe Roding** Essex
248 E1 **Ayton** Border
213 G2 **Ayton** Sundld
248 E1 **Ayton Castle** Border
330 H8 **Aywick** Shet
195 L7 **Azerley** N York

B

8 F1 **Babbacombe** Torbay
153 J5 **Babbington** Notts
148 F7 **Babbinswood** Shrops
84 D3 **Babbs Green** Herts
42 E8 **Babcary** Somset
92 D6 **Babel** Carmth
104 B4 **Babel Green** Suffk
162 B6 **Babell** Flints
13 K6 **Babeny** Devon
140 D6 **Babingley** Norfk
103 H3 **Babraham** Cambs
168 C4 **Babworth** Notts
325 N6 **Bac** W Isls
159 G4 **Bachau** IoA
111 K3 **Bache** Shrops
110 E1 **Bacheldre** Powys
36 F4 **Bachelor's Bump** E Susx
111 K2 **Bache Mill** Shrops
54 F1 **Bach-y-gwreiddyn** Swans
329 J8 **Backaland** Ork
328 G3 **Backaskaill** Ork
191 H4 **Backbarrow** Cumb
165 J2 **Backbower** Tamesd
291 J3 **Backburn** Abers
301 K2 **Backburn** Abers
72 B5 **Backe** Carmth
307 J5 **Backfolds** Abers
163 G6 **Backford** Ches
163 G6 **Backford Cross** Ches
306 D8 **Backhill** Abers
307 J8 **Backhill** Abers
307 G6 **Backhill of Clackriach** Abers
305 L5 **Backhill of Clunie** Abers
307 H7 **Backhill of Fortrie** Abers
290 E2 **Backhill of Trustach** Abers
315 K6 **Backies** Highld
311 Q4 **Backlands** Moray
319 L6 **Backlass** Highld
269 G6 **Backmuir of New Gilston** Fife
282 E4 **Back of Keppoch** Highld
151 L3 **Back o'th' Brook** Staffs
230 F2 **Back Rogerton** E Ayrs
104 B2 **Back Street** Suffk
58 C7 **Backwell** N Som
58 C6 **Backwell Common** N Som
58 C7 **Backwell Green** N Som
227 J5 **Backworth** N Tyne
85 J3 **Bacon End** Essex
85 J3 **Baconend Green** Essex
114 D2 **Bacon's End** Solhll
142 E4 **Baconsthorpe** Norfk
94 E7 **Bacton** Herefs
143 J5 **Bacton** Norfk
122 B6 **Bacton** Suffk
143 J5 **Bacton Green** Norfk
121 L6 **Bacton Green** Suffk
175 J3 **Bacup** Lancs
310 F3 **Badachonacher** Highld
308 C3 **Badachro** Highld
309 K6 **Badavanich** Highld
61 G4 **Badbury** Swindn
61 G4 **Badbury Wick** Swindn
99 J2 **Badby** Nhants
316 E5 **Badcall** Highld
312 G8 **Badcaul** Highld
151 H3 **Baddeley Edge** C Stke
151 H3 **Baddeley Green** C Stke
114 D5 **Baddesley Clinton** Warwks
130 F7 **Baddesley Ensor** Warwks
312 H2 **Baddidarach** Highld
288 E5 **Baddoch** Abers
85 L6 **Baddow Park** Essex
312 G5 **Badenscallie** Highld
306 B8 **Badenscoth** Abers
291 K2 **Badentoy Park** Abers
300 F5 **Badenyon** Abers
11 J4 **Badgall** Cnwll
135 J7 **Badgeney** Cambs
128 F7 **Badger** Shrops
2 D4 **Badger's Cross** Cnwll
97 H4 **Badger's Hill** Worcs
50 C1 **Badgers Mount** Kent
26 D3 **Badger Street** Somset
78 E3 **Badgeworth** Gloucs
41 L3 **Badgworth** Somset
11 K4 **Badharlick** Cnwll
294 E3 **Badicaul** Highld
123 G6 **Badingham** Suffk
52 D3 **Badlesmere** Kent
319 M7 **Badlipster** Highld
312 F8 **Badluarach** Highld
59 K4 **Badminton** S Glos
312 H2 **Badnaban** Highld
319 L10 **Badnagie** Highld
315 J8 **Badninish** Highld
312 H8 **Badrallach** Highld
97 J5 **Badsey** Worcs
255 L3 **Badshalloch** W Duns
47 L4 **Badshot Lea** Surrey
178 B4 **Badsworth** Wakefd
121 K6 **Badwell Ash** Suffk
121 L6 **Badwell Green** Suffk
7 L2 **Badworthy** Devon
32 C6 **Baffins** C Port
28 D4 **Bagber** Dorset
196 E5 **Bagby** N York
196 E5 **Bagby Grange** N York
171 G6 **Bag Enderby** Lincs
79 G5 **Bagendon** Gloucs
112 D3 **Bagginswood** Shrops
208 E5 **Baggrow** Cumb
322 G10 **Bàgh a Chàise** W Isls
320 D5 **Bàgh a' Chaisteil** W Isls
52 E3 **Bagham** Kent
321 M11 **Baghasdal** W Isls
321 Q3 **Bàgh Mòr** W Isls
320 D4 **Bàgh Shiarabhagh** W Isls
162 D5 **Bagillt** Flints
115 G5 **Baginton** Warwks
55 J3 **Baglan** Neath
185 K7 **Bagley** Leeds
127 J1 **Bagley** Shrops
42 C4 **Bagley** Somset
25 L3 **Bagley Green** Somset
149 G8 **Bagley Marsh** Shrops
47 G5 **Bagmore** Hants
151 H3 **Bagnall** Staffs
62 B7 **Bagnor** W Berk
59 K2 **Bagpath** Gloucs
78 D6 **Bagpath** Gloucs
165 L4 **Bagshaw** Derbys
64 B8 **Bagshot** Surrey
61 K7 **Bagshot** Wilts
48 B1 **Bagshot Heath** Surrey
175 J5 **Bagslate Moor** Rochdl
59 G3 **Bagstone** S Glos
140 F5 **Bagthorpe** Norfk
153 J3 **Bagthorpe** Notts
164 F3 **Baguley** Manch
21 H5 **Bagwich** IoW
131 J5 **Bagworth** Leics
76 E1 **Bagwyllydiart** Herefs
278 C1 **Bailanloan** P & K
325 M3 **Bail Àrd Bhuirgh** W Isls
59 J7 **Bailbrook** BaNES
185 H7 **Baildon** Brad
185 H7 **Baildon Green** Brad
322 F8 **Baile** W Isls
325 J10 **Baile Ailein** W Isls
321 N3 **Baile a' Mhanaich** W Isls
325 L4 **Baile an Truiseil** W Isls
297 J5 **Bailebeag** Highld
253 G6 **Baile Boidheach** Ag & B
321 N5 **Baile Gharbhaidh** W Isls
321 P3 **Baile Glas** W Isls
322 B10 **Baile Mhàrtainn** W Isls
322 E9 **Baile Mhic' Phàil** W Isls
270 H10 **Baile Mòr** Ag & B
320 D4 **Baile na Creige** W Isls
321 M4 **Baile nan Cailleach** W Isls
322 B11 **Baile Raghnill** W Isls
282 E7 **Bailetonach** Highld
32 C1 **Bailey Green** Hants
301 J1 **Bailiesward** Abers
321 P3 **Bail' Iochdrach** W Isls
256 F8 **Baillieston** C Glas
182 E3 **Bailrigg** Lancs
321 P2 **Bail Uachdraich** W Isls
325 P5 **Bail' Ur Tholastaidh** W Isls
194 D3 **Bainbridge** N York
257 K4 **Bainsford** Falk
302 B1 **Bainshole** Abers
134 B5 **Bainton** C Pete
188 E4 **Bainton** E R Yk
81 H1 **Bainton** Oxon
268 E7 **Baintown** Fife
235 G3 **Bairnkine** Border
51 J6 **Baker's Cross** Kent
84 D3 **Bakers End** Herts
77 H4 **Baker's Hill** Gloucs
66 F4 **Baker Street** Thurr
64 D3 **Baker's Wood** Bucks
22 C6 **Bakesdown** Cnwll
167 K5 **Bakestone Moor** Derbys
166 D7 **Bakewell** Derbys
147 H6 **Bala** Gwynd
292 J8 **Balachuirn** Highld
325 J10 **Balallan** W Isls
151 L7 **Balance Hill** Staffs
298 E8 **Balavil** Highld
297 J2 **Balbeg** Highld
297 J4 **Balbeg** Highld
268 B2 **Balbeggie** P & K
302 E5 **Balbithan** Abers
302 D7 **Balblair** Abers
310 C8 **Balblair** Highld
310 G4 **Balblair** Highld
269 J7 **Balbuthie** Fife
178 D7 **Balby** Donc
281 G7 **Balcathie** Angus
315 K10 **Balcherry** Highld
316 A10 **Balchladich** Highld
297 L2 **Balchraggan** Highld
310 C9 **Balchraggan** Highld
316 D4 **Balchrick** Highld
49 K7 **Balcombe** W Susx
49 K7 **Balcombe Lane** W Susx
269 L6 **Balcomie** Fife
268 E7 **Balcurvie** Fife
196 C6 **Baldersby** N York
196 C6 **Baldersby St James** N York
174 D1 **Balderstone** Lancs
175 K5 **Balderstone** Rochdl
163 G8 **Balderton** Ches
154 F3 **Balderton** Notts
3 K2 **Baldhu** Cnwll
175 G5 **Baldingstone** Bury
269 G5 **Baldinnie** Fife
102 B7 **Baldock** Herts
81 H6 **Baldon Row** Oxon
280 E8 **Baldovie** C Dund
172 g6 **Baldrine** IoM
36 F4 **Baldslow** E Susx
172 f6 **Baldwin** IoM
209 H3 **Baldwinholme** Cumb
150 E6 **Baldwin's Gate** Staffs
49 L6 **Baldwins Hill** W Susx
142 C4 **Bale** Norfk
270 B6 **Balemartine** Ag & B
322 B11 **Balemore** W Isls
270 C5 **Balephetrish** Ag & B
270 B6 **Balephuil** Ag & B
258 F7 **Balerno** C Edin
250 F4 **Baleromindubh** Ag & B
270 B5 **Balevullin** Ag & B
290 C8 **Balfield** Angus
328 G10 **Balfour** Ork
256 D3 **Balfron** Stirlg
256 C3 **Balfron Station** Stirlg
305 L7 **Balgaveny** Abers
280 F4 **Balgavies House** Angus
268 D7 **Balgeddie** Fife
258 C2 **Balgonar** Fife
302 F2 **Balgove** Abers
214 D5 **Balgowan** D & G
286 E3 **Balgowan** Highld
267 H3 **Balgowan** P & K
292 E9 **Balgown** Highld
292 F3 **Balgown** Highld
256 E5 **Balgrochan** E Duns
310 E8 **Balgunearie** Highld
310 E8 **Balgunloune** Highld
308 D7 **Balgy** Highld
302 E4 **Balhalgardy** Abers
65 J6 **Balham** Gt Lon
279 L5 **Balhary** P & K
330 K4 **Baliasta** Shet
318 D3 **Baligill** Highld
273 K6 **Baligrundle** Ag & B
253 G6 **Balimore** Ag & B
270 B6 **Balinoe** Ag & B
279 L3 **Balintore** Angus
311 K2 **Balintore** Highld
310 G3 **Balintraid** Highld
321 N3 **Balivanich** W Isls
280 B6 **Balkeerie** Angus
168 D4 **Balk Field** Notts
179 H2 **Balkholme** E R Yk
281 K4 **Balkiellie** Angus
218 E3 **Balkissock** S Ayrs
10 D7 **Ball** Cnwll
127 G1 **Ball** Shrops
172 d8 **Ballabeg** IoM
275 G3 **Ballachulish** Highld
175 H3 **Balladen** Lancs
172 c8 **Ballafesson** IoM
172 c8 **Ballakilpheric** IoM
172 d8 **Ballamodha** IoM
218 D3 **Ballantrae** S Ayrs
60 E4 **Ballard's Ash** Wilts
68 B2 **Ballards Gore** Essex
114 F1 **Ballard's Green** Warwks
172 d8 **Ballasalla** IoM
289 K2 **Ballater** Abers
172 e4 **Ballaugh** IoM
278 D4 **Ballechin** P & K
314 G10 **Balleigh** Highld
260 B5 **Ballencrieff** E Loth
258 B6 **Ballencrieff Toll** W Loth
278 C1 **Ballentoul** P & K
151 G3 **Ball Green** C Stke
151 J2 **Ball Haye Green** Staffs
22 D2 **Ballhill** Devon
62 B8 **Ball Hill** Hants
152 D3 **Ballidon** Derbys
240 D6 **Balliekine** N Ayrs
254 D4 **Balliemore** Ag & B
262 E2 **Balliemore** Ag & B
310 F9 **Ballifeary** Highld
253 L4 **Ballimore** Ag & B
263 K2 **Ballimore** Ag & B
265 J4 **Ballimore** Stirlg
251 C9 **Ballinaby** Ag & B
268 D2 **Ballindean** P & K
104 E5 **Ballingdon** Suffk
83 G4 **Ballingdon Bottom** Herts
104 E5 **Ballingdon Grove** Suffk
82 E6 **Ballinger Bottom** Bucks
82 E6 **Ballinger Bottom (South)** Bucks
82 E6 **Ballinger Common** Bucks
95 J7 **Ballingham** Herefs
95 J7 **Ballingham Hill** Herefs
258 F1 **Ballingry** Fife
278 E6 **Ballinlick** P & K
278 E4 **Ballinluig** P & K
279 H3 **Ballintuim** P & K
273 K6 **Balliveolan** Ag & B
314 E5 **Balloan** Highld
280 B3 **Balloch** Angus
310 G8 **Balloch** Highld
257 G6 **Balloch** N Lans
255 K4 **Balloch** W Duns
290 C3 **Ballochan** Abers
256 D3 **Ballochearn** Stirlg
254 D8 **Ballochgoy** Ag & B
239 H3 **Ballochroy** Ag & B
163 J3 **Ball o' Ditton** Halton
290 D2 **Ballogie** Abers
33 J1 **Balls Cross** W Susx
87 H2 **Balls Green** Essex
50 C6 **Balls Green** E Susx
78 D7 **Ball's Green** Gloucs
34 B2 **Balls Green** W Susx
129 K8 **Balls Hill** Sandw
272 B6 **Ballygown** Ag & B
251 F9 **Ballygrant** Ag & B
270 F3 **Ballyhaugh** Ag & B
253 J1 **Ballymeanoch** Ag & B
294 F3 **Balmacara** Highld
294 F3 **Balmacara Square** Highld
220 F4 **Balmaclellan** D & G
278 E4 **Balmacneil** P & K
292 G2 **Balmacqueen** Highld
216 E5 **Balmae** D & G
255 L2 **Balmaha** Stirlg
268 E6 **Balmalcolm** Fife
257 G5 **Balmalloch** N Lans
280 E5 **Balmashanner** Angus
292 E8 **Balmeanach** Highld
292 H3 **Balmeanach** Highld
293 J10 **Balmeanach** Highld
303 J5 **Balmedie** Abers
149 H7 **Balmer** Shrops
149 H7 **Balmer Heath** Shrops
30 E6 **Balmerlawn** Hants
240 E7 **Balmichael** N Ayrs
246 F6 **Balmoral** Border
256 E6 **Balmore** E Duns
292 D8 **Balmore** Highld
318 H3 **Balmore** Highld
269 G3 **Balmullo** Fife
310 G6 **Balmungie** Highld
219 G6 **Balmurrie** D & G
280 B1 **Balnaboth** Angus
315 L10 **Balnabruach** Highld
319 K11 **Balnabruich** Highld
315 K4 **Balnacoil** Highld
308 G8 **Balnacra** Highld
314 F5 **Balnadelson** Highld
298 C1 **Balnafoich** Highld
303 J8 **Balnagask** C Aber
278 D4 **Balnaguard** P & K
310 F3 **Balnaguisich** Highld
250 G3 **Balnahard** Ag & B
272 C8 **Balnahard** Ag & B
297 H2 **Balnain** Highld
316 H3 **Balnakeil** Highld
316 H3 **Balnakeil Craft Village** Highld
279 G2 **Balnakilly** P & K
292 G4 **Balnaknock** Highld
306 F4 **Balnamoon** Abers
280 F2 **Balnamoon** Angus
310 H4 **Balnapaling** Highld
178 D4 **Balne** N York
2 D3 **Balnoon** Cnwll
256 E7 **Balornock** C Glas
265 J3 **Balquhidder** Stirlg
114 E4 **Balsall** Solhll
114 E4 **Balsall Common** Solhll
114 B3 **Balsall Heath** Birm
114 E4 **Balsall Street** Solhll
98 E5 **Balscote** Oxon
103 J3 **Balsham** Cambs
67 G4 **Balstonia** Thurr
330 K4 **Baltasound** Shet
150 E4 **Balterley** Staffs
150 E3 **Balterley Green** Staffs
150 D3 **Balterley Heath** Staffs
306 E5 **Balthangie** Abers
268 F5 **Baltilly** Fife
42 D7 **Baltonsborough** Somset
310 C7 **Balvaird** Highld
279 G2 **Balvarran** P & K
304 E7 **Balvenie** Moray
262 D4 **Balvicar** Ag & B
298 F2 **Balvraid** Highld
310 C7 **Balvraid** Highld
2 F4 **Balwest** Cnwll
174 C2 **Bamber Bridge** Lancs
85 H2 **Bamber's Green** Essex
249 K6 **Bamburgh** Nthumb
279 K4 **Bamff** P & K
166 D4 **Bamford** Derbys
175 J5 **Bamford** Rochdl
78 D2 **Bamfurlong** Gloucs
174 C7 **Bamfurlong** Wigan
202 C4 **Bampton** Cumb
25 H2 **Bampton** Devon
80 C6 **Bampton** Oxon
202 C4 **Bampton Grange** Cumb
284 E6 **Banavie** Highld
99 G5 **Banbury** Oxon
72 F6 **Bancffosfelen** Carmth
290 F2 **Banchory** Abers
291 L1 **Banchory-Devenick** Abers
72 E6 **Bancycapel** Carmth
108 D3 **Banc-y-Darren** Cerdgn
72 C5 **Bancyfelin** Carmth
90 F8 **Bancyffordd** Carmth
65 J8 **Bandonhill** Gt Lon
190 F3 **Bandrake Head** Cumb
306 B3 **Banff** Abers
159 K6 **Bangor** Gwynd
149 G4 **Bangor on Dee** Wrexhm
22 C7 **Bangors** Cnwll
173 J6 **Bangor's Green** Lancs
90 E7 **Bangor Teifi** Cerdgn
122 B2 **Banham** Norfk
30 D5 **Bank** Hants
126 F4 **Bank** Powys
190 D3 **Bank End** Cumb
190 F2 **Bank End** Cumb
208 B6 **Bank End** Cumb
222 C6 **Bankend** D & G
174 F3 **Bank Fold** Bl w D
279 G7 **Bankfoot** P & K
230 F4 **Bankglen** E Ayrs
302 C7 **Bankhead** Abers
280 E7 **Bankhead** Angus
303 G7 **Bankhead** C Aber
257 J4 **Bankhead** Falk
244 F5 **Bankhead** S Lans
244 D5 **Bankhead** S Lans
242 C3 **Bankhead Moss** N Ayrs
174 E1 **Bank Hey** Bl w D
182 D4 **Bank Houses** Lancs
41 K8 **Bankland** Somset
175 H4 **Bank Lane** Bury
184 D4 **Bank Newton** N York
257 H5 **Banknock** Falk
224 D7 **Banks** Cumb
216 E4 **Banks** D & G
173 J3 **Banks** Lancs
113 K6 **Bank's Green** Worcs
111 G2 **Bankshead** Shrops
222 F3 **Bankshill** D & G
257 K4 **Bankside** Falk
112 C7 **Bank Street** Worcs
174 F5 **Bank Top** Lancs
185 J7 **Bank Top** Brad
176 E3 **Bank Top** Calder
151 G3 **Bank Top** C Stke
174 B6 **Bank Top** Lancs
226 E6 **Bank Top** N u Ty
130 B7 **Banners Gate** Birm
209 J7 **Bannest Hill** Cumb
143 G6 **Banningham** Norfk
85 K2 **Bannister Green** Essex
257 J2 **Bannockburn** Stirlg
4 B5 **Banns** Cnwll
49 H2 **Banstead** Surrey
257 K5 **Bantaskin** Falk
7 L6 **Bantham** Devon
257 H5 **Banton** N Lans
311 N8 **Bantrach** Moray
41 L2 **Banwell** N Som
123 G5 **Banyard's Green** Suffk
68 B8 **Bapchild** Kent
113 J2 **Baptist End** Dudley
44 C6 **Bapton** Wilts
325 L5 **Barabhas** W Isls
325 K5 **Barabhas Iarach** W Isls
282 E7 **Baramore** Highld
242 C7 **Barassie** S Ayrs
274 C7 **Baravullin** Ag & B
310 G3 **Barbaraville** Highld
257 L7 **Barbauchlaw** W Loth
166 B3 **Barber Booth** Derbys
191 H4 **Barber Green** Cumb
173 L4 **Barber's Moor** Lancs
325 L4 **Barbhas Uarach** W Isls
7 G4 **Barbican** C Plym
230 C3 **Barbieston** S Ayrs
193 H5 **Barbon** Cumb
96 D2 **Barbourne** Worcs
253 G3 **Barbreack** Ag & B
150 B2 **Barbridge** Ches
39 H4 **Barbrook** Devon
115 L5 **Barby** Nhants
116 B5 **Barby Nortoft** Nhants
274 E6 **Barcaldine** Ag & B
6 B4 **Barcelona** Cnwll
98 C6 **Barcheston** Warwks
223 L7 **Barclose** Cumb
35 H4 **Barcombe** E Susx
35 H3 **Barcombe Cross** E Susx
184 F7 **Barcroft** Brad
195 H3 **Barden** N York
50 E4 **Barden Park** Kent
103 K7 **Bardfield End Green** Essex
85 K1 **Bardfield Saling** Essex
331 E10 **Bardister** Shet
170 B7 **Bardney** Lincs
131 K4 **Bardon** Leics
225 H7 **Bardon Mill** Nthumb
256 D6 **Bardowie** E Duns
51 G8 **Bardown** E Susx
255 J6 **Bardrainney** Inver
191 G6 **Bardsea** Cumb
186 C6 **Bardsey** Leeds
175 K7 **Bardsley** Oldham
121 J5 **Bardwell** Suffk
182 E2 **Bare** Lancs
41 H7 **Bare Ash** Somset
248 D6 **Bareless** Nthumb
217 J2 **Barend** D & G
46 C8 **Bar End** Hants
200 C2 **Barepot** Cumb
3 K5 **Bareppa** Cnwll
47 K6 **Barford** Hants
138 C5 **Barford** Norfk
114 F7 **Barford** Warwks
98 F7 **Barford St John** Oxon
44 D7 **Barford St Martin** Wilts
98 F7 **Barford St Michael** Oxon
53 J3 **Barfrestone** Kent
256 B6 **Bargarran** Rens
153 G4 **Bargate** Derbys
256 F8 **Bargeddie** N Lancs
75 J7 **Bargoed** Caerph
219 K4 **Bargrennan** D & G
118 C4 **Barham** Cambs
53 H4 **Barham** Kent
106 C3 **Barham** Suffk
216 D3 **Barharrow** D & G
119 H7 **Bar Hill** Cambs
150 E5 **Bar Hill** Staffs
134 B4 **Barholm** Lincs
132 C5 **Barkby** Leics
132 C5 **Barkby Thorpe** Leics
149 K8 **Barkers Green** Shrops
29 G1 **Barkers Hill** Wilts
154 E7 **Barkestone-le-Vale** Leics
63 J7 **Barkham** Wokham
66 B4 **Barking** Gt Lon
105 J3 **Barking** Suffk
66 B3 **Barkingside** Gt Lon
105 J3 **Barking Tye** Suffk
176 D4 **Barkisland** Calder
4 B4 **Barkla Shop** Cnwll
155 H5 **Barkston** Lincs
186 E7 **Barkston Ash** N York
102 E6 **Barkway** Herts
43 G4 **Barlake** Somset
256 F8 **Barlanark** C Glas
110 F7 **Barland** Powys
54 E4 **Barland Common** Swans
151 G6 **Barlaston** Staffs
33 J3 **Barlavington** W Susx
167 J5 **Barlborough** Derbys
187 H8 **Barlby** N York
131 J5 **Barlestone** Leics
102 F6 **Barley** Herts
184 B6 **Barley** Lancs
102 F8 **Barleycroft End** Herts
82 F4 **Barley End** Bucks
184 B6 **Barley Green** Lancs
213 G3 **Barley Mow** Gatesd
133 G5 **Barleythorpe** Rutlnd
68 B3 **Barling** Essex
169 L6 **Barlings** Lincs
166 F6 **Barlow** Derbys
226 F7 **Barlow** Gatesd
178 E2 **Barlow** N York
164 F2 **Barlow Moor** Manch
187 L5 **Barmby Moor** E R Yk
178 F2 **Barmby on the Marsh** E R Yk
141 G5 **Barmer** Norfk
51 H2 **Barming Heath** Kent
226 E7 **Bar Moor** Gatesd
124 B3 **Barmouth** Gwynd
205 J4 **Barmpton** Darltn
189 J3 **Barmston** E R Yk
213 H2 **Barmston** Sundld
256 E7 **Barmulloch** C Glas
123 K4 **Barnaby Green** Suffk
134 B6 **Barnack** C Pete
115 H3 **Barnacle** Warwks
331 D9 **Barnafield** Shet
204 C4 **Barnard Castle** Dur
80 E4 **Barnard Gate** Oxon
104 B4 **Barnardiston** Suffk
96 C4 **Barnard's Green** Worcs
57 K3 **Barnardtown** Newpt
186 C7 **Barnbow Carr** Leeds
178 B7 **Barnburgh** Donc
123 K2 **Barnby** Suffk
178 E6 **Barnby Dun** Donc
154 F3 **Barnby in the Willows** Notts
168 C4 **Barnby Moor** Notts
243 L3 **Barncluith** S Lans
214 C6 **Barncorkrie** D & G
6 F3 **Barne Barton** C Plym
66 C5 **Barnehurst** Gt Lon
65 H5 **Barnes** Gt Lon
66 D5 **Barnes Cray** Gt Lon
166 F1 **Barnes Hall** Sheff
50 F4 **Barnes Street** Kent
83 L7 **Barnet** Gt Lon
180 D6 **Barnetby le Wold** N Linc
83 L7 **Barnet Gate** Gt Lon
150 B5 **Barnett Brook** Ches
113 H4 **Barnettbrook** Worcs
141 K5 **Barney** Norfk
85 J3 **Barnfield** Essex
52 B4 **Barnfield** Kent
94 F5 **Barnfields** Herefs
151 J2 **Barnfields** Staffs
121 H4 **Barnham** Suffk
33 J6 **Barnham** W Susx
138 B5 **Barnham Broom** Norfk
281 J3 **Barnhead** Angus
269 H1 **Barnhill** C Dund
149 J3 **Barnhill** Ches
311 Q6 **Barnhill** Moray
267 L3 **Barnhill** P & K
218 B5 **Barnhills** D & G
204 D5 **Barningham** Dur
121 K4 **Barningham** Suffk
142 E5 **Barningham Green** Norfk
253 H2 **Barnluasgan** Ag & B
114 D7 **Barnmoor Green** Warwks
181 G7 **Barnoldby le Beck** NE Lin
184 C5 **Barnoldswick** Lancs
193 J7 **Barnoldswick** N York
245 L6 **Barns** Border
133 H5 **Barnsdale** Rutlnd
34 B1 **Barns Green** W Susx
176 F6 **Barnside** Kirk
177 J6 **Barnsley** Barns
79 H5 **Barnsley** Gloucs
128 F8 **Barnsley** Shrops
53 J2 **Barnsole** Kent
38 D7 **Barnstaple** Devon
85 J3 **Barnston** Essex
162 E4 **Barnston** Wirral
154 D6 **Barnstone** Notts
113 L5 **Barnt Green** Worcs
258 F5 **Barnton** C Edin
164 B5 **Barnton** Ches
117 L3 **Barnwell** Nhants
78 D3 **Barnwood** Gloucs
269 H7 **Barnyards** Fife
95 G2 **Barons' Cross** Herefs
229 K8 **Barr** S Ayrs
26 B2 **Barr** Somset
215 J4 **Barrachan** D & G
256 F8 **Barrachnie** C Glas
306 F7 **Barrack** Abers
57 K3 **Barrack Hill** Newpt
324 G8 **Barraglom** W Isls
253 G4 **Barrahormid** Ag & B
262 F2 **Barran** Ag & B
270 B6 **Barrapol** Ag & B
203 J5 **Barras** Cumb
225 L5 **Barrasford** Nthumb
262 E6 **Barravullin** Ag & B
130 B6 **Barr Common** Wsall
172 e5 **Barregarrow** IoM
149 L2 **Barrets Green** Ches
243 G2 **Barrhead** E Rens
219 G3 **Barrhill** S Ayrs
102 E4 **Barrington** Cambs
26 F3 **Barrington** Somset
79 L4 **Barrington Park** Gloucs
3 G3 **Barripper** Cnwll
242 D3 **Barrmill** N Ayrs
262 E3 **Barnacarry** Ag & B
319 M2 **Barrock** Highld
78 D2 **Barrow** Gloucs
183 K7 **Barrow** Lancs
177 K8 **Barrow** Rothm
133 H3 **Barrow** Rutlnd
128 D6 **Barrow** Shrops
42 E5 **Barrow** Somset
120 F7 **Barrow** Suffk
136 B6 **Barroway Drove** Norfk
174 E5 **Barrow Bridge** Bolton
236 B4 **Barrowburn** Nthumb
155 G6 **Barrowby** Lincs
198 F4 **Barrowcliff** N York
58 D7 **Barrow Common** N Som
133 K6 **Barrowden** Rutlnd
184 B7 **Barrowford** Lancs
68 C8 **Barrow Green** Kent
58 D7 **Barrow Gurney** N Som
180 D3 **Barrow Hann** N Linc
180 D3 **Barrow Haven** N Linc
167 H5 **Barrow Hill** Derbys
18 E2 **Barrow Hill** Dorset
52 E6 **Barrowhill** Kent
190 D6 **Barrow-in-Furness** Cumb
190 D7 **Barrow Island** Cumb
163 J7 **Barrowmore Estate** Ches
173 K7 **Barrow Nook** Lancs
150 C2 **Barrows Green** Ches
192 F4 **Barrows Green** Cumb
163 K3 **Barrow's Green** Halton
153 J3 **Barrows Green** Notts
43 K7 **Barrow Street** Wilts
180 D3 **Barrow upon Humber** N Linc
132 B3 **Barrow upon Soar** Leics
152 F8 **Barrow upon Trent** Derbys
42 F1 **Barrow Vale** BaNES
78 E3 **Barrow Wake** Gloucs
280 F8 **Barry** Angus
56 E7 **Barry** V Glam
56 F7 **Barry Dock** V Glam
56 F7 **Barry Island** V Glam
132 D4 **Barsby** Leics
123 H2 **Barsham** Suffk
230 F3 **Barshare** E Ayrs
253 H1 **Barsloisnoch** Ag & B
67 H3 **Barstable** Essex
114 E4 **Barston** Solhll
95 J5 **Bartestree** Herefs
302 F2 **Barthol Chapel** Abers
85 L2 **Bartholomew Green** Essex
150 E3 **Barthomley** Ches
30 E4 **Bartley** Hants
113 L3 **Bartley Green** Birm
103 J4 **Bartlow** Cambs
102 F2 **Barton** Cambs
149 H3 **Barton** Ches
78 C3 **Barton** Gloucs
79 J1 **Barton** Gloucs
21 H4 **Barton** IoW
173 H6 **Barton** Lancs
182 F7 **Barton** Lancs
41 L2 **Barton** N Som
205 G6 **Barton** N York
81 G5 **Barton** Oxon
8 F1 **Barton** Torbay
97 K3 **Barton** Warwks
80 E2 **Barton Abbey** Oxon
136 E5 **Barton Bendish** Norfk
96 B5 **Barton Court** Herefs
78 C7 **Barton End** Gloucs
39 G5 **Barton Gate** Devon
130 D3 **Barton Gate** Staffs
130 D3 **Barton Green** Staffs
99 K7 **Barton Hartshorn** Bucks
58 F6 **Barton Hill** Bristl
187 K2 **Barton Hill** N York
153 K7 **Barton in Fabis** Notts
131 H5 **Barton in the Beans** Leics
101 J7 **Barton-le-Clay** Beds
197 K7 **Barton-le-Street** N York
187 K2 **Barton-le-Willows** N York
120 E5 **Barton Mills** Suffk
164 D1 **Barton Moss** Salfd
20 B3 **Barton on Sea** Hants
98 C7 **Barton-on-the-Heath** Warwks
42 D7 **Barton St David** Somset
117 H4 **Barton Seagrave** Nhants
95 H6 **Bartonsham** Herefs
46 B5 **Barton Stacey** Hants
39 G5 **Barton Town** Devon
143 K7 **Barton Turf** Norfk
130 E3 **Barton Turn** Staffs
130 D3 **Barton-under-Needwood** Staffs
180 C3 **Barton-upon-Humber** N Linc
175 G8 **Barton upon Irwell** Salfd
180 C3 **Barton Waterside** N Linc
177 J6 **Barugh** Barns
177 J6 **Barugh Green** Barns
325 L5 **Barvas** W Isls
119 L4 **Barway** Cambs
131 J7 **Barwell** Leics
65 G8 **Barwell** Gt Lon
23 K5 **Barwick** Devon
84 D3 **Barwick** Herts
27 K4 **Barwick** Somset
186 D7 **Barwick in Elmet** Leeds
127 J2 **Baschurch** Shrops
210 B4 **Bascodyke Head** Cumb
115 J7 **Bascote** Warwks
115 H7 **Bascote Heath** Warwks
121 L7 **Base Green** Suffk
111 H2 **Basford** Shrops
151 G4 **Basford** Staffs
151 J3 **Basford Green** Staffs
183 J6 **Bashall Eaves** Lancs
30 C7 **Bashley** Hants
20 B2 **Bashley Park** Hants
67 H3 **Basildon** Essex
46 E3 **Basingstoke** Hants
166 D6 **Baslow** Derbys
41 K4 **Bason Bridge** Somset
57 J3 **Bassaleg** Newpt
208 F7 **Bassenthwaite** Cumb
31 G3 **Bassett** C Sotn
166 E4 **Bassett** Sheff
31 G3 **Bassett Green** C Sotn
102 D5 **Bassingbourn** Cambs
154 B6 **Bassingfield** Notts
155 H2 **Bassingham** Lincs
155 J8 **Bassingthorpe** Lincs
84 B1 **Bassus Green** Herts
330 H7 **Basta** Shet
50 F2 **Basted** Kent
134 C4 **Baston** Lincs
96 D3 **Bastonford** Worcs
139 J3 **Bastwick** Norfk
129 J2 **Baswich** Staffs
41 K2 **Batch** Somset
111 K5 **Batchcott** Shrops
95 K4 **Batchfields** Herefs
113 L6 **Batchley** Worcs
64 E2 **Batchworth** Herts
64 E2 **Batchworth Heath** Herts
27 L6 **Batcombe** Dorset
43 G6 **Batcombe** Somset
164 C5 **Bate Heath** Ches
114 B4 **Bateman's Green** Worcs
71 G6 **Bateman's Hill** Pembks
167 G4 **Batemoor** Sheff
83 J3 **Batford** Herts
59 H7 **Bath** BaNES
59 J7 **Bathampton** BaNES
25 K2 **Bathealton** Somset
59 J7 **Batheaston** BaNES
59 J7 **Bathford** BaNES
258 B7 **Bathgate** W Loth
154 E2 **Bathley** Notts
11 K7 **Bathpool** Cnwll
26 D1 **Bathpool** Somset
106 E7 **Bath Side** Essex
165 G8 **Bath Vale** Ches
257 L7 **Bathville** W Loth
42 E3 **Bathway** Somset
59 J8 **Bathwick** BaNES
83 K7 **Batlers Green** Herts
177 G3 **Batley** Kirk
177 G3 **Batley Carr** Kirk
97 L7 **Batsford** Gloucs
8 B7 **Batson** Devon
24 E2 **Batsworthy** Devon
26 D3 **Batten's Green** Somset
113 G6 **Battenton Green** Worcs
206 D6 **Battersby** N York
65 J5 **Battersea** Gt Lon
105 J3 **Battisford** Suffk
105 H3 **Battisford Tye** Suffk
36 D3 **Battle** E Susx
93 H7 **Battle** Powys
78 F2 **Battledown** Gloucs
23 H5 **Battledown Cross** Devon
243 H1 **Battlefield** C Glas
127 L3 **Battlefield** Shrops
227 H6 **Battle Hill** N Tyne
67 J2 **Battlesbridge** Essex
78 E5 **Battlescombe** Gloucs
101 G8 **Battlesden** Beds
122 E4 **Battlesea Green** Suffk
25 G1 **Battleton** Somset
121 J7 **Battlies Green** Suffk
131 J5 **Battram** Leics
30 D7 **Battramsley** Hants
30 E7 **Battramsley Cross** Hants
47 K5 **Batt's Corner** Hants
176 F3 **Battyeford** Kirk
13 L4 **Batworthy** Devon
305 H2 **Bauds of Cullen** Moray
270 C6 **Baugh** Ag & B
96 E5 **Baughton** Worcs
46 E1 **Baughurst** Hants
61 K2 **Baulking** Oxon
170 D6 **Baumber** Lincs
79 G6 **Baunton** Gloucs
44 D7 **Baverstock** Wilts
138 C5 **Bawburgh** Norfk
137 L2 **Bawdeswell** Norfk
41 K6 **Bawdrip** Somset
107 G5 **Bawdsey** Suffk
136 D3 **Bawsey** Norfk
168 B2 **Bawtry** Donc
175 G2 **Baxenden** Lancs
130 F7 **Baxterley** Warwks
104 C2 **Baxter's Green** Suffk
28 E1 **Bay** Dorset
292 D6 **Bay** Highld
31 J2 **Baybridge** Hants
211 K3 **Baybridge** Nthumb
190 F6 **Baycliff** Cumb
61 J5 **Baydon** Wilts
84 C5 **Bayford** Herts
43 H8 **Bayford** Somset
183 K5 **Bay Gate** Lancs
182 E4 **Bay Horse** Lancs
210 F4 **Bayles** Cumb
50 D3 **Bayley's Hill** Kent
105 J3 **Baylham** Suffk
114 B5 **Baylis Green** Worcs
99 J8 **Baynard's Green** Oxon
96 E4 **Baynhall** Worcs
95 J8 **Baysham** Herefs
127 K5 **Bayston Hill** Shrops
65 J4 **Bayswater** Gt Lon
104 B5 **Baythorne End** Essex
156 D5 **Baythorpe** Lincs
112 D5 **Bayton** Worcs
112 E5 **Bayton Common** Worcs
68 D6 **Bay View** Kent
81 G6 **Bayworth** Oxon
59 G6 **Beach** S Glos
100 C6 **Beachampton** Bucks
136 F5 **Beachamwell** Norfk
239 G5 **Beacharr** Ag & B
112 E5 **Beach Hay** Worcs
36 C6 **Beachlands** E Susx
58 E2 **Beachley** Gloucs
3 G3 **Beacon** Cnwll
26 B6 **Beacon** Devon
26 C5 **Beacon** Devon
35 L2 **Beacon Down** E Susx
86 F2 **Beacon End** Essex
59 H7 **Beacon Hill** BaNES
64 B2 **Beacon Hill** Bucks
190 E6 **Beacon Hill** Cumb
18 F3 **Beacon Hill** Dorset
86 D4 **Beacon Hill** Essex
51 K7 **Beacon Hill** Kent
154 F3 **Beacon Hill** Notts
227 G4 **Beaconhill** Nthumb
106 E4 **Beacon Hill** Suffk
47 L6 **Beacon Hill** Surrey
227 H7 **Beacon Lough** Gatesd
82 B7 **Beacon's Bottom** Bucks
64 B2 **Beaconsfield** Bucks
129 J2 **Beaconside** Staffs
323 J6 **Beacrabhaic** W Isls
197 H5 **Beadlam** N York
101 K6 **Beadlow** Beds
249 L8 **Beadnell** Nthumb
23 K4 **Beaford** Devon
249 H5 **Beal** Nthumb
178 C2 **Beal** N York
254 B4 **Bealach Maim** Ag & B
6 E1 **Bealbury** Cnwll
51 J7 **Beal's Green** Kent
12 D6 **Bealsmill** Cnwll
111 L2 **Beambridge** Shrops
25 L3 **Beam Bridge** Somset
130 E1 **Beam Hill** Staffs
151 K6 **Beamhurst** Staffs
151 L6 **Beamhurst Lane** Staffs
27 H6 **Beaminster** Dorset
212 F3 **Beamish** Dur
82 E7 **Beamond End** Bucks
185 G4 **Beamsley** N York
66 E6 **Bean** Kent
60 B7 **Beanacre** Wilts
257 L5 **Beancross** Falk
100 E6 **Beanhill** M Keyn
236 F3 **Beanley** Nthumb
190 E4 **Beanthwaite** Cumb
328 C9 **Beaquoy** Ork
19 G2 **Bear Cross** Bmouth
42 F5 **Beard Hill** Somset
42 F5 **Beardly Batch** Somset
174 E2 **Beardwood** Bl w D
25 H6 **Beare** Devon
49 G5 **Beare Green** Surrey
114 D7 **Bearley** Warwks
114 D7 **Bearley Cross** Warwks
212 F5 **Bearpark** Dur
211 G2 **Bearsbridge** Nthumb
256 C6 **Bearsden** E Duns
51 J2 **Bearsted** Kent
150 D6 **Bearstone** Shrops
94 E2 **Bearwood** Herefs
19 G2 **Bearwood** Poole
113 L2 **Bearwood** Birm
150 F4 **Beasley** Staffs
232 F6 **Beattock** D & G
85 H4 **Beauchamp Roding** Essex
166 F4 **Beauchief** Sheff
226 C7 **Beauclerc** Nthumb
114 D6 **Beaudesert** Warwks
75 K4 **Beaufort** Blae G
30 F6 **Beaulieu** Hants
28 C5 **Beaulieu Wood** Dorset
310 C8 **Beauly** Highld
159 K5 **Beaumaris** IoA
209 H2 **Beaumont** Cumb
87 K2 **Beaumont** Essex
16 g7 **Beaumont** Jersey
64 C6 **Beaumont** W & M
205 H4 **Beaumont Hill** Darltn
132 B5 **Beaumont Leys** C Leic
87 K2 **Beaumont Quay** Essex
114 E5 **Beausale** Warwks
153 J4 **Beauvale** Notts
153 K4 **Beauvale** Notts
31 K1 **Beauworth** Hants
77 K2 **Beavan's Hill** Herefs
23 G7 **Beaworthy** Devon
104 B8 **Beazley End** Essex
163 G4 **Bebington** Wirral
227 H3 **Bebside** Nthumb
123 J2 **Beccles** Suffk
173 K3 **Becconsall** Lancs
190 F4 **Beck Bottom** Cumb
177 J3 **Beck Bottom** Wakefd
128 F6 **Beckbury** Shrops
65 L7 **Beckenham** Gt Lon
200 C6 **Beckermet** Cumb
194 C5 **Beckermonds** N York
42 C6 **Beckery** Somset
136 F7 **Beckett End** Norfk
193 H2 **Beck Foot** Cumb
200 F7 **Beckfoot** Cumb
208 C4 **Beckfoot** Cumb
97 G6 **Beckford** Worcs
60 E7 **Beckhampton** Wilts
191 J4 **Beck Head** Cumb
198 B1 **Beck Hole** N York
193 G2 **Beck Houses** Cumb
155 G3 **Beckingham** Notts
168 E2 **Beckingham** Lincs
43 J3 **Beckington** Somset
111 H4 **Beckjay** Shrops
37 G2 **Beckley** E Susx
19 L2 **Beckley** Hants
81 H4 **Beckley** Oxon
36 F2 **Beckley Furnace** E Susx
120 D4 **Beck Row** Suffk
190 E4 **Beck Side** Cumb
191 H4 **Beck Side** Cumb
193 H4 **Beckside** Cumb
66 B4 **Beckton** Gt Lon
185 L4 **Beckwith** N York
185 L4 **Beckwithshaw** N York
66 C3 **Becontree** Gt Lon
16 h6 **Becquet Vincent** Jersey
195 L4 **Bedale** N York
212 D7 **Bedburn** Dur
28 E3 **Bedchester** Dorset
56 D3 **Beddau** Rhondd
145 L4 **Beddgelert** Gwynd
35 H5 **Beddingham** E Susx
65 K7 **Beddington** Gt Lon
65 J7 **Beddington Corner** Gt Lon
122 E6 **Bedfield** Suffk
101 J4 **Bedford** Beds
174 E8 **Bedford** Wigan
65 H5 **Bedford Park** Gt Lon
51 H7 **Bedgebury Cross** Kent
82 C4 **Bedgrove** Bucks
33 K2 **Bedham** W Susx
32 C5 **Bedhampton** Hants
122 D6 **Bedingfield** Suffk
138 F8 **Bedingham Green** Norfk
185 L2 **Bedlam** N York
43 J4 **Bedlam** Somset
34 E3 **Bedlam Street** W Susx
85 G2 **Bedlar's Green** Essex
227 G3 **Bedlington** Nthumb
227 H3 **Bedlington Station** Nthumb
75 H6 **Bedlinog** Myr Td
58 E6 **Bedminster** Bristl
58 E7 **Bedminster Down** Bristl
83 H6 **Bedmond** Herts
129 K3 **Bednall** Staffs
129 K3 **Bednall Head** Staffs
235 G3 **Bedrule** Border
111 H4 **Bedstone** Shrops
57 G3 **Bedwas** Caerph
83 L2 **Bedwell** Herts
149 G4 **Bedwell** Wrexhm
75 K6 **Bedwellty** Caerph
75 J5 **Bedwellty Pits** Blae G
148 D6 **Bedwlwyn** Wrexhm
115 H2 **Bedworth** Warwks
115 G2 **Bedworth Heath** Warwks
115 G2 **Bedworth Woodlands** Warwks
132 D5 **Beeby** Leics
47 G6 **Beech** Hants
150 F6 **Beech** Staffs
151 G6 **Beechcliff** Staffs
185 G6 **Beechcliffe** Brad
59 H8 **Beechen Cliff** BaNES
63 G8 **Beech Hill** W Berk
174 C6 **Beech Hill** Wigan
44 E2 **Beechingstoke** Wilts
113 L2 **Beech Lanes** Birm
163 K5 **Beechwood** Halton
310 F9 **Beechwood** Highld
186 B7 **Beechwood** Leeds
57 K3 **Beechwood** Newpt
114 F4 **Beechwood** Solhll
83 G2 **Beecroft** Beds
62 C5 **Beedon** W Berk
62 C5 **Beedon Hill** W Berk
189 H4 **Beeford** E R Yk
166 E7 **Beeley** Derbys
181 G7 **Beelsby** NE Lin
62 E7 **Beenham** W Berk
63 K5 **Beenham's Heath** W & M
62 E7 **Beenham Stocks** W Berk
11 G3 **Beeny** Cnwll
15 L4 **Beer** Devon
42 B7 **Beer** Somset
26 E2 **Beer Crocombe** Somset
27 K4 **Beer Hackett** Dorset
8 D6 **Beesands** Devon
171 J4 **Beesby** Lincs
245 L1 **Beeslack** Mdloth
8 D6 **Beeson** Devon
101 L4 **Beeston** Beds
149 K2 **Beeston** Ches
137 J3 **Beeston** Norfk
153 K6 **Beeston** Notts
177 H1 **Beeston Hill** Leeds
177 H2 **Beeston Park Side** Leeds
142 F3 **Beeston Regis** Norfk
177 H1 **Beeston Royds** Leeds
139 G2 **Beeston St Lawrence** Norfk
221 K6 **Beeswing** D & G
192 E6 **Beetham** Cumb
26 D4 **Beetham** Somset
137 K3 **Beetley** Norfk
129 G3 **Beffcote** Staffs
57 H4 **Began** Cardif
80 F4 **Begbroke** Oxon
135 K5 **Begdale** Cambs
71 J5 **Begelly** Pembks
85 J6 **Beggar Hill** Essex
177 H3 **Beggarington Hill** Kirk
96 B6 **Beggars Ash** Herefs
34 C5 **Beggars Bush** W Susx
56 D7 **Beggars Pound** V Glam
40 D6 **Beggearn Huish** Somset
110 D4 **Beguildy** Powys
139 H5 **Beighton** Norfk
167 H4 **Beighton** Sheff
76 C4 **Beili-glas** Mons
325 M9 **Beinn Casgro** W Isls
242 C3 **Beith** N Ayrs
53 G2 **Bekesbourne** Kent
53 G2 **Bekesbourne Hill** Kent
209 J2 **Belah** Cumb
126 E6 **Belan** Powys
138 F3 **Belaugh** Norfk
30 F2 **Belbins** Hants
113 J4 **Belbroughton** Worcs
28 D5 **Belchalwell** Dorset
28 D5 **Belchalwell Street** Dorset
104 D5 **Belchamp Otten** Essex
104 C5 **Belchamp St Paul** Essex
104 D5 **Belchamp Walter** Essex
131 J5 **Belcher's Bar** Leics
170 E5 **Belchford** Lincs
307 J4 **Belfatton** Abers
175 K5 **Belfield** Rochdl
249 J7 **Belford** Nthumb
161 H5 **Belgrano** Conwy
149 G1 **Belgrave** Ches
132 B5 **Belgrave** C Leic
130 E6 **Belgrave** Staffs
260 F5 **Belhaven** E Loth
303 H5 **Belhelvie** Abers
301 J3 **Belhinnie** Abers
301 G6 **Bellabeg** Abers
256 C8 **Bellahouston** C Glas
219 G2 **Bellamore** S Ayrs
253 H2 **Bellanoch** Ag & B
245 L6 **Bellanrigg** Border
179 J2 **Bellasize** E R Yk
279 K3 **Bellaty** Angus
83 L6 **Bell Bar** Herts
268 F5 **Bellbrae** Fife
184 D3 **Bell Busk** N York
84 E6 **Bell Common** Essex
171 G5 **Belleau** Lincs
154 C2 **Belle Eau Park** Notts
177 K6 **Belle Green** Barns
300 C1 **Belleheiglash** Moray
177 J2 **Belle Isle** Leeds
113 J4 **Bell End** Worcs
195 H3 **Bellerby** N York
113 K3 **Belle Vale** Dudley
163 H3 **Belle Vale** Lpool
13 K6 **Bellever** Devon
208 D7 **Belle Vue** Cumb
209 J2 **Belle Vue** Cumb
178 D7 **Belle Vue** Donc
165 G1 **Belle Vue** Manch
127 K4 **Belle Vue** Shrops
177 J4 **Belle Vue** Wakefd
113 K5 **Bellevue** Worcs
242 E6 **Bellfield** E Ayrs
244 C6 **Bellfield** S Lans
48 C3 **Bellfields** Surrey
115 H3 **Bell Green** Covtry
65 L6 **Bell Green** Gt Lon
113 K4 **Bell Heath** Worcs
32 D2 **Bell Hill** Hants
281 G2 **Belliehill** Angus

95 L5	Catley Southfield Herefs
286 E3	Catloge Highld
224 B4	Catlowdy Cumb
109 G6	Catmere End Essex
62 B4	Catmore W Berk
14 B7	Caton Devon
182 F2	Caton Lancs
183 G1	Caton Green Lancs
13 K6	Caton Court Powys
230 E1	Catrine E Ayrs
57 L2	Cat's Ash Newpt
141 H5	Cat's Common Norfk
141 H5	Cats Edge Staffs
36 D4	Catsfield E Susx
36 D4	Catsfield Stream E Susx
27 J1	Catsgore Somset
42 E7	Catsham Somset
177 G7	Catshaw Barns
113 K5	Catthorpe Leics
130 B6	Catwall Wsall
150 F7	Cat's Hill Cross Staffs
233 L1	Catslackburn Border
63 H3	Catslip Oxon
128 E7	Catstree Shrops
186 D4	Cattal N York
105 K7	Cattawade Suffk
7 G4	Cattedown C Plym
182 E6	Catterall Lancs
195 K2	Catterick N York
195 K2	Catterick Bridge N York
195 J2	Catterick Garrison N York
209 L7	Catterlen Cumb
291 K6	Catterline Abers
186 F5	Catterton N York
48 C5	Catteshall Surrey
113 K5	Catthorpe Leics
27 K7	Cattistock Dorset
99 L5	Cattle End Nhants
211 H2	Catton Nthumb
196 C6	Catton N York
189 H5	Catwick E R Yk
118 B5	Catworth Cambs
78 E4	Caudle Green Gloucs
57 J6	Caudlesprings Norfk
101 G5	Caulcott Beds
234 D4	Caulcott Oxon
258 C5	Cauldcoats Holdings Falk
281 H5	Cauldcots Angus
255 E2	Cauldhame Stirlg
234 E3	Cauldmill Border
151 J4	Cauldon Staffs
151 L4	Cauldon Lowe Staffs
306 D4	Cauldwells Abers
217 K2	Caulkerbush D & G
223 L5	Caulside D & G
7 J5	Caundle Marsh Dorset
113 G3	Caunsall Worcs
154 D1	Caunton Notts
32 C4	Causeway Hants
32 C4	Causeway Hants
191 G4	Causeway End Cumb
192 E4	Causeway End Cumb
85 K3	Causeway End Essex
245 G6	Causewayend S Lans
60 C4	Causeway Foot Calder
176 D1	Causeway Foot Kirk
176 F5	Causeway Foot Kirk
113 K2	Causeway Green Sandw
257 H1	Causewayhead Stirlg
127 L7	Causewaywood Shrops
212 F2	Causey Dur
303 H5	Causeyend Abers
237 H8	Causey Park Bridge Nthumb
3 G4	Cautley Cumb
193 J2	Cautley Cumb
104 C4	Cavendish Suffk
153 H8	Cavendish Bridge Leics
124 F6	Cavenham Suffk
234 F1	Cavers Carre Border
81 H1	Caversfield Oxon
63 H5	Caversham Readg
63 H5	Caversham Heights Readg

151 J5	Caverswall Staffs
311 J7	Cawdor Highld
188 E4	Cawkeld E R Yk
170 E5	Cawkwell Lincs
187 G7	Cawood N York
6 F4	Cawsand Cnwll
142 E7	Cawston Norfk
115 K5	Cawston Warwks
177 H6	Cawthorne Barns
197 L4	Cawthorne N York
134 B2	Cawthorpe Lincs
197 H6	Cawton N York
102 D2	Caxton Cambs
111 L5	Caynham Shrops
155 H4	Caythorpe Lincs
199 G5	Cayton N York
322 B11	Ceann a Bhaigh W Isls
323 K6	Ceann a Bhaigh W Isls
323 M6	Ceann a Bhaigh W Isls
325 M8	Ceann a' Choinich Baghasdail W Isls
321 N11	Ceann a Deas Loch Baghasdail W Isls
323 L5	Ceann a' Gharaidh W Isls
325 M6	Ceann a-Muigh Chuil W Isls
325 N7	Ceann a-staigh Chuil W Isls
321 N10	Ceann a Tuath Loch Baghasdail W Isls
320 D5	Ceann Loch na Cleithe W Isls
325 M8	Ceann nam Buailtean W Isls
325 J11	Ceann Shiphoirt W Isls
320 C5	Ceann Tangabhal W Isls
324 H11	Ceann Tarabhaigh W Isls
325 K11	Cearsiadair W Isls
322 C9	Ceathramh Meadhanach W Isls
125 G2	Cedig Powys
57 J3	Cefn Newpt
126 F4	Cefn Powys
161 H7	Cefn Berain Conwy
147 H3	Cefn-brith Conwy
73 L6	Cefn-bryn-brain Carmth
54 E3	Cefn-bychan Swans
148 E3	Cefn-bychan Wrexhm
54 D2	Cefncaeau Carmth
54 D2	Cefn Canol Powys
160 F7	Cefn-coch Conwy
126 B6	Cefn Coch Powys
126 C5	Cefn-coch Powys
74 E5	Cefn Cribwr Brdgnd
148 E5	Cefn-mawr Wrexhm
158 F2	Cemaes IoA
125 G5	Cemmaes Powys
125 G5	Cemmaes Road Powys
90 C7	Cenarth Carmth
141 J5	Cenin Conwy
255 J2	Ceol na Mara Highld
273 G6	Ceos W Isls
23 B6	Ceres Fife
29 L8	Cerne Abbas Dorset
79 H7	Cerney Wick Gloucs
159 G6	Cerrigceinwen IoA
159 K6	Ceint IoA
73 G4	Celynen Powys
75 J6	Cefn Glas Brdgnd
92 E4	Cefn-gorwydd Powys
75 J7	Cefn hengoed Caerph
54 E5	Cefn-hengoed Swans
74 E5	Cefn Llwyd Cerdgn
148 E5	Cefn-mawr Wrexhm
148 F2	Cefnpennar Rhondd
74 E5	Cefn Rhigos Rhondd
148 E5	Cefn-y-bedd Flints
55 L1	Cefn-y-crib Swans
89 K7	Cefn-y-pant Carmth
75 L7	Cefn-crib Torfn
55 L5	Cefn Cross Brdgnd
147 H6	Cefn-ddwysarn Gwynd
110 F2	Cefn Einion Shrops
128 C5	Cefneithin Carmth
75 K7	Cefn Fforest Caerph
55 L5	Cefn Glas Brdgnd
55 J7	Cefn Golau Blae G
92 E4	Cefn-gorwydd Powys
162 D7	Cefn-mawr Wrexhm
54 E6	Cefneithin Carmth
158 F2	Cemaes IoA
125 G5	Cemmaes Powys
125 G5	Cemmaes Road Powys
90 C7	Cenarth Carmth
141 J5	Cenin Gwynd
255 J2	Ceol na Mara Highld
273 J2	Ceos W Isls
23 B6	Ceres Fife
29 L8	Cerne Abbas Dorset
79 H7	Cerney Wick Gloucs
159 G6	Cerrigceinwen IoA
146 E3	Cerrigydrudion Conwy

139 J3	Cess Norfk
235 J2	Cessford Border
145 K1	Ceunant Gwynd
96 E7	Chaceley Gloucs
78 E3	Chacewater Cnwll
96 E8	Chackmore Bucks
3 J2	Chacombe Nhants
99 L6	Chadbury Worcs
175 J6	Chadderton Oldham
175 J6	Chadderton Fold Oldham
60 C5	Chaddesden C Derb
113 G6	Chaddesley Corbett Worcs
12 E6	Chaddlehanger Devon
7 J3	Chaddlewood C Plym
61 L5	Chaddleworth W Berk
165 H3	Chadlington Oxon
80 C2	Chadshunt Warwks
129 K4	Chadsmoor Staffs
100 D2	Chadstone Nhants
113 L2	Chad Valley Birm
148 F7	Chadwell Leics
118 B6	Chadwell End Beds
66 C3	Chadwell Heath Gt Lon
66 F5	Chadwell St Mary Thurr
113 G6	Chadwick Worcs
114 E5	Chadwick End Solhll
174 B8	Chadwick Green St Hel
26 F4	Chaffcombe Somset
66 E5	Chafford Hundred Thurr
13 L4	Chagford Devon
35 G3	Chailey E Susx
135 J6	Chainbridge Cambs
156 F5	Chain Bridge Lincs
51 H4	Chainhurst Kent
29 J5	Chalbury Dorset
29 J5	Chalbury Common Dorset
49 K2	Chaldon Surrey
18 B5	Chaldon Herring or East Chaldon Dorset
21 G6	Chale IoW
21 G6	Chale Green IoW
33 G4	Chalfont Common Bucks
64 D2	Chalford Gloucs
64 C2	Chalfont Grove Bucks
64 D2	Chalfont St Giles Bucks
64 D2	Chalfont St Peter Bucks
78 E6	Chalford Gloucs
81 L6	Chalford Oxon
43 L3	Chalford Wilts
78 D6	Chalford Hill Gloucs
83 G1	Chalgrave Beds
81 J7	Chalgrove Oxon
67 G6	Chalk Kent
85 J4	Chalk End Essex
209 H4	Chalkfoot Cumb
137 H6	Chalkhill Norfk
81 H3	Chalton-on-Otmoor Oxon
28 F6	Charlton on the Hill Dorset
43 G5	Chalkshire Bucks
51 J6	Chalksole Kent
26 F5	Chalkway Somset
67 K3	Chalkwell Kent
49 L7	Challacombe Devon
47 G7	Challoch D & G
49 H5	Challock Kent
82 E3	Chalton Beds
32 B3	Chalton Hants
101 K4	Chalvey Slough
23 G4	Chalvington E Susx
64 C5	Chalvey Slough
167 G4	Chalvington E Susx
174 B4	Chamber End Essex
38 D4	Chamberhouse Devon
52 B5	Chambers Green Kent
16 D2	Chamberhayes Marsh Dorset
39 J8	Champson Devon
268 F5	Chance Inn Fife
108 B4	Chancery Cerdgn
96 B5	Chandler's Cross Herefs
96 C6	Chandler's Cross Herts
31 G7	Chandler's Ford Hants
47 H2	Chandlers Green Hants
215 G4	Change D & G
231 K6	Chanlockfoot D & G
101 K2	Channel's End Beds
333 F12	Channerwick Shet
43 J2	Chantry Devon
43 H4	Chantry Somset
106 C5	Chantry Suffk
4 D2	Chapel Cnwll
259 G2	Chapel Fife
186 B7	Chapel Allerton Leeds
41 L3	Chapel Allerton Somset
10 D6	Chapel Amble Cnwll
116 E6	Chapel Brampton Nhants
174 F5	Chapel Chorlton Staffs
40 D5	Chapel Cleeve Somset
36 B2	Chapel Cross E Susx
101 J5	Chapel End Beds
101 K2	Chapel End Beds
150 C5	Chapel End Ches
85 H1	Chapel End Essex
118 C2	Chapel End Warwks
131 L4	Chapel End Warwks
165 L4	Chapel-en-le-Frith Derbys
175 G6	Chapel Field Bury
143 K7	Chapel Field Norfk
187 G4	Chapel Fields Covtry
135 J2	Chapelgate Lincs
100 D7	Chapel Green Warwks
114 F2	Chapel Green Warwks
63 K7	Chapel Green Wokham
178 D2	Chapel Haddlesey N York
257 H8	Chapelhall N Lans
119 G3	Chapel Head Cambs
301 L1	Chapel Hill Abers
77 J6	Chapel Hill Flints
311 J3	Chapelhill Highld
156 C5	Chapel Hill Lincs
77 G7	Chapel Hill Mons
267 J1	Chapel Hill P & K
233 J3	Chapelhope Border
175 L6	Chapel Hope Border
59 L7	Chapelknowe D & G
62 E7	Chapel Knapp Wilts
81 L4	Chapel Lawn Shrops
193 K6	Chapel-le-Dale N York
40 F8	Chapel Leigh Somset
247 G6	Chapel Mains Border
165 L4	Chapel Milton Derbys
104 C2	Chapel of Ease Caerph
82 C3	Chapel of Garioch Abers
82 E2	Chapel Plaister Wilts
151 J3	Chapel Row Berks
303 G6	Chapel of Stonewood C Aber
247 H5	Chapel on Leader Border
41 H8	Chapel Plaister Wilts
64 F6	Chapel Row Berks
159 H2	Chapel Row E Susx
139 H7	Chapel Row Norfk
62 E7	Chapel Row W Berk
123 H4	Chapel St Leonards Lincs
79 G4	Chapel Stile Cumb
201 H3	Chapelthorpe Wakefd
177 J3	Chapelton Abers
291 K3	Chapelton Abers
175 H7	Chapelton Angus
243 K4	Chapelton Devon
174 F4	Chapeltown Bl w D
24 C4	Chapeltown Cnwll
23 F6	Chapeltown Devon
301 L6	Chapeltown Moray
153 G7	Chapeltown Sheff
44 C7	Chapmanslade Wilts
101 C2	Chapman's Hill Worcs
84 B1	Chapman's Town E Susx
36 B4	Chapman's Well Devon
85 L5	Chapmans Well Devon
111 K5	Chapmore End Herts
86 F3	Chappel Essex
166 B5	Charaton Cross Cnwll
12 C8	Charcott Kent
50 D4	Chard Somset
26 E5	Chard Junction Dorset
114 D2	Chardstock Devon
59 H2	Charfield S Glos

59 H2	Charfield Green S Glos
113 K6	Charfield Hill S Glos
78 E3	Chargrove Gloucs
52 B4	Charing Kent
52 B4	Charing Heath Kent
52 B3	Charing Hill Kent
97 L6	Charingworth Gloucs
80 D3	Charlbury Oxon
59 H7	Charlcombe BaNES
60 C5	Charlcutt Wilts
97 G7	Charlecote Warwks
129 L8	Charlemont Sandw
39 G7	Charles Devon
39 G7	Charles Bottom Devon
247 H8	Charlesfield Border
47 L5	Charleshill Surrey
280 C5	Charleston Rens
256 B8	Charleston Rens
307 J3	Charlestown Abers
185 J7	Charlestown Brad
291 L1	Charlestown C Aber
175 L2	Charlestown Manch
5 H4	Charlestown Cnwll
165 K2	Charlestown Derbys
17 J6	Charlestown Dorset
258 D4	Charlestown Fife
308 E8	Charlestown Highld
310 E8	Charlestown Highld
175 J7	Charlestown Manch
311 G4	Charlestown Salfd
175 H8	Charlestown Salfd
304 D7	Charlestown of Aberlour Moray
105 H3	Charlesworth Derbys
165 K2	Charlesworth Derbys
66 B5	Charlinch Somset
45 K4	Charlton Gt Lon
99 H6	Charlton Hants
225 J3	Charlton Nthumb
62 B3	Charlton Oxon
128 B4	Charlton Oxon
26 D1	Charlton Somset
42 F5	Charlton Somset
43 G3	Charlton Somset
64 E7	Charlton Surrey
60 C3	Charlton Wilts
97 H4	Charlton Worcs
113 C5	Charlton W Susx
33 G4	Charlton W Susx
79 G2	Charlton Abbots Gloucs
169 K6	Charlton Adam Somset
64 D7	Charlton-All-Saints Wilts
64 B3	Charlton-Horethorne Somset
166 F1	Charltonbrook Sheff
78 E2	Charlton Kings Gloucs
42 D8	Charlton Mackrell Somset
29 G6	Charlton Marshall Dorset
43 H7	Charlton Musgrove Somset
81 H3	Charlton-on-Otmoor Oxon
78 F2	Charlton Park Gloucs
206 E4	Charltons R & Cl
49 L7	Charlwood Hants
47 G7	Charlwood Surrey
31 K3	Charlwood Surrey
234 E1	Charlwood Surrey
17 K3	Charminster Bmouth
213 G4	Charmister C Derb
223 G2	Charmouth Dorset
119 K7	Charndon Bucks
134 C7	Charney Bassett Oxon
79 G6	Charnes Staffs
81 H2	Charney Bassett Oxon
128 F7	Charnock Green Lancs
150 F4	Charnock Hall Sheff
174 B4	Charnock Richard Lancs
106 C2	Charsfield Suffk
51 J3	Charter Corner Kent
46 E2	Charter Alley Hants
257 H3	Charterhouse Somset
80 C4	Charterville Allotments Oxon
52 F1	Chartham Kent
52 F2	Chartham Hatch Kent
51 J3	Chart Hill Kent
82 E6	Chartridge Bucks
51 J3	Chart Sutton Kent
97 H2	Charwelton Nhants

8 E2	Chelston Torbay
105 G4	Chelsworth Suffk
105 G4	Chelsworth Common Suffk
78 F2	Cheltenham Gloucs
117 K6	Chelveston Nhants
58 C7	Chelvey N Som
58 C7	Chelvey Batch N Som
42 F1	Chelwood BaNES
50 B8	Chelwood Common E Susx
60 C2	Chelworth Wilts
104 C4	Chelworth Street Suffk
115 H1	Chelworth Wilts
153 K6	Chelworth Lower Green Wilts
31 G3	Chelworth Upper Green Wilts
30 F3	Chelworth Old Village Wilts
43 G5	Chelynch Somset
111 J3	Cheney Longville Shrops
80 C6	Chimney Oxon
104 B4	Chimney-end Oxon
47 G2	Chineham Hants
65 L2	Chingford Gt Lon
65 L2	Chingford Green Gt Lon
165 K4	Chinley Derbys
81 L6	Chinnor Oxon
25 L2	Chipley Somset
114 B6	Chipnall Staffs
53 L5	Chippenham Cambs
197 J2	Chippenham Wilts
26 D6	Chippenham Cambs
38 E5	Chippenhall Green Suffk
43 J2	Chippenham Wilts
82 B2	Chipperfield Herts
102 E7	Chipping Herts
183 H6	Chipping Lancs
83 J7	Chipping Warden Nhants
97 L6	Chipping Campden Gloucs
86 C3	Chipping Hill Essex
80 C1	Chipping Norton Oxon
85 H6	Chipping Ongar Essex
59 H4	Chipping Sodbury S Glos
99 G4	Chipping Warden Nhants
25 J1	Chipstable Somset
49 J2	Chipstead Surrey
112 C5	Chirbury Shrops
148 E4	Chirk Wrexhm
148 E6	Chirk Bank Shrops
219 G4	Chirk Green Wrexhm
248 C2	Chirnside Border
227 J6	Chirton N Tyne
44 E2	Chirton Wilts
63 K3	Chisbridge Cross Bucks
61 J7	Chisbury Wilts
27 H3	Chiselborough Somset
61 G5	Chiseldon Swindn
81 H7	Chiselhampton Oxon
67 H6	Chiserley Calder
104 C5	Chislehurst Gt Lon
53 H2	Chislet Kent
71 J5	Chisworth Derbys
10 T6	Chilson Devon
209 J5	Chitcombe E Susx
166 F8	Chittering Cambs
32 F2	Chithurst W Susx
119 K5	Chittering Cambs
173 J4	Chitterne Wilts
179 H6	Chittlehamholt Devon
40 C6	Chittlehampton Devon
49 L3	Chitterne Wilts
56 E3	Chitts Hills Essex
167 L7	Chittoe Wilts
8 C7	Chivelstone Devon
38 C7	Chivenor Devon
83 G7	Chobham Surrey
82 E5	Cholderton Wilts
42 B5	Cholesbury Bucks
225 L5	Chollerford Nthumb
17 K7	Chollerton Nthumb
225 L5	Cholmondeston Ches
7 L3	Cholsey Oxon
150 B2	Cholstrey Herefs
62 E3	Cholwell BaNES
95 G2	Cholwell Devon
197 G2	Chop Gate N York
227 H3	Choppington Nthumb
212 D2	Chopwell Gatesd
149 L3	Chorley Ches
174 C4	Chorley Lancs
112 D3	Chorley Shrops
130 B4	Chorley Staffs
32 F1	Chorley Common Ches
77 G6	Chorleywood Herts
83 G7	Chorleywood Bottom Herts
83 G7	Chorleywood West Herts
150 D3	Choriton Ches
164 F2	Chorlton-cum-Hardy Manch
149 J2	Choriton Lane Ches
37 H6	Choulton Shrops
102 F6	Chowdene Gatesd
135 K7	Chowley Ches
321 M11	Chrishall Essex
102 F6	Christchurch Cambs
75 J7	Christchurch Gloucs
74 H4	Christchurch Gloucs
106 C4	Christchurch Newpt
106 D4	Christchurch Park Suffk

62 C3	Chilton Oxon
104 E5	Chilton Suffk
46 E5	Chilton Candover Hants
59 H7	Churchend S Glos
27 K2	Chilton Cantelo Somset
61 K6	Chilton Foliat Wilts
104 E5	Chilton Grove Suffk
213 G7	Chilton Lane Dur
90 B5	Chilton Polden Somset
41 L6	Chilton Polden Somset
104 C4	Chilton Street Suffk
25 L5	Chilton Trinity Somset
115 H1	Chilvers Coton Warwks
153 K6	Chilwell Notts
31 G3	Chilworth Hants
129 J8	Chilworth Surrey
44 F7	Chilworth Surrey
84 C6	Chingle Hants
84 F4	Chingford Green Gt Lon
15 K2	Chinley Devon
122 R1	Chinley Head Derbys
130 F3	Chinnor Oxon
80 E4	Chipley Staffs
165 K4	Chinnley Derbys
81 L6	Chinnor Oxon
25 L2	Chipley Somset
114 B6	Chipnall Staffs
120 C6	Chippenham Cambs
44 C5	Chippenham Wilts
82 B2	Chipperfield Herts
96 F3	Chippings Worcs
113 K4	Chippinghall Green Suffk
42 B1	Churchill Worcs
70 F4	Church Hill Pembks
129 K8	Church Hill Sandw
114 B6	Church Hill Staffs
53 J5	Church Hougham Kent
122 F4	Chippenhall Green Suffk
26 D6	Chippenham Cambs
38 E5	Churchill Devon
42 B2	Churchill N Som
80 D2	Churchill Oxon
96 F3	Churchill Worcs
113 H4	Churchill Worcs
42 B1	Churchill Green N Som
26 C4	Churchinford Somset
18 E5	Church Knowle Dorset
168 F5	Church Laneham Notts
116 F4	Church Lawford Warwks
150 F2	Church Lawton Ches
151 K6	Church Leigh Staffs
97 H3	Church Lench Worcs
152 C5	Church Mayfield Staffs
150 C1	Church Minshull Ches
111 H2	Churchmoor Rough Shrops
33 G7	Church Norton W Susx
71 J5	Churchtown Cnwll
10 T6	Churchtown Cnwll
301 K3	Churchtown Cnwll
21 G4	Churchtown Derbys
39 G5	Churchtown Devon
85 H5	Churchtown Devon
23 L1	Churchtown IoM
173 H3	Churchtown Lancs
40 C6	Churchtown Sefton
104 F5	Churchtown Somset
49 L3	Church Town Surrey
167 L7	Church Warsop Notts
114 D7	Church Westcote Gloucs
58 F7	Churchill N Som
84 E6	Churchwhitfield Kent
33 K3	Churchwood W Susx
151 J3	Churnet Grange Staffs
8 J8	Churscombe Torbay
59 J8	Churston Ferrers Torbay
47 L6	Churt Surrey
149 H2	Churton Ches
147 L5	Chute Cadley Wilts
45 K3	Chute Standen Wilts
160 E6	Chwefforld Conwy
145 H6	Chwilog Gwynd
2 D6	Chyandour Cnwll
3 H6	Chyanvounder Cnwll
171 H6	Chycoose Cnwll
2 E4	Chynoweth Cnwll
77 G6	Chyvarloe Cnwll
92 E4	Cicelyford Mons
88 C5	Cilau Pembks
162 C8	Cilcain Flints
91 H3	Cilcennin Cerdgn
92 E4	Cilfrew Neath
74 B6	Cilfynydd Rhondd
90 D7	Cilgerran Pembks
93 L3	Cilgwyn Carmth
145 G8	Cilgwyn Gwynd
91 H4	Ciliau-Aeron Cerdgn
306 B6	Cill Amhlaidh W Isls
321 N5	Cill Donnain W Isls
320 F2	Cille Bhrighde W Isls
321 P5	Cill Eireabhagh W Isls
321 M11	Cille Pheadair W Isls
129 L6	Cilmaengwyn Neath
73 L4	Cilmery Powys
93 H4	Cilsan Carmth
93 L5	Ciltwrch Powys
93 G3	Cilybebyll Neath
92 C6	Cilycwm Carmth
119 L2	Cim Gwynd
144 E5	Cinderford Gloucs
74 B6	Cinderhill Derbys
153 K5	Cinderhill C Nott
171 H3	Cinderhill Derbys
130 F5	Cinderhill Wolves
129 K8	Cinder Hill Wsall
50 D4	Cinder Hill W Susx
164 B2	Cinnamon Brow Warrtn
79 H4	Cippenham Slough
89 J3	Cippyn Pembks
78 D3	Cireboost W Isls
79 G6	Cirencester Gloucs
324 H6	Ciribhig W Isls
128 E3	Citadilla N York
110 E2	City Powys
175 J8	City of London
159 H3	City Dulas IoA
150 F5	Clabach Ag & B
262 D4	Clachaig Ag & B
262 D4	Clachaig Highld
288 B5	Clachan Ag & B
262 D4	Clachan Ag & B
239 J2	Clachan Ag & B
238 A6	Clachan Ag & B
293 K3	Clachan Highld
283 K10	Clachan Highld
313 K10	Clachan Highld
184 F2	Clachan-a-Luib W Isls
312 J8	Clachan na Luib W Isls
321 M7	Clachan of Campsie E Duns
256 E5	Clachan of Glendaruel Ag & B
262 C11	Clachan-Seil Ag & B
272 H11	Clachan Chnoc a Lin W Isls
321 M7	Clachan Iolairegin W Isls
262 B11	Clachbreck Ag & B
251 B12	Claddach Ag & B
322 C11	Claddach-knockline W Isls
322 C11	Claddach a' Bhale Shear W Isls
322 C11	Cladach Chirceboist W Isls
322 C11	Cladach Chnoc a Lin W Isls
321 N2	Clachan Iolaraigh W Isls
261 J5	Cladich Ag & B
241 G6	Cladswell Warwks
304 C4	Claggan Highld
289 J7	Claigan Highld
304 C4	Clanfield Hants
241 G6	Clandown BaNES
33 G3	Clanfield Hants
80 D4	Clanfield Oxon
45 K4	Clanville Hants
77 H5	Clapham Beds

135 L3	Church End Norfk
80 D5	Church End Oxon
98 D7	Church End Oxon
59 H7	Churchend S Glos
104 E6	Church End Suffk
114 F1	Church End Warwks
63 G6	Churchend Warwks
96 D5	Church End Worcs
80 D1	Church Enstone Oxon
36 B3	Churches Green E Susx
186 F7	Church Fenton N York
96 B4	Churchfield Herefs
129 L8	Churchfield Sandw
44 F7	Churchfields Wilts
84 C6	Churchgate Herts
84 F4	Churchgate Street Essex
15 K2	Church Green Devon
122 B1	Church Green Norfk
130 F3	Church Gresley Derbys
80 E4	Church Hanborough Oxon
70 F4	Church Hill Pembks
129 K8	Church Hill Sandw
114 B6	Church Hill Staffs
79 K3	Church Hougham Kent
65 L3	Church Houses N York
29 H7	Church Knowle Dorset
108 A5	Churchstanton Somset
14 B8	Churchstoke Powys
99 J2	Churchstow Devon
8 B5	Church Street Essex
104 C5	Church Street Kent
332 J4	Church Stretton Shrops
71 J5	Churchtown Cnwll
267 J3	Churchtown Cnwll
301 K3	Churchtown Cnwll
21 G4	Churchtown Derbys
166 E2	Churchtown Devon
22 D2	Churchtown IoM
39 G5	Churchtown Lancs
40 C6	Churchtown Sefton
56 F3	Churnet Grange Staffs
33 K3	Churscombe Torbay
99 J2	Churston Ferrers Torbay
8 J8	Churt Surrey
181 L4	Churton Ches
56 E5	Church Village Rhondd
267 K8	Church Warsop Notts
104 C5	Church Westcote Gloucs

42 F7	Clanville Somset
60 B5	Clanville Wilts
214 C6	Clanyard D & G
240 D2	Claonaig Ag & B
314 E6	Claonel Highld
84 E2	Clapgate Herts
101 H5	Clapham Beds
65 J5	Clapham Gt Lon
193 K8	Clapham Lancs
33 L5	Clapham W Susx
101 H3	Clapham Beds
185 K3	Clapham N York
68 F8	Clapham Hill Kent
129 K8	Clapham Park Gt Lon
52 E6	Clap Hill Kent
10 E7	Clapper Cnwll
51 K6	Clapper Hill Kent
26 D6	Clapton Somset
43 J5	Clapton Somset
58 E6	Clapton in Gordano N Som
79 K3	Clapton-on-the-Hill Gloucs
65 L3	Clapton Park Gt Lon
226 E7	Clara Vale Gatesd
71 G2	Clarbeston Pembks
71 G2	Clarbeston Road Pembks
168 B4	Clarborough Notts
319 K3	Clardon Highld
104 C4	Clare Suffk
221 H6	Clarebrand D & G
129 H6	Claregate Wolves
168 F5	Claremont Park Surrey
222 D6	Clarencefield D & G
41 K1	Clarence Park N Som
132 B6	Clarendon Park C Leic
70 E4	Clareston Pembks
71 G2	Clarbeston Road Pembks
71 G2	Clarbeston Pembks
97 J5	Clark's Hill Lincs
97 H5	Clark's Hill Worcs
247 H8	Clarkston E Rens
46 E3	Clarken Green Hants
165 K5	Clarke Green Ches
175 K7	Clarksfield Oldham
24 E4	Clark's Green Surrey
77 L2	Clifford's Mesne Gloucs
135 H2	Clash Highld
97 H5	Clark's Hill Worcs
97 L6	Clatford Wilts
264 E1	Clatt Abers
21 G4	Clatter Powys
85 H5	Clatterford IoW
85 H4	Clatterford End Essex
290 F6	Clatterin Brig Abers
269 G4	Clatto Fife
183 G1	Clatworthy Somset
40 E7	Claughton Lancs
183 G3	Claughton Lancs
162 F3	Claughton Wirral
98 D2	Claverdon Warwks
84 B6	Claverhambury Essex
58 D7	Claverham N Som
84 F4	Clavering Essex
128 F5	Claverley Shrops
59 H8	Claverton BaNES
59 J8	Claverton Down BaNES
56 E5	Clawdd-côch V Glam
147 L5	Clawdd-newydd Denbgs
57 J6	Clawdd Poncen Denbgs
204 D7	Clawton N York
12 C3	Clawton Devon
125 G4	Claxby Lincs
139 J4	Claxby Lincs
137 L4	Claxton N York
137 L4	Claxton Norfk
115 K2	Claybrooke Magna Leics
115 K2	Claybrooke Parva Leics
167 L8	Clay Common Suffk
323 K6	Clay Coton Nhants
116 B4	Clay Cross Derbys
154 F2	Clay Cross Derbys
117 L7	Claydon Oxon
164 D4	Claydon Suffk
72 C6	Clay End Herts
106 C2	Claygate D & G
50 F3	Claygate Kent
51 H5	Claygate Surrey
64 D5	Claygate Cross Kent
143 H2	Clayhall Gt Lon
25 K7	Clayhanger Devon
129 L6	Clayhanger Wsall
130 C7	Clayhanger Wsall
26 B5	Clayhidon Devon
92 E2	Clayhill E Susx
29 L5	Clay Hill Bristl
57 G5	Clayhill Hants
30 F5	Clay Hill Herts
167 H5	Clay Hill Wokingham
64 B4	Clay Hill Worcs
316 F5	Clayock Highld
79 J3	Claypit Hill Cambs
80 D5	Claypits Devon
78 B5	Claypits Gloucs
154 B2	Claypole Lincs
58 E5	Clays End BaNES
175 L8	Clayton Brad
176 E4	Clayton Donc
164 F5	Clayton Staffs
18 E4	Clayton W Susx
176 C7	Clayton Barns
174 D3	Clayton Brook Lancs
174 D4	Clayton Green Lancs
176 F4	Clayton Heights Brad
183 K5	Clayton-le-Dale Lancs
183 H8	Clayton-le-Moors Lancs
174 D5	Clayton-le-Woods Lancs
167 K5	Clayworth Notts
175 K4	Cleadale Highld
227 J7	Cleadon S Tyne
12 E6	Clearbrook Devon
95 H3	Clearwell Gloucs
205 H5	Cleasby N York
332 E5	Cleat Ork
204 B4	Cleatlam Dur
200 C4	Cleator Cumb
289 G7	Cleator Moor Cumb
246 F3	Cleekhimin N Lans
112 B2	Cleedownton Shrops
112 B3	Cleehill Shrops
114 F7	Cleekhimin N Lans
180 E2	Cleethorpes NE Lin
111 L4	Cleeton St Mary Shrops
58 C7	Cleeve N Som
62 B4	Cleeve Oxon
97 H4	Cleeve Hill Gloucs
279 E1	Cleeve Prior Worcs
72 E2	Cleghorn S Lans
159 K8	Clegyrnant Powys

66 D6	Clement Street Kent
61 G8	Clench Wilts
61 G7	Clench Common Wilts
96 B6	Clencher's Mill Herefs
236 C5	Clennell Nthumb
113 J4	Clent Worcs
112 D4	Cleobury Mortimer Shrops
112 C2	Cleobury North Shrops
239 G7	Cleongart Ag & B
311 J7	Clephanton Highld
311 J7	Clerkenwell Gt Lon
177 G3	Clerk Green Kirk
307 L6	Clerkhill Abers
234 E2	Clerklands Border
326 C5	Clestrain Ork
234 F4	Cleuch Head Border
222 D5	Cleughbrae D & G
255 K7	Clevancy Wilts
57 L6	Clevedon Bristl
182 A6	Cleveleys Lancs
42 B3	Clewer Somset
64 B5	Clewer Green W & M
64 B5	Clewer New Town W & M
142 C3	Cley next the Sea Norfk
320 D4	Cliad W Isls
323 J5	Cliasmol W Isls
330 K5	Clibberswick Shet
202 D3	Cliburn Cumb
46 F4	Cliddesden Hants
165 K3	Cliff Warwks
281 J6	Cliffburn Angus
113 J4	Cliffe N York
67 K5	Cliffe Medway
178 F1	Cliffe N York
204 B6	Cliffe N York
57 G4	Cliff End E Susx
67 H6	Cliffe Woods Medway
22 E2	Cliff Leics
94 B4	Clifford Herefs
186 D6	Clifford Leeds
95 K3	Clifford Warwks
27 L7	Clifford's Mesne Gloucs
50 B5	Cliff's End Kent
69 K8	Cliffs End Kent
113 H5	Clifton Beds
59 G6	Clifton Bristl
281 J6	Clifton C Nott
202 C2	Clifton Cumb
152 C5	Clifton Derbys
167 K1	Clifton Devon
185 G6	Clifton Donc
227 G3	Clifton Nthumb
175 G7	Clifton Oldham
187 G4	Clifton Salfd
130 F7	Clifton Worcs
227 G3	Clifton Campville Staffs
175 G7	Clifton Green Salfd
175 G7	Clifton Hampden Oxon
27 K4	Clifton Maybank Dorset
187 G3	Clifton Moor York
100 F3	Clifton Reynes M Keyn
116 E7	Clifton upon Dunsmore Warwks
112 E7	Clifton upon Teme Worcs
69 L6	Cliftonville Kent
257 G8	Cliftonville N Lans
143 J4	Cliftonville Norfk
33 L6	Climping W Susx
43 K8	Clink Somset
186 C3	Clint N York
185 J3	Clint N York
123 L2	Clint Green Norfk
137 G7	Clintmains Border
204 D7	Clints N York
122 B5	Cliobh W Isls
141 H4	Clipiau Gwynd
133 H8	Clippesby Norfk
137 L4	Clippings Green Norfk
115 J4	Clipsham Rutlnd
133 K8	Clipston Nhants
167 L5	Clipston Notts
137 K4	Clipstone Beds
154 E1	Clipstone Notts
183 K6	Clitheroe Lancs
101 H7	Cliton Manor Beds
53 L6	Cliuthar W Isls
57 L4	Clive Ches
164 C2	Clive Green Ches
330 M5	Clivocast Shet
180 E7	Clixby Lincs
60 C2	Cloatley Wilts
147 L3	Cloatley Cross Wilts
305 D2	Clochan Moray
163 K2	Clock Face St Hel
49 H1	Clock House Gt Lon
125 H6	Clockmill Border
311 H5	Cloddiau Powys
94 D6	Clodock Herefs
115 K2	Cloford Somset
146 D7	Clogwyn Cyrnau Conwy
72 E6	Cloigyn Carmth
307 L3	Clola Abers
126 D4	Clophill Beds
117 M3	Clopton Nhants
106 C2	Clopton Suffk
104 F3	Clopton Corner Suffk
104 E4	Clopton Green Suffk
121 K7	Clopton Green Suffk
223 H5	Closeburn D & G
221 J1	Closeburnmill D & G
172 C4	Closeclark IoM
22 E3	Close House Dur
27 K4	Closworth Somset
102 C7	Clothall Herts
102 C7	Clothall Common Herts
331 G9	Clother Shet
163 K8	Clotton Ches
163 K8	Clotton Common Ches
115 K2	Cloudesley Bush Warwks
95 J6	Clouds Herefs
151 L3	Cloud Side Staffs
176 F5	Clough Oldham
183 L2	Clough Rochdl
175 K5	Clough Oldham
175 H3	Clough Foot Calder
175 K4	Clough Head Calder
176 D2	Clough Head Calder
198 E2	Cloughton N York
198 E2	Cloughton Newlands N York
332 E5	Clousta Shet
326 C2	Clouston Ork
301 H4	Clova Abers
289 J7	Clova Angus
22 D5	Clovelly Devon
234 F4	Clovenfords Border
285 J7	Clovenstone Abers
300 E6	Clovullin Highld
165 J7	Clowne Derbys
112 D7	Clows Top Worcs
50 E3	Cloy Wrexhm
149 J5	Cluanie Inn Highld
301 G5	Clubworthy Cnwll
21 H3	Cluddley Wrexhm
110 E5	Cluanie Lodge Highld
110 F4	Clun Shrops
298 E2	Clunbury Shrops
111 H4	Clunas Highld
285 G3	Clunderwen Carmth
111 J3	Clune Highld
111 G4	Clungunford Shrops
72 D6	Clunderwen Carmth
72 C5	Clwt-y-bont Gwynd
159 L5	Clwydyfagwyr Myr Td

376 City, town and village index: Clydach - Crofts of Benachielt

75 L4 **Clydach** Mons
55 G1 **Clydach** Swans
75 K4 **Clydach Terrace** Blae G
56 C2 **Clydach Vale** Rhondd
256 B7 **Clydebank** W Duns
60 E5 **Clyffe Pypard** Wilts
255 G4 **Clynder** Ag & B
74 C6 **Clyne** Neath
315 L5 **Clynelish** Highld
145 H4 **Clynnog-Fawr** Gwynd
94 B5 **Clyro** Powys
14 F3 **Clyst Honiton** Devon
25 J6 **Clyst Hydon** Devon
14 F4 **Clyst St George** Devon
25 J6 **Clyst St Lawrence** Devon
14 F3 **Clyst St Mary** Devon
319 N9 **Clyth** Highld
76 D5 **Clytha Hill** Mons
76 D5 **Clytha Park** Mons
324 E7 **Cnip** W Isls
322 B11 **Cnoc a' Lin** W Isls
325 P7 **Cnoc Amhlaigh** W Isls
322 B11 **Cnoc an Torrain** W Isls
325 N6 **Cnoc an t-Solais** W Isls
252 B6 **Cnocbreac** Ag & B
325 L8 **Cnoc Màiri** W Isls
325 M8 **Cnoc nan Gobhar** W Isls
310 E3 **Cnoc Ruadh** Highld
108 D4 **Cnwch Coch** Cerdgn
11 K6 **Coad's Green** Cnwll
167 G4 **Coal Aston** Derbys
205 J3 **Coal Bank** Darltn
75 K5 **Coalbrookvale** Blae G
244 B7 **Coalburn** S Lans
226 E7 **Coalburns** Gatesd
211 H4 **Coalcleugh** Nthumb
78 B6 **Coaley** Gloucs
78 B6 **Coaley Peak** Gloucs
291 J2 **Coalford** Abers
230 C3 **Coalhall** E Ayrs
85 L7 **Coalhill** Essex
128 D5 **Coalmoor** Wrekin
115 H2 **Coalpit Field** Warwks
59 G4 **Coalpit Heath** S Glos
150 F3 **Coalpit Hill** Staffs
129 L6 **Coal Pool** Wsall
257 L1 **Coalsnaughton** Clacks
268 D8 **Coaltown of Balgonie** Fife
268 E6 **Coaltown of Burnturk** Fife
259 J1 **Coaltown of Wemyss** Fife
131 J4 **Coalville** Leics
77 H4 **Coalway** Gloucs
210 E2 **Coanwood** Nthumb
8 B4 **Coarsewell** Devon
27 G2 **Coat** Somset
257 G8 **Coatbridge** N Lans
257 H8 **Coatdyke** N Lans
61 G4 **Coate** Swindn
44 D1 **Coate** Wilts
135 G7 **Coates** Cambs
78 F6 **Coates** Gloucs
184 C5 **Coates** Lancs
245 L1 **Coates** Mdloth
168 F4 **Coates** Lincs
33 J3 **Coates** W Susx
206 D2 **Coatham** R & Cl
205 H4 **Coatham Mundeville** Darltn
232 F5 **Coatsgate** D & G
16 C3 **Cobb** Dorset
23 L1 **Cobbaton** Devon
96 C2 **Cobbler's Corner** Worcs
122 F1 **Cobbler's Green** Norfk
85 H4 **Cobbler's Pieces** Essex
76 F6 **Cobbler's Plain** Mons
164 B3 **Cobbs** Warrtn
96 C7 **Cobb's Cross** Gloucs
104 C7 **Cobbs Fenn** Essex
185 J3 **Cobby Syke** N York
78 F3 **Coberley** Gloucs
95 G6 **Cobhall Common** Herefs
67 G7 **Cobham** Kent
48 F1 **Cobham** Surrey
67 G7 **Cobham Park** Kent
139 L5 **Cobholm Island** Norfk
85 K3 **Cobler's Green** Essex
29 J2 **Cobley** Dorset
113 L5 **Cobley Hill** Worcs
111 K7 **Cobnash** Herefs
16 c2 **Cobo** Guern
151 G4 **Cobridge** C Stke
150 C6 **Cobscot** Shrops
167 H6 **Cock Alley** Derbys
197 H2 **Cockayne** N York
102 C4 **Cockayne Hatley** Beds
148 F4 **Cock Bank** Wrexhm
97 H3 **Cock Bevington** Warwks
300 D7 **Cock Bridge** Abers
261 H6 **Cockburnspath** Border
86 C6 **Cock Clarks** Essex
184 C8 **Cockden** Lancs
104 B3 **Cock & End** Suffk
259 K5 **Cockenzie and Port Seton** E Loth
173 L3 **Cocker Bar** Lancs
182 E4 **Cockerham** Lancs
208 D7 **Cockermouth** Cumb
83 J2 **Cockernhoe** Herts
177 G2 **Cockersdale** Leeds
205 H4 **Cockerton** Darltn
54 F3 **Cockett** Swans
204 E3 **Cockfield** Dur
104 F3 **Cockfield** Suffk
84 B7 **Cockfosters** Gt Lon
111 K6 **Cock Gate** Herefs
85 K3 **Cock Green** Essex
186 F3 **Cock Hill** N York
42 F7 **Cockhill** Somset
33 G3 **Cocking** W Susx
33 G3 **Cocking Causeway** W Susx
8 E2 **Cockington** Torbay
42 B4 **Cocklake** Somset
78 F4 **Cockleford** Gloucs
201 G7 **Cockley Beck** Cumb
136 F6 **Cockley Cley** Norfk
176 F4 **Cockley Hill** Kirk
37 G3 **Cock Marling** E Susx
18 E5 **Cocknowle** Dorset
63 J4 **Cockpole Green** Wokham
4 C4 **Cocks** Cnwll
104 E2 **Cocks Green** Suffk
91 K4 **Cockshead** Cerdgn
95 J6 **Cockshoot** Herefs
112 B3 **Cockshutford** Shrops
112 E3 **Cockshutt** Shrops
149 H8 **Cockshutt** Shrops
51 J3 **Cock Street** Kent
105 G6 **Cock Street** Suffk
141 K3 **Cockthorpe** Norfk
2 E4 **Cockwells** Cnwll
14 F5 **Cockwood** Devon
41 H5 **Cockwood** Somset
165 K5 **Cockyard** Derbys
94 F7 **Cockyard** Herefs
106 C3 **Coddenham** Suffk
105 K2 **Coddenham Green** Suffk
149 H2 **Coddington** Ches
96 B5 **Coddington** Herefs
154 F3 **Coddington** Notts
44 C6 **Codford St Mary** Wilts
44 C5 **Codford St Peter** Wilts
83 L3 **Codicote** Herts
83 L3 **Codicote Bottom** Herts
82 F6 **Codmore** Bucks
33 K2 **Codmore Hill** W Susx
153 H4 **Codnor** Derbys
153 H4 **Codnor Breach** Derbys
153 H3 **Codnor Gate** Derbys
153 H3 **Codnor Park** Derbys
59 H5 **Codrington** S Glos
129 H6 **Codsall** Staffs
129 G6 **Codsall Wood** Staffs
39 L6 **Codsend** Somset
75 L5 **Coedcae** Torfn
76 B5 **Coedcae** Torfn
76 E7 **Coed Cwnwr** Mons
146 E2 **Coedcynhelier** Conwy
56 D3 **Coedely** Rhondd
57 J2 **Coed Eva** Torfn
55 K5 **Coed Hirwaun** Neath
57 J4 **Coedkernew** Newpt
159 K6 **Coed Mawr** Gwynd
76 C4 **Coed Morgan** Mons
148 E3 **Coedpoeth** Wrexhm
148 E2 **Coed-talon** Flints
127 G4 **Coedway** Powys
90 D6 **Coed-y-bryn** Cerdgn
57 L2 **Coed-y-caerau** Newpt
76 E5 **Coed-y-fedw** Mons
124 D8 **Coed y Garth** Cerdgn
126 F1 **Coed y go** Shrops
76 C7 **Coed-y-paen** Mons
159 L7 **Coed-y-parc** Gwynd
75 K2 **Coed-yr-ynys** Powys
124 B2 **Coed Ystumgwern** Gwynd
126 E5 **Coed-y-wlad** Powys
74 C4 **Coelbren** Powys
100 E6 **Coffee Hall** M Keyn
14 D8 **Coffinswell** Devon
14 F5 **Cofton** Devon
113 L4 **Cofton Common** Birm
113 L4 **Cofton Hackett** Worcs
57 G7 **Cog** V Glam
57 G6 **Cogan** V Glam
117 G7 **Cogenhoe** Nhants
80 D5 **Cogges** Oxon
86 C2 **Coggeshall** Essex
86 D2 **Coggeshall Hamlet** Essex
50 F8 **Coggins Mill** E Susx
325 P1 **Coig Peighinnean** W Isls
325 L3 **Coig Peighinnean Bhuirgh** W Isls
289 J2 **Coilacriech** Abers
265 K6 **Coilantogle** Stirlg
263 J3 **Coillaig** Ag & B
320 F2 **Coilleag** W Isls
284 D1 **Coille Mhorgil** Highld
292 F9 **Coillore** Highld
324 H8 **Coire an Fhuarain** W Isls
167 H4 **Coisley Hill** Sheff
56 B4 **Coity** Brdgnd
102 E6 **Cokenach** Herts
130 F1 **Cokhay Green** Derbys
325 N7 **Col** W Isls
314 E4 **Colaboll** Highld
4 E2 **Colan** Cnwll
15 H4 **Colaton Raleigh** Devon
292 C7 **Colbost** Highld
195 J2 **Colburn** N York
202 F3 **Colby** Cumb
172 C8 **Colby** IoM
143 G5 **Colby** Norfk
87 G1 **Colchester** Essex
104 F2 **Colchester Green** Suffk
56 F7 **Colcot** V Glam
62 D6 **Cold Ash** W Berk
116 D4 **Cold Ashby** Nhants
47 K7 **Cold Ash Hill** Hants
59 J6 **Cold Ashton** S Glos
79 J3 **Cold Aston** Gloucs
317 N5 **Coldbackie** Highld
66 C6 **Coldblow** Gt Lon
51 K2 **Coldblow** Kent
71 J4 **Cold Blow** Pembks
100 F3 **Cold Brayfield** M Keyn
93 L6 **Coldbrook** Powys
84 D3 **Cold Christmas** Herts
193 K7 **Cold Cotes** N York
34 F5 **Coldean** Br & H
14 C6 **Coldeast** Devon
152 B2 **Coldeaton** Derbys
96 D7 **Cold Elm** Worcs
175 L2 **Colden** Calder
31 H2 **Colden Common** Hants
123 J7 **Coldfair Green** Suffk
135 J6 **Coldham** Cambs
129 H5 **Coldham** Staffs
103 G2 **Coldham's Common** Cambs
169 K4 **Cold Hanworth** Lincs
4 B5 **Coldharbour** Cnwll
25 K4 **Coldharbour** Devon
17 J5 **Coldharbour** Dorset
18 D4 **Cold Harbour** Dorset
77 H6 **Coldharbour** Gloucs
66 D5 **Coldharbour** Gt Lon
83 J3 **Cold Harbour** Herts
51 K2 **Coldharbour** Kent
67 L7 **Cold Harbour** Kent
155 J7 **Cold Harbour** Lincs
62 F5 **Cold Harbour** W & M
48 F5 **Coldharbour** Surrey
63 K5 **Cold Harbour** W & M
43 L2 **Cold Harbour** Wilts
43 L4 **Cold Harbour** Wilts
128 C2 **Cold Hatton** Wrekin
128 C2 **Cold Hatton Heath** Wrekin
213 K4 **Cold Hesledon** Dur
177 K5 **Cold Hiendley** Wakefd
99 L3 **Cold Higham** Nhants
261 L7 **Coldingham** Border
71 J5 **Cold Inn** Pembks
196 F5 **Cold Kirby** N York
151 G7 **Coldmeece** Staffs
150 E1 **Cold Moss Heath** Ches
132 E5 **Cold Newton** Leics
11 H4 **Cold Northcott** Cnwll
86 D6 **Cold Norton** Essex
266 C8 **Coldoch** Stirlg
133 G4 **Cold Overton** Leics
57 L3 **Coldra** Newpt
267 K7 **Coldrain** P & K
53 J4 **Coldred** Kent
24 B5 **Coldridge** Devon
182 C6 **Cold Row** Lancs
280 C7 **Coldstream** Angus
248 C6 **Coldstream** Border
5 G3 **Coldvreath** Cnwll
33 K3 **Coldwaltham** W Susx
130 B4 **Cold Well** Staffs
307 L7 **Coldwells** Abers
301 L4 **Coldwells Croft** Abers
43 G7 **Cole** Somset
111 G2 **Colebatch** Shrops
25 J5 **Colebrook** Devon
24 D7 **Colebrooke** Devon
155 J1 **Coleby** Lincs
179 K4 **Coleby** N Linc
103 J6 **Cole End** Essex
114 E2 **Cole End** Warwks
24 D6 **Coleford** Devon
77 H4 **Coleford** Gloucs
43 G4 **Coleford** Somset
40 F7 **Coleford Water** Somset
122 D2 **Colegate End** Norfk
102 F7 **Cole Green** Herts
114 C2 **Colehall** Birm
46 C3 **Cole Henley** Hants
29 J6 **Colehill** Dorset
83 K4 **Coleman Green** Herts
50 C7 **Coleman's Hatch** E Susx
149 H7 **Colemere** Shrops
47 H7 **Colemore** Hants
128 E7 **Colemore Green** Shrops
131 H3 **Coleorton** Leics
131 J3 **Coleorton Moor** Leics
65 G6 **Cole Park** Gt Lon
59 K6 **Colerne** Wilts
78 F4 **Colesbourne** Gloucs
43 J8 **Colesbrook** Dorset
8 C5 **Cole's Cross** Devon
26 F6 **Cole's Cross** Dorset
101 K2 **Colesden** Beds
105 J5 **Coles Green** Suffk
122 F7 **Cole's Green** Suffk
96 C3 **Coles Green** Worcs
82 E7 **Coleshill** Bucks
61 H2 **Coleshill** Oxon
114 E2 **Coleshill** Warwks
49 J3 **Coles Meads** Surrey
25 K6 **Colestocks** Devon
78 C4 **Colethrop** Gloucs
42 E2 **Coley** BaNES
176 E2 **Coley** Calder
63 H6 **Coley** Readg
49 H7 **Colgate** W Susx
255 J4 **Colgrain** Ag & B
64 E4 **Colham Green** Gt Lon
65 H3 **Colindale** Gt Lon
269 H7 **Colinsburgh** Fife
259 G7 **Colinton** C Edin
254 C6 **Colintraive** Ag & B
141 J6 **Colkirk** Norfk
268 C1 **Collace** P & K
77 K4 **Collafield** Gloucs
331 D9 **Collafirth** Shet
331 F12 **Collafirth** Shet
323 K6 **Collam** W Isls
11 H3 **Collamoor Head** Cnwll
8 B7 **Collaton** Devon
8 E2 **Collaton St Mary** Torbay
243 J2 **College Milton** S Lans
311 Q4 **College of Roseisle** Moray
47 L1 **College Town** Br For
242 C7 **Collennan** S Ayrs
268 D5 **Collessie** Fife
24 B3 **Colleton Mills** Devon
135 K5 **Collett's Br** Cambs
96 D3 **Collett's Green** Worcs
66 C2 **Collier Row** Gt Lon
36 E2 **Collier's Green** E Susx
85 G6 **Colliers Hatch** Essex
51 H4 **Collier Street** Kent
65 J6 **Collier's Wood** Gt Lon
213 H4 **Colliery Row** Sundld
303 K3 **Collieston** Abers
222 C4 **Collin** D & G
45 H3 **Collingbourne Ducis** Wilts
45 H2 **Collingbourne Kingston** Wilts
186 C5 **Collingham** Leeds
154 F1 **Collingham** Notts
112 C7 **Collington** Herefs
100 B2 **Collingtree** Nhants
100 B2 **Collingtree Park** Nhants
227 H4 **Collingwood** Nthumb
63 G5 **Collins End** Oxon
163 L2 **Collins Green** Warrtn
96 B2 **Collins Green** Worcs
25 H4 **Collipriest** Devon
281 H5 **Colliston** Angus
25 K6 **Colliton** Devon
25 K6 **Colliton Cross** Devon
115 H2 **Collycroft** Warwks
268 D7 **Collydean** Fife
175 H8 **Collyhurst** Manch
302 F1 **Collynie** Abers
133 K6 **Collyweston** Nhants
218 E2 **Colmonell** S Ayrs
247 G6 **Colmslie** Border
247 G5 **Colmsliehill** Border
101 J2 **Colmworth** Beds
300 E7 **Colnabaichin** Abers
64 D5 **Colnbrook** Slough
119 H4 **Colne** Cambs
184 C7 **Colne** Lancs
184 C6 **Colne Edge** Lancs
104 E7 **Colne Engaine** Essex
119 H4 **Colnefields** Cambs
138 D5 **Colney** Norfk
65 J2 **Colney Hatch** Gt Lon
79 H5 **Coln Rogers** Gloucs
79 J5 **Coln St Aldwyns** Gloucs
79 H4 **Coln St Dennis** Gloucs
306 C6 **Colp** Abers
211 L2 **Colpitts Grange** Nthumb
302 B2 **Colpy** Abers
22 F4 **Colscott** Devon
165 K7 **Colshaw** Staffs
195 H5 **Colsterdale** N York
133 J2 **Colsterworth** Lincs
256 D7 **Colston** E Duns
8 C2 **Colston** Devon
88 F7 **Colston** Pembks
154 D7 **Colston Bassett** Notts
63 J3 **Colstrope** Bucks
311 Q5 **Coltfield** Moray
47 H3 **Colt Hill** Hants
201 K8 **Colthouse** Cumb
62 D7 **Colthrop** W Berk
138 F2 **Coltishall** Norfk
244 C2 **Coltness** N Lans
191 G3 **Colton** Cumb
186 C8 **Colton** Leeds
138 C5 **Colton** Norfk
186 F6 **Colton** N York
129 L2 **Colton** Staffs
121 H6 **Colton** Suffk
129 J7 **Colton Hills** Wolves
190 F6 **Colt Park** Cumb
59 H4 **Colt's Green** S Glos
50 F5 **Colt's Hill** Kent
325 N7 **Col Uarach** W Isls
213 H2 **Columbia** Sundld
25 H7 **Columbjohn** Devon
94 B3 **Colva** Powys
217 J3 **Colvend** D & G
330 H6 **Colvister** Shet
96 B5 **Colwall** Herefs
96 C5 **Colwall Green** Herefs
96 C5 **Colwall Stone** Herefs
20 D4 **Colwell** IoW
225 L4 **Colwell** Nthumb
129 L2 **Colwich** Staffs
154 B5 **Colwick** Notts
56 B5 **Colwinston** V Glam
33 H6 **Colworth** W Susx
117 K7 **Colworth Ho** Beds
160 F5 **Colwyn Bay** Conwy
16 B3 **Colyford** Devon
15 L3 **Colyton** Devon
235 K8 **Comb** Nthumb
7 H4 **Combe** Devon
8 B7 **Combe** Devon
50 F8 **Combe** E Susx
111 G7 **Combe** Herefs
80 E3 **Combe** Oxon
42 B8 **Combe** Somset
45 L1 **Combe** W Berk
29 H7 **Combe Almer** Dorset
12 F4 **Combebow** Devon
48 B6 **Combe Common** Surrey
43 J1 **Combe Down** BaNES
8 D2 **Combe Fishacre** Devon
40 F7 **Combe Florey** Somset
43 H2 **Combe Hay** BaNES
14 E7 **Combeinteignhead** Devon
38 E4 **Combe Martin** Devon
111 H7 **Combe Moor** Herefs
8 F1 **Combe Pafford** Torbay
26 B6 **Combe Raleigh** Devon
164 B5 **Comberbach** Ches
130 D5 **Comberford** Staffs
102 E2 **Comberton** Cambs
111 K6 **Comberton** Herefs
113 G4 **Comberton** Worcs
26 E4 **Combe St Nicholas** Somset
28 C2 **Combe Throop** Somset
16 B3 **Combpyne** Devon
38 D7 **Combrew** Devon
151 L6 **Combridge** Staffs
98 D3 **Combrook** Warwks
165 K5 **Combs** Derbys
177 G4 **Combs** Kirk
105 H2 **Combs** Suffk
105 J2 **Combs Ford** Suffk
41 H5 **Combwich** Somset
302 C7 **Comers** Abers
3 L2 **Come-to-Good** Cnwll
26 B2 **Comeytrowe** Somset
3 J3 **Comford** Cnwll
3 J5 **Comfort** Cnwll
113 G6 **Comhampton** Worcs
108 C3 **Comins Coch** Cerdgn
259 G7 **Comiston** C Edin
127 K7 **Comley** Shrops
119 L7 **Commercial End** Cambs
161 L8 **Commins** Denbgs
125 G6 **Commins Coch** Powys
57 K2 **Common Cefn-llwyn** Mons
206 E5 **Commondale** N York
182 B8 **Common Edge** Lancs
200 C3 **Common End** Cumb
167 H8 **Common End** Derbys
95 J7 **Common Hill** Herefs
11 J8 **Common Moor** Cnwll
60 F3 **Common Platt** Wilts
163 K6 **Commonside** Ches
163 L7 **Common Side** Ches
152 D5 **Commonside** Notts
153 H4 **Common Side** Derbys
153 J2 **Commonside** Derbys
166 F5 **Common Side** Derbys
83 G6 **Commonwood** Herts
149 J8 **Commonwood** Shrops
149 G3 **Commonwood** Wrexhm
58 B3 **Common-y-coed** Mons
50 F2 **Comp** Kent
41 J7 **Compass** Somset
165 J2 **Compstall** Stockp
7 G3 **Compton** C Plym
152 C4 **Compton** Derbys
8 E2 **Compton** Devon
31 H1 **Compton** Hants
45 K8 **Compton** Hants
186 C6 **Compton** Leeds
113 G3 **Compton** Staffs
47 L4 **Compton** Wolves
48 C4 **Compton** Surrey
62 D4 **Compton** W Berk
44 F3 **Compton** Wilts
129 H7 **Compton** Wolves
28 F3 **Compton Abbas** Dorset
79 H3 **Compton Abdale** Gloucs
60 D6 **Compton Bassett** Wilts
61 J3 **Compton Beauchamp** Oxon
41 L2 **Compton Bishop** Somset
44 D8 **Compton Chamberlayne** Wilts
58 F8 **Compton Common** BaNES
58 F8 **Compton Dando** BaNES
42 C7 **Compton Dundon** Somset
27 G3 **Compton Durville** Somset
31 H1 **Compton End** Hants
96 B8 **Compton Green** Gloucs
58 E4 **Compton Greenfield** S Glos
42 D2 **Compton Martin** BaNES
27 L1 **Compton Pauncefoot** Somset
17 H3 **Compton Valence** Dorset
258 C3 **Comrie** Fife
266 D3 **Comrie** P & K
178 B8 **Conanby** Rothm
254 C3 **Conchra** Ag & B
213 H2 **Concord** Sundld
167 G2 **Concord Park** Sheff
279 G6 **Concraigie** P & K
182 E3 **Conder Green** Lancs
97 G6 **Conderton** Worcs
97 K8 **Condicote** Gloucs
257 G6 **Condorrat** N Lans
127 K5 **Condover** Shrops
16 F3 **Coneygar** Dorset
65 L8 **Coney Hall** Gt Lon
78 C3 **Coney Hill** Gloucs
34 B2 **Coneyhurst** W Susx
197 J7 **Coneysthorpe** N York
186 C3 **Coneythorpe** N York
121 J4 **Coney Weston** Suffk
47 K7 **Conford** Hants
11 K6 **Congdon's Shop** Cnwll
221 K6 **Congeith** D & G
51 G4 **Congelow** Kent
131 H5 **Congerstone** Leics
140 E7 **Congham** Norfk
165 G8 **Congleton** Ches
151 G1 **Congleton Edge** Ches
146 D5 **Congl-y-wal** Gwynd
58 B8 **Congresbury** N Som
129 J4 **Congreve** Staffs
58 F6 **Conham** S Glos
311 M7 **Conicavel** Moray
156 D2 **Coningsby** Lincs
118 D2 **Conington** Cambs
178 C8 **Conisbrough** Donc
251 D10 **Conisby** Ag & B
171 G1 **Conisholme** Lincs
201 J8 **Coniston** Cumb
189 J7 **Coniston** E R Yk
184 D4 **Coniston Cold** N York
184 E1 **Conistone** N York
43 J1 **Conkwell** Wilts
162 E7 **Connah's Quay** Flints
274 D8 **Connel** Ag & B
231 G4 **Connel Park** E Ayrs
100 D5 **Conniburrow** M Keyn
292 G2 **Connista** Highld
5 L2 **Connon** Cnwll
2 F3 **Connor Downs** Cnwll
44 E2 **Conock** Wilts
310 C7 **Conon Bridge** Highld
184 E5 **Cononley** N York
184 E5 **Cononley Woodside** N York
281 G5 **Cononsyth** Angus
292 J9 **Conordan** Highld
128 D3 **Conquermoor Heath** Wrekin
151 J4 **Consall** Staffs
212 C3 **Consett** Dur
195 J3 **Constable Burton** N York
175 H3 **Constable Lee** Lancs
3 J5 **Constantine** Cnwll
10 B7 **Constantine Bay** Cnwll
310 A6 **Contin** Highld
291 J1 **Contlaw** C Aber
160 D5 **Conwy** Conwy
68 C8 **Conyer** Kent
121 H6 **Conyer's Green** Suffk
36 D5 **Cooden** E Susx
23 G5 **Cookbury** Devon
22 F5 **Cookbury Wick** Devon
63 L4 **Cookham** W & M
63 L4 **Cookham Dean** W & M
63 L4 **Cookham Rise** W & M
97 H2 **Cookhill** Worcs
225 L5 **Cooklaw** Nthumb
123 H4 **Cookley** Suffk
113 G3 **Cookley** Worcs
63 G2 **Cookley Green** Oxon
291 K3 **Cookney** Abers
185 K6 **Cookridge** Leeds
35 H4 **Cooksbridge** E Susx
113 J6 **Cooksey Corner** Worcs
113 H6 **Cooksey Green** Worcs
87 K3 **Cook's Green** Essex
105 G3 **Cook's Green** Suffk
151 H5 **Cookshill** Staffs
5 J1 **Cooksland** Cnwll
85 J5 **Cooksmill Green** Essex
163 L6 **Cooksongreen** Ches
34 B2 **Coolham** W Susx
49 G8 **Coolhurst Wood** W Susx
67 J5 **Cooling** Medway
53 H6 **Coolinge** Kent
67 H6 **Cooling Street** Medway
82 C5 **Coombe** Bucks
3 G2 **Coombe** Cnwll
3 K2 **Coombe** Cnwll
3 L2 **Coombe** Cnwll
4 F4 **Coombe** Cnwll
6 B2 **Coombe** Cnwll
22 C4 **Coombe** Cnwll
14 E7 **Coombe** Devon
15 J3 **Coombe** Dorset
25 J3 **Coombe** Devon
16 D2 **Coombe** Dorset
59 J2 **Coombe** Gloucs
65 G6 **Coombe** Gt Lon
32 C2 **Coombe** Hants
53 J2 **Coombe** Kent
27 G5 **Coombe** Somset
28 F2 **Coombe** Wilts
44 F3 **Coombe** Wilts
29 L1 **Coombe Bissett** Wilts
58 D5 **Coombe Dingle** Bristl
78 D1 **Coombe Hill** Gloucs
18 C5 **Coombe Keynes** Dorset
15 H2 **Coombelake** Devon
34 C5 **Coombes** W Susx
150 E6 **Coombesdale** Staffs
113 K2 **Coombeswood** Dudley
67 G8 **Coomb Hill** Kent
59 H4 **Coombs End** S Glos
26 E5 **Coombses** Somset
84 F6 **Coopersale Common** Essex
50 C4 **Cooper's Corner** Kent
35 J2 **Cooper's Green** E Susx
83 K5 **Cooper's Green** Herts
101 H6 **Cooper's Hill** Beds
64 C6 **Cooper's Hill** Surrey
53 K2 **Cooper Street** Kent
174 D6 **Cooper Turning** Bolton
33 L4 **Cootham** W Susx
113 H7 **Copcut** Worcs
105 K5 **Copdock** Suffk
60 E4 **Coped Hall** Wilts
161 J7 **Copenhagen** Denbgs
86 E2 **Copford** Essex
86 E2 **Copford Green** Essex
186 B2 **Copgrove** N York
331 G10 **Copister** Shet
307 L6 **Coplandhill** Abers
101 K4 **Cople** Beds
176 D3 **Copley** Calder
204 D2 **Copley** Dur
176 B8 **Copley** Tamesd
177 G2 **Copley Hill** Kirk
166 C5 **Coplow Dale** Derbys
187 G5 **Copmanthorpe** York
150 F8 **Copmere End** Staffs
32 C6 **Copnor** C Port
182 D7 **Copp** Lancs
22 C6 **Coppathorne** Cnwll
150 D2 **Coppenhall** Ches
129 J3 **Coppenhall** Staffs
150 D2 **Coppenhall Moss** Ches
2 F3 **Copperhouse** Cnwll
175 K7 **Coppice** Oldham
112 E3 **Coppicegate** Shrops
118 D3 **Coppingford** Cambs
52 B4 **Coppins Corner** Kent
40 B7 **Coppleham** Somset
24 D6 **Copplestone** Devon
174 C5 **Coppull** Lancs
174 C5 **Coppull Moor** Lancs
34 C2 **Copsale** W Susx
65 H6 **Copse Hill** Gt Lon
183 J8 **Copster Green** Lancs
115 K2 **Copston Magna** Warwks
53 J2 **Cop Street** Kent
114 D6 **Copt Green** Warwks
84 E6 **Copthall Green** Essex
114 D4 **Copt Heath** Solhll
196 B7 **Copt Hewick** N York
211 J5 **Copthill** Dur
150 B5 **Copthorne** Ches
11 K3 **Copthorne** Cnwll
127 K4 **Copthorne** Shrops
49 K6 **Copthorne** W Susx
149 H6 **Coptiviney** Shrops
131 K4 **Copt Oak** Leics
52 D2 **Copton** Kent
141 J4 **Copy's Green** Norfk
30 E4 **Copythorne** Hants
287 J2 **Corarnstilbeg** Highld
66 E3 **Corbets Tey** Gt Lon
16 f7 **Corbiere** Jersey
226 B7 **Corbridge** Nthumb
167 H7 **Corbriggs** Derbys
117 H2 **Corby** Nhants
133 L1 **Corby Glen** Lincs
209 L2 **Corby Hill** Cumb
241 G7 **Cordon** N Ayrs
138 C8 **Cordwell** Norfk
112 C5 **Coreley** Shrops
64 B3 **Cores End** Bucks
26 C3 **Corfe** Somset
18 F5 **Corfe Castle** Dorset
18 F2 **Corfe Mullen** Dorset
263 J1 **Corfhouse** Ag & B
111 K3 **Corfton** Shrops
111 K2 **Corfton Bache** Shrops
300 E7 **Corgarff** Abers
5 H2 **Corgee** Cnwll
31 K3 **Corhampton** Hants
231 H7 **Corlae** D & G
55 J3 **Corlannau** Neath
114 F2 **Corley** Warwks
114 F2 **Corley Ash** Warwks
114 F3 **Corley Moor** Covtry
251 E13 **Cornabus** Ag & B
270 B5 **Cornaigbeg** Ag & B
270 B5 **Cornaigmore** Ag & B
104 E5 **Cornard Tye** Suffk
245 L1 **Cornbank** Mdloth
112 C4 **Cornbrook** Shrops
182 D7 **Corner Row** Lancs
95 J4 **Cornett** Herefs
190 C2 **Corney** Cumb
213 H7 **Cornforth** Dur
305 K4 **Cornhill** Abers
303 H7 **Cornhill** C Aber
151 G3 **Cornhill** C Stke
314 E8 **Cornhill** Highld
93 K5 **Cornhill** Powys
248 D6 **Cornhill on Tweed** Nthumb
175 J2 **Cornholme** Calder
103 L6 **Cornish Hall End** Essex
327 M5 **Cornquoy** Ork
211 H5 **Cornriggs** Dur
212 D5 **Cornsay** Dur
212 E5 **Cornsay Colliery** Dur
257 H1 **Cornton** Stirlg
310 D6 **Corntown** Highld
56 B5 **Corntown** V Glam
80 B1 **Cornwell** Oxon
7 K3 **Cornwood** Devon
8 D3 **Cornworthy** Devon
284 D6 **Corpach** Highld
142 E6 **Corpusty** Norfk
274 F2 **Corran** Highld
295 G7 **Corran** Highld
172 h5 **Corrany** IoM
241 G5 **Corrie** N Ayrs
223 G2 **Corrie Common** D & G
228 C2 **Corriecravie** N Ayrs
220 F3 **Corriedoo** D & G
309 P5 **Corriemoillie** Highld
298 E4 **Corrievorrie** Highld
328 D10 **Corrigall** Ork
297 G2 **Corrimony** Highld
169 G2 **Corringham** Lincs
67 H4 **Corringham** Thurr
124 F5 **Corris** Gwynd
124 E5 **Corris Uchaf** Gwynd
264 B7 **Corrow** Ag & B
294 B4 **Corry** Highld
279 H1 **Corrydon** P & K
316 H11 **Corrykinloch** Highld
278 C8 **Corrymuckloch** P & K
272 F6 **Corrynachenchy** Ag & B
310 B8 **Corry of Ardnagrask** Highld
319 M2 **Corsback** Highld
13 J2 **Corscombe** Devon
27 J5 **Corscombe** Dorset
305 K7 **Corse** Abers
96 C8 **Corse** Gloucs
96 D7 **Corse Lawn** Worcs
59 L7 **Corsham** Wilts
267 L3 **Corsiehill** P & K
302 C7 **Corsindae** Abers
43 K4 **Corsley** Wilts
43 K4 **Corsley Heath** Wilts
221 H4 **Corsock** D & G
59 G7 **Corston** BaNES
60 B4 **Corston** Wilts
259 G6 **Corstorphine** C Edin
280 C3 **Cortachy** Angus
139 L7 **Corton** Suffk
44 B5 **Corton** Wilts
27 L2 **Corton Denham** Somset
177 L8 **Cortworth** Rothm
147 L5 **Corwen** Denbgs
22 F3 **Cory** Devon
17 J4 **Coryates** Dorset
56 F4 **Coryton** Cardif
12 F5 **Coryton** Devon
26 D7 **Coryton** Devon
67 H4 **Coryton** Thurr
131 L7 **Cosby** Leics
62 D3 **Coscote** Oxon
129 J8 **Coseley** Dudley
115 K4 **Cosford** Warwks
100 C5 **Cosgrove** Nhants
32 C5 **Cosham** C Port
252 F4 **Coshandrochaid** Ag & B
70 F6 **Cosheston** Pembks
57 G7 **Cosmeston** V Glam
28 B5 **Cosmore** Dorset
153 J5 **Cossall** Notts
153 J5 **Cossall Marsh** Notts
132 C4 **Cossington** Leics
41 L5 **Cossington** Somset
328 D8 **Costa** Ork
138 D4 **Costessey** Norfk
138 D4 **Costessey Park** Norfk
167 L3 **Costhorpe** Notts
10 E7 **Costislost** Cnwll
132 B1 **Costock** Notts
133 H2 **Coston** Leics
138 B5 **Coston** Norfk
3 G3 **Coswinsawsin** Cnwll
80 D6 **Cote** Oxon
41 K5 **Cote** Somset
34 B5 **Cote** W Susx
163 L7 **Cotebrook** Ches
202 F7 **Cotegill** Cumb
209 L3 **Cotehill** Cumb
192 E4 **Cotes** Cumb
132 B2 **Cotes** Leics
150 F7 **Cotes** Staffs
115 L3 **Cotesbach** Leics
150 F7 **Cotes Heath** Staffs
153 H3 **Cotes Park** Derbys
15 J3 **Cotford** Devon
154 B6 **Cotgrave** Notts
303 G5 **Cothall** Abers
58 E6 **Cotham** Bristl
154 E4 **Cotham** Notts
41 G7 **Cothelstone** Somset
96 C3 **Cotheridge** Worcs
204 C4 **Cotherstone** Dur
80 F7 **Cothill** Oxon
77 G6 **Cotland** Mons
26 B6 **Cotleigh** Devon
153 J5 **Cotmanhay** Derbys
60 E5 **Cotmarsh** Wilts
15 J4 **Cotmaton** Devon
102 F2 **Coton** Cambs
116 D5 **Coton** Nhants
149 K7 **Coton** Shrops
129 G2 **Coton** Staffs
130 D6 **Coton** Staffs
151 J7 **Coton** Staffs
129 H2 **Coton Clanford** Staffs
151 J7 **Coton Hayes** Staffs
127 K4 **Coton Hill** Shrops
151 J7 **Coton Hill** Staffs
152 C8 **Coton in the Clay** Staffs
130 E3 **Coton in the Elms** Derbys
130 F3 **Coton Park** Derbys
149 K6 **Cotonwood** Shrops
129 G2 **Cotonwood** Staffs
79 G7 **Cotswold Community** Wilts
8 C2 **Cott** Devon
182 F8 **Cottam** Lancs
168 F5 **Cottam** Notts
299 K2 **Cottartown** Highld
119 J6 **Cottenham** Cambs
65 H7 **Cottenham Park** Gt Lon
194 B3 **Cotterdale** N York
102 D8 **Cottered** Herts
167 L4 **Cotterhill Woods** Rothm
113 L3 **Cotteridge** Birm
117 L1 **Cotterstock** Nhants
116 D5 **Cottesbrooke** Nhants
133 J4 **Cottesmore** Rutlnd
25 G4 **Cotteylands** Devon
180 C1 **Cottingham** E R Yk
117 G1 **Cottingham** Nhants
185 H7 **Cottingley** Brad
99 J7 **Cottisford** Oxon
151 L4 **Cotton** Staffs
122 B6 **Cotton** Suffk
101 J4 **Cotton End** Beds
100 B2 **Cotton End** Nhants
280 D7 **Cotton of Brighty** Angus
281 G5 **Cotton of Gardyne** Angus
176 C3 **Cotton Stones** Calder
184 D7 **Cotton Tree** Lancs
45 L6 **Cottonworth** Hants
301 K3 **Cottown** Abers
302 E5 **Cottown** Abers
306 E7 **Cottown** Abers
268 C3 **Cottown** P & K
6 F1 **Cotts** Devon
23 L4 **Cottwood** Devon
128 C3 **Cotwall** Wrekin
151 H7 **Cotwalton** Staffs
328 E10 **Coubister** Ork
46 D7 **Couch Green** Hants
5 K3 **Couch's Mill** Cnwll
77 H2 **Coughton** Herefs
114 B7 **Coughton** Warwks
97 J2 **Coughton Fields** Warwks
308 G8 **Coulags** Highld
206 C5 **Coulby Newham** Middsb
200 B6 **Coulderton** Cumb
308 H6 **Coulin Lodge** Highld
301 K8 **Coull** Abers
292 G7 **Coulnacraggan** Highld
310 B7 **Coul of Fairburn** Highld
255 G3 **Coulport** Ag & B
49 J2 **Coulsdon** Gt Lon
44 C3 **Coulston** Wilts
245 G7 **Coulter** S Lans
41 H5 **Coultings** Somset
197 H7 **Coulton** N York
128 B6 **Cound** Shrops
128 B6 **Coundlane** Shrops
128 B6 **Coundmoor** Shrops
115 G3 **Coundon** Covtry
205 G2 **Coundon** Dur
205 G2 **Coundongate** Dur
205 G2 **Coundon Grange** Dur
83 G5 **Counters End** Herts
194 D4 **Countersett** N York
104 E7 **Countess Cross** Essex
14 E3 **Countess Wear** Devon
132 B7 **Countesthorpe** Leics
39 H4 **Countisbury** Devon
279 K6 **Coupar Angus** P & K
174 C2 **Coup Green** Lancs
203 G4 **Coupland** Cumb
248 E7 **Coupland** Nthumb
239 K4 **Cour** Ag & B
222 D1 **Courance** D & G
40 F7 **Coursley** Somset
52 E6 **Court-at-Street** Kent
14 C4 **Court Barton** Devon
55 L5 **Court Colman** Brdgnd
46 F2 **Court Corner** Hants
282 F2 **Courteachan** Highld
100 C3 **Courteenhall** Nhants
73 H4 **Court Henry** Carmth
163 H2 **Court Hey** Knows
115 H3 **Court House Green** Covtry
16 F3 **Court Orchard** Dorset
68 D2 **Courtsend** Essex
41 H7 **Courtway** Somset
259 K7 **Cousland** Mdloth
51 G7 **Cousley Wood** E Susx
332 F7 **Cova** Shet
255 G4 **Cove** Ag & B
261 H6 **Cove** Border
25 H3 **Cove** Devon
47 K2 **Cove** Hants
312 C8 **Cove** Highld
291 L1 **Cove Bay** C Aber
123 K4 **Cove Bottom** Suffk
123 L3 **Covehithe** Suffk
129 J5 **Coven** Staffs
95 K5 **Covender** Herefs
119 K3 **Coveney** Cambs
170 F2 **Covenham St Bartholomew** Lincs
170 F2 **Covenham St Mary** Lincs
129 J5 **Coven Heath** Staffs
129 H5 **Coven Lawn** Staffs
115 G4 **Coventry** Covtry
3 K7 **Coverack** Cnwll
3 H4 **Coverack Bridges** Cnwll
195 H4 **Coverham** N York
304 B1 **Covesea** Moray
61 G4 **Covingham** Swindn
118 B5 **Covington** Cambs
244 F6 **Covington** S Lans
193 H6 **Cowan Bridge** Lancs
183 J5 **Cow Ark** Lancs
36 B4 **Cowbeech** E Susx
36 B4 **Cowbeech Hill** E Susx
134 F3 **Cowbit** Lincs
156 F4 **Cowbridge** Lincs
56 C6 **Cowbridge** V Glam
176 E4 **Cowcliffe** Kirk
50 C5 **Cowden** Kent
266 D3 **Cowden** P & K
258 F2 **Cowdenbeath** Fife
192 E2 **Cowen Head** Cumb
152 F4 **Cowers Lane** Derbys
21 G2 **Cowes** IoW
196 E3 **Cowesby** N York
30 D2 **Cowesfield Green** Wilts
87 H1 **Cowey Green** Essex
34 D2 **Cowfold** W Susx
193 L4 **Cowgill** Cumb
122 B6 **Cow Green** Suffk
29 H7 **Cowgrove** Dorset
153 G4 **Cowhill** Derbys
183 G8 **Cow Hill** Lancs
58 E2 **Cowhill** S Glos
59 G6 **Cowhorn Hill** S Glos
291 K4 **Cowie** Abers
257 J3 **Cowie** Stirlg
256 E7 **Cowlairs** C Glas
3 L2 **Cowlands** Cnwll
80 C6 **Cowleaze Corner** Oxon
166 F5 **Cowley** Derbys
14 D2 **Cowley** Devon
78 F4 **Cowley** Gloucs
64 E4 **Cowley** Gt Lon
81 G6 **Cowley** Oxon
25 H4 **Cowleymoor** Devon
64 E4 **Cowley Peachy** Gt Lon
174 C4 **Cowling** Lancs
184 E6 **Cowling** N York
195 K4 **Cowling** N York
104 B3 **Cowlinge** Suffk
165 L6 **Cowlow** Derbys
176 F4 **Cowmes** Kirk
175 H3 **Cowpe** Lancs
227 H3 **Cowpen** Nthumb
206 B3 **Cowpen Bewley** S on T
32 C4 **Cowplain** Hants
82 F4 **Cow Roast** Herts
211 J5 **Cowshill** Dur
42 C1 **Cowslip Green** N Som
258 C2 **Cowstrandburn** Fife
186 D4 **Cowthorpe** N York
111 H5 **Coxall** Herefs
150 C5 **Coxbank** Ches
153 G5 **Coxbench** Derbys
42 D6 **Coxbridge** Somset
123 H3 **Cox Common** Suffk
257 H2 **Coxet Hill** Stirlg
11 H2 **Coxford** Cnwll
30 F4 **Coxford** C Sotn
141 G6 **Coxford** Norfk
174 F5 **Cox Green** Bolton
112 F2 **Coxgreen** Staffs
48 E7 **Cox Green** Surrey
63 L5 **Cox Green** W & M
51 H3 **Coxheath** Kent
3 J2 **Cox Hill** Cnwll
213 H6 **Coxhoe** Dur
42 D5 **Coxley** Somset
177 H4 **Coxley** Wakefd
42 D5 **Coxley Wick** Somset
227 G6 **Coxlodge** N u Ty
153 K2 **Cox Moor** Notts
12 D7 **Coxpark** Cnwll
85 H7 **Coxtie Green** Essex
196 F6 **Coxwold** N York
56 B5 **Coychurch** Brdgnd
230 C2 **Coylton** S Ayrs
299 H6 **Coylumbridge** Highld
301 H7 **Coynach** Abers
301 J2 **Coynachie** Abers
55 L4 **Coytrahên** Brdgnd
49 K6 **Crabbet Park** W Susx
53 J5 **Crabble** Kent
113 L7 **Crabbs Cross** Worcs
102 F8 **Crabbs Green** Herts
142 D6 **Crabgate** Norfk
29 K5 **Crab Orchard** Dorset
7 H3 **Crabtree** C Plym
34 D1 **Crabtree** W Susx
148 F5 **Crabtree Green** Wrexhm
202 F3 **Crackenthorpe** Cumb
11 G2 **Crackington Haven** Cnwll
150 F3 **Crackley** Staffs
114 F5 **Crackley** Warwks
128 F4 **Crackleybank** Shrops
30 F4 **Cracknore Hard** Hants
194 E2 **Crackpot** N York
121 L4 **Crackthorn Corner** Suffk
184 E2 **Cracoe** N York
150 E4 **Cracow Moss** Staffs
25 K4 **Craddock** Devon
324 D8 **Cradhlastadh** W Isls
185 G7 **Cradle Edge** Brad
84 F2 **Cradle End** Herts
113 J3 **Cradley** Dudley
96 B4 **Cradley** Herefs
113 J2 **Cradley Heath** Sandw
93 H7 **Cradoc** Powys
6 E4 **Crafthole** Cnwll
82 D3 **Crafton** Bucks
251 E14 **Cragabus** Ag & B
192 E7 **Crag Bank** Lancs
192 E7 **Crag Foot** Lancs
299 K3 **Craggan** Highld
265 K3 **Craggan** Stirlg
300 C1 **Cragganmore** Moray
315 L3 **Craggie** Highld
176 C3 **Cragg Vale** Calder
212 F3 **Craghead** Dur
3 H4 **Crahan** Cnwll
74 D2 **Crai** Powys
305 H4 **Craibstone** Moray
280 E5 **Craichie** Angus
220 F4 **Craig** D & G
308 H8 **Craig** Highld
75 H7 **Craig Berthlwyd** Myr Td
73 K8 **Craig-cefn-parc** Swans
268 D2 **Craigdallie** P & K
302 F2 **Craigdam** Abers
231 G5 **Craigdarroch** E Ayrs
310 A6 **Craigdarroch** Highld
262 E6 **Craigdhu** Ag & B
215 J5 **Craigdhu** D & G
233 K2 **Craig Douglas** Border
302 D6 **Craigearn** Abers
304 D7 **Craigellachie** Moray
281 G7 **Craigend** Angus
246 F4 **Craigend** Border
256 F7 **Craigend** C Glas
267 L3 **Craigend** P & K
257 H3 **Craigend** Stirlg
255 J4 **Craigendoran** Ag & B
255 L7 **Craigends** Rens
251 D9 **Craigens** Ag & B
230 F3 **Craigens** E Ayrs
259 H5 **Craigentinny** C Edin
245 L6 **Craigerne** Border
291 J3 **Craiggie Cat** Abers
279 J5 **Craighall** P & K
256 B4 **Craighat** Stirlg
305 H7 **Craighead** Abers
252 C7 **Craighouse** Ag & B
303 H5 **Craigie** Abers
269 G1 **Craigie** C Dund
267 L3 **Craigie** P & K
279 H6 **Craigie** P & K
229 L2 **Craigie** S Ayrs
242 E7 **Craigie** S Ayrs
303 G7 **Craigiebuckler** C Aber
258 F5 **Craigiehall** C Edin
259 L5 **Craigielaw** E Loth
233 J2 **Craigierig** Border
259 G6 **Craigleith** C Edin
73 L7 **Craig Llangiwg** Neath
148 D8 **Craig-llwyn** Shrops
259 G6 **Craiglockhart** C Edin
230 D8 **Craigmalloch** E Ayrs
306 F4 **Craigmaud** Abers
281 G7 **Craigmill** Angus
257 J1 **Craigmill** Stirlg
259 H6 **Craigmillar** C Edin
254 E7 **Craigmore** Ag & B
148 E6 **Craignant** Wrexhm
244 B2 **Craigneuk** N Lans
257 H7 **Craigneuk** N Lans
273 H7 **Craignure** Ag & B
281 J2 **Craigo** Angus
267 K6 **Craigow** P & K
310 E8 **Craigrory** Highld
268 F5 **Craigrothie** Fife
265 H3 **Craigruie** Stirlg
104 B6 **Craig's End** Essex
247 H6 **Craigsford Mains** Border
258 D7 **Craigshill** W Loth
212 D6 **Craigside** Dur
280 B4 **Craigton** Angus
280 F7 **Craigton** Angus
291 J1 **Craigton** C Aber
256 C8 **Craigton** C Glas
310 F8 **Craigton** Highld
314 F7 **Craigton** Highld
318 E5 **Craigtown** Highld
159 K6 **Craig-y-don** IoA
73 L8 **Craig-y-Duke** Neath
74 C3 **Craig-y-nos** Powys
124 C8 **Craig-y-penrhyn** Cerdgn
57 G3 **Craig-y-Rhacca** Caerph
233 L5 **Craik** Border
269 L6 **Crail** Fife
235 H2 **Crailing** Border
235 J2 **Crailinghall** Border
195 K3 **Crakehall** N York
196 D7 **Crakehill** N York
151 L6 **Crakemarsh** Staffs
233 H2 **Cramalt** Border
187 K2 **Crambe** N York
187 K1 **Crambeck** N York
48 B5 **Cramhurst** Surrey
227 H4 **Cramlington** Nthumb
258 F5 **Cramond** C Edin
258 F5 **Cramond Bridge** C Edin
30 F2 **Crampmoor** Hants
164 D7 **Cranage** Ches
150 F6 **Cranberry** Staffs
29 K4 **Cranborne** Dorset
64 B6 **Cranbourne** Br For
46 F3 **Cranbourne** Hants
66 B3 **Cranbrook** Gt Lon
51 J6 **Cranbrook** Kent
51 J6 **Cranbrook Common** Kent
177 J7 **Crane Moor** Barns
67 H2 **Cranes** Essex
137 J4 **Crane's Corner** Norfk
101 G5 **Cranfield** Beds
22 E2 **Cranford** Devon
64 F5 **Cranford** Gt Lon
117 J4 **Cranford St Andrew** Nhants
117 J4 **Cranford St John** Nhants
78 D4 **Cranham** Gloucs
66 E3 **Cranham** Gt Lon
256 E7 **Cranhill** C Glas
97 K3 **Cranhill** Warwks
174 B8 **Crank** St Hel
174 D7 **Crankwood** Wigan
48 E6 **Cranleigh** Surrey
122 D5 **Cranley** Suffk
65 J3 **Cranley Gardens** Gt Lon
304 D4 **Cranloch** Moray
121 L5 **Cranmer Green** Suffk
20 E3 **Cranmore** IoW
43 G5 **Cranmore** Somset
305 H5 **Crannoch** Moray
132 F7 **Cranoe** Leics
123 G7 **Cransford** Suffk
247 K1 **Cranshaws** Border
172 h2 **Cranstal** IoM
188 F4 **Cranswick** E R Yk
4 C2 **Crantock** Cnwll
155 K4 **Cranwell** Lincs
136 F7 **Cranwich** Norfk
137 K6 **Cranworth** Norfk
262 D6 **Craobh Haven** Ag & B
13 G8 **Crapstone** Devon
254 B1 **Crarae** Ag & B
317 Q4 **Crask** Highld
301 K7 **Craskins** Abers
310 B9 **Crask of Aigas** Highld
237 K3 **Craster** Nthumb
94 C7 **Craswall** Herefs
112 E2 **Crateford** Shrops
129 J5 **Crateford** Staffs
123 G4 **Cratfield** Suffk
291 H2 **Crathes** Abers
289 H2 **Crathie** Abers
286 D3 **Crathie** Highld
205 L6 **Crathorne** N York
111 J3 **Craven Arms** Shrops
226 E7 **Crawcrook** Gatesd
173 L7 **Crawford** Lancs
232 D2 **Crawford** S Lans
244 D4 **Crawforddyke** S Lans
232 B2 **Crawfordjohn** S Lans
231 K4 **Crawick** D & G
26 D5 **Crawley** Devon
46 B7 **Crawley** Hants
80 C4 **Crawley** Oxon
49 J6 **Crawley** W Susx
49 K6 **Crawley Down** W Susx
102 F6 **Crawley End** Essex
47 L2 **Crawley Hill** Surrey
211 L5 **Crawleyside** Dur
177 G5 **Crawshaw** Kirk
175 H2 **Crawshawbooth** Lancs
291 K6 **Crawton** Abers
332 C5 **Crawton** Shet
194 D6 **Cray** N York
279 H2 **Cray** P & K
66 D6 **Crayford** Gt Lon
197 G7 **Crayke** N York
142 C5 **Craymere Beck** Norfk
67 H2 **Crays Hill** Essex
62 F4 **Cray's Pond** Oxon
63 J4 **Crazies Hill** Wokham
24 E3 **Creacombe** Devon
274 E6 **Creagan** Ag & B
262 E7 **Creaganterve Mhòr** Ag & B
321 P5 **Creagastrom** W Isls
321 N5 **Creag Ghoraidh** W Isls
278 F2 **Creag na Cuinneige** P & K
149 K7 **Creamore Bank** Shrops
2 B6 **Crean** Cnwll
116 E5 **Creaton** Nhants
223 G5 **Creca** D & G
94 F5 **Credenhill** Herefs
24 E6 **Crediton** Devon
219 L6 **Creebridge** D & G
18 E5 **Creech** Dorset
18 E5 **Creech Bottom** Dorset
26 D1 **Creech Heathfield** Somset
26 D1 **Creech St Michael** Somset
4 F5 **Creed** Cnwll
331 J12 **Creediknowe** Shet
3 J2 **Creegbrawse** Cnwll
18 F3 **Creekmoor** Poole
66 C4 **Creekmouth** Gt Lon
86 E7 **Creeksea** Essex
105 K2 **Creeting Bottoms** Suffk
105 J2 **Creeting St Mary** Suffk
105 J2 **Creeting St Peter** Suffk
133 L2 **Creeton** Lincs
215 L2 **Creetown** D & G
263 K7 **Creggans** Ag & B
172 b9 **Cregneash** IoM
172 f6 **Cregny Baa** IoM
93 K3 **Cregrina** Powys
271 J10 **Creich** Ag & B
268 E3 **Creich** Fife
76 F7 **Creigau** Mons
151 L6 **Creighton** Staffs
56 E4 **Creigiau** Cardif
3 H4 **Crelly** Cnwll
6 F4 **Cremyll** Cnwll
29 K4 **Crendell** Dorset
292 G7 **Crepkill** Highld
82 C2 **Creslow** Bucks
128 B6 **Cressage** Shrops
166 C6 **Cressbrook** Derbys
71 H5 **Cresselly** Pembks
63 K2 **Cressex** Bucks
78 B6 **Cress Green** Gloucs
86 B3 **Cressing** Essex
237 K8 **Cresswell** Nthumb
151 J6 **Cresswell** Staffs
71 H5 **Cresswell Quay** Pembks
167 K6 **Creswell** Derbys
129 J2 **Creswell** Staffs
130 B4 **Creswell Green** Staffs
122 E7 **Cretingham** Suffk
253 G7 **Cretshengan** Ag & B
150 D3 **Crewe** Ches
149 H3 **Crewe-by-Farndon** Ches
210 D7 **Crewgarth** Cumb
127 G3 **Crewgreen** Powys
27 G5 **Crewkerne** Somset
84 C6 **Crews Hill** Gt Lon
58 F6 **Crew's Hole** Bristl
153 G7 **Crewton** C Derb
264 F2 **Crianlarich** Stirlg
58 E4 **Cribbs Causeway** S Glos
175 G3 **Cribden Side** Lancs
91 H5 **Cribyn** Cerdgn
145 J6 **Criccieth** Gwynd
153 G3 **Crich** Derbys
152 F3 **Crich Carr** Derbys
307 G7 **Crichie** Abers
246 D1 **Crichton** Mdloth
58 C2 **Crick** Mons
116 B5 **Crick** Nhants
93 J5 **Crickadarn** Powys
47 K2 **Cricket Hill** Hants
26 F4 **Cricket Malherbie** Somset
26 F5 **Cricket St Thomas** Somset
42 B4 **Crickham** Somset
126 F2 **Crickheath** Shrops
126 F2 **Crickheath Wharf** Shrops
75 L3 **Crickhowell** Powys
60 E2 **Cricklade** Wilts
65 H3 **Cricklewood** Gt Lon
150 C8 **Crickmery** Shrops
95 K3 **Crick's Green** Herefs
30 B4 **Criddlestyle** Hants
178 C3 **Cridling Stubbs** N York
21 G5 **Cridmore** IoW
266 F3 **Crieff** P & K
5 H2 **Criggan** Cnwll
126 F4 **Criggion** Powys
177 J4 **Crigglestone** Wakefd
175 J5 **Crimble** Rochdl
26 E5 **Crimchard** Somset
213 L6 **Crimdon Park** Dur
307 J4 **Crimond** Abers
307 J4 **Crimonmogate** Abers
22 C3 **Crimp** Cnwll
136 C6 **Crimplesham** Norfk
98 B4 **Crimscote** Warwks
253 H2 **Crinan** Ag & B
253 H2 **Crinan Ferry** Ag & B
57 K3 **Crindau** Newpt
244 C2 **Crindledyke** N Lans
138 D5 **Cringleford** Norfk
184 F5 **Cringles** Brad
245 L5 **Cringletie** Border
71 J4 **Crinow** Pembks
104 D7 **Cripple Corner** Essex
2 E3 **Cripplesease** Cnwll
29 K4 **Cripplestyle** Dorset
36 E2 **Cripp's Corner** E Susx
165 K4 **Crist** Derbys
30 D1 **Critchell's Green** Hants
43 J4 **Critchill** Somset
47 L7 **Critchmere** Surrey
51 J7 **Crit Hall** Kent
94 F7 **Crizeley** Herefs
10 E7 **Croanford** Cnwll
200 D4 **Croasdale** Cumb
66 D7 **Crockenhill** Kent
63 H3 **Crocker End** Oxon
31 K5 **Crockerhill** Hants
33 H5 **Crockerhill** W Susx
14 B3 **Crockernwell** Devon
38 E6 **Crockers** Devon
77 G3 **Crocker's Ash** Herefs
43 K5 **Crockerton** Wilts
43 K5 **Crockerton Green** Wilts
221 J5 **Crocketford** D & G
187 H5 **Crockey Hill** York
62 B8 **Crockham Heath** W Berk
50 B3 **Crockham Hill** Kent
50 F5 **Crockhurst Street** Kent
87 G1 **Crockleford Heath** Essex
326 H6 **Crockness** Ork
26 E4 **Crock Street** Somset
148 D8 **Croesau Bach** Shrops
74 D7 **Croeserw** Neath
88 C6 **Croes-goch** Pembks
76 C4 **Croes-Hywel** Mons
90 E7 **Croes-lan** Cerdgn
76 C5 **Croes Llanfair** Mons
146 B5 **Croesor** Gwynd
75 K7 **Croespenmaen** Caerph
161 L6 **Croes-wian** Flints
72 E5 **Croesyceiliog** Carmth
76 B7 **Croesyceiliog** Torfn
57 K2 **Croes-y-mwyalch** Torfn
76 C6 **Croes y pant** Mons
145 K2 **Croesywaun** Gwynd
23 G7 **Croft** Devon
111 K6 **Croft** Herefs
131 L7 **Croft** Leics
157 K1 **Croft** Lincs
164 B2 **Croft** Warrtn
256 B3 **Croftamie** Stirlg
243 H1 **Croftfoot** C Glas
277 K5 **Croftgarrow** P & K
3 J2 **Crofthandy** Cnwll
190 F5 **Croftlands** Cumb
257 L8 **Croftmalloch** W Loth
3 H3 **Croft Mitchell** Cnwll
310 E8 **Croftnacriech** Highld
209 H3 **Crofton** Cumb
66 B7 **Crofton** Gt Lon
177 K4 **Crofton** Wakefd
61 J8 **Crofton** Wilts
205 H6 **Croft-on-Tees** N York
268 C7 **Croft Outerly** Fife
164 E1 **Crofts Bank** Traffd
319 L9 **Crofts of Benachielt** Highld

378 City, town and village index: Drakeland Corner - Elton

7 J3 **Drakeland Corner** Devon
113 G3 **Drakelow** Worcs
307 H8 **Drakemyre** Abers
242 B3 **Drakemyre** N Ayrs
96 F4 **Drakes Broughton** Worcs
114 B4 **Drakes Cross** Worcs
105 G4 **Drakestone Green** Suffk
12 E7 **Drakewalls** Cnwll
116 F4 **Draughton** Nhants
184 F4 **Draughton** N York
5 L1 **Drawbridge** Cnwll
178 F2 **Drax** N York
81 J5 **Draycot** Oxon
60 B5 **Draycot Cerne** Wilts
115 J6 **Draycote** Warwks
60 F8 **Draycot Fitz Payne** Wilts
61 G5 **Draycot Foliat** Swindn
153 H7 **Draycott** Derbys
78 B6 **Draycott** Gloucs
97 L6 **Draycott** Gloucs
129 G8 **Draycott** Shrops
27 J2 **Draycott** Somset
42 C3 **Draycott** Somset
96 E4 **Draycott** Worcs
152 C8 **Draycott in the Clay** Staffs
151 J5 **Draycott in the Moors** Staffs
24 D4 **Drayford** Devon
32 C5 **Drayton** C Port
117 G1 **Drayton** Leics
156 D6 **Drayton** Lincs
116 B7 **Drayton** Nhants
138 D4 **Drayton** Norfk
62 C2 **Drayton** Oxon
98 F5 **Drayton** Oxon
27 G2 **Drayton** Somset
27 H3 **Drayton** Somset
97 L2 **Drayton** Warwks
113 J4 **Drayton** Worcs
130 D6 **Drayton Bassett** Staffs
82 E4 **Drayton Beauchamp** Bucks
100 D8 **Drayton Parslow** Bucks
81 H7 **Drayton St Leonard** Oxon
185 G3 **Drebley** N York
172 h4 **Dreemskerry** IoM
70 E4 **Dreenhill** Pembks
72 B4 **Drefach** Carmth
73 G6 **Drefach** Carmth
73 K5 **Dre-fach** Carmth
90 E8 **Drefach** Carmth
90 E8 **Drefelin** Carmth
299 K3 **Dreggie** Highld
259 G7 **Dreghorn** C Edin
242 C6 **Dreghorn** N Ayrs
161 L7 **Dre-gôch** Denbgs
53 H5 **Drellingore** Kent
260 C5 **Drem** E Loth
151 H5 **Dresden** C Stke
321 N7 **Dreumasdal** W Isls
13 L3 **Drewsteignton** Devon
171 G6 **Driby** Lincs
188 F3 **Driffield** E R Yk
79 H7 **Driffield** Gloucs
2 C5 **Drift** Cnwll
200 D8 **Drigg** Cumb
177 G2 **Drighlington** Leeds
253 G4 **Drimnagall** Ag & B
272 E4 **Drimnin** Highld
27 G6 **Drimpton** Dorset
264 B7 **Drimsynie** Ag & B
189 H3 **Dringhoe** E R Yk
187 G5 **Dringhouses** York
323 L6 **Drinisiadar** W Isls
121 K7 **Drinkstone** Suffk
121 K7 **Drinkstone Green** Suffk
27 K5 **Drive End** Dorset
294 C4 **Drochaid Lusa** Highld
129 L1 **Drointon** Staffs
113 H7 **Droitwich** Worcs
316 D5 **Droman** Highld
267 L4 **Dron** P & K
167 G5 **Dronfield** Derbys
166 F5 **Dronfield Woodhouse** Derbys
230 C3 **Drongan** E Ayrs
280 B7 **Dronley** Angus
28 D5 **Droop** Dorset
56 F5 **Drope** V Glam
167 G2 **Dropping Well** Rothm
31 K3 **Droxford** Hants
175 J8 **Droylsden** Tamesd
176 F2 **Drub** Kirk
96 C6 **Druggers End** Worcs
147 K5 **Druid** Denbgs
70 D3 **Druidston** Pembks
284 D7 **Druimarbin** Highld
274 F6 **Druimavuic** Ag & B
253 G6 **Druimdrishaig** Ag & B
282 F5 **Druimindarroch** Highld
310 B10 **Druimkinnerras** Highld
259 J7 **Drum** C Edin
267 J7 **Drum** P & K
244 E6 **Drumalbin** S Lans
316 C10 **Drumbeg** Highld
305 K7 **Drumblade** Abers
305 L7 **Drumblair** Abers
214 C5 **Drumbreddan** D & G
220 D3 **Drumbuie** D & G
294 E2 **Drumbuie** Highld
209 G2 **Drumburgh** Cumb
256 C6 **Drumchapel** C Glas
310 D9 **Drumchardine** Highld
312 D9 **Drumchork** Highld
243 J6 **Drumclog** S Lans
305 K8 **Drumdollo** Abers
269 G7 **Drumeldrie** Fife
245 J7 **Drumelzier** Border
294 C5 **Drumfearn** Highld
257 H7 **Drumgelloch** N Lans
280 D4 **Drumgley** Angus
287 H2 **Drumguish** Highld
300 C2 **Drumin** Moray
230 E7 **Drumjohn** D & G
302 B7 **Drumlassie** Abers
238 C4 **Drumlemble** Ag & B
303 H5 **Drumligair** Abers
291 H5 **Drumlithie** Abers
173 J5 **Drummersdale** Lancs
215 J4 **Drummodie** D & G
310 D4 **Drummond** Highld
310 F9 **Drummond** Highld
215 L6 **Drummoral** D & G
214 D6 **Drummore** D & G
315 K7 **Drummuie** Highld
304 F7 **Drummuir** Moray
281 G6 **Drummygar** Angus
297 K3 **Drumnadrochit** Highld
305 J5 **Drumnagorrach** Moray
291 H2 **Drumoak** Abers
257 G7 **Drumpellier** N Lans
219 G7 **Drumphail** D & G
220 F5 **Drumrash** D & G
313 K5 **Drumrunie** Highld
256 C6 **Drumry** W Duns
303 J4 **Drums** Abers
283 L6 **Drumsallie** Highld
229 K4 **Drumshang** S Ayrs
221 L5 **Drumsleet** D & G
310 E8 **Drumsmittal** Highld
280 E7 **Drumsturdy** Angus
215 J4 **Drumtroddan** D & G
292 G7 **Drumuie** Highld
299 H4 **Drumuillie** Highld
266 B7 **Drumvaich** Stirlg
303 H1 **Drumwhindle** Abers
281 J5 **Drunkendub** Angus
162 E8 **Drury** Flints
137 J6 **Drurylane** Norfk
149 J5 **Drury Lane** Wrexhm
137 H3 **Drury Square** Norfk
202 F4 **Drybeck** Cumb
305 G3 **Drybridge** Moray
242 C6 **Drybridge** N Ayrs
77 J3 **Drybrook** Gloucs
247 H7 **Dryburgh** Border
234 D2 **Dryden** Border
155 G4 **Dry Doddington** Lincs
119 H7 **Dry Drayton** Cambs
46 F6 **Dry Hill** Hants
50 C3 **Dryhill** Kent
233 K2 **Dryhope** Border
259 G5 **Drylaw** C Edin
3 G4 **Drym** Cnwll
256 B3 **Drymen** Stirlg
136 F5 **Drymere** Norfk
307 G6 **Drymuir** Abers
43 L2 **Drynham** Wilts
310 D7 **Drynie Park** Highld
293 G10 **Drynoch** Highld
80 F6 **Dry Sandford** Oxon
73 G4 **Dryslwyn** Carmth
67 H3 **Dry Street** Essex
128 B5 **Dryton** Shrops
316 D9 **Duartmore Bridge** Highld
12 D3 **Dubbs Cross** Devon
306 D3 **Dubford** Abers
303 H6 **Dubford** C Aber
310 E3 **Dublin** Highld
122 D6 **Dublin** Suffk
281 G4 **Dubton** Angus
208 E7 **Dubwath** Cumb
313 P3 **Duchally Lodge** Highld
107 H4 **Duck Corner** Suffk
101 G3 **Duck End** Beds
101 J5 **Duck End** Beds
82 B1 **Duck End** Bucks
118 E7 **Duck End** Cambs
85 G2 **Duck End** Essex
85 K1 **Duck End** Essex
103 L7 **Duck End** Essex
85 L2 **Duckend Green** Essex
58 F2 **Duckhole** S Glos
149 J3 **Duckington** Ches
80 D5 **Ducklington** Oxon
167 H6 **Duckmanton** Derbys
101 K2 **Duck's Cross** Beds
83 L7 **Ducks Island** Gt Lon
96 D6 **Duckswich** Worcs
78 C6 **Dudbridge** Gloucs
65 H3 **Dudden Hill** Gt Lon
103 G6 **Duddenhoe End** Essex
259 H6 **Duddingston** C Edin
133 K6 **Duddington** Nhants
26 C2 **Duddlestone** Somset
50 C8 **Duddleswell** E Susx
112 D3 **Duddlewick** Shrops
248 E5 **Duddo** Nthumb
163 K7 **Duddon** Ches
190 D3 **Duddon Bridge** Cumb
163 K7 **Duddon Common** Ches
148 F6 **Dudleston** Shrops
149 G6 **Dudleston Grove** Shrops
149 G6 **Dudleston Heath** Shrops
113 J2 **Dudley** Dudley
227 H5 **Dudley** N Tyne
176 F1 **Dudley Hill** Brad
113 K1 **Dudley Port** Sandw
129 K6 **Dudley's Fields** Wsall
113 J2 **Dudley Wood** Dudley
164 B4 **Dudlows Green** Warrtn
29 K7 **Dudsbury** Dorset
82 F5 **Dudswell** Herts
70 D2 **Dudwells** Pembks
22 E3 **Duerdon** Devon
152 F5 **Duffield** Derbys
153 G5 **Duffieldbank** Derbys
74 C7 **Duffryn** Neath
57 J3 **Duffryn** Newpt
110 E3 **Duffryn** Shrops
291 L2 **Duff's Hill** Abers
304 E7 **Dufftown** Moray
304 B2 **Duffus** Moray
202 F2 **Dufton** Cumb
188 C1 **Duggleby** N York
294 E2 **Duirinish** Highld
294 D6 **Duisdalebeg** Highld
294 D6 **Duisdalemore** Highld
284 C6 **Duisky** Highld
114 E2 **Duke End** Warwks
211 K2 **Dukesfield** Nthumb
75 J4 **Dukestown** Blae G
165 H1 **Dukinfield** Tamesd
159 H3 **Dulas** IoA
42 E5 **Dulcote** Somset
25 K5 **Dulford** Devon
278 B5 **Dull** P & K
257 G5 **Dullatur** N Lans
103 K2 **Dullingham** Cambs
103 K2 **Dullingham Ley** Cambs
299 J4 **Dulnain Bridge** Highld
258 E3 **Duloch** Fife
118 D7 **Duloe** Beds
6 B3 **Duloe** Cnwll
311 L9 **Dulsie** Highld
40 B8 **Dulverton** Somset
65 K6 **Dulwich** Gt Lon
65 K6 **Dulwich Village** Gt Lon
255 L5 **Dumbarton** W Duns
97 H6 **Dumbleton** Gloucs
256 D8 **Dumbreck** C Glas
233 G6 **Dumcrieff** D & G
222 B4 **Dumfries** D & G
256 C4 **Dumgoyne** Stirlg
46 E4 **Dummer** Hants
32 F2 **Dumpford** W Susx
23 G5 **Dumpinghill** Devon
137 L4 **Dumpling Green** Norfk
164 E1 **Dumplington** Traffd
69 L7 **Dumpton** Kent
281 J3 **Dun** Angus
277 K3 **Dunalastair** P & K
253 J2 **Dunamuck** Ag & B
293 K11 **Dunan** Highld
300 D7 **Dunandhu** Abers
253 J2 **Dunans** Ag & B
254 C2 **Dunans** Ag & B
41 J5 **Dunball** Somset
260 F5 **Dunbar** E Loth
319 L10 **Dunbeath** Highld
274 C8 **Dunbeg** Ag & B
266 D7 **Dunblane** Stirlg
268 D4 **Dunbog** Fife
292 B6 **Dun Boreraig** Highld
30 E1 **Dunbridge** Hants
333 F10 **Duncansclett** Shet
310 D6 **Duncanston** Highld
301 L3 **Duncanstone** Abers
324 G6 **Dùn Charlabhaigh** W Isls
14 D4 **Dunchideock** Devon
115 K5 **Dunchurch** Warwks
292 C7 **Dùn Colbost** Highld
182 E7 **Duncombe** Lancs
99 L3 **Duncote** Nhants
222 B3 **Duncow** D & G
267 L6 **Duncrievie** P & K
33 J3 **Duncton** W Susx
269 G1 **Dundee** C Dund
220 D2 **Dundeugh** D & G
42 C7 **Dundon** Somset
259 G2 **Dundonald** Fife
242 D7 **Dundonald** S Ayrs
242 C7 **Dundonald Camp** N Ayrs
42 C7 **Dundon Hayes** Somset
312 H9 **Dundonnell** Highld
208 F4 **Dundraw** Cumb
296 F6 **Dundreggan** Highld
216 F4 **Dundrennan** D & G
31 K3 **Dundridge** Hants
58 D7 **Dundry** N Som
266 E5 **Dunduff** P & K
257 G8 **Dundyvan** N Lans
302 E7 **Dunecht** Abers
278 D3 **Dunfallandy** P & K
258 E3 **Dunfermline** Fife
79 J7 **Dunfield** Gloucs
176 E7 **Dunford Bridge** Barns
321 N3 **Dun Gainmhich** W Isls
52 B2 **Dungate** Kent
43 L3 **Dunge** Wilts
37 L3 **Dungeness** Kent
166 E3 **Dungworth** Sheff
163 J6 **Dunham-on-the-Hill** Ches
168 F6 **Dunham on Trent** Notts
113 J7 **Dunhampstead** Worcs
113 G6 **Dunhampton** Worcs
164 D3 **Dunham Town** Traffd
164 D3 **Dunham Woodhouses** Traffd
169 K5 **Dunholme** Lincs
269 J5 **Dunino** Fife
257 J4 **Dunipace** Falk
266 C3 **Dunira** P & K
278 F6 **Dunkeld** P & K
280 C5 **Dunkenny** Angus
43 H2 **Dunkerton** BaNES
25 L5 **Dunkeswell** Devon
185 L5 **Dunkeswick** N York
119 L2 **Dunkirk** Cambs
163 G6 **Dunkirk** Ches
153 K6 **Dunkirk** C Nott
52 E3 **Dunkirk** Kent
142 F6 **Dunkirk** Norfk
59 J3 **Dunkirk** S Glos
150 F3 **Dunkirk** Staffs
44 C1 **Dunkirk** Wilts
50 F3 **Dunk's Green** Kent
290 D8 **Dunlappie** Angus
46 B3 **Dunley** Hants
112 F6 **Dunley** Worcs
242 E4 **Dunlop** E Ayrs
10 F8 **Dunmere** Cnwll
239 J1 **Dunmore** Ag & B
257 K3 **Dunmore** Falk
310 C8 **Dunmore** Highld
190 D5 **Dunnerholme** Cumb
319 M2 **Dunnet** Highld
280 F5 **Dunnichen** Angus
259 H2 **Dunnikier** Fife
267 J5 **Dunning** P & K
189 J4 **Dunnington** E R Yk
97 J3 **Dunnington** Warwks
187 J4 **Dunnington** York
190 D4 **Dunningwell** Cumb
175 H2 **Dunnockshaw** Lancs
21 J6 **Dunnose** IoW
127 K3 **Dunnsheath** Shrops
51 J1 **Dunn Street** Kent
52 C4 **Dunn Street** Kent
262 F1 **Dunollie** Ag & B
254 F5 **Dunoon** Ag & B
311 N8 **Dunphail** Moray
214 E2 **Dunragit** D & G
253 G4 **Dunrostan** Ag & B
166 D6 **Dunsa** Derbys
248 B3 **Duns** Border
20 E5 **Dunsbury** IoW
134 C1 **Dunsby** Lincs
174 F5 **Dunscar** Bolton
221 K3 **Dunscore** D & G
178 E6 **Dunscroft** Donc
206 E4 **Dunsdale** R & Cl
63 H5 **Dunsden Green** Oxon
22 E5 **Dunsdon** Devon
48 D6 **Dunsfold Common** Surrey
48 D6 **Dunsfold Green** Surrey
14 C4 **Dunsford** Devon
48 D6 **Dunsford** Surrey
268 D5 **Dunshalt** Fife
153 J1 **Dunsill** Notts
279 J8 **Dunsinnan** P & K
11 K7 **Dunslea** Cnwll
207 K5 **Dunsley** N York
113 H3 **Dunsley** Staffs
82 C5 **Dunsmore** Bucks
115 L4 **Dunsmore** Warwks
183 J4 **Dunsop Bridge** Lancs
83 G2 **Dunstable** Beds
130 B1 **Dunstal** Staffs
130 D2 **Dunstall** Staffs
96 E5 **Dunstall Common** Worcs
120 E7 **Dunstall Green** Suffk
129 J6 **Dunstall Hill** Wolves
237 J3 **Dunstan** Nthumb
40 C5 **Dunster** Somset
99 G8 **Duns Tew** Oxon
167 G6 **Dunston** Derbys
227 G7 **Dunston** Gatesd
169 L8 **Dunston** Lincs
138 E6 **Dunston** Norfk
129 J3 **Dunston** Staffs
7 J4 **Dunstone** Devon
8 C6 **Dunstone** Devon
129 J3 **Dunston Heath** Staffs
227 G7 **Dunston Hill** Gatesd
178 E6 **Dunsville** Donc
189 G7 **Dunswell** E R Yk
245 H4 **Dunsyre** S Lans
12 D6 **Dunterton** Devon
98 E8 **Dunthrop** Oxon
78 F5 **Duntisbourne Abbots** Gloucs
78 F5 **Duntisbourne Leer** Gloucs
78 F5 **Duntisbourne Rouse** Gloucs
28 B5 **Duntish** Dorset
256 B6 **Duntocher** W Duns
102 B5 **Dunton** Beds
82 C2 **Dunton** Bucks
141 H5 **Dunton** Norfk
115 L1 **Dunton Bassett** Leics
50 D2 **Dunton Green** Kent
141 H5 **Dunton Patch** Norfk
66 F2 **Dunton Wayletts** Essex
292 G2 **Duntulm** Highld
229 K3 **Dunure** S Ayrs
54 E3 **Dunvant** Swans
292 D7 **Dunvegan** Highld
10 D7 **Dunveth** Cnwll
41 K7 **Dunwear** Somset
123 K5 **Dunwich** Suffk
151 H2 **Dunwood** Staffs
5 H4 **Duporth** Cnwll
209 J3 **Durdar** Cumb
268 C3 **Durdie** P & K
3 K5 **Durgan** Cnwll
50 F7 **Durgates** E Susx
213 G5 **Durham** Dur
232 B6 **Durisdeer** D & G
232 B6 **Durisdeermill** D & G
177 J4 **Durkar** Wakefd
41 J6 **Durleigh** Somset
32 E2 **Durleighmarsh** W Susx
31 J3 **Durley** Hants
61 H8 **Durley** Wilts
31 J3 **Durley Street** Hants
53 J2 **Durlock** Kent
95 K6 **Durlow Common** Herefs
20 B3 **Durlston Court** Hants
175 K4 **Durn** Rochdl
312 G8 **Durnamuck** Highld
317 J3 **Durness** Highld
27 H2 **Durnfield** Somset
302 D3 **Durno** Abers
30 D7 **Durns Town** Hants
274 E3 **Duror** Highld
319 L4 **Durran** Highld
51 L6 **Durrant Green** Kent
32 D5 **Durrants** Hants
44 F5 **Durrington** Wilts
34 B6 **Durrington** W Susx
34 B6 **Durrington-on-Sea** W Susx
328 E9 **Durrisdale** Ork
291 H2 **Durris Ho** Abers
77 L7 **Dursley** Gloucs
43 L3 **Dursley** Wilts
77 K2 **Dursley Cross** Gloucs
41 J8 **Durston** Somset
28 F5 **Durweston** Dorset
332 H4 **Dury** Shet
14 E3 **Duryard** Devon
116 F7 **Duston** Nhants
67 J4 **Dutch Village** Essex
299 H4 **Duthil** Highld
110 E4 **Dutlas** Powys
85 J1 **Duton Hill** Essex
12 C4 **Dutson** Cnwll
163 L5 **Dutton** Ches
103 G4 **Duxford** Cambs
80 D7 **Duxford** Oxon
111 J4 **Duxmoor** Shrops
160 C5 **Dwygyfylchi** Conwy
159 G7 **Dwyran** IoA
126 B6 **Dwyrhiw** Powys
303 G6 **Dyce** C Aber
41 G5 **Dyche** Somset
211 K2 **Dye House** Nthumb
58 D4 **Dyer's Common** S Glos
102 D4 **Dyer's Green** Cambs
55 K3 **Dyffryn** Brdgnd
72 C4 **Dyffryn** Carmth
90 C5 **Dyffryn** Cerdgn
88 E5 **Dyffryn** Pembks
56 E6 **Dyffryn** V Glam
124 B2 **Dyffryn Ardudwy** Gwynd
90 C5 **Dyffryn-bern** Cerdgn
73 K3 **Dyffryn Ceidrych** Carmth
74 C5 **Dyffryn Cellwen** Neath
134 C2 **Dyke** Lincs
311 M6 **Dyke** Moray
280 C2 **Dykehead** Angus
244 D2 **Dykehead** N Lans
265 K8 **Dykehead** Stirlg
279 K3 **Dykend** Angus
306 C7 **Dykeside** Abers
125 H8 **Dylife** Powys
52 F8 **Dymchurch** Kent
95 L7 **Dymock** Gloucs
59 H5 **Dyrham** S Glos
259 J2 **Dysart** Fife
161 J5 **Dyserth** Denbgs

E

292 E9 **Eabost** Highld
292 E8 **Eabost West** Highld
53 J2 **Each End** Kent
113 K4 **Eachway** Worcs
226 E5 **Eachwick** Nthumb
324 D8 **Eadar Dha Fhadhail** W Isls
182 D6 **Eagland Hill** Lancs
169 G7 **Eagle** Lincs
169 G7 **Eagle Barnsdale** Lincs
169 G7 **Eagle Moor** Lincs
205 L4 **Eaglescliffe** S on T
200 D2 **Eaglesfield** Cumb
223 G5 **Eaglesfield** D & G
243 H3 **Eaglesham** E Rens
100 E6 **Eaglestone** M Keyn
118 B1 **Eaglethorpe** Nhants
166 D8 **Eagle Tor** Derbys
174 F5 **Eagley** Bolton
172 d7 **Eairy** IoM
154 C1 **Eakring** Notts
179 H5 **Ealand** N Linc
65 G5 **Ealing** Gt Lon
210 E2 **Eals** Nthumb
202 C2 **Eamont Bridge** Cumb
184 C5 **Earby** Lancs
174 E3 **Earcroft** Bl w D
112 E1 **Eardington** Shrops
94 F2 **Eardisland** Herefs
94 D4 **Eardisley** Herefs
127 H2 **Eardiston** Shrops
112 D6 **Eardiston** Worcs
119 H4 **Earith** Cambs
236 D1 **Earle** Nthumb
163 L1 **Earlestown** St Hel
63 J6 **Earley** Wokham
138 D5 **Earlham** Norfk
292 F4 **Earlish** Highld
117 H7 **Earls Barton** Nhants
104 E8 **Earls Colne** Essex
97 G2 **Earl's Common** Worcs
96 E5 **Earl's Croome** Worcs
115 G4 **Earlsdon** Covtry
36 B3 **Earl's Down** E Susx
269 H8 **Earlsferry** Fife
65 J6 **Earlsfield** Gt Lon
155 G6 **Earlsfield** Lincs
302 F2 **Earlsford** Abers
121 L6 **Earl's Green** Suffk
131 K7 **Earl Shilton** Leics
122 E7 **Earl Soham** Suffk
165 L7 **Earl Sterndale** Derbys
247 H6 **Earlston** Border
242 E6 **Earlston** E Ayrs
46 C1 **Earlstone Common** Hants
105 K2 **Earl Stonham** Suffk
220 E3 **Earlstoun** D & G
76 E7 **Earlswood** Mons
114 C5 **Earlswood** Warwks
49 J4 **Earlswood** Surrey
32 F7 **Earnley** W Susx
243 K3 **Earnock** S Lans
174 B3 **Earnshaw Bridge** Lancs
320 D5 **Earsairidh** W Isls
227 J5 **Earsdon** N Tyne
232 E6 **Earshaig** D & G
123 G2 **Earsham** Norfk
122 E4 **Earsham Street** Suffk
187 H3 **Earswick** York
33 H5 **Eartham** W Susx
58 F3 **Earthcott Green** S Glos
206 D6 **Easby** N York
262 C4 **Easdale** Ag & B
33 G2 **Easebourne** W Susx
115 K4 **Easenhall** Warwks
48 B5 **Eashing** Surrey
81 K4 **Easington** Bucks
213 K5 **Easington** Dur
181 L4 **Easington** E R Yk
183 J4 **Easington** Lancs
249 J6 **Easington** Nthumb
81 K7 **Easington** Oxon
98 F6 **Easington** Oxon
207 G4 **Easington** R & Cl
213 K5 **Easington Colliery** Dur
213 J4 **Easington Lane** Sundld
196 F8 **Easingwold** N York
35 K3 **Eason's Green** E Susx
280 B5 **Eassie** Angus
56 D7 **East Aberthaw** V Glam
38 D8 **Eastacombe** Devon
23 L2 **Eastacott** Devon
65 H4 **East Acton** Gt Lon
99 G6 **East Adderbury** Oxon
8 C5 **East Allington** Devon
24 F1 **East Anstey** Devon
45 L4 **East Anton** Hants
195 K2 **East Appleton** N York
177 H2 **East Ardsley** Leeds
32 F5 **East Ashling** W Susx
46 B4 **East Aston** Hants
302 F7 **East Auchronie** Abers
198 E4 **East Ayton** N York
281 G7 **East Balmirmer** Angus
75 L5 **East Bank** Blae G
170 C4 **East Barkwith** Lincs
51 H3 **East Barming** Kent
207 J5 **East Barnby** N York
65 J2 **East Barnet** Gt Lon
141 J5 **East Barsham** Norfk
121 J6 **East Barton** Suffk
33 G8 **East Beach** W Susx
142 F3 **East Beckham** Norfk
64 E6 **East Bedfont** Gt Lon
228 D2 **East Bennan** N Ayrs
105 J7 **East Bergholt** Suffk
137 J3 **East Bilney** Norfk
211 J6 **East Blackdene** Dur
35 J7 **East Blatchington** E Susx
18 D3 **East Bloxworth** Dorset
227 K7 **East Boldon** S Tyne
30 F6 **East Boldre** Hants
205 H5 **Eastbourne** Darltn
36 B7 **Eastbourne** E Susx
41 K6 **East Bower** Somset
41 K3 **East Brent** Somset
123 K6 **Eastbridge** Suffk
154 C5 **East Bridgford** Notts
204 B4 **East Briscoe** Dur
26 C2 **Eastbrook** Somset
57 G6 **Eastbrook** V Glam
315 L6 **East Brora** Highld
39 G7 **East Buckland** Devon
15 H5 **East Budleigh** Devon
188 E3 **Eastburn** E R Yk
64 B4 **East Burnham** Bucks
332 F5 **East Burrafirth** Shet
18 C4 **East Burton** Dorset
64 E2 **Eastbury** Herts
61 K5 **Eastbury** W Berk
212 D4 **East Butsfield** Dur
25 H5 **East Butterleigh** Devon
179 J6 **East Butterwick** N Linc
184 F4 **Eastby** N York
290 F6 **East Cairnbeg** Abers
258 D7 **East Calder** W Loth
138 D6 **East Carleton** Norfk
185 K6 **East Carlton** Leeds
117 G2 **East Carlton** Nhants
61 L3 **East Challow** Oxon
8 C6 **East Charleton** Devon
27 K5 **East Chelborough** Dorset
35 G4 **East Chiltington** E Susx
27 H4 **East Chinnock** Somset
44 F3 **East Chisenbury** Wilts
45 J4 **East Cholderton** Hants
68 C6 **Eastchurch** Kent
48 E3 **East Clandon** Surrey
81 L1 **East Claydon** Bucks
58 B6 **East Clevedon** N Som
315 L6 **East Clyne** Highld
27 J4 **East Coker** Somset
78 D6 **Eastcombe** Gloucs
41 G7 **East Combe** Somset
178 E1 **East Common** N York
28 F3 **East Compton** Dorset
42 F5 **East Compton** Somset
8 D3 **East Cornworthy** Devon
64 F3 **Eastcote** Gt Lon
99 L3 **Eastcote** Nhants
114 D4 **Eastcote** Solhll
64 F3 **Eastcote Village** Gt Lon
22 D3 **Eastcott** Cnwll
44 D2 **Eastcott** Wilts
187 K6 **East Cottingwith** E R Yk
101 J4 **Eastcotts** Beds
45 H1 **Eastcourt** Wilts
60 C2 **Eastcourt** Wilts
21 H2 **East Cowes** IoW
178 F3 **East Cowick** E R Yk
205 J7 **East Cowton** N York
227 H4 **East Cramlington** Nthumb
43 G5 **East Cranmore** Somset
18 E5 **East Creech** Dorset
298 C3 **East Croachy** Highld
299 H5 **East Croftmore** Highld
209 H4 **East Curthwaite** Cumb
301 J7 **East Davoch** Abers
35 L7 **East Dean** E Susx
77 K2 **East Dean** Gloucs
30 D1 **East Dean** Hants
33 H4 **East Dean** W Susx
167 H2 **East Dene** Rothm
280 E7 **East Denside** Angus
226 F6 **East Denton** N u Ty
164 F2 **East Didsbury** Manch
14 F6 **Eastdon** Devon
8 D5 **Eastdown** Devon
38 F5 **East Down** Devon
50 D1 **Eastdown** Kent
168 E5 **East Drayton** Notts
65 K6 **East Dulwich** Gt Lon
58 E7 **East Dundry** N Som
180 D2 **East Ella** C KuH
101 G5 **East End** m keyn
101 K2 **East End** Beds
82 C3 **East End** Bucks
29 H7 **East End** Dorset
180 F1 **East End** E R Yk
181 H2 **East End** E R Yk
189 J3 **East End** E R Yk
84 E4 **Eastend** Essex
87 G5 **East End** Essex
79 K6 **East End** Gloucs
20 E2 **East End** Hants
32 C2 **East End** Hants
46 B1 **East End** Hants
103 G8 **East End** Herts
51 K6 **East End** Kent
51 L5 **East End** Kent
68 C6 **East End** Kent
100 F5 **East End** M Keyn
101 G5 **East End** M Keyn
58 C6 **East End** N Som
80 C2 **Eastend** Oxon
80 D4 **East End** Oxon
80 E3 **East End** Oxon
98 E7 **East End** Oxon
99 G6 **East End** Oxon
27 L1 **East End** Somset
42 E3 **East End** Somset
43 G4 **East End** Somset
59 J6 **East End** S Glos
105 K6 **East End** Suffk
106 D2 **East End** Suffk
297 L5 **Easter Aberchalder** Highld
310 E3 **Easter Ardross** Highld
268 B7 **Easter Balgedie** P & K
289 G3 **Easter Balmoral** Abers
288 E8 **Easter Binzian** P & K
297 K4 **Easter Boleskine** Highld
58 E4 **Easter Compton** S Glos
279 H6 **Easter Essendy** P & K
314 F9 **Easter Fearn** Highld
300 B4 **Easter Fodderletter** Moray
311 J8 **Easter Galcantray** Highld
33 H5 **Eastergate** W Susx
256 F7 **Easterhouse** C Glas
247 G6 **Easter Housebyres** Border
259 G8 **Easter Howgate** Mdloth
268 D5 **Easter Kilwhiss** Fife
310 D6 **Easter Kinkell** Highld
268 E4 **Easter Kinsleith** Fife
281 G7 **Easter Knox** Angus
247 G6 **Easter Langlee** Border
280 B2 **Easter Lednathie** Angus
280 E5 **Easter Meathie** Angus
114 F4 **Eastern Green** Covtry
302 F8 **Easter Ord** C Aber
327 M4 **Easter Park** Ork
333 G9 **Easter Quarff** Shet
206 B4 **Easter Skeld** Shet
332 E7 **Easter Skeld** Shet
247 L7 **Easter Softlaw** Border
44 D2 **Easterton** Wilts
44 D2 **Easterton Sands** Wilts
41 K3 **Eastertown** Somset
305 L2 **Easter Whyntie** Abers
45 G3 **East Everleigh** Wilts
65 H8 **East Ewell** Surrey
51 H3 **East Farleigh** Kent
116 E3 **East Farndon** Nhants
120 C5 **East Fen Common** Cambs
179 J8 **East Ferry** Lincs
247 G8 **Eastfield** Border
58 E5 **Eastfield** Bristl
134 D6 **Eastfield** C Pete
257 G6 **Eastfield** N Lans
257 K8 **Eastfield** S Lans
227 H4 **Eastfield** Nthumb
198 F5 **Eastfield** N York
243 J1 **Eastfield** S Lans
237 J5 **Eastfield Hall** Nthumb
62 C7 **East Fields** W Berk
268 D8 **East Finglassie** Fife
169 K3 **East Firsby** Lincs
17 J6 **East Fleet** Dorset
186 D8 **East Garforth** Leeds
61 L5 **East Garston** W Berk
134 C5 **Eastgate** C Pete
211 K6 **Eastgate** Dur
142 E7 **Eastgate** Norfk
227 H7 **East Gateshead** Gatesd
62 B3 **East Ginge** Oxon
86 D2 **East Gores** Essex
132 C4 **East Goscote** Leics
45 J1 **East Grafton** Wilts
47 J5 **East Green** Hants
103 L3 **East Green** Suffk
123 J6 **East Green** Suffk
45 H8 **East Grimstead** Wilts
49 L6 **East Grinstead** W Susx
37 H2 **East Guldeford** E Susx
116 D6 **East Haddon** Nhants
62 D3 **East Hagbourne** Oxon
83 K2 **Easthall** Herts
180 E4 **East Halton** N Linc
66 B4 **East Ham** Gt Lon
163 G4 **Eastham** Wirral
112 D6 **Eastham** Worcs
163 G4 **Eastham Ferry** Wirral
33 H5 **East Hampnett** W Susx
63 L7 **Easthampstead** Br For
111 J7 **Easthampton** Herefs
62 B2 **East Hanney** Oxon
86 B6 **East Hanningfield** Essex
178 B4 **East Hardwick** Wakefd
121 K2 **East Harling** Norfk
196 D2 **East Harlsey** N York
42 E2 **East Harptree** BaNES
227 H4 **East Hartford** Nthumb
32 E3 **East Harting** W Susx
44 B8 **East Hatch** Wilts
102 C3 **East Hatley** Cambs
138 B3 **Easthaugh** Norfk
195 J3 **East Hauxwell** N York
281 G7 **East Haven** Angus
63 J7 **Eastheath** Wokham
156 C5 **East Heckington** Lincs
212 D5 **East Hedleyhope** Dur
315 P3 **East Helmsdale** Highld
62 C3 **East Hendred** Oxon
167 J2 **East Herringthorpe** Rothm
213 J3 **East Herrington** Sundld
198 D6 **East Heslerton** N York
57 L8 **East Hewish** N Som
50 E1 **East Hill** Kent
280 F5 **East Hills** Angus
35 K3 **East Hoathly** E Susx
18 D4 **East Holme** Dorset
18 F3 **East Holton** Dorset
227 J5 **East Holywell** N Tyne
128 B7 **Easthope** Shrops
128 B7 **Easthopewood** Shrops
66 F3 **East Horndon** Essex
86 E2 **Easthorpe** Essex
154 F6 **Easthorpe** Leics
154 D3 **Easthorpe** Notts
42 D3 **East Horrington** Somset
48 E3 **East Horsley** Surrey
249 G7 **East Horton** Nthumb
332 F7 **Easthouse** Shet
259 J7 **Easthouses** Mdloth
19 H2 **East Howe** Bmouth
41 K4 **East Huntspill** Somset
83 J3 **East Hyde** Beds
39 H4 **East Ilkerton** Devon
62 C4 **East Ilsley** W Berk
329 N2 **Easting** Ork
24 C5 **Eastington** Devon
78 B5 **Eastington** Gloucs
79 J4 **Eastington** Gloucs
171 G8 **East Keal** Lincs
60 F7 **East Kennett** Wilts
186 C6 **East Keswick** Leeds
243 K3 **East Kilbride** S Lans
23 H7 **East Kimber** Devon
33 L6 **East Kingston** W Susx
156 F1 **East Kirkby** Lincs
198 C6 **East Knapton** N York
18 C4 **East Knighton** Dorset
24 E2 **East Knowstone** Devon
43 L7 **East Knoyle** Wilts
212 E3 **East Kyo** Dur
27 G3 **East Lambrook** Somset
314 H11 **East Lamington** Highld
32 C4 **Eastland Gate** Hants
53 K4 **East Langdon** Kent
116 E1 **East Langton** Leics
314 H5 **East Langwell** Highld
33 G4 **East Lavant** W Susx
33 H3 **East Lavington** W Susx
212 C3 **East Law** Dur
204 F5 **East Layton** N York
79 L5 **Eastleach Martin** Gloucs
79 K5 **Eastleach Turville** Gloucs
132 B1 **East Leake** Notts
248 D6 **East Learmouth** Nthumb
7 L4 **East Leigh** Devon
24 B5 **East Leigh** Devon
38 C8 **Eastleigh** Devon
31 H3 **Eastleigh** Hants
137 H3 **East Lexham** Norfk
236 E2 **East Lilburn** Nthumb
52 C2 **Eastling** Kent
260 D5 **East Linton** E Loth
47 J8 **East Liss** Hants
62 B3 **East Lockinge** Oxon
207 G4 **East Loftus** R & Cl
6 C4 **East Looe** Cnwll
179 H8 **East Lound** N Linc
14 B7 **East Lounston** Devon
18 D5 **East Lulworth** Dorset
198 D8 **East Lutton** N York
41 G8 **East Lydeard** Somset
42 E7 **East Lydford** Somset
41 K8 **East Lyng** Somset
290 F2 **East Mains** Abers
280 B7 **East Mains** Angus
247 H4 **East Mains** Border
243 J3 **East Mains** S Lans
280 F4 **East Mains of Burnside** Angus
51 H2 **East Malling** Kent
51 G2 **East Malling Heath** Kent
280 D7 **East March** Angus
32 F4 **East Marden** W Susx
168 D6 **East Markham** Notts
181 H5 **East Marsh** NE Lin
29 K3 **East Martin** Hants
184 D4 **East Marton** N York
28 F2 **East Melbury** Dorset
32 C2 **East Meon** Hants
25 H3 **East Mere** Devon
87 H4 **East Mersea** Essex
319 P2 **East Mey** Highld
64 F7 **East Molesey** Surrey
177 J3 **East Moor** Wakefd
57 H5 **East Moors** Cardif
18 E2 **East Morden** Dorset
185 G6 **East Morton** Brad
232 B6 **East Morton** D & G
34 F5 **East Moulsecoomb** Br & H
197 J6 **East Ness** N York
280 B6 **East Nevay** Angus
189 L7 **East Newton** E R Yk
197 H6 **East Newton** N York
32 C7 **Eastney** C Port
96 B6 **Eastnor** Herefs
132 F6 **East Norton** Leics
26 B2 **East Nynehead** Somset
46 E4 **East Oakley** Hants
179 J4 **Eastoft** N Linc
14 C7 **East Ogwell** Devon
32 D7 **Eastoke** Hants
58 F6 **Easton** Bristl
118 C5 **Easton** Cambs
209 G2 **Easton** Cumb
223 L5 **Easton** Cumb
7 L5 **Easton** Devon
13 L4 **Easton** Devon
17 K7 **Easton** Dorset
46 D7 **Easton** Hants
20 D4 **Easton** IoW
133 J1 **Easton** Lincs
138 C4 **Easton** Norfk
42 D4 **Easton** Somset
106 F2 **Easton** Suffk
62 B6 **Easton** W Berk
59 L6 **Easton** Wilts
59 L3 **Easton Grey** Wilts
58 D5 **Easton-in-Gordano** N Som
100 E2 **Easton Maudit** Nhants
133 L6 **Easton on the Hill** Nhants
45 H1 **Easton Royal** Wilts
42 F7 **Easton Town** Somset
59 L3 **Easton Town** Wilts
28 E3 **East Orchard** Dorset
248 F3 **East Ord** Nthumb
41 K6 **Eastover** Somset
12 D3 **East Panson** Devon
29 K7 **East Parley** Dorset
51 G4 **East Peckham** Kent
42 E6 **East Pennard** Somset
118 D6 **East Perry** Cambs
5 G6 **East Portholland** Cnwll
8 B7 **East Portlemouth** Devon
8 C7 **East Prawle** Devon
217 L2 **East Preston** D & G
33 L6 **East Preston** W Susx
28 C5 **East Pulham** Dorset
22 F3 **East Putford** Devon
40 F5 **East Quantoxhead** Somset
213 H4 **East Rainton** Sundld
181 G8 **East Ravendale** NE Lin
141 H6 **East Raynham** Norfk
134 F7 **Eastrea** Cambs
223 H6 **Eastriggs** D & G
186 C6 **East Rigton** Leeds
179 H1 **Eastrington** E R Yk
59 K6 **Eastrip** Wilts
41 L1 **East Rolstone** N Som
46 F5 **Eastrop** Hants
205 L7 **East Rounton** N York
24 B7 **East Rowden** Devon
141 G6 **East Rudham** Norfk
142 F3 **East Runton** Norfk
143 J6 **East Ruston** Norfk
53 K3 **Eastry** Kent
260 B7 **East Saltoun** E Loth
65 H5 **East Sheen** Gt Lon
333 F14 **Eastshore** Shet
327 L6 **Eastside** Ork
221 J2 **East Skelston** D & G
227 H3 **East Sleekburn** Nthumb
139 K2 **East Somerton** Norfk
212 F3 **East Stanley** Dur
168 E2 **East Stockwith** Lincs
18 D4 **East Stoke** Dorset
154 D4 **East Stoke** Notts
27 H3 **East Stoke** Somset
28 E2 **East Stour** Dorset
28 E2 **East Stour Common** Dorset
53 J1 **East Stourmouth** Kent
23 L1 **East Stowford** Devon
46 D6 **East Stratton** Hants
53 K2 **East Street** Kent
42 D6 **East Street** Somset
53 K4 **East Studdal** Kent
293 K10 **East Suisnish** Highld
5 L2 **East Taphouse** Cnwll
23 H1 **East-the-Water** Devon
247 J6 **East Third** Border
237 H7 **East Thirston** Nthumb
67 G5 **East Tilbury** Thurr
47 H7 **East Tisted** Hants
170 B4 **East Torrington** Lincs
40 F7 **East Town** Somset
42 F5 **East Town** Somset
43 L2 **East Town** Wilts
71 G7 **East Trewent** Pembks
138 B4 **East Tuddenham** Norfk
45 J8 **East Tytherley** Hants
60 C5 **East Tytherton** Wilts
24 E6 **East Village** Devon
56 C6 **East Village** V Glam
58 F5 **Eastville** Bristl
157 H2 **Eastville** Lincs
127 L8 **East Wall** Shrops
136 E3 **East Walton** Norfk
42 D3 **East Water** Somset
13 K3 **East Week** Devon
154 E8 **Eastwell** Leics
30 E2 **East Wellow** Hants
52 D4 **Eastwell Park** Kent
259 J1 **East Wemyss** Fife
258 B8 **East Whitburn** W Loth
279 J7 **East Whitefield** P & K
84 E4 **Eastwick** Herts
331 E10 **Eastwick** Shet
66 C5 **East Wickham** Gt Lon
71 J6 **East Williamston** Pembks
136 D3 **East Winch** Norfk
45 H7 **East Winterslow** Wilts
32 E7 **East Wittering** W Susx
195 H4 **East Witton** N York
175 L2 **Eastwood** Calder
95 K5 **Eastwood** Herefs
153 J4 **Eastwood** Notts
167 H2 **Eastwood** Rothm
67 K3 **Eastwood** Sthend
225 K2 **East Woodburn** Nthumb
135 J8 **Eastwood End** Cambs
153 J4 **Eastwood Hall** Notts
46 B1 **East Woodhay** Hants
43 J5 **East Woodlands** Somset
47 H6 **East Worldham** Hants
24 D4 **East Worlington** Devon
34 C6 **East Worthing** W Susx
121 J1 **East Wretham** Norfk
22 D3 **East Youlstone** Devon
115 H6 **Eathorpe** Warwks
163 L8 **Eaton** Ches
165 G7 **Eaton** Ches
95 H2 **Eaton** Herefs
154 E8 **Eaton** Leics
138 E5 **Eaton** Norfk
168 D5 **Eaton** Notts
80 E6 **Eaton** Oxon
111 H2 **Eaton** Shrops
111 L1 **Eaton** Shrops
94 F6 **Eaton Bishop** Herefs
82 F2 **Eaton Bray** Beds
128 B5 **Eaton Constantine** Shrops
118 D7 **Eaton Ford** Cambs
149 H1 **Eaton Hall** Ches
80 B7 **Eaton Hastings** Oxon
127 L5 **Eaton Mascott** Shrops
101 L2 **Eaton Socon** Cambs
128 D2 **Eaton upon Tern** Shrops
136 B3 **Eau Brink** Norfk
95 H5 **Eau Withington** Herefs
114 F3 **Eaves Green** Solhll
195 K8 **Eavestone** N York
23 K3 **Ebberly Hill** Devon
198 C5 **Ebberston** N York
29 H2 **Ebbesbourne Wake** Wilts
29 L5 **Ebblake** Dorset
75 K5 **Ebbw Vale** Blae G
212 D5 **Ebchester** Dur
57 L8 **Ebdon** N Som
48 C8 **Ebernoe** W Susx
14 F4 **Ebford** Devon
78 C6 **Ebley** Gloucs
149 J4 **Ebnal** Ches
95 G2 **Ebnall** Herefs
127 L3 **Ebreywood** Shrops
97 L5 **Ebrington** Gloucs
46 D1 **Ecchinswell** Hants
261 H7 **Ecclaw** Border
222 F5 **Ecclefechan** D & G
190 E3 **Eccle Riggs** Cumb
248 B5 **Eccles** Border
51 H1 **Eccles** Kent
175 G8 **Eccles** Salfd
166 F4 **Ecclesall** Sheff
166 F2 **Ecclesfield** Sheff
281 K1 **Ecclesgreig** Abers
150 F8 **Eccleshall** Staffs
185 J7 **Eccleshill** Brad
258 D6 **Ecclesmachan** W Loth
143 L6 **Eccles on Sea** Norfk
121 L1 **Eccles Road** Norfk
149 H1 **Eccleston** Ches
174 B4 **Eccleston** Lancs
163 J1 **Eccleston** St Hel
163 J2 **Eccleston Park** St Hel
28 E1 **Eccliffe** Dorset
185 L6 **Eccup** Leeds
302 D7 **Echt** Abers
235 J1 **Eckford** Border
235 J1 **Eckfordmoss** Border
167 H5 **Eckington** Derbys
96 F5 **Eckington** Worcs
35 K4 **Eckington Corner** E Susx
177 G7 **Ecklands** Barns
23 G3 **Eckworthy** Devon
117 G7 **Ecton** Nhants
151 L2 **Ecton** Staffs
117 G7 **Ecton Brook** Nhants
166 B3 **Edale** Derbys
166 C3 **Edale End** Derbys
41 H5 **Edbrook** Somset
34 D4 **Edburton** W Susx
208 D4 **Edderside** Cumb
314 H9 **Edderton** Highld
69 G7 **Eddington** Kent
61 K7 **Eddington** W Berk
245 L4 **Eddleston** Border
243 L3 **Eddlewood** S Lans
50 B4 **Edenbridge** Kent
175 H4 **Edenfield** Lancs
210 C7 **Edenhall** Cumb
134 B2 **Edenham** Lincs
191 J5 **Eden Mount** Cumb
65 L7 **Eden Park** Gt Lon
166 D7 **Edensor** Derbys
255 J2 **Edentaggart** Ag & B
178 E6 **Edenthorpe** Donc
209 J2 **Edentown** Cumb
213 K6 **Eden Vale** Dur
43 L3 **Eden Vale** Wilts
262 F7 **Ederline** Ag & B
144 E6 **Edern** Gwynd
43 G4 **Edford** Somset
42 D6 **Edgarley** Somset
114 B3 **Edgbaston** Birm
99 H4 **Edgcote** Nhants
81 K2 **Edgcott** Bucks
39 K6 **Edgcott** Somset
3 J4 **Edgcumbe** Cnwll
78 C5 **Edge** Gloucs
127 H5 **Edge** Shrops
128 B2 **Edgebolton** Shrops
77 H4 **Edge End** Gloucs
183 K8 **Edge End** Lancs
142 D5 **Edgefield** Norfk
142 D5 **Edgefield Street** Norfk
174 F4 **Edge Fold** Bolton
174 E6 **Edge Fold** Bolton
149 J3 **Edge Green** Ches
121 L3 **Edge Green** Norfk
174 C8 **Edge Green** Wigan
163 G3 **Edge Hill** Lpool
98 E4 **Edgehill** Warwks
130 E7 **Edge Hill** Warwks
165 G3 **Edgeley** Stockp
166 E2 **Edge Mount** Sheff
127 G3 **Edgerley** Shrops
235 H4 **Edgerston** Border
176 E4 **Edgerton** Kirk
175 H3 **Edgeside** Lancs
78 E5 **Edgeworth** Gloucs
8 E1 **Edginswell** Torbay
113 L7 **Edgiock** Worcs
128 E3 **Edgmond** Wrekin
128 E2 **Edgmond Marsh** Wrekin
111 H2 **Edgton** Shrops
65 G2 **Edgware** Gt Lon
115 G3 **Edgwick** Covtry
174 F4 **Edgworth** Bl w D
130 B5 **Edial** Staffs
265 K5 **Edinample** Stirlg
292 E6 **Edinbane** Highld
259 H5 **Edinburgh** C Edin
130 E4 **Edingale** Staffs
154 C2 **Edingley** Notts
143 J5 **Edingthorpe** Norfk
143 J5 **Edingthorpe Green** Norfk
41 L6 **Edington** Somset
44 B3 **Edington** Wilts
41 L3 **Edingworth** Somset
22 C2 **Edistone** Devon
41 K4 **Edithmead** Somset
133 J5 **Edith Weston** Rutlnd
152 C5 **Edlaston** Derbys
82 F3 **Edlesborough** Bucks
237 G5 **Edlingham** Nthumb
170 D6 **Edlington** Lincs
29 J4 **Edmondsham** Dorset
212 F4 **Edmondsley** Dur
56 D2 **Edmondstown** Rhondd
133 H3 **Edmondthorpe** Leics
245 H5 **Edmonston** S Lans
328 H9 **Edmonstone** Ork
10 D7 **Edmonton** Cnwll
65 K2 **Edmonton** Gt Lon
212 B3 **Edmundbyers** Dur
247 L6 **Ednam** Border
152 D5 **Ednaston** Derbys
85 K6 **Edney Common** Essex
278 C4 **Edradynate** P & K
248 C2 **Edrom** Border
149 K7 **Edstaston** Shrops
114 D7 **Edstone** Warwks
95 L2 **Edvin Loach** Herefs
153 L6 **Edwalton** Notts
104 F5 **Edwardstone** Suffk
75 H7 **Edwardsville** Myr Td
73 J2 **Edwinsford** Carmth
168 B7 **Edwinstowe** Notts
102 B5 **Edworth** Beds
95 K2 **Edwyn Ralph** Herefs
290 E8 **Edzell** Angus
74 C6 **Efail-fâch** Neath
56 E4 **Efail Isaf** Rhondd
145 G6 **Efailnewydd** Gwynd
126 D1 **Efail-rhyd** Powys
89 J7 **Efailwen** Carmth
148 B2 **Efenechtyd** Denbgs
48 F3 **Effingham** Surrey
332 E6 **Effirth** Shet
234 E3 **Effledge** Border
130 D3 **Efflinch** Staffs
10 B7 **Efflins** Cnwll
7 G3 **Efford** C Plym
24 F6 **Efford** Devon
46 B3 **Egbury** Hants
96 F3 **Egdon** Worcs
174 F5 **Egerton** Bolton
52 B4 **Egerton** Kent
51 L4 **Egerton Forstal** Kent
149 K3 **Egerton Green** Ches
43 J4 **Egford** Somset
12 C4 **Eggbeare** Cnwll
178 C3 **Eggborough** N York
7 H3 **Eggbuckland** C Plym
24 B4 **Eggesford** Devon
82 E2 **Eggington** Beds
152 E8 **Egginton** Derbys
152 E8 **Egginton Common** Derbys
204 B3 **Egglesburn** Dur
205 L5 **Egglescliffe** S on T
204 C3 **Eggleston** Dur
64 C6 **Egham** Surrey
64 D6 **Egham Hythe** Surrey
64 C7 **Egham Wick** Surrey
133 H5 **Egleton** Rutlnd
237 G3 **Eglingham** Nthumb
10 E7 **Egloshayle** Cnwll
11 K4 **Egloskerry** Cnwll
160 E6 **Eglwysbach** Conwy
56 D7 **Eglwys-Brewis** V Glam
149 J5 **Eglwys Cross** Wrexhm
124 D7 **Eglwys Fach** Cerdgn
89 K5 **Eglwyswen** Pembks
89 J5 **Eglwyswrw** Pembks
168 D7 **Egmanton** Notts
141 H4 **Egmere** Norfk
200 B5 **Egremont** Cumb
162 F2 **Egremont** Wirral
207 J6 **Egton** N York
207 J6 **Egton Bridge** N York
185 G8 **Egypt** Brad
64 C3 **Egypt** Bucks
46 C5 **Egypt** Hants
62 B5 **Egypt** W Berk
86 E1 **Eight Ash Green** Essex
213 G2 **Eighton Banks** Gatesd
95 H6 **Eign Hill** Herefs
294 F5 **Eilanreach** Highld
247 H7 **Eildon** Border
274 F8 **Eilean Duirinnis** Ag & B
324 F9 **Einacleit** W Isls
323 P2 **Eisgein** W Isls
146 B7 **Eisingrug** Gwynd
226 F5 **Eland Green** Nthumb
109 J6 **Elan Village** Powys
58 F3 **Elberton** S Glos
41 L2 **Elborough** N Som
127 H2 **Elbridge** Shrops
33 H6 **Elbridge** W Susx
7 H4 **Elburton** C Plym
113 L7 **Elcock's Brook** Worcs
78 B7 **Elcombe** Gloucs
60 F4 **Elcombe** Swindn
61 L7 **Elcot** W Berk
61 G4 **Eldene** Swindn
135 G7 **Eldernell** Cambs
96 D7 **Eldersfield** Worcs
255 L8 **Elderslie** Rens
103 J7 **Elder Street** Essex
205 G2 **Eldon** Dur
205 G2 **Eldon Lane** Dur
183 L1 **Eldroth** N York
185 H6 **Eldwick** Brad
213 J4 **Elemore Vale** Sundld
249 K7 **Elford** Nthumb
130 D4 **Elford** Staffs
119 L5 **Elford Closes** Cambs
304 C3 **Elgin** Moray
293 J14 **Elgol** Highld
53 G5 **Elham** Kent
258 C7 **Eliburn** W Loth
269 H8 **Elie** Fife
158 F4 **Elim** IoA
30 F4 **Eling** Hants
62 D5 **Eling** W Berk
236 B7 **Elishaw** Nthumb
168 C5 **Elkesley** Notts
116 C4 **Elkington** Nhants
85 J6 **Elkins Green** Essex
78 F4 **Elkstone** Gloucs
8 F2 **Ellacombe** Torbay
299 G4 **Ellan** Highld
176 E3 **Elland** Calder
176 E3 **Elland Lower Edge** Calder
253 G5 **Ellary** Ag & B
152 B5 **Ellastone** Staffs
182 E3 **Ellel** Lancs
247 L1 **Ellemford** Border
262 C4 **Ellenabeich** Ag & B
208 B6 **Ellenborough** Cumb
4 C3 **Ellenglaze** Cnwll
129 G1 **Ellenhall** Staffs
48 E6 **Ellen's Green** Surrey
196 D2 **Ellerbeck** N York
198 B5 **Ellerburn** N York
207 J5 **Ellerby** N York
128 C2 **Ellerdine** Wrekin
128 C2 **Ellerdine Heath** Wrekin
25 H6 **Ellerhayes** Devon
274 F5 **Elleric** Ag & B
179 L2 **Ellerker** E R Yk
187 K7 **Ellerton** E R Yk
195 L2 **Ellerton** N York
128 E1 **Ellerton** Shrops
82 C5 **Ellesborough** Bucks
149 G7 **Ellesmere** Shrops
175 G8 **Ellesmere Park** Salfd
163 H5 **Ellesmere Port** Ches
40 C5 **Ellicombe** Somset
29 L5 **Ellingham** Hants
139 H8 **Ellingham** Norfk
237 H1 **Ellingham** Nthumb
195 J5 **Ellingstring** N York
118 D5 **Ellington** Cambs
227 H1 **Ellington** Nthumb
118 D5 **Ellington Thorpe** Cambs
281 H7 **Elliot** Angus
43 J4 **Elliots Green** Somset
75 K6 **Elliot's Town** Caerph
46 F4 **Ellisfield** Hants
292 J3 **Ellishadder** Highld
251 B12 **Ellister** Ag & B
247 H8 **Elliston** Border
131 J4 **Ellistown** Leics
303 J2 **Ellon** Abers
209 K6 **Ellonby** Cumb
123 J2 **Ellough** Suffk
179 L2 **Elloughton** E R Yk
77 H5 **Ellwood** Gloucs
135 K5 **Elm** Cambs
78 D3 **Elmbridge** Gloucs
113 J6 **Elmbridge** Worcs
48 E2 **Elm Corner** Surrey
60 F5 **Elm Cross** Wilts
103 G6 **Elmdon** Essex
114 D3 **Elmdon** Solhll
114 D3 **Elmdon Heath** Solhll
33 J6 **Elmer** W Susx
65 L7 **Elmers End** Gt Lon
173 L6 **Elmers Green** Lancs
47 L8 **Elmers Marsh** W Susx
131 K7 **Elmesthorpe** Leics
21 K3 **Elmfield** IoW
28 E1 **Elm Hill** Dorset
82 C3 **Elmhurst** Bucks
130 C4 **Elmhurst** Staffs
97 G5 **Elmley Castle** Worcs
113 H6 **Elmley Lovett** Worcs
78 B4 **Elmore** Gloucs
78 B3 **Elmore Back** Gloucs
66 D3 **Elm Park** Gt Lon
22 C2 **Elmscott** Devon
105 J4 **Elmsett** Suffk
95 H2 **Elms Green** Herefs
112 E6 **Elms Green** Worcs
192 E6 **Elmslack** Lancs
87 H1 **Elmstead** Essex
66 B6 **Elmstead** Gt Lon
87 H2 **Elmstead Heath** Essex
87 H1 **Elmstead Market** Essex
87 H2 **Elmstead Market** Essex
52 F4 **Elmsted** Kent
53 J1 **Elmstone** Kent
78 E1 **Elmstone Hardwicke** Gloucs
188 E3 **Elmswell** E R Yk
121 K7 **Elmswell** Suffk
167 K6 **Elmton** Derbys
313 L4 **Elphin** Highld
259 K6 **Elphinstone** E Loth
302 F7 **Elrick** Abers
215 H4 **Elrig** D & G
225 K7 **Elrington** Nthumb
94 D3 **Elsdon** Herefs
236 C8 **Elsdon** Nthumb
177 K7 **Elsecar** Barns
85 G1 **Elsenham** Essex
81 G4 **Elsfield** Oxon
180 C5 **Elsham** N Linc
138 B3 **Elsing** Norfk
184 D5 **Elslack** N York
31 L6 **Elson** Hants
149 G6 **Elson** Shrops
245 H5 **Elsrickle** S Lans
48 B5 **Elstead** Surrey
32 F3 **Elsted** W Susx
205 J3 **Elstob** Dur
24 D6 **Elston** Devon
154 E4 **Elston** Notts
44 E5 **Elston** Wilts
24 E5 **Elstone** Devon
101 J4 **Elstow** Beds
83 K7 **Elstree** Herts
181 G1 **Elstronwick** E R Yk
182 D7 **Elswick** Lancs
227 G7 **Elswick** N u Ty
182 D7 **Elswick Leys** Lancs
119 G7 **Elsworth** Cambs
201 J7 **Elterwater** Cumb
66 B6 **Eltham** Gt Lon
102 C2 **Eltisley** Cambs
175 G5 **Elton** Bury
134 B8 **Elton** Cambs
163 J5 **Elton** Ches

City, town and village index: Elton - Frithelstock 379

152 D1 **Elton** Derbys
77 K4 **Elton** Gloucs
111 K5 **Elton** Herefs
154 E6 **Elton** Notts
205 L4 **Elton** S on T
163 H5 **Elton Green** Ches
95 G5 **Elton's Marsh** Herefs
226 D7 **Eltringham** Nthumb
232 D3 **Elvanfoot** S Lans
153 H7 **Elvaston** Derbys
121 G4 **Elveden** Suffk
213 G5 **Elvet Hill** Dur
260 B6 **Elvingston** E Loth
53 J3 **Elvington** Kent
187 J5 **Elvington** York
39 G7 **Elwell** Devon
17 K5 **Elwell** Dorset
213 L7 **Elwick** Hartpl
249 J6 **Elwick** Nthumb
150 D1 **Elworth** Ches
40 E7 **Elworthy** Somset
120 B4 **Ely** Cambs
56 F5 **Ely** Cardif
100 E4 **Emberton** M Keyn
208 E7 **Embleton** Cumb
205 L2 **Embleton** Dur
237 J2 **Embleton** Nthumb
315 K8 **Embo** Highld
42 F3 **Emborough** Somset
315 J8 **Embo Street** Highld
184 F4 **Embsay** N York
66 D3 **Emerson Park** Gt Lon
59 G5 **Emerson's Green** S Glos
100 D7 **Emerson Valley** M Keyn
30 D5 **Emery Down** Hants
177 G5 **Emley** Kirk
63 J7 **Emmbrook** Wokham
63 H5 **Emmer Green** Readg
167 H5 **Emmett Carr** Derbys
81 L6 **Emmington** Oxon
135 K5 **Emneth** Norfk
135 L5 **Emneth Hungate** Norfk
135 L2 **Emorsgate** Norfk
133 K5 **Empingham** Rutlnd
47 H7 **Empshott** Hants
47 H7 **Empshott Green** Hants
114 F6 **Emscote** Warwks
127 L4 **Emstrey** Shrops
32 D5 **Emsworth** Hants
62 B7 **Enborne** W Berk
62 B8 **Enborne Row** W Berk
127 L7 **Enchmarsh** Shrops
131 L7 **Enderby** Leics
192 F5 **Endmoor** Cumb
151 H3 **Endon** Staffs
151 H3 **Endon Bank** Staffs
56 F3 **Energlyn** Caerph
84 C7 **Enfield** Gt Lon
113 L6 **Enfield** Worcs
84 D7 **Enfield Highway** Gt Lon
84 D7 **Enfield Lock** Gt Lon
84 C7 **Enfield Town** Gt Lon
84 D7 **Enfield Wash** Gt Lon
44 F3 **Enford** Wilts
332 D5 **Engamoor** Shet
158 F5 **Engedi** IoA
59 G4 **Engine Common** S Glos
62 F6 **Englefield** W Berk
64 C6 **Englefield Green** Surrey
150 D3 **Englesea-brook** Ches
77 H3 **English Bicknor** Gloucs
59 H8 **Englishcombe** BaNES
149 H8 **English Frankton** Shrops
10 B8 **Engollan** Cnwll
45 L4 **Enham Alamein** Hants
41 H7 **Enmore** Somset
111 K7 **Enmore Field** Herefs
28 F2 **Enmore Green** Dorset
200 D4 **Ennerdale Bridge** Cumb
5 G3 **Enniscaven** Cnwll
279 G2 **Enochdhu** P & K
271 K5 **Ensay** Ag & B
19 H2 **Ensbury** Bmouth
19 H3 **Ensbury Park** Bmouth
127 J3 **Ensdon** Shrops
23 K1 **Ensis** Devon
80 F3 **Enslow** Oxon
80 D2 **Enstone** Oxon
232 B6 **Enterkinfoot** D & G
206 B6 **Enterpen** N York
48 C5 **Enton Green** Surrey
113 G2 **Enville** Staffs
320 D3 **Eòlaigearraidh** W Isls
271 K10 **Eorabus** Ag & B
325 P2 **Eòropaidh** W Isls
78 B4 **Epney** Gloucs
154 C4 **Epperstone** Notts
84 F6 **Epping** Essex
84 E5 **Epping Green** Essex
84 B5 **Epping Green** Herts
84 E6 **Epping Upland** Essex
204 F5 **Eppleby** N York
180 C1 **Eppleworth** E R Yk
49 G1 **Epsom** Surrey
98 E5 **Epwell** Oxon
179 H7 **Epworth** N Linc
179 H7 **Epworth Turbary** N Linc
149 G5 **Erbistock** Wrexhm
294 E3 **Erbusaig** Highld
309 R9 **Erchless Castle** Highld
114 C1 **Erdington** Birm
263 H6 **Eredine** Ag & B
317 J5 **Eriboll** Highld
232 F4 **Ericstane** D & G
50 E6 **Eridge Green** E Susx
253 K5 **Erines** Ag & B
274 D6 **Eriska** Ag & B
120 E4 **Eriswell** Suffk
66 D5 **Erith** Gt Lon
44 C3 **Erlestoke** Wilts
169 J6 **Ermine** Lincs
7 K4 **Ermington** Devon
6 F3 **Ernesettle** C Plym
142 F5 **Erpingham** Norfk
52 B2 **Erriottwood** Kent
297 L4 **Errogie** Highld
268 D3 **Errol** P & K
256 B6 **Erskine** Rens
255 L6 **Erskine Bridge** Rens
218 B6 **Ervie** D & G
106 E7 **Erwarton** Suffk
93 J5 **Erwood** Powys
205 J6 **Eryholme** N York
148 D2 **Eryrys** Denbgs
204 F2 **Escomb** Dur
40 E6 **Escott** Somset
187 H6 **Escrick** N York
72 D3 **Esgair** Carmth
124 F5 **Esgairgeiliog** Powys
160 E5 **Esgyryn** Conwy
212 E5 **Esh** Dur
64 F8 **Esher** Surrey
246 B6 **Eshiels** Border
185 J6 **Esholt** Brad
237 J7 **Eshott** Nthumb
184 D3 **Eshton** N York
212 E5 **Esh Winning** Dur
310 B10 **Eskadale** Highld
259 J7 **Eskbank** Mdloth
200 E7 **Eskdale Green** Cumb
233 J7 **Eskdalemuir** D & G
181 K8 **Eskham** Lincs
178 E4 **Eskholme** Donc
251 F10 **Esknish** Ag & B
207 J7 **Esk Valley** N York
236 E4 **Eslington Park** Nthumb
204 E3 **Esperley Lane Ends** Dur
182 D7 **Esprick** Lancs
133 L4 **Essendine** Rutlnd
84 B5 **Essendon** Herts
310 E10 **Essich** Highld
129 K6 **Essington** Staffs
303 H2 **Esslemont** Abers
206 D4 **Eston** R & Cl
7 H3 **Estover** C Plym
13 H3 **Estrayer Park** Devon
332 H6 **Eswick** Shet
248 E6 **Etal** Nthumb
44 D1 **Etchilhampton** Wilts
36 C1 **Etchingham** E Susx
53 G6 **Etchinghill** Kent
129 L3 **Etchinghill** Staffs
35 K2 **Etchingwood** E Susx
204 F2 **Etherley Dene** Dur
281 J5 **Ethie Mains** Angus
137 L4 **Etling Green** Norfk
77 K5 **Etloe** Gloucs
64 C5 **Eton** W & M
64 C5 **Eton Wick** W & M
151 G4 **Etruria** C Stke
127 H6 **Etsell** Shrops
209 J2 **Etterby** Cumb
286 F3 **Etteridge** Highld
203 K2 **Ettersgill** Dur
150 D1 **Ettiley Heath** Ches
129 J7 **Ettingshall** Wolves
129 J8 **Ettingshall Park** Wolves
98 C4 **Ettington** Warwks
134 C5 **Etton** C Pete
188 E6 **Etton** E R Yk
233 K4 **Ettrick** Border
234 B2 **Ettrickbridge** Border
233 K4 **Ettrickhill** Border
152 E7 **Etwall** Derbys
152 E7 **Etwall Common** Derbys
112 D2 **Eudon Burnell** Shrops
112 D2 **Eudon George** Shrops
121 H4 **Euston** Suffk
174 C4 **Euxton** Lancs
56 C3 **Evanstown** Brdgnd
310 D4 **Evanton** Highld
155 L4 **Evedon** Lincs
113 J1 **Eve Hill** Dudley
315 J8 **Evelix** Highld
96 B5 **Evendine** Herefs
110 F7 **Evenjobb** Powys
99 J7 **Evenley** Nhants
98 B8 **Evenlode** Gloucs
95 J6 **Even Pits** Herefs
60 F4 **Even Swindon** Swindn
204 E3 **Evenwood** Dur
204 F3 **Evenwood Gate** Dur
329 L8 **Everbay** Ork
42 F6 **Evercreech** Somset
99 J2 **Everdon** Nhants
188 B6 **Everingham** E R Yk
45 G3 **Everleigh** Wilts
198 E4 **Everley** N York
101 G7 **Eversholt** Beds
27 K6 **Evershot** Dorset
67 H3 **Eversley** Essex
47 J1 **Eversley** Hants
47 J1 **Eversley Centre** Hants
47 J1 **Eversley Cross** Hants
179 L1 **Everthorpe** E R Yk
101 L3 **Everton** Beds
20 C3 **Everton** Hants
163 G2 **Everton** Lpool
168 C2 **Everton** Notts
223 K4 **Evertown** D & G
95 L4 **Evesbatch** Herefs
97 H5 **Evesham** Worcs
132 C6 **Evington** C Leic
52 F5 **Evington** Kent
208 B6 **Ewanrigg** Cumb
166 E1 **Ewden Village** Sheff
49 H1 **Ewell** Surrey
53 J5 **Ewell Minnis** Kent
62 F2 **Ewelme** Oxon
78 F7 **Ewen** Gloucs
56 B5 **Ewenny** V Glam
156 B4 **Ewerby** Lincs
156 B4 **Ewerby Thorpe** Lincs
223 K1 **Ewes** D & G
48 E5 **Ewhurst** Surrey
36 E2 **Ewhurst Green** E Susx
48 E6 **Ewhurst Green** Surrey
162 E7 **Ewloe** Flints
162 E7 **Ewloe Green** Flints
174 E2 **Ewood** Bl w D
175 G3 **Ewood Bridge** Lancs
12 E3 **Eworthy** Devon
47 K4 **Ewshot** Hants
94 E8 **Ewyas Harold** Herefs
23 L6 **Exbourne** Devon
31 G6 **Exbury** Hants
35 K7 **Exceat** E Susx
25 G2 **Exebridge** Somset
195 L4 **Exelby** N York
14 D3 **Exeter** Devon
39 K6 **Exford** Somset
127 J5 **Exfords Green** Shrops
97 K3 **Exhall** Warwks
115 H2 **Exhall** Warwks
63 G4 **Exlade Street** Oxon
176 D3 **Exley** Calder
184 F6 **Exley Head** Brad
14 E4 **Exminster** Devon
15 G6 **Exmouth** Devon
333 F14 **Exnaboe** Shet
120 C6 **Exning** Suffk
53 G5 **Exted** Kent
14 F4 **Exton** Devon
31 L2 **Exton** Hants
133 J4 **Exton** Rutlnd
40 B7 **Exton** Somset
14 D3 **Exwick** Devon
166 D5 **Eyam** Derbys
99 H3 **Eydon** Nhants
134 E6 **Eye** C Pete
111 K7 **Eye** Herefs
122 C5 **Eye** Suffk
134 E6 **Eye Green** C Pete
261 L8 **Eyemouth** Border
102 B4 **Eyeworth** Beds
51 K3 **Eyhorne Street** Kent
107 G3 **Eyke** Suffk
101 L2 **Eynesbury** Cambs
293 F11 **Eynort** Highld
66 D8 **Eynsford** Kent
80 E5 **Eynsham** Oxon
16 E3 **Eype** Dorset
16 E3 **Eype's Mouth** Dorset
292 G6 **Eyre** Highld
293 K10 **Eyre** Highld
132 B7 **Eyres Monsell** C Leic
53 J4 **Eythorne** Kent
111 K7 **Eyton** Herefs
111 H2 **Eyton** Shrops
127 H4 **Eyton** Shrops
148 F5 **Eyton** Wrexhm
128 B5 **Eyton on Severn** Shrops
128 C3 **Eyton upon the Weald Moors** Wrekin

F

45 J3 **Faberstown** Hants
45 L2 **Faccombe** Hants
206 B7 **Faceby** N York
159 J7 **Fachell** Gwynd
145 L1 **Fachwen** Gwynd
175 J4 **Facit** Lancs
153 J1 **Fackley** Notts
149 L3 **Faddiley** Ches
197 J4 **Fadmoor** N York
55 G1 **Faerdre** Swans
185 J8 **Fagley** Brad
73 K8 **Fagwyr** Swans
285 H1 **Faichem** Highld
256 C6 **Faifley** W Duns
58 D6 **Failand** N Som
230 D1 **Failford** S Ayrs
175 J7 **Failsworth** Oldham
124 C4 **Fairbourne** Gwynd
51 L3 **Fairbourne Heath** Kent
178 B2 **Fairburn** N York
66 C4 **Fair Cross** Gt Lon
175 H5 **Fairfield** Bury
257 K2 **Fairfield** Clacks
165 L6 **Fairfield** Derbys
37 J1 **Fairfield** Kent
163 G2 **Fairfield** Lpool
165 G1 **Fairfield** Tamesd
205 L4 **Fairfield** S on T
97 H5 **Fairfield** Worcs
113 G4 **Fairfield** Worcs
113 J4 **Fairfield** Worcs
59 H7 **Fairfield Park** BaNES
96 B7 **Fairfields** Gloucs
79 K6 **Fairford** Gloucs
136 D3 **Fair Green** Norfk
173 H2 **Fairhaven** Lancs
240 E4 **Fairhaven** N Ayrs
210 B7 **Fair Hill** Cumb
243 L3 **Fairhill** S Lans
48 C3 **Fairlands** Surrey
21 H3 **Fairlee** IoW
241 L2 **Fairlie** N Ayrs
37 G4 **Fairlight** E Susx
37 G4 **Fairlight Cove** E Susx
66 C2 **Fairlop** Gt Lon
19 J3 **Fairmile** Dorset
48 F1 **Fairmile** Surrey
259 G7 **Fairmilehead** C Edin
226 F2 **Fair Moor** Nthumb
75 K7 **Fairoak** Caerph
31 H3 **Fair Oak** Hants
46 D1 **Fair Oak** Hants
183 H5 **Fair Oak** Lancs
150 E7 **Fairoak** Staffs
47 G1 **Fair Oak Green** Hants
50 F1 **Fairseat** Kent
86 B3 **Fairstead** Essex
136 C3 **Fairstead** Norfk
78 F2 **Fairview** Gloucs
35 J1 **Fairwarp** E Susx
56 F5 **Fairwater** Cardif
57 J2 **Fairwater** Torfn
43 L3 **Fairwood** Wilts
23 G2 **Fairy Cross** Devon
141 J5 **Fakenham** Norfk
121 H4 **Fakenham Magna** Suffk
246 E1 **Fala** Mdloth
246 E1 **Fala Dam** Mdloth
246 D2 **Falahill** Border
95 J7 **Falcon** Herefs
130 C7 **Falcon Lodge** Birm
66 B5 **Falconwood** Gt Lon
99 J5 **Falcutt** Nhants
169 L4 **Faldingworth** Lincs
247 G7 **Faldonside** Border
16 j6 **Faldouet** Jersey
59 G2 **Falfield** S Glos
106 F6 **Falkenham** Suffk
106 F6 **Falkenham Sink** Suffk
257 K5 **Falkirk** Falk
268 D6 **Falkland** Fife
235 J4 **Falla** Border
152 F1 **Fallgate** Derbys
257 J2 **Fallin** Stirlg
166 E7 **Fallinge** Derbys
129 K7 **Fallings Heath** Wsall
164 F2 **Fallowfield** Manch
243 L1 **Fallside** N Lans
35 G5 **Falmer** E Susx
3 K4 **Falmouth** Cnwll
234 B5 **Falnash** Border
198 F4 **Falsgrave** N York
258 B7 **Falside** W Loth
225 G2 **Falstone** Nthumb
316 D7 **Fanagmore** Highld
101 H8 **Fancott** Beds
310 B9 **Fanellan** Highld
197 G3 **Fangdale Beck** N York
187 L4 **Fangfoss** E R Yk
257 H4 **Fankerton** Falk
272 B6 **Fanmore** Ag & B
85 K4 **Fanner's Green** Essex
247 J5 **Fans** Border
165 G6 **Fanshowe** Ches
51 H3 **Fant** Kent
191 J5 **Far Arnside** Cumb
178 E5 **Far Bank** Donc
173 K3 **Far Banks** Lancs
134 E8 **Farcet** Cambs
131 H6 **Far Coton** Leics
100 B2 **Far Cotton** Nhants
112 B4 **Farden** Shrops
31 K5 **Fareham** Hants
201 H8 **Far End** Cumb
130 B4 **Farewell** Staffs
112 E5 **Far Forest** Worcs
170 F5 **Farforth** Lincs
78 B6 **Far Green** Gloucs
167 G8 **Farhill** Derbys
130 C2 **Far Hoarcross** Staffs
80 B7 **Faringdon** Oxon
174 B3 **Farington** Lancs
174 B3 **Farington Moss** Lancs
210 C2 **Farlam** Cumb
165 L3 **Farlands Booth** Derbys
315 J5 **Farlary** Highld
153 G4 **Far Laund** Derbys
58 C7 **Farleigh** N Som
49 L1 **Farleigh** Surrey
49 L2 **Farleigh Court** Surrey
51 H3 **Farleigh Green** Kent
43 K2 **Farleigh Hungerford** Somset
46 F4 **Farleigh Wallop** Hants
59 K8 **Farleigh Wick** Wilts
171 J6 **Farlesthorpe** Lincs
192 F5 **Farleton** Cumb
183 G1 **Farleton** Lancs
152 E1 **Farley** Derbys
58 B6 **Farley** N Som
127 H5 **Farley** Shrops
128 C6 **Farley** Shrops
128 F7 **Far Ley** Staffs
151 L5 **Farley** Staffs
45 H8 **Farley** Wilts
104 B3 **Farley Green** Suffk
48 E4 **Farley Green** Surrey
63 J8 **Farley Hill** Wokham
78 B3 **Farleys End** Gloucs
32 C5 **Farlington** C Port
197 H8 **Farlington** N York
112 C3 **Farlow** Shrops
43 G1 **Farmborough** BaNES
85 J4 **Farmbridge End** Essex
97 J8 **Farmcote** Gloucs
112 F1 **Farmcote** Shrops
79 J3 **Farmington** Gloucs
80 E5 **Farmoor** Oxon
174 B7 **Far Moor** Wigan
3 H4 **Farms Common** Cnwll
131 H3 **Farm Town** Leics
305 J5 **Farmtown** Moray
152 F4 **Farnah Green** Derbys
66 B8 **Farnborough** Gt Lon
47 K3 **Farnborough** Hants
98 F4 **Farnborough** Warwks
62 B4 **Farnborough** W Berk
47 L2 **Farnborough Green** Hants
47 L2 **Farnborough Park** Hants
47 L2 **Farnborough Street** Hants
48 C4 **Farncombe** Surrey
117 J7 **Farndish** Beds
149 H3 **Farndon** Ches
154 E3 **Farndon** Notts
281 H3 **Farnell** Angus
29 H3 **Farnham** Dorset
84 F2 **Farnham** Essex
186 B2 **Farnham** N York
107 H2 **Farnham** Suffk
47 K4 **Farnham** Surrey
64 C3 **Farnham Common** Bucks
84 F1 **Farnham Green** Essex
64 C4 **Farnham Park** Bucks
64 C4 **Farnham Royal** Bucks
184 F5 **Farnhill** N York
66 D7 **Farningham** Kent
177 H1 **Farnley** Leeds
185 K5 **Farnley** N York
176 F5 **Farnley Bank** Kirk
176 F5 **Farnley Tyas** Kirk
154 C2 **Farnsfield** Notts
174 F6 **Farnworth** Bolton
163 J3 **Farnworth** Halton
78 E6 **Far Oakridge** Gloucs
298 C2 **Farr** Highld
317 Q4 **Farr** Highld
297 L4 **Farraline** Highld
15 G3 **Farringdon** Devon
213 J3 **Farringdon** Sundld
28 E3 **Farrington** Dorset
42 F2 **Farrington Gurney** BaNES
177 H1 **Far Royds** Leeds
191 H1 **Far Sawrey** Cumb
185 K7 **Farsley** Leeds
86 C6 **Farther Howegreen** Essex
67 K8 **Farthing Corner** Medway
51 K4 **Farthing Green** Kent
99 H6 **Farthinghoe** Nhants
53 J5 **Farthingloe** Kent
99 K3 **Farthingstone** Nhants
78 D6 **Far Thrupp** Gloucs
15 K2 **Farway** Devon
26 E6 **Farway Marsh** Devon
292 B7 **Fasach** Highld
308 E6 **Fasag** Highld
282 B7 **Fascadale** Highld
278 D2 **Faskally** P & K
255 G3 **Faslane Port** Ag & B
274 F5 **Fasnacloich** Ag & B
290 E6 **Fasque** Abers
284 C6 **Fassfern** Highld
213 H3 **Fatfield** Sundld
305 L4 **Fattahead** Abers
258 D6 **Faucheldean** W Loth
210 B3 **Faugh** Cumb
210 B4 **Faugh Head** Cumb
247 G7 **Faughill** Border
152 C8 **Fauld** Staffs
244 E1 **Fauldhouse** W Loth
234 C1 **Fauldshope** Border
86 B3 **Faulkbourne** Essex
43 H3 **Faulkland** Somset
149 L7 **Fauls** Shrops
205 H4 **Faverdale** Darltn
52 C1 **Faversham** Kent
300 E2 **Favillar** Moray
196 D7 **Fawdington** N York
236 E3 **Fawdon** Nthumb
227 G6 **Fawdon** N u Ty
165 L8 **Fawfieldhead** Staffs
66 E7 **Fawkham Green** Kent
61 K3 **Fawler** Oxon
80 D3 **Fawler** Oxon
63 J3 **Fawley** Bucks
31 H6 **Fawley** Hants
61 L4 **Fawley** W Berk
63 H3 **Fawley Bottom** Bucks
95 J8 **Fawley Chapel** Herefs
179 K3 **Faxfleet** E R Yk
49 H7 **Faygate** W Susx
163 G1 **Fazakerley** Lpool
130 E6 **Fazeley** Staffs
286 D3 **Feagour** Highld
195 J5 **Fearby** N York
311 J2 **Fearn** Highld
277 K6 **Fearnan** P & K
308 B6 **Fearnbeg** Highld
164 B2 **Fearnhead** Warrtn
308 B5 **Fearnmore** Highld
186 B7 **Fearnville** Leeds
129 J6 **Featherstone** Staffs
177 L3 **Featherstone** Wakefd
113 L7 **Feckenham** Worcs
159 K4 **Fedw Fawr** IoA
86 D2 **Feering** Essex
194 E2 **Feetham** N York
151 G3 **Fegg Hayes** C Stke
183 L1 **Feizor** N York
49 L6 **Felbridge** Surrey
143 G4 **Felbrigg** Norfk
49 L5 **Felcourt** Surrey
83 G5 **Felden** Herts
53 K2 **Felderland** Kent
164 C5 **Feldy** Ches
111 J2 **Felhampton** Shrops
74 D2 **Felin-Crai** Powys
56 C4 **Felindre** Rhondd
72 F6 **Felindre** Carmth
73 G4 **Felindre** Carmth
73 K3 **Felindre** Carmth
90 D8 **Felindre** Carmth
75 K2 **Felindre** Powys
110 D3 **Felindre** Powys
126 D6 **Felindre** Powys
73 J8 **Felindre** Swans
89 H5 **Felindre Farchog** Pembks
91 H4 **Felinfach** Cerdgn
93 J7 **Felinfach** Powys
54 D1 **Felinfoel** Carmth
73 G4 **Felingwmisaf** Carmth
73 G4 **Felingwmuchaf** Carmth
91 L8 **Felin Newydd** Carmth
93 K6 **Felin-newydd** Powys
148 D8 **Felin Newydd** Powys
148 F4 **Felin Puleston** Wrexhm
90 D6 **Felin-Wnda** Cerdgn
196 E5 **Felixkirk** N York
107 G7 **Felixstowe** Suffk
107 G6 **Felixstowe Ferry** Suffk
248 E5 **Felkington** Nthumb
177 K5 **Felkirk** Wakefd
200 D4 **Felldyke** Cumb
193 K2 **Fell End** Cumb
227 J7 **Fellgate** S Tyne
202 F5 **Fell Head** Cumb
227 H7 **Felling** Gatesd
227 H7 **Felling Shore** Gatesd
184 F6 **Fell Lane** Brad
209 H6 **Fell Side** Cumb
212 E2 **Fellside** Gatesd
101 G2 **Felmersham** Beds
143 G6 **Felmingham** Norfk
67 H3 **Felmore** Essex
33 J6 **Felpham** W Susx
104 F2 **Felsham** Suffk
85 K3 **Felsted** Essex
64 E6 **Feltham** Gt Lon
26 C3 **Feltham** Somset
64 E6 **Felthamhill** Surrey
138 D3 **Felthorpe** Norfk
95 J4 **Felton** Herefs
58 D7 **Felton** N Som
237 H6 **Felton** Nthumb
127 H3 **Felton Butler** Shrops
120 D1 **Feltwell** Norfk
176 F4 **Fenay Bridge** Kirk
184 B7 **Fence** Lancs
213 H3 **Fence Houses** Sundld
81 H3 **Fencott** Oxon
278 C1 **Fenderbridge** P & K
119 K7 **Fen Ditton** Cambs
119 G6 **Fen Drayton** Cambs
134 E2 **Fen End** Lincs
114 E5 **Fen End** Solhll
134 E7 **Fengate** C Pete
142 F7 **Fengate** Norfk
227 G6 **Fenham** N u Ty
156 D5 **Fenhouses** Lincs
174 D2 **Feniscliffe** Bl w D
174 D3 **Feniscowles** Bl w D
25 K7 **Feniton** Devon
101 J4 **Fenlake** Beds
112 F3 **Fenn Green** Shrops
41 G8 **Fennington** Somset
149 K6 **Fenn's Bank** Wrexhm
67 J5 **Fenn Street** Medway
152 C3 **Fenny Bentley** Derbys
25 L7 **Fenny Bridges** Devon
98 F3 **Fenny Compton** Warwks
131 H7 **Fenny Drayton** Leics
100 E7 **Fenny Stratford** M Keyn
226 F1 **Fenrother** Nthumb
156 F2 **Fen Side** Lincs
119 G6 **Fenstanton** Cambs
104 D3 **Fenstead End** Suffk
122 B3 **Fen Street** Suffk
121 K4 **Fen Street** Suffk
122 B4 **Fen Street** Suffk
119 G4 **Fenton** Cambs
151 G5 **Fenton** C Stke
209 L2 **Fenton** Cumb
155 G3 **Fenton** Lincs
168 F5 **Fenton** Lincs
248 F7 **Fenton** Nthumb
10 F6 **Fentonadle** Cnwll
260 C4 **Fenton Barns** E Loth
151 G4 **Fenton Low** C Stke
5 J2 **Fenton Pits** Cnwll
178 D4 **Fenwick** Donc
242 F5 **Fenwick** E Ayrs
226 C5 **Fenwick** Nthumb
249 H5 **Fenwick** Nthumb
238 E6 **Feochaig** Ag & B
3 L3 **Feock** Cnwll
251 G9 **Feolin Ferry** Ag & B
292 D8 **Feorlig** Highld
256 B8 **Ferguslie Park** Rens
294 B7 **Ferindonald** Highld
292 B6 **Feriniquarrie** Highld
16 d3 **Fermain Bay** Guern
280 E2 **Fern** Angus
63 L3 **Fern** Bucks
176 B8 **Fern Bank** Tamesd
50 E5 **Ferndale** Kent
74 F7 **Ferndale** Rhondd
29 K7 **Ferndown** Dorset
29 G2 **Ferne** Wilts
311 M9 **Ferness** Highld
191 J1 **Ferney Green** Cumb
61 J2 **Fernham** Oxon
175 H5 **Fernhill** Bury
75 G7 **Fernhill** Rhondd
104 D4 **Fern Hill** Suffk
49 J5 **Fernhill** W Susx
174 E6 **Fernhill Gate** Bolton
96 E2 **Fernhill Heath** Worcs
48 B8 **Fernhurst** W Susx
268 E4 **Fernie** Fife
243 L3 **Ferniegair** S Lans
246 E5 **Ferniehirst** Border
293 F10 **Fernilea** Highld
165 K5 **Fernilee** Derbys
3 K2 **Fernsplatt** Cnwll
186 C2 **Ferrensby** N York
180 B3 **Ferriby Sluice** N Linc
33 L6 **Ferring** W Susx
178 B3 **Ferrybridge** Wakefd
281 K3 **Ferryden** Angus
303 H7 **Ferryhill** C Aber
119 H3 **Ferry Hill** Cambs
213 G7 **Ferryhill** Dur
213 G7 **Ferryhill Station** Dur
72 D7 **Ferryside** Carmth
122 B3 **Fersfield** Norfk
285 K6 **Fersit** Highld
299 G8 **Feshiebridge** Highld
48 F2 **Fetcham** Surrey
307 H5 **Fetterangus** Abers
290 E7 **Fettercairn** Abers
310 D7 **Fettes** Highld
99 H8 **Fewcott** Oxon
185 J4 **Fewston** N York
185 J4 **Fewston Bents** N York
73 J4 **Ffairfach** Carmth
108 E6 **Ffair-Rhos** Cerdgn
91 K7 **Ffaldybrenin** Carmth
91 L7 **Ffarmers** Carmth
75 L3 **Ffawyddog** Powys
162 B8 **Ffordd-las** Denbgs
94 B6 **Fforddlas** Powys
55 L5 **Ffordd-y-Gyfraith** Brdgnd
73 H8 **Fforest** Carmth
54 F2 **Fforest-fach** Swans
55 H1 **Fforest Gôch** Neath
108 C6 **Ffoshelyg** Cerdgn
90 E6 **Ffostrasol** Cerdgn
75 H5 **Ffos-y-frân** Myr Td
148 F3 **Ffos-y-go** Wrexhm
126 D7 **Ffridd** Powys
145 L3 **Ffridd Uchaf** Gwynd
148 E2 **Ffrith** Flints
72 C5 **Ffynnon** Carmth
72 E4 **Ffynnon-ddrain** Carmth
88 E7 **Ffynnon Gron** Pembks
162 B4 **Ffynnongroyw** Flints
93 L5 **Ffynnon Gynydd** Powys
314 C2 **Fiag Bridge** Highld
49 L1 **Fickleshole** Surrey
271 J10 **Fidden** Ag & B
291 J5 **Fiddes** Abers
96 F7 **Fiddington** Gloucs
41 H5 **Fiddington** Somset
44 D3 **Fiddington Sands** Wilts
28 E4 **Fiddleford** Dorset
173 J3 **Fiddler's Ferry** Sefton
163 L3 **Fiddler's Ferry** Warrtn
307 K3 **Fiddler's Green** Abers
78 E2 **Fiddler's Green** Gloucs
95 J6 **Fiddler's Green** Herefs
137 L7 **Fiddlers' Green** Norfk
84 F6 **Fiddlers Hamlet** Essex
325 Q7 **Fidigeadh** W Isls
94 D3 **Field** Herefs
42 F5 **Field** Somset
151 K7 **Field** Staffs
80 C4 **Field Assarts** Oxon
191 H4 **Field Broughton** Cumb
64 F7 **Field Common** Surrey
142 C4 **Field Dalling** Norfk
51 J7 **Field Green** Kent
131 K5 **Field Head** Leics
83 G5 **Fields End** Herts
94 F3 **Field's Place** Herefs
28 D2 **Fifehead Magdalen** Dorset
28 D4 **Fifehead Neville** Dorset
28 D4 **Fifehead St Quintin** Dorset
305 G5 **Fife Keith** Moray
79 L3 **Fifield** Oxon
64 B5 **Fifield** W & M
44 F3 **Fifield** Wilts
29 J1 **Fifield Bavant** Wilts
45 G4 **Figheldean** Wilts
60 B3 **Filands** Wilts
139 K4 **Filby** Norfk
139 K4 **Filby Heath** Norfk
80 F5 **Filchampstead** Oxon
35 L6 **Filching** E Susx
199 H5 **Filey** N York
16 E2 **Filford** Dorset
100 E4 **Filgrave** M Keyn
7 K3 **Filham** Devon
79 L6 **Filkins** Oxon
24 C4 **Filleigh** Devon
39 G8 **Filleigh** Devon
169 H3 **Fillingham** Lincs
114 F2 **Fillongley** Warwks
47 G8 **Filmore Hill** Hants
58 E5 **Filton** S Glos
58 E7 **Filwood Park** Bristl
188 C2 **Fimber** E R Yk
280 E3 **Finavon** Angus
263 G7 **Finchairn** Ag & B
163 H2 **Fincham** Lpool
136 D5 **Fincham** Norfk
63 J8 **Finchampstead** Wokham
32 D4 **Finchdean** Hants
103 L7 **Finchingfield** Essex
65 J2 **Finchley** Gt Lon
268 F3 **Fincraigs** Fife
152 F7 **Findern** Derbys
311 N5 **Findhorn** Moray
305 H2 **Findochty** Moray
267 J3 **Findo Gask** P & K
291 L2 **Findon** Abers
34 B5 **Findon** W Susx
310 E5 **Findon Mains** Highld
34 B5 **Findon Valley** W Susx
117 J5 **Finedon** Nhants
94 D6 **Fine Street** Herefs
122 E6 **Fingal Street** Suffk
302 E3 **Fingask** Abers
112 E5 **Fingerpost** Worcs
63 J2 **Fingest** Bucks
195 J4 **Finghall** N York
209 G2 **Fingland** Cumb
231 K3 **Fingland** D & G
53 K3 **Finglesham** Kent
87 G2 **Fingringhoe** Essex
115 G4 **Finham** Covtry
177 J8 **Finkle Street** Barns
277 G8 **Finlarig** Stirlg
99 K7 **Finmere** Bucks
276 F3 **Finnart** P & K
165 G4 **Finney Green** Ches
150 E4 **Finney Green** Staffs
122 B6 **Finningham** Suffk
178 F8 **Finningley** Donc
305 L5 **Finnygaud** Abers
323 J7 **Finsbay** W Isls
65 K4 **Finsbury** Gt Lon
65 K3 **Finsbury Park** Gt Lon
113 K6 **Finstall** Worcs
191 H3 **Finsthwaite** Cumb
80 D3 **Finstock** Oxon
328 D11 **Finstown** Ork
306 D5 **Fintry** Abers
280 D8 **Fintry** C Dund
256 E3 **Fintry** Stirlg
114 D6 **Finwood** Warwks
290 E3 **Finzean** Abers
271 J10 **Fionnphort** Ag & B
323 J7 **Fionnsabhagh** W Isls
193 H3 **Firbank** Cumb
167 L3 **Firbeck** Rothm
187 K1 **Firby** N York
195 L4 **Firby** N York
175 K5 **Firgrove** Rochdl
310 E4 **Firhill** Highld
35 J5 **Firle** E Susx
171 J8 **Firsby** Lincs
45 H7 **Firsdown** Wilts
174 D7 **Firs Lane** Wigan
312 E8 **First Coast** Highld
164 F2 **Firswood** Traffd
234 E2 **Firth** Border
328 E11 **Firth** Ork
331 F11 **Firth** Shet
205 J5 **Firth Moor** Darltn
281 G6 **Firth Muir of Boysack** Angus
167 G2 **Firth Park** Sheff
52 B5 **Fir Toll** Kent
212 D7 **Fir Tree** Dur
167 G2 **Fir Vale** Sheff
174 F5 **Firwood Fold** Bolton
21 J3 **Fishbourne** IoW
32 F6 **Fishbourne** W Susx
213 J7 **Fishburn** Dur
257 L1 **Fishcross** Clacks
302 C1 **Fisherford** Abers
100 E6 **Fishermead** M Keyn
259 J6 **Fisherrow** E Loth
34 E5 **Fishersgate** W Susx
31 H2 **Fisher's Pond** Hants
48 C7 **Fisherstreet** W Susx
310 G7 **Fisherton** Highld
229 K3 **Fisherton** S Ayrs
44 D6 **Fisherton de la Mere** Wilts
311 K6 **Fishertown** Highld
130 D5 **Fisherwick** Staffs
63 L4 **Fishery** W & M
88 F5 **Fishguard** Pembks
178 F5 **Fishlake** Donc
23 J5 **Fishleigh** Devon
23 K5 **Fishleigh Castle** Devon
139 J4 **Fishley** Norfk
129 K6 **Fishley** Wsall
156 E6 **Fishmere End** Lincs
26 F7 **Fishpond Bottom** Dorset
58 F5 **Fishponds** Bristl
175 H6 **Fishpool** Bury
95 L8 **Fishpool** Gloucs
185 K5 **Fishpool** N York
110 D6 **Fishpools** Powys
157 G5 **Fishtoft** Lincs
156 F4 **Fishtoft Drove** Lincs
248 E3 **Fishwick** Border
174 C2 **Fishwick** Lancs
293 E10 **Fiskavaig** Highld
169 K6 **Fiskerton** Lincs
154 D3 **Fiskerton** Notts
189 K8 **Fitling** E R Yk
44 F4 **Fittleton** Wilts
33 K3 **Fittleworth** W Susx
135 J4 **Fitton End** Cambs
175 K7 **Fitton Hill** Oldham
127 J3 **Fitz** Shrops
40 F8 **Fitzhead** Somset
177 L4 **Fitzwilliam** Wakefd
272 F5 **Fiunary** Highld
77 H4 **Five Acres** Gloucs
35 J2 **Five Ash Down** E Susx
35 L2 **Five Ashes** E Susx
40 E5 **Five Bells** Somset
95 K4 **Five Bridges** Herefs
163 K5 **Fivecrosses** Ches
26 F2 **Fivehead** Somset
20 F4 **Five Houses** IoW
182 F4 **Five Lane Ends** Lancs
11 J5 **Fivelanes** Cnwll
58 C2 **Five Lanes** Mons
50 F4 **Five Oak Green** Kent
16 i7 **Five Oaks** Jersey
48 E8 **Five Oaks** W Susx
72 F7 **Five Roads** Carmth
114 E6 **Five Ways** Warwks
51 K3 **Five Wents** Kent
176 E3 **Fixby** Kirk
37 G2 **Flackley Ash** E Susx
86 B3 **Flack's Green** Essex
63 L3 **Flackwell Heath** Bucks
97 G4 **Fladbury** Worcs
97 G4 **Fladbury Cross** Worcs
333 G10 **Fladdabister** Shet
166 B7 **Flagg** Derbys
95 K3 **Flaggoners Green** Herefs
199 K7 **Flamborough** E R Yk
83 H4 **Flamstead** Herts
84 C6 **Flamstead End** Herts
33 J6 **Flansham** W Susx
177 J3 **Flanshaw** Wakefd
185 G7 **Flappit Spring** Brad
184 D3 **Flasby** N York
165 K7 **Flash** Staffs
292 F6 **Flashader** Highld
33 J2 **Flathurst** W Susx
83 G6 **Flaunden** Herts
154 E5 **Flawborough** Notts
186 E1 **Flawith** N York
58 D7 **Flax Bourton** N Som
186 C3 **Flaxby** N York
152 F5 **Flaxholme** Derbys
138 C8 **Flaxlands** Norfk
77 K3 **Flaxley** Gloucs
175 G3 **Flax Moss** Lancs
40 F6 **Flaxpool** Somset
187 J2 **Flaxton** N York
132 C8 **Fleckney** Leics
115 L7 **Flecknoe** Warwks
168 F6 **Fledborough** Notts
17 J5 **Fleet** Dorset
32 D6 **Fleet** Hants
47 K3 **Fleet** Hants
135 H2 **Fleet** Lincs
66 E6 **Fleet Downs** Kent
31 J5 **Fleetend** Hants
135 H1 **Fleet Hargate** Lincs
31 K6 **Fleetlands** Hants
184 E2 **Fleets** N York
19 G3 **Fleet's Corner** Poole
182 B5 **Fleetwood** Lancs
139 J4 **Fleggburgh** Norfk
325 P7 **Fleisirin** W Isls
213 J5 **Fleming Field** Dur
53 J2 **Flemings** Kent
56 D6 **Flemingston** V Glam
243 J2 **Flemington** S Lans
243 L5 **Flemington** S Lans
121 G6 **Flempton** Suffk
323 J7 **Fleoideabhagh** W Isls
5 J1 **Fletchersbridge** Cnwll
50 D3 **Fletcher's Green** Kent
208 E5 **Fletchertown** Cumb
35 H2 **Fletching** E Susx
35 H2 **Fletching Common** E Susx
315 J8 **Fleuchary** Highld
75 K7 **Fleur-de-lis** Caerph
22 C5 **Flexbury** Cnwll
31 G2 **Flexford** Hants
48 B4 **Flexford** Surrey
208 B7 **Flimby** Cumb
51 H7 **Flimwell** E Susx
162 E6 **Flint** Flints
102 F5 **Flint Cross** Cambs
154 D4 **Flintham** Notts
212 E3 **Flint Hill** Dur
162 D6 **Flint Mountain** Flints
189 K7 **Flinton** E R Yk
114 F3 **Flint's Green** Solhll
94 D2 **Flintsham** Herefs
51 J6 **Flishinghurst** Kent
140 E6 **Flitcham** Norfk
203 H5 **Flitholme** Cumb
101 J6 **Flitton** Beds
101 H7 **Flitwick** Beds
179 K4 **Flixborough** N Linc
179 K5 **Flixborough Stather** N Linc
198 F6 **Flixton** N York
123 G2 **Flixton** Suffk
164 D2 **Flixton** Traffd
177 G5 **Flockton** Kirk
177 H4 **Flockton Green** Kirk
177 G5 **Flockton Moor** Kirk
321 P3 **Flodaigh** W Isls
248 E6 **Flodden** Nthumb
292 H2 **Flodigarry** Highld
94 C2 **Floodgates** Herefs
135 H8 **Flood's Ferry** Cambs
29 L3 **Flood Street** Hants
191 H5 **Flookburgh** Cumb
138 D7 **Flordon** Norfk
99 K2 **Flore** Nhants
151 H5 **Florence** C Stke
236 D6 **Flotterton** Nthumb
82 C7 **Flowers Bottom** Bucks
36 B4 **Flowers Green** E Susx
165 H1 **Flowery Field** Tamesd
105 J4 **Flowton** Suffk
256 D6 **Fluchter** E Duns
331 G13 **Flugarth** Shet
331 G10 **Flukes Hole** Shet
176 E6 **Flush House** Kirk
307 J6 **Flushing** Abers
3 L4 **Flushing** Cnwll
15 H3 **Fluxton** Devon
97 G3 **Flyford Flavell** Worcs
122 F5 **Foals Green** Suffk
67 H4 **Fobbing** Thurr
304 E4 **Fochabers** Moray
75 J5 **Fochriw** Caerph
179 J4 **Fockerby** N Linc
136 C5 **Fodderstone Gap** Norfk
310 C6 **Fodderty** Highld
42 E8 **Foddington** Somset
125 K4 **Foel** Powys
73 G6 **Foel-gastell** Carmth
280 D5 **Foffarty** Angus
187 L7 **Foggathorpe** E R Yk
165 H3 **Foggbrook** Stockp
248 B4 **Fogo** Border
332 C5 **Fogrigarth** Shet
304 C4 **Fogwatt** Moray
316 D7 **Foindle** Highld
279 J2 **Folda** Angus
175 J4 **Fold Head** Lancs
157 J3 **Fold Hill** Lincs
166 E2 **Foldrings** Sheff
151 K6 **Fole** Staffs
115 H3 **Foleshill** Covtry
113 G4 **Foley Park** Worcs
28 B4 **Folke** Dorset
53 H6 **Folkestone** Kent
155 L7 **Folkingham** Lincs
35 K6 **Folkington** E Susx
118 C1 **Folksworth** Cambs
198 F6 **Folkton** N York
302 D2 **Folla Rule** Abers
128 F7 **Folley** Shrops
186 B4 **Follifoot** N York
227 J7 **Follingsby** Gatesd
28 C6 **Folly** Dorset
70 E2 **Folly** Pembks
23 G5 **Folly Cross** Devon
23 K7 **Folly Gate** Devon
86 B1 **Folly Green** Essex
56 D7 **Fonmon** V Glam
11 J3 **Fonston** Cnwll
44 B7 **Fonthill Bishop** Wilts
44 B7 **Fonthill Gifford** Wilts
28 F3 **Fontmell Magna** Dorset
28 E4 **Fontmell Parva** Dorset
33 J5 **Fontwell** W Susx
56 D7 **Font-y-gary** V Glam
268 F4 **Foodieash** Fife
166 C5 **Foolow** Derbys
97 H8 **Footbridge** Gloucs
130 B6 **Footherley** Staffs
112 D5 **Footrid** Worcs
66 C6 **Foots Cray** Gt Lon
301 G6 **Forbestown** Abers
191 G2 **Force Forge** Cumb
50 B2 **Force Green** Kent
191 G2 **Force Mills** Cumb
204 F5 **Forcett** N York
13 G3 **Forda** Devon
38 C6 **Forda** Devon
262 F7 **Ford** Ag & B
82 B5 **Ford** Bucks
7 G3 **Ford** C Plym
167 H4 **Ford** Derbys
7 K4 **Ford** Devon
8 C6 **Ford** Devon
23 G2 **Ford** Devon
26 C6 **Ford** Devon
97 J8 **Ford** Gloucs
95 H2 **Ford** Herefs
69 H7 **Ford** Kent
248 E6 **Ford** Nthumb
88 F7 **Ford** Pembks
173 H8 **Ford** Sefton
127 J4 **Ford** Shrops
40 E8 **Ford** Somset
42 E3 **Ford** Somset
151 L3 **Ford** Staffs
45 G7 **Ford** Wilts
59 K6 **Ford** Wilts
33 K6 **Ford** W Susx
114 D2 **Fordbridge** Solhll
50 D5 **Fordcombe** Kent
267 L5 **Fordel** P & K
258 F3 **Fordell** Fife
126 E6 **Forden** Powys
85 K3 **Ford End** Essex
102 F7 **Ford End** Essex
6 F3 **Forder** Cnwll
14 B8 **Forder Green** Devon
41 K7 **Fordgate** Somset
151 G3 **Ford Green** C Stke
182 E5 **Ford Green** Lancs
120 C5 **Fordham** Cambs
104 F8 **Fordham** Essex
136 C7 **Fordham** Norfk
86 E1 **Fordham Heath** Essex
127 J4 **Ford Heath** Shrops
248 F6 **Ford Hill** Nthumb
129 J6 **Fordhouses** Wolves
266 D3 **Fordie** P & K
29 L3 **Fordingbridge** Hants
171 H6 **Fordington** Lincs
227 H5 **Fordley** N Tyne
199 G6 **Fordon** E R Yk
291 G6 **Fordoun** Abers
35 H1 **Ford's Green** E Susx
122 B6 **Ford's Green** Suffk
86 E1 **Fordstreet** Essex
26 B3 **Ford Street** Somset
24 E7 **Fordton** Devon
26 E6 **Fordwater** Devon
80 B4 **Fordwells** Oxon
53 G2 **Fordwich** Kent
305 K3 **Fordyce** Abers
129 J2 **Forebridge** Staffs
194 B8 **Foredale** N York
299 G3 **Foregin** Highld
229 L2 **Forehill** S Ayrs
21 K4 **Foreland Fields** IoW
131 G1 **Foremark** Derbys
16 c4 **Forest** Guern
183 L4 **Forest Becks** Lancs
236 F7 **Forestburn Gate** Nthumb
76 B2 **Forest Coal Pit** Mons
49 L1 **Forestdale** Gt Lon
66 B3 **Forest Gate** Gt Lon
32 B4 **Forest Gate** Hants
78 C6 **Forest Green** Gloucs
48 F5 **Forest Green** Surrey
227 H6 **Forest Hall** N Tyne
210 C2 **Forest Head** Cumb
65 L6 **Forest Hill** Gt Lon
81 H5 **Forest Hill** Oxon
61 H7 **Forest Hill** Wilts
175 H2 **Forest Holme** Lancs
203 K2 **Forest-in-Teesdale** Dur
186 B3 **Forest Lane Head** N York
257 L2 **Forest Mill** Clacks
186 B3 **Forest Moor** N York
22 F4 **Forestreet** Devon
50 B6 **Forest Row** E Susx
21 G4 **Forest Side** IoW
32 E4 **Forestside** W Susx
153 L1 **Forest Town** Notts
43 K1 **Forewoods Common** Wilts
280 E4 **Forfar** Angus
267 K4 **Forgandenny** P & K
3 H1 **Forge** Cnwll
124 F7 **Forge** Powys
76 B7 **Forge Hammer** Torfn
75 L5 **Forge Side** Torfn
243 L2 **Forgewood** N Lans
304 F5 **Forgie** Moray
305 L6 **Forgue** Abers
113 L4 **Forhill** Worcs
173 G6 **Formby** Sefton
138 C8 **Forncett End** Norfk
138 D8 **Forncett St Mary** Norfk
138 D8 **Forncett St Peter** Norfk
279 G5 **Forneth** P & K
121 G6 **Fornham All Saints** Suffk
121 H6 **Fornham St Genevieve** Suffk
121 G6 **Fornham St Martin** Suffk
10 F3 **Forrabury** Cnwll
311 N6 **Forres** Moray
257 K7 **Forrestfield** N Lans
104 C7 **Forry's Green** Essex
151 J5 **Forsbrook** Staffs
319 M10 **Forse** Highld
114 B5 **Forshaw Heath** Warwks
318 E8 **Forsinard** Highld
51 H2 **Forstal** Kent
17 K2 **Forston** Dorset
297 G7 **Fort Augustus** Highld
279 J2 **Forter** Angus
267 K4 **Forteviot** P & K
310 H6 **Fort George** Highld
244 E3 **Forth** S Lans
96 E7 **Forthampton** Gloucs
77 L7 **Forthay** Gloucs
16 c2 **Fort Hommet** Guern
258 E5 **Forth Road Bridge** C Edin
277 K5 **Fortingall** P & K
65 J3 **Fortis Green** Gt Lon
16 e1 **Fort le Marchant** Guern
255 H5 **Fort Matilda** Inver
31 L6 **Forton** Hants
46 B5 **Forton** Hants
182 E4 **Forton** Lancs
127 J3 **Forton** Shrops
26 E5 **Forton** Somset
128 E2 **Forton** Staffs
127 J3 **Forton Heath** Shrops
306 B6 **Fortrie** Abers
307 H7 **Fortrie** Abers
310 G6 **Fortrose** Highld
17 K7 **Fortuneswell** Dorset
284 E7 **Fort William** Highld
64 B2 **Forty Green** Bucks
82 B6 **Forty Green** Bucks
84 C7 **Forty Hill** Gt Lon
122 B7 **Forward Green** Suffk
78 D6 **Forwood** Gloucs
45 K2 **Fosbury** Wilts
80 B2 **Foscot** Oxon
100 B6 **Foscote** Bucks
99 L4 **Foscote** Nhants
59 L5 **Foscote** Wilts
156 F7 **Fosdyke** Lincs
156 F7 **Fosdyke Bridge** Lincs
277 L3 **Foss** P & K
79 H5 **Foss Cross** Gloucs
79 H4 **Fossebridge** Gloucs
90 F3 **Foss-y-ffin** Cerdgn
52 E1 **Fostall** Kent
51 K6 **Fosten Green** Kent
178 F5 **Fosterhouses** Donc
99 L3 **Foster's Booth** Nhants
113 K6 **Foster's Green** Worcs
84 F5 **Foster Street** Essex
152 C7 **Foston** Derbys
132 C8 **Foston** Leics
155 G5 **Foston** Lincs
187 J1 **Foston** N York
189 H3 **Foston on the Wolds** E R Yk
170 F2 **Fotherby** Lincs
208 B7 **Fothergill** Cumb
134 B8 **Fotheringhay** Nhants
327 M4 **Foubister** Ork
135 K3 **Foul Anchor** Cambs
209 K4 **Foulbridge** Cumb
248 E2 **Foulden** Border
136 F7 **Foulden** Norfk
130 E7 **Foul End** Warwks
30 B5 **Foulford** Hants
36 B3 **Foul Mile** E Susx
35 L6 **Foulride Green** E Susx
184 C6 **Foulridge** Lancs
142 C7 **Foulsham** Norfk
2 F3 **Foundry** Cnwll
142 D6 **Foundry Hill** Norfk
55 L5 **Fountain** Brdgnd
246 E4 **Fountainhall** Border
82 D7 **Four Ashes** Bucks
114 C4 **Four Ashes** Solhll
113 G2 **Four Ashes** Staffs
129 J5 **Four Ashes** Staffs
121 L5 **Four Ashes** Suffk
16 c3 **Four Cabots** Guern
125 L5 **Four Crosses** Powys
126 F3 **Four Crosses** Powys
129 K5 **Four Crosses** Staffs
148 D3 **Four Crosses** Wrexhm
26 D5 **Four Elms** Devon
50 C4 **Four Elms** Kent
42 E7 **Four Foot** Somset
41 H6 **Four Forks** Somset
174 D6 **Four Gates** Bolton
135 J3 **Four Gotes** Cambs
62 F7 **Four Houses Corner** W Berk
177 H7 **Four Lane End** Barns
174 E2 **Four Lane Ends** Bury
185 H8 **Four Lane Ends** Brad
175 G5 **Four Lane Ends** Bury
3 H3 **Four Lanes** Cnwll
150 F2 **Fourlanes End** Ches
47 G6 **Four Marks** Hants
158 D5 **Four Mile Bridge** IoA
78 C4 **Four Mile Elm** Gloucs
37 G2 **Four Oaks** E Susx
95 L8 **Four Oaks** Gloucs
52 C1 **Four Oaks** Kent
114 E3 **Four Oaks** Birm
130 C7 **Four Oaks Park** Birm
315 K8 **Fourpenny** Highld
62 E5 **Four Points** W Berk
97 H5 **Four Pools** Worcs
72 F7 **Four Roads** Carmth
225 K6 **Fourstones** Nthumb
51 J8 **Four Throws** Kent
85 J4 **Four Wantz** Essex
51 J6 **Four Wents** Kent
51 J7 **Four Wents** Kent
44 D8 **Fovant** Wilts
303 J4 **Foveran** Abers
5 K4 **Fowey** Cnwll
41 K6 **Fowler's Plot** Somset
164 C1 **Fowley Common** Warrtn
280 B8 **Fowlis** Angus
267 G3 **Fowlis Wester** P & K
102 F4 **Fowlmere** Cambs
95 J7 **Fownhope** Herefs
105 J7 **Foxash Estate** Essex
242 F1 **Foxbar** Rens
66 B6 **Foxbury** Gt Lon
80 F6 **Foxcombe Hill** Oxon
100 F8 **Fox Corner** Beds
48 C3 **Fox Corner** Surrey
79 G3 **Foxcote** Gloucs
43 H2 **Foxcote** Somset
172 d7 **Foxdale** IoM
46 D3 **Foxdown** Hants
104 D5 **Foxearth** Essex
67 G7 **Foxendown** Kent
190 E3 **Foxfield** Cumb
115 G3 **Foxford** Covtry
60 C5 **Foxham** Wilts
85 H7 **Fox Hatch** Essex
59 J8 **Fox Hill** BaNES
95 L4 **Fox Hill** Herefs
30 E4 **Foxhills** Hants
5 G4 **Foxhole** Cnwll
11 K2 **Foxhole** Cnwll
138 E7 **Foxhole** Norfk
54 E4 **Fox Hole** Swans
198 F7 **Foxholes** N York
43 L5 **Fox Holes** Wilts
35 K3 **Foxhunt Green** E Susx
47 L2 **Fox Lane** Hants
94 F4 **Foxley** Herefs
137 L2 **Foxley** Norfk
150 E3 **Foxley** Staffs
59 L3 **Foxley** Wilts
113 L6 **Foxlydiate** Worcs
177 G4 **Fox Royd** Kirk
105 H8 **Fox Street** Essex
151 K4 **Foxt** Staffs
102 F4 **Foxton** Cambs
205 K3 **Foxton** Dur
116 E2 **Foxton** Leics
196 D2 **Foxton** N York
194 C6 **Foxup** N York
164 B7 **Foxwist Green** Ches
112 C4 **Foxwood** Shrops
95 J8 **Foy** Herefs
297 J4 **Foyers** Highld
2 F4 **Fraddam** Cnwll
4 F3 **Fraddon** Cnwll
130 C4 **Fradley** Staffs
130 C4 **Fradley Junction** Staffs
130 D4 **Fradley South** Staffs
151 J7 **Fradswell** Staffs
189 J2 **Fraisthorpe** E R Yk
35 J2 **Framfield** E Susx
138 F6 **Framingham Earl** Norfk
138 F6 **Framingham Pigot** Norfk
122 F7 **Framlingham** Suffk
17 J2 **Frampton** Dorset
156 F6 **Frampton** Lincs
59 G4 **Frampton Cotterell** S Glos
97 H7 **Frampton Court** Gloucs
59 G4 **Frampton End** S Glos
78 E6 **Frampton Mansell** Gloucs
77 L5 **Frampton on Severn** Gloucs
156 E5 **Frampton West End** Lincs
106 D2 **Framsden** Suffk
213 G5 **Framwellgate Moor** Dur
78 E6 **France Lynch** Gloucs
113 G4 **Franche** Worcs
164 B5 **Frandley** Ches
162 D3 **Frankby** Wirral
143 H7 **Frankfort** Norfk
95 H4 **Franklands Gate** Herefs
113 K3 **Frankley** Worcs
113 K3 **Frankley Green** Worcs
113 K4 **Frankley Hill** Worcs
93 K2 **Frank's Bridge** Powys
115 J5 **Frankton** Warwks
127 K4 **Frankwell** Shrops
138 B4 **Frans Green** Norfk
50 E6 **Frant** E Susx
307 J2 **Fraserburgh** Abers
87 H2 **Frating** Essex
87 H2 **Frating Green** Essex
32 C6 **Fratton** C Port
130 E7 **Freasley** Warwks
6 E4 **Freathy** Cnwll
167 G4 **Frecheville** Sheff
120 D5 **Freckenham** Suffk
173 K2 **Freckleton** Lancs
49 G3 **Fredley** Surrey
166 F6 **Freebirch** Derbys
133 G3 **Freeby** Leics
46 C4 **Freefolk** Hants
151 K5 **Freehay** Staffs
80 E4 **Freeland** Oxon
256 B7 **Freeland** Rens
138 D3 **Freeland Corner** Norfk
30 F4 **Freemantle** C Sotn
258 C8 **Freeport Village** W Loth
332 G6 **Freester** Shet
139 J5 **Freethorpe** Norfk
175 H5 **Free Town** Bury
4 F5 **Freewater** Cnwll
84 D7 **Freezy Water** Gt Lon
157 G5 **Freiston** Lincs
157 G5 **Freiston Shore** Lincs
38 D7 **Fremington** Devon
194 F2 **Fremington** N York
58 F5 **Frenchay** S Glos
13 K4 **Frenchbeer** Devon
85 L2 **Frenches Green** Essex
45 J8 **Frenchmoor** Hants
50 C3 **French Street** Kent
174 B2 **Frenchwood** Lancs
47 K5 **Frensham** Surrey
122 C3 **Frenze** Norfk
318 F3 **Fresgoe** Highld
60 F4 **Freshbrook** Swindn
173 G6 **Freshfield** Sefton
43 J1 **Freshford** BaNES
20 D4 **Freshwater** IoW
20 D4 **Freshwater Bay** IoW
71 G7 **Freshwater East** Pembks
122 E4 **Fressingfield** Suffk
106 D6 **Freston** Suffk
319 Q3 **Freswick** Highld
77 L5 **Fretherne** Gloucs
138 E3 **Frettenham** Norfk
268 D6 **Freuchie** Fife
279 K2 **Freuchies** Angus
70 E4 **Freystrop** Pembks
41 G6 **Friarn** Somset
129 L8 **Friar Park** Sandw
19 K3 **Friars Cliff** Dorset
50 C7 **Friar's Gate** E Susx
37 G4 **Friar's Hill** E Susx
267 L3 **Friarton** P & K
17 J4 **Friar Waddon** Dorset
135 K5 **Friday Bridge** Cambs
65 L2 **Friday Hill** Gt Lon
107 G3 **Friday Street** Suffk
123 H7 **Friday Street** Suffk
48 F4 **Friday Street** Surrey
188 C3 **Fridaythorpe** E R Yk
65 J2 **Friern Barnet** Gt Lon
270 F4 **Friesland** Ag & B
169 L4 **Friesthorpe** Lincs
155 H4 **Frieston** Lincs
63 J3 **Frieth** Bucks
26 C1 **Frieze Hill** Somset
153 J3 **Friezeland** Notts
80 E7 **Frilford** Oxon
80 E7 **Frilford Heath** Oxon
62 D6 **Frilsham** W Berk
47 L2 **Frimley** Surrey
47 L2 **Frimley Green** Surrey
47 L2 **Frimley Ridge** Surrey
67 H7 **Frindsbury** Medway
140 E5 **Fring** Norfk
99 J8 **Fringford** Oxon
51 K2 **Friningham** Kent
104 B6 **Frinkle Green** Essex
51 L2 **Frinsted** Kent
87 L3 **Frinton-on-Sea** Essex
281 G5 **Friockheim** Angus
124 C4 **Friog** Gwynd
132 D6 **Frisby** Leics
132 D3 **Frisby on the Wreake** Leics
157 J2 **Friskney** Lincs
157 J2 **Friskney Eaudyke** Lincs
157 J3 **Friskney Tofts** Lincs
35 K7 **Friston** E Susx
123 J7 **Friston** Suffk
153 G3 **Fritchley** Derbys
52 B2 **Frith** Kent
30 C4 **Fritham** Hants
156 F4 **Frith Bank** Lincs
112 D6 **Frith Common** Worcs
23 H3 **Frithelstock** Devon

382 City, town and village index: Hatherton - Hoghton Bottoms

150 C4 **Hatherton** Ches
129 J4 **Hatherton** Staffs
102 C3 **Hatley St George** Cambs
327 K2 **Hatson** Ork
6 E2 **Hatt** Cnwll
165 J2 **Hattersley** Tamesd
30 E1 **Hatt Hill** Hants
46 F6 **Hattingley** Hants
303 L1 **Hatton** Abers
152 D7 **Hatton** Derbys
170 C5 **Hatton** Lincs
111 K1 **Hatton** Shrops
163 L4 **Hatton** Warrtn
114 E6 **Hatton** Warwks
306 D6 **Hatton Castle** Abers
302 F4 **Hattoncrook** Abers
128 F6 **Hatton Grange** Shrops
149 J1 **Hatton Heath** Ches
64 B8 **Hatton Hill** Surrey
245 L4 **Hattonknowe** Border
302 F5 **Hatton of Fintray** Abers
280 C6 **Hatton of Ogilvie** Angus
117 H6 **Hatton Park** Nhants
230 D1 **Haugh** E Ayrs
171 H5 **Haugh** Lincs
175 K5 **Haugh** Rochdl
170 F4 **Haugham** Lincs
246 C6 **Haugh-head** Border
236 E1 **Haugh Head** Nthumb
121 L7 **Haughley** Suffk
121 L7 **Haughley Green** Suffk
121 L7 **Haughley New Street** Suffk
305 G8 **Haugh of Glass** Moray
221 J6 **Haugh of Urr** D & G
149 L2 **Haughton** Ches
168 C6 **Haughton** Notts
127 G3 **Haughton** Powys
127 H1 **Haughton** Shrops
128 B3 **Haughton** Shrops
128 D7 **Haughton** Shrops
128 E5 **Haughton** Shrops
129 H2 **Haughton** Staffs
165 H2 **Haughton Green** Tamesd
205 J4 **Haughton le Skerne** Darltn
46 E1 **Haughurst Hill** Hants
84 C2 **Haultwick** Herts
271 J5 **Haunn** Ag & B
320 F2 **Haunn** W Isls
130 E4 **Haunton** Staffs
16 h5 **Hautes Croix** Jersey
102 F3 **Hauxton** Cambs
165 G8 **Havannah** Ches
32 D5 **Havant** Hants
94 F3 **Haven** Herefs
95 J4 **Haven** Herefs
156 D3 **Haven Bank** Lincs
21 J4 **Havenstreet** IoW
177 K5 **Havercroft** Wakefd
70 E4 **Haverfordwest** Pembks
103 L4 **Haverhill** Suffk
190 D5 **Haverigg** Cumb
66 D2 **Havering-atte-Bower** Gt Lon
138 D3 **Haveringland** Norfk
100 D5 **Haversham** M Keyn
191 G4 **Haverthwaite** Cumb
206 B3 **Haverton Hill** S on T
51 H4 **Haviker Street** Kent
42 D6 **Havyatt** Somset
42 C1 **Havyatt Green** N Som
162 F7 **Hawarden** Flints
96 F4 **Hawbridge** Worcs
86 B2 **Hawbush Green** Essex
190 E6 **Hawcoat** Cumb
96 C7 **Hawcross** Gloucs
124 D3 **Hawddamor** Gwynd
90 D6 **Hawen** Cerdgn
194 C4 **Hawes** N York
138 E7 **Hawes' Green** Norfk
182 B8 **Hawes Side** Bpool
113 G7 **Hawford** Worcs
128 C1 **Hawgreen** Shrops
234 E4 **Hawick** Border
26 E6 **Hawkchurch** Devon
104 C3 **Hawkedon** Suffk
50 E6 **Hawkenbury** Kent
51 J5 **Hawkenbury** Kent
43 L3 **Hawkeridge** Wilts
15 H4 **Hawkerland** Devon
95 H4 **Hawkersland Cross** Herefs
115 H3 **Hawkesbury** Warwks
59 J3 **Hawkesbury** S Glos
59 J3 **Hawkesbury Upton** S Glos
114 F3 **Hawkes End** Covtry
113 L4 **Hawkesley** Birm
165 J3 **Hawk Green** Stockp
200 C2 **Hawk Hill** Cumb
237 J4 **Hawkhill** Nthumb
225 G2 **Hawkhope** Nthumb
51 H7 **Hawkhurst** Kent
35 K3 **Hawkhurst Common** E Susx
53 H6 **Hawkinge** Kent
103 L7 **Hawkin's Hill** Essex
47 H8 **Hawkley** Hants
174 C7 **Hawkley** Wigan
39 L7 **Hawkridge** Somset
209 J4 **Hawksdale** Cumb
129 K4 **Hawks Green** Staffs
175 G4 **Hawkshaw** Bury
201 J8 **Hawkshead** Cumb
201 J8 **Hawkshead Hill** Cumb
64 B3 **Hawks Hill** Bucks
49 G2 **Hawk's Hill** Surrey
244 C6 **Hawksland** S Lans
103 K7 **Hawkspur Green** Essex
175 K2 **Hawks Stones** Calder
194 E7 **Hawkswick** N York
185 J6 **Hawksworth** Leeds
154 E5 **Hawksworth** Notts
67 L2 **Hawkwell** Essex
47 K2 **Hawley** Hants
66 D6 **Hawley** Kent
26 C6 **Hawley Bottom** Devon
47 L2 **Hawley Lane** Hants
79 H2 **Hawling** Gloucs
196 F4 **Hawnby** N York
113 K3 **Hawne** Dudley
184 F7 **Haworth** Brad
191 G1 **Haws Bank** Cumb
104 D2 **Hawstead** Suffk
104 E2 **Hawstead Green** Suffk
213 K4 **Hawthorn** Dur
47 G7 **Hawthorn** Hants
56 E3 **Hawthorn** Rhondd
69 H7 **Hawthorn Corner** Kent
156 D2 **Hawthorn Hill** Lincs
63 L6 **Hawthorn Hill** Br For
155 K8 **Hawthorpe** Lincs
154 E3 **Hawton** Notts
187 G3 **Haxby** York
179 H8 **Haxey** N Linc
179 H7 **Haxey Carr** N Linc
50 B4 **Haxted** Surrey
45 G4 **Haxton** Wilts
10 D7 **Hay** Cnwll
112 C5 **Haybridge** Shrops
42 D4 **Haybridge** Somset
128 D4 **Haybridge** Wrekin
78 D2 **Hayden** Gloucs
163 L1 **Haydock** St Hel
43 G3 **Haydon** BaNES
28 B3 **Haydon** Dorset
26 D2 **Haydon** Somset
42 E4 **Haydon** Somset
60 F3 **Haydon** Swindn
225 J7 **Haydon Bridge** Nthumb
60 F3 **Haydon Wick** Swindn
12 C7 **Haye** Cnwll
64 E4 **Hayes** Gt Lon
65 L7 **Hayes** Gt Lon
151 L1 **Hayes** Staffs
64 E4 **Hayes End** Gt Lon
60 F2 **Hayes Knoll** Wilts
165 K3 **Hayfield** Derbys
178 E8 **Hay Field** Donc
259 H2 **Hayfield** Fife
178 E8 **Hayfield Green** Donc
128 C4 **Haygate** Wrekin
26 C2 **Haygrass** Somset
85 H6 **Hay Green** Essex
102 D6 **Hay Green** Herts
135 L3 **Hay Green** Norfk
230 D3 **Hayhill** E Ayrs
280 F6 **Hayhillock** Angus
21 J3 **Haylands** IoW
2 F3 **Hayle** Cnwll
113 J3 **Hayley Green** Dudley
114 C3 **Hay Mills** Birm
26 E1 **Haymoor End** Somset
150 C3 **Haymoor Green** Ches
24 F5 **Hayne** Devon
101 K5 **Haynes** Beds
101 J5 **Haynes Church End** Beds
101 J5 **Haynes West End** Beds
94 B5 **Hay-on-Wye** Herefs
88 D7 **Hayscastle** Pembks
88 E7 **Hayscastle Cross** Pembks
70 E2 **Haysford** Pembks
281 H6 **Hayshead** Angus
256 E6 **Hayston** E Duns
246 B6 **Haystoun** Border
84 D1 **Hay Street** Herts
29 J5 **Haythorne** Dorset
303 H7 **Hayton** C Aber
208 D5 **Hayton** Cumb
210 B2 **Hayton** Cumb
188 B5 **Hayton** E R Yk
168 D4 **Hayton** Notts
111 L3 **Hayton's Bent** Shrops
14 B6 **Haytor Vale** Devon
22 F4 **Haytown** Devon
34 F2 **Haywards Heath** W Susx
178 D5 **Haywood** Donc
244 F3 **Haywood** S Lans
154 B2 **Haywood Oaks** Notts
36 C4 **Hazard's Green** E Susx
244 C5 **Hazelbank** S Lans
70 E6 **Hazelbeach** Pembks
28 C5 **Hazelbury Bryan** Dorset
86 C6 **Hazeleigh** Essex
84 F2 **Hazel End** Essex
47 H2 **Hazeley** Hants
47 H2 **Hazeley Bottom** Hants
47 J2 **Hazeley Heath** Hants
47 H2 **Hazeley Lea** Hants
165 H3 **Hazel Grove** Stockp
175 G4 **Hazelhurst** Bury
20 C2 **Hazelhurst** Hants
175 G7 **Hazelhurst** Salfd
175 L7 **Hazelhurst** Tamesd
249 H7 **Hazelrigg** Nthumb
192 E6 **Hazelslack** Cumb
129 L4 **Hazelslade** Staffs
51 G6 **Hazel Street** Kent
51 L2 **Hazel Street** Kent
103 K4 **Hazel Stub** Suffk
268 E3 **Hazelton Walls** Fife
152 F4 **Hazelwood** Derbys
8 B4 **Hazelwood** Devon
50 B1 **Hazelwood** Gt Lon
176 F7 **Hazlehead** Barns
82 D7 **Hazlemere** Bucks
127 K8 **Hazler** Shrops
227 G5 **Hazlerigg** N Tyne
151 J4 **Hazles** Staffs
151 K4 **Hazlescross** Staffs
79 H3 **Hazleton** Gloucs
185 G4 **Hazlewood** N York
237 H6 **Hazon** Nthumb
140 D4 **Heacham** Norfk
46 C7 **Headbourne Worthy** Hants
94 D2 **Headbrook** Herefs
51 K5 **Headcorn** Kent
185 L7 **Headingley** Leeds
81 G5 **Headington** Oxon
81 G5 **Headington Hill** Oxon
204 F4 **Headlam** Dur
191 H5 **Headless Cross** Cumb
113 L6 **Headless Cross** Worcs
46 D1 **Headley** Hants
47 K6 **Headley** Hants
49 H3 **Headley** Surrey
47 K6 **Headley Down** Hants
114 B4 **Headley Heath** Worcs
58 E7 **Headley Park** Bristl
257 J4 **Head of Muir** Falk
22 F6 **Headon** Devon
168 D5 **Headon** Notts
243 L4 **Heads** S Lans
234 D2 **Headshaw** Border
209 L2 **Heads Nook** Cumb
64 F3 **Headstone** Gt Lon
258 D3 **Headwell** Fife
153 G3 **Heage** Derbys
194 F2 **Healaugh** N York
165 G3 **Heald Green** Stockp
175 J6 **Healds Green** Oldham
38 F4 **Heale** Devon
26 C3 **Heale** Somset
26 F1 **Heale** Somset
43 G5 **Heale** Somset
212 B2 **Healey** Nthumb
195 J5 **Healey** N York
175 J4 **Healey** Rochdl
177 H4 **Healey** Wakefd
237 G6 **Healey Cote** Nthumb
212 C4 **Healeyfield** Dur
212 B2 **Healey Hall** Nthumb
181 G5 **Healing** NE Lin
2 D4 **Heamoor** Cnwll
201 L8 **Heaning** Cumb
270 C6 **Heanish** Ag & B
153 H4 **Heanor** Derbys
153 H4 **Heanor Gate** Derbys
38 D6 **Heanton Punchardon** Devon
175 H5 **Heap Bridge** Rochdl
169 G3 **Heapham** Lincs
47 K6 **Hearn** Hants
51 K4 **Hearnden Green** Kent
233 G1 **Hearthstane** Border
152 F2 **Hearthstone** Derbys
51 L1 **Hearts Delight** Kent
39 H7 **Heasley Mill** Devon
294 B5 **Heaste** Highld
57 G5 **Heath** Cardif
167 H7 **Heath** Derbys
163 K4 **Heath** Halton
100 F8 **Heath and Reach** Beds
174 C5 **Heath Charnock** Lancs
34 B4 **Heath Common** W Susx
152 B1 **Heathcote** Derbys
150 C8 **Heathcote** Shrops
115 G7 **Heathcote** Warwks
13 L2 **Heath Cross** Devon
14 C3 **Heath Cross** Devon
82 D7 **Heath End** Hants
82 F5 **Heath End** Bucks
46 B1 **Heath End** Hants
46 E1 **Heath End** Hants
131 H2 **Heath End** Leics
59 G3 **Heath End** S Glos
47 K4 **Heath End** Surrey
114 E7 **Heath End** Warwks
129 L6 **Heath End** Wsall
33 J3 **Heath End** W Susx
131 H4 **Heather** Leics
13 L5 **Heathercombe** Devon
292 H8 **Heatherfield** Highld
47 H3 **Heather Row** Hants
48 B2 **Heatherside** Surrey
102 F4 **Heathfield** Cambs
14 C6 **Heathfield** Devon
35 L2 **Heathfield** E Susx
77 L7 **Heathfield** Gloucs
31 K5 **Heathfield** Hants
170 B2 **Heathfield** Lincs
255 J8 **Heathfield** Rens
229 L2 **Heathfield** S Ayrs
26 B1 **Heathfield** Somset
81 G3 **Heathfield Village** Oxon
46 F6 **Heath Green** Hants
114 B5 **Heath Green** Worcs
129 L4 **Heath Hayes** Staffs
128 F4 **Heath Hill** Shrops
42 B4 **Heath House** Somset
63 K7 **Heathlands** Wokham
128 C2 **Heath Lanes** Wrekin
66 D3 **Heath Park** Gt Lon
303 G7 **Heathryfold** C Aber
66 D6 **Heath Side** Kent
26 C6 **Heathstock** Devon
113 G1 **Heathton** Shrops
152 D7 **Heathtop** Derbys
129 J7 **Heath Town** Wolves
201 L8 **Heathwaite** Cumb
206 B7 **Heathwaite** N York
130 B1 **Heatley** Staffs
164 D3 **Heatley** Traffd
174 E6 **Heaton** Bolton
185 H7 **Heaton** Brad
182 D2 **Heaton** Lancs
227 H6 **Heaton** N u Ty
165 J8 **Heaton** Staffs
165 G2 **Heaton Chapel** Stockp
165 G2 **Heaton Mersey** Stockp
165 G2 **Heaton Moor** Stockp
165 G2 **Heaton Norris** Stockp
185 H7 **Heaton Royds** Brad
173 K5 **Heaton's Bridge** Lancs
27 L2 **Heaven's Door** Somset
50 E2 **Heaverham** Kent
165 H3 **Heaviley** Stockp
14 E3 **Heavitree** Devon
227 J7 **Hebburn** S Tyne
227 J6 **Hebburn Colliery** S Tyne
227 H7 **Hebburn New Town** S Tyne
184 F2 **Hebden** N York
176 B2 **Hebden Bridge** Calder
164 B8 **Hebden Green** Ches
84 C2 **Hebing End** Herts
89 K7 **Hebron** Carmth
159 H4 **Hebron** IoA
226 F2 **Hebron** Nthumb
222 D3 **Heck** D & G
168 E1 **Heckdyke** Notts
47 H1 **Heckfield** Hants
122 D4 **Heckfield Green** Suffk
86 E2 **Heckfordbridge** Essex
139 H7 **Heckingham** Norfk
156 B5 **Heckington** Lincs
177 G3 **Heckmondwike** Kirk
60 C7 **Heddington Wick** Wilts
327 J2 **Heddle** Ork
39 G8 **Heddon** Devon
226 E6 **Heddon-on-the-Wall** Nthumb
139 G8 **Hedenham** Norfk
28 E5 **Hedge End** Dorset
31 J4 **Hedge End** Hants
156 E4 **Hedgehog Bridge** Lincs
64 C3 **Hedgerley** Bucks
64 C3 **Hedgerley Green** Bucks
64 C3 **Hedgerley Hill** Bucks
41 J8 **Hedging** Somset
212 D5 **Hedley Hill** Dur
212 C2 **Hedley on the Hill** Nthumb
129 L4 **Hednesford** Staffs
180 F2 **Hedon** E R Yk
64 B3 **Hedsor** Bucks
227 J7 **Hedworth** S Tyne
100 D6 **Heelands** M Keyn
167 G4 **Heeley** Sheff
95 J3 **Hegdon Hill** Herefs
203 J5 **Heggerscales** Cumb
209 J6 **Heggle Lane** Cumb
332 F6 **Heglibister** Shet
205 H3 **Heighington** Darltn
169 K7 **Heighington** Lincs
150 E4 **Heighley** Staffs
175 G3 **Height End** Lancs
112 F5 **Heightington** Worcs
175 L6 **Heights** Oldham
310 C5 **Heights of Brae** Highld
309 J5 **Heights of Kinlochewe** Highld
317 K5 **Heilam** Highld
247 L7 **Heiton** Border
203 H4 **Helbeck** Cumb
12 C3 **Hele** Devon
13 L7 **Hele** Devon
25 H6 **Hele** Devon
38 D4 **Hele** Devon
26 B2 **Hele** Somset
8 F1 **Hele** Torbay
22 C6 **Helebridge** Cnwll
255 J4 **Helensburgh** Ag & B
3 J5 **Helford** Cnwll
3 K5 **Helford Passage** Cnwll
84 D3 **Helham Green** Herts
141 H6 **Helhoughton** Norfk
103 K5 **Helions Bumpstead** Essex
167 K2 **Hellaby** Rothm
10 F7 **Helland** Cnwll
26 E2 **Helland** Somset
4 F5 **Helland Barton** Cnwll
10 F7 **Hellandbridge** Cnwll
61 L8 **Hell Corner** W Berk
138 E4 **Hellesdon** Norfk
2 E2 **Hellesveor** Cnwll
99 H2 **Hellidon** Nhants
184 C3 **Hellifield** N York
184 C3 **Hellifield Green** N York
35 L4 **Hellingly** E Susx
139 G6 **Hellington** Norfk
332 F7 **Hellister** Shet
85 H3 **Hellman's Cross** Essex
194 D3 **Helm** N York
234 B2 **Helmburn** Border
99 J5 **Helmdon** Nhants
176 D5 **Helme** Kirk
106 D2 **Helmingham** Suffk
212 E6 **Helmington Row** Dur
315 P4 **Helmsdale** Highld
175 G3 **Helmshore** Lancs
193 J4 **Helmside** Cumb
197 G5 **Helmsley** N York
196 D7 **Helperby** N York
198 E7 **Helperthorpe** N York
156 B5 **Helpringham** Lincs
134 C5 **Helpston** C Pete
163 J5 **Helsby** Ches
163 J5 **Helsby** Ches
22 C6 **Helscott** Cnwll
171 K6 **Helsey** Lincs
3 H5 **Helston** Cnwll
10 F5 **Helstone** Cnwll
3 K2 **Helston Water** Cnwll
202 C3 **Helton** Cumb
194 B8 **Helwith Bridge** N York
139 G4 **Hemblington** Norfk
139 G4 **Hemblington Corner** Norfk
42 E6 **Hembridge** Somset
83 H6 **Hemel Hempstead** Herts
7 J3 **Hemerdon** Devon
127 G6 **Hemford** Shrops
151 G5 **Hem Heath** C Stke
178 F1 **Hemingbrough** N York
170 D6 **Hemingby** Lincs
177 K7 **Hemingfield** Barns
118 F5 **Hemingford Abbots** Cambs
118 F5 **Hemingford Grey** Cambs
106 C3 **Hemingstone** Suffk
153 J8 **Hemington** Leics
118 B2 **Hemington** Nhants
43 H3 **Hemington** Somset
106 F5 **Hemley** Suffk
206 B5 **Hemlington** Middsb
123 H6 **Hemp Green** Suffk
189 G4 **Hempholme** E R Yk
138 E8 **Hempnall** Norfk
138 E8 **Hempnall Green** Norfk
311 Q5 **Hempriggs** Moray
104 F8 **Hemp's Green** Essex
153 K5 **Hempshill Vale** C Nott
103 K6 **Hempstead** Essex
67 J8 **Hempstead** Medway
142 D4 **Hempstead** Norfk
143 L6 **Hempstead** Norfk
78 C3 **Hempsted** Gloucs
141 J6 **Hempton** Norfk
98 F7 **Hempton** Oxon
82 B6 **Hempton Wainhill** Oxon
139 K3 **Hemsby** Norfk
52 F5 **Hemsted** Kent
169 H2 **Hemswell** Lincs
169 J3 **Hemswell Cliff** Lincs
29 H5 **Hemsworth** Dorset
167 G4 **Hemsworth** Sheff
177 L5 **Hemsworth** Wakefd
25 L4 **Hemyock** Devon
22 C3 **Henaford** Devon
159 K6 **Hen Bentref Llandegfan** IoA
113 J6 **Henbrook** Worcs
58 E5 **Henbury** Bristl
165 G6 **Henbury** Ches
29 H7 **Henbury** Dorset
247 L6 **Hendersyde Park** Border
126 E7 **Hendomen** Powys
65 H3 **Hendon** Gt Lon
213 K2 **Hendon** Sundld
2 F5 **Hendra** Cnwll
3 H4 **Hendra** Cnwll
3 J3 **Hendra** Cnwll
3 J7 **Hendra** Cnwll
4 F3 **Hendra** Cnwll
5 G2 **Hendra** Cnwll
5 G4 **Hendra** Cnwll
10 F5 **Hendra** Cnwll
6 C1 **Hendrabridge** Cnwll
11 G4 **Hendraburnick** Cnwll
4 C3 **Hendra Croft** Cnwll
162 C7 **Hendre** Flints
124 B5 **Hendre** Gwynd
125 K7 **Hendre** Powys
160 F7 **Hendre-ddu** Conwy
56 F3 **Hendredenny Park** Caerph
56 C3 **Hendreforgan** Rhondd
161 L8 **Hendrerwydd** Denbgs
73 J7 **Hendrewen** Swans
73 H8 **Hendy** Carmth
56 D4 **Hendy** Rhondd
161 K8 **Hên-efail** Denbgs
159 G5 **Heneglwys** IoA
59 G5 **Henfield** S Glos
34 D3 **Henfield** W Susx
12 D3 **Henford** Devon
43 L5 **Henfords Marsh** Wilts
91 G3 **Henfynyw** Cerdgn
75 J7 **Hengoed** Caerph
147 L2 **Hengoed** Denbgs
94 B3 **Hengoed** Powys
148 E7 **Hengoed** Shrops
138 C3 **Hengrave** Norfk
121 G6 **Hengrave** Suffk
58 F7 **Hengrove** Bristl
58 E7 **Hengrove Park** Bristl
103 H8 **Henham** Essex
67 G7 **Henhurst** Kent
126 C5 **Heniarth** Powys
26 D2 **Henlade** Somset
58 E5 **Henleaze** Bristl
28 B6 **Henley** Dorset
78 E3 **Henley** Gloucs
111 K2 **Henley** Shrops
111 L4 **Henley** Shrops
42 B7 **Henley** Somset
106 C3 **Henley** Suffk
45 K2 **Henley** Wilts
59 K7 **Henley** Wilts
33 G1 **Henley** W Susx
33 G1 **Henley Common** W Susx
115 H3 **Henley Green** Covtry
114 C6 **Henley-in-Arden** Warwks
63 H4 **Henley-on-Thames** Oxon
48 B3 **Henley Park** Surrey
36 D4 **Henley's Down** E Susx
67 G7 **Henley Street** Kent
90 D7 **Henllan** Cerdgn
161 J7 **Henllan** Denbgs
71 K3 **Henllan Amgoed** Carmth
148 F7 **Henlle** Shrops
57 J2 **Henllys** Torfn
57 J2 **Henllys Vale** Torfn
101 L6 **Henlow** Beds
14 C5 **Hennock** Devon
104 E6 **Henny Street** Essex
160 D6 **Henryd** Conwy
89 G7 **Henry's Moat** Pembks
178 D3 **Hensall** N York
185 K6 **Henshaw** Leeds
225 H7 **Henshaw** Nthumb
200 B4 **Hensingham** Cumb
80 F3 **Hensington** Oxon
123 K2 **Henstead** Suffk
31 H2 **Hensting** Hants
38 E5 **Henstridge** Devon
28 C3 **Henstridge** Somset
28 C2 **Henstridge Ash** Somset
28 B2 **Henstridge Bowden** Somset
28 C2 **Henstridge Marsh** Somset
82 B6 **Henton** Oxon
42 C4 **Henton** Somset
11 K7 **Henwood** Cnwll
80 F6 **Henwood** Oxon
80 F6 **Henwood and Lamborough Hill** Oxon
50 F5 **Henwood Green** Kent
332 H8 **Heogan** Shet
72 F8 **Heol-ddu** Carmth
54 F2 **Heol-ddu** Swans
75 G5 **Heolgerrig** Myr Td
56 B4 **Heol-laethog** Brdgnd
56 B4 **Heol-las** Brdgnd
55 G2 **Heol Las** Swans
74 E2 **Heol Senni** Powys
56 B4 **Heol-y-Cyw** Brdgnd
93 L6 **Heol-y-gaer** Powys
55 L7 **Heol-y-mynydd** V Glam
236 F2 **Hepburn** Nthumb
236 D6 **Hepple** Nthumb
227 G3 **Hepscott** Nthumb
167 G8 **Hepthorne Lane** Derbys
175 L2 **Heptonstall** Calder
176 F6 **Hepworth** Kirk
121 K4 **Hepworth** Suffk
70 D5 **Herbrandston** Pembks
95 H6 **Hereford** Herefs
292 D7 **Heribost** Highld
292 G2 **Heribusta** Highld
246 D3 **Heriot** Border
258 F7 **Hermiston** C Edin
234 E7 **Hermitage** Border
27 L5 **Hermitage** Dorset
62 D6 **Hermitage** W Berk
32 E5 **Hermitage** W Susx
164 B2 **Hermitage Green** Warrtn
177 J7 **Hermit Hill** Barns
72 D2 **Hermon** Carmth
158 F7 **Hermon** IoA
89 L6 **Hermon** Pembks
8 C3 **Hernaford** Devon
69 G7 **Herne** Kent
69 G7 **Herne Bay** Kent
69 G8 **Herne Common** Kent
65 K6 **Herne Hill** Gt Lon
51 G3 **Herne Pound** Kent
23 K1 **Herner** Devon
52 E1 **Hernhill** Kent
3 J4 **Herniss** Cnwll
6 B2 **Herodsfoot** Cnwll
53 J3 **Heronden** Kent
66 F2 **Herongate** Essex
218 E3 **Heronsford** S Ayrs
64 D2 **Heronsgate** Herts
35 J1 **Heron's Ghyll** E Susx
42 D2 **Herons Green** BaNES
56 B5 **Heronston** V Glam
330 J7 **Herra** Shet
47 G4 **Herriard** Hants
139 K7 **Herringfleet** Suffk
101 J5 **Herring's Green** Beds
120 E6 **Herringswell** Suffk
167 H2 **Herringthorpe** Rothm
53 G1 **Hersden** Kent
22 C5 **Hersham** Cnwll
64 F8 **Hersham** Surrey
36 B4 **Herstmonceux** E Susx
19 G6 **Herston** Dorset
327 K6 **Herston** Ork
84 C4 **Hertford** Herts
84 D4 **Hertford Heath** Herts
84 C4 **Hertingfordbury** Herts
173 K3 **Hesketh Bank** Lancs
183 H6 **Hesketh Lane** Lancs
173 K3 **Hesketh Moss** Lancs
209 H6 **Hesket Newmarket** Cumb
174 B4 **Heskin Green** Lancs
213 K6 **Hesleden** Dur
225 J3 **Hesleyside** Nthumb
187 H4 **Heslington** York
186 F4 **Hessay** York
6 D3 **Hessenford** Cnwll
121 J7 **Hessett** Suffk
180 C2 **Hessle** E R Yk
177 L4 **Hessle** Wakefd
332 D6 **Hestaford** Shet
182 E1 **Hest Bank** Lancs
78 E2 **Hester's Way** Gloucs
333 F14 **Hestingott** Shet
332 D7 **Hestinsetter** Shet
64 F5 **Heston** Gt Lon
328 C10 **Hestwall** Ork
162 E4 **Heswall** Wirral
99 J8 **Hethe** Oxon
138 D6 **Hethel** Norfk
96 C8 **Hethelpit Cross** Gloucs
138 C6 **Hethersett** Norfk
224 B6 **Hethersgill** Cumb
223 L6 **Hetherside** Cumb
149 K4 **Hetherson Green** Ches
248 D8 **Hethpool** Nthumb
213 G6 **Hett** Dur
184 E3 **Hetton** N York
213 J4 **Hetton Downs** Sundld
213 J4 **Hetton-le-Hill** Sundld
213 J4 **Hetton-le-Hole** Sundld
226 D5 **Heugh** Nthumb
301 G6 **Heugh-head** Abers
123 G5 **Heveningham** Suffk
50 C5 **Hever** Kent
192 E5 **Heversham** Cumb
138 D2 **Hevingham** Norfk
5 G5 **Hewas Water** Cnwll
77 H6 **Hewelsfield** Gloucs
77 G6 **Hewelsfield Common** Gloucs
209 J6 **Hewer Hill** Cumb
185 K3 **Hew Green** N York
58 B8 **Hewish** N Som
27 G5 **Hewish** Somset
26 F6 **Hewood** Dorset
227 H7 **Heworth** Gatesd
187 H4 **Heworth** York
225 L7 **Hexham** Nthumb
66 D6 **Hextable** Kent
178 D7 **Hexthorpe** Donc
101 K7 **Hexton** Herts
13 J7 **Hexworthy** Devon
184 C6 **Hey** Lancs
85 J7 **Heybridge** Essex
86 D5 **Heybridge** Essex
86 D5 **Heybridge Basin** Essex
7 H5 **Heybrook Bay** Devon
102 F5 **Heydon** Cambs
142 E6 **Heydon** Norfk
155 K6 **Heydour** Lincs
176 C5 **Hey Green** Kirk
176 B7 **Heyheads** Tamesd
173 H2 **Hey Houses** Lancs
270 B6 **Heylipol** Ag & B
331 C9 **Heylor** Shet
110 E5 **Heyop** Powys
175 L8 **Heyrod** Tamesd
182 C2 **Heysham** Lancs
185 J2 **Heyshaw** N York
33 G3 **Heyshott** W Susx
33 G3 **Heyshott Green** W Susx
175 K6 **Heyside** Oldham
44 B5 **Heytesbury** Wilts
98 E8 **Heythrop** Oxon
175 H5 **Heywood** Rochdl
43 L3 **Heywood** Wilts
180 B7 **Hibaldstow** N Linc
104 E3 **Hibb's Green** Suffk
104 C5 **Hickford Hill** Essex
178 B7 **Hickleton** Donc
143 L7 **Hickling** Norfk
154 C8 **Hickling** Notts
143 L7 **Hickling Green** Norfk
143 L7 **Hickling Heath** Norfk
154 C8 **Hickling Pastures** Notts
52 E2 **Hickmans Green** Kent
69 G8 **Hicks Forstal** Kent
58 F7 **Hicks Gate** BaNES
3 K2 **Hick's Mill** Cnwll
34 E3 **Hickstead** W Susx
97 L5 **Hidcote Bartrim** Gloucs
97 L5 **Hidcote Boyce** Gloucs
128 E7 **Hifnal** Shrops
175 K6 **Higginshaw** Oldham
177 L4 **High Ackworth** Wakefd
153 G2 **Higham** Derbys
67 H6 **Higham** Kent
184 B7 **Higham** Lancs
105 H6 **Higham** Suffk
120 E6 **Higham** Suffk
177 J6 **Higham Common** Barns
226 E4 **Higham Dykes** Nthumb
117 K6 **Higham Ferrers** Nhants
101 K7 **Higham Gobion** Beds
65 L2 **Higham Hill** Gt Lon
131 H7 **Higham on the Hill** Leics
23 H6 **Highampton** Devon
65 L2 **Highams Park** Gt Lon
50 F4 **Higham Wood** Kent
226 D2 **High Angerton** Nthumb
214 C4 **High Ardwell** D & G
210 C5 **High Bankhill** Cumb
257 G5 **High Banton** N Lans
171 G8 **High Barn** Lincs
83 L7 **High Barnet** Gt Lon
84 E7 **High Beach** Essex
193 J8 **High Bentham** N York
23 L2 **High Bickington** Devon
193 G6 **High Biggins** Cumb
194 B6 **High Birkwith** N York
185 K3 **High Birstwith** N York
243 K2 **High Blantyre** S Lans
257 J5 **High Bonnybridge** Falk
166 E2 **High Bradfield** Sheff
184 F5 **High Bradley** N York
39 G7 **High Bray** Devon
209 J5 **Highbridge** Cumb
31 H2 **Highbridge** Hants
284 F5 **Highbridge** Highld
41 J4 **Highbridge** Somset
129 L6 **Highbridge** Wsall
49 L7 **Highbrook** W Susx
50 E5 **High Brooms** Kent
78 D4 **High Brotheridge** Gloucs
23 J2 **High Bullen** Devon
176 F5 **Highburton** Kirk
32 C6 **Highbury** C Port
65 K3 **Highbury** Gt Lon
43 G4 **Highbury** Somset
153 K5 **Highbury Vale** C Nott
237 J5 **High Buston** Nthumb
226 F5 **High Callerton** Nthumb
191 H4 **High Cark** Cumb
193 H6 **High Casterton** Cumb
187 K4 **High Catton** E R Yk
226 F2 **High Church** Nthumb
46 B2 **Highclere** Hants
166 D5 **Highcliffe** Derbys
19 L3 **Highcliffe** Dorset
80 D5 **High Cogges** Oxon
137 K5 **High Common** Norfk
205 G4 **High Coniscliffe** Darltn
175 K5 **High Crompton** Oldham
102 F2 **High Cross** Cambs
3 J5 **High Cross** Cnwll
50 E8 **High Cross** E Susx
32 D1 **High Cross** Hants
83 J7 **High Cross** Herts
84 D3 **High Cross** Herts
57 J3 **High Cross** Newpt
114 D6 **High Cross** Warwks
34 D3 **High Cross** W Susx
243 J1 **High Crosshill** S Lans
191 H2 **High Cunsey** Cumb
240 D6 **High Dougarie** N Ayrs
213 H4 **High Dubmire** Sundld
204 B2 **High Dyke** Dur
85 J4 **High Easter** Essex
178 D3 **High Eggborough** N York
195 J5 **High Ellington** N York
232 B6 **High Enoch** D & G
43 G5 **Higher Alham** Somset
28 D6 **Higher Ansty** Dorset
14 D4 **Higher Ashton** Devon
174 E2 **Higher Audley** Bl w D
4 B4 **Higher Bal** Cnwll
173 J1 **Higher Ballam** Lancs
182 F8 **Higher Bartle** Lancs
162 F3 **Higher Bebington** Wirral
101 G7 **Higher Berry End** Beds
175 H7 **Higher Blackley** Manch
175 J6 **Higher Boarshaw** Rochdl
17 L3 **Higher Bockhampton** Dorset
2 B4 **Higher Bojewyan** Cnwll
2 B4 **Higher Boscaswell** Cnwll
8 F3 **Higher Brixham** Torbay
175 H7 **Higher Broughton** Salfd
27 G2 **Higher Burrow** Somset
25 J7 **Higher Burrowtown** Devon
149 K2 **Higher Burwardsley** Ches
128 B3 **High Ercall** Wrekin
27 K6 **Higher Chalmington** Dorset
25 L6 **Higher Cheriton** Devon
26 F4 **Higher Chillington** Somset
165 J2 **Higher Chisworth** Derbys
6 B3 **Highercliff** Cnwll
22 E2 **Higher Clovelly** Devon
3 H3 **Higher Condurrow** Cnwll
11 H2 **Higher Crackington** Cnwll
10 D8 **Higher Cransworth** Cnwll
174 E2 **Higher Croft** Bl w D
64 D3 **Higher Denham** Bucks
165 K1 **Higher Dinting** Derbys
165 J4 **Higher Disley** Ches
2 F4 **Higher Downs** Cnwll
13 L6 **Higher Dunstone** Devon
41 J8 **Higher Durston** Somset
174 B7 **Higher End** Wigan
16 E3 **Higher Eype** Dorset
174 E7 **Higher Folds** Wigan
184 C6 **Higherford** Lancs
14 E8 **Higher Gabwell** Devon
174 F7 **Higher Green** Wigan
27 J5 **Higher Halstock Leigh** Dorset
182 D2 **Higher Heysham** Lancs
175 J3 **Higher Hogshead** Lancs
28 B1 **Higher Holton** Somset
165 H5 **Higher Hurdsfield** Ches
27 J7 **Higher Kingcombe** Dorset
148 F1 **Higher Kinnerton** Flints
28 C2 **Higher Marsh** Somset
28 C6 **Higher Melcombe** Dorset
5 H3 **Higher Menadew** Cnwll
15 H3 **Higher Metcombe** Devon
39 H7 **Higher Molland** Devon
38 E6 **Higher Muddiford** Devon
28 C2 **Higher Nyland** Dorset
174 B2 **Higher Penwortham** Lancs
43 L6 **Higher Pertwood** Wilts
5 H4 **Higher Porthpean** Cnwll
165 H4 **Higher Poynton** Ches
12 D2 **Higher Prestacott** Devon
101 G7 **Higher Rads End** Beds
149 G7 **Higher Ridge** Shrops
14 D8 **Higher Rocombe Barton** Devon
29 J6 **Higher Row** Dorset
163 K4 **Higher Runcorn** Halton
27 L3 **Higher Sandford** Dorset
162 F7 **Higher Shotton** Flints
164 C6 **Higher Shurlach** Ches
14 B7 **Higher Sigford** Devon
38 D4 **Higher Slade** Devon
40 F5 **Higher Street** Somset
25 K6 **Higher Tale** Devon
4 E1 **Higher Tolcarne** Cnwll
27 L5 **Higher Totnell** Dorset
3 L2 **Highertown** Cnwll
5 H2 **Higher Town** Cnwll
11 G5 **Highertown** Cnwll
2 d1 **Higher Town** IoS
40 C4 **Higher Town** Somset
11 J8 **Higher Tremarcoombe** Cnwll
40 F6 **Higher Vexford** Somset
12 F7 **Higher Walreddon** Devon
174 C2 **Higher Walton** Lancs
163 L3 **Higher Walton** Warrtn
26 D5 **Higher Wambrook** Somset
38 C4 **Higher Warcombe** Devon
25 J5 **Higher Weaver** Devon
28 E6 **Higher Whatcombe** Dorset
174 D3 **Higher Wheelton** Lancs
164 B4 **Higher Whitley** Ches
164 C5 **Higher Wincham** Ches
18 B4 **Higher Woodsford** Dorset
27 K6 **Higher Wraxall** Dorset
149 J5 **Higher Wych** Ches
204 F2 **High Etherley** Dur
157 G4 **High Ferry** Lincs
174 F6 **Highfield** Bolton
31 G4 **Highfield** C Sotn
187 K7 **Highfield** E R Yk
212 D2 **Highfield** Gatesd
77 J6 **Highfield** Gloucs
83 H5 **Highfield** Herts
50 D1 **Highfield** Kent
183 K4 **High Field** Lancs
242 C3 **Highfield** N Ayrs
81 H2 **Highfield** Oxon
166 F3 **Highfield** Sheff
174 B7 **Highfield** Wigan
102 E2 **Highfields** Cambs
132 B6 **Highfields** C Leic
167 H7 **Highfields** Derbys
178 C6 **Highfields** Donc
86 D3 **Highfields** Essex
78 B7 **Highfields** Gloucs
248 F3 **Highfields** Nthumb
129 J2 **Highfields** Staffs
212 F3 **High Forge** Dur
212 E2 **High Friarside** Dur
256 E6 **High Gallowhill** E Duns
86 B1 **High Garrett** Essex
114 B2 **Highgate** Birm
50 B7 **Highgate** E Susx
65 J3 **Highgate** Gt Lon
51 J7 **Highgate** Kent
126 C7 **Highgate** Powys
212 E7 **High Grange** Dur
195 K7 **High Grantley** N York
201 K7 **High Green** Cumb
176 F5 **High Green** Kirk
137 J4 **High Green** Norfk
137 J5 **High Green** Norfk
138 C5 **High Green** Norfk
166 F1 **High Green** Sheff
112 E3 **High Green** Shrops
121 H7 **High Green** Suffk
96 E4 **High Green** Worcs
51 L6 **High Halden** Kent
67 J5 **High Halstow** Medway
42 B7 **High Ham** Somset
212 F3 **High Handenhold** Dur
200 C2 **High Harrington** Cumb
186 B3 **High Harrogate** N York
213 J5 **High Haswell** Dur
128 C2 **High Hatton** Shrops
237 K6 **High Hauxley** Nthumb
207 L6 **High Hawsker** N York
150 C8 **High Heath** Shrops
129 L6 **High Heath** Wsall
209 L5 **High Hesket** Cumb
213 L6 **High Hesleden** Dur
201 H3 **High Hill** Cumb
85 K4 **High Houses** Essex
194 B4 **High Houses** N York
177 H6 **High Hoyland** Barns
188 E7 **High Hunsley** E R Yk
35 J1 **High Hurstwood** E Susx
197 L8 **High Hutton** N York
208 F6 **High Ireby** Cumb
142 E3 **High Kelling** Norfk
196 F6 **High Kilburn** N York
311 K9 **Highland Boath** Highld
16 E3 **Highlands** Dorset
105 J7 **Highlands** Suffk
165 G7 **Highlane** Ches
167 H4 **Highlane** Derbys
112 D7 **High Lane** Herefs
165 H3 **High Lane** Stockp
2 F3 **High Lanes** Cnwll
10 B7 **Highlanes** Cnwll
150 E7 **Highlanes** Staffs
85 G5 **High Laver** Essex
208 D4 **Highlaws** Cumb
78 B2 **Highleadon** Gloucs
164 D4 **High Legh** Ches
32 F7 **Highleigh** W Susx
206 B5 **High Leven** S on T
112 E3 **Highley** Shrops
42 F2 **High Littleton** BaNES
208 F4 **High Longthwaite** Cumb
200 F2 **High Lorton** Cumb
215 K6 **High Mains** D & G
198 B6 **High Marishes** N York
168 F6 **High Marnham** Notts
178 C7 **High Melton** Donc
226 D7 **High Mickley** Nthumb
209 G4 **Highmoor** Cumb
167 J5 **High Moor** Derbys
174 B5 **High Moor** Lancs
63 H3 **Highmoor** Oxon
167 J4 **High Moor** Rothm
63 G4 **Highmoor Cross** Oxon
58 C3 **Highmoor Hill** Mons
213 H4 **High Moorsley** Sundld
78 B3 **Highnam** Gloucs
78 B2 **Highnam Green** Gloucs
77 H4 **High Nash** Gloucs
191 J4 **High Newton** Cumb
237 J1 **High Newton-by-the-Sea** Nthumb
190 F3 **High Nibthwaite** Cumb
138 B6 **Highoak** Norfk
193 H3 **High Oaks** Cumb
128 F1 **High Offley** Staffs
85 H6 **High Ongar** Essex
129 G3 **High Onn** Staffs
129 G3 **High Onn Wharf** Staffs
192 F3 **High Park** Cumb
173 J4 **High Park** Sefton
58 E7 **Highridge** Bristl
179 L5 **High Risby** N Linc
176 D2 **Highroad Well Moor** Calder
85 J3 **High Roding** Essex
121 J7 **High Rougham** Suffk
201 K3 **High Row** Cumb
209 J6 **High Row** Cumb
183 H2 **High Salter** Lancs
34 B5 **High Salvington** W Susx
208 E4 **High Scales** Cumb
200 C7 **High Sellafield** Cumb
194 C3 **High Shaw** N York
227 K6 **High Shields** S Tyne
213 G5 **High Shincliffe** Dur
208 F7 **High Side** Cumb
213 J2 **High Southwick** Sundld
212 D2 **High Spen** Gatesd
207 K5 **High Stakesby** N York
69 H7 **Highstead** Kent
51 L1 **Highsted** Kent
212 D5 **High Stoop** Dur
5 G4 **High Street** Cnwll
51 H7 **High Street** Kent
52 E1 **Highstreet** Kent
71 K3 **High Street** Carmth
71 K4 **High Street** Pembks
107 J2 **High Street** Suffk
123 H3 **High Street** Suffk
123 J5 **High Street** Suffk
104 C7 **Highstreet Green** Essex
105 H2 **High Street Green** Suffk
48 C6 **Highstreet Green** Surrey
246 F7 **High Sunderland** Border
222 D4 **Hightae** D & G
114 B4 **Highter's Heath** Birm
213 L7 **High Throston** Hartpl
151 G1 **Hightown** Ches
31 H4 **Hightown** C Sotn
30 B5 **Hightown** Hants
83 H2 **High Town** Luton
173 H7 **Hightown** Sefton
128 E8 **High Town** Shrops
129 K4 **High Town** Staffs
148 F4 **Hightown** Wrexhm
105 G2 **Hightown Green** Suffk
170 E7 **High Toynton** Lincs
236 E5 **High Trewhitt** Nthumb
212 F3 **High Urpeth** Dur
258 C3 **High Valleyfield** Fife
200 B5 **High Walton** Cumb
225 L6 **High Warden** Nthumb
201 J8 **High Water Head** Cumb
3 J2 **Highway** Cnwll
95 G4 **Highway** Herefs
27 H2 **Highway** Somset
63 L4 **Highway** W & M
60 D6 **Highway** Wilts
14 C7 **Highweek** Devon
212 D2 **High Westwood** Dur
209 H3 **High Whinnow** Cumb
25 L5 **Highwood** Devon
18 D4 **Highwood** Dorset
30 B5 **Highwood** Hants
112 D6 **Highwood** Worcs
65 H2 **Highwood Hill** Gt Lon
77 H7 **High Woolaston** Gloucs
205 K6 **High Worsall** N York
61 H2 **Highworth** Swindn
23 G5 **Highworthy** Devon
201 K8 **High Wray** Cumb
84 F4 **High Wych** Herts
63 L2 **High Wycombe** Bucks
137 G6 **Hilborough** Norfk
78 F3 **Hilcot** Gloucs
153 J2 **Hilcote** Derbys
79 H6 **Hilcot End** Gloucs
44 F2 **Hilcott** Wilts
50 E4 **Hildenborough** Kent
50 E4 **Hilden Park** Kent
103 H4 **Hildersham** Cambs
77 J2 **Hildersley** Herefs
151 H7 **Hilderstone** Staffs
189 J1 **Hilderthorpe** E R Yk
27 L6 **Hilfield** Dorset
136 C7 **Hilgay** Norfk
130 C7 **Hill** Birm
77 J7 **Hill** S Glos
115 K6 **Hill** Warwks
178 C2 **Hillam** N York
71 G4 **Hillblock** Pembks
69 H7 **Hillborough** Kent
62 F5 **Hill Bottom** Oxon
19 G3 **Hillbourne** Poole
302 E4 **Hillbrae** Abers
305 K6 **Hillbrae** Abers
32 E1 **Hill Brow** W Susx
29 H6 **Hillbutts** Dorset
150 F6 **Hill Chorlton** Staffs
164 B3 **Hillcliffe** Warrtn
152 E4 **Hillcliffiane** Derbys
143 L7 **Hill Common** Norfk
25 L1 **Hillcommon** Somset
43 K4 **Hill Corner** Somset
96 E5 **Hill Croome** Worcs
152 F7 **Hillcross** C Derb
173 L5 **Hill Dale** Lancs
43 L5 **Hill Deverill** Wilts
156 F4 **Hilldyke** Lincs
280 E5 **Hillend** Angus
212 B6 **Hill End** Dur
258 C1 **Hill End** Fife
258 E4 **Hillend** Fife
96 E6 **Hill End** Gloucs
64 E2 **Hill End** Gt Lon
257 J7 **Hillend** N Lans
41 L2 **Hillend** N Som
185 G4 **Hill End** N York
129 G8 **Hillend** Shrops
27 J4 **Hill End** Somset
54 B3 **Hillend** Swans
113 J7 **Hill End** Worcs
95 L8 **Hillend Green** Gloucs
77 H4 **Hillersland** Gloucs
24 C7 **Hillerton** Devon
99 L8 **Hillesden** Bucks
99 L7 **Hillesden Hamlet** Bucks
59 J3 **Hillesley** Gloucs
26 B2 **Hillfarrance** Somset
8 D4 **Hillfield** Devon
114 C4 **Hillfield** Solhll
58 F6 **Hillfields** Bristl
115 G4 **Hillfields** Covtry
185 K8 **Hillfoot** Leeds
101 K7 **Hillfoot End** Beds
97 G4 **Hill Furze** Worcs
76 F1 **Hill Gate** Herefs
103 G7 **Hill Green** Essex
67 K8 **Hill Green** Kent
62 C5 **Hillgreen** W Berk
48 B8 **Hillgrove** W Susx
95 J4 **Hillhampton** Herefs
302 E4 **Hillhead** Abers
302 E6 **Hillhead** Abers
5 J2 **Hillhead** Cnwll
8 F4 **Hillhead** Devon
242 E6 **Hillhead** S Ayrs
31 J6 **Hill Head** Hants
230 C3 **Hillhead** S Ayrs
307 G4 **Hillhead of Auchentumb** Abers
307 K7 **Hillhead of Cocklaw** Abers
306 B5 **Hillhead of Mountblairy** Abers
50 C5 **Hill Hoath** Kent
130 B6 **Hill Hook** Birm
112 C4 **Hill Houses** Shrops
130 C4 **Hilliard's Cross** Staffs
319 L4 **Hilliclay** Highld
64 E4 **Hillingdon** Gt Lon
64 E4 **Hillingdon Heath** Gt Lon
140 E6 **Hillington** Norfk
256 C8 **Hillington** C Glas
21 G3 **Hillis Corner** IoW
25 L4 **Hillmoor** Devon
115 L5 **Hillmorton** Warwks
70 F5 **Hill Mountain** Pembks
301 G7 **Hillockhead** Abers
175 G2 **Hillock Vale** Lancs
258 E2 **Hill of Beath** Fife
257 H1 **Hill of Drip** Stirlg
315 K11 **Hill of Fearn** Highld
306 B5 **Hill of Mountblairy** Abers
31 J5 **Hill Park** Hants
50 B2 **Hill Park** Kent
113 H4 **Hillpool** Worcs
31 K3 **Hillpound** Hants
130 B3 **Hill Ridware** Staffs
166 F2 **Hillsborough** Sheff
291 L2 **Hillside** Angus
281 J2 **Hillside** Angus
177 G7 **Hill Side** Barns
7 L2 **Hillside** Devon
26 B5 **Hillside** Devon
32 E1 **Hill Side** Hants
47 J3 **Hillside** Hants
176 F4 **Hill Side** Kirk
327 L5 **Hillside** Ork
328 D9 **Hillside** Ork
173 H5 **Hillside** Sefton
331 F13 **Hillside** Shet
112 B2 **Hillside** Shrops
60 E2 **Hillside** Wilts
112 F7 **Hill Side** Worcs
152 B7 **Hill Somersal** Derbys
167 J7 **Hills Town** Derbys
30 E3 **Hillstreet** Hants
52 F4 **Hill Street** Kent
331 C10 **Hillswick** Shet
177 H6 **Hill Top** Barns
75 K5 **Hilltop** Blae G
185 G8 **Hill Top** Brad
82 F6 **Hilltop** Bucks
166 F8 **Hilltop** Derbys
167 G5 **Hill Top** Derbys
167 J1 **Hill Top** Donc
204 B3 **Hill Top** Dur
212 E3 **Hill Top** Dur
212 F5 **Hill Top** Dur
31 G6 **Hill Top** Hants
176 D5 **Hill Top** Kirk
185 L8 **Hill Top** Leeds
153 J4 **Hill Top** Notts
185 J2 **Hill Top** N York
185 L2 **Hill Top** N York
167 G2 **Hill Top** Rothm
174 F7 **Hill Top** Salfd
129 K8 **Hill Top** Sandw
166 E3 **Hill Top** Sheff
129 H5 **Hill Top** Staffs
114 F1 **Hill Top** Warwks
115 H1 **Hill Top** Warwks
33 G2 **Hill Top** W Susx
268 F1 **Hilltown** C Dund
18 F2 **Hill View** Dorset
213 J3 **Hillview** Sundld
21 K4 **Hillway** IoW
333 F14 **Hillwell** Shet
130 C6 **Hill Wood** Birm
115 G6 **Hill Wootton** Warwks
30 F3 **Hillyfields** Hants
267 K3 **Hillyland** P & K
60 D5 **Hilmarton** Wilts
43 L2 **Hilperton** Wilts
43 L1 **Hilperton Marsh** Wilts
32 C6 **Hilsea** C Port
189 L8 **Hilston** E R Yk
31 G2 **Hiltingbury** Hants
303 H2 **Hilton** Abers
248 D3 **Hilton** Border
303 H7 **Hilton** C Aber
118 F6 **Hilton** Cambs
203 G3 **Hilton** Cumb
152 D7 **Hilton** Derbys
28 D6 **Hilton** Dorset
204 F3 **Hilton** S on T
310 F9 **Hilton** Highld
315 J10 **Hilton** Highld
315 M9 **Hilton** Highld
128 F7 **Hilton** Shrops
130 B6 **Hilton** Staffs
206 B5 **Hilton** S on T
174 D6 **Hilton House** Bolton
311 K2 **Hilton of Cadboll** Highld
175 H7 **Hilton Park** Bury
96 F2 **Himbleton** Worcs
113 H1 **Himley** Staffs
192 F5 **Hincaster** Cumb
65 G8 **Hinchley Wood** Surrey
176 E6 **Hinchliffe Mill** Kirk
97 K7 **Hinchwick** Gloucs
131 J8 **Hinckley** Leics
16 F2 **Hincknowle** Dorset
328 D11 **Hindatown** Ork
121 L4 **Hinderclay** Suffk
162 F5 **Hinderton** Ches
207 H4 **Hinderwell** N York
148 F7 **Hindford** Shrops
47 L6 **Hindhead** Surrey
183 K8 **Hindle Fold** Lancs
212 B2 **Hindley** Nthumb
174 D7 **Hindley** Wigan
174 D7 **Hindley Green** Wigan
96 E2 **Hindlip** Worcs
142 C6 **Hindolveston** Norfk
44 B7 **Hindon** Wilts
190 D7 **Hindpool** Cumb
141 K4 **Hindringham** Norfk
174 E7 **Hindsford** Wigan
137 L6 **Hingham** Norfk
128 D1 **Hinstock** Shrops
105 J5 **Hintlesham** Suffk
105 J5 **Hintlesham Park** Suffk
77 K6 **Hinton** Gloucs
19 L2 **Hinton** Hants
94 D6 **Hinton** Herefs
99 H3 **Hinton** Nhants
59 H5 **Hinton** S Glos
127 J5 **Hinton** Shrops
27 K2 **Hinton** Somset
46 F8 **Hinton Ampner** Hants
42 E2 **Hinton Blewett** BaNES
43 J2 **Hinton Charterhouse** BaNES
97 H5 **Hinton Cross** Worcs
99 J6 **Hinton-in-the-Hedges** Nhants
29 J5 **Hinton Martell** Dorset
97 H6 **Hinton on the Green** Worcs
29 H6 **Hinton Parva** Dorset
61 H4 **Hinton Parva** Swindn
27 G4 **Hinton St George** Somset
28 D3 **Hinton St Mary** Dorset
80 D7 **Hinton Waldrist** Oxon
112 C4 **Hints** Shrops
130 D6 **Hints** Staffs
117 J7 **Hinwick** Beds
127 H5 **Hinwood** Shrops
52 D5 **Hinxhill** Kent
103 G4 **Hinxton** Cambs
102 B5 **Hinxworth** Herts
176 E2 **Hipperholme** Calder
96 B2 **Hipplecote** Worcs
237 J4 **Hipsburn** Nthumb
195 J2 **Hipswell** N York
159 K6 **Hirael** Gwynd
71 K2 **Hiraeth** Carmth
291 G1 **Hirn** Abers
126 B2 **Hirnant** Powys
257 K8 **Hirst** N Lans
227 H2 **Hirst** Nthumb
178 E3 **Hirst Courtney** N York
148 B1 **Hirwaen** Denbgs
74 E5 **Hirwaun** Rhondd
56 B4 **Hirwaun Common** Brdgnd
23 J1 **Hiscott** Devon
234 B6 **Hislop** Border
43 L4 **Hisomley** Wilts
119 J7 **Histon** Cambs
105 G3 **Hitcham** Suffk
222 E6 **Hitchill** D & G
102 B8 **Hitchin** Herts
101 L8 **Hitchin Hill** Herts
43 K5 **Hitcombe Bottom** Wilts
65 L6 **Hither Green** Gt Lon
13 L2 **Hittisleigh** Devon
13 L2 **Hittisleigh Barton** Devon
179 J1 **Hive** E R Yk
129 L1 **Hixon** Staffs
53 J2 **Hoaden** Kent
76 D2 **Hoaldalbert** Mons
130 C2 **Hoar Cross** Staffs
95 H8 **Hoarwithy** Herefs
69 H8 **Hoath** Kent
50 C5 **Hoath Corner** Kent
111 G4 **Hobarris** Shrops
327 J3 **Hobbister** Ork
129 L5 **Hobble End** Staffs
104 B3 **Hobbles Green** Suffk
84 F4 **Hobbs Cross** Essex
84 F7 **Hobbs Cross** Essex
43 G2 **Hobbs Wall** BaNES
149 J3 **Hob Hill** Ches
234 F4 **Hobkirk** Border
165 K2 **Hobroyd** Derbys
212 E2 **Hobson** Dur
132 D3 **Hoby** Leics
40 F8 **Hoccombe** Somset
66 C7 **Hockenden** Gt Lon
84 F2 **Hockerill** Herts
138 B4 **Hockering** Norfk
138 B4 **Hockering Heath** Norfk
154 D2 **Hockerton** Notts
26 B2 **Hockholler** Somset
26 B2 **Hockholler Green** Somset
165 H4 **Hockley** Ches
67 K2 **Hockley** Essex
87 G5 **Hockley** Essex
52 C2 **Hockley** Kent
114 F4 **Hockley** Covtry
130 E6 **Hockley** Staffs
114 D5 **Hockley Heath** Solhll
82 F1 **Hockliffe** Beds
120 E2 **Hockwold cum Wilton** Norfk
25 J3 **Hockworthy** Devon
31 G2 **Hocombe** Hants
84 C5 **Hoddesdon** Herts
174 F3 **Hoddlesden** Bl w D
222 E5 **Hoddom Mains** D & G
97 J4 **Hoden** Worcs
151 H3 **Hodgefield** Staffs
114 C2 **Hodgehill** Birm
164 F7 **Hodgehill** Ches
71 G7 **Hodgeston** Pembks
281 H5 **Hodgeton** Angus
110 D1 **Hodley** Powys
150 B8 **Hodnet** Shrops
150 B8 **Hodnetheath** Shrops
168 B3 **Hodsock** Notts
66 F8 **Hodsoll Street** Kent
61 G4 **Hodson** Swindn
167 K5 **Hodthorpe** Derbys
31 K3 **Hoe** Hants
137 K3 **Hoe** Norfk
48 E4 **Hoe** Surrey
62 B7 **Hoe Benham** W Berk
31 L4 **Hoe Gate** Hants
202 F4 **Hoff** Cumb
156 D6 **Hoffleet Stow** Lincs
331 D10 **Hogaland** Shet
51 L2 **Hogbarn** Kent
52 D2 **Hogben's Hill** Kent
256 E7 **Hogganfield** C Glas
104 E2 **Hoggard's Green** Suffk
82 C1 **Hoggeston** Bucks
43 K2 **Hoggington** Wilts
114 E1 **Hoggrill's End** Warwks
322 A10 **Hogha Gearraidh** W Isls
47 K4 **Hog Hatch** Surrey
202 B2 **Hoghouse Hill** Cumb
174 D2 **Hoghton** Lancs
174 D2 **Hoghton Bottoms** Lancs

388 City, town and village index: Milltown of Edinvillie - Newcastleton or Copshaw Holm

304 D7 Milltown of Edinvillie Moray
301 J5 Milltown of Kildrummy Abers
305 J6 Milltown of Rothiemay Moray
301 H6 Milltown of Towie Abers
65 L5 Millwall Gt Lon
26 E7 Millway Rise Devon
310 F4 Milnafua Highld
267 L7 Milnathort P & K
163 J8 Milners Heath Ches
256 C6 Milngavie E Duns
257 J5 Milnquarter Falk
175 K5 Milnrow Rochdl
174 F2 Milnshaw Lancs
192 E5 Milnthorpe Cumb
177 J4 Milnthorpe Wakefd
243 L2 Milnwood N Lans
73 H5 Milo Carmth
292 B7 Milovaig Highld
112 C5 Milson Shrops
52 B2 Milstead Kent
45 G4 Milston Wilts
99 J4 Milthorpe Nhants
280 C5 Milton Angus
177 K7 Milton Barns
119 K7 Milton Cambs
256 D7 Milton C Glas
32 C7 Milton C Port
151 H3 Milton C Stke
192 F5 Milton Cumb
224 D7 Milton Cumb
214 F3 Milton D & G
221 J5 Milton D & G
131 G1 Milton Derbys
297 J2 Milton Highld
299 G6 Milton Highld
308 B9 Milton Highld
309 P6 Milton Highld
310 D8 Milton Highld
310 H3 Milton Highld
311 M7 Milton Highld
319 P6 Milton Highld
67 G6 Milton Kent
300 C5 Milton Moray
305 J3 Milton Moray
57 L3 Milton Newpt
168 D6 Milton Notts
41 K1 Milton N Som
62 C2 Milton Oxon
98 F6 Milton Oxon
267 H5 Milton P & K
278 D7 Milton P & K
71 G6 Milton Pembks
94 B3 Milton Powys
27 H2 Milton Somset
265 J7 Milton Stirlg
255 L6 Milton W Duns
43 L7 Milton Wilts
28 E6 Milton Abbas Dorset
12 E6 Milton Abbot Devon
246 B1 Milton Bridge Mdloth
101 G7 Milton Bryan Beds
43 G6 Milton Clevedon Somset
307 H8 Milton Coldwells Abers
7 G1 Milton Combe Devon
81 K6 Milton Common Oxon
22 F4 Milton Damerel Devon
304 B3 Miltonduff Moray
77 L4 Milton End Gloucs
79 J6 Milton End Gloucs
101 H2 Milton Ernest Beds
149 H2 Milton Green Ches
12 E6 Milton Green Devon
62 C2 Milton Heights Oxon
14 E6 Milton Hill Devon
62 C2 Milton Hill Oxon
100 C6 Milton Keynes M Keyn
100 E6 Milton Keynes Village M Keyn
45 G1 Milton Lilbourne Wilts
100 B2 Milton Malsor Nhants
277 H7 Milton Morenish P & K
301 L8 Milton of Auchinhove Abers
268 E7 Milton of Balgonie Fife
255 L2 Milton of Buchanan Stirlg
290 E1 Milton of Campfield Abers
256 E5 Milton of Campsie E Duns
302 C7 Milton of Corsindae Abers
266 F3 Milton of Cultoquhey P & K
301 K6 Milton of Cushnie Abers
278 E4 Milton of Dalcapon P & K
291 G5 Milton of Dellavaird Abers
278 E3 Milton of Edradour P & K
280 E3 Milton of Finavon Angus
310 H7 Milton of Gollanfield Highld
301 J3 Milton of Lesmore Abers
310 F9 Milton of Leys Highld
291 K1 Milton of Murtle C Aber
301 J3 Milton of Noth Abers
280 C6 Milton of Ogilvie Angus
289 K2 Milton of Tullich Abers
43 K8 Milton on Stour Dorset
62 C2 Milton Park Oxon
67 L7 Milton Regis Kent
35 K6 Milton Street E Susx
79 L3 Milton under Wychwood Oxon
25 L1 Milverton Somset
115 G6 Milverton Warwks
151 J7 Milwich Staffs
162 C6 Milwr Flints
48 C1 Mimbridge Surrey
254 B1 Minard Ag & B
254 B2 Minard Castle Ag & B
29 H4 Minchington Dorset
78 D6 Minchinhampton Gloucs
248 C7 Mindrum Nthumb
40 C4 Minehead Somset
148 E3 Minera Wrexhm
11 H2 Mineshope Cnwll
60 D2 Minety Wilts
124 E4 Minffordd Gwynd
146 B6 Minffordd Gwynd
159 K6 Minffordd Gwynd
282 F8 Mingarrypark Highld
321 M9 Mingearraidh W Isls
4 B5 Mingoose Cnwll
170 F8 Miningsby Lincs
11 K7 Minions Cnwll
229 L4 Minishant S Ayrs
47 K2 Minley Manor Hants
125 G4 Minllyn Gwynd
303 H4 Minnes Abers
219 L6 Minnigaff D & G
306 D3 Minnonie Abers
85 L4 Minnow End Essex
150 C1 Minshull Vernon Ches
186 C2 Minskip N York
30 D4 Minstead Hants
33 G2 Minsted W Susx
68 B6 Minster Kent
69 J8 Minster Kent
212 B2 Minsteracres Nthumb
127 H6 Minsterley Shrops
80 C4 Minster Lovell Oxon
78 B3 Minsterworth Gloucs
27 L6 Minterne Magna Dorset
28 B6 Minterne Parva Dorset
170 C6 Minting Lincs
307 J6 Mintlaw Abers
307 H6 Mintlaw Station Abers
234 F2 Minto Border
234 E2 Minto Kames Border
111 J1 Minton Shrops
192 F3 Mintsfeet Cumb
71 G4 Minwear Pembks
114 D1 Minworth Birm
328 D10 Mirbister Ork
200 B4 Mirehouse Cumb
319 P4 Mireland Highld
176 F4 Mirfield Kirk
78 E5 Miserden Gloucs
122 F2 Misery Corner Norfk
56 D4 Miskin Rhondd
75 G7 Miskin Rhondd
29 J2 Misselfore Wilts
168 C2 Misson Notts
116 B3 Misterton Leics
168 E2 Misterton Notts
27 G5 Misterton Somset
168 E1 Misterton Soss Notts
105 K7 Mistley Essex
105 K7 Mistley Heath Essex
65 J7 Mitcham Gt Lon
77 K3 Mitcheldean Gloucs
4 E4 Mitchell Cnwll
245 H7 Mitchell Hill Border
232 D7 Mitchellslacks D & G
246 F4 Mitchelston Border
76 F4 Mitchel Troy Mons
190 B1 Mite Houses Cumb
226 F2 Mitford Nthumb
4 B4 Mithian Cnwll
4 B5 Mithian Downs Cnwll
96 F7 Mitton Gloucs
129 H3 Mitton Staffs
99 K7 Mixbury Oxon
176 D2 Mixenden Calder
151 K2 Mixon Staffs
5 K4 Mixtow Cnwll
330 H5 Moarfield Shet
223 L5 Moat Cumb
280 D7 Moatmill Angus
105 H2 Moats Tye Suffk
164 E5 Mobberley Ches
151 K5 Mobberley Staffs
150 C5 Moblake Ches
82 D6 Mobwell Bucks
94 D5 Moccas Herefs
160 E5 Mochdre Conwy
110 B2 Mochdre Powys
215 H4 Mochrum D & G
30 B5 Mockbeggar Hants
52 F5 Mockbeggar Kent
67 H6 Mockbeggar Medway
200 D3 Mockerkin Cumb
7 L4 Modbury Devon
151 H6 Moddershall Staffs
167 K6 Model Village Derbys
115 J7 Model Village Warwks
50 E5 Modest Corner Kent
6 F2 Moditonham Quay Cnwll
317 P4 Modsarie Highld
161 H6 Moelfre Conwy
159 J3 Moelfre IoA
148 C8 Moelfre Powys
145 K2 Moel Tryfan Gwynd
162 C7 Moel-y-crio Flints
232 F5 Moffat D & G
257 H8 Moffat Mills N Lans
49 H3 Mogador Surrey
101 K4 Moggerhanger Beds
24 F3 Mogworthy Devon
131 G3 Moira Leics
93 L5 Moity Powys
52 D3 Molash Kent
293 G14 Mol-chlach Highld
162 D8 Mold Flints
85 H2 Molehill Green Essex
85 L3 Molehill Green Essex
188 F6 Molescroft E R Yk
226 E3 Molesden Nthumb
118 B4 Molesworth Cambs
5 H3 Molinnis Cnwll
293 K10 Moll Highld
39 K8 Molland Devon
163 G7 Mollington Ches
98 F4 Mollington Oxon
257 G6 Mollinsburn N Lans
159 G6 Mona IoA
91 H3 Monachty Cerdgn
265 H4 Monachyle Stirlg
110 E6 Monaughty Powys
291 G6 Monboddo Abers
267 L4 Moncreiffe P & K
127 G5 Mondaytown Shrops
291 H6 Mondynes Abers
277 G8 Monemore Stirlg
106 E2 Monewden Suffk
242 E3 Moneyacres E Ayrs
267 K2 Moneydie P & K
64 D2 Moneyhill Herts
131 H3 Money Hill Leics
63 L5 Moneyrow Green W & M
151 K4 Moneystone Staffs
3 K4 Mongleath Cnwll
221 H1 Moniaive D & G
269 J1 Monifieth Angus
280 E7 Monikie Angus
268 D5 Monimail Fife
89 J4 Monington Pembks
177 K6 Monk Bretton Barns
205 H5 Monk End N York
83 L7 Monken Hadley Gt Lon
178 C2 Monk Fryston N York
213 K6 Monk Hesleden Dur
95 K5 Monkhide Herefs
209 H2 Monkhill Cumb
178 B3 Monkhill Wakefd
128 C8 Monkhopton Shrops
95 G2 Monkland Herefs
23 H2 Monkleigh Devon
127 L4 Monkmoor Shrops
56 B6 Monknash V Glam
23 K5 Monkokehampton Devon
12 D7 Monkscross Cnwll
227 J5 Monkseaton N Tyne
105 G4 Monks Eleigh Suffk
105 G4 Monks Eleigh Tye Suffk
49 H8 Monk's Gate W Susx
164 F6 Monk's Heath Ches
46 F2 Monk Sherborne Hants
306 D7 Monkshill Abers
51 L5 Monks Hill Kent
40 E6 Monksilver Somset
115 K3 Monks Kirby Warwks
104 D6 Monks Lodge Essex
122 E6 Monk Soham Suffk
65 L7 Monks Orchard Gt Lon
59 L7 Monk's Park Wilts
114 C4 Monkspath Solhll
82 B6 Monks Risborough Bucks
171 H7 Monksthorpe Lincs
100 E6 Monkston Park M Keyn
268 D6 Monkstown Fife
103 K8 Monk Street Essex
186 B7 Monkswood Leeds
259 J8 Monkswood Mdloth
76 C6 Monkswood Mons
26 B6 Monkton Devon
69 J7 Monkton Kent
70 F6 Monkton Pembks
242 D8 Monkton S Ayrs
227 J7 Monkton S Tyne
56 B6 Monkton V Glam
43 J1 Monkton Combe BaNES
43 L6 Monkton Deverill Wilts
59 K7 Monkton Farleigh Wilts
259 J6 Monktonhall E Loth
26 D1 Monkton Heathfield Somset
29 J4 Monkton Up Wimborne Dorset
16 C2 Monkton Wyld Dorset
213 J2 Monkwearmouth Sundld
27 G7 Monkwood Dorset
47 G7 Monkwood Hants
96 D2 Monkwood Green Worcs
95 H4 Monmarsh Herefs
129 J7 Monmore Green Wolves
76 F4 Monmouth Mons
76 D1 Monmouth Cap Mons
94 E5 Monnington on Wye Herefs
215 J5 Monreith D & G
215 J5 Monreith Mains D & G
27 H3 Montacute Somset
174 E5 Montcliffe Bolton
254 E8 Montford Ag & B
127 J4 Montford Shrops
127 J3 Montford Bridge Shrops
301 L5 Montgarrie Abers
230 E1 Montgarswood E Ayrs
126 E7 Montgomery Powys
47 L3 Montgomery Lines Hants
242 C5 Montgreenan N Ayrs
175 G8 Monton Salfd
58 E6 Montpelier Bristl
268 F6 Montrave Fife
281 K3 Montrose Angus
87 G7 Montsale Essex
114 F1 Monwode Lea Warwks
45 K5 Monxton Hants
166 C7 Monyash Derbys
302 C5 Monymusk Abers
266 F3 Monzie P & K
256 F6 Moodiesburn N Lans
26 F4 Moolham Somset
37 G1 Moon's Green Kent
114 B6 Moon's Moat Worcs
268 E4 Moonzie Fife
27 G3 Moor Somset
44 C7 Mooray Wilts
16 E2 Moorbath Dorset
170 E8 Moorby Lincs
200 B2 Moorclose Cumb
175 J6 Moorclose Rochdl
63 K2 Moor Common Bucks
94 E2 Moorcot Herefs
29 H5 Moor Crichel Dorset
7 K3 Moor Cross Devon
19 H3 Moordown Bmouth
163 L4 Moore Halton
185 G7 Moor Edge Brad
177 H7 Moor End Barns
63 K2 Moor End Bucks
82 F3 Moor End Beds
176 C2 Moor End Calder
102 E4 Moor End Cambs
209 H3 Moorend Cumb
223 G5 Moorend D & G
152 D4 Moorend Derbys
24 B5 Moorend Devon
213 G5 Moor End Dur
188 B7 Moor End E R Yk
77 L6 Moorend Gloucs
78 D4 Moorend Gloucs
78 F2 Moor End Gloucs
182 C6 Moor End Lancs
186 D5 Moor End Leeds
186 C2 Moor End N York
187 G7 Moor End N York
58 F5 Moorend S Glos
165 J3 Moorend Stockp
96 F2 Moor End Worcs
187 J3 Moor End York
96 B4 Moorend Cross Herefs
196 D8 Moor End Field N York
178 F4 Moorends Donc
165 K2 Moorfield Derbys
142 F6 Moorgate Norfk
167 H2 Moorgate Rothm
114 B3 Moor Green Birm
31 H3 Moorgreen Hants
84 C1 Moor Green Herts
153 J4 Moorgreen Notts
151 J5 Moor Green Staffs
59 L7 Moor Green Wilts
167 K8 Moorhaigh Notts
130 C7 Moor Hall Birm
166 F6 Moorhall Derbys
94 E4 Moorhampton Herefs
7 L3 Moorhaven Village Devon
26 C5 Moorhayne Devon
185 H7 Moorhead Brad
177 G5 Moor Head Kirk
177 G2 Moor Head Leeds
175 K7 Moorhey Oldham
167 H4 Moorhole Sheff
209 G3 Moorhouse Cumb
209 H2 Moorhouse Cumb
178 B5 Moorhouse Donc
168 E7 Moorhouse Notts
50 B3 Moorhouse Bank Surrey
156 E2 Moorhouses Lincs
24 E7 Moorlake Devon
42 E1 Moorledge BaNES
42 B6 Moorlinch Somset
186 F3 Moor Monkton N York
186 F3 Moor Monkton Moor N York
302 C6 Moor of Balvack Abers
311 P6 Moor of Granary Moray
208 C6 Moor Park Cumb
95 G5 Moor Park Herefs
64 E2 Moor Park Herts
47 L4 Moor Park Surrey
200 C5 Moor Row Cumb
208 F4 Moor Row Cumb
206 F5 Moorsholm R & Cl
176 F2 Moor Side Brad
162 E5 Moorside Ches
28 D3 Moorside Dorset
212 C4 Moorside Dur
182 D8 Moor Side Lancs
182 E7 Moor Side Lancs
185 K7 Moorside Leeds
156 D2 Moor Side Lincs
175 L6 Moorside Oldham
175 G7 Moorside Salfd
52 F6 Moorstock Kent
67 K7 Moor Street Medway
6 B2 Moorswater Cnwll
178 B5 Moorthorpe Wakefd
176 F3 Moor Top Kirk
12 C2 Moortown Devon
13 G7 Moortown Devon
23 J3 Moortown Devon
30 B6 Moortown Hants
20 F5 Moortown IoW
180 D8 Moortown Lincs
128 C3 Moortown Wrekin
315 J10 Morangie Highld
282 F3 Morar Highld
153 H6 Moravian Settlement Derbys
158 D4 Môrawelon IoA
118 C1 Morborne Cambs
24 D5 Morchard Bishop Devon
24 D6 Morchard Road Devon
16 D3 Morcombelake Dorset
133 J6 Morcott Rutlnd
148 E8 Morda Shrops
18 E2 Morden Dorset
65 J7 Morden Gt Lon
102 C5 Morden Green Cambs
65 H7 Morden Park Gt Lon
95 J6 Mordiford Herefs
248 E2 Mordington Holdings Border
205 J2 Mordon Dur
111 G1 More Shrops
25 G1 Morebath Devon
235 K2 Morebattle Border
182 D2 Morecambe Lancs
60 F3 Moredon Swindn
259 H7 Moredun C Edin
313 J7 Morefield Highld
53 H6 Morehall Kent
8 C4 Moreleigh Devon
277 G7 Morenish P & K
200 C4 Moresby Parks Cumb
31 J1 Morestead Hants
18 B4 Moreton Dorset
85 G5 Moreton Essex
111 K7 Moreton Herefs
80 E6 Moreton Oxon
81 K6 Moreton Oxon
128 F3 Moreton Staffs
152 B8 Moreton Staffs
162 E2 Moreton Wirral
127 L2 Moreton Corbet Shrops
13 L4 Moretonhampstead Devon
98 B7 Moreton-in-Marsh Gloucs
95 J4 Moreton Jeffries Herefs
98 D2 Moreton Morrell Warwks
95 H4 Moreton on Lugg Herefs
98 D3 Moreton Paddox Warwks
99 J4 Moreton Pinkney Nhants
150 B7 Moreton Say Shrops
78 B5 Moreton Valence Gloucs
150 B6 Moretonwood Shrops
54 D2 Morfa Carmth
73 H6 Morfa Carmth
90 D5 Morfa Cerdgn
144 C7 Morfa Gwynd
54 D2 Morfa Bacas Carmth
72 D6 Morfa Bach Carmth
145 K6 Morfa Bychan Gwynd
145 H2 Morfa Dinlle Gwynd
74 D5 Morfa Glas Neath
144 E5 Morfa Nefyn Gwynd
148 B4 Morfydd Denbgs
56 F4 Morganstown Cardif
30 B2 Morgan's Vale Wilts
108 C4 Moriah Cerdgn
77 H5 Mork Gloucs
202 D3 Morland Cumb
164 F4 Morley Ches
153 G5 Morley Derbys
204 E2 Morley Dur
177 H2 Morley Leeds
164 F4 Morley Green Ches
153 G5 Morleymoor Derbys
153 G4 Morley Park Derbys
138 B7 Morley St Botolph Norfk
153 G5 Morley Smithy Derbys
12 C7 Mornick Cnwll
259 G6 Morningside C Edin
244 C2 Morningside N Lans
122 E1 Morningthorpe Norfk
227 G2 Morpeth Nthumb
281 K2 Morphie Abers
130 C3 Morrey Staffs
151 K3 Morridge Side Staffs
151 J6 Morrilow Heath Staffs
55 G2 Morriston Swans
57 G6 Morristown V Glam
142 C3 Morston Norfk
38 C4 Mortehoe Devon
167 J3 Morthen Rothm
62 F8 Mortimer W Berk
111 J7 Mortimer's Cross Herefs
62 F8 Mortimer West End Hants
65 H5 Mortlake Gt Lon
177 J8 Mortomley Sheff
209 J3 Morton Cumb
209 K6 Morton Cumb
153 G1 Morton Derbys
21 K4 Morton IoW
134 C2 Morton Lincs
168 F2 Morton Lincs
169 G8 Morton Lincs
138 C3 Morton Norfk
154 D3 Morton Notts
58 F2 Morton S Glos
126 F2 Morton Shrops
114 C7 Morton Bagot Warwks
126 F2 Morton Common Shrops
232 B7 Morton Mains D & G
128 B2 Morton Mill Shrops
196 B3 Morton-on-Swale N York
97 H3 Morton Spirt Worcs
204 F3 Morton Tinmouth Dur
97 H2 Morton Underhill Worcs
2 B3 Morvah Cnwll
6 C3 Morval Cnwll
295 J4 Morvich Highld
315 J6 Morvich Highld
128 D8 Morville Shrops
128 D8 Morville Heath Shrops
12 E8 Morwellham Quay Devon
22 C3 Morwenstow Cnwll
167 H4 Mosborough Sheff
242 F5 Moscow E Ayrs
112 F1 Mose Shrops
209 J7 Mosedale Cumb
114 B3 Moseley Birm
129 J7 Moseley Wolves
96 D2 Moseley Worcs
174 F6 Moses Gate Bolton
174 F7 Mosley Common Wigan
270 B6 Moss Ag & B
178 D5 Moss Donc
282 F8 Moss Highld
148 F3 Moss Wrexhm
301 J5 Mossat Abers
163 K3 Moss Bank Halton
331 F10 Mossbank Shet
174 B8 Moss Bank St Hel
200 B2 Mossbay Cumb
230 C2 Mossblown S Ayrs
164 D3 Mossbrow Traffd
235 H3 Mossburnford Border
220 E5 Mossdale D & G
224 B6 Mossedge Cumb
182 D5 Moss Edge Lancs
182 D6 Moss Edge Lancs
63 L6 Moss End Br For
164 C5 Moss End Ches
244 B1 Mossend N Lans
200 E3 Mosser Cumb
200 E2 Mosser Mains Cumb
151 H6 Mossgate Staffs
242 F8 Mossgiel E Ayrs
247 G6 Mosshouses Border
165 G6 Moss Houses Ches
280 D4 Mosside Angus
165 H6 Moss Lane Ches
151 G1 Mossley Ches
175 L7 Mossley Tamesd
163 G3 Mossley Hill Lpool
164 F3 Moss Nook St Hel
163 K2 Moss Nook St Hel
304 C3 Moss of Barmuckity Moray
256 C8 Mosspark C Glas
129 J2 Moss Pit Staffs
208 E3 Moss Side Cumb
311 K7 Moss-side Highld
163 H1 Moss Side Knows
173 J1 Moss Side Sefton
174 B3 Moss Side Lancs
164 F1 Moss Side Manch
305 J5 Moss-side Moray
173 J7 Moss Side Sefton
305 L8 Moss-side of Monellie Abers
304 E3 Mosstodloch Moray
280 F6 Mosston Angus
174 B5 Mossy Lea Lancs
27 G5 Mosterton Dorset
163 G6 Moston Ches
175 J7 Moston Manch
128 B1 Moston Shrops
150 D1 Moston Green Ches
162 B4 Mostyn Flints
28 E1 Motcombe Dorset
7 J5 Mothecombe Devon
201 L2 Motherby Cumb
244 B2 Motherwell N Lans
65 H7 Motspur Park Gt Lon
66 B6 Mottingham Gt Lon
30 E1 Mottisfont Hants
20 E5 Mottistone IoW
165 J1 Mottram in Longdendale Tamesd
165 J1 Mottram Rise Tamesd
165 G5 Mottram St Andrew Ches
85 G3 Mott's Green Essex
50 D6 Mott's Mill E Susx
16 c3 Mouilpied Guern
163 K6 Mouldsworth Ches
278 D3 Moulin P & K
34 F5 Moulsecoomb Br & H
62 E4 Moulsford Oxon
85 L5 Moulsham Essex
100 F5 Moulsoe M Keyn
164 C7 Moulton Ches
134 F2 Moulton Lincs
116 F6 Moulton Nhants
205 G7 Moulton N York
120 D7 Moulton Suffk
56 E6 Moulton V Glam
134 F3 Moulton Chapel Lincs
135 G3 Moulton Eaugate Lincs
116 F7 Moulton Park Nhants
139 H5 Moulton St Mary Norfk
135 G1 Moulton Seas End Lincs
289 H6 Moulzie Angus
4 C3 Mount Cnwll
11 G8 Mount Cnwll
158 C4 Mountain IoA
75 J5 Mountain Air Blae G
75 H7 Mountain Ash Rhondd
59 K5 Mountain Bower Wilts
245 J4 Mountain Cross Border
52 E3 Mountain Street Kent
3 J2 Mount Ambrose Cnwll
58 C3 Mount Ballan Mons
233 K1 Mountbenger Border
233 K1 Mountbengerburn Border
256 B6 Mountblow W Duns
67 K2 Mount Bovers Essex
104 E7 Mount Bures Essex
5 H4 Mount Charles Cnwll
10 E8 Mount Charles Cnwll
45 J3 Mount Cowdown Wilts
84 F6 Mount End Essex
35 J3 Mount Ephraim E Susx
28 D3 Mounters Dorset
36 D2 Mountfield E Susx
310 D5 Mountgerald Highld
7 G4 Mount Gould C Plym
4 B5 Mount Hawke Cnwll
3 J7 Mount Hermon Cnwll
48 C2 Mount Hermon Surrey
310 F5 Mount High Highld
59 G6 Mount Hill S Glos
4 E2 Mountjoy Cnwll
12 D2 Mount Lane Devon
85 J7 Mountnessing Essex
58 D2 Mounton Mons
99 L7 Mount Pleasant Bucks
150 F2 Mount Pleasant Ches
5 H2 Mount Pleasant Cnwll
151 G5 Mount Pleasant C Stke
130 F3 Mount Pleasant Derbys
131 G1 Mount Pleasant Derbys
152 F4 Mount Pleasant Derbys
26 B6 Mount Pleasant Devon
211 H5 Mount Pleasant Dur
213 G7 Mount Pleasant Dur
35 H3 Mount Pleasant E Susx
35 J6 Mount Pleasant E Susx
162 D6 Mount Pleasant Flints
227 H7 Mount Pleasant Gatesd
64 D2 Mount Pleasant Gt Lon
319 K3 Mountpleasant Highld
69 J7 Mount Pleasant Kent
206 C5 Mount Pleasant Middsb
75 H7 Mount Pleasant Myr Td
74 B7 Mount Pleasant Neath
137 K8 Mount Pleasant Norfk
71 G5 Mount Pleasant Pembks
127 K4 Mount Pleasant Shrops
205 L3 Mount Pleasant S on T
104 B4 Mount Pleasant Suffk
115 H2 Mount Pleasant Warwks
97 H6 Mount Pleasant Worcs
113 K7 Mount Pleasant Worcs
8 C5 Mounts Devon
148 E3 Mount Sion Wrexhm
80 D3 Mount Skippett Oxon
307 G4 Mountsolie Abers
132 B4 Mountsorrel Leics
29 J2 Mount Sorrel Wilts
176 D2 Mount Tabor Calder
256 F8 Mount Vernon C Glas
6 F4 Mount Wise C Plym
48 B5 Mousehill Surrey
2 D5 Mousehole Cnwll
249 J7 Mousen Nthumb
114 E6 Mousley End Warwks
222 D5 Mouswald D & G
22 D1 Mouth Mill Devon
182 D8 Mowbreck Lancs
151 G2 Mow Cop Staffs
205 H4 Mowden Darltn
86 B4 Mowden Essex
235 L2 Mowhaugh Border
132 B5 Mowmacre Hill C Leic
50 C4 Mowshurst Kent
116 C2 Mowsley Leics
187 G1 Moxby N York
129 K7 Moxley Wsall
285 L5 Moy Highld
298 E2 Moy Highld
304 C3 Moycroft Moray
298 E1 Moy Hall Highld
89 J4 Moylgrove Pembks
243 H1 Mt Florida C Glas
239 G5 Muasdale Ag & B
291 L3 Muchalls Abers
95 H7 Much Birch Herefs
95 K4 Much Cowarne Herefs
95 G7 Much Dewchurch Herefs
27 G2 Muchelney Somset
27 G2 Muchelney Ham Somset
84 E3 Much Hadham Herts
173 L3 Much Hoole Lancs
173 L3 Much Hoole Moss Houses Lancs
173 L3 Much Hoole Town Lancs
6 B3 Muchlarnick Cnwll
95 L7 Much Marcle Herefs
296 E2 Muchrachd Highld
128 C6 Much Wenlock Shrops
67 G4 Mucking Thurr
17 J3 Muckleford Dorset
150 D6 Mucklestone Staffs
141 G4 Muckleton Norfk
128 B2 Muckleton Shrops
301 L4 Muckletown Abers
128 C7 Muckley Shrops
130 B5 Muckley Corner Staffs
128 C7 Muckley Cross Shrops
171 G4 Muckton Lincs
171 G4 Muckton Bottom Lincs
317 L9 Mudale Highld
165 J2 Mudd Tamesd
38 E6 Muddiford Devon
38 D7 Muddlebridge Devon
35 K4 Muddles Green E Susx
19 K3 Mudeford Dorset
27 K3 Mudford Somset
27 K3 Mudford Sock Somset
42 B4 Mudgley Somset
256 D5 Mugdock Stirlg
292 G9 Mugeary Highld
152 E5 Mugginton Derbys
152 E5 Muggintonlane End Derbys
49 J3 Mugswell Surrey
314 G6 Muie Highld
288 D4 Muir Abers
247 G4 Muircleugh Border
306 C5 Muirden Abers
281 G7 Muirdrum Angus
268 E8 Muiredge Fife
243 H2 Muirend C Glas
280 B8 Muirhead Angus
268 D6 Muirhead Fife
256 F7 Muirhead N Lans
242 C7 Muirhead S Ayrs
259 G5 Muirhouse C Edin
244 B3 Muirhouse N Lans
280 C3 Muirhouses Angus
258 C4 Muirhouses Falk
268 D3 Muirhouses P & K
231 H1 Muirkirk E Ayrs
301 K5 Muir of Alford Abers
310 B7 Muir of Fairburn Highld
301 L6 Muir of Fowlis Abers
304 E3 Muir of Lochs Moray
310 C7 Muir of Ord Highld
280 D7 Muir of Pert Angus
310 C7 Muir of Tarradale Highld
284 E5 Muirshearlich Highld
291 J2 Muirskie Abers
306 E6 Muirtack Abers
307 H8 Muirtack Abers
310 G5 Muirton Highld
267 G5 Muirton P & K
267 L2 Muirton P & K
310 B7 Muirton Mains Highld
279 J6 Muirton of Ardblair P & K
281 J2 Muirton of Ballochy Angus
306 D5 Muiryfold Abers
194 D2 Muker N York
138 D6 Mulbarton Norfk
304 F5 Mulben Moray
5 H1 Mulberry Cnwll
2 D4 Mulfra Cnwll
251 F11 Mulindry Ag & B
324 H6 Mullach Chàrlabhaigh W Isls
38 D5 Mullacott Cross Devon
45 J4 Mullenspond Hants
3 H7 Mullion Cnwll
3 H7 Mullion Cove Cnwll
54 F4 Mumbles Hill Swans
171 K6 Mumby Lincs
175 K6 Mumps Oldham
95 L3 Munderfield Row Herefs
95 L3 Munderfield Stocks Herefs
143 J4 Mundesley Norfk
137 G8 Mundford Norfk
139 G7 Mundham Norfk
86 D6 Mundon Essex
303 H6 Mundurno C Aber
52 B4 Mundy Bois Kent
296 E8 Munerigie Highld
330 K5 Muness Shet
312 F8 Mungasdale Highld
209 J7 Mungrisdale Cumb
310 E7 Munlochy Highld
95 L5 Munsley Herefs
111 L2 Munslow Shrops
95 H5 Munstone Herefs
57 G6 Murch V Glam
13 K4 Murchington Devon
97 J5 Murcot Worcs
81 H3 Murcott Oxon
60 C2 Murcott Wilts
266 B8 Murdieston Stirlg
163 L4 Murdishaw Halton
258 D8 Murieston W Loth
319 L3 Murkle Highld
284 C3 Murlaggan Highld
285 J5 Murlaggan Highld
326 F4 Murra Ork
259 G6 Murrayfield C Edin
222 E5 Murraythwaite D & G
47 H2 Murrell Green Hants
78 B2 Murrell's End Gloucs
96 B7 Murrell's End Gloucs
96 B8 Murrell's End Gloucs
280 E7 Murroes Angus
135 H5 Murrow Cambs
100 D8 Mursley Bucks
68 B8 Murston Kent
280 E3 Murthill Angus
279 G7 Murthly P & K
203 G3 Murton Cumb
213 J4 Murton Dur
248 F4 Murton Nthumb
227 J5 Murton N Tyne
54 E4 Murton Swans
187 J4 Murton York
196 F4 Murton Grange N York
8 B3 Murtwell Devon
16 B3 Musbury Devon
19 H2 Muscliff Bmouth
197 J5 Muscoates N York
116 C7 Muscott Nhants
263 G3 Musdale Ag & B
113 J2 Mushroom Green Dudley
259 J6 Musselburgh E Loth
70 C5 Musselwick Pembks
139 J3 Mustard Hyrn Norfk
154 F6 Muston Leics
199 G6 Muston N York
113 H5 Mustow Green Worcs
65 J2 Muswell Hill Gt Lon
216 E4 Mutehill D & G
123 K2 Mutford Suffk
266 F4 Muthill P & K
25 J6 Mutterton Devon
35 L2 Mutton Hall E Susx
128 E4 Muxton Wrekin
162 C5 Mwdwl-eithin Flints
162 C7 Mwynbwll Flints
319 L6 Mybster Highld
92 C7 Myddfai Carmth
127 K2 Myddle Shrops
127 K2 Myddlewood Shrops
73 J6 Myddyn-fych Carmth
91 G4 Mydroilyn Cerdgn
182 E7 Myerscough Lancs
174 D1 Myerscough Smithy Lancs
3 L3 Mylor Bridge Cnwll
3 L4 Mylor Churchtown Cnwll
57 G5 Mynachdy Cardif
75 G7 Mynachdy Rhondd
89 J6 Mynachlog-ddu Pembks
111 H5 Mynd Shrops
111 H2 Myndtown Shrops
108 E4 Mynydd Bach Cerdgn
58 C2 Mynydd-bach Mons
54 F2 Mynydd-Bach Swans
54 F2 Mynydd-bach-y-glo Swans
159 H3 Mynydd Bodafon IoA
144 d3 Mynydd Gilan Gwynd
162 D8 Mynydd Isa Flints
57 G2 Mynyddislwyn Caerph
162 B6 Mynydd-llan Flints
159 L7 Mynydd Llandegai Gwynd
160 F5 Mynydd Marian Conwy
158 F3 Mynydd Mechell IoA
159 G4 Mynydd-Mwyn IoA
159 G4 Mynydd Mwyn Mawr IoA
158 E4 Mynydd-y-gôf IoA
158 E4 Mynydd-yr-eithin IoA
144 F7 Mynytho Gwynd
291 G2 Myrebird Abers
319 N5 Myrelandhorn Highld
92 C7 Myrtle Hill Carmth
47 L2 Mytchett Surrey
47 L2 Mytchett Place Surrey
175 L2 Mytholm Calder
176 C2 Mytholmroyd Calder
182 C8 Mythop Lancs
114 F7 Myton Warwks
186 D1 Myton Hall N York
186 D1 Myton-on-Swale N York
127 J3 Mytton Shrops

N

312 C10 Naast Highld
176 F4 Nab Hill Kirk
174 D2 Nab's Head Lancs
322 H6 Na Buirgh W Isls
187 G5 Naburn York
185 H7 Nab Wood Brad
52 D5 Naccolt Kent
53 G3 Nackington Kent
106 E5 Nacton Suffk
14 D3 Nadderwater Devon
189 G3 Nafferton E R Yk
324 G6 Na Gearrannan W Isls
78 D7 Nag's Head Gloucs
162 C5 Naid-y-march Flints
77 J3 Nailbridge Gloucs
41 H8 Nailsbourne Somset
58 C7 Nailsea N Som
131 J5 Nailstone Leics
43 H1 Nailwell BaNES
311 K6 Nairn Highld
49 H4 Nalderswood Surrey
2 E4 Nanceddan Cnwll
3 G4 Nancegollan Cnwll
2 F2 Nancemellin Cnwll
3 J5 Nancenoy Cnwll
2 D3 Nancledra Cnwll
175 H4 Nangreaves Bury
144 E7 Nanhoron Gwynd
124 E2 Nannau Gwynd
162 C7 Nannerch Flints
131 L3 Nanpantan Leics
5 G3 Nanpean Cnwll
2 B5 Nanquidno Cnwll
5 H1 Nanstallon Cnwll
72 E5 Nant Carmth
148 C2 Nant Denbgs
148 E7 Nant Shrops
162 C7 Nant Alyn Flints
75 G4 Nant-ddu Powys
90 E4 Nanternis Cerdgn
72 F4 Nantgaredig Carmth
56 F3 Nantgarw Rhondd
72 D2 Nantgerdinen Carmth
109 K7 Nant Glas Powys
147 K1 Nantglyn Denbgs
109 K4 Nantgwyn Powys
3 H6 Nantithet Cnwll
145 K3 Nantlle Gwynd
162 E8 Nant Mawr Flints
126 E2 Nantmawr Shrops
109 L6 Nantmel Powys
146 B4 Nantmor Gwynd
145 L2 Nant Peris Gwynd
109 K5 Nantserth Powys
150 B3 Nantwich Ches
92 C5 Nant-y-Bai Carmth
75 J4 Nant-y-Bwch Blae G
74 C5 Nant-y-cafn Neath
72 F5 Nantycaws Carmth
126 F1 Nant y Caws Shrops
57 H3 Nant-y-ceisiad Caerph
76 C5 Nant-y-derry Mons
160 B6 Nant-y-felin Conwy
73 H2 Nant-y-ffân Carmth
55 L3 Nantyffyllon Brdgnd
75 K4 Nantyglo Blae G
148 D8 Nant-y-gollen Shrops
56 B2 Nant-y-moel Brdgnd
160 B6 Nant-y-pandy Conwy
146 F2 Nant-y-Rhiw Conwy
320 F2 Na Pairceanan W Isls
53 K4 Napchester Kent
82 D7 Naphill Bucks
96 E4 Napleton Worcs
150 D6 Napley Staffs
150 D6 Napley Heath Staffs
184 B4 Nappa N York
194 E3 Nappa Scar N York
115 K7 Napton on the Hill Warwks
71 H4 Narberth Pembks
71 H4 Narberth Bridge Pembks
131 L7 Narborough Leics
136 E4 Narborough Norfk
26 D5 Narfords Devon
6 D3 Narkurs Cnwll
263 G5 Narrachan Ag & B
22 F3 Narracott Devon
139 J4 Narrowgate Corner Norfk
145 J4 Nasareth Gwynd
116 D4 Naseby Nhants
320 C5 Nasg W Isls
100 C7 Nash Bucks
66 B8 Nash Gt Lon
111 G7 Nash Herefs
53 J2 Nash Kent
57 K4 Nash Newpt
112 C5 Nash Shrops
27 J4 Nash Somset
78 D5 Nashend Gloucs
112 F3 Nash End Worcs
47 G4 Nashes Green Hants
82 C5 Nash Lee Bucks
35 L4 Nash Street E Susx
66 F7 Nash Street Kent
133 L7 Nassington Nhants
78 B5 Nastend Gloucs
84 D2 Nasty Herts
22 D2 Natcott Devon
203 H6 Nateby Cumb
182 E6 Nateby Lancs
47 H3 Nately Scures Hants
192 F4 Natland Cumb
96 F7 Natton Gloucs
105 H4 Naughton Suffk
79 J2 Naunton Gloucs
96 E6 Naunton Worcs
97 G3 Naunton Beauchamp Worcs
48 B8 Navant Hill W Susx
155 J2 Navenby Lincs
85 G7 Navestock Heath Essex
85 H7 Navestock Side Essex
315 P3 Navidale Highld
197 J5 Nawton N York
105 G7 Nayland Suffk
84 E5 Nazeing Essex
84 E5 Nazeing Gate Essex
84 E6 Nazeing Long Green Essex
84 D5 Nazeing Mead Essex
19 K2 Neacroft Hants
209 H3 Nealhouse Cumb
115 G3 Neal's Green Warwks
52 D2 Neames Forstal Kent
332 H5 Neap Shet
185 H1 Near Hardcastle N York
191 H1 Near Sawrey Cumb
82 C1 Nearton End Bucks
65 H3 Neasden Gt Lon
205 J5 Neasham Darltn
80 D2 Neat Enstone Oxon
74 B7 Neath Neath
55 H2 Neath Abbey Neath
47 H5 Neatham Hants
100 E5 Neath Hill M Keyn
139 G2 Neatishead Norfk
180 F1 Neat Marsh E R Yk
137 J6 Neaton Norfk
91 H2 Nebo Cerdgn
146 F2 Nebo Conwy
145 J3 Nebo Gwynd
159 H2 Nebo IoA
97 L5 Nebsworth Warwks
114 B2 Nechells Birm
137 H5 Necton Norfk
316 C10 Nedd Highld
227 G3 Nedderton Nthumb
42 E3 Nedge Hill Somset
105 G4 Nedging Suffk
105 H4 Nedging Tye Suffk
122 E3 Needham Norfk
85 G3 Needham Green Essex
105 J2 Needham Market Suffk
120 E6 Needham Street Suffk
119 G5 Needingworth Cambs
130 D2 Needwood Staffs
4 D3 Neeham Cnwll
112 D4 Neen Savage Shrops
112 D5 Neen Sollars Shrops
112 C2 Neenton Shrops
148 F6 Nefod Shrops
144 F5 Nefyn Gwynd
42 F4 Neighbourne Somset
96 F2 Neight Hill Worcs
242 F2 Neilston E Rens
98 F5 Neithrop Oxon
75 J7 Nelson Caerph
184 C7 Nelson Lancs
227 H4 Nelson Village Nthumb
244 C5 Nemphlar S Lans
42 D1 Nempnett Thrubwell N Som
134 F5 Nene Terrace Lincs
211 G4 Nenthall Cumb
211 G5 Nenthead Cumb
247 K6 Nenthorn Border
24 D7 Neopardy Devon
34 B5 Nepcote W Susx
200 D2 Nepgill Cumb
34 D3 Nep Town W Susx
251 C11 Nerabus Ag & B
148 D1 Nercwys Flints
243 J2 Nerston S Lans
248 F7 Nesbit Nthumb
162 F5 Ness Ches
127 H3 Nesscliffe Shrops
162 F5 Nessholt Ches
329 N3 Nesstoun Ork
162 E5 Neston Ches
59 L7 Neston Wilts
114 B2 Netchells Green Birm
58 F6 Netham Bristl
244 C4 Nethanfoot S Lans
164 F5 Nether Alderley Ches
44 F4 Netheravon Wilts
247 G5 Nether Blainslie Border
166 B3 Nether Booth Derbys
306 D4 Netherbrae Abers
328 C10 Netherbrough Ork
132 D1 Nether Broughton Leics
244 C4 Netherburn S Lans
193 H6 Nether Burrow Lancs
152 E6 Nether Burrows Derbys
27 H7 Netherbury Dorset
223 K5 Netherby Cumb
186 B5 Netherby N York
233 J6 Nether Cassock D & G
28 B7 Nether Cerne Dorset
166 F6 Nether Chanderhill Derbys
26 C2 Netherclay Somset
217 K2 Nether Clifton D & G
27 K3 Nether Compton Dorset
99 G5 Nethercote Oxon
115 L7 Nethercote Warwks
12 D2 Nethercott Devon
38 C6 Nethercott Devon
80 F2 Nethercott Oxon
40 F7 Nethercott Somset
302 F4 Nether Crimond Abers
304 F3 Nether Dallachy Moray
281 J4 Nether Dysart Angus
166 F4 Nether Edge Sheff
166 E6 Nether End Derbys
77 H7 Netherend Gloucs
177 G6 Nether End Kirk
132 E4 Nether End Leics
25 G7 Nether Exe Devon
36 D3 Netherfield E Susx
100 E6 Netherfield M Keyn
154 B5 Netherfield Notts
232 C4 Nether Fingland S Lans
142 D6 Nethergate Norfk
132 C5 Nether Hall C Leic
44 F8 Netherhampton Wilts
167 H5 Nether Handley Derbys
280 C6 Nether Handwick Angus
167 H1 Nether Haugh Rothm
168 D5 Nether Headon Notts
153 G3 Nether Heage Derbys
99 L2 Nether Heyford Nhants
246 C6 Nether Horsburgh Border
328 D10 Netherhouse Ork
232 E4 Nether Howecleuch D & G
192 F8 Nether Kellet Lancs
245 L5 Nether Kidston Border
307 J7 Nether Kinmundy Abers
242 F2 Nether Kirkton E Rens
152 B7 Netherland Green Staffs
167 K6 Nether Langwith Notts
216 F4 Netherlaw D & G
27 G5 Netherlay Dorset
303 K2 Nether Leask Abers
243 H2 Netherlee E Rens
291 K3 Netherley Abers
176 C5 Netherley Kirk
163 H3 Netherley Lpool
166 F7 Nether Loads Derbys
222 C2 Nethermill D & G
305 J5 Nethermills Moray
167 G7 Nether Moor Derbys
306 F7 Nethermuir Abers
49 J2 Netherne on-the-Hill Surrey
166 E5 Nether Padley Derbys
243 G2 Netherplace E Rens
187 G3 Nether Poppleton York
234 E2 Netherraw Border
304 C6 Nether Ringorm Moray
209 H6 Nether Row Cumb
130 F4 Netherseal Derbys
246 E4 Nether Shiels Border
196 E3 Nether Silton N York
110 F5 Nether Skyborry Shrops
121 J7 Nether St Suffk
27 J5 Netherstoke Dorset
130 C4 Nether Stowe Staffs
41 G6 Nether Stowey Somset
85 H4 Nether Street Essex
84 E3 Nether Street Herts
230 F3 Netherthird E Ayrs
176 E6 Netherthong Kirk
167 H6 Netherthorpe Derbys
280 F3 Netherton Angus
163 K5 Netherton Ches
11 K7 Netherton Cnwll
208 B6 Netherton Cumb
14 D7 Netherton Devon
113 J2 Netherton Dudley
79 K6 Netherton Gloucs
45 L2 Netherton Hants
77 G1 Netherton Herefs
176 E5 Netherton Kirk
244 B3 Netherton N Lans
236 D5 Netherton Nthumb
279 H4 Netherton P & K
173 J7 Netherton Sefton
112 E3 Netherton Shrops
256 D5 Netherton Stirlg
177 H4 Netherton Wakefd
97 G5 Netherton Worcs
200 B6 Nethertown Cumb
319 P1 Nethertown Highld
183 K7 Nethertown Lancs
130 C3 Nethertown Staffs
268 B6 Nether Urquhart Fife
45 K6 Nether Wallop Hants
225 L6 Nether Warden Nthumb
200 E7 Nether Wasdale Cumb
209 J4 Nether Welton Cumb
79 L2 Nether Westcote Gloucs
130 E8 Nether Whitacre Warwks
81 L4 Nether Winchendon or Lower Winchendon Bucks
226 E1 Netherwitton Nthumb
243 J8 Netherwood E Ayrs
98 F7 Nether Worton Oxon
299 K4 Nethy Bridge Highld
31 G5 Netley Hants
31 H4 Netley Hill Hants
30 E4 Netley Marsh Hants
25 G7 Nettacott Devon
84 E4 Netteswell Essex
63 G3 Nettlebed Oxon
43 G4 Nettlebridge Somset
17 G2 Nettlecombe Dorset
21 H6 Nettlecombe IoW
83 G4 Nettleden Herts
169 K5 Nettleham Lincs
51 G3 Nettlestead Kent
105 J4 Nettlestead Suffk
51 G3 Nettlestead Green Kent
21 K3 Nettlestone IoW
212 F4 Nettlesworth Dur
78 E4 Nettleton Gloucs
180 D7 Nettleton Lincs
59 K5 Nettleton Wilts
59 K5 Nettleton Green Wilts
59 K5 Nettleton Shrub Wilts
180 E8 Nettleton Top Lincs
44 F6 Netton Wilts
73 K4 Neuadd Carmth
67 H2 Nevendon Essex
89 H4 Nevern Pembks
213 G5 Nevilles Cross Dur
133 G8 Nevill Holt Leics
222 B6 New Abbey D & G
306 F3 New Aberdour Abers
65 L8 New Addington Gt Lon
185 K5 Newall Leeds
164 F3 Newall Green Manch
46 E7 New Alresford Hants
279 K5 New Alyth P & K
134 E6 Newark C Pete
329 M5 Newark Ork
154 F3 Newark-on-Trent Notts
114 F2 New Arley Warwks
188 F6 New Arram E R Yk
244 B2 Newarthill N Lans
66 F7 New Ash Green Kent
154 F3 New Balderton Notts
169 L5 Newball Lincs
53 G6 Newbarn Kent
66 F7 New Barn Kent
84 B7 New Barnet Gt Lon
180 D5 New Barnetby N Linc
190 E6 Newbarns Cumb
117 H7 New Barton Nhants
153 L5 New Basford C Nott
259 J7 Newbattle Mdloth
56 D6 New Beaupre V Glam
65 L6 New Beckenham Gt Lon
236 F2 New Bewick Nthumb
222 F6 Newbie D & G
190 B2 Newbiggin Cumb
190 F7 Newbiggin Cumb
193 G6 Newbiggin Cumb
202 B2 Newbiggin Cumb
202 E2 Newbiggin Nthumb
210 C4 Newbiggin Cumb
203 L2 Newbiggin Dur
212 D4 Newbiggin Dur
211 K4 Newbiggin Nthumb
194 E3 Newbiggin N York
194 E4 Newbiggin N York
227 J2 Newbiggin-by-the-sea Nthumb
279 L6 Newbigging Angus
280 D7 Newbigging Angus
280 E7 Newbigging Angus
235 J3 Newbigging Border
258 E5 Newbigging C Edin
245 G4 Newbigging S Lans
329 L5 Newbiggings Ork
226 F6 Newbiggin Hall Estate N u Ty
203 G6 Newbiggin-on-Lune Cumb
115 K4 New Bilton Warwks
167 G6 Newbold Derbys
131 J3 Newbold Leics
132 F5 Newbold Leics
175 K5 Newbold Rochdl
131 J6 Newbold Heath Leics
115 K4 Newbold on Avon Warwks
98 B4 Newbold-on-Stour Warwks
98 C2 Newbold Pacey Warwks
129 J6 Newbolds Wolves
131 J6 Newbold Verdon Leics
156 E2 New Bolingbroke Lincs
167 J6 New Bolsover Derbys
134 E5 Newborough C Pete
130 C1 Newborough Staffs
163 L1 New Boston St Hel
80 F5 New Botley Oxon
99 H6 Newbottle Nhants
213 H3 Newbottle Sundld
169 J6 New Boultham Lincs
106 F5 Newbourne Suffk
100 D5 New Bradwell M Keyn
212 F5 New Brancepeth Dur
59 H7 Newbridge BaNES
75 L7 Newbridge Caerph
258 E6 Newbridge C Edin
2 C4 Newbridge Cnwll
3 K2 Newbridge Cnwll
12 C8 Newbridge Cnwll
222 B4 Newbridge D & G
50 B7 Newbridge E Susx
30 D3 Newbridge Hants
20 F4 Newbridge IoW
184 B7 Newbridge Lancs
198 B4 Newbridge N York
80 D6 Newbridge Oxon
126 F1 Newbridge Shrops
129 H7 Newbridge Wolves
148 E5 Newbridge Wrexhm
96 D6 Newbridge Green Worcs
57 L2 Newbridge on Usk Mons
93 H2 Newbridge-on-Wye Powys
185 H7 New Brighton Brad
162 D7 New Brighton Flints
32 E5 New Brighton Hants
162 E2 New Brighton Wirral
148 E3 New Brighton Wrexhm
167 G6 New Brimington Derbys
153 J3 New Brinsley Notts
206 F3 New Brotton R & Cl
225 K6 Newbrough Nthumb
148 F3 New Broughton Wrexhm
122 B1 New Buckenham Norfk
43 G2 New Buildings BaNES
24 D6 Newbuildings Devon
18 F5 New Buildings Dorset
303 J4 Newburgh Abers
268 C4 Newburgh Fife
173 L5 Newburgh Lancs
226 F6 Newburn N u Ty
174 F6 New Bury Bolton
52 B1 Newbury Kent
43 G3 Newbury Somset
62 C7 Newbury W Berk
43 K5 Newbury Wilts
202 D3 Newby Cumb
184 B5 Newby Lancs
185 L5 Newby N York
193 K7 Newby N York
196 C8 Newby N York
198 F3 Newby N York
206 C5 Newby N York
191 H3 Newby Bridge Cumb
193 K7 Newby Cote N York
209 L2 Newby East Cumb
202 D3 Newby Head Cumb
306 E5 New Byth Abers
209 J3 Newby West Cumb
196 C4 Newby Wiske N York
55 L5 Newcastle Brdgnd
76 E3 Newcastle Mons
110 E3 Newcastle Shrops
90 C7 Newcastle Emlyn Carmth
224 B2 Newcastleton or Copshaw Holm Border

City, town and village index: Perranwell Station - Ratfyn 391

3 K3 Perranwell Station Cnwll
3 K3 Perran Wharf Cnwll
4 C4 Perranzabuloe Cnwll
79 G5 Perrott's Brook Gloucs
130 B8 Perry Birm
24 F5 Perry Devon
53 J2 Perry Kent
114 B1 Perry Barr Birm
130 B8 Perry Beeches Birm
130 B8 Perry Common Birm
130 E6 Perry Crofts Staffs
113 J5 Perryfields Worcs
166 B4 Perryfoot Derbys
86 C2 Perry Green Essex
84 E3 Perry Green Herts
41 J6 Perry Green Somset
60 C3 Perry Green Wilts
59 H8 Perrymead BaNES
95 K8 Perrystone Hill Herefs
66 F6 Perry Street Kent
26 E5 Perry Street Somset
52 D2 Perrywood Kent
150 F8 Pershall Staffs
96 F4 Pershore Worcs
281 H1 Pert Angus
118 B6 Pertenhall Beds
267 K3 Perth P & K
75 G7 Perthcelyn Rhondd
149 G7 Perthy Shrops
95 J5 Perton Herefs
129 H7 Perton Staffs
36 E3 Pestalozzi Children's Village E Susx
52 D3 Pested Kent
134 E6 Peterborough C Pete
312 A10 Peterburn Highld
94 E6 Peterchurch Herefs
291 J1 Peterculter C Aber
307 L6 Peterhead Abers
213 K5 Peterlee Dur
257 H8 Petersburn N Lans
32 D2 Petersfield Hants
12 D4 Peter's Finger Devon
83 J3 Peter's Green Herts
23 H4 Peters Marland Devon
57 J4 Peterstone Wentlooge Newpt
56 E5 Peterston-super-Ely V Glam
77 H2 Peterstow Herefs
13 G6 Peter Tavy Devon
326 G4 Petertown Ork
4 B4 Peterville Cnwll
52 F3 Petham Kent
11 K4 Petherwin Gate Cnwll
23 J5 Petrockstowe Devon
100 E4 Petsoe End M Keyn
37 G4 Pett E Susx
106 D2 Pettaugh Suffk
52 F5 Pett Bottom Kent
53 G3 Pett Bottom Kent
51 G5 Petteridge Kent
244 F5 Pettinain S Lans
66 F8 Pettings Kent
106 F3 Pettistree Suffk
37 G4 Pett Level E Susx
25 J2 Petton Devon
127 J1 Petton Shrops
66 B7 Petts Wood Gt Lon
302 E1 Petty Abers
59 J3 Petty France S Glos
303 H4 Pettymuick Abers
142 D7 Pettywell Norfk
33 J2 Petworth W Susx
36 C6 Pevensey E Susx
36 B6 Pevensey Bay E Susx
7 G3 Peverell C Plym
45 G1 Pewsey Wilts
45 G1 Pewsey Wharf Wilts
164 B4 Pewterspear Warrtn
260 D5 Phantassie E Loth
328 F4 Pharays Park Ork
85 J2 Pharisee Green Essex
63 J3 Pheasants Bucks
63 J3 Pheasant's Hill Bucks
130 B7 Pheasey Wsall
96 F2 Phepson Worcs
213 H3 Philadelphia Sundld
22 D2 Philham Devon
246 E8 Philiphaugh Border
2 F3 Phillack Cnwll
4 E7 Philleigh Cnwll
75 J6 Phillip's Town Caerph
85 J3 Philpot End Essex
258 C5 Philpstoun W Loth
77 J1 Phocle Green Herefs
47 H2 Phoenix Green Hants
204 F2 Phoenix Row Dur
27 G1 Pibsbury Somset
72 E5 Pibwrlwyd Carmth
200 C3 Pica Cumb
177 L8 Piccadilly Rothm
130 E7 Piccadilly Warwks
122 F2 Piccadilly Corner Norfk
83 H5 Piccotts End Herts
178 C6 Pickburn Donc
96 D5 Picken End Worcs
197 L5 Pickering N York
212 E2 Pickering Nook Dur
281 G4 Pickerton Angus
30 B5 Picket Hill Hants
45 L4 Picket Piece Hants
30 B5 Picket Post Hants
114 F3 Pickford Covtry
114 F3 Pickford Green Covtry
196 B5 Pickhill N York
77 L1 Picklenash Gloucs
127 J7 Picklescott Shrops
184 F7 Pickles Hill Brad
174 E7 Pickley Green Wigan
164 C5 Pickmere Ches
41 G8 Pickney Somset
128 E2 Pickstock Wrekin
174 F3 Pickup Bank Bl w D
38 C5 Pickwell Devon
132 F4 Pickwell Leics
59 L6 Pickwick Wilts
176 D3 Pickwood Scar Calder
155 K7 Pickworth Lincs
133 K4 Pickworth Rutlnd
163 H6 Picton Ches
161 L4 Picton Flints
205 L6 Picton N York
42 B8 Pict's Hill Somset
35 H6 Piddinghoe E Susx
63 J2 Piddington Bucks
100 D3 Piddington Nhants
81 J3 Piddington Oxon
17 L2 Piddlehinton Dorset
119 G4 Pidley Cambs
28 C5 Pidney Dorset
3 H3 Piece Cnwll
112 C7 Pie Corner Herefs
204 F4 Piercebridge Darlt
84 F7 Piercing Hill Essex
328 F4 Pierowall Ork
78 E1 Piff's Elm Gloucs
226 F2 Pigdon Nthumb
41 H6 Pightley Somset
29 J6 Pig Oak Dorset
85 J5 Pigstye Green Essex
176 C4 Pike End Calder
152 C2 Pikehall Derbys
175 J1 Pike Hill Lancs
176 C4 Pike Law Calder
30 D5 Pikeshill Hants
95 H4 Pikestye Herefs
29 J6 Pilford Dorset
85 H7 Pilgrims Hatch Essex
169 G2 Pilham Lincs
166 D7 Pilhough Derbys
58 D5 Pill N Som
70 E5 Pill Pembks
6 E2 Pillaton Cnwll
129 J4 Pillaton Staffs
98 D4 Pillerton Hersey Warwks
98 C4 Pillerton Priors Warwks
110 F6 Pilleth Powys
177 J7 Pilley Barns
78 F3 Pilley Gloucs
30 E7 Pilley Hants
30 E7 Pilley Bailey Hants
57 K3 Pillgwenlly Newpt
182 D5 Pilling Lancs
182 C5 Pilling Lane Lancs
23 H2 Pillmouth Devon
77 J5 Pillowell Gloucs
96 C8 Pillows Green Gloucs
28 D3 Pillwell Dorset
234 D4 Pilmuir Border
311 N6 Pilmuir Moray
58 E3 Pilning S Glos
259 H5 Pilrig C Edin
166 B8 Pilsbury Derbys
27 G7 Pilsdon Dorset
134 B5 Pilsgate C Pete
153 H1 Pilsley Derbys
166 D6 Pilsley Derbys
153 H1 Pilsley Green Derbys
139 H4 Pilson Green Norfk
35 H2 Piltdown E Susx
259 G5 Pilton C Edin
38 D7 Pilton Devon
117 L3 Pilton Nhants
133 J6 Pilton Rutlnd
42 E5 Pilton Somset
54 B4 Pilton Green Swans
42 E6 Piltown Somset
175 H5 Pimhole Bury
65 J5 Pimlico Gt Lon
83 H5 Pimlico Herts
183 L6 Pimlico Lancs
27 K5 Pimperne Dorset
28 F5 Pimperne Dorset
134 E1 Pinchbeck Lincs
134 E2 Pinchbeck West Lincs
178 F4 Pincheon Green Donc
206 D5 Pinchinthorpe R & Cl
59 K8 Pinckney Green Wilts
174 B4 Pincock Lancs
53 K4 Pineham Kent
100 E5 Pineham M Keyn
60 F3 Pinehurst Swindn
78 C6 Pinfarthings Gloucs
173 J5 Pinfold Lancs
177 H7 Pinfold Hill Barns
100 F7 Pinfoldpond Beds
104 E2 Pinford End Suffk
72 E8 Pinged Carmth
63 G7 Pingewood W Berk
83 L1 Pin Green Herts
14 F3 Pinhoe Devon
114 F3 Pinkett's Booth Covtry
114 B6 Pink Green Worcs
259 K6 Pinkie Braes E Loth
59 L3 Pinkney Wilts
63 K4 Pinkneys Green W & M
25 L3 Pinksmoor Somset
114 E6 Pinley Green Warwks
219 G1 Pinmore S Ayrs
84 E5 Pinnacles Essex
64 F3 Pinner Gt Lon
64 F2 Pinner Green Gt Lon
64 F2 Pinnerwood Park Gt Lon
96 D4 Pin's Green Worcs
149 L4 Pinsley Green Ches
111 K2 Pinstones Shrops
96 F4 Pinvin Worcs
131 G6 Pinwall Leics
218 F2 Pinwherry S Ayrs
153 H3 Pinxton Derbys
95 H5 Pipe and Lyde Herefs
111 K5 Pipe Aston Herefs
150 D5 Pipe Gate Shrops
130 B5 Pipehill Staffs
43 J2 Pipehouse BaNES
311 K7 Piperhill Highld
130 B3 Pipe Ridware Staffs
163 H7 Piper's Ash Ches
96 D7 Piper's End Worcs
111 K7 Piper's Hill Worcs
11 K5 Pipers Pool Cnwll
117 G2 Pipewell Nhants
38 D6 Pippacott Devon
174 C3 Pippin Street Lancs
67 G3 Pipps Hill Essex
51 J7 Pipsden Kent
48 B2 Pirbright Surrey
48 B2 Pirbright Camp Surrey
240 D5 Pirnmill N Ayrs
101 L7 Pirton Herts
96 E4 Pirton Worcs
108 D4 Pisgah Cerdgn
266 D7 Pisgah Stirlg
63 H5 Pishill Oxon
63 H2 Pishill Bank Oxon
167 G2 Pismire Hill Sheff
144 F5 Pistyll Gwynd
76 D5 Pit Mons
278 B1 Pitagowan P & K
307 H2 Pitblae Abers
267 K2 Pitcairngreen P & K
311 J3 Pitcalnie Highld
302 D3 Pitcaple Abers
78 C5 Pitchcombe Gloucs
82 B2 Pitchcott Bucks
104 F2 Pitcher's Green Suffk
127 L6 Pitchford Shrops
82 B6 Pitch Green Bucks
48 C5 Pitch Place Surrey
47 L6 Pitch Place Surrey
43 G7 Pitcombe Somset
258 E3 Pitcorthie Fife
43 G4 Pitcot Somset
55 L7 Pitcot V Glam
260 E5 Pitcox E Loth
279 K7 Pitcur P & K
280 C8 Pitempton C Dund
302 C5 Pitfichie Abers
291 J6 Pitforthie Abers
315 J8 Pitgrudy Highld
280 F4 Pitkennedy Angus
268 E6 Pitlessie Fife
278 D3 Pitlochry P & K
310 H2 Pitmaduthy Highld
303 G3 Pitmedden Abers
26 C3 Pitminster Somset
281 G5 Pitmuies Angus
302 C5 Pitmunie Abers
42 C8 Pitney Somset
280 C7 Pitpointie Angus
280 E5 Pitreuchie Angus
269 G5 Pitscottie Fife
67 H3 Pitsea Essex
175 K7 Pitses Oldham
116 F6 Pitsford Nhants
40 F7 Pitsford Hill Somset
167 G3 Pitsmoor Sheff
82 E3 Pitstone Bucks
82 E4 Pitstone Hill Bucks
46 C8 Pitt Hants
78 B7 Pitt Court Gloucs
304 B3 Pittendreich Moray
314 H6 Pittentrail Highld
269 K7 Pittenweem Fife
268 D8 Pitteuchar Fife
213 H5 Pittington Dur
54 B4 Pitton Swans
45 H7 Pitton Wilts
151 G3 Pitts Hill C Stke
307 H2 Pittulie Abers
78 E2 Pittville Gloucs
10 C6 Pityme Cnwll
213 G4 Pity Me Dur
122 E4 Pixey Green Suffk
96 D4 Pixham Worcs
95 L6 Pixley Herefs
128 D1 Pixley Shrops
51 G3 Pizien Well Kent
198 C7 Place Newton N York
306 C5 Plaidy Abers
6 C4 Plaidy Cnwll
2 E4 Plain-an-Gwarry Cnwll
3 H2 Plain-an-Gwarry Cnwll
71 H3 Plain Dealings Pembks
257 H7 Plains N Lans
41 G6 Plainsfield Somset
153 J3 Plain Spot Notts
10 D6 Plain Street Cnwll
127 L7 Plaish Shrops
65 L4 Plaistow Gt Lon
65 L6 Plaistow Gt Lon
48 D7 Plaistow W Susx
104 D8 Plaistow Green Essex
30 D3 Plaitford Wilts
30 D2 Plaitford Green Hants
174 D7 Plank Lane Wigan
192 E2 Plantation Bridge Cumb
233 G8 Plantationfoot D & G
129 G2 Plardiwick Staffs
127 H2 Plasau Shrops
148 C5 Plâs Berwyn Denbgs
148 F3 Plas Coch Wrexhm
109 L2 Plas Dinam Powys
72 F3 Plas Fawr Carmth
108 C3 Plas Gogerddan Cerdgn
146 B3 Plas Gwynant Gwynd
66 B4 Plashet Gt Lon
72 B7 Plashett Carmth
126 B6 Plasiolyn Powys
124 F6 Plâs Llwyngwern Powys
125 J7 Plas Llysyn Powys
126 D7 Plas Meredydd Powys
148 C6 Plas Nantyr Wrexhm
125 K7 Plasnewydd Powys
159 H5 Plas Penmynydd IoA
42 D1 Plaster's Green BaNES
46 D1 Plastow Green Hants
51 H2 Platt Kent
174 D7 Platt Bridge Wigan
149 K6 Platt Lane Shrops
177 K7 Platts Common Barns
51 L3 Platt's Heath Kent
213 G4 Plawsworth Dur
50 F3 Plaxtol Kent
37 H2 Playden E Susx
106 E4 Playford Suffk
63 H5 Play Hatch Oxon
3 L2 Playing Place Cnwll
96 C7 Playley Green Gloucs
127 J5 Plealey Shrops
25 L3 Pleamore Cross Somset
257 J3 Plean Stirlg
71 J5 Pleasant Valley Pembks
174 D2 Pleasington Bl w D
167 K8 Pleasley Derbys
167 K8 Pleasleyhill Notts
28 C4 Pleck Dorset
28 D3 Pleck Dorset
129 K7 Pleck Wsall
174 E1 Pleckgate Bl w D
28 D6 Pleck or Little Ansty Dorset
85 H1 Pledgdon Green Essex
177 J4 Pledwick Wakefd
16 d2 Pleinheaume Guern
16 f5 Plemont Jersey
163 J6 Plemstall Ches
235 J4 Plenderleith Border
225 G7 Plenmeller Nthumb
85 K4 Pleshey Essex
294 F2 Plockton Highld
323 L6 Plocrapol W Isls
42 D7 Plot Gate Somset
42 D6 Plot Street Somset
131 G8 Plough Hill Warwks
111 H2 Plowden Shrops
127 H6 Ploxgreen Shrops
52 B4 Pluckley Kent
52 B5 Pluckley Thorne Kent
69 J8 Plucks Gutter Kent
208 E6 Plumbland Cumb
167 H4 Plumbley Sheff
52 C2 Plumford Kent
164 D5 Plumley Ches
77 K3 Plump Hill Gloucs
209 L6 Plumpton Cumb
35 G4 Plumpton E Susx
182 C8 Plumpton Lancs
99 J4 Plumpton Nhants
100 B4 Plumpton End Nhants
209 L6 Plumpton Foot Cumb
35 G3 Plumpton Green E Susx
210 B6 Plumpton Head Cumb
66 B5 Plumstead Gt Lon
142 E5 Plumstead Norfk
66 B5 Plumstead Common Gt Lon
142 E5 Plumstead Green Norfk
154 B7 Plumtree Notts
51 K4 Plumtree Green Kent
154 B7 Plumtree Park Notts
154 E7 Plungar Leics
11 K6 Plusha Cnwll
28 C6 Plush Dorset
12 C7 Plushabridge Cnwll
77 H7 Plusterwine Gloucs
90 E5 Plwmp Cerdgn
7 G3 Plymouth C Plym
7 H3 Plympton C Plym
7 H4 Plymstock C Plym
25 J6 Plymtree Devon
176 C6 Pobgreen Oldham
75 K5 Pochin Houses Blae G
164 B1 Pocket Nook Wigan
197 H4 Pockley N York
188 B5 Pocklington E R Yk
137 J7 Pockthorpe Norfk
138 B3 Pockthorpe Norfk
141 G6 Pockthorpe Norfk
142 C7 Pockthorpe Norfk
134 E2 Pode Hole Lincs
27 J2 Podimore Somset
117 J7 Podington Beds
113 H5 Podmoor Worcs
137 K4 Podmore Norfk
150 E6 Podmore Staffs
78 C3 Podsmead Gloucs
80 D4 Poffley End Oxon
177 J6 Pogmoor Barns
87 H3 Point Clear Essex
156 B7 Pointon Lincs
19 J3 Pokesdown Bmouth
320 E2 Pol a' Charra W Isls
219 H5 Polbae D & G
6 D3 Polbathic Cnwll
258 C8 Polbeth W Loth
6 E2 Polborder Cnwll
10 E8 Polbrock Cnwll
232 F6 Poldean D & G
118 B2 Polebrook Nhants
96 D4 Pole Elm Worcs
35 L6 Polegate E Susx
176 D4 Pole Moor Kirk
315 J8 Poles Highld
25 K2 Poleshill Somset
43 K3 Pole's Hole Wilts
130 F6 Polesworth Warwks
3 H3 Polgear Cnwll
2 B6 Polgigga Cnwll
312 G5 Polglass Highld
5 G4 Polgooth Cnwll
33 K6 Poling W Susx
33 K5 Poling Corner W Susx
5 J4 Polkerris Cnwll
316 H6 Polla Highld
3 G4 Polladras Cnwll
103 K6 Pollards Cross Essex
143 J5 Pollard Street Norfk
51 L3 Pollhill Kent
162 E4 Poll Hill Wirral
179 E4 Pollington E R Yk
283 H8 Polloch Highld
243 G1 Pollok C Glas
243 H1 Pollokshaws C Glas
256 D8 Pollokshields C Glas
292 B7 Pollosgan Highld
243 H1 Polmadie C Glas
297 J2 Polmally Highld
3 J3 Polmarth Cnwll
5 G5 Polmassick Cnwll
5 J4 Polmear Cnwll
257 L5 Polmont Falk
10 D7 Polmorla Cnwll
230 C4 Polnessan E Ayrs
283 G5 Polnish Highld
117 L4 Polopit Nhants
3 J5 Polpenwith Cnwll
2 E3 Polpeor Cnwll
6 B4 Polperro Cnwll
5 K4 Polruan Cnwll
42 D5 Polsham Somset
231 H6 Polskeoch D & G
14 E3 Polsloe Devon
105 G5 Polstead Suffk
105 G6 Polstead Heath Suffk
253 J1 Poltalloch Ag & B
3 J7 Poltesco Cnwll
14 F2 Poltimore Devon
259 H7 Polton Mdloth
247 L3 Polwarth Border
3 J5 Polwheveral Cnwll
11 K5 Polyphant Cnwll
10 C6 Polzeath Cnwll
245 L2 Pomathorn Mdloth
166 B7 Pomeroy Derbys
7 H4 Pomphlett C Plym
148 E4 Ponciau Wrexhm
40 F8 Pond Close Somset
93 K6 Ponde Powys
118 E1 Pondersbridge Cambs
84 D7 Ponders End Gt Lon
82 F6 Pond Park Bucks
103 G6 Pond Street Essex
21 K3 Pondwell IoW
2 C3 Poniou Cnwll
3 J5 Ponjeravah Cnwll
3 J3 Ponsanooth Cnwll
25 H5 Ponsford Devon
200 C6 Ponsonby Cumb
3 K7 Ponsongath Cnwll
13 L7 Ponsworthy Devon
5 K4 Pont Cnwll
16 j8 Pontac Jersey
73 J6 Pontamman Carmth
72 E6 Pontantwn Carmth
73 K8 Pontardawe Swans
73 H8 Pontarddulais Swans
73 G4 Pont-ar-gothi Carmth
74 D1 Pont ar Hydfer Powys
73 L4 Pont-ar-llechau Carmth
72 E3 Pontarsais Carmth
148 E1 Pontblyddyn Flints
73 K4 Pontbren Araeth Carmth
57 G5 Pontcanna Cardif
91 H5 Pont Creuddyn Cerdgn
125 H7 Pont Crugnant Powys
146 D2 Pont Cyfyng Conwy
148 E5 Pont Cysyllte Denbgs
125 L8 Pontdolgoch Powys
178 B3 Pontefract Wakefd
226 F5 Ponteland Nthumb
108 E3 Ponterwyd Cerdgn
127 J5 Pontesbury Shrops
127 H5 Pontesbury Hill Shrops
127 J5 Pontesford Shrops
148 D6 Pontfadog Wrexhm
89 G6 Pontfaen Pembks
93 G7 Pont-faen Powys
148 E6 Pont-Faen Shrops
90 D5 Pontgarreg Cerdgn
127 G3 Ponthen Shrops
72 F7 Pont Henri Carmth
57 K2 Ponthir Torfn
90 C6 Ponthirwaun Cerdgn
158 C4 Pont Hwfa IoA
88 E5 Pontiago Pembks
95 L6 Pontithel Powys
75 K7 Pontllanfraith Caerph
54 F1 Pontlliw Swans
125 L3 Pont Llogel Powys
145 H3 Pontllyfni Gwynd
75 J5 Pontlottyn Caerph
74 E5 Pontneddfechan Powys
72 E7 Pont-newydd Carmth
162 C7 Pont-newydd Flints
76 B7 Pontnewydd Torfn
76 B6 Pontnewynydd Torfn
146 B1 Pont Pen-y-benglog Conwy
108 E6 Pontrhydfendigaid Cerdgn
109 G3 Pont Rhydgaled Powys
93 G6 Pont Rhyd-y-berry Powys
55 L4 Pont Rhyd-y-cyff Brdgnd
55 J3 Pontrhydyfen Neath
108 E5 Pont-rhyd-y-groes Cerdgn
76 B7 Pontrhydyrun Torfn
159 J8 Pont-Rhythallt Gwynd
94 F8 Pontrilas Herefs
126 B4 Pontrobert Powys
159 J8 Pont-rug Gwynd
36 C3 Ponts Green E Susx
77 J2 Pontshill Herefs
90 F6 Pont-Siân Cerdgn
56 E2 Pont Siôn Norton Rhondd
75 G4 Pontsticill Myr Td
74 D5 Pont-Walby Neath
72 F7 Pontyates Carmth
73 G6 Pontyberew Carmth
148 F6 Pont-y-blew Shrops
148 E2 Pontybodkin Flints
56 D4 Pontyclun Rhondd
55 L3 Pontycymer Brdgnd
89 J5 Pontyglasier Pembks
56 D2 Pontygwaith Rhondd
57 H2 Pontymister Caerph
76 B6 Pontymoel Torfn
146 D3 Pont-y-pant Conwy
76 B6 Pontypool Torfn
56 D3 Pontypridd Rhondd
88 E7 Pont-yr-hafod Pembks
56 B3 Pont-y-rhyl Brdgnd
161 K8 Pont-Ystrad Denbgs
93 K6 Pont-y-wal Powys
57 H2 Pontywaun Caerph
30 F4 Pooksgreen Hants
3 H2 Pool Cnwll
2 c2 Pool IoS
185 K6 Pool Leeds
96 C5 Poolbrook Worcs
312 D10 Pool Crofts Highld
178 B2 Poole N York
19 G4 Poole Poole
25 L2 Poole Somset
151 J2 Poolend Staffs
28 C3 Poolestown Dorset
312 C10 Poolewe Highld
202 B3 Pooley Bridge Cumb
122 B3 Pooley Street Norfk
151 G2 Poolfold Staffs
95 H3 Pool Head Herefs
149 J7 Poolhead Shrops
173 J4 Pool Hey Lancs
96 B8 Poolhill Gloucs
77 H2 Poolmill Herefs
267 H7 Pool of Muckhart Clacks
126 F4 Pool Quay Powys
167 H6 Poolsbrook Derbys
174 C7 Poolstock Wigan
40 C6 Pooltown Somset
50 C4 Pootings Kent
70 E4 Pope Hill Pembks
77 K4 Pope's Hill Gloucs
63 K7 Popeswood Br For
39 H7 Popham Devon
46 E5 Popham Hants
65 L4 Poplar Gt Lon
171 H1 Poplar Grove Lincs
84 B2 Poplars Herts
46 F3 Popley Hants
153 L5 Porchester Notts
20 F3 Porchfield IoW
138 F6 Poringland Norfk
3 H4 Porkellis Cnwll
39 L4 Porlock Somset
39 L4 Porlockford Somset
39 L4 Porlock Weir Somset
239 J2 Portachoillan Ag & B
294 E2 Port-an-eorna Highld
253 L3 Port Ann Ag & B
274 D5 Port Appin Ag & B
333 F9 Port Arthur Shet
44 C7 Portash Wilts
251 G9 Port Askaig Ag & B
253 L7 Portavadie Ag & B
254 D7 Port Bannatyne Ag & B
259 H2 Port Brae Fife
8 E3 Port Bridge Devon
58 D6 Portbury N Som
223 G7 Port Carlisle Cumb
251 D11 Port Charlotte Ag & B
31 K5 Portchester Hants
297 H6 Portclair Highld
206 B3 Port Clarence S on T
254 B6 Port Driseach Ag & B
256 D7 Port Dundas C Glas
10 D6 Porteath Cnwll
258 E5 Port Edgar C Edin
251 F13 Port Ellen Ag & B
302 E5 Port Elphinstone Abers
218 C5 Portencalzie D & G
241 K4 Portencross N Ayrs
256 B7 Porterfield Rens
172 b9 Port Erin IoM
303 L1 Port Erroll Abers
83 K3 Porter's End Herts
17 H4 Portesham Dorset
305 G2 Portessie Moray
172 h4 Port e Vullen IoM
54 C4 Port-Eynon Swans
27 G1 Portfield Somset
33 G6 Portfield W Susx
70 E3 Portfield Gate Pembks
12 E4 Portgate Devon
10 E5 Port Gaverne Cnwll
255 J5 Port Glasgow Inver
304 F3 Portgordon Moray
315 N4 Portgower Highld
4 D2 Porth Cnwll
56 D2 Porth Rhondd
3 K6 Porthallow Cnwll
6 B4 Porthallow Cnwll
55 J6 Porthcawl Brdgnd
144 C7 Port Colmon Gwynd
10 A7 Porthcothan Cnwll
2 B6 Porthcurno Cnwll
88 C6 Portheiddy Pembks
308 B3 Port Henderson Highld
88 C6 Porthgain Pembks
2 B6 Porthgwarra Cnwll
63 G3 Port Hill Oxon
127 K4 Porthill Shrops
10 C6 Porthilly Cnwll
3 L6 Porth Kea Cnwll
56 E7 Porthkerry V Glam
3 G5 Porthleven Cnwll
159 G2 Porthllechog IoA
2 c2 Porthloo IoS
145 K6 Porthmadog Gwynd
2 C3 Porthmeor Cnwll
3 J5 Porth Navas Cnwll
3 L6 Porthoustock Cnwll
4 A5 Porthtowan Cnwll
158 C4 Porth-y-felin IoA
73 G5 Porthyrhyd Carmth
92 B6 Porthyrhyd Carmth
126 E2 Porth-y-waen Shrops
163 J2 Portico St Hel
252 D6 Portincaple Ag & B
16 f5 Portinfer Jersey
12 E6 Portington Devon
179 H1 Portington E R Yk
263 H5 Portinnisherrich Ag & B
201 G3 Portinscale Cumb
10 D5 Port Isaac Cnwll
58 B5 Portishead N Som
255 H4 Portkil Ag & B
305 H2 Portknockie Moray
42 C6 Portland Somset
291 L2 Portlethen Abers
291 L2 Portlethen Village Abers
217 J3 Portling D & G
70 F5 Port Lion Pembks
4 F7 Portloe Cnwll
214 C5 Port Logan D & G
6 B4 Portlooe Cnwll
315 L10 Portmahomack Highld
54 F2 Port Mead Swans
5 H6 Portmellon Cnwll
325 Q7 Port Mholair W Isls
282 A6 Port Mòr Highld
20 D2 Portmore Hants
207 H4 Port Mulgrave N York
274 D5 Portnacroish Ag & B
325 P7 Portnaguran W Isls
251 B12 Portnahaven Ag & B
293 F9 Portnalong Highld
282 E4 Portnaluchaig Highld
317 J4 Portnancon Highld
325 P7 Port nan Giuran W Isls
322 E9 Port nan Long W Isls
325 P2 Port Nis W Isls
259 J6 Portobello C Edin
213 G2 Portobello Gatesd
129 J7 Portobello Wolves
265 K7 Port of Menteith Stirlg
45 G6 Porton Wilts
319 L11 Portormin Highld
214 A3 Portpatrick D & G
10 D5 Port Quin Cnwll
206 B4 Portrack S on T
274 C5 Port Ramsay Ag & B
3 H1 Portreath Cnwll
292 H8 Portree Highld
241 K2 Portrye N Ayrs
172 c9 Port St Mary IoM
4 E7 Portscatho Cnwll
32 B6 Portsea C Port
325 P2 Port Sgiogarstaigh W Isls
318 E3 Portskerra Highld
58 C3 Portskewett Mons
34 E5 Portslade Br & H
34 D6 Portslade-by-Sea Br & H
34 D5 Portslade Village Br & H
214 A2 Portslogan D & G
32 C7 Portsmouth C Port
175 J2 Portsmouth Calder
172 e8 Port Soderick IoM
31 L5 Port Solent C Port
263 K3 Portsonachan Ag & B
305 K2 Portsoy Abers
162 F4 Port Sunlight Wirral
135 K2 Port Sutton Bridge Lincs
31 G4 Portswood C Sotn
55 H4 Port Talbot Neath
304 F3 Porttannachy Moray
55 G3 Port Tennant Swans
272 B1 Portuairk Highld
317 M4 Portvasgo Highld
18 C4 Portway Dorset
95 G4 Portway Herefs
95 G6 Portway Herefs
113 K2 Portway Sandw
27 G1 Portway Somset
42 C6 Portway Somset
96 C7 Portway Worcs
114 B5 Portway Warwks
251 B12 Port Wemyss Ag & B
215 H5 Port William D & G
165 H2 Portwood Stockp
6 E4 Portwrinkle Cnwll
216 E5 Portyerrock D & G
128 C6 Posenhall Shrops
104 C4 Poslingford Suffk
256 D7 Possil Park C Glas
245 K7 Posso Border
13 J6 Postbridge Devon
81 L7 Postcombe Oxon
18 E3 Post Green Dorset
52 F6 Postling Kent
79 G1 Postlip Gloucs
138 F5 Postwick Norfk
290 D2 Potarch Abers
105 K6 Potash Suffk
47 H3 Potbridge Hants
48 B5 Pot Common Surrey
51 L8 Potman's Heath Kent
101 G7 Potsgrove Beds
83 G5 Potten End Herts
69 J7 Potten Street Kent
198 E6 Potter Brompton N York
122 D1 Pottergate Street Norfk
169 L7 Potterhanworth Lincs
169 L7 Potterhanworth Booths Lincs
139 J3 Potter Heigham Norfk
177 J8 Potter Hill Sheff
132 E2 Potter Hill Leics
44 C2 Potterne Wilts
44 C2 Potterne Wick Wilts
83 L6 Potters Bar Herts
182 E4 Potters Brook Lancs
52 C5 Potters Corner Kent
83 J5 Potters Crouch Herts
51 L4 Potter's Forstal Kent
115 H3 Potter's Green Covtry
35 K2 Potter's Green E Susx
83 L3 Pottersheath Herts
58 D7 Potters Hill N Som
131 K7 Potters Marston Leics
152 B6 Potter Somersal Derbys
100 C5 Potterspury Nhants
84 F5 Potter Street Essex
303 H5 Potterton Abers
186 D7 Potterton Leeds
177 J1 Pottery Field Leeds
137 J2 Potthorpe Norfk
38 D7 Pottington Devon
206 B7 Potto N York
102 B4 Potton Beds
136 E2 Pott Row Norfk
165 H5 Pott Shrigley Ches
83 G5 Pouchen End Herts
22 C5 Poughill Cnwll
24 F5 Poughill Devon
30 B5 Poulner Hants
44 C2 Poulshot Wilts
149 G2 Poulton Ches
79 J6 Poulton Gloucs
162 E2 Poulton Wirral
162 F4 Poulton Wirral
182 B7 Poulton-le-Fylde Lancs
27 G3 Pound Somset
96 C4 Pound Bank Worcs
112 E5 Pound Bank Worcs
17 K3 Poundbury Dorset
54 E3 Poundffald Swans
50 D7 Poundfield E Susx
35 L2 Poundford E Susx
35 K2 Pound Green E Susx
46 E2 Pound Green Hants
20 D4 Pound Green IoW
104 B3 Pound Green Suffk
63 G7 Poundgreen Wokham
112 F4 Pound Green Worcs
49 J6 Pound Hill W Susx
218 F2 Poundland S Ayrs
81 J1 Poundon Bucks
50 D5 Poundsbridge Kent
13 L7 Poundsgate Devon
22 B7 Poundstock Cnwll
46 C1 Pound Street Hants
35 K2 Pounsley E Susx
215 L4 Pouton D & G
66 C7 Poverest Gt Lon
49 J5 Povey Cross Surrey
236 F3 Powburn Nthumb
14 F5 Powderham Devon
50 E4 Powder Mills Kent
86 B3 Powers Hall End Essex
17 G2 Powerstock Dorset
222 E6 Powfoot D & G
95 L5 Pow Green Herefs
208 F2 Powhill Cumb
96 D3 Powick Worcs
22 F3 Powler's Piece Devon
267 J8 Powmill P & K
164 F4 Pownall Park Ches
47 H5 Powntley Copse Hants
17 L5 Poxwell Dorset
64 D5 Poyle Slough
34 E4 Poynings W Susx
27 L3 Poyntington Dorset
165 H4 Poynton Ches
128 B3 Poynton Wrekin
128 B3 Poynton Green Wrekin
70 F3 Poyston Pembks
70 F3 Poyston Cross Pembks
105 G2 Poystreet Green Suffk
2 F5 Praa Sands Cnwll
292 G7 Prabost Highld
51 H2 Prating Street Kent
50 C1 Pratt's Bottom Gt Lon
3 G3 Praze-an-Beeble Cnwll
149 L7 Prees Shrops
182 C5 Preesall Lancs
182 C5 Preesall Park Lancs
149 L7 Prees Green Shrops
148 E6 Preesgweene Shrops
149 L6 Prees Heath Shrops
148 F7 Preeshenlle Shrops
149 L6 Prees Higher Heath Shrops
149 L7 Prees Lower Heath Shrops
149 L7 Prees Wood Shrops
162 E8 Prenbrigog Flints
70 B2 Prendergast Pembks
70 F3 Prendergast Pembks
248 E2 Prenderguest Border
236 E4 Prendwick Nthumb
90 F7 Pren-gwyn Cerdgn
145 L5 Prenteg Gwynd
162 F3 Prenton Wirral
163 J2 Prescot St Hel
25 K4 Prescott Devon
97 G8 Prescott Gloucs
112 D3 Prescott Shrops
127 J2 Prescott Shrops
84 D4 Presdales Herts
305 G3 Preshome Moray
279 J1 Presnerb Angus
167 G7 Press Derbys
248 C6 Pressen Nthumb
161 K4 Prestatyn Denbgs
165 G5 Prestbury Ches
78 F2 Prestbury Gloucs
111 G7 Presteigne Powys
128 B7 Presthope Shrops
42 F5 Prestleigh Somset
175 G6 Prestolee Bolton
248 B2 Preston Border
34 F5 Preston Br & H
14 D7 Preston Torbay
17 K5 Preston Dorset
259 K6 Preston E Loth
260 D5 Preston E Loth
180 F1 Preston E R Yk
79 G6 Preston Gloucs
95 L7 Preston Gloucs
65 G3 Preston Gt Lon
83 K2 Preston Herts
52 D1 Preston Kent
53 J1 Preston Kent
174 C2 Preston Lancs
237 H1 Preston Nthumb
227 J6 Preston N Tyne
133 H6 Preston Rutlnd
8 E2 Preston Torbay
60 D5 Preston Wilts
61 J6 Preston Wilts
114 D6 Preston Bagot Warwks
99 L8 Preston Bissett Bucks
25 L1 Preston Bowyer Somset
127 L2 Preston Brockhurst Shrops
163 L4 Preston Brook Halton
46 F5 Preston Candover Hants
99 J3 Preston Capes Nhants
62 F2 Preston Crowmarsh Oxon
100 C2 Preston Deanery Nhants
259 H6 Prestonfield C Edin
114 D6 Preston Fields Warwks
227 J5 Preston Grange N Tyne
114 D6 Preston Green Warwks
127 K3 Preston Gubbals Shrops
205 J3 Preston-le-Skerne Dur
95 J4 Preston Marsh Herefs
217 L2 Prestonmill D & G
127 J4 Preston Montford Shrops
97 L4 Preston on Stour Warwks
205 L4 Preston-on-Tees S on T
163 L4 Preston on the Hill Halton
94 E5 Preston on Wye Herefs
259 K6 Prestonpans E Loth
27 J3 Preston Plucknett Somset
104 F3 Preston St Mary Suffk
195 G3 Preston-under-Scar N York
128 D3 Preston upon the Weald Moors Wrekin
95 J4 Preston Wynne Herefs
175 H7 Prestwich Bury
226 F5 Prestwick Nthumb
229 L1 Prestwick S Ayrs
132 B2 Prestwold Leics
82 D6 Prestwood Bucks
113 H2 Prestwood Staffs
152 B5 Prestwood Staffs
48 C2 Prey Heath Surrey
56 B2 Price Town Brdgnd
120 B3 Prickwillow Cambs
42 D3 Priddy Somset
23 G5 Priestacott Devon
166 B6 Priestcliffe Derbys
166 B6 Priestcliffe Ditch Derbys
58 F8 Priest Down BaNES
129 J7 Priestfield Wolves
96 D5 Priestfield Worcs
234 D6 Priesthaugh Border
243 G1 Priesthill C Glas
192 F7 Priest Hutton Lancs
243 H6 Priestland E Ayrs
176 E2 Priestley Green Calder
247 G8 Priestlon Border
222 E6 Priestside D & G
126 F7 Priest Weston Shrops
63 L7 Priestwood Br For
66 F8 Priestwood Kent
66 F8 Priestwood Green Kent
131 L8 Primethorpe Leics
227 J7 Primrose S Tyne
139 G4 Primrose Corner Norfk
138 B3 Primrose Green Norfk
59 H7 Primrose Hill BaNES
113 J2 Primrose Hill Dudley
65 J4 Primrose Hill Gt Lon
173 J5 Primrose Hill Lancs
199 H6 Primrose Valley N York
113 H7 Primsland Worcs
150 D5 Prince Hill Ches
279 K6 Princeland P & K
176 E4 Prince Royd Kirk
129 K8 Princes End Sandw
71 J4 Princes Gate Pembks
32 E1 Prince's Marsh Hants
163 G3 Princes Park Lpool
82 C6 Princes Risborough Bucks
115 J5 Princethorpe Warwks
75 J5 Princetown Caerph
13 H7 Princetown Devon
32 E5 Prinsted W Susx
50 D1 Printstile Kent
147 L1 Prion Denbgs
269 J5 Prior Muir Fife
248 F3 Prior Park Nthumb
224 B6 Prior Rigg Cumb
95 J6 Prior's Frome Herefs
111 K4 Priors Halton Shrops
99 G2 Priors Hardwick Warwks
128 E4 Priorslee Wrekin
99 G2 Priors Marston Warwks
78 D2 Prior's Norton Gloucs
96 E7 Priors Park Gloucs
26 C1 Priorswood Somset
70 D5 Priory Pembks
104 F5 Priory Green Suffk
106 D5 Priory Heath Suffk
94 C4 Priory Wood Herefs
56 D5 Prisk V Glam
23 J1 Pristacott Devon
43 G1 Priston BaNES
122 C2 Pristow Green Norfk
67 L3 Prittlewell Sthend
31 K7 Privett Hants
32 C1 Privett Hants
38 D6 Prixford Devon
4 E5 Probus Cnwll
315 J8 Proncy Highld
208 D5 Prospect Cumb
129 L4 Prospect Village Staffs
3 G4 Prospidnick Cnwll
256 E7 Provanmill C Glas
4 F2 Providence Cnwll
24 E5 Prowse Devon
226 D7 Prudhoe Nthumb
2 F5 Prussia Cove Cnwll
58 F8 Publow BaNES
84 D2 Puckeridge Herts
26 F3 Puckington Somset
59 G5 Pucklechurch S Glos
30 F2 Pucknall Hants
96 E6 Puckrup Gloucs
78 C5 Puckshole Gloucs
8 C2 Puddaven Devon
164 D7 Puddinglake Ches
182 F7 Pudding Pie Nook Lancs
162 F6 Puddington Ches
24 E4 Puddington Devon
5 J3 Puddle Cnwll
26 E4 Puddlebridge Somset
50 C3 Puddledock Kent
50 E3 Puddledock Kent
122 B1 Puddledock Norfk
17 L3 Puddletown Dorset
26 E4 Pudleigh Somset
95 J2 Pudleston Herefs
175 K2 Pudsey Calder
185 K8 Pudsey Leeds
33 K3 Pulborough W Susx
176 D2 Pule Hill Calder
128 E2 Puleston Wrekin
149 G2 Pulford Ches
28 B5 Pulham Dorset
122 D2 Pulham Market Norfk
122 E2 Pulham St Mary Norfk
58 F2 Pullens Green S Glos
127 K5 Pulley Shrops
51 K7 Pullington Kent
101 J7 Pulloxhill Beds
262 E2 Pulpit Hill Ag & B
127 J6 Pulverbatch Shrops
258 D7 Pumpherston W Loth
91 L7 Pumsaint Carmth
89 G7 Puncheston Pembks
17 G4 Puncknowle Dorset
36 B2 Punnett's Town E Susx
32 C5 Purbrook Hants
19 K5 Purewell Dorset
66 E5 Purfleet Thurr
41 K5 Puriton Somset
86 C6 Purleigh Essex
49 K1 Purley Gt Lon
62 F5 Purley on Thames W Berk
297 L1 Purlie Lodge Highld
110 F4 Purlogue Shrops
59 L7 Purlpit Wilts
119 K2 Purls Bridge Cambs
41 K2 Purn N Som
28 B3 Purse Caundle Dorset
111 H3 Purslow Shrops
177 L4 Purston Jaglin Wakefd
26 F5 Purtington Somset
77 K6 Purton Gloucs
62 C5 Purton W Berk
60 E3 Purton Wilts
60 E3 Purton Common Wilts
60 E2 Purton Stoke Wilts
102 B8 Purwell Herts
100 B4 Pury End Nhants
80 D7 Pusey Oxon
95 K6 Putley Herefs
95 K6 Putley Common Herefs
95 L6 Putley Green Herefs
78 B5 Putloe Gloucs
65 H6 Putney Gt Lon
101 J3 Putnoe Beds
38 B5 Putsborough Devon
95 H5 Putson Herefs
82 D4 Puttenham Herts
48 B4 Puttenham Surrey
104 C5 Puttock End Essex
85 H2 Puttock's End Essex
17 J5 Putton Dorset
28 D4 Puxey Dorset
100 C5 Puxley Nhants
58 B8 Puxton N Som
54 C1 Pwll Carmth
126 D6 Pwll Powys
162 C6 Pwll-clai Flints
70 E6 Pwllcrochan Pembks
148 B3 Pwll-glâs Denbgs
93 H7 Pwllgloyw Powys
145 G7 Pwllheli Gwynd
57 H5 Pwll-Mawr Cardif
162 C6 Pwll-melyn Flints
58 D2 Pwllmeyric Mons
72 B5 Pwll-trap Carmth
55 J3 Pwll-y-glaw Neath
57 G3 Pwllypant Caerph
153 H3 Pye Bridge Derbys
34 E4 Pyecombe W Susx
25 G7 Pye Corner Devon
51 L4 Pye Corner Kent
57 J3 Pye Corner Newpt
58 F5 Pye Corner S Glos
129 K4 Pye Green Staffs
153 H3 Pye Hill Notts
181 G5 Pyewipe NE Lin
55 K5 Pyle Brdgnd
21 G6 Pyle IoW
54 E4 Pyle Swans
31 H3 Pylehill Hants
48 C2 Pyle Hill Surrey
40 F7 Pyleigh Somset
42 F6 Pylle Somset
119 K2 Pymoor Cambs
16 F3 Pymore Dorset
114 C1 Pype Hayes Birm
48 D2 Pyrford Surrey
48 D2 Pyrford Green Surrey
48 D2 Pyrford Village Surrey
26 C1 Pyrland Somset
81 K7 Pyrton Oxon
117 H5 Pytchley Nhants
22 E6 Pyworthy Devon

Q

110 E3 Quabbs Shrops
50 B7 Quabrook E Susx
156 D7 Quadring Lincs
156 D7 Quadring Eaudike Lincs
33 G2 Quags Corner W Susx
81 L3 Quainton Bucks
75 H7 Quaker's Yard Myr Td
212 E3 Quaking Houses Dur
200 B4 Quality Corner Cumb
78 D6 Quarhouse Gloucs
45 J5 Quarley Hants
176 E4 Quarmby Kirk
152 F5 Quarndon Derbys
152 F5 Quarndon Common Derbys
242 E1 Quarrelton Rens
82 C3 Quarrendon Bucks
21 J3 Quarr Hill IoW
255 K7 Quarriers Village Inver
155 K5 Quarrington Lincs
213 H6 Quarrington Hill Dur
163 K7 Quarrybank Ches
113 J2 Quarry Bank Dudley
314 H10 Quarryhill Highld
130 E6 Quarry Hill Staffs
267 L2 Quarrymill P & K
304 B3 Quarrywood Moray
243 L3 Quarter S Lans
267 G3 Quarterbank P & K
112 E1 Quatford Shrops
328 E10 Quatquoy Ork
112 F2 Quatt Shrops
212 E5 Quebec Dur
32 E2 Quebec W Susx
78 C4 Quedgeley Gloucs
328 C8 Queena Ork
120 B3 Queen Adelaide Cambs
67 L6 Queenborough Kent
27 K2 Queen Camel Somset
58 F7 Queen Charlton BaNES
24 E3 Queen Dart Devon
96 D6 Queenhill Worcs
43 J7 Queen Oak Wilts
21 J5 Queen's Bower IoW
176 D1 Queensbury Brad
65 G3 Queensbury Gt Lon
32 F1 Queen's Corner W Susx
162 E7 Queensferry Flints
258 E5 Queensferry W Loth
127 G1 Queen's Head Shrops
256 F7 Queenslie C Glas
101 H4 Queen's Park Beds
174 E2 Queen's Park Bl w D
163 H7 Queen's Park Ches
85 K7 Queen's Park Essex
116 F7 Queen's Park Nhants
182 B7 Queenstown Bpool
51 G4 Queen Street Kent
268 D7 Queensway Fife
256 F5 Queenzieburn N Duns
60 D7 Quemerford Wilts
333 F14 Quendale Shet
103 H7 Quendon Essex
132 C4 Queniborough Leics
79 J6 Quenington Gloucs
182 F2 Quernmore Lancs
130 B8 Queslett Birm
6 D2 Quethiock Cnwll
331 F12 Quhamm Shet
328 B11 Quholm Ork
175 L7 Quick Edge Tamesd
62 E5 Quick's Green W Berk
121 L2 Quidenham Norfk
46 D3 Quidhampton Hants
44 F7 Quidhampton Wilts
306 F8 Quilquox Abers
149 K7 Quina Brook Shrops
99 K3 Quinbury End Nhants
327 K6 Quindry Ork
113 K3 Quinton Dudley
100 C3 Quinton Nhants
4 E2 Quintrell Downs Cnwll
152 B5 Quixhill Staffs
12 E2 Quoditch Devon
266 E3 Quoig P & K
149 K4 Quoisley Ches
4 F2 Quoit Cnwll
132 B3 Quorn (Quorndon) Leics
244 F6 Quothquan S Lans
328 B9 Quoyloo Ork
326 G4 Quoyness Ork
332 F7 Quoyness Shet
330 K3 Quoys Shet
332 H4 Quoys Shet
332 G6 Quoys of Catfirth Shet

R

51 J4 Rabbit's Cross Kent
62 F2 Rabbits Hill Oxon
83 L3 Rableyheath Herts
208 E3 Raby Cumb
162 F5 Raby Wirral
106 D5 Racecourse Suffk
45 J5 Racedown Hants
245 J7 Rachan Mill Border
159 L7 Rachub Gwynd
80 E6 Rack End Oxon
24 E3 Rackenford Devon
33 L4 Rackham W Susx
138 F4 Rackheath Norfk
41 L3 Rackley Somset
222 C5 Racks D & G
326 F5 Rackwick Ork
328 F4 Rackwick Ork
152 E6 Radbourne Derbys
175 G6 Radcliffe Bury
237 K6 Radcliffe Nthumb
154 B5 Radcliffe on Trent Notts
99 L7 Radclive Bucks
80 B7 Radcot Oxon
310 G6 Raddery Highld
25 J1 Raddington Somset
25 G6 Raddon Devon
269 H6 Radernie Fife
68 F8 Radfall Kent
68 B8 Radfield Kent
43 G2 Radford BaNES
153 L5 Radford C Nott
115 G3 Radford Covtry
80 E2 Radford Oxon
97 H2 Radford Worcs
80 D2 Radfordbridge Oxon
115 G7 Radford Semele Warwks
17 K5 Radipole Dorset
41 H6 Radlet Somset
83 J7 Radlett Herts
81 G7 Radley Oxon
85 J5 Radley Green Essex
81 G7 Radley Park Oxon
127 J5 Radlith Shrops
167 K8 Radmanthwaite Notts
128 C2 Radmoor Shrops
149 L2 Radmore Green Ches
130 B1 Radmore Wood Staffs
82 B7 Radnage Bucks
3 J2 Radnor Cnwll
256 B6 Radnor Park W Duns
43 G2 Radstock BaNES
99 J5 Radstone Nhants
98 E4 Radway Warwks
150 E2 Radway Green Ches
101 G2 Radwell Beds
102 B6 Radwell Herts
103 K6 Radwinter Essex
103 K6 Radwinter End Essex
56 F4 Radyr Cardif
232 F8 Raehills D & G
262 E3 Raera Ag & B
47 L2 Rafborough Hants
143 H7 RAF Coltishall Norfk
311 P6 Rafford Moray
330 G7 Raga Shet
132 D2 Ragdale Leics
111 K1 Ragdon Shrops
176 D1 Raggalds Brad
45 K4 Ragged Appleshaw Hants
319 P8 Raggra Highld
2 D5 Raginnis Cnwll
76 E5 Raglan Mons
122 B1 Ragmere Norfk
61 K6 Ragnal W Berk
168 F6 Ragnall Notts
255 G3 Rahane Ag & B
166 E3 Rails Sheff
332 H6 Railsbrough Shet
96 D2 Rainbow Hill Worcs
173 L7 Rainford St Hel
173 L7 Rainford Junction St Hel
66 D4 Rainham Medway
67 K7 Rainham Medway
163 J2 Rainhill St Hel
163 J2 Rainhill Stoops St Hel
165 J5 Rainow Ches
165 H5 Rainowlow Ches
175 H4 Rain Shore Rochdl
175 H7 Rainsough Bury
196 C6 Rainton N York
213 H4 Rainton Bridge Sundld
213 H4 Rainton Gate Dur
153 L2 Rainworth Notts
202 E6 Raisbeck Cumb
210 F4 Raise Cumb
268 C2 Rait P & K
170 E4 Raithby Lincs
171 G7 Raithby by Spilsby Lincs
47 J8 Rake W SUSX
32 E1 Rake Common Hants
130 B3 Rake End Staffs
175 H3 Rake Head Lancs
151 L5 Rakes Dale Staffs
151 K5 Rakeway Staffs
175 K5 Rakewood Rochdl
38 E7 Raleigh Devon
54 D3 Ralit Swans
91 J6 Ram Carmth
331 E10 Ramah Shet
61 H8 Ram Alley Wilts
292 B8 Ramasaig Highld
3 J4 Rame Cnwll
6 F5 Rame Cnwll
59 G4 Ram Hill S Glos
52 C4 Ram Lane Kent
330 K5 Ramnageo Shet
27 K6 Rampisham Dorset
190 E7 Rampside Cumb
119 J6 Rampton Cambs
168 E5 Rampton Notts
175 G4 Ramsbottom Bury
305 K5 Ramsburn Moray
61 J6 Ramsbury Wilts
319 K11 Ramscraigs Highld
32 D2 Ramsdean Hants
46 E2 Ramsdell Hants
66 C7 Ramsden Gt Lon
80 C3 Ramsden Oxon
96 F4 Ramsden Worcs
67 H2 Ramsden Bellhouse Essex
85 L7 Ramsden Heath Essex
175 K3 Ramsden Wood Calder
118 F2 Ramsey Cambs
106 E7 Ramsey Essex
172 h4 Ramsey IoM
233 K4 Ramseycleuch Border
119 G2 Ramsey Forty Foot Cambs
118 F3 Ramsey Heights Cambs
86 E5 Ramsey Island Essex
118 F2 Ramsey Mereside Cambs
118 F2 Ramsey St Mary's Cambs
69 L8 Ramsgate Kent
195 H7 Ramsgill N York
204 E2 Ramshaw Dur
211 L4 Ramshaw Dur
107 G5 Ramsholt Suffk
151 L4 Ramshorn Staffs
13 J3 Ramsley Devon
50 E6 Ramslye Kent
48 C7 Ramsnest Common Surrey
325 L9 Ranais W Isls
170 D5 Ranby Lincs
168 C4 Ranby Notts
169 L5 Rand Lincs
78 C5 Randwick Gloucs
255 K8 Ranfurly Rens
130 D2 Rangemore Staffs
59 G3 Rangeworthy S Glos
230 D4 Rankinston E Ayrs
86 B3 Rank's Green Essex
166 F3 Ranmoor Sheff
48 F3 Ranmore Common Surrey
283 J5 Ranochan Highld
168 B3 Ranskill Notts
129 H2 Ranton Staffs
129 G2 Ranton Green Staffs
139 H4 Ranworth Norfk
325 M8 Raon na Cruadha W Isls
48 F7 Rapkyns W Susx
257 H2 Raploch Stirlg
328 H5 Rapness Ork
26 E3 Rapps Somset
188 B7 Rascal Moor E R Yk
217 G4 Rascarrel D & G
254 E4 Rashfield Ag & B
256 B6 Rashielee Rens
113 J6 Rashwood Worcs
196 E7 Raskelf N York
75 K4 Rassau Blae G
176 E3 Rastrick Calder
295 H5 Ratagan Highld
131 L5 Ratby Leics
131 G7 Ratcliffe Culey Leics
153 J8 Ratcliffe on Soar Notts
132 C4 Ratcliffe on the Wreake Leics
60 C6 Ratford Wilts
70 D4 Ratford Bridge Pembks
45 G5 Ratfyn Wilts

3 K6 St Keverne Cnwll
10 E6 St Kew Cnwll
10 E6 St Kew Highway Cnwll
6 B2 St Keyne Cnwll
5 H1 St Lawrence Cnwll
86 F6 St Lawrence Essex
21 H6 St Lawrence IoW
16 h6 St Lawrence Jersey
69 L7 St Lawrence Kent
82 E5 St Leonards Bucks
29 L6 St Leonards Dorset
36 E5 St Leonards E Susx
243 J3 Saint Leonards S Lans
51 G2 St Leonard's Street Kent
2 B6 St Levan Cnwll
152 F6 St Luke's C Derb
56 F6 St Lythans V Glam
10 E7 St Mabyn Cnwll
268 B3 St Madoes P & K
94 E7 St Margarets Herefs
53 L5 St Margaret's at Cliffe Kent
327 K6 St Margaret's Hope Ork
123 G3 St Margaret South Elmham Suffk
78 E2 St Mark's Gloucs
172 d8 St Marks IoM
3 J6 St Martin Cnwll
6 C3 St Martin Cnwll
16 d3 St Martin Guern
16 j6 St Martin Jersey
267 L1 St Martins P & K
148 F6 St Martin's Shrops
148 F6 St Martin's Moor Shrops
16 g6 St Mary Jersey
46 B3 St Mary Bourne Hants
8 F1 St Marychurch Torbay
66 C7 St Mary Cray Gt Lon
56 C5 St Mary Hill V Glam
67 K5 St Mary Hoo Medway
52 E8 St Mary in the Marsh Kent
2 d2 St Mary's IoS
327 L4 St Mary's Ork
52 E8 St Mary's Bay Kent
76 F3 St Maughans Mons
76 F3 St Maughans Green Mons
3 L4 St Mawes Cnwll
4 E1 St Mawgan Cnwll
6 E1 St Mellion Cnwll
57 H4 St Mellons Cardif
10 B7 St Merryn Cnwll
5 G4 St Mewan Cnwll
5 G6 St Michael Caerhays Cnwll
4 E6 St Michael Penkevil Cnwll
269 G3 St Michaels Fife
51 L6 St Michaels Kent
8 E3 St Michaels Torbay
112 B6 St Michaels Worcs
163 G3 St Michael's Hamlet Lpool
182 E6 St Michael's on Wyre Lancs
123 G3 St Michael South Elmham Suffk
10 D6 St Minver Cnwll
269 J7 St Monans Fife
11 H8 St Neot Cnwll
101 L2 St Neots Cambs
4 D3 St Newlyn East Cnwll
83 L1 St Nicholas Herts
88 D5 St Nicholas Pembks
56 E6 St Nicholas V Glam
69 J7 St Nicholas at Wade Kent
134 E3 St Nicholas House Lincs
123 G3 St Nicholas South Elmham Suffk
131 H8 St Nicolas Park Warwks
257 J2 St Ninians Stirlg
139 K7 St Olaves Norfk
87 J3 St Osyth Essex
87 J3 St Osyth Heath Essex
16 g6 St Ouen Jersey
77 G2 St Owen's Cross Herefs
78 C3 St Paul's Gloucs
66 C7 St Paul's Cray Gt Lon
83 K2 St Paul's Walden Herts
16 g6 St Peter Jersey
16 d2 St Peter Port Guern
78 E2 St Peter's Gloucs
69 L7 St Peter's Kent
227 H7 St Peter's N u Ty
123 G3 St Peter South Elmham Suffk
96 E3 St Peter The Great Worcs
70 F7 St Petrox Pembks
16 b3 St Pierre du Bois Guern
6 B2 St Pinnock Cnwll
230 B2 St Quivox S Ayrs
3 J8 St Ruan Cnwll
16 d2 St Sampson Guern
16 c3 St Saviour Guern
16 i7 St Saviour Jersey
50 D5 Saint's Hill Kent
4 F4 St Stephen Cnwll
12 C4 St Stephens Cnwll
83 J5 St Stephens Herts
10 F5 St Teath Cnwll
14 E3 St Thomas Devon
55 G3 St Thomas Swans
10 F6 St Tudy Cnwll
70 E7 St Twynnells Pembks
5 K3 St Veep Cnwll
281 H6 St Vigeans Angus
66 E2 St Vincent's Hamlet Essex
5 G2 St Wenn Cnwll
76 F2 St Weonards Herefs
5 K3 St Winnow Cnwll
56 E5 St y-Nyll V Glam
162 B5 Saith ffynnon Flints
8 B7 Salcombe Devon
15 J4 Salcombe Regis Devon
86 E4 Salcott-cum-Virley Essex
100 D8 Salden Bucks
164 F2 Sale Manch
171 J5 Saleby Lincs
96 F2 Sale Green Worcs
36 D2 Salehurst E Susx
73 J3 Salem Carmth
108 D3 Salem Cerdgn
3 J2 Salem Cnwll
272 E6 Salen Ag & B
273 G2 Salen Highld
176 E4 Salendine Nook Kirk
234 D2 Salenside Border
174 E1 Salesbury Lancs
96 F2 Saleway Worcs
100 F6 Salford Beds
98 C8 Salford Oxon
175 H8 Salford Salfd
100 F6 Salford Ford Beds
97 J3 Salford Priors Warwks
49 J4 Salfords Surrey
138 F4 Salhouse Norfk
258 C2 Saline Fife
45 G7 Salisbury Wilts
210 B6 Salkeld Dykes Cumb
295 H2 Sallachy Highld
314 D5 Sallachy Highld
142 E7 Salle Norfk
50 D5 Salmans Kent
170 F6 Salmonby Lincs
281 G7 Salmond's Muir Angus
24 E7 Salmonhutch Devon
79 H2 Salperton Gloucs
79 H3 Salperton Park Gloucs
101 J3 Salph End Beds
244 C1 Salsburgh N Lans
208 C4 Salta Cumb
151 J8 Salt Staffs
6 E3 Saltash Cnwll
310 G4 Saltburn Highld
206 F3 Saltburn-by-the-sea R & Cl
133 H1 Saltby Leics
208 E3 Salt Coates Cumb
190 B1 Saltcoats Cumb
260 B4 Saltcoats E Loth
241 L5 Saltcoats N Ayrs
173 J2 Saltcotes Lancs
35 G6 Saltdean E Susx
180 F2 Salt End E R Yk
200 B2 Salterbeck Cumb
184 C5 Salterforth Lancs
46 F2 Salters Heath Hants
150 B8 Saltershill Shrops
136 B6 Salters Lode Norfk
114 C5 Salter Street Solhll
164 B7 Salterswall Ches
44 F6 Salterton Wilts
171 J2 Saltfleet Lincs
171 J2 Saltfleetby All Saints Lincs
171 H2 Saltfleetby St Clement Lincs
171 H3 Saltfleetby St Peter Lincs
59 G7 Saltford BaNES
64 C4 Salt Hill Slough
190 E7 Salthouse Cumb
142 D3 Salthouse Norfk
114 B2 Saltley Birm
57 K4 Saltmarsh Newpt
179 H3 Saltmarshe E R Yk
326 G6 Saltness Ork
163 G8 Saltney Flints
197 K6 Salton N York
23 H2 Saltrens Devon
227 G7 Saltwell Gatesd
226 F3 Saltwick Nthumb
53 G6 Saltwood Kent
270 D5 Salum Ag & B
34 B5 Salvington W Susx
113 H7 Salwarpe Worcs
16 E2 Salwayash Dorset
113 L7 Sambourne Warwks
43 L5 Sambourne Wilts
128 E2 Sambrook Wrekin
321 N2 Samhla W Isls
174 C1 Samlesbury Lancs
174 D2 Samlesbury Bottoms Lancs
25 L3 Sampford Arundel Somset
40 E5 Sampford Brett Somset
23 L6 Sampford Chapple Devon
23 L6 Sampford Courtenay Devon
25 L3 Sampford Moor Somset
25 J4 Sampford Peverell Devon
13 G7 Sampford Spiney Devon
329 L8 Samsonslane Ork
68 C3 Samuel's Corner Essex
260 B6 Samuelston E Loth
308 D9 Sanachan Highld
250 C8 Sanaigmore Ag & B
2 C5 Sancreed Cnwll
188 D7 Sancton E R Yk
312 E8 Sand Highld
332 E7 Sand Shet
42 B4 Sand Somset
270 A6 Sandaig Ag & B
283 G1 Sandaig Highld
208 F5 Sandale Cumb
177 J4 Sandal Magna Wakefd
282 B5 Sandavore Highld
150 D1 Sandbach Ches
150 E1 Sandbach Heath Ches
254 F4 Sandbank Ag & B
19 G4 Sandbanks Poole
87 G5 Sandbeach Essex
130 C3 Sandborough Staffs
180 E7 Sandbraes Lincs
305 J2 Sandend Abers
49 K1 Sanderstead Gt Lon
55 H3 Sandfields Neath
130 C5 Sandfields Staffs
203 G4 Sandford Cumb
24 E6 Sandford Devon
18 E4 Sandford Dorset
30 B6 Sandford Hants
21 H5 Sandford IoW
42 B2 Sandford N Som
127 G2 Sandford Shrops
149 L7 Sandford Shrops
243 L5 Sandford S Lans
96 E4 Sandford Worcs
42 B2 Sandford Batch N Som
307 L7 Sandfordhill Abers
81 G6 Sandford-on-Thames Oxon
27 L2 Sandford Orcas Dorset
80 E1 Sandford St Martin Oxon
191 H5 Sand Gate Cumb
53 H7 Sandgate Kent
216 C3 Sandgreen D & G
307 H2 Sandhaven Abers
214 D3 Sandhead D & G
177 L6 Sandhill Barns
81 L1 Sandhill Bucks
120 B2 Sandhill Cambs
27 K6 Sandhills Dorset
28 B4 Sandhills Dorset
186 C7 Sandhills Leeds
162 F2 Sandhills Lpool
81 H5 Sandhills Oxon
48 B6 Sandhills Surrey
226 B6 Sandhoe Nthumb
263 J8 Sandhole Ag & B
187 L7 Sand Hole E R Yk
179 J1 Sandholme E R Yk
156 F6 Sandholme Lincs
47 L1 Sandhurst Br For
78 C2 Sandhurst Gloucs
51 J8 Sandhurst Kent
51 J8 Sandhurst Cross Kent
187 K3 Sand Hutton N York
196 C5 Sandhutton N York
153 J6 Sandiacre Derbys
171 K4 Sandilands Lincs
244 D6 Sandilands S Lans
164 B6 Sandiway Ches
29 L4 Sandleheath Hants
51 J2 Sandling Kent
164 E7 Sandlow Green Ches
332 B5 Sandness Shet
85 L6 Sandon Essex
102 D7 Sandon Herts
151 H8 Sandon Staffs
151 H8 Sandonbank Staffs
21 K5 Sandown IoW
50 F5 Sandown Park Kent
27 G6 Sandpit Dorset
96 D8 Sandpits Gloucs
83 K4 Sandridge Herts
140 D6 Sandringham Norfk
63 K2 Sands Bucks
65 J5 Sands End Gt Lon
207 K5 Sandsend N York
190 E4 Sand Side Cumb
190 F5 Sandside Cumb
192 E5 Sandside Cumb
216 E4 Sand Side D & G
182 D4 Sand Side Lancs
332 F7 Sandsound Shet
179 G6 Sandtoft N Linc
330 E7 Sandvoe Shet
51 L3 Sandway Kent
113 L2 Sandwell Sandw
53 K2 Sandwich Kent
53 L2 Sandwich Bay Estate Kent
201 L4 Sandwick Cumb
327 K7 Sandwick Ork
332 J4 Sandwick Shet
333 G12 Sandwick Shet
325 M8 Sandwick W Isls
200 B5 Sandwith Cumb
200 B5 Sandwith Newtown Cumb
101 L4 Sandy Beds
54 C1 Sandy Carmth
156 E2 Sandy Bank Lincs
328 H7 Sandybank Ork
213 J5 Sandy Carrs Dur
162 F7 Sandycroft Flints
35 L3 Sandy Cross E Susx
47 L4 Sandy Cross Surrey
30 E7 Sandy Down Hants
151 G3 Sandyford C Stke
233 H8 Sandyford D & G
14 D7 Sandygate Devon
14 F3 Sandy Gate Devon
172 f3 Sandygate IoM
166 F3 Sandygate Sheff
70 C5 Sandy Haven Pembks
217 J2 Sandyhills D & G
5 K2 Sandylake Cnwll
182 D2 Sandylands Lancs
25 L2 Sandylands Somset
185 H7 Sandy Lane Brad
54 D4 Sandylane Swans
60 C7 Sandy Lane Wilts
149 H5 Sandy Lane Wrexhm
22 F7 Sandymoor Cross Devon
223 K6 Sandysike Cumb
21 G5 Sandy Way IoW
130 C5 Sandyway Staffs
317 J3 Sangobeg Highld
316 H3 Sangomore Highld
61 K7 Sanham Green W Berk
163 L3 Sankey Bridges Warrtn
112 F6 Sankyns Green Worcs
282 A8 Sanna Highld
321 P6 Sanndabhaig W Isls
325 M8 Sanndabhaig W Isls
241 G4 Sannox N Ayrs
231 K5 Sanquhar D & G
127 L2 Sansaw Heath Shrops
200 D7 Santon Cumb
172 e8 Santon IoM
179 L5 Santon N Linc
200 E7 Santon Bridge Cumb
121 G2 Santon Downham Suffk
131 K8 Sapcote Leics
96 B2 Sapey Bridge Herefs
112 E7 Sapey Common Herefs
121 J4 Sapiston Suffk
118 E5 Sapley Cambs
152 C7 Sapperton Derbys
78 E6 Sapperton Gloucs
155 K7 Sapperton Lincs
156 F8 Saracen's Head Lincs
319 P8 Sarclet Highld
73 H7 Sardis Carmth
71 J5 Sardis Pembks
31 J5 Sarisbury Hants
56 B4 Sarn Brdgnd
161 L5 Sarn Flints
110 E1 Sarn Powys
72 C5 Sarnau Carmth
90 D5 Sarnau Cerdgn
147 J6 Sarnau Gwynd
93 H7 Sarnau Powys
126 E3 Sarnau Powys
144 e2 Sarn Bach Gwynd
94 E3 Sarnesfield Herefs
144 D7 Sarn Meyllteyrn Gwynd
73 H6 Saron Carmth
90 E8 Saron Carmth
147 K1 Saron Denbgs
145 J2 Saron Gwynd
159 J7 Saron Gwynd
83 G7 Sarratt Herts
83 G7 Sarratt Bottom Herts
69 J7 Sarre Kent
80 B2 Sarsden Oxon
80 B2 Sarsden Halt Oxon
316 H4 Sarsgrum Highld
127 J4 Sascott Shrops
212 D5 Satley Dur
53 J6 Satmar Kent
293 G10 Satran Highld
194 D2 Satron N York
24 B2 Satterleigh Devon
191 G2 Satterthwaite Cumb
63 G4 Satwell Oxon
302 C6 Sauchen Abers
279 J8 Saucher P & K
257 L2 Sauchie Clacks
290 F8 Sauchieburn Abers
229 L4 Sauchrie S Ayrs
163 G6 Saughall Ches
162 D3 Saughall Massie Wirral
258 F6 Saughton C Edin
234 F7 Saughtree Border
77 L5 Saul Gloucs
168 E3 Saundby Notts
71 J6 Saundersfoot Pembks
82 B6 Saunderton Bucks
82 B7 Saunderton Lee Bucks
38 B6 Saunton Devon
171 G7 Sausthorpe Lincs
314 E5 Saval Highld
272 F5 Savary Highld
3 K2 Saveock Cnwll
151 J6 Saverley Green Staffs
176 D3 Savile Park Calder
177 G3 Savile Town Kirk
115 L6 Sawbridge Warwks
84 F3 Sawbridgeworth Herts
198 D5 Sawdon N York
153 J7 Sawley Derbys
183 L5 Sawley Lancs
195 K8 Sawley N York
184 F8 Sawood Brad
103 G4 Sawston Cambs
118 D3 Sawtry Cambs
26 B2 Sawyer's Hill Somset
60 D2 Sawyers Hill Wilts
133 G3 Saxby Leics
169 K3 Saxby Lincs
33 J6 Saxby W Susx
180 B4 Saxby All Saints N Linc
132 E2 Saxelbye Leics
122 B7 Saxham Street Suffk
169 H5 Saxilby Lincs
142 C4 Saxlingham Norfk
138 E7 Saxlingham Green Norfk
138 E7 Saxlingham Nethergate Norfk
123 H7 Saxmundham Suffk
154 C6 Saxondale Notts
103 L2 Saxon Street Cambs
122 F6 Saxtead Suffk
122 F7 Saxtead Green Suffk
122 F6 Saxtead Little Green Suffk
142 E5 Saxthorpe Norfk
186 E7 Saxton N York
34 E3 Sayers Common W Susx
197 H7 Scackleton N York
323 L6 Scadabhagh W Isls
168 C2 Scaftworth Notts
198 B7 Scagglethorpe N York
175 G2 Scaitcliffe Lancs
250 F4 Scalasaig Ag & B
179 J2 Scalby E R Yk
198 E4 Scalby N York
198 F3 Scalby Mills N York
101 J2 Scald End Beds
116 F5 Scaldwell Nhants
223 L7 Scaleby Cumb
223 L7 Scaleby Hill Cumb
182 E2 Scale Hall Lancs
210 C4 Scale Houses Cumb
190 F6 Scales Cumb
201 J2 Scales Cumb
210 C5 Scales Cumb
132 F2 Scalford Leics
207 G5 Scaling R & Cl
207 G5 Scaling Dam N York
273 G7 Scallastle Ag & B
333 F9 Scalloway Shet
170 E5 Scamblesby Lincs
187 L6 Scamland E R Yk
283 J7 Scamodale Highld
198 C6 Scampston N York
169 J5 Scampton Lincs
327 K3 Scapa Ork
176 D4 Scapegoat Hill Kirk
329 L4 Scar Ork
199 G4 Scarborough N York
4 F4 Scarcewater Cnwll
167 J7 Scarcliffe Derbys
186 C6 Scarcroft Leeds
309 M7 Scardroy Highld
331 B9 Scarff Shet
319 N2 Scarfskerry Highld
204 C5 Scargill Dur
190 F2 Scar Head Cumb
270 C6 Scarinish Ag & B
173 J5 Scarisbrick Lancs
208 F7 Scarness Cumb
137 J4 Scarning Norfk
154 D5 Scarrington Notts
173 K6 Scarth Hill Lancs
186 E7 Scarthingwell N York
181 H6 Scartho NE Lin
332 D8 Scarvister Shet
328 B9 Scarwell Ork
333 F14 Scatness Shet
331 E11 Scatsta Shet
180 B6 Scawby N Linc
178 C7 Scawsby Donc
178 D6 Scawthorpe Donc
197 G5 Scawton N York
35 G2 Scayne's Hill W Susx
75 J1 Scethrog Powys
150 F2 Scholar Green Ches
176 E1 Scholemoor Brad
184 F7 Scholes Kirk
176 F2 Scholes Kirk
176 F6 Scholes Kirk
186 C7 Scholes Leeds
167 G1 Scholes Rothm
205 G3 School Aycliffe Dur
164 B8 School Green Ches
104 B7 School Green Essex
20 D4 School Green IoW
63 H7 Schoolgreen Wokham
291 L2 Schoolhill Abers
302 E8 Schoolhill Abers
26 F6 School House Dorset
200 B4 Scilly Bank Cumb
177 H5 Scissett Kirk
88 E6 Scleddau Pembks
7 K5 Scobbiscombe Devon
168 B4 Scofton Notts
122 D4 Scole Norfk
122 C3 Scole Common Norfk
322 B9 Scolpaig W Isls
267 L2 Scone P & K
293 J10 Sconser Highld
268 F7 Scoonie Fife
267 L3 Scoonieburn P & K
271 L11 Scoor Ag & B
155 L2 Scopwick Lincs
312 G7 Scoraig Highld
188 F5 Scorborough E R Yk
3 J2 Scorrier Cnwll
13 K8 Scorriton Devon
182 F5 Scorton Lancs
205 H7 Scorton N York
138 F2 Sco Ruston Norfk
321 P3 Scotbheinn W Isls
209 K3 Scotby Cumb
204 F6 Scotch Corner N York
152 F4 Scotches Derbys
182 E3 Scotforth Lancs
176 E5 Scotgate Kirk
150 F4 Scot Hay Staffs
169 K5 Scothern Lincs
131 H2 Scotland Leics
132 D7 Scotland Leics
155 K8 Scotland Lincs
62 E7 Scotland W Berk
98 D7 Scotland End Oxon
227 H3 Scotland Gate Nthumb
129 J6 Scotlands Wolves
105 G6 Scotland Street Suffk
268 B7 Scotlandwell P & K
174 D6 Scot Lane End Bolton
174 D6 Scot Lane End Wigan
310 G2 Scotsburn Highld
269 G2 Scotscraig Fife
226 C2 Scots' Gap Nthumb
291 G7 Scotston Abers
278 D6 Scotston P & K
256 C7 Scotstoun C Glas
273 K2 Scotstown Highld
227 G7 Scotswood N u Ty
64 B7 Scotswood W & M
283 G1 Scottas Highld
179 K7 Scotter Lincs
179 K7 Scotterthorpe Lincs
179 K8 Scotton Lincs
186 B3 Scotton N York
195 J2 Scotton N York
143 H7 Scottow Norfk
155 L6 Scott Willoughby Lincs
260 E4 Scoughall E Loth
241 J2 Scoulag Ag & B
137 K6 Scoulton Norfk
151 L8 Scounslow Green Staffs
316 D8 Scourie Highld
316 C8 Scourie More Highld
333 F13 Scousburgh Shet
177 G6 Scout Dike Barns
202 D6 Scout Green Cumb
175 L6 Scouthead Oldham
77 H4 Scowles Gloucs
319 K2 Scrabster Highld
235 H3 Scraesburgh Border
170 F7 Scrafield Lincs
51 K1 Scragged Oak Kent
236 D5 Scrainwood Nthumb
157 G5 Scrane End Lincs
68 B6 Scrapsgate Kent
132 D5 Scraptoft Leics
26 D4 Scrapton Somset
139 L3 Scratby Norfk
187 K2 Scrayingham N York
5 H4 Scredda Cnwll
155 L5 Scredington Lincs
25 K1 Screedy Somset
171 H7 Scremby Lincs
249 G4 Scremerston Nthumb
154 D5 Screveton Notts
170 E7 Scrivelsby Lincs
186 B3 Scriven N York
182 D5 Scronkey Lancs
168 B2 Scrooby Notts
152 C7 Scropton Derbys
156 D2 Scrub Hill Lincs
196 B3 Scruton N York
126 D2 Scrwgan Powys
223 L5 Scuggate Cumb
180 D1 Sculcoates C KuH
141 H5 Sculthorpe Norfk
179 L5 Scunthorpe N Linc
54 C4 Scurlage Swans
26 E4 Sea Somset
27 G5 Seaborough Dorset
150 F5 Seabridge Staffs
53 G7 Seabrook Kent
213 J2 Seaburn Sundld
162 F2 Seacombe Wirral
51 H7 Seacox Heath E Susx
186 B7 Seacroft Leeds
157 L1 Seacroft Lincs
156 F6 Seadyke Lincs
257 H6 Seafar N Lans
303 H8 Seafield C Aber
259 G8 Seafield Mdloth
229 L2 Seafield S Ayrs
330 H7 Seafield Shet
258 C7 Seafield W Loth
35 J7 Seaford E Susx
162 F1 Seaforth Sefton
132 C3 Seagrave Leics
60 C4 Seagry Heath Wilts
213 K4 Seaham Dur
249 L7 Seahouses Nthumb
50 E2 Seal Kent
162 F7 Sealand Flints
47 L4 Seale Surrey
198 F5 Seamer N York
206 B5 Seamer N York
190 F7 Sea Mill Cumb
241 K4 Seamill N Ayrs
58 D5 Sea Mills Bristl
10 C7 Sea Mills Cnwll
143 L6 Sea Palling Norfk
180 D6 Searby Lincs
68 E7 Seasalter Kent
200 C7 Seascale Cumb
268 D3 Seaside P & K
171 L7 Seathorne Lincs
190 E1 Seathwaite Cumb
201 G5 Seathwaite Cumb
191 H4 Seatle Cumb
201 G5 Seatoller Cumb
281 J6 Seaton Angus
303 H7 Seaton C Aber
6 D4 Seaton Cnwll
208 B7 Seaton Cumb
15 L3 Seaton Devon
189 J5 Seaton E R Yk
53 H2 Seaton Kent
227 J4 Seaton Dur
133 H7 Seaton Rutlnd
213 J3 Seaton Sundld
227 G5 Seaton Burn N Tyne
206 C2 Seaton Carew Hartpl
227 J4 Seaton Delaval Nthumb
15 L2 Seaton Junction Devon
187 L6 Seaton Ross E R Yk
227 J4 Seaton Sluice Nthumb
16 E3 Seatown Dorset
304 C1 Seatown Moray
305 G2 Seatown Moray
3 J3 Seaureaugh Moor Cnwll
206 D7 Seave Green N York
21 K3 Seaview IoW
208 E3 Seaville Cumb
26 F4 Seavington St Mary Somset
27 G3 Seavington St Michael Somset
87 J4 Seawick Essex
76 B7 Sebastopol Torfn
209 H5 Sebergham Cumb
130 F5 Seckington Warwks
312 E8 Second Coast Highld
26 E7 Sector Devon
193 H3 Sedbergh Cumb
58 D2 Sedbury Gloucs
194 C3 Sedbusk N York
101 L4 Seddington Beds
97 H6 Sedgeberrow Worcs
155 G6 Sedgebrook Lincs
205 K2 Sedgefield Dur
140 E4 Sedgeford Norfk
43 L8 Sedgehill Wilts
114 E4 Sedgemere Solhll
129 J8 Sedgley Dudley
175 H7 Sedgley Park Bury
192 F4 Sedgwick Cumb
36 E3 Sedlescombe E Susx
82 B4 Sedrup Bucks
52 B2 Seed Kent
174 C2 Seed Lee Lancs
175 G8 Seedley Salfd
44 B1 Seend Wilts
44 B1 Seend Cleeve Wilts
44 B1 Seend Head Wilts
64 C2 Seer Green Bucks
139 G7 Seething Norfk
65 G7 Seething Wells Gt Lon
332 E6 Sefster Shet
173 J7 Sefton Sefton
163 G3 Sefton Park Lpool
31 J5 Segensworth Hants
227 H5 Seghill Nthumb
111 K3 Seifton Shrops
129 H2 Seighford Staffs
323 J5 Seilebost W Isls
159 J7 Seion Gwynd
129 G8 Seisdon Staffs
325 P8 Seisiadar W Isls
148 E7 Selattyn Shrops
47 H7 Selborne Hants
178 E1 Selby N York
52 D2 Selgrove Kent
33 H2 Selham W Susx
65 K7 Selhurst Gt Lon
246 F8 Selkirk Border
77 H1 Sellack Herefs
95 J8 Sellack Boat Herefs
330 H6 Sellafirth Shet
2 C4 Sellan Cnwll
329 M5 Sellibister Ork
26 C3 Sellick's Green Somset
52 F6 Sellindge Kent
52 D2 Selling Kent
44 B1 Sells Green Wilts
207 K6 Selly Hill N York
113 L3 Selly Oak Birm
113 L3 Selly Park Birm
35 K5 Selmeston E Susx
49 L1 Selsdon Gt Lon
33 G8 Selsey W Susx
192 F2 Selside Cumb
193 L6 Selside N York
78 C6 Selsley Gloucs
32 D7 Selsmore Hants
53 K2 Selson Kent
53 H5 Selsted Kent
153 J3 Selston Notts
153 J3 Selston Common Notts
153 H3 Selston Green Notts
40 B4 Selworthy Somset
332 E6 Semblister Shet
105 H4 Semer Suffk
28 F1 Sem Hill Wilts
43 L1 Semington Wilts
28 F1 Semley Wilts
156 B7 Sempringham Lincs
48 D2 Send Surrey
48 D3 Send Grove Surrey
48 D2 Send Marsh Surrey
56 F2 Senghenydd Caerph
2 B5 Sennen Cnwll
2 B5 Sennen Cove Cnwll
92 F8 Sennybridge Powys
168 B3 Serlby Notts
44 E6 Serrington Wilts
196 D6 Sessay N York
136 C4 Setchey Norfk
30 E6 Setley Hants
259 L6 Seton E Loth
259 L5 Seton Mains E Loth
331 G9 Setter Shet
332 F6 Setter Shet
332 J8 Setter Shet
328 E10 Settiscarth Ork
184 B2 Settle N York
198 B7 Settrington N York
41 G7 Seven Ash Somset
79 G2 Sevenhampton Gloucs
61 G2 Sevenhampton Swindn
66 C3 Seven Kings Gt Lon
50 D3 Sevenoaks Kent
50 D3 Sevenoaks Common Kent
50 D3 Sevenoaks Weald Kent
74 C5 Seven Sisters Neath
78 F3 Seven Springs Gloucs
86 E1 Seven Star Green Essex
7 L5 Seven Stones Cross Devon
58 D4 Severn Beach S Glos
96 D5 Severn Stoke Worcs
101 J3 Sevick End Beds
52 D5 Sevington Kent
103 J6 Sewards End Essex
84 D7 Sewardstone Essex
84 D7 Sewardstonebury Essex
82 F2 Sewell Beds
199 J8 Sewerby E R Yk
3 J4 Seworgan Cnwll
133 H2 Sewstern Leics
206 B6 Sexhow N York
97 L7 Sezincote Gloucs
320 D5 Sgallairidh W Isls
322 H6 Sgarasta Bheag W Isls
322 H6 Sgarasta Mhor W Isls
316 D6 Sgeir Iosal Highld
325 P2 Sgiogarstaigh W Isls
292 C4 Sgoir Beag Highld
250 F3 Sgreadan Ag & B
81 K5 Shabbington Bucks
78 E3 Shab Hill Gloucs
129 G5 Shackerley Shrops
131 H5 Shackerstone Leics
153 H7 Shacklecross Derbys
48 B4 Shackleford Surrey
176 B2 Shackleton Calder
65 K3 Shacklewell Gt Lon
175 K3 Shade Calder
213 H5 Shadforth Dur
123 J3 Shadingfield Suffk
52 C6 Shadoxhurst Kent
174 F2 Shadsworth Bl w D
78 B7 Shadwell Gloucs
65 L4 Shadwell Gt Lon
186 B7 Shadwell Leeds
121 J3 Shadwell Norfk
151 J3 Shaffalong Staffs
102 F6 Shaftenhoe End Herts
28 F2 Shaftesbury Dorset
177 K5 Shafton Barns
177 K5 Shafton Two Gates Barns
18 C5 Shaggs Dorset
150 C8 Shakeford Shrops
174 E7 Shakerley Wigan
95 L7 Shakesfield Gloucs
61 K8 Shalbourne Wilts
20 E4 Shalcombe IoW
47 G5 Shalden Hants
47 G5 Shalden Green Hants
14 E7 Shaldon Devon
20 F4 Shalfleet IoW
104 B8 Shalford Essex
43 H7 Shalford Somset
48 D4 Shalford Surrey
104 B8 Shalford Green Essex
39 G8 Shallowford Devon
39 H5 Shallowford Devon
151 G8 Shallowford Staffs
52 E3 Shalmsford Street Kent
99 K6 Shalstone Bucks
48 D5 Shamley Green Surrey
255 H3 Shandon Ag & B
311 K3 Shandwick Highld
132 E7 Shangton Leics
227 H4 Shankhouse Nthumb
21 J5 Shanklin IoW
291 K1 Shannaburn Abers
228 D2 Shannochie N Ayrs
265 J8 Shannochill Stirlg
301 K1 Shanquhar Abers
202 D5 Shap Cumb
77 K3 Shapridge Gloucs
29 G6 Shapwick Dorset
42 B6 Shapwick Somset
44 F2 Sharcott Wilts
114 C2 Shard End Birm
153 H7 Shardlow Derbys
129 J5 Shareshill Staffs
177 K4 Sharlston Wakefd
177 K4 Sharlston Common Wakefd
114 C4 Sharmans Cross Solhll
67 J6 Sharnal Street Medway
101 G2 Sharnbrook Beds
175 J3 Sharneyford Lancs
115 K1 Sharnford Leics
28 C5 Sharnhill Green Dorset
182 F8 Sharoe Green Lancs
196 B7 Sharow N York
101 J7 Sharpenhoe Beds
236 D6 Sharperton Nthumb
174 F5 Sharples Bolton
151 J6 Sharpley Heath Staffs
77 K6 Sharpness Gloucs
35 H2 Sharpsbridge E Susx
35 L3 Sharp's Corner E Susx
43 J2 Sharpstone BaNES
139 H2 Sharp Street Norfk
49 L7 Sharpthorne W Susx
11 K7 Sharptor Cnwll
113 J6 Sharpway Gate Worcs
142 C4 Sharrington Norfk
166 F3 Sharrow Sheff
164 F3 Sharston manch
112 F3 Shatterford Worcs
53 J2 Shatterling Kent
166 C4 Shatton Derbys
7 H2 Shaugh Prior Devon
150 D3 Shavington Ches
184 F7 Shaw Brad
175 K6 Shaw Oldham
60 F3 Shaw Swindn
62 C7 Shaw W Berk
59 L7 Shaw Wilts
111 K3 Shawbank Shrops
128 C4 Shawbirch Wrekin
324 H5 Shawbost W Isls
127 L2 Shawbury Shrops
175 J5 Shawclough Rochdl
77 K1 Shaw Common Gloucs
236 F4 Shawdon Hall Nthumb
115 L3 Shawell Leics
175 J5 Shawfield Rochdl
151 L1 Shawfield Staffs
185 L4 Shawfield Head N York
31 H2 Shawford Hants
43 J3 Shawford Somset
175 J3 Shawforth Lancs
102 C7 Shaw Green Herts
174 B4 Shaw Green Lancs
185 L4 Shaw Green N York
221 K4 Shawhead D & G
257 G8 Shawhead N Lans
164 E5 Shaw Heath Ches
165 G3 Shaw Heath Stockp
243 H1 Shawlands C Glas
185 K2 Shaw Mills N York
244 B3 Shawsburn S Lans
175 K6 Shaw Side Oldham
243 K4 Shawton S Lans
243 K4 Shawtonhill S Lans
222 C6 Shearington D & G
116 C1 Shearsby Leics
41 J7 Shearston Somset
23 G5 Shebbear Devon
128 F1 Shebdon Staffs
318 H4 Shebster Highld
243 H2 Sheddens E Rens
215 L6 Sheddock D & G
303 G7 Sheddocksley C Aber
31 J4 Shedfield Hants
152 B1 Sheen Staffs
167 G6 Sheepbridge Derbys
61 K5 Sheepdrove W Berk
328 G4 Sheepheight Ork
212 E2 Sheep Hill Dur
100 F7 Sheeplane Beds
63 L3 Sheepridge Bucks
176 F4 Sheepridge Kirk
78 D4 Sheepscombe Gloucs
13 H8 Sheepstor Devon
23 H5 Sheepwash Devon
227 G2 Sheepwash Nthumb
58 C5 Sheepway N Som
131 G6 Sheepy Magna Leics
131 G6 Sheepy Parva Leics
85 G4 Sheering Essex
68 B5 Sheerness Kent
48 D1 Sheerwater Surrey
32 E2 Sheet Hants
111 L5 Sheet Shrops
48 B2 Sheets Heath Surrey
2 D5 Sheffield Cnwll
166 F3 Sheffield Sheff
62 F6 Sheffield Bottom W Berk
35 H1 Sheffield Green E Susx
167 G3 Sheffield Park Sheff
101 K6 Shefford Beds
61 L6 Shefford Woodlands W Berk
316 D4 Sheigra Highld
244 B2 Sheildmuir N Lans
128 C6 Sheinton Shrops
111 J4 Shelderton Shrops
114 D3 Sheldon Birm
166 C7 Sheldon Derbys
25 L5 Sheldon Devon
52 D2 Sheldwich Kent
52 D2 Sheldwich Lees Kent
56 B4 Shelf Brdgnd
176 E2 Shelf Calder
122 B3 Shelfanger Norfk
114 C7 Shelfield Warwks
129 L6 Shelfield Wsall
114 C7 Shelfield Green Warwks
100 B2 Shelfleys Nhants
154 C5 Shelford Notts
115 J2 Shelford Warwks
97 G2 Shell Worcs
121 L7 Shelland Suffk
131 G3 Shellbrook Leics
85 G5 Shelley Essex
177 G5 Shelley Kirk
105 H6 Shelley Suffk
177 G5 Shelley Woodhouse Kirk
163 K3 Shell Green Halton
61 K2 Shellingford Oxon
85 J5 Shellow Bowells Essex
49 G4 Shellwood Cross Surrey
112 E7 Shelsley Beauchamp Worcs
112 E7 Shelsley Walsh Worcs
131 L3 Shelthorpe Leics
117 L6 Shelton Beds
151 G4 Shelton C Stke
122 E1 Shelton Norfk
154 E5 Shelton Notts
127 K4 Shelton Shrops
122 E1 Shelton Green Norfk
153 G7 Shelton Lock C Derb
150 F6 Shelton under Harley Staffs
127 G7 Shelve Shrops
26 B6 Shelvin Devon
69 H7 Shelvingford Kent
95 H5 Shelwick Herefs
95 H5 Shelwick Green Herefs
66 E2 Shenfield Essex
98 E5 Shenington Oxon
83 K6 Shenley Herts
100 D6 Shenley Brook End M Keyn
83 K6 Shenleybury Herts
100 D6 Shenley Church End M Keyn
113 L3 Shenley Fields Birm
100 D6 Shenley Lodge M Keyn
100 D6 Shenley Wood M Keyn
94 E6 Shenmore Herefs
219 J7 Shennanton D & G
130 C6 Shenstone Staffs
113 H5 Shenstone Worcs
130 C6 Shenstone Woodend Staffs
131 H6 Shenton Leics
297 G3 Shenval Highld
300 D3 Shenval Moray
135 G4 Shepeau Stow Lincs
84 B2 Shephall Herts
65 H4 Shepherd's Bush Gt Lon
136 B3 Shepherd's Gate Norfk
63 H4 Shepherd's Green Oxon
48 B7 Shepherd's Hill Surrey
77 L6 Shepherd's Patch Gloucs
140 D5 Shepherd's Port Norfk
53 J4 Shepherdswell or Sibertswold Kent
176 F6 Shepley Kirk
77 J7 Shepperdine S Glos
64 E7 Shepperton Surrey
102 E4 Shepreth Cambs
131 K3 Shepshed Leics
27 G3 Shepton Beauchamp Somset
42 F5 Shepton Mallet Somset
43 G7 Shepton Montague Somset
51 J3 Shepway Kent
213 K7 Sheraton Dur
13 J7 Sherberton Devon
27 L3 Sherborne Dorset
79 K4 Sherborne Gloucs
42 E2 Sherborne Somset
46 F2 Sherborne St John Hants
114 F7 Sherbourne Warwks
104 F5 Sherbourne Street Suffk
213 H5 Sherburn Dur
198 D6 Sherburn N York
213 H5 Sherburn Grange Dur
213 H5 Sherburn Hill Dur
186 E8 Sherburn in Elmet N York
48 E4 Shere Surrey
141 H6 Shereford Norfk
30 D2 Sherfield English Hants
47 G2 Sherfield on Loddon Hants
175 G2 Sherfin Lancs
8 C6 Sherford Devon
18 E3 Sherford Dorset
26 C2 Sherford Somset
128 F4 Sheriffhales Shrops
227 H7 Sheriff Hill Gatesd
187 J1 Sheriff Hutton N York
97 H4 Sheriff's Lench Worcs
142 F3 Sheringham Norfk
100 E4 Sherington M Keyn
142 F3 Sheringwood Norfk
34 D3 Shermanbury W Susx
113 J7 Shernal Green Worcs
140 E5 Shernborne Norfk
96 C4 Sherrard's Green Worcs
83 L4 Sherrardspark Herts
44 C6 Sherrington Wilts
59 L3 Sherston Wilts
153 L5 Sherwood C Nott
23 K2 Sherwood Green Devon
50 F5 Sherwood Park Kent
256 E8 Shettleston C Glas
174 B6 Shevington Wigan
174 B5 Shevington Moor Wigan
174 B6 Shevington Vale Wigan
6 E3 Sheviock Cnwll
242 C6 Shewalton N Ayrs
176 D2 Shibden Head Brad
21 H4 Shide IoW
295 H5 Shiel Bridge Highld
308 C3 Shieldaig Highld
308 D7 Shieldaig Highld
256 C7 Shieldhall C Glas
222 C3 Shieldhill D & G
257 K5 Shieldhill Falk
245 G5 Shieldhill S Lans
212 F3 Shield Row Dur
282 F7 Shielfoot Highld
280 D3 Shielhill Angus
278 C2 Shierglas P & K
128 F5 Shifnal Shrops
237 H5 Shilbottle Nthumb
237 J5 Shilbottle Grange Nthumb
205 G2 Shildon Dur
242 E2 Shillford E Rens
321 M7 Shilligarry W Isls
25 H2 Shillingford Devon
62 E2 Shillingford Oxon
14 E4 Shillingford Abbot Devon
14 D4 Shillingford St George Devon
28 E4 Shillingstone Dorset
101 K7 Shillington Beds
236 B5 Shillmoor Nthumb
80 B5 Shilton Oxon
115 J3 Shilton Warwks
17 J5 Shilvinghampton Dorset
226 F3 Shilvington Nthumb
122 D3 Shimpling Norfk
104 E3 Shimpling Suffk
104 E3 Shimpling Street Suffk
213 G5 Shincliffe Dur
213 H3 Shiney Row Sundld
63 H7 Shinfield Wokham
102 D4 Shingay Cambs
136 F5 Shingham Norfk
107 H5 Shingle Street Suffk
8 C2 Shinner's Bridge Devon
50 E3 Shipbourne Kent
137 J5 Shipdham Norfk
42 B2 Shipham Somset
8 E1 Shiphay Torbay
63 J5 Shiplake Oxon
63 G4 Shiplake Bottom Oxon
63 H5 Shiplake Row Oxon
41 L2 Shiplate N Som
245 L4 Shiplaw Border
185 J7 Shipley Brad
153 H4 Shipley Derbys
129 G7 Shipley Shrops
34 B2 Shipley W Susx
49 K5 Shipley Bridge Surrey
153 H5 Shipley Common Derbys
246 F4 Shipley Gate Border
123 H1 Shipmeadow Suffk
71 J5 Shipping Pembks
80 F7 Shippon Oxon
98 C5 Shipston-on-Stour Warwks
82 B1 Shipton Bucks
79 G3 Shipton Gloucs
187 G3 Shipton N York
112 B1 Shipton Shrops
45 H4 Shipton Bellinger Hants
16 F3 Shipton Gorge Dorset
32 F7 Shipton Green W Susx
81 L2 Shipton Lee Bucks
59 L3 Shipton Moyne Gloucs
79 G3 Shipton Oliffe Gloucs
80 F3 Shipton-on-Cherwell Oxon
79 G3 Shipton Solers Gloucs
188 C6 Shiptonthorpe E R Yk
80 B3 Shipton under Wychwood Oxon
81 K7 Shirburn Oxon
173 J5 Shirdley Hill Lancs
167 K7 Shirebrook Derbys
166 F2 Shirecliffe Sheff
167 G2 Shiregreen Sheff
58 D5 Shirehampton Bristl
227 J5 Shiremoor N Tyne
58 C2 Shirenewton Mons
129 L6 Shire Oak Wsall
165 L4 Shireoaks Derbys
167 K4 Shireoaks Rothm
258 C3 Shires Mill Notts
52 B6 Shirkoak Kent
153 G2 Shirland Derbys
128 D7 Shirlett Shrops
31 G4 Shirley C Sotn
152 D5 Shirley Derbys
65 L7 Shirley Gt Lon
30 B7 Shirley Hants
114 C4 Shirley Solhll
114 C4 Shirley Heath Solhll
30 D7 Shirley holms Hants
30 F4 Shirley Warren C Sotn
94 F2 Shirl Heath Herefs
31 K4 Shirrell Heath Hants
38 E6 Shirwell Devon
240 E8 Shiskine N Ayrs
18 C3 Shitterton Dorset
111 H7 Shobdon Herefs
30 B5 Shobley Hants
130 E2 Shobnall Staffs
24 F6 Shobrooke Devon
132 D2 Shoby Leics
149 H4 Shocklach Ches
149 H4 Shocklach Green Ches
68 B4 Shoeburyness Sthend
53 L3 Sholden Kent
31 H4 Sholing C Sotn
31 H4 Sholing Common C Sotn
175 K6 Sholver Oldham
30 E2 Shootash Hants
82 F5 Shootersway Herts
127 J4 Shoot Hill Shrops
10 B7 Shop Cnwll
22 C4 Shop Cnwll
22 F4 Shop Devon
106 E7 Shop Corner Suffk
224 D5 Shopford Cumb
41 G7 Shopnoller Somset
48 B8 Shopp Hill W Susx
33 G6 Shopwyke W Susx
175 K2 Shore Calder
175 K4 Shore Rochdl
26 C6 Shore Bottom Devon
65 K4 Shoreditch Gt Lon
26 C2 Shoreditch Somset
203 H7 Shoregill Cumb
50 D1 Shoreham Kent
34 D6 Shoreham Beach W Susx
34 D6 Shoreham-by-Sea W Susx
248 F4 Shoresdean Nthumb
80 D4 Shores Green Oxon
248 E4 Shoreswood Nthumb
310 E5 Shoreton Highld
31 K1 Shorley Hants
53 G6 Shorncliffe Camp Kent
79 G7 Shorncote Gloucs
67 G6 Shorne Kent
67 G6 Shorne Ridgeway Kent
67 G6 Shorne West Kent
13 G4 Shortacombe Devon
6 C3 Shortacross Cnwll
35 H2 Shortbridge E Susx
113 K3 Short Cross Dudley
47 K5 Shortfield Common Surrey
35 J3 Shortgate E Susx
122 B2 Short Green Norfk
80 C3 Shorthampton Oxon
130 B8 Short Heath Birm
131 G4 Short Heath Derbys
47 J6 Shortheath Hants
47 K5 Shortheath Surrey
129 K6 Short Heath Wsall
127 J5 Shorthill Shrops
65 L7 Shortlands Gt Lon
4 D5 Shortlanesend Cnwll
242 E6 Shortlees E Ayrs
26 C6 Shortmoor Devon
27 H6 Shortmoor Dorset
8 E2 Shorton Torbay
256 B7 Shortroods Rens
77 H4 Shortstanding Gloucs
101 J4 Shortstown Beds
43 K4 Short Street Wilts
78 C7 Shortwood Gloucs
59 G5 Shortwood S Glos
21 G5 Shorwell IoW
43 G2 Shoscombe BaNES
43 G2 Shoscombe Vale BaNES
127 H2 Shotatton Shrops
138 F7 Shotesham Norfk
67 J2 Shotgate Essex
133 J7 Shotley Nhants
106 E6 Shotley Suffk
212 C3 Shotley Bridge Dur
212 C3 Shotleyfield Nthumb
106 E7 Shotley Gate Suffk
52 D3 Shottenden Kent
47 L7 Shottermill Surrey
97 L3 Shottery Warwks
98 F4 Shotteswell Warwks
107 G5 Shottisham Suffk
152 F4 Shottle Derbys
152 F4 Shottlegate Derbys
205 K2 Shotton Dur
213 K6 Shotton Dur
162 E7 Shotton Flints
227 G4 Shotton Nthumb
248 C7 Shotton Nthumb
213 K5 Shotton Colliery Dur
244 D1 Shotts N Lans
162 F6 Shotwick Ches
136 D5 Shouldham Norfk
136 D5 Shouldham Thorpe Norfk
96 D2 Shoulton Worcs
50 F7 Shover's Green E Susx
150 E4 Shraleybrook Staffs
127 J3 Shrawardine Shrops
112 F7 Shrawley Worcs
64 D4 Shreding Green Bucks
114 E6 Shrewley Warwks
127 L4 Shrewsbury Shrops
44 E5 Shrewton Wilts
33 H6 Shripney W Susx
61 H3 Shrivenham Oxon
137 K8 Shropham Norfk
86 F2 Shrub End Essex
64 C7 Shrubs Hill Surrey
95 J5 Shucknall Herefs
103 K5 Shudy Camps Cambs
292 H8 Shulishadermor Highld
292 G2 Shulista Highld
78 E3 Shurdington Gloucs
63 K6 Shurlock Row W & M
113 L7 Shurnock Worcs
318 H5 Shurrery Highld
41 H5 Shurton Somset
114 E1 Shustoke Warwks
24 F6 Shute Devon
26 C7 Shute Devon
45 G8 Shute End Wilts
98 E5 Shutford Oxon
129 H2 Shut Heath Staffs
96 E6 Shuthonger Gloucs
100 B4 Shutlanger Nhants
6 C4 Shutta Cnwll
129 H5 Shutt Green Staffs
130 F5 Shuttington Warwks
53 G5 Shuttlesfield Kent
167 J6 Shuttlewood Derbys
175 H4 Shuttleworth Bury
77 J1 Shutton Herefs
55 L4 Shwt Brdgnd
324 H5 Siabost W Isls
325 J5 Siabost bho Dheas W Isls
325 J5 Siabost bho Thuath W Isls
325 L4 Siadar W Isls
325 L4 Siadar Iarach W Isls
325 L4 Siadar Uarach W Isls
222 E2 Sibbaldbie D & G
116 D3 Sibbertoft Nhants
111 J3 Sibdon Carwood Shrops
98 E6 Sibford Ferris Oxon
98 E6 Sibford Gower Oxon
104 C7 Sible Hedingham Essex
103 K8 Sibley's Green Essex
157 G3 Sibsey Lincs
156 F3 Sibsey Fen Side Lincs
134 B7 Sibson Cambs
131 H6 Sibson Leics
154 E4 Sibthorpe Notts
168 D6 Sibthorpe Notts
123 H6 Sibton Suffk
121 H7 Sicklesmere Suffk
186 C5 Sicklinghall N York
15 J4 Sid Devon
41 J8 Sidbrook Somset
15 J3 Sidbury Devon
112 D2 Sidbury Shrops
42 B2 Sidcot N Som
66 C6 Sidcup Gt Lon
176 E3 Siddal Calder
208 B7 Siddick Cumb
164 F6 Siddington Ches
79 G7 Siddington Gloucs
164 F6 Siddington Heath Ches
113 K5 Sidemoor Worcs
174 F5 Side of the Moor Bolton
143 H4 Sidestrand Norfk
151 G5 Sideway C Stke
15 J3 Sidford Devon
33 G7 Sidlesham W Susx
33 G6 Sidlesham Common W Susx
36 D5 Sidley E Susx
49 J4 Sidlow Surrey
15 J4 Sidmouth Devon
150 E6 Sidway Staffs
14 B7 Sigford Devon
189 J5 Sigglesthorne E R Yk
258 F6 Sighthill C Edin
256 D7 Sighthill C Glas
56 C6 Sigingstone V Glam
79 L4 Signet Oxon
27 L2 Sigwells Somset
46 F1 Silchester Hants
325 J11 Sildinis W Isls
132 C3 Sileby Leics
190 C4 Silecroft Cumb
138 C7 Silfield Norfk
38 B8 Silford Devon
91 J5 Silian Cerdgn
31 G2 Silkstead Hants
177 H6 Silkstone Barns
177 H7 Silkstone Common Barns
155 L5 Silk Willoughby Lincs
268 F7 Sillerhole Fife
208 D3 Silloth Cumb
305 J5 Sillyearn Moray
92 B6 Siloh Carmth
198 E3 Silpho N York
184 F5 Silsden Brad
101 J6 Silsoe Beds
43 J8 Silton Dorset
291 G2 Silverbank Abers
245 L1 Silverburn Mdloth
192 E6 Silverdale Lancs
150 F4 Silverdale Staffs
192 E7 Silverdale Green Lancs
113 J2 Silver End Dudley
86 C3 Silver End Essex
306 D3 Silverford Abers
142 F6 Silvergate Norfk
138 F8 Silver Green Norfk
36 D1 Silver Hill E Susx
36 E4 Silverhill E Susx
36 E4 Silverhill Park E Susx
28 B2 Silver Knap Somset
258 F5 Silverknowes C Edin
122 F4 Silverley's Green Suffk
244 E4 Silvermuir S Lans
99 L5 Silverstone Nhants
78 B6 Silver Street Gloucs
51 L1 Silver Street Kent
42 D7 Silver Street Somset
114 B4 Silver Street Worcs
25 H6 Silverton Devon
255 L5 Silverton W Duns
243 L3 Silvertonhill S Lans
66 B5 Silvertown Gt Lon
4 B5 Silverwell Cnwll
112 C4 Silvington Shrops
332 D8 Silwick Shet
177 H7 Sim Hill Barns
175 H6 Simister Bury
165 K2 Simmondley Derbys
163 K3 Simm's Cross Halton
174 B7 Simm's Lane End St Hel
225 K5 Simonburn Nthumb
39 J6 Simonsbath Somset
25 L3 Simonsburrow Devon
227 J7 Simonside S Tyne
183 L8 Simonstone Lancs
194 C3 Simonstone N York
248 D4 Simprim Border
100 E6 Simpson M Keyn
70 D3 Simpson Pembks
70 D3 Simpson Cross Pembks
248 C3 Sinclair's Hill Border
230 D3 Sinclairston E Ayrs
259 H2 Sinclairtown Fife
196 B5 Sinderby N York
211 H3 Sinderhope Nthumb
164 D2 Sinderland Green Traffd
63 J7 Sindlesham Wokham
152 F7 Sinfin C Derb
153 G7 Sinfin Moor C Derb
100 C7 Singleborough Bucks
43 H2 Single Hill Somset
182 C7 Singleton Lancs
33 G4 Singleton W Susx
66 F6 Singlewell Kent
148 F2 Singret Wrexhm
51 K5 Sinkhurst Green Kent
301 J6 Sinnahard Abers
197 K4 Sinnington N York
113 G7 Sinton Worcs
113 G7 Sinton Green Worcs
59 H7 Sion Hill BaNES
64 E5 Sipson Gt Lon

398 City, town and village index: Walton - Whaw

116 B2 **Walton** Leics
163 G2 **Walton** Lpool
100 E6 **Walton** M Keyn
94 B2 **Walton** Powys
111 K4 **Walton** Shrops
42 C6 **Walton** Somset
151 G7 **Walton** Wrekin
151 G8 **Walton** Staffs
106 F6 **Walton** Suffk
177 K4 **Walton** Wakefd
98 C3 **Walton** Warwks
128 B3 **Walton** Wrekin
96 F7 **Walton Cardiff** Gloucs
82 C4 **Walton Court** Bucks
71 G2 **Walton East** Pembks
28 D3 **Walton Elm** Dorset
99 H7 **Walton Grounds** Nhants
31 L5 **Walton Heath** Hants
135 K4 **Walton Highway** Norfk
58 B6 **Walton in Gordano** N Som
174 C2 **Walton-le-Dale** Lancs
81 G5 **Walton Manor** Oxon
64 F7 **Walton-on-Thames** Surrey
129 K2 **Walton-on-the-Hill** Staffs
49 H2 **Walton on the Hill** Surrey
87 M2 **Walton on the Naze** Essex
132 B3 **Walton on the Wolds** Leics
130 E3 **Walton-on-Trent** Derbys
113 J4 **Walton Pool** Worcs
103 J5 **Waltons** Essex
58 B6 **Walton St Mary** N Som
174 C2 **Walton Summit** Lancs
136 E3 **Walton Warren** Norfk
70 D4 **Walton West** Pembks
161 L5 **Walwen** Flints
162 C6 **Walwen** Flints
162 D5 **Walwen** Flints
225 L5 **Walwick** Nthumb
205 G4 **Walworth** Darltn
65 K5 **Walworth** Gt Lon
205 G3 **Walworth Gate** Darltn
70 D4 **Walwyn's Castle** Pembks
26 D5 **Wambrook** Somset
208 F3 **Wampool** Cumb
48 B4 **Wanborough** Surrey
61 H4 **Wanborough** Swindn
232 C1 **Wandel** S Lans
232 D1 **Wandel Dyke** S Lans
65 K7 **Wandle Park** Gt Lon
83 J2 **Wandon End** Herts
65 J6 **Wandsworth** Gt Lon
123 K4 **Wangford** Suffk
132 C4 **Wanlip** Leics
232 B4 **Wanlockhead** D & G
35 L6 **Wannock** E Susx
134 B7 **Wansford** C Pete
189 G3 **Wansford** E R Yk
51 J4 **Wanshurst Green** Kent
22 B6 **Wanson** Cnwll
66 B3 **Wanstead** Gt Lon
43 H5 **Wanstrow** Somset
77 K6 **Wanswell** Gloucs
62 B3 **Wantage** Oxon
96 B2 **Wants Green** Worcs
59 H5 **Wapley** S Glos
115 H6 **Wappenbury** Warwks
99 K4 **Wappenham** Nhants
65 K4 **Wapping** Gt Lon
36 B3 **Warbleton** E Susx
32 D5 **Warblington** Hants
62 E2 **Warborough** Oxon
119 G3 **Warboys** Cambs
182 B7 **Warbreck** Bpool
11 J3 **Warbstow** Cnwll
11 J3 **Warbstow Cross** Cnwll
164 C3 **Warburton** Traffd
164 E4 **Warburton Green** Traffd
203 G4 **Warcop** Cumb
68 D6 **Warden** Kent
225 L6 **Warden** Nthumb
110 F7 **Warden** Powys
114 C2 **Ward End** Birm
78 E2 **Warden Hill** Gloucs
20 D4 **Warden Point** IoW
101 K5 **Warden Street** Beds
177 J7 **Ward Green** Barns
121 L7 **Ward Green** Suffk
183 H7 **Ward Green Cross** Lancs
101 J6 **Wardhedges** Beds
329 K8 **Wardhill** Ork
99 G4 **Wardington** Oxon
233 K3 **Wardlaw** Border
150 B2 **Wardle** Ches
175 K4 **Wardle** Rochdl
150 B2 **Wardle Bank** Ches
227 H7 **Wardley** Gatesd
133 G7 **Wardley** Rutlnd
175 G7 **Wardley** Salfd
47 K8 **Wardley** W Susx
166 C6 **Wardlow** Derbys
29 G1 **Wardour** Wilts
257 H5 **Wardpark** N Lans
82 C6 **Wardrobes** Bucks
165 H4 **Wardsend** Ches
119 K3 **Wardy Hill** Cambs
16 C3 **Ware** Devon
84 D4 **Ware** Herts
53 J1 **Ware** Kent
18 E4 **Wareham** Dorset
52 C7 **Warehorne** Kent
249 J8 **Warenford** Nthumb
249 J7 **Waren Mill** Nthumb
249 H7 **Warenton** Nthumb
84 D3 **Wareside** Herts
102 C3 **Waresley** Cambs
113 G6 **Waresley** Worcs
51 K2 **Ware Street** Kent
63 L6 **Warfield** Br For
8 E4 **Warfleet** Devon
156 D7 **Wargate** Lincs
163 L2 **Wargrave** St Hel
63 J5 **Wargrave** Wokham
95 G6 **Warham** Herefs
141 J3 **Warham** Norfk
165 J1 **Warhill** Tamesd
114 C5 **Waring's Green** Solhll
225 K4 **Wark** Nthumb
248 C6 **Wark** Nthumb
248 C6 **Wark Common** Nthumb
23 L2 **Warkleigh** Devon
117 H3 **Warkton** Nhants
99 G5 **Warkworth** Nhants
237 K5 **Warkworth** Nthumb
196 B3 **Warlaby** N York
175 K3 **Warland** Calder
11 H8 **Warleggan** Cnwll
59 J8 **Warleigh** BaNES
66 E2 **Warley** Essex
176 C2 **Warley Town** Calder
113 L2 **Warley Woods** Sandw
49 K2 **Warlingham** Surrey
152 E3 **Warmbrook** Derbys
177 K3 **Warmfield** Wakefd
150 C1 **Warmingham** Ches
34 B3 **Warminghurst** W Susx
118 B1 **Warmington** Nhants
98 F4 **Warmington** Warwks
43 L4 **Warminster** Wilts
43 L5 **Warminster Common** Wilts
51 K4 **Warmlake** Kent
59 G6 **Warmley** S Glos
58 F6 **Warmley Hill** S Glos
59 G6 **Warmley Tower** S Glos
117 K6 **Warmonds Hill** Nhants
178 C7 **Warmsworth** Donc
18 B4 **Warmwell** Dorset
47 H3 **Warnborough Green** Hants
96 E2 **Warndon** Worcs
83 G5 **Warners End** Herts
31 L2 **Warnford** Hants
49 G7 **Warnham** W Susx
33 K5 **Warningcamp** W Susx
34 E1 **Warninglid** W Susx
81 J7 **Warpsgrove** Oxon
165 G6 **Warren** Ches
18 D3 **Warren** Dorset
70 E7 **Warren** Pembks
167 G1 **Warren** Sheff
206 D3 **Warrenby** R & Cl
47 H8 **Warren Corner** Hants
47 K4 **Warren Corner** Hants
106 E5 **Warren Heath** Suffk
63 K4 **Warren Row** W & M
102 C8 **Warren's Green** Herts
52 B3 **Warren Street** Kent
100 E3 **Warrington** M Keyn
164 B3 **Warrington** Warrtn
259 H5 **Warriston** C Edin
31 H5 **Warsash** Hants
319 P2 **Warse** Highld
185 K1 **Warsill** N York
151 L2 **Warslow** Staffs
167 L7 **Warsop Vale** Notts
114 B4 **Warstock** Birm
129 K5 **Warstone** Staffs
188 C4 **Warter** E R Yk
195 J6 **Warthermarske** N York
187 J3 **Warthill** N York
36 C5 **Wartling** E Susx
132 D2 **Wartnaby** Leics
173 K2 **Warton** Lancs
192 F7 **Warton** Lancs
236 D6 **Warton** Nthumb
130 F6 **Warton** Warwks
173 J2 **Warton Bank** Lancs
114 F6 **Warwick** Warwks
209 L2 **Warwick Bridge** Cumb
209 L2 **Warwick-on-Eden** Cumb
223 L4 **Warwicksland** Cumb
49 K3 **Warwick Wold** Surrey
328 E7 **Wasbister** Ork
200 F6 **Wasdale Head** Cumb
165 L4 **Wash** Derbys
102 F7 **Washall Green** Herts
10 E8 **Washaway** Cnwll
8 C4 **Washbourne** Devon
42 B3 **Washbrook** Somset
105 K5 **Washbrook** Suffk
105 K5 **Washbrook Street** Suffk
62 B8 **Wash Common** W Berk
135 L3 **Wash Dyke** Norfk
151 H4 **Washerwall** Staffs
25 G3 **Washfield** Devon
204 D7 **Washfold** N York
40 E5 **Washford** Somset
114 B6 **Washford** Worcs
24 E4 **Washford Pyne** Devon
169 K6 **Washingborough** Lincs
118 C2 **Washingley** Cambs
213 H2 **Washington** Sundld
34 B4 **Washington** W Susx
213 H2 **Washington Village** Sundld
104 F4 **Washmere Green** Suffk
176 E6 **Washpit** Kirk
62 B8 **Wash Water** W Berk
114 B2 **Washwood Heath** Birm
62 E8 **Wasing** W Berk
212 C4 **Waskerley** Dur
98 C2 **Wasperton** Warwks
49 K4 **Wasp Green** Surrey
169 L8 **Wasps Nest** Lincs
196 F6 **Wass** N York
114 E6 **Waste Green** Warwks
7 K5 **Wastor** Devon
26 C7 **Watchcombe** Devon
40 E5 **Watchet** Somset
61 H2 **Watchfield** Oxon
41 K4 **Watchfield** Somset
192 F2 **Watchgate** Cumb
208 E5 **Watchhill** Cumb
85 K2 **Watch House Green** Essex
223 G6 **Watchill** D & G
8 F1 **Watcombe** Torbay
201 H4 **Watendlath** Cumb
14 B5 **Water** Devon
175 H2 **Water** Lancs
119 K7 **Waterbeach** Cambs
33 G5 **Waterbeach** W Susx
223 G4 **Waterbeck** D & G
83 J6 **Waterdale** Herts
141 H4 **Waterden** Norfk
19 K2 **Waterditch** Hants
100 E7 **Water Eaton** M Keyn
81 G4 **Water Eaton** Oxon
101 J6 **Water End** Beds
101 K4 **Water End** Beds
102 B4 **Water End** Beds
82 B7 **Waterend** Bucks
200 E3 **Waterend** Cumb
187 L7 **Water End** E R Yk
103 J5 **Water End** Essex
78 B4 **Waterend** Gloucs
47 G3 **Water End** Hants
83 G4 **Water End** Herts
83 K4 **Waterend** Herts
83 L6 **Water End** Herts
151 L3 **Waterfall** Staffs
239 K6 **Waterfoot** Ag & B
202 B3 **Waterfoot** Cumb
175 H3 **Waterfoot** Lancs
243 H3 **Waterfoot** S Lans
20 D3 **Waterford** Hants
84 C4 **Waterford** Herts
178 B2 **Water Fryston** Wakefd
190 D7 **Water Garth Nook** Cumb
6 B4 **Watergate** Cnwll
11 G5 **Watergate** Cnwll
27 G3 **Watergore** Somset
85 G7 **Waterhales** Essex
68 E8 **Waterham** Kent
60 E2 **Waterhay** Wilts
201 K7 **Waterhead** Cumb
7 L5 **Waterhead** Devon
230 E4 **Waterhead** E Ayrs
245 L3 **Waterheads** Border
139 J8 **Waterheath** Norfk
212 E5 **Waterhouses** Dur
194 C8 **Water Houses** N York
151 L3 **Waterhouses** Staffs
51 G3 **Wateringbury** Kent
78 E6 **Waterlane** Gloucs
43 G5 **Waterlip** Somset
174 E2 **Waterloo** Tamesd
57 G3 **Waterloo** Caerph
11 G7 **Waterloo** Cnwll
167 H8 **Waterloo** Derbys
94 D4 **Waterloo** Herefs
294 C4 **Waterloo** Highld
244 C3 **Waterloo** N Lans
122 C4 **Waterloo** Norfk
138 E3 **Waterloo** Norfk
279 G7 **Waterloo** P & K
70 F6 **Waterloo** Pembks
19 G3 **Waterloo** Poole
173 H8 **Waterloo** Sefton
149 K7 **Waterloo** Shrops
175 K7 **Waterloo** Tamesd
173 H8 **Waterloo Park** Sefton
159 H8 **Waterloo Port** Gwynd
32 C5 **Waterlooville** Hants
51 K5 **Waterman Quarter** Kent
78 D3 **Watermead** Gloucs
232 D4 **Watermeetings** S Lans
36 D4 **Watermill** E Susx
201 L3 **Watermillock** Cumb
79 G6 **Watermoor** Gloucs
134 C7 **Water Newton** Cambs
114 D1 **Water Orton** Warwks
81 J5 **Waterperry** Oxon
25 J1 **Waterrow** Somset
33 K3 **Watersfield** W Susx
175 K6 **Watersheddings** Oldham
174 F3 **Waterside** Bl w D
82 F6 **Waterside** Bucks
208 F4 **Waterside** Cumb
165 K4 **Waterside** Derbys
178 F5 **Waterside** Donc
230 C5 **Waterside** E Ayrs
242 F5 **Waterside** E Ayrs
256 F6 **Waterside** E Rens
243 G1 **Waterside** E Rens
49 L4 **Waterside** Surrey
192 E6 **Waterslack** Lancs
174 E6 **Water's Nook** Bolton
292 A7 **Waterstein** Highld
81 J5 **Waterstock** Oxon
70 E5 **Waterston** Pembks
99 L7 **Water Stratford** Bucks
128 C3 **Waters Upton** Wrekin
167 H4 **Waterthorpe** Sheff
303 J2 **Waterton** Abers
56 B5 **Waterton** V Glam
190 F3 **Water Yeat** Cumb
83 H7 **Watford** Herts
116 B6 **Watford** Nhants
130 C6 **Watford Gap** Birm
64 F2 **Watford Heath** Herts
56 F3 **Watford Park** Caerph
202 F6 **Wath** Cumb
195 H8 **Wath** N York
196 B6 **Wath** N York
197 J6 **Wath** N York
200 C5 **Wath Brow** Cumb
246 E4 **Watherston** Border
177 L7 **Wath Upon Dearne** Rothm
78 C6 **Watledge** Gloucs
59 G4 **Watley's End** S Glos
136 C4 **Watlington** Norfk
63 G2 **Watlington** Oxon
153 K4 **Watnall** Notts
200 B5 **Watson Hill** Cumb
319 M6 **Watten** Highld
121 L5 **Wattisfield** Suffk
105 H3 **Wattisham** Suffk
105 G3 **Wattisham Stone** Suffk
138 C7 **Wattlefield** Norfk
127 G4 **Wattlesborough Heath** Shrops
16 F3 **Watton** Dorset
188 F4 **Watton** E R Yk
137 J6 **Watton** Norfk
84 C3 **Watton at Stone** Herts
85 G7 **Watton's Green** Essex
257 H7 **Wattston** N Lans
56 D2 **Wattstown** Rhondd
57 H2 **Wattsville** Caerph
281 H5 **Waulkmill** Angus
215 K4 **Waulkmill** D & G
267 L2 **Waulkmill** P & K
281 H6 **Waulkmills** Angus
159 K8 **Waun** Gwynd
54 E3 **Waunarlwydd** Swans
88 B7 **Waun Beddau** Pembks
108 C3 **Waun Fawr** Cerdgn
145 K2 **Waunfawr** Gwynd
90 D8 **Waungilwen** Carmth
54 E1 **Waungron** Swans
75 K5 **Waun-Lwyd** Blae G
72 E8 **Waun y Clyn** Carmth
55 K4 **Waun y Gilfach** Brdgnd
100 F6 **Wavendon** M Keyn
100 F6 **Wavendon Gate** M Keyn
208 F4 **Waverbridge** Cumb
163 J8 **Waverton** Ches
208 F4 **Waverton** Cumb
163 G3 **Wavertree** Lpool
61 L7 **Wawcott** W Berk
189 G7 **Wawne** E R Yk
143 L6 **Waxham** Norfk
181 J2 **Waxholme** E R Yk
69 K7 **Way** Kent
14 B7 **Waye** Devon
96 B6 **Wayend Street** Herefs
67 J8 **Wayfield** Medway
26 F5 **Wayford** Somset
149 L5 **Waymills** Shrops
76 E3 **Wayne Green** Mons
164 B7 **Way's Green** Ches
22 F2 **Waytown** Devon
38 E7 **Waytown** Devon
27 H7 **Waytown** Dorset
24 F4 **Way Village** Devon
41 L1 **Way Wick** N Som
305 L4 **Weachyburn** Abers
40 F5 **Weacombe** Somset
80 C6 **Weald** Oxon
65 G3 **Wealdstone** Gt Lon
6 F3 **Wearde** Cnwll
185 L6 **Weardley** Leeds
42 B3 **Weare** Somset
23 H2 **Weare Giffard** Devon
211 J6 **Wearhead** Dur
42 B8 **Wearne** Somset
202 F7 **Weasdale** Cumb
137 G2 **Weasenham All Saints** Norfk
141 H7 **Weasenham St Peter** Norfk
175 G8 **Weaste** Salfd
49 K5 **Weatherhill** Surrey
114 B5 **Weatheroak Hill** Worcs
164 B6 **Weaverham** Ches
51 J2 **Weavering Street** Kent
130 C3 **Weaverslake** Staffs
198 E7 **Weaverthorpe** N York
41 L2 **Webbington** Somset
113 L6 **Webheath** Worcs
127 K2 **Webscott** Shrops
32 C4 **Wecock** Hants
303 G2 **Wedderlairs** Abers
53 J2 **Weddington** Kent
131 H8 **Weddington** Warwks
44 E2 **Wedhampton** Wilts
42 B4 **Wedmore** Somset
129 K7 **Wednesbury** Sandw
129 K8 **Wednesbury Oak** Sandw
129 J6 **Wednesfield** Wolves
168 F7 **Weecar** Notts
82 C3 **Weedon** Bucks
99 K2 **Weedon Bec** Nhants
99 K4 **Weedon Lois** Nhants
130 C6 **Weeford** Staffs
8 C2 **Week** Devon
12 F5 **Week** Devon
23 K1 **Week** Devon
24 C3 **Week** Devon
24 D5 **Weeke** Devon
46 C7 **Weeke** Hants
11 J2 **Week Green** Cnwll
117 H3 **Weekley** Nhants
25 L2 **Weekmoor** Somset
21 J3 **Weeks** IoW
22 C7 **Week St Mary** Cnwll
189 G7 **Weel** E R Yk
87 J2 **Weeley** Essex
87 K2 **Weeley Heath** Essex
181 H6 **Weelsby** NE Lin
278 C4 **Weem** P & K
129 J2 **Weeping Cross** Staffs
97 J2 **Weethley** Warwks
97 H3 **Weethley Bank** Warwks
97 J3 **Weethley Bank** Warwks
97 H3 **Weethley Gate** Warwks
120 F2 **Weeting** Norfk
181 K3 **Weeton** E R Yk
182 C8 **Weeton** Lancs
185 L5 **Weeton** N York
185 L7 **Weetwood** Leeds
163 K7 **Weetwood Common** Ches
67 J3 **Weir** Essex
175 J2 **Weir** Lancs
127 G2 **Weirbrook** Shrops
6 F2 **Weir Quay** Cnwll
332 F6 **Weisdale** Shet
167 L6 **Welbeck Abbey** Notts
138 B5 **Welborne** Norfk
155 J3 **Welbourn** Lincs
138 B5 **Welbourne Common** Norfk
197 J5 **Welburn** N York
197 K8 **Welburn** N York
205 K7 **Welbury** N York
155 J6 **Welby** Lincs
119 K2 **Welches Dam** Cambs
22 C3 **Welcombe** Devon
174 C4 **Weld Bank** Lancs
117 J2 **Weldon** Nhants
237 G7 **Weldon** Nthumb
116 C3 **Welford** Nhants
61 L6 **Welford** W Berk
97 K3 **Welford-on-Avon** Warwks
116 F1 **Welham** Leics
168 D4 **Welham** Notts
43 G7 **Welham** Somset
187 L8 **Welhambridge** E R Yk
83 L5 **Welham Green** Herts
47 J4 **Well** Hants
171 H6 **Well** Lincs
195 L5 **Well** N York
96 C6 **Welland** Worcs
96 D6 **Welland Stone** Worcs
280 E7 **Wellbank** Angus
175 G3 **Well Bank** Lancs
29 G3 **Well Bottom** Dorset
35 L1 **Wellbrook** E Susx
222 F6 **Welldale** D & G
63 L3 **Well End** Bucks
83 K7 **Well End** Herts
50 D5 **Weller's Town** Kent
98 C2 **Wellesbourne** Warwks
164 E3 **Well Green** Traffd
101 L8 **Well Head** Herts
185 G8 **Well Heads** Brad
66 C8 **Well Hill** Kent
62 D6 **Wellhouse** W Berk
66 C5 **Welling** Gt Lon
117 H6 **Wellingborough** Nhants
137 H2 **Wellingham** Norfk
155 J2 **Wellingore** Lincs
200 D7 **Wellington** Cumb
95 G4 **Wellington** Herefs
25 L2 **Wellington** Somset
128 C4 **Wellington** Wrekin
95 L5 **Wellington Heath** Herefs
186 C7 **Wellington Hill** Leeds
25 K2 **Wellisford** Somset
43 H2 **Wellow** BaNES
20 E4 **Wellow** IoW
181 H6 **Wellow** NE Lin
168 C7 **Wellow** Notts
30 D2 **Wellow Wood** Hants
62 F3 **Well Place** Oxon
84 E2 **Wellpond Green** Herts
185 K7 **Wellroyd** Leeds
42 E4 **Wells** Somset
131 H6 **Wellsborough** Leics
150 C3 **Wells Green** Ches
141 J3 **Wells-next-the-sea** Norfk
26 C1 **Wellsprings** Somset
51 G2 **Well Street** Kent
85 J3 **Wellstye Green** Essex
8 F2 **Wellswood** Torbay
5 K1 **Welltown** Cnwll
25 G5 **Well Town** Devon
258 D3 **Wellwood** Fife
135 L8 **Welney** Norfk
22 D2 **Welsford** Devon
149 H7 **Welshampton** Shrops
77 H3 **Welsh Bicknor** Gloucs
149 K6 **Welsh End** Shrops
149 G7 **Welsh Frankton** Shrops
65 H3 **Welsh Harp** Gt Lon
88 E7 **Welsh Hook** Pembks
76 F3 **Welsh Newton** Herefs
77 G3 **Welsh Newton Common** Herefs
126 E5 **Welshpool** Powys
56 D5 **Welsh St Donats** V Glam
87 G1 **Welshwood Park** Essex
13 L7 **Welstor** Devon
43 G3 **Welton** BaNES
209 J5 **Welton** Cumb
230 E1 **Welton** E Ayrs
180 B2 **Welton** E R Yk
169 K5 **Welton** Lincs
116 B6 **Welton** Nhants
169 K4 **Welton Hill** Lincs
171 J7 **Welton le Marsh** Lincs
170 E3 **Welton le Wold** Lincs
181 J3 **Welwick** E R Yk
83 L3 **Welwyn** Herts
84 B4 **Welwyn Garden City** Herts
149 K8 **Wem** Shrops
41 J6 **Wembdon** Somset
65 G4 **Wembley** Gt Lon
7 H5 **Wembury** Devon
24 B5 **Wembworthy** Devon
254 F7 **Wemyss Bay** Inver
108 D5 **Wenallt** Cerdgn
124 E3 **Wenallt** Gwynd
147 J5 **Wenallt** Gwynd
103 H6 **Wendens Ambo** Essex
81 H3 **Wendlebury** Oxon
137 J4 **Wendling** Norfk
82 D5 **Wendover** Bucks
82 D5 **Wendover Dean** Bucks
3 H4 **Wendron** Cnwll
102 D4 **Wendy** Cambs
10 F7 **Wenfordbridge** Cnwll
123 J4 **Wenhaston** Suffk
123 J4 **Wenhaston Black Heath** Suffk
118 E4 **Wennington** Cambs
66 D4 **Wennington** Gt Lon
193 H7 **Wennington** Lancs
152 E1 **Wensley** Derbys
195 G3 **Wensley** N York
178 B4 **Wentbridge** Wakefd
111 H1 **Wentnor** Shrops
119 K4 **Wentworth** Cambs
177 K8 **Wentworth** Rothm
56 F6 **Wenvoe** V Glam
94 E3 **Weobley** Herefs
94 F3 **Weobley Marsh** Herefs
113 L3 **Weoley Castle** Birm
33 K5 **Wepham** W Susx
162 E7 **Wepre** Flints
136 D6 **Wereham** Norfk
136 D6 **Wereham Row** Norfk
150 E3 **Wereton** Staffs
129 H6 **Wergs** Wolves
145 K6 **Wern** Gwynd
75 J3 **Wern** Powys
126 F2 **Wern** Powys
126 F4 **Wern** Powys
148 E7 **Wern** Shrops
54 D3 **Wern** Swans
126 E1 **Wern ddu** Shrops
175 K7 **Werneth** Oldham
165 J2 **Werneth Low** Tamesd
54 D3 **Wernffrwd** Swans
76 C2 **Wern-Gifford** Mons
127 G2 **Wernlas** Shrops
54 E2 **Wern-olau** Swans
76 D4 **Wernrheolydd** Mons
56 C4 **Wern Tarw** Brdgnd
76 D5 **Wern-y-cwrt** Mons
162 D7 **Wern-y-gaer** Flints
12 C4 **Werrington** Cnwll
134 D6 **Werrington** C Pete
151 H4 **Werrington** Staffs
163 H6 **Wervin** Ches
185 L5 **Wescoe Hill** N York
182 D8 **Wesham** Lancs
153 G2 **Wessington** Derbys
153 G2 **Wessington Green** Derbys
56 D7 **West Aberthaw** V Glam
38 E7 **Westacott** Devon
136 F3 **West Acre** Norfk
65 G4 **West Acton** Gt Lon
99 G6 **West Adderbury** Oxon
248 F4 **West Allerdean** Nthumb
227 J5 **West Allotment** N Tyne
8 B6 **West Alvington** Devon
44 F5 **West Amesbury** Wilts
39 K8 **West Anstey** Devon
195 K3 **West Appleton** N York
177 H2 **West Ardsley** Leeds
242 F2 **West Arthurlie** E Rens
170 E6 **West Ashby** Lincs
38 D6 **West Ashford** Devon
32 F5 **West Ashling** W Susx
43 L2 **West Ashton** Wilts
204 F2 **West Auckland** Dur
198 E5 **West Ayton** N York
41 G7 **West Bagborough** Somset
281 G7 **West Balmirmer** Angus
75 L5 **West Bank** Blae G
163 K4 **West Bank** Halton
170 C4 **West Barkwith** Lincs
207 J5 **West Barnby** N York
65 H7 **West Barnes** Gt Lon
260 E5 **West Barns** E Loth
141 H5 **West Barsham** Norfk
16 F3 **West Bay** Dorset
142 E4 **West Beckham** Norfk
64 E6 **West Bedfont** Surrey
257 K8 **West Benhar** N Lans
228 D2 **West Bennan** N Ayrs
53 G1 **Westbere** Kent
86 F1 **West Bergholt** Essex
17 G4 **West Bexington** Dorset
136 E3 **West Bilney** Norfk
211 J6 **West Blackdene** Dur
12 F5 **West Blackdown** Devon
34 E5 **West Blatchington** Br & H
246 D6 **West Bold** Border
227 K7 **West Boldon** S Tyne
155 G5 **Westborough** Lincs
19 H3 **Westbourne** Bmouth
106 C4 **Westbourne** Suffk
32 E5 **Westbourne** W Susx
65 J4 **Westbourne Green** Gt Lon
43 J8 **West Bourton** Dorset
176 F1 **West Bowling** Brad
183 K6 **West Bradford** Lancs
42 E6 **West Bradley** Somset
177 H5 **West Bretton** Wakefd
153 L6 **West Bridgford** Notts
65 J5 **West Brompton** Gt Lon
113 L1 **West Bromwich** Sandw
94 C5 **Westbrook** Herefs
69 K6 **Westbrook** Kent
48 C5 **Westbrook** Surrey
163 L3 **Westbrook** Warrtn
62 B6 **Westbrook** W Berk
60 C7 **Westbrook** Wilts
122 C3 **Westbrook Green** Norfk
83 G5 **Westbrook Hay** Herts
152 B7 **West Broughton** Derbys
39 G7 **West Buckland** Devon
26 B2 **West Buckland** Somset
243 K1 **Westburn** S Lans
290 F7 **West Burnside** Abers
332 D5 **West Burrafirth** Shet
194 F4 **West Burton** N York
33 J4 **West Burton** W Susx
99 K6 **Westbury** Bucks
127 H5 **Westbury** Shrops
43 L3 **Westbury** Wilts
43 L3 **Westbury Leigh** Wilts
77 L4 **Westbury-on-Severn** Gloucs
58 E5 **Westbury on Trym** Bristl
42 D4 **Westbury-sub-Mendip** Somset
212 D5 **West Butsfield** Dur
179 J6 **West Butterwick** N Linc
173 J1 **Westby** Lancs
155 J8 **Westby** Lincs
48 D1 **West Byfleet** Surrey
139 L4 **West Caister** Norfk
258 C8 **West Calder** W Loth
27 K2 **West Camel** Somset
185 K6 **West Carlton** Leeds
180 D1 **West Carr** C KuH
179 G6 **West Carr** N Linc
61 L3 **West Challow** Oxon
8 C6 **West Charleton** Devon
27 J5 **West Chelborough** Dorset
237 J7 **West Chevington** Nthumb
33 L3 **West Chiltington** W Susx
33 L3 **West Chiltington Common** W Susx
27 H4 **West Chinnock** Somset
227 J6 **West Chirton** N Tyne
44 F3 **West Chisenbury** Wilts
48 D3 **West Clandon** Surrey
19 H3 **West Cliff** Bmouth
207 K5 **West Cliff** N York
53 K5 **West Cliffe** Kent
67 L4 **Westcliff-on-Sea** Sthend
315 L5 **West Clyne** Highld
27 J4 **West Coker** Somset
8 C2 **Westcombe** Devon
42 C8 **Westcombe** Somset
43 G6 **Westcombe** Somset
31 G6 **West Common** Hants
17 H3 **West Compton** Dorset
42 E5 **West Compton** Somset
213 H7 **West Cornforth** Dur
61 K3 **Westcot** Oxon
132 B6 **Westcotes** C Leic
81 L3 **Westcott** Bucks
25 J6 **Westcott** Devon
127 H6 **Westcott** Shrops
48 F4 **Westcott** Surrey
80 E1 **Westcott Barton** Oxon
45 H1 **Westcourt** Wilts
178 E3 **West Cowick** E R Yk
100 D7 **Westcroft** M Keyn
129 J6 **Westcroft** Wolves
51 K7 **West Cross** Kent
54 F4 **West Cross** Swans
60 B2 **West Crudwell** Wilts
11 K3 **West Curry** Cnwll
209 H4 **West Curthwaite** Cumb
35 K7 **Westdean** E Susx
30 C1 **West Dean** Hants
33 G4 **West Dean** W Susx
134 C5 **West Deeping** Lincs
70 E4 **West Denant** Pembks
34 E5 **Westdene** Br & H
280 E7 **West Denside** Angus
226 F6 **West Denton** N u Ty
163 G2 **West Derby** Lpool
136 D6 **West Dereham** Norfk
164 F2 **West Didsbury** Manch
237 G2 **West Ditchburn** Nthumb
38 D5 **West Down** Devon
45 L6 **West Down** Hants
44 D4 **Westdown Camp** Wilts
5 H2 **West Downs** Cnwll
10 E5 **Westdowns** Cnwll
64 E5 **West Drayton** Gt Lon
168 D6 **West Drayton** Notts
319 M2 **West Dunnet** Highld
65 G4 **West Ealing** Gt Lon
166 F8 **West Edge** Derbys
180 C2 **West Ella** E R Yk
101 G3 **West End** Beds
118 B7 **West End** Beds
63 L6 **West End** W & M
75 L7 **West End** Caerph
209 H2 **West End** Cumb
178 F6 **West End** Donc
28 F6 **West End** Dorset
179 L1 **West End** E R Yk
180 F2 **West End** E R Yk
181 H2 **West End** E R Yk
188 F2 **West End** E R Yk
189 J3 **West End** E R Yk
78 D7 **West End** Gloucs
145 G7 **West End** Gwynd
31 H4 **West End** Hants
31 K5 **West End** Surrey
46 F6 **West End** Hants
84 B5 **West End** Herts
52 B2 **West End** Kent
69 G7 **West End** Kent
176 F2 **West End** Kirk
174 F2 **West End** Lancs
182 D2 **West End** Lancs
185 K7 **West End** Leeds
131 J3 **West End** Leics
157 G4 **West End** Lincs
181 K8 **West End** Lincs
76 E7 **West End** Mons
137 J5 **West End** Norfk
139 L4 **West End** Norfk
58 C7 **West End** N Som
185 H3 **West End** N York
186 F6 **West End** N York
187 G7 **West End** N York
62 E3 **West End** Oxon
80 C2 **Westend** Oxon
80 E6 **West End** Worcs
58 E2 **Westend** S Glos
59 H3 **West End** S Glos
244 F4 **West End** S Lans
42 E3 **West End** Somset
43 G7 **West End** Somset
123 K3 **West End** Suffk
47 K5 **West End** Surrey
48 B1 **West End** Surrey
64 F8 **West End** Surrey
63 K6 **West End** W & M
29 G2 **West End** Wilts
29 H2 **West End** Wilts
60 C5 **West End** Wilts
97 J6 **West End** Worcs
34 C3 **West End** W Susx
47 G1 **West End Green** Hants
225 H6 **Westend Town** Nthumb
56 B7 **West-end Town** V Glam
52 F6 **Westenhanger** Kent
297 K5 **Wester Aberchalder** Highld
315 L10 **Wester Arboll** Highld
256 E6 **Wester Auchinloch** N Lans
268 B7 **Wester Balgedie** P & K
260 F5 **Wester Broomhouse** E Loth
305 L3 **Wester Culbeuchly** Abers
319 K6 **Westerdale** Highld
206 F6 **Westerdale** N York
258 C6 **Wester Dechmont** W Loth
233 L2 **Wester Deloraine** Border
280 B6 **Wester Denoon** Angus
289 J7 **Wester Eggie** Angus
279 H6 **Wester Essendy** P & K
234 C2 **Wester Essenside** Border
332 F6 **Westerfield** Shet
106 D4 **Westerfield** Suffk
302 F5 **Wester Fintray** Abers
300 B4 **Wester Fodderletter** Moray
280 D5 **Wester Foffarty** Angus
33 H5 **Westergate** W Susx
306 D3 **Wester Greenskares** Abers
314 D8 **Wester Gruinards** Highld
259 G7 **Wester Hailes** C Edin
50 B3 **Westerham** Kent
226 F6 **Westerhope** N u Ty
247 G6 **Wester Housebyres** Border
234 B1 **Wester Kershope** Border
310 E3 **Wester Lealty** Highld
59 G5 **Westerleigh** S Glos
59 H5 **Westerleigh Hill** S Glos
280 E5 **Wester Meathie** Angus
208 F4 **Western Bank** Cumb
269 G6 **Wester Newburn** Fife
53 K5 **Western Heights** Kent
213 G5 **Western Hill** Dur
132 B6 **Western Park** C Leic
222 C2 **Wester Parkgate** D & G
333 G9 **Wester Quarff** Shet
332 D8 **Wester Skeld** Shet
281 J4 **Westerton** Angus
212 F7 **Westerton** Dur
33 G5 **Westerton** W Susx
288 E8 **Westerton of Runavey** P & K
332 D8 **Westerwick** Shet
65 H8 **West Ewell** Surrey
51 H3 **West Farleigh** Kent
99 H3 **West Farndon** Nhants
127 G1 **West Felton** Shrops
269 G1 **West Ferry** C Dund
280 D5 **Westfield** Angus
43 G3 **Westfield** BaNES
185 J6 **Westfield** Leeds
200 B2 **Westfield** Cumb
36 F3 **Westfield** E Susx
32 D7 **Westfield** Hants
96 B4 **Westfield** Herefs
319 J4 **Westfield** Highld
177 G3 **Westfield** Kirk
257 G6 **Westfield** W Loth
180 E4 **West Field** N Linc
137 K5 **Westfield** Norfk
206 D3 **Westfield** R & Cl
167 H4 **Westfield** Sheff
48 D2 **Westfield** Surrey
257 L6 **Westfield** W Loth
187 G4 **West Field** York
28 C5 **Westfields** Dorset
95 G5 **Westfields** Herefs
62 C7 **West Fields** W Berk
279 J5 **Westfields of Rattray** P & K
51 J1 **Westfield Sole** Kent
35 J5 **West Firle** E Susx
249 K8 **West Fleetham** Nthumb
248 E7 **West Flodden** Nthumb
310 E4 **Westford** Highld
25 L2 **Westford** Somset
186 C8 **West Garforth** Leeds
210 C5 **Westgarth Hill** Cumb
211 K6 **Westgate** Dur
179 H6 **Westgate** N Linc
141 K3 **Westgate** Norfk
177 G2 **Westgate Hill** Brad
69 K6 **Westgate on Sea** Kent
138 D2 **Westgate Street** Norfk
62 B3 **West Ginge** Oxon
165 G1 **West Gorton** Manch
45 H1 **West Grafton** Wilts
177 K6 **West Green** Barns
65 K3 **West Green** Gt Lon
47 H2 **West Green** Hants
49 J6 **West Green** W Susx
30 C1 **West Grimstead** Wilts
34 C2 **West Grinstead** W Susx
178 D2 **West Haddlesey** N York
116 C5 **West Haddon** Nhants
62 D3 **West Hagbourne** Oxon
113 J4 **West Hagley** Worcs
302 C3 **Westhall** Abers
123 J3 **Westhall** Suffk
153 H5 **West Hallam** Derbys
79 L4 **Westhall Hill** Oxon
179 L3 **West Halton** N Linc
17 K6 **Westham** Dorset
36 B6 **Westham** E Susx
65 L4 **West Ham** Gt Lon
46 F3 **West Ham** Hants
42 B4 **Westham** Somset
33 G5 **Westhampnett** W Susx
65 H3 **West Hampstead** Gt Lon
167 G5 **West Handley** Derbys
61 L2 **West Hanney** Oxon
85 L7 **West Hanningfield** Essex
177 L4 **West Hardwick** Wakefd
121 K2 **West Harling** Norfk
196 D2 **West Harlsey** N York
42 E2 **West Harptree** BaNES
64 F3 **West Harrow** Gt Lon
32 E2 **West Harting** W Susx
227 K7 **West Harton** S Tyne
26 D2 **West Hatch** Somset
44 B8 **West Hatch** Wilts
42 B5 **Westhay** Somset
173 K6 **Westhead** Lancs
136 B5 **West Head** Norfk
113 L4 **West Heath** Birm
164 F8 **West Heath** Ches
66 C5 **West Heath** Gt Lon
46 E2 **West Heath** Hants
47 L2 **West Heath** Hants
315 P3 **West Helmsdale** Highld
65 H3 **West Hendon** Gt Lon
62 B3 **West Hendred** Oxon
331 B10 **West Heogaland** Shet
213 H3 **West Herrington** Sundld
198 D6 **West Heslerton** N York
57 L8 **West Hewish** N Som
95 J5 **Westhide** Herefs
302 F7 **Westhill** Abers
15 H3 **West Hill** Devon
189 J1 **West Hill** E R Yk
189 K7 **Westhill** E R Yk
36 F4 **West Hill** E Susx
65 H6 **West Hill** Gt Lon
310 G9 **Westhill** Highld
58 C5 **West Hill** N Som
43 H8 **West Hill** Somset
59 L7 **West Hill** Wilts
49 K7 **West Hill** W Susx
280 F6 **West Hills** Angus
49 L7 **West Hoathly** W Susx
18 D4 **West Holme** Dorset
227 J5 **West Holywell** N Tyne
204 C6 **West Hope** Dur
95 G3 **Westhope** Herefs
111 K2 **Westhope** Shrops
66 F3 **West Horndon** Essex
99 H3 **Westhorp** Nhants
156 D7 **Westhorpe** Lincs
154 C3 **Westhorpe** Notts
121 L6 **Westhorpe** Suffk
42 E4 **West Horrington** Somset
48 E3 **West Horsley** Surrey
249 G7 **West Horton** Nthumb
53 J5 **West Hougham** Kent
174 D6 **Westhoughton** Bolton
332 D6 **West Houlland** Shet
193 J7 **Westhouse** N York
153 H2 **Westhouses** Derbys
156 F3 **West Houses** Lincs
19 G2 **West Howe** Bmouth
40 B6 **West Howetown** Somset
49 G3 **Westhumble** Surrey
41 K5 **West Huntspill** Somset
19 J2 **West Hurn** Dorset
64 D2 **West Hyde** herts
270 B7 **West Hynish** Ag & B
52 F7 **West Hythe** Kent
39 H4 **West Ilkerton** Devon
62 C4 **West Ilsley** W Berk
330 J4 **Westing** Shet
97 K6 **Westington** Gloucs
32 E6 **West Itchenor** W Susx
227 G6 **West Jesmond** N u Ty
171 G8 **West Keal** Lincs
60 F7 **West Kennett** Wilts
65 H5 **West Kensington** Gt Lon
241 L4 **West Kilbride** N Ayrs
50 E1 **West Kingsdown** Kent
33 L6 **West Kingston** W Susx
59 K5 **West Kington** Wilts
59 K5 **West Kington Wick** Wilts
162 D3 **West Kirby** Wirral
198 C6 **West Knapton** N York
17 L4 **West Knighton** Dorset
43 L7 **West Knoyle** Wilts
212 E3 **West Kyo** Dur
7 K4 **Westlake** Devon
27 G3 **West Lambrook** Somset
84 E2 **Westland Green** Herts
150 F5 **Westlands** Staffs
113 H7 **Westlands** Worcs
53 K4 **West Langdon** Kent
314 G5 **West Langwell** Highld
44 C3 **West Lavington** Wilts
33 G2 **West Lavington** W Susx
204 E6 **West Layton** N York
213 K4 **West Lea** Dur
227 G3 **Westlea** Nthumb
60 F4 **Westlea** Swindn
131 L1 **West Leake** Notts
248 C6 **West Learmouth** Nthumb
24 B5 **West Leigh** Devon
25 K3 **Westleigh** Devon
38 C8 **Westleigh** Devon
32 D5 **West Leigh** Hants
40 F7 **West Leigh** Somset
174 D7 **Westleigh** Wigan
123 J6 **Westleton** Suffk
137 G3 **West Lexham** Norfk
127 H5 **Westley** Shrops
121 G7 **Westley** Suffk
67 G3 **Westley Heights** Essex
103 K2 **Westley Waterless** Cambs
187 H1 **West Lilling** N York
82 B4 **Westlington** Bucks
245 K3 **West Linton** Border
223 K7 **Westlinton** Cumb
47 J8 **West Liss** Hants
59 J5 **West Littleton** S Glos
62 B3 **West Lockinge** Oxon
6 B4 **West Looe** Cnwll
40 B4 **West Luccombe** Somset
18 C5 **West Lulworth** Dorset
198 D8 **West Lutton** N York
42 E7 **West Lydford** Somset
95 J5 **West Lydiatt** Herefs
39 H4 **West Lyn** Devon
41 K8 **West Lyng** Somset
136 C2 **West Lynn** Norfk
247 H4 **West Mains** Border
243 J3 **West Mains** S Lans
244 F4 **West Mains** S Lans
51 G2 **West Malling** Kent
96 C4 **West Malvern** Worcs
96 F6 **Westmancote** Worcs
32 E4 **West Marden** W Susx
36 E5 **West Marina** E Susx
168 D6 **West Markham** Notts
53 J1 **Westmarsh** Kent
181 H5 **West Marsh** NE Lin
184 C4 **West Marton** N York
28 F2 **West Melbury** Dorset
177 L7 **West Melton** Rothm
32 B2 **West Meon** Hants
32 B1 **West Meon Woodlands** Hants
87 G4 **West Mersea** Essex
34 F4 **Westmeston** E Susx
84 D1 **Westmill** Herts
101 L7 **Westmill** Herts
17 G2 **West Milton** Dorset
65 J5 **Westminster** Gt Lon
68 B6 **West Minster** Kent
64 F7 **West Molesey** Surrey
227 J5 **West Monkseaton** N Tyne
41 J8 **West Monkton** Somset
227 H5 **West Moor** N Tyne
208 D6 **Westmoor End** Cumb
29 K6 **West Moors** Dorset
18 E2 **West Morden** Dorset
185 G6 **West Morton** Brad
27 K2 **West Mudford** Somset
280 C4 **Westmuir** Angus
281 G2 **West Muir** Angus
197 J6 **West Ness** N York
328 E8 **Westness** Ork
208 D5 **Westnewton** Cumb
189 J7 **West Newton** E R Yk
140 D6 **West Newton** Norfk
248 E7 **Westnewton** Nthumb
41 J8 **West Newton** Somset
65 K6 **West Norwood** Gt Lon
13 K2 **West Nymph** Devon
227 K6 **Westoe** S Tyne
14 C7 **West Ogwell** Devon
59 H7 **Weston** BaNES
150 D3 **Weston** Halton
165 G6 **Weston** Ches
31 G5 **Weston** C Sotn
15 K4 **Weston** Devon
25 L6 **Weston** Devon
17 K7 **Weston** Dorset
27 J5 **Weston** Dorset
163 K4 **Weston** Halton
32 D2 **Weston** Hants
94 E2 **Weston** Shrops
102 C7 **Weston** Herts
134 F2 **Weston** Lincs
99 J4 **Weston** Nhants
168 E7 **Weston** Notts
185 J5 **Weston** N York
71 G4 **Weston** Pembks
111 G5 **Weston** Shrops
126 F1 **Weston** Shrops
128 B8 **Weston** Shrops
149 L8 **Weston** Shrops
245 G4 **Weston** S Lans
129 K1 **Weston** Staffs
123 J2 **Weston** Suffk
61 L6 **Weston** W Berk
27 L1 **Weston Bampfylde** Somset
95 J5 **Weston Beggard** Herefs
59 L3 **Westonbirt** Gloucs
116 F1 **Weston by Welland** Nhants
46 D6 **Weston Colley** Hants
103 K3 **Weston Colville** Cambs
31 H4 **Weston Common** C Sotn
127 J1 **Westoncommon** Shrops
47 G4 **Weston Corbett** Hants
120 D4 **Weston Ditch** Suffk
116 F7 **Weston Favell** Nhants
103 K3 **Weston Green** Cambs
138 C4 **Weston Green** Norfk
65 G7 **Weston Green** Surrey
128 F4 **Weston Heath** Shrops
134 F2 **Weston Hills** Lincs
115 H2 **Weston in Arden** Warwks
101 H7 **Westoning** Beds
58 C6 **Weston in Gordano** N Som
128 F2 **Weston Jones** Staffs
138 C3 **Weston Longville** Norfk
127 J1 **Weston Lullingfields** Shrops
20 D4 **Weston Manor** IoW
7 G3 **Weston Mill** C Plym
97 L3 **Weston-on-Avon** Warwks
81 G3 **Weston-on-the-Green** Oxon
153 G8 **Weston-on-Trent** Derbys
47 G4 **Weston Patrick** Hants
163 J4 **Weston Point** Ches
148 E6 **Weston Rhyn** Shrops
97 L3 **Weston Sands** Warwks
97 K5 **Weston-Sub-Edge** Gloucs
41 J1 **Weston-super-Mare** Somset
43 H5 **Weston Town** Somset
82 C4 **Weston Turville** Bucks
129 G4 **Weston-under-Lizard** Staffs
77 J2 **Weston under Penyard** Herefs
115 H6 **Weston under Wetherley** Warwks
152 E5 **Weston Underwood** Derbys
100 E3 **Weston Underwood** M Keyn
127 J1 **Westonwharf** Shrops
41 L6 **Westonzoyland** Somset
28 E3 **West Orchard** Dorset
60 F7 **West Overton** Wilts
187 L1 **Westow** N York
40 F7 **Westowe** Somset
25 L4 **Westown** Devon
268 C2 **Westown** P & K
12 C3 **West Panson** Devon
180 D2 **West Park** C KuH
213 L7 **West Park** Hartpl
185 L7 **West Park** Leeds
163 J1 **West Park** St Hel
227 K6 **West Park** S Tyne
29 K7 **West Parley** Dorset
203 L3 **West Pasture** Dur
50 F3 **West Peckham** Kent
212 F3 **West Pelton** Dur
42 D6 **West Pennard** Somset
4 C2 **West Pentire** Cnwll
118 C6 **West Perry** Cambs
76 B7 **West Pontnewydd** Torfn
138 F6 **West Poringland** Norfk
39 L4 **West Porlock** Somset
26 F3 **Westport** Somset
4 F6 **West Portholland** Cnwll
255 L6 **West Porton** Rens
28 C5 **West Pulham** Dorset
22 F3 **West Putford** Devon
40 F5 **West Quantoxhead** Somset
257 L5 **Westquarter** Falk
56 F6 **Westra** V Glam
213 H4 **West Rainton** Dur
169 K3 **West Rasen** Lincs
181 G8 **West Ravendale** NE Lin
141 H6 **West Raynham** Norfk
168 C4 **West Retford** Notts
62 E4 **Westridge Green** W Berk
257 L7 **Westrigg** W Loth
214 C4 **West Ringuinea** D & G
78 C5 **Westrip** Gloucs
59 L6 **Westrop** Wilts
62 D6 **Westrop Green** W Berk
205 L7 **West Rounton** N York
120 D4 **West Row** Suffk
141 G6 **West Rudham** Norfk
64 E3 **West Ruislip** Gt Lon
180 C6 **Westrum** Lincs
142 F3 **West Runton** Norfk
247 J4 **Westruther** Border
135 J7 **Westry** Cambs
260 B7 **West Saltoun** E Loth
24 E6 **West Sandford** Devon
330 F8 **West Sandwick** Shet
176 D1 **West Scholes** Brad
195 G5 **West Scrafton** N York
42 F5 **West Shepton** Somset
291 K2 **Westside** Abers
75 K5 **West Side** Blae G
328 H7 **West Side** Ork
221 J2 **West Skelston** D & G
227 H2 **West Sleekburn** Nthumb
139 K3 **West Somerton** Norfk
19 J3 **West Southbourne** Bmouth
17 L4 **West Stafford** Dorset
168 E1 **West Stockwith** Notts
13 K7 **West Stoke** Devon
27 H3 **West Stoke** Somset
32 F5 **West Stoke** W Susx
203 K7 **West Stonesdale** N York
42 B4 **West Stoughton** Somset
28 D2 **West Stour** Dorset
69 H8 **West Stourmouth** Kent
121 G5 **West Stow** Suffk
44 F1 **West Stowell** Wilts
317 M4 **West Strathan** Highld
46 D5 **West Stratton** Hants
51 L3 **West Street** Kent
53 K3 **West Street** Kent
67 H5 **West Street** Medway
121 K5 **West Street** Suffk
195 L6 **West Tanfield** N York
5 L2 **West Taphouse** Cnwll
253 J7 **West Tarbert** Ag & B
34 B6 **West Tarring** W Susx
247 J6 **West Third** Border
237 H6 **West Thirston** Nthumb
32 E6 **West Thorney** W Susx
167 H5 **Westthorpe** Derbys
66 E5 **West Thurrock** Thurr
67 G5 **West Tilbury** Thurr
47 G8 **West Tisted** Hants
137 G8 **West Tofts** Norfk
279 H8 **West Tofts** P & K
3 H2 **West Tolgus** Cnwll
170 B4 **West Torrington** Lincs
14 D2 **West Town** Devon
22 E2 **West Town** Devon
32 D7 **West Town** Hants
111 J7 **West Town** Herefs
42 D1 **West Town** Somset
58 C7 **West Town** N Som
42 D6 **West Town** Somset
34 E3 **West Town** W Susx
45 J7 **West Tytherley** Hants
176 D3 **West Vale** Calder
173 J8 **Westvale** Knows
213 L6 **West View** Hartpl
56 C6 **West Village** V Glam
8 B6 **Westville** Devon
153 K4 **Westville** Notts
135 K4 **West Walton** Norfk
209 G5 **Westward** Cumb
38 B8 **Westward Ho!** Devon
5 L4 **West Watergate** Cnwll
83 J7 **West Watford** Herts
12 E3 **Westweekmoor** Devon
52 C4 **Westwell** Kent
79 L4 **Westwell** Oxon
52 C4 **Westwell Leacon** Kent
30 D3 **West Wellow** Hants
59 L7 **Westwells** Wilts
259 J2 **West Wemyss** Fife
279 J8 **West Whitefield** P & K
119 J6 **Westwick** Cambs
204 D4 **Westwick** Dur
143 H6 **Westwick** Norfk
41 L1 **West Wick** N Som
103 K4 **West Wickham** Cambs
65 L7 **West Wickham** Gt Lon
71 G5 **West Williamston** Pembks
155 J5 **West Willoughby** Lincs
136 C3 **West Winch** Norfk
45 H7 **West Winterslow** Wilts
32 E7 **West Wittering** W Susx
195 G4 **West Witton** N York
134 D7 **Westwood** C Pete
14 F5 **Westwood** Devon
25 J7 **Westwood** Devon
21 H3 **Westwood** IoW
53 G4 **Westwood** Kent
69 L7 **Westwood** Kent
153 H3 **Westwood** Notts
243 J3 **Westwood** S Lans
43 K2 **Westwood** Wilts
44 F7 **Westwood** Wilts
225 K2 **West Woodburn** Nthumb
61 L8 **West Woodhay** W Berk
114 F4 **Westwood Heath** Covtry
43 J5 **West Woodlands** Somset
105 G7 **Westwood Park** Essex
175 G8 **Westwood Park** Salfd
179 G8 **Westwoodside** N Linc
47 H6 **West Worldham** Hants
24 D4 **West Worlington** Devon
34 B6 **West Worthing** W Susx
103 J3 **West Wratting** Cambs
63 K2 **West Wycombe** Bucks
226 E7 **West Wylam** Nthumb
164 B3 **Westy** Warrtn
59 K5 **West Yatton** Wilts
331 G9 **West Yell** Shet
41 K7 **West Yeo** Somset
66 E8 **West Yoke** Kent
22 D3 **West Youlstone** Cnwll
67 K7 **Wetham Green** Kent
209 K3 **Wetheral** Cumb
209 L2 **Wetheral Plain** Cumb
186 D5 **Wetherby** Leeds
121 L7 **Wetherden** Suffk
121 L6 **Wetherden Upper Town** Suffk
122 C6 **Wetheringsett** Suffk
104 B7 **Wethersfield** Essex
331 E12 **Wethersta** Shet
122 C7 **Wetherup Street** Suffk
151 J4 **Wetley Rocks** Staffs
130 F2 **Wetmore** Staffs
150 B1 **Wettenhall** Ches
150 B1 **Wettenhall Green** Ches
111 J2 **Wettles** Shrops
152 B2 **Wetton** Staffs
188 D3 **Wetwang** E R Yk
150 E7 **Wetwood** Staffs
45 J2 **Wexcombe** Wilts
64 C4 **Wexham Street** Bucks
142 E3 **Weybourne** Norfk
47 L4 **Weybourne** Surrey
122 E3 **Weybread** Suffk
64 E7 **Weybridge** Surrey
26 E6 **Weycroft** Devon
319 K3 **Weydale** Highld
45 K4 **Weyhill** Hants
17 K6 **Weymouth** Dorset
94 B2 **Weythel** Powys
100 D7 **Whaddon** Bucks
102 E4 **Whaddon** Cambs
78 C4 **Whaddon** Gloucs
78 F2 **Whaddon** Gloucs
30 B1 **Whaddon** Wilts
43 L1 **Whaddon** Wilts
102 D4 **Whaddon Gap** Cambs
202 C3 **Whale** Cumb
167 K6 **Whaley** Derbys
165 K4 **Whaley Bridge** Derbys
167 K6 **Whaley Thorns** Notts
319 P8 **Whaligoe** Highld
183 K7 **Whalley** Lancs
183 K7 **Whalley Banks** Lancs
164 F2 **Whalley Range** Manch
173 L6 **Whalleys** Lancs
226 E3 **Whalton** Nthumb
183 L2 **Wham** N York
135 G2 **Whaplode** Lincs
135 G4 **Whaplode Drove** Lincs
135 G2 **Whaplode St Catherine** Lincs
98 F3 **Wharf** Warwks
193 L8 **Wharfe** N York
182 D7 **Wharles** Lancs
100 F5 **Wharley End** Beds
225 K6 **Wharmley** Nthumb
166 E2 **Wharncliffe Side** Sheff
188 C1 **Wharram le Street** N York
164 C7 **Wharton** Ches
95 G2 **Wharton** Herefs
168 F2 **Wharton** Lincs
164 C7 **Wharton Green** Ches
204 F6 **Whashton** N York
192 E5 **Whasset** Cumb
28 E6 **Whatcombe** Dorset
98 D5 **Whatcote** Warwks
130 E7 **Whateley** Warwks
105 H4 **Whatfield** Suffk
26 F5 **Whatley** Somset
43 H4 **Whatley** Somset
36 E3 **Whatlington** E Susx
112 C5 **Whatmore** Shrops
52 F5 **Whatsole Street** Kent
152 F3 **Whatstandwell** Derbys
154 D6 **Whatton** Notts
215 K4 **Whauphill** D & G
204 B7 **Whaw** N York